Cognitive Models of Speech Processing: The Second Sperlonga Meeting

edited by

Gerry T.M. Altmann
University of Sussex, Brighton, UK

Richard Shillcock
Edinburgh University, UK

T0347152

Ψ **Psychology** Press
Taylor & Francis Group

LONDON AND NEW YORK

First published 1993 by Lawrence Erlbaum Associates Ltd.

Published 2014 by Psychology Press
27 Church Road, Hove, East Sussex, BN3 2FA

and by Psychology Press
711 Third Avenue, New York, NY 10017

First issued in paperback 2014

Psychology Press is an imprint of the Taylor & Francis Group, an informa business

British Library Cataloguing in Publication Data
Cognitive Models of Speech Processing:
Second Sperlonga Meeting
I. Altmann, Gerry   II. Shillcock, Richard
153.6

ISBN 13: 978-1-138-87700-9 (pbk)
ISBN 13: 978-0-86377-302-0 (hbk)

Typeset in the United Kingdom by J&L Composition Ltd, Filey, North Yorkshire

Contents

List of First Authors

Dr Gerry T.M. Altmann, Laboratory of Experimental Psychology, University of Sussex, Brighton BN1 9QG, UK.

Dr Ellen Bard, Human Communication Research Centre, University of Edinburgh, 2 Buccleuch Place, Edinburgh, UK.

Dr Andrew Barss, Department of Linguistics, University of Arizona, Tuscon, AZ 85721, USA.

Dott. Cristina Burani, Istituto di Psicologia, CNR, Viale Marx, 15, 00156 Roma, Italy.

Professor Rachel Clifton, Department of Psychology, University of Massachusetts, Tobin Hall, Amherst, MA 01003, USA.

Dr Anne Cutler, MRC Applied Psychology Unit, 15 Chaucer Road, Cambridge CB2 2EF, UK.

Dr Emmanuel Dupoux, Laboratoire Psycholinguisitique, 54 Boulevard Raspail, F-57 Paris 6e, France.

Professor Janet Fodor, Graduate Centre, CUNY, 32 West 42nd Street, New York, NY 10036. USA.

Professor Ken Forster, Department of Psychology, University of Arizona, Tuscon, Arizona 85721, USA.

Professor Peter Jusczyk, Department of Psychology, State University of New York at Buffalo, Buffalo, NY 14260, USA.

Professor William Marslen-Wilson, Birkbeck College, Department of Psychology, Malet Street, London WC1E 7HX, UK.

Dr Janet Nicol, Department of Psychology, University of Arizona, Tuscon, Arizona 85721, USA.

Dr Dennis Norris, MRC Applied Psychology Unit, 15 Chaucer Road, Cambridge CB2 2EF, UK.

Dr Juan Segui, Psychologie Experiméntale, CNRS, 28 rue Serpente, 75006 Paris, France.

Dr Richard Shillcock, Human Communication Research Centre, Edinburgh University, 2 Buccleuch Place, Edinburgh, UK.

Dott. Patrizia Tabossi, Dipartimento di Psicologia, Universitá di Bologna, Viale Berti-Pichat, 5, 40127 Bologna, Italy.

Professor Mike Tanenhaus, Department of Psychology, University of Rochester, River Station, Rochester, NY 14627, USA.

Dr. Lorraine K. Tyler, Department of Psychology, Birkbeck College, Mallet Street, London WC1E 7HX, UK.

Professor Janet Werker, Department of Psychology, University of British Columbia, 2136 West Mall, Vancouver BC, Canada V6T 1Y7.

Acknowledgements

The Second Sperlonga Workshop was held between 4th and 8th June, 1990. Thirty participants took part in the five days of psycholinguistic discussion. The First Sperlonga Workshop[1] had taken place two years previously, and this second meeting provided an opportunity to assess the progress that has been made in the intervening time. This volume represents the bulk of the work presented to the workshop in 1990, and we are grateful to the authors for the time and effort they have put into their contributions.

The Sperlonga Workshop would not have been possible without the generous support of British Telecom. In particular, we thank John Matthews and Fred Stentiford for recognising the importance of a workshop that not only enables broad discussion between leading academics, but which also ensures that the results of these discussions can be disseminated, via this volume, to a wider audience. Thanks are also due to Mr and Mrs Cosmo di Mille, whose Park Hotel Fiorelle provided the perfect environment in which to satisfy our intellectual, and gastronomic, appetites. In addition, the Sperlonga council and the local Tourist Board were very helpful in providing transport and other local amenities.

Finally, our thanks to the journal *Language and Cognitive Processes*, which provided editorial support during the production of this volume. Each chapter underwent a review procedure similar to that used for

---

[1] Altmann, G.T.M. (Ed.). 1990. *Cognitive models of speech processing: Psycholinguistic and computational perspectives*. Cambridge, MA: MIT Press.

academic journals. This has enabled us to ensure that the content is of the highest standard. We are grateful to the following people, as well as the authors themselves, for reviewing the chapters making up this volume: Alan Garnham, Judith Henstra, Laurie Stowe, Patricia Kuhl, Paul Warren, Peter Sells, Wayne Murray, Marcus Taft, Gordon Brown, Simon Garrod, Anne Anderson, Kerry Kilborn, Geoff Lindsey, and Nick Chater.

G.T.M.A.
R.C.S.

1

Overview

Richard Shillcock
Centre for Cognitive Science, University of Edinburgh, UK.

Gerry T.M. Altmann
Laboratory of Experimental Psychology, University of Sussex, Brighton, UK.

INTRODUCTION

The chapters in this volume reflect many of the general theoretical concerns that have motivated research on speech and language processing over the past decade—modularity in language processing, interaction between bottom-up and top-down processing, the significance of connectionist modelling, the processing of languages other than English—as well as more specific concerns such as the nature of the lexical representations onto which the speech input is mapped, the mapping process itself, and the processes that operate over the lexical representations to yield ultimately the meaning of the spoken sentence. These issues of representation and process can be studied with reference to acquisition of language processing in infancy, its deployment by normal adults, and its breakdown in language–disordered individuals. Moreover, each can be studied with reference to production or perception, and to processing across different languages. A further perspective is provided by models of language behaviour, in terms either of implemented computational models or of formal theories of language. In recent years, we have seen that attempts to address these concerns have led to increasing interaction across different disciplines. One of the aims of this series on Cognitive Models of Speech Processing, has been to bring together examples of such interactions. Thus, in this second volume,[1] Marslen-Wilson draws on current phonological

---

[1] Many of the chapters in this second volume explore themes that were developed in the first volume, *Cognitive models of speech processing: Psycholinguistic and computational approaches* (Altmann, Ed. 1990), to which the reader is referred.

theory to inform the study of processing issues in lexical access; Nicol employs formal syntactic theory to develop and test hypotheses about parsing and sentence processing; Fodor, Barss, and Sag have as their main concern the relationship between formal syntax and the human sentence processor. And so on. In virtually every chapter we see the important distinction between *representation* and *process*. It is scarcely possible to proceed at all in modelling speech processes without critical assumptions concerning the most appropriate representations to use—syllables, phonemes, phonetic features, graphemes, morphemes, words . . . Nor is it possible to proceed very far without confronting implications for the more global aspects of cognition and the functional architecture that underpins it.

The purpose of this overview is to provide the reader with an illustrative summary of the concerns of each of the chapters, in chronological order; to furnish a sketch of some of the relevant background, issues, and connections; and to set the context within which cognitive models of speech processing are being developed. This chapter is not intended as an introduction to speech processing *per se*, but is intended instead to arm the reader with sufficient context by which to assess the individual contributions within the volume.

We have attempted to order the chapters to reflect some of the main commonalities between the papers, but, given the nature of language research, virtually any ordering might generate thought-provoking contrasts or comparisons. Sometimes the relationship between successive chapters stems from a common objective, experimental paradigm or field of study, and we have provided a general title for each such group of chapters in the list of contents. Sometimes one chapter was explicitly elicited as a commentary on the adjacent chapter(s), reflecting the roles of speakers and discussants in the original conference and the continuing interaction between the authors. The commentaries are sometimes short and applied, sometimes longer and more discursive. Any chapter may be read independently, but by reading adjacent chapters a broadening picture emerges of the overall progress in our understanding of speech and language processing.

MODELLING ACQUISITION

A key concern of those researching the development of language skills has been to assess the actual perceptual abilities of infants at different ages, with the goal of determining how the language processor progresses from its biologically given starting point to its experientially defined adult state. Adult speakers of different languages employ, and are sensitive to, different collections of speech sounds. How is this sensitivity developed for certain contrasts between speech sounds, and lost for others? How does sensitivity change over time? And on what basis do these changes occur; are they irreversible, for instance? The notion of a biologically given starting point may be misleading; sensitivity to (low frequency) auditory stimuli begins *in utero* when the foetus is between six and seven months old. Further, the relationship between perceptual development and neural development in the early months remains to be explicated; the acquisition of speech processing capacity may well reflect a biologically given time-table of development, which weakens the notion of a biologically given starting point, and as a consequence different sorts of information may have different effects as development occurs. What is clear, however, is that very young infants show a preference for hearing the full complexity of natural connected speech (Mehler, Bertonocini, Barriere, & Jassik-Gerschenfeld, 1978), and that newborns are adept at discriminating between speech sounds (Streeter, 1976). Considerable changes in perceptual abilities occur over the first year and more, however. Of crucial importance in the adult processor is the ability to ignore acoustic–phonetic differences that are of no relevance in the specific language that has been learned. At this point in the development of the field, the principal concern is with establishing the timetable of events, the raw data for a theory of the development of speech processing.

Measures of discrimination in infant speech perception typically rely on increased sucking of a non-nutritive nipple to elicit 'interesting' (i.e. non-monotonous, contrasting) stimuli, or on the infant learning to orientate to a rewarding stimulus on perception of a specific cue. The use of such approaches has revealed surprising abilities of discrimination in very young infants; this ability to distinguish particular contrasts begins to be lost in the first year, under the influence of the ambient language, but the pattern of loss, and its potential reversibility, sheds light on the construction of the adult speech processor. For instance, the vulnerability to loss of a particular contrast depends in part on its relationship to the other contrasts present in the adult phonological system. Peter Jusczyk presents a valuable review of two decades of research into infant speech perception, addressing questions concerning the innate endowment that the infant brings to the problem, and the effect of exposure to the particular language of the community in which the infant is reared. He proposes the WRAPSA model as a theoretical framework in which to pursue these questions. The infant is seen as bringing general perceptual processes to bear on the acoustic input; with experience, these are attuned to the contrasts used in the ambient language. Juscyzk sees the syllable as the critical unit in the development of segmentation and pattern extraction (cf. Mehler, Dupoux, & Segui, 1990). Finally, and perhaps most at odds with the view of adult lexical access reported in many chapters in this volume, Jusczyk eschews any role in his model of the infant lexicon for abstract prototypical representations of the constituents of words, preferring instead a model in which multiple traces of a particular word reside in longterm memory. He proposes that 'lexical access' for infants involves matching to these multiple traces.

The theoretical concerns encountered in Jusczyk's chapter recur in Janet Werker's contribution, together with the methodological problems of assessing the perceptual capabilities of infants. In contrast to Jusczyk's approach, however, Werker is more willing to consider the possibility of speech processing being special, as opposed to emerging from general perceptual abilities. The notion that humans are evolutionarily endowed for speech processing has often proved attractive, as in early claims made for the speech-specificity of categorical perception, for instance. A more conservative approach involves attempting to account for the data using more general perceptual mechanisms, while still allowing that the human may be evolutionarily adapted for language use (thus, profoundly deaf individuals taught to sign from birth may develop the same complexity of communicative skills as speaking individuals.) Werker demonstrates the value of cross-linguistic research when she describes experiments requiring infants and adults to categorise speech stimuli from a non-native language. After presenting evidence bearing on the level—acoustic, phonetic, phonemic—at which subjects' responses are driven, she goes on to question some of the implications for the proposed modularity of processing; is phonetic analysis performed by a dedicated perceptual module? What makes Werker's and Jusczyk's contributions particularly relevant is that they converge on issues of representation and process, while employing very different sets of assumptions concerning the 'speech is special' debate.

In both Jusczyk and Werker's chapters, various assumptions are made concerning the most appropriate levels of representation for the interpretation of the data. Recent work on the nature of the representations that are constructed prior to contacting the mental lexicon has stressed the role of the syllable and the potential for cross-linguistic comparison, both of which are topics that recur in the Jusczyk and Werker chapters. Recent work on speech segmentation strategies reveals that these two topics may be intimately linked, with the syllable being a more salient processing unit in some languages than in others (e.g. Cutler, Mehler, Norris, & Segui, 1986; Sebastián-Gallés, Dupoux, Segui, & Mehler, 1992). A recurrent theme is that the study of apparently language-specific processing behaviour is allowing testable hypotheses to be made about language-independent universal processing structures; indeed, this issue is addressed explicitly by Anne Cutler, although the reader may ponder the potential for cross-linguistic comparison in each of the topics encountered in this volume.

PRE-LEXICAL PROCESSING AND LEXICAL REPRESENTATION

Central to modelling speech processing is the need to establish the perceptual role of particular patterns in the input. Jusczyk, for instance, attributes an important role to the syllable during the acquisition stage. The role of the syllable is also central to recent work by Emmanuel Dupoux, who presents detailed evidence from a series of experiments aimed at establishing the perceptual status of the syllable. Using monitoring techniques, together with exhaustive manipulations of the consonant/vowel structure of the stimulus materials, Dupoux reports data that lead to a qualification of the original Syllabic Hypothesis—that there is pre-lexical segmentation of the speech stream into syllables (e.g. Mehler, Domergues, Frauenfelder, & Segui, 1981; Segui, Dupoux, & Mehler, 1990). He goes on to discuss alternative accounts of the hypothesis, principally involving the demisyllable. Dupoux demonstrates some of the problems of interpreting the relevant experimental results; in this analysis, absolute reaction times are taken into account in order to argue for differential interpretations of subjects' responses. Of the range of experimental techniques described in this volume, perhaps phoneme-monitoring is the technique that has engendered the most experiments aimed, partly or wholly, at clarifying the technique itself, and elucidating the nature of the judgement being made by the subject. In contrast, the cross-modal priming technique, which features in many chapters, has been relatively free of this sort of attention and has thus accumulated fewer constraints on the nature of the stimulus materials that can be used with the technique.

Anne Cutler reviews cross-linguistic research using the syllable-monitoring task, and claims that the apparent contradictions within and between languages can be resolved by admitting language-specific processing differences in the context of a universal initial cognitive endowment. Specifically, Cutler claims that languages differ in terms of which aspect of the speech signal is the most appropriate in facilitating segmentation prior to lexical access; thus, although the syllable is taken to be a salient aspect of language structure in French, a syllable-timed language, this is definitely not the case in English, a stress-timed language (cf. Cutler, et al., 1986). This is a very different enterprise from seeking to determine language-independent 'units of perception', and it moves attention towards the principles that govern the emergence of language-specific differences and towards potential 'parameter setting' in infancy. Note that both enterprises assume some segmentation of the speech stream into an appropriate form for lexical access to be attempted; in this they differ from the connectionist approach of McClelland and Elman (1986), for instance, who see segmentation as a by-product of lexical access and not as a necessary goal of the processor.

Concern about prelexical representation and lexical access necessarily leads to concern about the form of the representations in the mental lexicon itself, a longstanding central issue in psycholinguistics. The orthodox approach has been to assume that each word has a unique lexical entry, access to which provides information concerning that word's orthography, phonology, syntax, and semantics. This entry is seen as central, and modality independent. Much of the current debate revolves around an alternative to the orthodox approach—the connectionist claim that a lexical entry is no more than the ensemble of mappings between orthographic, phonological, and semantic representations (Seidenberg & McClelland, 1989). The study of the representation of complex words—words containing more than one morpheme—represents a challenge to both approaches. The formal study of morphology reveals the rule-governed structure of complex words, together with its interaction with other levels of description; how is this structure reflected in the storage and processing of these words, in their lexical entries?

Lorraine Tyler and colleagues consider this question from the orthodox perspective of abstract lexical entries with internal structure (stems and affixes) (see Seidenberg (1989) for a review of the reading of complex words from an alternative, connectionist, approach). In this general area progress has, until recently, been relatively limited, perhaps because of the lack of sufficiently sensitive experimental techniques, or perhaps simply because of the lack of the critical data necessary to distinguish between alternative models. Research generated by the 'classical' (i.e. non-connectionist) models has concentrated on derivational morphology, revealing a relationship in storage between related words (e.g. Bradley, 1980) and suggesting a variety of processing architectures to reflect this fact (e.g. Taft, 1991). Recently, further progress has been made, and this is exemplified by Tyler et al.'s contribution to this volume, and by Cristina Burani's commentary. The former makes use of *repetition priming*: a cross-modal priming technique in which, for instance, the word *friendly* is heard and at its offset a lexical decision to the visual word *friend* is measured. Tyler et al. present data in the context of the Cohort model (e.g. Marslen-Wilson, 1987; Marslen-Wilson & Tyler, 1980; Marslen-Wilson, this volume), in which the processor attempts to isolate the discrete abstract representation of one (complex) word from the rest of the words in the lexicon—the most relevant competitors in the cases considered by Tyler being morphologically related words. At issue here are central, modality-independent lexical representations—the entries in the mental lexicon—rather than input representations that are specific to the spoken or written language.

The strength of Tyler's approach is in the comprehensive manipulation of semantic transparency and phonological relatedness. Researchers approaching morphology from a connectionist perspective (e.g. Rumelhart & McClelland, 1986; Seidenberg & McClelland, 1989; see also Taft, 1991), and who eschew discrete abstract lexical entries, will find no initial comfort in some of the data presented here, notably the finding that there is no priming between derived words that share a stem (such as *confessor* and *confession*). At first sight this apparent insulation of the semantics of same-stem derived words is surprising, given that so much of their meaning is similar if not identical. From the perspective of diachronic language change, however, semantic drift between morphologically related words (*committee, commission, commit, committal* . . .) is common and we should perhaps expect processing to reflect or allow this. Tyler et al.'s model of the storage of complex words (that is, their central lexical entries, not the modality specific access representations) involves shared stems, and accommodates these data by assuming inhibitory connections between suffixes. Thus there is priming between words when one is a stem, but priming is disallowed when both are derived words. The speed and sensitivity of the processor are once again in evidence, with the apparently immediate deactivation of inappropriate semantic representations on the strength of a spoken suffix alone. These data establish the merits of the repetition priming technique in investigating morphology, and should provoke the interest of those concerned with formal accounts of morphology and its computational modelling. Crucial representational issues are also raised, such as the status of shared stems when different semantics are implied by the suffix.

Burani, in her commentary on the chapter by Tyler et al., provides a wide-ranging discussion of aspects of the relationship between formal linguistic accounts of morphology and psychological accounts of the processing of derived words. She considers, for instance, the relationship between the productivity of a particular suffix and the actual number of words in the lexicon manifesting that suffix; the relationship between the two is not simply predictable. Burani emphasises the usefulness of detailed statistics concerning the occurrence of particular affixes and affix-like strings in the language (perhaps prefiguring an explicit computational account), and the need to take such statistics into account when generating stimulus materials for psycholinguistic experiments. Burani also contrasts the decompositional model proposed by Tyler et al. with the predictions of a non-decompositional model. It could be argued that in representing complex words, decomposition along morphological lines must be reflected at some level (even if it is in terms of the weighted relationships between stored complex forms). It seems inescapable that there is more structure in the behaviour of derived words than is sketched out in the initial experiments reported by Tyler; it remains to be seen whether the metaphors of discrete storage and decomposition are sufficient to capture this behaviour in interesting ways.

Both Tyler et al. and Burani concentrate on the processing of derived words (*confession, courteous, friendly*), but there are clear implications for the processing of inflected word forms (*confessing, walked*) as well. The chapter by Richard Shillcock and Ellen Bard is relevant in this regard: they claim that the results of processing the syntactic context are available in the early stages of the recognition of function words. It is only a short step to making the same claim for the perception of inflectional affixes, and possibly also the perception of derivational affixes. A comprehensive model of the representation of complex words will need to address the relationship between such representations and syntactic processes.

INTERACTION AND VARIATION IN LEXICAL PROCESSING

The chapters in this section deal with issues of competition among candidates at a lexical level of representation. The concern is principally with the architecture of the processor and with the nature of the representations. Word recognition may be seen as the matching of some pattern in the input against a representation among the, perhaps, 50,000 words in the mental lexicon. This matching is usually synchronous with the left-to-right accumulation of the critical information in the input (Marslen-Wilson, 1985). What sort of processing architecture could subserve this? Given that lexical representations mediate between sublexical and post-lexical (syntactic, semantic, etc.) processing, how might this be reflected in the representation of each individual word?

Shillcock and Bard address these issues in the context of claims for modularity in language processing, and in particular the informational encapsulation of lexical access from syntax. The last decade of psycholinguistic research has been dominated by the issue of modularity (see, for instance, Garfield, 1987): the notion that the language processor is composed of modules, each of which is responsible for a strictly defined function and is only allowed access to strictly defined sorts of information (Fodor, 1983). This notion is also observed in formal linguistics and in philosophical approaches to cognition. Of all of the proposed characteristics of modules (speed, automaticity, mandatory processing, fixed neural architectures . . .) the one that has most attracted the attention of psycholinguists has been that of informational encapsulation: the proposal that each module has a clearly defined input and output, and any other type of information simply has no access to the internal workings of that module. The paradigmatic example is the lexical access module, which has been demonstrated to be surprisingly immune to anything but the acoustic input. Thus, for instance, there is a robust finding that all of the meanings of *rose* ('flower', 'stood') are activated on hearing *they all rose*; information about the syntactic context of *rose* is apparently ignored in lexical access, and may only be brought to bear subsequently to select one of the meanings of the ambiguous word that has been activated (Swinney, 1979; Tannenhaus, Leiman, & Seidenberg, 1979). A goal of many studies over the last few years has been to devise stimulus materials that nonetheless show that the lexical access module *does* have limited access to information other than that contained within the auditory input. Few experiments have permitted claims that the informational encapsulation of lexical access is not complete (e.g. Blütner & Sommer, 1988; Tabossi, 1988).

Shillcock and Bard demonstrate that lexical access is apparently informed by higher-level processing at least in the case of closed-class words—that is, the grammatical words such as *would* and *you*—or more specifically, those homophones like *wood/would* or *mine/mine* where one of the candidates is a closed-class word. When *would* is heard, it simply does not access *wood* if the sentential context effectively selects a closed-class word. Attention naturally turns to the computational nature of the architecture that allows this limited interaction. In fact, the experiments reported were prompted by the suggestion by Tanenhaus and Lucas (1987) that informational encapsulation simply reflects the fact that a particular interaction is computationally unattractive: if higher-level processing selects for a noun, then this information is of little initial use given the enormous number of nouns in the lexicon, but if it selects for a pronoun, then this is very useful information—there are only a few pronouns, and it potentially allows the listener to distinguish *you* from *ewe*.

This chapter, as well as those by Tyler et al. and Marslen-Wilson, presents data involving the sudden and complete suppression of the semantic activation corresponding to a particular word. Past models, such as TRACE (McClelland & Elman, 1986) have represented such data in terms of lateral inhibition within a level of representation, and excitatory connections between different levels. Shillcock and Bard propose a model in which information encapsulation is broached by excitatory connections from higher-level processing into the lexicon, supporting a particular closed-class lexical candidate. Marslen-Wilson, in contrast, proposes direct inhibitory connections between sub-lexical and lexical levels, capable of quickly quashing the activation of a lexical candidate. He also presents data that argue against lateral inhibition within the lexical level. An issue for the future will be to clarify the role of inhibition within models employing the activation metaphor. Nevertheless these chapters demonstrate that it is possible for single psycholinguistic experiments to address wider issues in the functional architecture of cognition in a surprisingly direct way.

The second contribution in this section focuses explicitly on the mapping between acoustic input and lexical representations. This chapter, by William Marslen-Wilson, continues recent work on issues of representation and process in lexical access (cf. Marslen-Wilson, 1989), asking how it is that one can resolve the dilemma of requiring lexical access to behave robustly in the face of lawful phonological variation (*handbag* may be produced as *hambag*, for instance) and random noise in the speech signal, but still be sensitive to phonological mismatch between the input and stored lexical representations. Marslen-Wilson reports results demonstrating that the processor is surprisingly rapid in deactivating semantic representations when the speech input departs only marginally from the expected pronunciation of the word: an incomplete word, such as /fli/ activates *fleet*, but a minimal departure from the required pronunciation, as in pronouncing *sausage* as *sausis*, produces no semantic activation of the distorted word's associates by the end of that word. Marslen-Wilson offers a solution to the earlier dilemma by suggesting a model that allows immediate inhibition of the representation of a word by the mismatching input, and in which the phonological representation of the word is *underspecified*—default phonological information is simply not represented in the specification of a lexical entry. This continues earlier work by Lahiri and Marslen-Wilson (1991) and offers answers to the question 'What is a lexical representation actually like?'. A challenge emerges for connectionist models of lexical access to capture both the underspecified representations suggested by Marslen-Wilson and Lahiri, and the fast inhibition due to mismatch. The model poses a dilemma, however: on the one hand, the lexical representation of *sweet* is required to be underspecified with respect to the place of articulation of the /t/, thus permitting activation of *sweet* by /swik/ as in *sweet girl* (in which assimilation may turn the /t/ into a /k/); on the other hand, data is presented showing that *streak* (possibly representing an assimilated token of *street*) does not prime *road*. Perhaps the processor employs a finer grain representation than the phonemes used here to represent assimilation; perhaps different processing strategies emerge when recognising words in continuous speech (as opposed to isolated words), with some complex interaction (currently unspecified in the model) between the adjacent (subsequent) context and the activation/inhibition of the previous critical word.

Marslen-Wilson's data are relevant to any model of word recognition that views recognition as coming about through the accumulation of evidence in left-to-right fashion as the speech signal is processed. Tabossi, in her commentary on recent related work by Marslen-Wilson and colleagues, considers in more detail some consequences of such left-to-right processing, and presents data on the circumstances in which *mis*-segmentation of the speech stream occurs. Her data, from Italian-speaking subjects, suggest that the processor cannot necessarily recognise word junctures, and consequently the material following the juncture may be used both to select among the cohort of candidates initiated some time before the juncture, and to initiate a *new* cohort of candidates whose onsets are compatible with this post-juncture material. These data pose a challenge to strictly left-to-right models because a degree of parallelism is required in order to capture the dual function of the speech input (that is, its function in constraining existing hypotheses and spawning new ones).

In this volume, Marslen-Wilson develops the Cohort model by consigning competition between activated lexical entries to a later decision stage, and by introducing a distinction between first-pass and second-pass processing. Both these additions have implications for the interpretation of lexical access data. For instance, when we hear the distorted word *apricod* it is apparent that it is derived from *apricot*, yet it is suggested that we should regard this recognition as a second-pass effect; the first pass effect (a surprising absence of semantic priming) is the one that current models of lexical access should strive to reflect. The suggestion is that TRACE confounds first- and second-pass processing. The second-pass processes—perhaps involving a loosening of the criteria for recognition—may not necessarily fall out of existing models of (first-pass) lexical access, and perhaps should be characterised by the directing of conscious attention to the process. A further implication of the revisions to the model would seem to be that absolute reaction times in experiments with auditory stimuli may assume the same importance as in experiments in reading, with differences in absolute time reflecting a difference in the processes being tapped (cf. the chapters in this volume by Dupoux, and by Segui and Grainger). Finally, perhaps the late recognition phenomenon (Bard, Shillcock, & Altmann, 1989) should be reassessed in the light of this distinction between first- and second-pass recognition.

Dennis Norris is similarly concerned with the properties of particular implementations of process models. He presents a detailed exploration of some of the properties of simple connectionist models of word recognition, including a model of lexical access that was presented at the first Sperlonga workshop (Norris, 1990). Some of the properties of these models are demonstrated as part of an important discussion of claims for 'top-down' activation in psychological models, notably the word superiority effect, and Elman and McClelland's (1988) demonstration of phoneme restoration in conjunction with the compensation for coarticulation effect. Norris demonstrates that it is possible to obtain apparent top-down behaviour from a connectionist model that contains only feedforward and delay connections. Because such models learn, it is impossible in practice to prevent 'low level' processes (e.g. phoneme identification) developing sensitivity to structure in the training data that might more parsimoniously be described at a higher level of representation (e.g. lexical context, morphological structure). These simulations force attention to the issues of levels of description and processing, and demonstrate that traditional box-and-arrow models may not trivially be transformed into connectionist models without a careful reappraisal of how the learning process effectively redistributes their functional architecture. They also demonstrate the difficulty of determining the precise generalisations that are acquired by even small connectionist networks of the sort employed by Norris. Patrizia Tabossi, in her commentary on this chapter, questions whether terms such as 'bottom-up', 'top-down', and 'interactive' can usefully be applied to such networks, while agreeing that the simulations do illuminate the original data.

Interpretation of the relationship between a model and real data is more difficult in the case of very small scale simulations. Stronger claims may be made for models in which at least one dimension reflects the true size and complexity of the real world problem, such as the number of entities available at a particular level of representation, or the richness of the training corpus (cf. Seidenberg & McClelland, 1989; Shillcock, Lindsey, Levy & Chater, 1992). Bard and Shillcock suggest that studying the nature of the real world problem (that is, the discriminations that would be required given the actual words in the lexicon) is a necessary prerequisite to building the most parsimonious model of a psychological process. This analysis of the real world problem, which has generally been more explicit in work on vision, for instance, has particular attractions for the study of lexical access, where computerised lexica provide approximate descriptions of one aspect of the real world problem. Identifying one word from tens of thousands of different words is something that can be studied using computerised dictionaries, and there have been an increasing number of such studies over the past decade (see Altmann, 1990, for a review). Bard and Shillcock assess claims about spoken word recognition by looking at the typical cohorts of competitors formed by the entries in a phonemically transcribed dictionary. Various models of word recognition have been advanced to account for observed patterns of competition between activated hypotheses. The authors demonstrate that the typical cohort of words contains a very large proportion of very low frequency words, with fewer and fewer higher frequency words and, very often, an isolated high-frequency outliner. This observation, concerning the typical frequency profile of a word-initial cohort, allows the comprehensive exploration of a minimal model of lexical access in which representations of individual words are activated in proportion to their frequency. This model, together with the observed facts about cohorts, makes a number of predictions about lexical access which were previously captured by special features of the functional architecture of models of word recognition. Of course, care must be taken when generalising from the idealised lexicon inferred from a dictionary. As Tabossi points out in her chapter, it is likely that such dictionaries over-estimate the number of words in any one competitor set, and that, as a consequence, the frequency profile of the psychological cohort may be rather different from that found in the computer simulation. Nonetheless, the data provided by Bard and Shillcock provide an important new perspective on how the structure in the contents of the mental lexicon can constrain the class of model required to explain word recognition phenomena.

SENTENCE-LEVEL PROCESSING

The emphasis thus far has been on studies of some of those components of speech processing that match patterns in the acoustic input against patterns stored in the mental lexicon. The result of this matching process is loosely defined as 'word recognition'. In this section we focus on 'what happens next'. It is a moot point whether processing proceeds by first identifying individual words, and then identifying the syntactic/semantic relations between the words as a prelude to establishing a final representation of the meaning of the utterance, or whether processing proceeds by building partial syntactic/semantic hypotheses on the basis of partial lexical hypotheses (see Thompson & Altmann, 1990, for further discussion). Nonetheless, some higher level representation *is* constructed, and the studies described by Mike Tanenhaus and colleagues, and by Janet Nicol, consider one particular aspect of this construction process.[2] Paradoxically, whereas the studies described earlier have focused on identifying words on the basis of what appears in the speech wave, these studies focus more on those constituents that *do not* appear in a particular part of the input sequence.

Janet Nicol reviews recent work employing cross-modal priming to study sentence processing, and in particular the semantic priming observed at positions which, in some syntactic theories, are defined as containing phonetically null constituents that relate to other constituents in the sentence. The relevant constructions are ones such as *Which boy did you see?* The verb *see* would canonically be followed by the noun that is the object of *see*. In fact, the sentence is analysed as having a null constituent located after *see* ([which boy]$_1$ did you see $_1$?). This particular application of cross-modal priming—apparently demonstrating semantic reactivation of the filler at the point of the gap—has made some of the most provocative

---

[2] In some respects it may be useful to read the chapter by Nicol before that of Tanenhaus et al. The order of the two chapters reflects the close connection between the chapter by Nicol and those by Fodor and by Barss.

recent connections between formal syntactic theory and psycholinguistic studies of processing (cf. Fodor, 1989). Nicol presents data from two new experiments, and draws the controversial conclusion that semantic reactivation in sentence processing may be a function of the assignment of the argument structure (theta roles) of the verb. She points out that in most previous studies the locations of the verb and the trace, or null constituent, were typically adjacent in the stimulus materials, thus making the interpretation of the data particularly difficult with respect to investigating their distinct roles in the processing. She goes on to speculate about some of the precise properties of the stimulus materials that may determine reactivation. The chapter shows very clearly the productivity of this line of research, and suggests its potential to reveal still more about the role of the verb in sentence processing. At the same time, however, what seemed like an attractively simple and concrete relationship between formal syntax and studies of processing—the syntactic gap being almost visibly filled—has apparently become a more complex state of affairs in which it is becoming increasingly difficult to say very much about the initial assignment of constituent structure.

Many of Nicol's conclusions are reinforced by Tanenhaus, Boland, Mauner and Carlson, who present a comprehensive review of sentence processing studies which support the view that access to the argument structure of the verb underlies semantic reactivation phenomena. The claim is that as soon as a verb is recognised the listener/reader has access to the structure of thematic roles usually associated with it. Thus syntactic gaps can be filled in advance (e.g. Tanenhaus, Carlson, & Trueswell, 1989; Tanenhaus, Garnsey, & Boland, 1990). A further claim is that unexpressed, syntactically null arguments will also be incorporated into the interpretation. Tanenhaus and colleagues present evidence that implicit arguments may function anaphorically within discourse. Many of the results referred to have been obtained using self-paced reading in which the subject is required to press a button as soon as the sentence appears to have stopped making sense. The authors discuss the relative merits of this 'low-tech' technique, defending it on the grounds that it gives results that are consonant with a battery of more elaborate techniques.

ISSUES OF PROCESS IN FORMAL LINGUISTICS

The contributions in the previous section by Nicol, and by Tanenhaus et al., address experimental psycholinguistic processing issues in terms of categories from formal linguistics. Indeed, both rely on certain assumptions about the role of formal linguistic descriptions in process models. This relationship—between linguistic description and theories of process—is considered explicitly in the chapters by Janet Fodor, and Andy Barss. Fodor presents an extensive discussion of the syntactic argumentation necessary to interpret the body of data on semantic reactivation by empty categories and, more generally, to frame a testable hypothesis concerning syntactic processing. Specifically, she discusses the possibilities of capturing observed priming differences between different sorts of empty categories in terms of the levels of structure recognised by Government Binding (GB) theory; the central claim is that *wh*-traces, unlike the other empty categories, are realised at the level of Phonetic Form. *Wh*-traces give the most robust reactivation effects of any of the null constituents, and they also, alone of the null constituents, veto *wanna*-contraction—the (lexicalised) phonological reduction of a closed-class word (*want to* being reduced, for instance, to *wanna*). Fodor's chapter demonstrates the rigour necessary to frame a hypothesis that potentially provides data for or against a particular formal analysis. Specifically, she suggests that subject *wh*-traces in subordinate clauses offer critical data that will arbitrate between GB and Generalised Phrase Structure Grammar analyses.

Fodor's position assumes that there is a more or less transparent relationship between the processor and the grammar, so that any observable isomorphism between the processing data and a particular formal analysis would be evidence in favour of that analysis, compared to some alternative analysis for which no isomorphism exists. The importance she attaches to the relationship between psycholinguistic experimentation and formal syntax is echoed in the extensive commentary on her chapter by Barss, who examines closely each part of the syntactic argumentation, with particular emphasis on function word contraction. He argues, contrary to Fodor, that GB theory has a better account of the data than GPSG. The final chapter in this section, by Ivan Sag and Janet Fodor, defends Fodor's initial claim concerning GPSG and the empty category data, and in doing so, provides further insight into the nature of the debates that drive linguistic theory.

As stated at the outset, one of the aims of this series has been to highlight examples of constructive interaction across the disciplines. The dialogue between Fodor, Barss, and Sag, based on the empirical data concerning the progressing of simple categories, is an example of such interaction. What started as empirical evidence concerning the psychological reality of empty categories, rapidly became the focus for a re-examination of formal linguistic theory. This led, in turn, to new insights, which have spawned novel empirical predictions. Taken together, these chapters provide the reader with a stimulating insight into the relationship between experimental psycholinguistics and formal syntax, with the contrast between the GPSG and GB perspectives providing a sobering note on the possibility of using psycholinguistic data to arbitrate between different grammatical formalisms.

PROCESSING WRITTEN WORDS

It is unsurprising that in a volume primarily concerned with the processing of speech, the majority of chapters address issues of *spoken* language. However, consideration of written language can never be far away: the ubiquitous cross-modal priming task relies on the identification of a *written* stimulus: there are phonological effects in reading—that is, the spoken form of a word influences recognition of the written form (Meyer, Schvaneveldt, & Ruddy, 1974); the issue of competition between similar lexical candidates straddles the two modalities (the subject of considerable discussion in the first Cognitive Models volume). Moreover, there is a continuing debate on whether a 'lexical entry' should be seen as a modality-independent abstract entity, or as no more than the collection of mappings between orthographic, phonological, and semantic representations. This volume closes with two chapters which primarily address effects in visual word recognition. Ken Forster reviews form priming and interference effects in the reading of single words preceded by a rapidly presented single word or nonword. He concentrates on the often conflicting data on lexical neighbourhood density effects: the extent to which the perception of a word is conditioned by the number of closely similar words in the lexicon. A number of experiments are reported, which tease apart the different levels of representation at which the effects potentially occur, from low-level spatial representations, to more abstract graphemic representations, to lexical representations themselves.

The same issue of neighbourhood effects is addressed in the final chapter by Juan Segui and Jonathan Grainger: first in the course of an investigation into the reading of single, isolated words, and second in a consideration of word priming studies. They conclude that an interactive-activation framework (McClelland & Rumelhart, 1981) best describes data from a very wide range of visual word recognition and priming studies, but with certain exceptions. In general, however, their perspective coincides with the basic models of spoken word recognition advanced in previous chapters, in which competition between similar lexical hypotheses is determined by the precise degree of similarity, and by word frequency. Although neither contribution is primarily concerned with models of speech processing, the considerable overlap in issues is clear, as is the common use of the activation metaphor in processing. In the discussion of neighbourhood effects, reference may usefully be made to the chapter by Bard and Shillcock on the distribution of word frequencies within the lexicon.

Is there any unifying theme that emerges from the chapters reviewed here? A pervasive concern in many of the chapters is with the principled competition between entities within a particular level of representation.

Thus, for instance, in the chapter by Marslen-Wilson specific claims are made about the absence of lateral inhibitory connections between the representations of words at the lexical level; one particular representation of a word comes to dominate the others as a result of the inhibition of the opposition by lower-level information. In the chapters addressing morphology, the focus narrows down on the interaction of morphologically related words. There is a similar concern with interlexical competition in the chapters by Bard and Shillcock on closed-class words and the nature of typical cohorts. The two chapters on visual word recognition are centrally concerned with the functional architectures that underlie priming and interference effects. In the chapters on infant speech perception, there is interest in the way in which the emerging representation of the phonology of the ambient language may condition which perceptual contrasts survive, and which are assimilated to the developing system. Finally, the chapter by Norris is directly concerned with understanding interaction within and between levels of representation. For the most part, such discussions envisage interactive-activation architectures in which there exist simple inhibitory links between local representations. The chapter by Norris demonstrates the difficulties involved in moving to distributed representations and then investigating the resulting functional architecture. When the data suggest that there are influences external to the level in question, then the issue moves from one of specifying the details of intra-level competition, and becomes one of modularity and informational encapsulation: do other levels of representation influence the level in question?

The remaining chapters, which fall outside this theme, are all nonetheless intimately concerned with levels of representation. Dupoux and Cutler discuss whether a syllabic level of prelexical representation should be established. Nicol, and Tanenhaus, et al., in the sentence-processing contributions, suggest the early involvement in parsing of information concerning the argument structure of a verb. Barss, Fodor, and Sag, debate the level of formal grammatical description at which certain processing phenomena should be captured. These converging concerns underline the increasing interaction between the different disciplines involved, and they indicate the progress that has been made in the development of, as well as the direction of future research in, cognitive models of speech processing.

REFERENCES

Altmann, G.T.M. (1990). Lexical statistics and cognitive models of speech processing. In G.T.M. Altmann (Ed.), *Cognitive models of speech processing: Psycholinguistic and computational perspectives.* Cambridge, MA: MIT Press/Bradford Books.

Bard, E.G., Shillcock, R.C., & Altmann, G.T.M. (1989). The recognition of words after their acoustic offset: Effect of subsequent context. *Perception and Psychophysics, 44,* 395–408.

Blutner, R., & Sommer, R. (1988). Sentence processing and lexical access: The influence of the focus-identifying task. *Journal of Memory and Language, 27,* 359–367.

Bradley, D. (1980). Lexical representation of derivational relation. In M. Aronoff & M-L Kean (Eds), *Juncture.* Saratoga, CA: Anma Libri.

Cutler, A., Mehler, J., Norris, D., & Segui, J. (1986). The syllable's differing role in the segmentation of French and English. *Journal of Memory and Language, 25,* 385–400.

Elman, J., & McClelland, J.L. (1988). Cognitive penetration of the mechanisms of perception: Compensation for coarticulation of lexically restored phonemes. *Journal of Memory and Language, 27,* 143–165.

Fodor, J.A. (1983). Modularity of mind. Cambridge, MA: MIT Press.

Fodor, J.D. (1989). Empty categories in sentence processing. *Language and Cognitive Processes, 4*(3/4), SI 155–210.

Garfield, J. (Ed.). (1987). *Modularity in knowledge representation and natural language understanding.* Cambridge, MA: MIT Press.

Lahiri, A., & Marslen-Wilson, W.D. (1991). The mental representation of lexical form: A phonological approach to the recognition lexicon. *Cognition, 38,* 245–294.

Marslen-Wilson, W.D. (1985). Speed shadowing and speech comprehension. *Speech Communication, 4,* 55–73.

Marslen-Wilson, W.D. (:1987). Functional parallelism in spoken word recognition. *Cognition, 25,* 71–102.

Marlsen-Wilson, W.D. (Ed.). (1989). *Lexical representation and process.* Cambridge, MA: MIT Press.

Marslen-Wilson, W.D., & Tyler, L.K. (1980). The temporal structure of spoken language understanding. *Cognition, 8,* 1–71.

McClelland, J.L., & Elman, J.L. (1986). The TRACE model of speech perception. *Cognitive Psychology, 18,* 1–86.

McClelland, J.L., & Rumelhart, D.E. (1981). An interactive-activation model of context effects in letter perception. Part 1: An account of basic findings. *Psychological Review, 88,* 375–405.

Mehler, J., Bertoncini, J., Barriere, M., & Jassik-Gerschenfeld, D. (1978). Infant recognition of mother's voice. *Perception, 7,* 491–7.

Mehler, J., Domergues, J.Y., Frauenfelder, U., & Segui, J. (1981). The syllable's role in speech segmentation. *Journal of Verbal Learning and Verbal Behaviour, 20,* 298–305.

Mehler, J., Dupoux, E., & Segui, J. (1990). Constraining models of lexical access: The onset of word recognition. In G.T.M. Altmann (Ed.), *Cognitive models of speech processing* (pp. 236–262). Cambridge, MA: MIT Press.

Meyer, D.M., Schvaneveldt, R.W., & Ruddy, M.G. (1974). Functions of graphemic and phonemic codes in visual word recognition. *Memory & Cognition, 2,* 309–321.

Norris, D. (1990). A Dynamic-Net model of human speech recognition. In G.T.M. Altmann (Ed.), *Cognitive models of speech processing.* Cambridge, MA: MIT Press.

Sebastián-Gallés, N., Dupoux, E., Segui, J., & Mehler, J. (1992). Contrasting syllabic effects in Catalan and Spanish. *Journal of Memory and Language, 31,* 18–32.

Segui, J., Dupoux, E., & Mehler, J. (1990). The role of the syllable in speech segmentation, phoneme identification, and lexical access. In G.T.M. Altmann (Ed.), *Cognitive models of speech processing* (pp. 263–280). Cambridge, MA: MIT Press.

Seidenberg, M.S. (1989). Reading complex words. In G. Carlson & M. Tanenhaus (Eds.), *Linguistic structure in language processing.* Dordrecht, The Netherlands: Kluwer.

Seidenberg, M.S., & McClelland, J.L. (1989). A distributed, developmental model of word recognition and naming. *Psychological Review, 96,* 523–568.

Shillcock, R.C., Lindsey, G., Levy, J., & Chater, N. (1992). A phonologically motivated input representation for the modelling of auditory word perception in continuous speech. *Proceedings of the Cognitive Science Society Conference*. Hillsdale, NJ: Lawrence Erlbaum Associates Inc.

Streeter, L.A. (1976). Language perception of two-month old infants shows effects of both innate mechanisms and experience. *Nature, 259*, 39–41.

Swinney, D.A. (1979). Lexical access during sentence comprehension: (Re)considerations of context effects. *Journal of Verbal Learning and Verbal Behavior, 18*, 645–659.

Taft, M. (1991). *Reading and the mental lexicon*. Hove, UK: Lawrence Erlbaum Associates Ltd.

Tanenhaus, M.K., Carlson, G., & Trueswell, J.C. (1989). The role of thematic structures in interpretation and parsing. *Language and Cognitive Processes, 4*,(3/4), SI 211–234.

Tanenhaus, M.K., Garnsey, S.M., & Boland, J. (1990). Combinatory lexical information and language comprehension. In G.T.M. Altmann (Ed.), *Cognitive models of speech processing: Psycholinguistic and computational perspectives* Cambridge, MA: MIT Press/ Bradford Books.

Tanenhaus, M.K., Leiman, J.M., & Seidenberg, M.S. (1979). Syntactic context and lexical access. *Quarterly Journal of Experimental Psychology, 36A*, 649–661.

Tanenhaus, M.K., & Lucas, M.M. (1987). Context effects in lexical processing. *Cognition, 25*, 213–234.

Thompson, H.S., & Altmann, G.T.M. (1990). Modularity compromised—Selecting partial hypotheses. In G.T.M. Altmann (Ed.), *Cognitive models of speech processing: Psycholinguistic and computational perspectives*, Cambridge, MA: MIT Press/Bradford Books.

Modelling Acquisition

2

Introduction to the Chapters by Werker and Jusczyk

Rachel K. Clifton
Department of Psychology, University of Massachusetts, USA.

The two decades of research on infant speech perception (1971–1991) have moved us from almost total ignorance to a solid basis for understanding the origin and development of this important ability. The classic paper by Eimas and colleagues (Eimas, Siqueland, Jusczyk, & Vigorito, 1971) not only presented startling data concerning very young infants' discriminative abilities, but also raised many of the issues that have occupied researchers ever since. For example, one unexpected finding was the absence of age differences in performance between 1 and 4 months; the younger group was equally adept at discriminating the contrasts. In the present decade the age range has been extended to newborns, and they too show remarkable powers of discrimination (Bertoncini, Bijeljac-Babic, Blumstein, & Mehler, 1987). In retrospect, we should not have been surprised that this ability developed early because the human auditory system is remarkably mature at birth (Bredburg, 1985), and begins to function *in utero* at around 30 weeks gestation (for a review, see Rubel, Born, Deitch, & Durham, 1984).

Perhaps the most surprising aspect of infant speech perception emerged when researchers began to fill in the details of infants' basic abilities. Eimas and colleagues chose VOT as the departure point, but by the end of the first decade we knew that infants could discriminate contrasts from languages to which they had never been exposed. This result had two telling implications: it destroyed the notion that exposure to speech contrasts was necessary to induce and foster discriminative abilities, and it raised several questions concerning the subsequent loss of these abilities. It is readily observed that adults have lost the ability to make some non-native discriminations (though under certain manipulations, described in Werker's chapter in this volume, discrimination is possible). Werker and Jusczyk have led the field in posing and answering such questions as: When are the early abilities lost? Is the loss truly permanent? What is the nature of the loss? What produces the loss? Werker and colleagues have established two notable characteristics of this loss; first, it takes place very early in life, as young as 10 months of age, and second, the loss is fairly abrupt within an individual, taking place over a period of about three months. This pattern of loss in discriminative abilities suggests that an active, but still unspecified, process interferes with the maintenance of the discrimination. A gradual fading of discrimination over several years would have implied a natural waning of unused abilities, in much the same way that motor skills decline if unused. Werker's term 'perceptual reorganisation' captures the sense of this rapid shift in the ability to detect differences in non-native contrasts.

When considering this loss, we should remember (and Werker reminds us) that not every non-native contrast gets 'reorganised' in the same way. The work of Best and colleagues with Zulu clicks is a theoretically interesting example (Best, McRoberts, & Sithole, 1988). These authors suggested that this discrimination is not lost because it is not assimilable to English phonology, and is therefore spared because it is not processed as speech. In a critical review of the cross-language literature, Burnham (1986) proposed that some contrasts, which he labelled 'fragile', are lost in infancy if they are not experienced at that time, whereas other contrasts, labelled 'robust', are not lost until early childhood (4–8 years). Furthermore, the latter can easily be retrained at older ages, whereas the former cannot. Burnham suggested that robust contrasts may have more distinct psychoacoustic cues, as well as participation in more allophonic variation in the person's native language. Whether or not one agrees with Burnham, his distinction stresses that care must be taken in selecting the particular non-native contrasts in cross-language research, because general conclusions cannot be drawn on the basis of one or two contrasts.

An aspect of the early loss that bears investigation is whether early retraining in the second or third year of life would resurrect even the 'fragile' contrasts normally lost by 12 months. Werker and colleagues have found ingenious ways to show that adults' ability to discriminate certain non-native contrasts is not lost forever, but rather is dependent on context (phonemic, phonetic, acoustic), and short-term memory load (Werker & Tees, 1984). Nevertheless, adults do show a permanent loss in phonemic discrimination of certain non-native contrasts. Given that a discriminative loss is apparent by 12–14 months of age, the question arises as to whether early retraining during the preschool years might reverse the trend and prevent the permanent loss seen in adults. If so, a description of the type and amount of exposure necessary to retrain preschoolers could aid our understanding of what the nature of the early loss is, and what produces it.

Both Werker and Jusczyk propose reasonable processes that constrain and manipulate perceptual reorganisation. Werker evaluates four alternative mechanisms, which are not mutually exclusive. Of these, cognitive recategorisation seems to be both the most difficult to prove, and the most difficult to rule out; these qualities can mislead researchers for years along unprofitable lines of study, so caution is advised. The claim is that perceptual reorganisation of speech contrasts is related to, and perhaps dependent on, other emerging cognitive abilities. Lalonde and Werker (described in Werker's chapter in this volume) tested 40 9-month-olds and found that the same infants were apt to pass an object search task and a visual categorisation task, and to fail at discrimination of non-native contrasts. However, this coincidence does not prove that these tasks are based on a common cognitive process; these three abilities could emerge from independent processes that have similar maturational timetables. On the other hand, articulatory mediation, for which Werker finds some support, should be reconsidered in light of a recent report in *Science* (Petitto & Marentette, 1991) showing that articulatory mechanisms are not necessary for language acquisition in infancy. Deaf children of deaf parents begin signing around 10–14 months of age, displaying 'manual babbling' at around the same age as verbal babbling appears in hearing children. These new data will impact on our theorising about language acquisition, although they do not preclude a role for articulatory mediation in the hearing child's language acquisition.

Both Werker and Jusczyk support the view that general auditory abilities, either alone or in concert with broad phonetic abilities, are responsible for the remarkable discriminative powers of the very young infant. Werker does not rule out any of the four alternatives she discusses, while Jusczyk develops a model that emphasises the importance of infants' sensitivity to the sound structure of the native language. One strength of Jusczyk's WRAPSA model is that it makes the step toward explaining how the infant segments and recognises words in the sound stream. There has been a great need for models that carry development beyond the initial stages, and one can only applaud the efforts being made toward this goal. Surely the third decade of infant speech perception research will close the gap in explaining how these infant abilities are related to language acquisition and production.

REFERENCES

Bertoncini, J., Bijeljac-Babic, R., Blumstein, S., & Mehler, J. (1987). Discrimination in neonates of very short CVs. *Journal of The Acoustical Society of America, 82*, 31–37.

Best, C., McRoberts, G., & Sithole, N. (1988). The phonological basis of perceptual loss for non-native contrasts: Maintenance of discrimination among Zulu clicks by English-speaking adults and infants. *Journal of Experimental Psychology: Human Perception & Performance, 14*, 345–360.

Bredberg, G. (1985). The anatomy of the developing ear. In S.E. Trehub & B. Schneider (Eds.), *Auditory development in infancy*, (pp. 3–20). New York: Plenum Press.

Burnham, D. (1986). Developmental loss of speech perception: Exposure to and experience with a first language. *Applied Psycholinguistics, 7*, 207–240.

Eimas, P., Siqueland, S., Jusczyk, P., & Vigorito, J. (1971). Speech perception in infants. *Science, 171*, 303–306.

Petitto, L., & Marentette, P. (1991). Babbling in the manual mode: Evidence for the ontogeny of language. *Science, 251*, 1493–1496.

Rubel, E., Born, E., Deitch, J., & Durham, O. (1984). Recent advances toward understanding auditory system development. In C. Berlin (Ed.), *Hearing science: Recent advances*, (pp. 109–157). San Diego, CA: College Hill Press.

Werker, J., & Tees, R. (1984). Phonemic and phonetic factors in adult cross-language speech perception. *Journal of The Acoustical Society of America, 75*, 1866–1878.

3

How Word Recognition May Evolve from Infant Speech Perception Capacities

Peter W. Jusczyk
Department of Psychology, State University of New York at Buffalo, Buffalo, NY 14260, USA.

INTRODUCTION

When the field of infant speech perception research began, a little over 20 years ago, the central questions concerned the nature of the basic perceptual capacities. Could nonspeaking infants even perceive differences between speech sounds? If so, then how does their sensitivity to speech contrasts compare to adults? What role does experience with learning a particular language play in perceiving speech? The answer to the first of these questions came from the very first studies in the area, which demonstrated that infants are capable of perceiving contrasts between syllables that differ in as little as a single phonetic feature (e.g. Eimas, Siqueland, Jusczyk, & Vigorito, 1971; Moffit, 1971; Morse, 1972; Trehub, 1973). In the interim, considerable information has been gained about the second of these issues as well. For example, it has been shown that infants are able to adjust to changes in speaking voice (e.g. Kuhl, 1979; 1983) and speaking rate (Eimas & Miller, 1981) at a very early age and can detect contrasts in different positions within utterances (e.g. Goodsitt, Morse, Ver Hoove, & Cowan, 1984; Jusczyk, 1977; Jusczyk & Thompson, 1978). Although current methodology does not permit a detailed comparison of just how sensitive infants' capacities in these domains are relative to adults', there seems to be reasonable match at a gross level.

The third question, concerning the role of experience, has shifted ground since the earliest studies. Initially, interest in the role of experience in speech perception came up in discussions of whether infant speech perception capacities were innate or not. This issue was addressed by examining the ability of infants to perceive contrasts from foreign languages (e.g. Aslin, Pisoni, Hennessy, & Perey, 1981; Cutting & Eimas, 1975; Lasky, Syrdal-Lasky, & Klein, 1975; Streeter, 1976; Trehub, 1976; Werker, Gilbert, Humphrey, & Tees, 1981). These studies along with ones demonstrating that newborn infants could discriminate speech contrasts (e.g. Bertoncini, Bijeljac-Babic, Blumstein, & Mehler, 1987), suggested that the basic capacities function without a prior period of prolonged exposure to language input. More recently, discussions of the role of experience have shifted to a consideration of the impact that the native language has on the development of speech perception capacities (e.g. Best, McRoberts, & Sithole, 1988; Jusczyk, 1985, 1986; Werker, 1991). Because the sound structures of different languages are not the same, infants need to learn about the regularities that characterise their native language. These regularities are important in determining how sounds can be combined to make possible words in the language, in distinguishing among different words, and in specifying boundaries between different words—all of which are needed in order to become a fluent speaker/hearer of the language. Moreover, in normal conversations, speech is transmitted at a much more rapid rate than is typical in most speech perception experiments with infants (where items are often presented in isolation). There is some reason to believe that knowledge of regularities in the sound structure of the native language is critical for segmenting speech and recognising words (e.g. Church, 1987). Therefore, even though speech perception may rely initially on innate capacities, such capacities must eventually be keyed to the sound structure of the native language.

How and when is information about the sound structure of the native language integrated with basic speech perception capacities? Results of the recent studies from our laboratory and other laboratories around the world suggest that, during the first year, sensitivity may develop to the kinds of structural regularities that could support word recognition in the native language. In considering how various components of word recognition could develop from underlying speech perception capacities, I have found it useful to formulate a model that relates the components and how they evolve as language is acquired.

OVERVIEW OF THE WRAPSA MODEL

My focus is on the way that speech perception capacities develop to support word recognition from fluent, continuous speech. I assume that phonological categories evolve as part of the process of learning to recognise words in the native language. Consequently, I have named the model WRAPSA, which is an acronym for *Word Recognition and Phonological Structure Acquisition*. The model itself has two purposes. One is to deal with the various stages of recognising words from the acoustic input. Thus it provides a hypothetical description of what occurs when a mature listener decodes the acoustic signal into words. The other purpose of the model is to provide a framework for investigating the way that word recognition develops in the language learner. The framework stands as an indication of the endpoint of the developmental continuum. Given a description of the initial capacities of the infant, one can then ask about how and when the various elements of the framework become functional during the course of development.

A visual description of the model is shown in Fig. 3.1. The incoming speech signal first undergoes a preliminary analysis by the auditory system. The auditory analysers provide a description of the signal in terms of a set of spectral and temporal features. The analysers always provide a description of the acoustic characteristics of the input. This description is

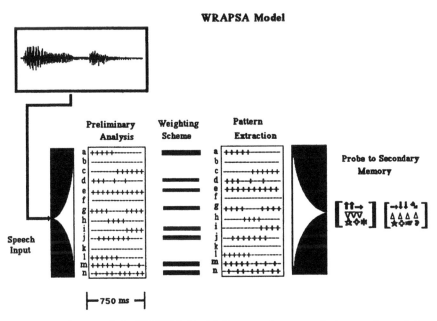

FIG. 3.1   Diagram of the WRAPSA Model. Input to the system is the waveform of the English utterance 'baby'. First stage of processing involves a preliminary analysis of the signal by the analytic processes, which for purposes of description are labelled from 'a' to 'n'. Because the processes are constantly monitoring the input, a continuous reading of the presence of activity is available for a given timeslice, here 750msec. Certain of these processes are more closely monitored than others due to the Weighting Scheme associated with the native language (designated by the bold bars). The sound pattern is extracted from the emphasised processes (in bold face) and then serves as a probe to secondary memory. The bold brackets indicate the stressed syllable, the symbols inside are meant to indicate that some featural description of the sound structure is present, but not one that is explicitly segmented into phones.

neutral with respect to the language spoken. However, once a language has been acquired, then the output of these analysers will be weighted to give prominence to those features that are most critical to making meaningful distinctions between words in that language.

The weighting scheme is essentially a means of setting the attentional focus to these features, and to ignoring ones that do not typically distinguish between words in the language that has been acquired. The weighted input then undergoes a pattern extraction process which further refines the description and attempts to segment it into word-sized units. No attempt is made at this point to recover a description of individual phonetic segments. Instead, the resulting representation of the sound structure of a lexical item is more global. It is marked as to prosodic structure, and to syllables and their prominent characteristics. This representation serves as a probe to the lexicon in secondary memory, where it seeks a match to the representation of the sound structure of a previously stored utterance. If a match is obtained, then its meaning can be accessed and the word is identified. If no match occurs, then the input may be reprocessed, or if the context supplies sufficient information about the meaning of the candidate item, then the representation itself may be stored as a new lexical item. It should be noted that WRAPSA assumes that representations of sound structure of items in the lexicon are not abstract prototypes. Instead, they are representations of items actually encountered in various contexts. Thus, instead of a single abstract description of the sound structure of a lexical item, there are multiple traces of individual instances of the item and matching of candidates is done on the basis of the best fit with these traces.

This description gives a brief indication of how the WRAPSA model is organised. In what follows, the main features of the model are described along with the findings that have led to its development.

PRELIMINARY ANALYSIS OF THE SPEECH SIGNAL

Processing begins when the speech signal is picked up by the auditory system. At this stage, speech sounds are treated no differently than are other kinds of acoustic signals. The signal is transformed by the peripheral auditory system, and passed through an array of analytic processes that yield decisions about the acoustic properties that are present in the signal. These analytic processes provide a description of the signal split into spectral and temporal features. The extraction of these features is spectrally specific in that the auditory analysers are tuned to particular frequency regions (see also Sawusch, 1986).

What kind of analysis of speech is provided at this level? The auditory analysers extract information such as whether or not there is noise present in some region of the spectrum at a given moment of time. Hence, they indicate at what frequencies there is evidence of acoustic energy. They also provide information about the nature of the noise source—whether it is periodic or aperiodic. Durations and intensities of the components of the noise, and their relative bandwidths are also noted. In addition, the analysers are sensitive to the presence, direction and degree of any spectral changes. Extraction of features takes place independently for each spectrally specific analyser. However some temporal tagging of features that occur in the same syllable-sized unit also takes place. In effect, the syllables constitute the elementary temporal slices for the input.

As Mehler, Dupoux, and Segui (1990) have noted, temporal normalisation of speech is crucial to categorising distinctions that depend on durational cues. They argue further that it is hard to see how to account for temporal normalisation of speech without assuming that syllables are the basic processing units. They point out that one could arrive at an indication of speaking rate by averaging the duration of syllables. By factoring out speaking rate, the listener could then correctly identify such items as [ba] and [wa] that depend on durational differences in initial positions. Moreover, the notion that syllables are basic units of organisation in perception also has empirical support in studies with adults (e.g. Cutler, Mehler, Norris & Segui, 1986; Mehler, Dommergues, Frauenfelder, & Segui, 1981) and with infants (e.g. Bertoncini & Mehler, 1981; Bertoncini et al., 1988). Finally, it is interesting to note that many theorists have argued that the syllable plays a pivotal role in the way that prosodic variables (such as rhythm, stress, and tone) are organised in speech (e.g. Goldsmith, 1976; Liberman & Prince, 1977; Selkirk, 1984).

The analytic processes provide a great deal of fine-grained information that can be used in discriminating different sounds. These processes serve as the most basic level of analysis. As such, they constitute sensory limits on the perception of speech and nonspeech sounds. They provide the dimensions along which acoustic signals can be arranged and classified. They are an important part of the infant's innate endowment for speech perception. It is these capacities that are usually tapped in speech perception experiments with young infants. In fact, most of the results with infants six months of age or younger can be explained with reference to such mechanisms (Jusczyk, 1986; Studdert-Kennedy, 1986). For example, consider the well-known capacities of infants to make fine distinctions between different speech syllables (e.g. Eimas et al., 1971; Eimas, 1974, 1975). It is not necessary that an infant perceive the syllable, [ba], as consisting of two phonetic segments, [b] and [a], and the syllable, [pa], as [p] and [a], and then conclude that there is a difference in the initial segments. Rather, to register a distinction between two syllables, it is sufficient to detect a mismatch in the way in which some of the auditory analysers react to each of the sounds. Moreover, given the results of studies showing that infants can discriminate contrasts that do not occur in the ambient language of their home environment (e.g. Lasky et al., 1975; Streeter, 1976), it is clear that the perceptual capacities with which they are endowed must be general enough to encompass any natural language. Finally, many of the capacities that have been noted for the infant's perception of speech (e.g. Eimas et al., 1971; Eimas & Miller, 1981; Hirsh-Pasek et al., 1987), apparently have counterparts in the perception of nonspeech (e.g. Jusczyk & Krumhansl, 1991; Jusczyk, Rosner, Reed & Kennedy, 1989; Jusczyk et al., 1983; Krumhansl & Jusczyk, 1990). Consequently, it seems likely that general auditory mechanisms such as the analytic processes, underlie the perception of speech and nonspeech sounds in this early period of development.

The operation of what I am calling the analytic processes makes it possible to account for several other findings in the adult speech perception literature. For instance, it is well-known that the perception of certain speech contrasts (e.g. stop consonants) is categorical, in the sense that listeners are readily able to perceive fine distinctions between sounds from different phoneme categories, like /ba/ and /pa/, but are not able to perceive distinctions between variants from within the same phoneme category, such as two different /pa/'s (e.g. Liberman, Cooper, Shankweiler, & Studdert-Kennedy, 1967; Repp, 1984). At first glance, categorical perception appears to be the result of some sort of sensory limitation on the listener's capacities to resolve within-category differences. Nevertheless, there are situations in which it can be demonstrated that within-category differences are not only detected by the auditory system, but can actually be accessed by the perceiver. Pisoni and Tash (1974) used a same/different reaction time task in which subjects were presented with pairs of items that were: (1) identical; (2) from within the same phonemic category; or (3) from different phonemic categories. Even though subjects were unable to discriminate the within-category pairs, their reaction times for 'same' responses to these items were significantly slower than they were for the identical pairs. This suggests that information about within-category differences was detected by the auditory system, even though subjects were not able to access it to label the items as different. Other researchers have found that there are circumstances in which listeners can access within-category differences. Samuel (1977) used extensive training with his subjects and found that they could learn to resolve very fine distinctions between within-category pairs. Carney, Widin, and Veimeister (1977) obtained similar results when they used a psychophysical test procedure that greatly reduced uncertainty about the stimulus pairs.

The three studies described here show that even though within-category differences are not detected under normal listening conditions, these differences are picked up at some level of auditory processing. It is also clear that information about such differences decays rapidly and is not available for further processing unless extraordinary means are taken. Of course, in the typical conversational situation, one wants to identify the correct phonemic categories as rapidly as possible, and this means ignoring any within-category variation. So it is not surprising that within-category differences do not remain in the system for very long. WRAPSA attributes the capacity to resolve within-category differences to the operation of the analytic processes. Categorisation occurs at the level of pattern extraction.

THE WEIGHTING SCHEME

The analytic processes provide a description of the input. However, because these processes are monitoring an input that is continually changing, the descriptions that they provide are necessarily very short-lived. In addition, because the analytic processes must provide the foundation for the many possible ways in which acoustic signals can be classified by humans, the number of these processes is likely to be great. This places pressure on the perceptual system to recode the input in a more efficient manner. Of course, the most efficient recoding of the signal would be one that preserved only the information critical to making meaningful distinctions in the language, and discarded the rest. In other words, one wants to focus attentional resources on the properties that are relevant for distinguishing among lexical items in the native language. Consequently, during the first few months of life, one expects to find that the processing that occurs for speech and nonspeech is very general and language-neutral. In effect, any pattern extraction that the perceptual system performs on the information available from the analytic processes is done with default settings. One important effect of experience is to refine these settings so as to reflect the structural properties of the native language.

There is evidence to suggest that infants begin to develop a sensitivity to the structural properties of the native language during the first year of life. As noted earlier, Werker and her colleagues report that discriminability of certain foreign language contrasts declines between 6 and 12 months of age. In addition, there are data that suggest that even newborns are sensitive to certain features of their mothers' native language. Mehler and colleagues (1988) found that newborn infants preferred to listen to passages spoken in their mothers' native language as opposed to ones spoken in a foreign language. In this case, it appears that the infants were responding to prosodic characteristics of speech such as the rhythm, intonation, and stress patterns because they showed the same pattern of responding even for low-pass filtered speech. The filtering removed the phonetic content of the speech while leaving the prosody intact. Hence, sensitivity to the prosodic features of the mother's native language may even develop prenatally.

In a setting in which several different languages are spoken, being attuned to the prosodic characteristics of the mother's speech would help to orient the infant to the right sort of input for acquiring the native language. It helps to keep utterances from different languages separate from those of the native language. This may ensure that the infant attends to the right input in trying to learn the structure of the native language. Naturally, the infant must learn more about the actual categories used in the language. With respect to the sound structure of the language, the infant must learn what kinds of sounds can be used to form words in the language, and any constraints that exist on the ordering of constituent sounds in words (i.e. phonotactic constraints). Because the constituent sounds and phonotactic constraints differ from language to language, the infant must discover the ones that apply in the native language.

Results from a recent study in our laboratory (Jusczyk, Friederici, & Wessels, in press) suggest that infants begin the process of learning the nature of the sound categories and phonotactic constraints in the native language during the first year. To explore this issue, we investigated whether and when infants show a preference for listening to unfamiliar items that are potential words in their native language. We used a listening preference procedure (Fernald, 1984; Hirsh-Pasek et al., 1987) to present infants with pre-recorded spoken lists of low-frequency abstract words. From a loudspeaker on one side of the room, the infants heard lists of words from their native language, English, whereas on the other side of the room the words were from an unfamiliar language, Dutch (see Table 3.1 for examples of the lists used). The items were two- or three-syllable words recorded by a bilingual Dutch/English talker. Unfamiliar abstract words were used to ensure that infants would respond to the sound properties of the items rather than to their recognisability. On a given trial, an infant could hear up to 15 different words. More than half of these items were not permissible words in the other language, either because they contained sound categories that could not appear in the other language (e.g. dipthongs are not permissible in Dutch) or because they violated phonotactic constraints in the other language (e.g. the sequence [kn] does not initiate syllables in spoken English, although it does in Dutch). Infants' listening preferences were determined by measuring the average amount of time that they listened to the Dutch and English lists.

Six-month-old American infants showed no clear preference for either type of list. Their average listening times were 9.39sec. for English and 9.14sec for Dutch. However, by 9 months, the American infants displayed a significant preference for the English lists (8.93sec.) over the Dutch lists

TABLE 3.1
Sample Word Lists for Phonotactic Study

English	Dutch
vacate	structuur
avoid	waardig
lengthen	geslacht
brutal	oprecht
jostle	nerveus
trustworthy	efferent
admission	revolutie
thistle	hersteld
exotic	uitsteeksel
lavish	woestyn
abundant	obstructie
jury	eggen
fluctuate	anderzins
usage	verwant
impact	lading

Mean duration (English) = 28.05sec. Mean duration (Dutch) = 28.28sec.

(5.03sec.). As a check to ensure that the infants were responding on the basis of phonetic and phonotactic information, rather than prosodic differences between the English and Dutch words, we ran an additional experiment with low-pass filtered speech. The low-pass filtering left the prosody intact but removed the distinctive phonetic and phonotactic cues. Under these circumstances, the 9-month-olds failed to show a significant preference for the English words. Thus, infants in the original study appear to have been responding to the phonetic and phonotactic features of the utterances. In a third experiment, new lists of English and Dutch words were used. These new lists contained only words that violated the phonotactic constraints of the other language (i.e. the words consisted of sounds that are permissible in the other language—only the sequence of the sounds is impermissible). Once again, the 9-month-old American infants displayed a significant preference for the English (8.67sec.) over the Dutch (6.44sec.) lists. Hence, by 9 months of age, infants appear to have picked up considerable information about the sound properties of potential words in their native language. This information about the sound properties of words in the language is exactly what one needs to be able to extract rapidly from the speech signal.

Thus, although initially the analytic processes provide much fine-grained acoustic detail about the input, the perceptual system is tuned to weigh certain properties more heavily than others in categorising the signal. This tuning of the perceptual system to the structural features of the input language is what I refer to as the 'weighting scheme'. The weighting scheme is a formula or automatic means of setting the focus of attention to properties that are relevant for signalling meaningful distinctions in the language. For instance, in English, voiceless stop consonants occurring in syllable initial positions (e.g. [pa]) are aspirated, whereas voiced stops are not (e.g. [ba]). Thus, attention to whether aspiration is present or not can serve as a cue for distinguishing voiced from voiceless stops. Analytic processes related to the detection of acoustic correlates of aspiration would be among those weighted heavily in the interpretive schemes of English listeners. By comparison, English does not have a distinction between different 'ch' sounds, like the one in Polish between the hard [cz] and soft [ć]. Consequently, analytic processes relating to this distinction would not be weighted heavily in the interpretive schemes of English listeners (though they would receive heavy weightings in interpretive schemes of Polish listeners).

This role for selective attention is similar to one proposed by Nosofsky (1986, 1987; Nosofsky, Clark, & Shin, 1989). Nosofsky's Generalised Context Model for category representation accounts for various phenomena associated with classification behaviour, including recognition judgments and rule-based categorisations. The model claims that selectively attending to a particular dimension distorts the overall psychological space by stretching or shrinking perceptual distances. Distances between points along an attended dimension are stretched (making them more discriminable), whereas distances along unattended dimensions are shrunk (making them less discriminable). Figure 3.2 illustrates how perceptual space may be distorted when comparing some simple figures along a particular dimension.

The notions of stretching and shrinking perceptual space when attending to particular dimensions are very similar to what I have in mind when I refer to weighting the information returned to the analytic processes. In particular, information that is weighted most heavily is that which is attended to most closely in categorising the input. The perceptual system is most sensitive to fine-grained differences reported by these processes. Conversely, information that is available through the other analytic processes is not closely attended to, hence, distinctions available through these analytic processes may go unnoticed. In other words, a bigger difference may be necessary in order to register distinctions available through unattended analytic processes. The weighting scheme, then, is a means of automatically focusing attention on those analytic processes that are most likely to provide information about the properties that are critical for categorising words in the language. When a language is acquired, the weighting scheme supplies default settings for perceptually categorising speech input. When a new language is acquired, the perceiver must

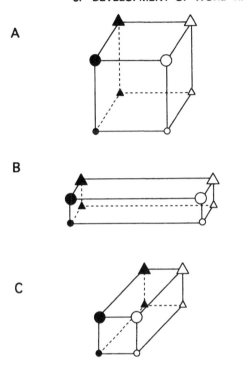

FIG. 3.2. (After Nosofsky) Schematic illustration of the way that selective attention may modify the perceptual spacing of stimuli on categorisation tasks. (A) Represents a neutral case where attention is not focused on a particular dimension. (B) Shows the situation in which the subject focuses on the colour distinction: note that the perceptual distance along the colour dimension is stretched, whereas the spacing of the stimuli is compressed on the shape and size dimensions. (C) Displays the comparable changes that occur when shape is attended to, and colour and size differences are ignored.

learn a new weighting scheme for utterances in that language. This new weighting scheme is an alternative to the one used for the native language. Although some of the categorisations made in the second language may have the same basis as in the native language, others will not. Consequently, learning the new weighting scheme involves overcoming the tendency to fall back automatically on those settings that are used for the native language. In much the same way, the listener who learns to perceive within-category differences in a speech perception experiment, must somehow learn to by-pass the weightings normally used for perceiving speech in that language.

There is some indication that altering the focus of attention in infants can have a big impact on the way in which they perceive speech. Jusczyk et al., (1990) attempted to manipulate the attentional focus of 4-day old and 2-month-old infants. They exposed their subjects to sets of items that were either distantly related or very closely clustered in perceptual space. By presenting closely clustered items, they hoped to focus infants' attention on fine-grained distinctions among items. Conversely, by presenting items that were greatly separated in perceptual space, they aimed to have infants focus on gross distinctions and to ignore finer-grained ones. Their manipulation succeeded. Whereas previous research had shown that newborns are sensitive to vowel changes (e.g. Bertoncini et al., 1988), Jusczyk et al. found that when 4-day-olds were exposed to a set of widely separated vowel contrasts (e.g. [bi], [ba], [bu]), they gave no evidence of detecting the addition of a new syllable ([bʌ]) that was very similar to one of the familiar ones (i.e. [ba]). Most importantly, the failure of the infants to detect the new item is not the result of their inability to discriminate the contrast, because newborns tested on the [ba]/[bʌ] contrast did discriminate these items. Rather, focusing infants' attention on grosser distinctions appears to have played the significant role. Further support for this view comes from an additional experiment in which Jusczyk et al. used closely clustered items (e.g. [pa], [ta], [ka]) during the initial familiarisation phase, and then added a new item that differed in its initial consonant (e.g. [ma]). Previous research had reported that newborns did not readily detect such changes (Bertoncini et al., 1988). However, the Bertoncini et al. study had used a familiarisation set that consisted of items that were perceptually very distant. Jusczyk et al. found that when closely clustered items were used in the familiarisation phase, the newborns did detect the novel item in the test phase. Hence, this study provides support for the view that the setting of the attentional focus does have an impact on how likely infants are to pick up certain distinctions.

One interesting implication of the Jusczyk et al. (1990) study is that there may be a passive component to the way in which the weighting scheme is derived during language acquisition. Distributional properties of the input could play some role in determining which of the analytic processing receives greater weighting—at least during the early phases of development. Thus, although it is certainly true, as MacKain (1982) has claimed, that an infant exposed to English may hear some proportion of tokens that would include features, such as prevoicing, which are irrelevant to English distinctions, it is highly likely that the frequency of these is probably insignificant compared to tokens that embody information important for English contrasts. Therefore, exposure to the input corpus could help tune the perceptual system. However, in addition, as the infant becomes preoccupied with the task of attaching meaning to sequences of sounds, there may be a more active tuning of the weighting scheme, in order to give most importance to those acoustic properties that are most critical to making meaningful distinctions in the target language. Here, feedback in the form of responses to misperceptions may play some role in adjusting the weighting scheme, to ensure a more accurate decoding of the speech stream into the correct lexical items.

Aside from the common sense arguments that the perceptual system is best served by taking into account the structural regularities that exist in the input, is there any reason to believe that fluent speech perception involves the development of a weighting scheme? As noted earlier, it appears to be the case that young infants from different cultures categorise speech contrasts in more or less the same ways, whereas native speakers of different languages exhibit significant differences in the way that they categorise the same sounds. Clearly, learning the sound structure of a language has an impact on perceptual categorisation. Moreover, although sensitivity to contrasts outside the native language may decline towards the end of the first year, this process is evidently not irreversible. Listeners can be re-trained to perceive foreign language contrasts (e.g. Flege, 1992; Logan, Lively, & Pisoni, 1989; McClasky, Pisoni, & Carrell, 1980; Pisoni, Aslin, Perey, & Hennessy, 1982; Werker & Tees, 1984). Consequently, one interpretation of these declines in perception is that they stem from shifts of attention away from dimensions that distinguish foreign language contrasts, and the concomitant re-organisation of the psychological spacing of the sounds.

Other evidence suggesting that something like a weighting scheme is involved in speech perception by fluent speakers comes from studies demonstrating that the same acoustic information can be perceived in more than one way. For example, Carden, Levitt, Jusczyk, and Walley (1981) showed that merely changing the instructions for listeners (by telling them to label sounds as either stops or fricatives) was sufficient to induce shifts in perceptual category boundaries. These shifts, which occurred in both identification and discrimination tests, were comparable to those observed when frication noises were either added or subtracted from the stimuli. Similarly, studies using sinewave analogues to speech have shown significant shifts in how such stimuli are perceived, depending on whether subjects are instructed to hear the sounds as speech or nonspeech (Bailey, Summerfield, & Dorman, 1977; Gagnon & Sawusch, 1990; Grunke & Pisoni, 1982; Remez, Rubin, Pisoni, & Carrell, 1981; Schwab, 1981). It has been suggested that the effect of engaging phonetic processing in these tasks is to induce changes in the perceptual sensitivity of listeners (Nusbaum & Schwab, 1986). Finally, it appears that bilingual speakers classify the same speech token differently depending on the language used in an accompanying carrier phase. Elman, Diehl, and Buchwald (1977) reported that Spanish–English bilinguals changed the voicing category associated with a particular token depending on whether the carrier phase was in English or Spanish.

In all these cases, the physical properties of the stimuli did not change. Rather, what changed was the nature of the perceptual set induced by the instructions. Consequently, it seems reasonable to suppose that it is the weight given to the information available in the acoustic signal that induced the perceptual changes that were reported. Given the task demands associated with fluent word recognition, such as the number of categorisations that must be made in short timespans, it would be valuable to preset attention to the portions of the signal with the highest information value to the listener. This is the role that the weighting scheme plays in speech perception.

PATTERN EXTRACTION

The weighting scheme gives emphasis to the information provided by some subset of the analytic processes. However, the task of extracting candidate words from the continuous input in fluent speech still remains. Specifically, the perceptual system has to make some determination of word boundaries and provide a description of the way that the information returned by the analytic processes is structured within these candidate words. The resulting description constitutes the representation that is used to make contact with previously stored lexical items to identify the word and obtain its meaning.

One important facet of the pattern extraction process has to do with the integration of information returned by the analytic processes. In particular, successful word recognition depends on a correct description of the way that information in the analytic processes is interrelated and organised. For example, information relevant to determining the presence of stop closures, vowels, nasal resonances, frication, glide-like transitions, etc., must be correctly integrated and sequenced to yield an accurate description of the input—one that is sufficient to distinguish a string like [sno] from [nos] or [ons]. There is some evidence that 2- to 3-month-olds have at least some rudimentary ability to integrate such features into the correct sequences. Thus, Miller and Eimas (1979; Eimas & Miller, 1981) found that infants were able to detect changes in the integration of information about manner and place (i.e. they discriminated sequences like [ba]–[na] from [da]–[ma]). Just how precise the infant's ability is in this domain, when word recognition begins, is hard to say. Certainly, there are many examples in the child phonology literature (e.g. Ferguson, 1986; Vihman & Elbert, 1987) that suggest that children often misplace features in their early productions of words.

Another very important aspect of the pattern extraction process has to do with correctly segmenting the input into component words. How does the infant arrive at the correct segmentation of the input? One potential solution to this problem that is sometimes suggested (e.g. Suomi, submitted) is that infants may continually match the input against familiar words in their lexicon. In effect, the infant is looking for familiar words in the input, and whenever such items are found they serve to break up the input into islands of known and unknown items. This approach suggests that infants may learn to recognise the individual words in isolation first, and after acquiring some number of these, may then begin to segment the speech stream.

Although familiarity with certain lexical items could play some role in segmenting speech, it is not sufficient to account for it. First of all, there are simply too many items that infants are unlikely to hear presented in isolation (e.g. words like 'over', 'the', 'did', and 'of'). Second, some words that might be heard in isolation also can appear as syllables in larger words (e.g. 'can' also occurs in 'candle', 'pecan', 'cannibal', 'uncanny', 'candidate', etc.). Segmenting around these items would lead to an incorrect segmentation of the input. Third, the acoustic characteristics of a word spoken in isolation are often very different from those that are present when the word is spoken in a fluent speech context in which the surrounding items influence its pronunciation (e.g. the words 'did' and 'you' when put together in a phrase like 'did you take it?').

What other sources of information could infants exploit to segment speech? One possibility that has been suggested (Gleitman, Gleitman, Landau, & Wanner, 1988; Hirsh-Pasek et al., 1987; Jusczyk, 1991) concerns prosodic cues. For example, some languages like Czech and Polish have very regular stress patterns. In such languages, locating the main stresses could provide useful information about the location of word boundaries. Even in a language like English, which permits many different stress patterns in words, there appears to be a predominant pattern. Cutler and Carter (1987) found that a very high proportion of words in fluent speech contexts actually follow a strong-weak stress pattern. Cutler and Norris (1988) have suggested that a listening strategy of locating word boundaries before strong stressed syllables could prove to be an effective first step in segmenting fluent speech into words.

Could attentiveness to prosody serve the language learner as a means of segmenting speech into words? If so, then it might play an important role in the pattern extraction process. Not only could prosody serve to segment the stream into candidate lexical units, but it could also provide a frame for organising the information that is obtained through the weighted analytic processes (i.e. information could be tagged as to whether it occurred in conjunction with a strong or weak stress).

Certainly, it is well-known that infants are sensitive to the prosodic features of language from a very early age (DeCasper & Fifer, 1980; Fernald, 1984; Jusczyk & Thompson, 1978; Mehler et al., 1988). More-over, there are indications that infants, as young as $4\frac{1}{2}$ months of age, are sensitive to prosodic markers of syntactic units such as clauses (Hirsh-Pasek et al., 1987; Jusczyk, 1989) and phrases (Jusczyk, Kemler Nelson,

Hirsh-Pasek, Kennedy, 1992; Kemler Nelson, 1989). Whether sensitivity to prosodic cues also serves to segment phrasal units into discrete words is not clear at present. Recent studies in our laboratory (Kemler Nelson, 1989; Woodward et al., in preparation) suggest that American 11-month olds are sensitive to word boundaries. Specifically, these infants listen significantly longer to samples of speech that are interrupted at word boundaries as opposed to in the middle of words. However, the basis for this sensitivity has not yet been established.

Another alternative basis for segmentation of speech into words that has been suggested (e.g. Church, 1987) is sensitivity to allophonic constraints. Certain allophones occur only in specific contexts within syllables. For example, in English, aspirated /t/, occurs only in syllable-initial positions, whereas retroflexed /t/ occurs only in clusters with /r/'s within the same syllables. Sensitivity to the possible positions that allophones can occupy could thus provide clues to boundaries between syllables and words. Once one learns the contexts in which the allophone can appear, then it may be possible to rely on this knowledge to help in segmentation of known, and even unknown, words from the input. However, it is difficult to see how one could gain knowledge of what the contextual constraints are for these allophones, unless one could generalise across a set of words already stored in the lexicon. In other words, the only way to gain information about the contexts would be by pulling the regularities out of items already existing in the lexicon. This implies that at least some of the lexical entries were segmented from speech by some means other than allophonic constraints. Thus, with respect to the way that segmentation skills develop, it is hard to see how allophonic constraints could play much more than a supplementary role.

To summarise, the pattern extraction process involves segmenting the input into word-sized units, and providing some description of the overall organisation of the information in such units. I have suggested that sensitivity to prosody may be an important factor both in segmenting the speech wave and in organising the information available through the analytic processes.

RECOGNISING WORDS AND STORING REPRESENTATIONS

The representation that results from the pattern extraction process is not a fully developed phonetic representation of the speech signal. Instead, it is much more global than this. As noted earlier, the representation is marked with respect to its overall prosodic pattern, such as its stress and tonal characteristics. One consequence of this is that since the units on which stress and tone are carried are syllables (e.g. Goldsmith, 1976; Halle

& Vergnaud, 1987; Hayes, 1982; Liberman & Prince, 1977; Selkirk, 1984), the representation is structured according to the number of syllables that it contains. The information included in these syllabic units is that which has been made available through the analytic processes favoured by the weighting scheme. Nevertheless, although this information has the highest priority for being included in the representation, it is not necessarily the case that all of it is encoded into the representation. In addition, information from other analytic processes may be present, but has a much lower probability of being included in the representation. Some information is available from the pattern extraction process about the organisation of information from the analytic processes, but there is nothing like a representation structured into phonetic segments. One consequence of gaining fluency with the language is that the listener gets better at including the critical information from the analytic processes in the representation, and provides a more complete description of its organisation. Nevertheless, there is reason to believe that the kind of global representation described here could suffice for word recognition during the early stages of acquisition. Charles-Luce and Luce (1990) calculated the number of near neighbours (perceptually similar words) for words in children's lexicons at various ages. They found that a typical 7-year-old's vocabulary contains a much lower proportion of confusable items than does that of an average adult. Hence, for children who do not know many words, a much less complete description of the sound properties may serve to distinguish different items in the lexicon.

One claim made in the model is that the representation is structured in terms of syllabic segments rather than phonetic ones (see also Mehler et al., 1990, for discussion of this point). This claim is based on the results of a number of investigations that we have carried out on the representation of speech by infants. In several studies, we sought to determine whether infants' representations of syllables are structured as a series of phonetic segments (Bertoncini et al., 1988; Jusczyk & Derrah, 1987). One indication of this would be if infants perceived syllables containing the same segment as more similar than ones containing different segmets. Newborns and 2-month-olds were familiarised with a series of syllables containing a common phonetic segment (e.g. [bi], [ba], [bo], [bɚ]). A new test item was added to the set, which either shared (e.g. [bu]) or did not share (e.g. [du]) the common segment. There was no indication that the infants perceived the new item with the common segment as more similar to the familiar items. In fact, the infants treated both the [bu] and [du] as equally novel.

More recently, we have received additional empirical support for our contention that infants' representations are structured according to syllabic, rather than phonetic, segments. In one study, Jusczyk, Kennedy and

Jusczyk (in preparation) examined whether the presence of a common phonetic segment would enhance 2-month-olds' memory for a series of syllabic stimuli. Infants were familiarised with a set of syllables that either shared (e.g. [bi], [ba], [bu]), or did not share ([si], [ba], [tu]), a common phonetic segment. A two-minute delay period was imposed, then testing resumed with either the original set of syllables, or with one in which the identity of one of the syllables had changed (e.g. [ba] was changed to [da]). Infants who had been exposed to the series with the common segment performed no better than their counterparts who heard the syllables without common segments. In contrast, when a similar type of study was conducted with bisyllabic stimuli that either contained (e.g. [ba'zi], [ba'lo], [ba'mIt]) or did not contain (e.g. [pae'zi], [nɛ'lo], [ko'mIt]) a common syllabic segment, very different results were obtained (Jusczyk, Kennedy, Jusczyk, Schomberg, & Koenig, in preparation). Only those infants who heard the sets containing the common syllable were able to detect changes to the sets after the two-minute delay period. Apparently, the existence of the common syllable facilitated the way that the infants were able to encode the stimuli for later recall. Further indication that it is the syllable that is serving as a representational unit, comes from an additional experiment that we conducted. This time, infants were exposed to familiar-isation sets that included two common phonetic segments but in different syllables (e.g. [za'bi], [la'bo], (ma'bIt]. Even though the same number of common phonetic segments were present as in the syllable condition of the previous experiment, the infants did not detect changes to the familiarisation set after the delay period. Thus, although there is some evidence to suggest that infants' representations are structured in terms of syllabic units, a comparable case cannot be made for phonetic segments.

Assuming that an infant processes the input and arrives at the kind of representation that is described here, some sort of matching process must take place to establish the identity of the lexical item and access its meaning. The usual account of this process is to say that the representation of the input is matched against some abstract representation of the sound patterns of different lexical items, whereby the closest match will be accepted. Indeed, I proposed such an account in an earlier version of the present model (Jusczyk, 1985; 1986). One reason for assuming that the access route to the lexicon is via some sort of abstract prototypical representation of the sound structure, is to deal with the fact that each utterance of the same word will vary in its acoustic characteristics, especially when produced by different talkers. The prototype is simply an average of all these different variations. Hence, how we recognise the utterance of a particular word by a talker that we have never heard before is simply that its representation is closer to this prototype than it is to any other one. Thus, by this view, the description of the sound structure of a lexical item in memory is a general one, as opposed to a particular one that corresponds to an utterance that has actually been encountered.

The view that lexical representations are stored as prototypes carries with it the assumption that there is some sort of generic memory system in which representations of categories are stored (Tulving, 1983). Recently, the assumption of the existence of a generic memory system has been challenged and an alternative view has been put forward of how category information is recognised and remembered (e.g. Hintzman, 1986, 1988; Jacoby & Brooks, 1984; Nosofsky, 1988). This alternative position states that a more accurate view of how we deal with category information is by storing representations of individual exemplars that we actually experience, rather than by storing away prototypical representations of objects and events. The basic idea behind these models is that one only stores away traces of individual episodes, and that the category as a whole is represented by an aggregate of traces acting in concert at the time of retrieval. Hintzman's Minerva 2 Model (1986) operates in this way, and demonstrates that computing a local average from stored instances can serve as an effective recognition routine. Jacoby and Brooks (1984) have also noted that when representations are of specific episodes, generality can be achieved by treating similar situations analogously. Word recognition could be explained by what they call 'nonanalytic generalization' (Jacoby & Brooks, 1984, p. 3): 'A word could be identified by reference to a previous occurrence of a word in a similar context, from a similar source and in a similar format, rather than by reference to a generalized description of the word . . .'.

Recognition in a multiple trace system like this occurs when a new input, or probe, is broadcast simultaneously to all traces in secondary memory. Each trace is activated according to its similarity to the probe. Those traces with the greatest overlap to the probe are most strongly activated. The reply that is received from secondary memory has been described by Hintzman (1986) as an 'echo'. All of the traces in secondary memory contribute to this echo. However, traces most similar to the probe produce a more intense response. Consequently, they contribute more to the echo. If several traces are very strongly activated, then the content of the echo will primarily reflect their common properties. This ensures that characteristics distinguishing one trace from another will tend to be masked in the echo. Thus, even though no prototype is actually stored in secondary memory, the echo may behave in much the same way. In comparing the echo to the probe, the echo might be used to fill in gaps that exist in the information supplied by the probe. Phenomena like phonemic restoration effects (e.g. Samuel, 1981 a,b, 1986; Warren, 1970) might be explained in this way.

Multiple trace models have certain advantages that make them appealing for explaining certain facts about word recognition. First of all, these models can account for many of the important findings that are associated with prototype models (e.g. differential forgetting of prototypes and old instances, typicality, and category size effects). Moreover, the multiple trace models are also better able to handle facets that are not easily accounted for by prototype models. For example, context-dependent effects have been reported in the memory and concept-learning literature (e.g. Craik & Kirsner, 1974; Jacoby, 1983; Osgood & Hoosain, 1974; Potter & Faulconer, 1979; Roth & Schoben, 1983). These effects are connected with the fact that performance on tasks such as recognition memory is better when the test probe is identical to the previously experienced item. For instance, Craik & Kirsner (1974) found that their subjects were faster and more accurate in recognising items when they were repeated by the same talker who spoke the original item. Moreover, Logan (1988) has recently demonstrated that an instance-based model can account for automaticity in skill learning. This demonstration may have important ramifications for theorising about fluent word recogniton because, as Logan notes, automatic processing is fast, effortless, autonomous, and unavailable to consciousness. The same properties are characteristic of fluent speech recognition. Hence, demonstrating that such automaticity can be derived from a system that stores only individual instances opens the door to considering instance-based accounts ot word recognition.

From a developmental perspective, it may be advantageous to view word recognition as involving representations of previously encountered instances rather than abstract prototypes. For example, a multiple trace model could provide a clearer account of how knowledge of the sound structure is modified by experience. Consider what happens when a memory trace is stored according to the WRAPSA model. The trace itself preserves the overall organisation of properties in the perceptual representation. Naturally, not every utterance that an infant hears will be stored as an episodic trace. Although some random storage of the sound structure of processed input may occur, in general, storing sound patterns requires that some extra effort is given to processing the sounds. This may involve rehearsing the perceptual representation, an effort to associate it with the meaning or context, or some other such process. The role of experience is not to modify previously stored traces. Rather, new traces are added to those already in secondary memory. Thus, the additions of a new trace modifies the way that the whole memory system behaves. The more that a trace differs from preceding ones, the greater is the change in the behaviour of the memory system during subsequent efforts at identifying new items. Hence, a system like this can more easily account for the way that small changes in input can produce the kinds of large-scaled reorganisations of categories that are often observed in development.

The structure of the representation that serves as the probe determines which combination of traces will contribute most heavily to the echo returned from secondary memory. Depending on how specific the probe is, the set of traces most strongly activated will be large or small. The weighting scheme helps in constraining the perceptual representation that serves as the probe. Initially, before any meaningful encoding of speech sounds occurs, one might expect that the configuration of properties that appear in speech probes will vary more or less randomly. However, once the infant begins to establish a weighting scheme, there should be more stability in the configuration of properties that are found in the probes for a particular word. So as development proceeds, the features most likely to be included in the probe will be ones most relevant to drawing meaningful distinctions in the language being acquired. Nevertheless, the probe is not necessarily a complete description of all the pertinent properties for identifying a word in all contexts. At least during the earliest stages of the development of the lexicon, a probe may include only a partial description of a word's sound structure (e.g. its stress pattern, and a few of its key phonetic features). A partial description of this sort could suffice when vocabulary is small, and contains few items with highly similar sound patterns (Charles-Luce & Luce, 1990). Indeed, recent evidence suggests that 3-year-olds (Echols, 1988; Peters, 1977), and even adults (Lahiri & Marslen-Wilson, 1991) may have only partially specified representations.

One of the biggest attractions of multiple-trace memory models is that they seem to offer a straightforward solution to the question of why performance should be better in recognising a previously encountered instance rather than some arbitrary member of the same category. The answer is that the match to the memory trace is better when the previously encountered instance serves as the probe. Still, one might ask whether there is any reason to postulate that infants are storing traces of particular instances that they hear. A study recently conducted by Jusczyk, Pisoni, and Mullennix (1992) provides some suggestive evidence on this point. The study was conducted to examine the consequences of talker variability on the way that 2-month olds process speech sounds.

Previous work with adult subjects (e.g. Martin, Mullennix, Pisoni, & Summers, 1989; Mullennix & Pisoni, 1990; Mullennix, Pisoni & Martin, 1989) indicated that continually switching between different talkers' voices can affect early stages of perceptual encoding, and even disrupt memory processes. Jusczyk et al. investigated whether similar effects ensue when 2-month-olds are exposed to speech produced by many different talkers. In a series of experiments, they contrasted the effects of presenting infants with tokens of the words 'bug' and 'dug', produced either by a single talker or by 12 different talkers (6 males and 6 females). Previous research by Kuhl (e.g. 1979; 1983) had shown that 6-month-old infants were able to continue to discriminate a similar contrast, in spite of changes in speaking voices. Jusczyk et al. replicated this result with their 2-month-old subjects. However, in addition, they examined how the changes in speaking voices affected the infants' memory for what they heard. Specifically, after familiarising the infants with a particular stimulus set, they introduced a two-minute delay period prior to the test period. In one condition (single talker), the infants hear the same token (e.g. 'bug') throughout the familiarisation phase. Then, after the delay period, half of the subjects (control group) heard the same token, and the other half (experimental group) heard the other token (e.g. 'dug'). A second condition (multiple talkers) was identical to the first, except that, rather than hearing just a single token during the familiarisation and test phases, the infants heard tokens produced by 12 different talkers. The subjects in the single talker condition easily discriminated the contrast between 'bug' and 'dug' even after the two-minute delay period. By comparison, infants in the multiple-talker condition gave no evidence of discriminating the contrast after the delay period, even though their counterparts in the earlier experiment without the delay had been able to do so. Hence, the changes in speaking voice seem to affect encoding processes related to the infants' memory for speech sounds.

One possible explanation for the results obtained by Jusczyk et al. is that the differences in speaking voices may have prevented infants from forming an abstract prototype representation of the word from the different instances. Instead, they may have tried to form representations for each individual instance, and been overloaded in doing so. Perhaps the discrepancies in the voices were so great that this may have confused the infants. If so, then the infants might be better able to form prototypes when the set of voices is more restricted. Of course, the most restrictive set would be one that consisted of repetitions of the words that were produced by the same talker. For this reason, Jusczyk et al. conducted additional experiments in which infants were exposed to 12 tokens of a word in the familiarisation phase (e.g. 'bug'), and either the same 12 tokens (control group) or 12 tokens of a different word (e.g. 'dug') during the test phase. The results of this investigation are shown in Fig. 3.3. When the infants were tested without a delay period, they successfully discriminated the phonetic change from 'bug' to 'dug'. However, when a two-minute delay period was imposed between the familiarisation and test phases, the infants were unable to discriminate the same contrast. Therefore, even when the variation stems from differences among the tokens produced by the same talker, there is evidence that it disrupts infants' memory for speech. Certainly, further study is needed before we can conclude that encoding of speech by infants takes the form of multiple

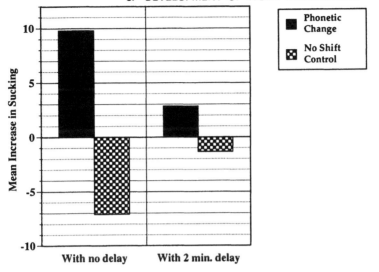

FIG. 3.3. The mean increase in sucking observed during the test period for subjects who heard multiple tokens of a given syllable during the familiarisation phase, and then multiple tokens of either a different syllable (Phonetic Change) or the same syllable (NoShift Control). Note that the difference between the Phonetic Change and NoShift Controls is significant only in the NoDelay Condition.

traces, rather than abstract prototypes. However, the pattern of results observed here fits with the view that infants may encode individual instances in memory, and that lexical access may involve matching to multiple traces.

SUMMARY AND CONCLUSIONS

The WRAPSA model is proposed as a framework for viewing the way that word recognition develops from underlying speech perception capacities. In describing the model, I have tried to indicate the important components associated with recognising words in fluent speech, their origins in the perceptual capacities of infants, and their evolution as a native language is acquired. In its present form, the model makes a number of claims about the basic processes underlying word recognition. Its key assumptions can be summarised as follows:

1. Infants come equipped with a general set of perceptual analysers, or analytic processes, that underlie auditory perception of both speech and nonspeech signals.
2. As language is acquired, the infant develops a scheme for weighting the information returned by the analytic processes.

3. The weighting scheme reflects the important structural properties of words in the native language. It is particular to this language, and is the locus of any language–specific effects observed in processing speech.
4. Pattern extraction which involves segmenting words from the speech stream is conducted on the weighted information.
5. The representations that result from the pattern extraction processes are structured into syllable-sized units and contain loosely organised featural information from the analysers along with some prosodic marking.
6. These representations serve as the probes to secondary memory, where they are matched against traces of previously encountered utterances, rather than against abstract prototype representations of the sound structure of words.

In conclusion, the WRAPSA model is intended as a working hypothesis about the way that word recognition processes develop during the course of language acquisition. As further information is gained about the nature of word recognition processes, some of the assumptions made will undoubtedly have to be revised. In addition, many aspects of the model will have to be made much more precise for the model to be taken seriously as an explanation of how word recognition develops. For the time being, the model is one means of organising a number of interesting facts that have been discovered about the development of speech perception capacities during the last 20 years.

ACKNOWLEDGEMENTS

The occasion for writing this chapter was the conference on Cognitive Models of Speech Processing held in Sperlonga, Italy, in June 1990. I would like to express my gratitude to the conference organisers for a stimulating week of scientific discussions, and to the sponsor British Telecom International for its generous support. The chapter was written while the author was supported by a research grant from NICHD (#15795).

REFERENCES

Aslin, R.N., Pisoni, D.B., Hennessy, B.L., & Perey, A.J. (1981). Discrimination of voice onset time by human infants: New findings and implications for the effects of early experience. *Child Development*, *52*, 1135–1145.
Bailey, P.J., Summerfield, A.Q., & Dorman, M.F. (1977). On the identification of sine-wave analogs of certain speech sounds. *Status Report on Speech Research*, (SR-51-52), New Haven, CT: Haskins Laboratories.

Bertoncini, J., Bijeljac-Babic, R., Blumstein, S.E., & Mehler, J. (1987). Discrimination in neonates of very short CVs. *Journal of the Acoustical Society of America*, *82*, 31–37.

Bertoncini, J., Bijeljac-Babic, R., Jusczyk, P.W., Kennedy, L.J., & Mehler, J. (1988). An investigation of young infants' perceptual representations of speech sounds. *Journal of Experimental Psychology: General*, *117*, 21–33.

Bertoncini, J., & Mehler, J. (1981). Syllables as units in infant speech perception. *Infant Behavior and Development*, *4*, 247–260.

Best, C.T., McRoberts, G.W., & Sithole, N.M. (1988). Examination of the perceptual reorganization for speech contrasts: Zulu click discrimination by English-speaking adults and infants. *Journal of Experimental Psychology: Human Perception and Performance*, *14*, 245–360.

Carden, G.C., Levitt, A., Jusczyk, P.W., & Walley, A.C. (1981). Evidence for phonetic processing of cues to place of articulation: Perceived manner affects perceived place. *Perception & Psychophysics*, *29*, 26–36.

Carney, A.E., Widin, G.P., & Veimeister, N.F. (1977). Noncategorical perception of stop consonants differing in VOT. *Journal of the Acoustical Society of America*, *62*, 961–970.

Charles-Luce, J., & Luce, P.A. (1990). Similarity neighborhoods of words in young children's lexicons. *Journal of Child Language*, *17*, 205–215.

Church, K. (1987). Phonological parsing and lexical retrieval. *Cognition*, *25*, 53–69.

Craik, F.I.M., & Kirsner, K. (1974). The effect of speaker's voice on word recognition. *Quarterly Journal of Experimental Psychology*, *26*, 274–284.

Cutler, A., & Carter, D.M. (1987). The predominance of strong initial syllables in the English vocabulary. *Computer Speech and Language*, *2*, 133–142.

Cutler, A., Mehler, J., Norris, D.G., & Segui, J. (1986). The syllable's differing role in the segmentation of French and English. *Journal of Memory and Language*, *25*, 385–400.

Cutler, A., & Norris, D.G. (1989). The role of strong syllables in segmentation for lexical access. *Journal of Experimental Psychology: Human Perception and Performance*, *14*, 113–121.

Cutler, A., & Norris, D.G. (1988). The role of strong syllables in segmentation for lexical access. *Journal of Experimental Psychology: Human Perception and Performance*, *14*, 113–121

Cutting, J.E., & Eimas, P.D. (1975). Phonetic feature analyzers and the processing of speech in infants. In J.F. Kavanaugh & J.E. Cutting (Eds.), *The role of speech in language*. Cambridge, MA: MIT Press.

DeCasper, A.J., & Fifer, W.P. (1980). Of Human Bonding: Newborns prefer their mothers' voices. *Science*, *208*, 1174–1176.

Echols, C.H. (1988). The role of stress, position and intonation in the representation and identification of early words. *Papers and Reports on Child Language Development*, *27*, 39–46.

Eimas, P.D. (1974). Auditory and linguistic units of processing of cues for place of articulation by infants. *Perception & Psychophysics*, *16*. 513–521.

Eimas, P.D. (1975). Auditory and phonetic coding of the cues of speech: Discrimination of the [r-l] distinction by young infants. *Perception & Psychophysics*, *18*, 341–347.

Eimas, P.D., & Miller, J.L. (1981). Organization in the perception of segmental and suprasegmental information by infants. *Infant Behavior and Development*, *4*, 395–399.

Eimas, P.D., Siqueland, E.R., Jusczyk, P.W., & Vigorito, J. (1971). Speech perception in infants. *Science*, *171*, 303–306.

Elman, J.L., Diehl, R.L., & Buchwald, S.E. (1977). Perceptual switching in bilinguals. *Journal of the Acoustical Society of America*, *62*, 971–974.

Ferguson, C.A. (1986). Discovering sound units and constructing sound systems: It's child's play. In J. Perkell & D.H. Klatt (Eds.), *Invariance and variability in speech processes* (pp. 36–51). Hillsdale, NJ: Lawrence Erlbaum Associates Inc.

Fernald, A. (1984). Expanded intonation contours in mothers' speech to newborns. *Developmental Psychology*, *20*, 104–113.

Flege, J.E. (1992). Perception and production: The relevance of phonetic input to L2 phonological learning. In C.A. Ferguson & T. Heubner (Eds.), *Crosscurrents in second language acquisition and linguistic theories.* Philadelphia: John Benjamins.

Gagnon, D.A., & Sawusch, J.R. (1990, November). *Rediscovering auditory coherence in phonetic patterns.* Paper presented at the 120th meeting of the Acoustical Society of America, San Diego, CA.

Gleitman, L., Gleitman, H., Landau, B., & Wanner, E. (1988). Where learning begins: Initial representations for language learning. In F. Newmeyer (Ed.), *The Cambridge linguistic survey,* Vol. III. Cambridge, MA: Harvard University Press.

Goldsmith, J. (1976). An overview of autosegmental phonology. *Linguistic Analysis, 2,* 23–68.

Goodsitt, J.V., Morse, P.A., Ver Hoove, J.N., & Cowan, N. (1984). Infant speech perception in multisyllabic contexts. *Child Development, 55,* 903–910.

Grunke, M.E., & Pisoni, D.B. (1982). Some experiments on perceptual learning of mirror-image acoustic patterns. *Perception & Psychophysics, 31,* 210–218.

Halle, M., & Vergnaud, J.R. (1987). *An essay on stress.* Cambridge, MA: MIT Press.

Hayes, B. (1982). Extrametricality and English stress. *Linguistic Inquiry, 13,* 227–276.

Hintzman, D.L. (1986). 'Schema Abstraction' in a multiple-trace memory model. *Psychological Review, 93,* 411–428.

Hintzman, D.L. (1988). Judgments of frequency and recognition memory in a multiple-trace memory model. *Psychological Review, 95,* 528–551.

Hirsh-Pasek, K., Kemler Nelson, D.G., Jusczyk, P.W., Wright Cassidy, K., Druss, B., & Kennedy, L.J. (1987). Clauses are perceptual units for young infants. *Cognition, 26,* 269–286.

Jacoby, L.L. (1983). Perceptual enhancement: Persistent effects of an experience. *Journal of Experimental Psychology: Learning, Memory and Cognition, 9,* 21–38.

Jacoby, L.L. & Brooks, L.R. (1984). Nonanalytic cognition: Memory, perception, and concept learning. In G.H. Bower (Ed.), *The psychology of learning and motivation.* (vol. 18, pp. 1–47). New York: Academic Press.

Jusczyk, P.W. (1977). Perception of syllable-final stops by two-month-old infants. *Perception and Psychophysics, 21,* 450–454.

Jusczyk, P.W. (1985). On characterizing the development of speech perception. In J. Mehler & R. Fox (Eds.), *Neonate cognition: Beyond the blooming, buzzing confusion* (pp. 199–229). Hillsdale, NJ: Lawrence Erlbaum Associates Inc.

Jusczyk, P.W. (1986). Towards a model for the development of speech perception. In J. Perkell & D.H. Klatt (Eds.), *Invariance and variability in speech processes* (pp. 1–19). Hillsdale, NJ: Lawrence Erlbaum Associates Inc.

Jusczyk, P.W. (1989, April). *Perception of cues to clausal units in native and non-native languages.* Paper presented at the biennial meeting of the Society for Research in Child Development, Kansas City.

Jusczyk, P.W. (1991). Undoing Hockett's Wringer: Discovering the sound patterns of the native language. *Papers and Reports on Child Language Development, 30,* 1–16.

Jusczyk, P.W., Bertoncini, J., Bijeljac-Babic, R., Kennedy, L.J., & Mehler, J. (1990). The role of attention in speech perception by infants. *Cognitive Development, 5,* 265–286.

Jusczyk, P.W., & Derrah, C. (1987). Representation of speech sounds by young infants. *Developmental Psychology, 23,* 648–654.

Jusczyk, P.W., Friederici, A.D., Wessels, J.M.I., Svenkerud, V.Y., & Jusczyk, A.M. (in press). Infants' sensitivity to the sound patterns of native language words. *Journal of Memory and Language.*

Jusczyk, P.W., Kemler Nelson, D.G., Hirsh-Pasek, K., Kennedy, L., Woodward, A., & Piwoz, J. (1992). Perception of acoustic correlates of major phrasal units by young infants. *Cognitive Psychology, 24,* 252–293.

Jusczyk, P.W., Kennedy, L.J., & Jusczyk, A.M. (in preparation). *Young infants' memory for information in speech syllables.*

Jusczyk, P.W., Kennedy, L., Jusczyk, A.M., Schomberg, T., & Koenig, N. (in preparation). *An investigation of the infant's representation of information in bisyllabic utterances.*

Jusczyk, P.W., & Krumhansl, C.L. (1991, April). *Infants' sensitivity to musical phrase structure.* Paper presented at the biennial meeting of the Society for Research in Child Development, Seattle.

Jusczyk, P.W., Pisoni, D.B., Reed, M., Fernald, A., & Myers, M. (1983). Infants' discrimination of the duration of a rapid spectrum change in nonspeech signals. *Science, 222,* 175–177.

Jusczyk, P.W., Pisoni, D.B., & Mullennix, J. (1992). Some consequences of stimulus variability on speech processing by 2-month-old infants. *Cognition, 43,* 253–291.

Jusczyk, P.W., Rosner, B.S., Reed, M., & Kennedy, L.J. (1989). Could temporal order differences underlie 2-month-olds' discrimination of English voicing contrasts? *Journal of the Acoustical Society of America, 85,* 1741–1749.

Jusczyk, P.W., & Thompson, E.J. (1978). Perception of a phonetic contrast in multisyllabic utterances by two-month-old infants. *Perception & Psychophysics, 23,* 105–109.

Kemler Nelson, D.G. (1989). *Developmental trends in infants' sensitivity to prosodic cues correlated with linguistic units.* Paper presented at the biennial meeting of the Society for Research in Child Development, Kansas City.

Krumhansl, C.L., & Jusczyk, P.W. (1990). Infants' perception of phrase structure in music. *Psychological Science, 1,* 70–73.

Kuhl, P.K. (1979). Speech perception in early infancy: Perceptual constancy for spectrally dissimilar vowel categories. *Journal of the Acoustical Society of America, 66,* 1668–1679.

Kuhl, P.K. (1983). Perception of auditory equivalence classes for speech in early infancy. *Infant Behavior and Development, 6,* 263–285.

Lahiri, A., & Marslen-Wilson, W. (1991). The mental representation of lexical form: A phonological approach to the recognition lexicon. *Cognition, 38,* 245–294.

Lasky, R.E., Syrdal-Lasky, A., & Klein, R.E. (1975). VOT discrimination by four to six and a half month old infants from Spanish environments. *Journal of Experimental Child Psychology, 20,* 215–225.

Liberman, A.M., Cooper, F.S., Shankweiler, D.P., & Studdert-Kennedy, M. (1967). Perception of the speech code. *Psychological Review, 74,* 431–461.

Liberman, M., & Prince, A. (1977). On stress and linguistic rhythm. *Linguistic Inquiry, 8,* 249–336.

Logan, G.D. (1988). Toward an instance theory of automatization. *Psychological Review, 95,* 492–527.

Logan, J.S., Lively, S.E., & Pisoni, D.B. (1989). Training Japanese listeners to identify /r/ and /l/. *Journal of the Acoustical Society of America, 85,* S137–138.

MacKain, K.S. (1982). Assessing the role of experience on infants' speech discrimination. *Journal of Child Language, 9,* 527–542.

Martin, C.S., Mullennix, J.W., Pisoni, D.B., & Summers, W.V. (1989). Effects of talker variability on recall of spoken word lists. *Journal of Experimental Psychology: Learning, Memory, and Cognition, 15,* 676–684.

McClasky, C.L., Pisoni, D.B., & Carrell, T.D. (1980). Effects of transfer of training on identification of a new linguistic contrast in voicing. In *Research on Speech Perception, Progress Report No. 6,* Bloomington, IN: Indiana University.

Mehler, J., Dommergues, J.Y., Frauenfelder, U., & Segui, J. (1981). The syllable's role in speech segmentation. *Journal of Verbal Learning and Verbal Behavior, 20,* 298–305.

Mehler, J., Dupoux, E., & Segui, J. (1990). Constraining models of lexical access: The onset of word recognition. In G.T.M. Altmann (Ed.), *Cognitive models of speech processing* (pp. 236–262). Hillsdale, NJ: Lawrence Erlbaum Associates Inc.

Mehler, J., Jusczyk, P.W., Lambertz, G., Halsted, N., Bertoncini, J., & Amiel-Tison, C. (1988). A precursor of language acquisition in young infants. *Cognition, 29*, 143–178.

Miller, J.L., & Eimas, P.D. (1979). Organization in infant speech perception. *Canadian Journal of Psychology, 33*, 353–367.

Moffitt, A.R. (1971). Consonant cue perception by twenty- to twenty-four-week old infants. *Child Development, 42*, 717–731.

Morse, P.A. (1972). The discrimination of speech and nonspeech stimuli in early infancy. *Journal of Experimental Child Psychology, 13*, 477–492.

Mullennix, J.W. & Pisoni, D.B. (1990). Detailing the nature of talker normalization in speech perception. *Perception & Psychophysics, 47*, 379–390.

Mullennix, J.W., Pisoni, D.B., & Martin, C.S. (1989). Some effects of talker variability on spoken word recognition. *Journal of the Acoustical Society of America, 85*, 365–378.

Nosofsky, R.M. (1986). Attention, similarity, and the identification–categorization relationship. *Journal of Experimental Psychology: General, 115*, 39–57.

Nosofsky, R.M. (1987). Attention and learning processes in the identification and categorization of integral stimuli. *Journal of Experimental Psychology: Learning, Memory & Cognition, 15*, 700–708.

Nosofsky, R.M. (1988). Exemplar-based accounts of relations between classification, recognition, and typicality. *Journal of Experimental Psychology: Learning, Memory & Cognition, 15*, 282–304.

Nosofsky, R.M., Clark, S.E., & Shin, H.J. (1989). Rules and exemplars in categorization, identification and recognition. *Journal of Experimental Psychology: Learning, Memory & Cognition, 15*, 282–304.

Nusbaum, H.C., & Schwab, E.C. (1986). The role of attention and active processing in speech perception. In E.C. Schwab & H.C. Nusbaum (Eds.), *Pattern recognition by humans and machines, Vol. 1: Speech perception* (pp. 113–157). New York: Academic Press.

Osgood, C.E., & Hoosain, R. (1974). Salience of the word as a unit in the perception of language. *Perception & Psychophysics, 15*, 168–192.

Peters, A.M. (1977). Language learning strategies: Does the whole equal the sum of the parts? *Language, 53*, 560–573.

Pisoni, D.B., Aslin, R.N., Perey, A.J., & Hennessy, B.L. (1982). Some effects of laboratory training on identification and discrimination of voicing contrasts in stop consonants. *Journal of Experimental Psychology: Human Perception and Performance, 8*, 297–314.

Pisoni, D.B., & Tash, J. (1974). Reaction times to comparisons within and across phonetic categories. *Perception & Psychophysics, 15*, 285–290.

Potter, M.C., & Faulconer, B.A. (1979). Understanding noun phrases. *Journal of Verbal Learning and Verbal Behavior, 18*, 509–521.

Remez, R.E., Rubin, P.E., Pisoni, D.B., & Carrell, T.D. (1981). Speech perception without traditional cues. *Science, 212*, 947–950.

Repp, B.H. (1984). Categorical perception: Issues, methods, findings. In N.J. Lass (Ed.), *Speech and language: Advances in basic research and practice*, Vol. 10. New York: Academic Press.

Roth, E.M., & Schoben, E.J. (1983). The effect of context on the structure of categories. *Cognitive Psychology, 15*, 346–378.

Samuel, A.G. (1977). The effect of discrimination training on speech perception: Non-categorical perception. *Perception & Psychophysics, 22*, 321–330.

Samuel, A.G. (1981a). Phonemic restoration: Insights from a new methodology. *Journal of Experimental Psychology: General, 110*, 474–494.

Samuel, A.G. (1981b). The role of bottom-up confirmation in the phonemic restoration illusion. *Journal of Experimental Psychology: Human Perception and Performance, 7,* 1124–1131.

Samuel, A.G. (1986). The role of the lexicon in speech perception. In E.C. Schwab & H.C. Nusbaum (Eds.), *Pattern recognition by humans and machines: Vol. 1, Speech perception* (pp. 89–111). New York: Academic Press.

Sawusch, J.R. (1986). Auditory and phonetic coding of speech. In E.C. Schwab & H.C. Nusbaum (Eds.), *Pattern recognition by humans and machines: Vol. 1, Speech perception* (pp. 51–88). New York: Academic Press.

Schwab, E.C. (1981). *Auditory and phonetic processing for tone analogs of speech.* Unpublished doctoral dissertation. State University of New York at Buffalo.

Selkirk, E.O. (1984). *Phonology and syntax: The relation between sound and structure.* Cambridge, MA: MIT Press.

Streeter, L.A. (1976). Language perception of 2-month old infants shows effects of both innate mechanisms and experience. *Nature, 259,* 39–41.

Suomi, K. (submitted). *An outline of a developmental model of adult phonological organization and behavior.*

Studdert-Kennedy, M. (1986). Sources of variability in early speech development. In J. Perkell & D.H. Klatt (Eds.), *Invariance and variability in speech processes* (pp. 58–76). Hillsdale, NJ: Lawrence Erlbaum Associates Inc.

Trehub, S.E. (1973). Infants' sensitivity to vowel and tonal contrasts. *Developmental Psychology, 9,* 91–96.

Trehub, S.E. (1976). The discrimination of foreign speech contrasts by infants and adults. *Child Development, 47,* 466–472.

Tulving, E. (1983). *Elements of episodic memory.* New York: Oxford University Press.

Vihman, M.M., & Elbert, M. (1987). Phonological development. In J.E. Bernthal & N.W. Bankson (Eds.), *Articulation disorders.* Englewood Cliffs, NJ: Prentice Hall.

Warren, R.M. (1970). Phonemic restoration of missing speech sounds. *Science, 167,* 392–393.

Werker, J.F. (1991). The ontogeny of speech perception. In I.G. Mattingley & M. Studdert-Kennedy (Eds.), *Modularity and the motor theory of speech perception.* (pp. 91–109). Hillsdale, NJ: Lawrence Erlbaum Associates Inc.

Werker, J.F., Gilbert, J.H., Humphrey, K., & Tees, R.C. (1981). Developmental aspects of cross-language speech perception. *Child Development, 52,* 349–355.

Werker, J.F., & Tees, R.C. (1984). Phonemic and phonetic factors in adult cross-language speech perception. *Journal of the Acoustical Society of America, 75,* 1866–1878.

Woodward, A., Kemler Nelson, D., Jusczyk, P.W., Hirsh-Pasek, K., Kennedy, L.J., & Jusczyk, A.M. (in preparation). *Infants' sensitivity to word boundaries in fluent speech.*

Developmental Changes in Cross-language Speech Perception: Implications for Cognitive Models of Speech Processing

4

Janet F. Werker
University of British Columbia, Vancouver, Canada.

INTRODUCTION

Developmental research in cross-language speech perception provides a unique perspective on cognitive models of speech processing, by permitting the simultaneous consideration of both universal and language-specific aspects of speech perception. Universal aspects of speech perception can be identified by studying the behaviour of the young infant prior to extensive exposure to any one language, thus allowing at least an estimate of what the parameters of the initial state might be. Studies of cross-language speech perception in adults can augment this search for universals, by identifying phonetic sensitivities that remain robust irrespective of supportive language experience. Perhaps most importantly, cross-language studies of infants, children, and adults can reveal the ways in which linguistic sensitivities change as a function of differential language exposure. In this endeavour it is possible to empirically manipulate factors of variation such as the range of experience, age, the testing context, etc., in order to help identify the mechanisms that underlie how language-specific experience shapes initial abilities. The goal of this chapter is to highlight developmental research in cross-language speech perception, and to evaluate cognitive models of speech processing in the light of this research.

INITIAL INFANT SENSITIVITIES

Much of the research in speech perception has been designed to help resolve the theoretical controversy concerning whether speech is processed via a specialised linguistic or a generalised auditory mechanism. Although many variations of specialised *vs* general models have been posited, for years the most influential specialised model has ben the modified motor theory of speech perception (Liberman & Mattingly, 1985). However, given the ascendancy of domain-specific conceptions of cognitive and perceptual processing across many other content domains (see Carey & Gelman, 1991), it is likely that there will be a proliferation of alternative specialised models of speech perception.

In contrast to these models advocating 'special' processes in the analysis of speech, many general auditory processing models of speech perception have been proposed. According to these models, speech is described as being processed in a step-wise, linear fashion. In the first stage, the signal is analysed using the same general auditory processes that are used in the analysis of any other complex signal. On the basis of this initial analysis, the signal is secondarily assigned to a phonetic category.

In 1971, Eimas, Siqueland, Jusczyk, and Vigorito attempted to address the controversy of general *vs* specialised mechanisms for speech perception by studying speech perception abilities in prelinguistic infants, presumably before they had years of practice listening to speech.[1] The results of this study indicated that young infants, like adults, show elevated discrimination of speech stimuli from contrasting phonetic categories. At the time of publication, these results were widely interpreted as verifying the existence of a specialised phonetic processing capability that is functional from birth, and specific to humans listening to human-language phones. The results of this initial publication were replicated in numerous studies using many different phonetic continua (for reviews of this early work, see Eimas, 1975; Kuhl, 1979).

Within four years of the initial report by Eimas and colleagues, Kuhl and Miller (1975) published a study revealing that chinchillas, like human infants, also show categorical-like perception for voiced *vs* voiceless stop consonants. This study raised the very real possibility that categorical-like perception in the human infant reveals the way in which the mammalian auditory system works, and thus may not require an explanation in terms of 'specialised' processing mechanisms for speech. Similarly, reports that young human infants also show categorical perception of certain timing characteristics of nonspeech stimuli[2] (Jusczyk, Pisoni, Walley, & Murray, 1980) began to undermine the strength of the specificity interpretation.

---

[1] It is now believed that much of the information in the speech signal (at least the low frequency information) may be available to the foetus for some time prior to birth, possibly even as early as the 26th week of gestation, when the auditory system begins to function. Thus the expectation that a newborn infant is a 'naive' subject with respect to speech may be incorrect.

[2] The stimuli used were two-component, tone-onset-tone stimuli in which the relative onset of low frequency (first formant) information varied relative to the onset of higher frequency energy.

Studies of cross-language speech perception in young infants greatly enriched the debate. Young infants' ability to discriminate speech sounds according to phonetically significant boundaries was shown to extend to non-native as well as native contrasts. For example, in a now classic study, Streeter (1976) showed that young Kikuyu-learning infants are able to discriminate the English voiced/voiceless distinction even though this distinction is not used contrastively in the Kikuyu language. Similar demonstrations of sensitivity to non-native phonetic contrasts were reported in many other studies (e.g. Trehub, 1976. For reviews, see Best, in press; MacKain, 1982; Strange, 1986). The cross-language work made it abundantly clear that human infants are endowed with the ability, irrespective of its origins, to discriminate phonetic information in CV syllables in a way that will facilitate language processing, and the eventual acquisition of meaning. Thus although the cross-language work was unable to put the general vs specific debate to rest, it made clear that the important issues extend beyond this theoretical debate.

In the last 10 years, the area of inquiry in speech perception research has broadened to include many more aspects of speech processing than categorical perception. For example, it is now known that human infants as young as 3-months of age show a left hemisphere advantage for the perception of human speech (Best, Hoffman, & Glanville, 1982; see also Bertoncini et al., 1989; Molfese & Molfese, 1979). It is also known that human infants show the same pattern of trading relations in the perception of speech (Miller & Eimas, 1983) as do adults (Miller, 1981), and that the infants, like adults, are sensitive to the bimodal nature of human speech (Kuhl & Meltzhoff, 1982; MacKain, Studdert-Kennedy, Spieker, & Stern, 1983). In order to determine if these abilities which facilitate speech processing are part of the infant's initial endowment, or whether they develop through experience with human speech, it would be useful to extend this work using non-native speech contrasts as stimuli.

In addition to studies of discrimination, there have been a number of studies examining whether infants 'categorise' speech stimuli. Categorisation, as defined in the infancy literature, refers to the ability to treat discriminably different stimuli as equivalent (Kuhl, 1979). It is still controversial whether phonetic categorisation is evident in infants younger than 4-months of age. For example, Kuhl and Miller (1982) report that infants of 4- and 16-weeks can categorise stimuli according to vowel colour, over and above discriminable differences in pitch. However, in other studies it has been reported that although infants of both 2-days and 4-months can have difficulty 'categorising' sets of same-consonant, different-vowel stimuli on the basis of the repeating initial consonant while ignoring the variability in the following vowel (Bertoncini et al., 1988; Jusczyk & Derrah, 1987). Nevertheless, by 6-months of age infants can categorise discriminably different, but phonetically equivalent sounds across several non-phonetic dimensions (see Kuhl, 1987 for a review). Indeed, recent research suggests that phonetic categories may be organised around prototypes by 6-months of age (Greiser & Kuhl, 1989).

Whether infants can categorise speech is probably more relevant to understanding the relationship between speech perception and language processing than is any other aspect of infant speech perception. It is this ability to treat discriminable variability as equivalent that is required eventually to map sound on to meaning. It has been suggested that although infant *discrimination* abilities may be explained by discontinuities in auditory sensitivities (and can thus be attributed to general auditory mechanisms), the organisation of perceptual *categories* might belie the availability of a specifically phonetic mode of perception (albeit at a more abstract level of processing) even in the very young infant (Kuhl, 1988). It is thus of extreme importance to conduct cross-language investigations of whether infants can categorise non-native stimuli. In our cross-language research, which is reviewed here, we have begun to address the issue of categorisation, but additional work is still required.

CROSS-LANGUAGE SPEECH PERCEPTION RESEARCH

As mentioned earlier, the phonetic relevance of infant perception extends to non-native contrasts. It is clear that young infants are endowed with the ability to discriminate CV syllables according to phonetically relevant boundaries. In contrast to this broad-based ability in young infants, over 20 years of research has shown that adults have more difficulty in discriminating and categorising many non-native phonetic contrasts than they do in discriminating and categorising equally acoustically distinct phonetic contrasts that have functional phonemic status in their native language.

Our work has shown that this developmental change from broad-based to language-specific phonetic perception is evident as early as 10–12 months of age. In an early experiment, English-speaking adults, Hindu-speaking adults, and English-learning infants aged 6–8 months were compared on their ability to discriminate two Hindi speech contrasts: the retroflex/dental place-of-articulation contrast, /Ta/-/ta/, and the voiceless aspirated *vs* breathy voiced dental stops, /t^ha/-/d^ha/. Natural rather than synthetic stimuli were used in this original study to allow us to access discrimination and categorisation of phonetic categories within the context of at least some naturally occurring variation. A native Hindi speaker was recorded producing over 100 repetitions of each syllable type. Several exemplars from each category were selected, such that the distribution of non-phonetic acoustic cues (duration, intensity, fundamental frequency, etc.) overlapped between categories. It was hoped that this would force infants and adults to categorise the stimuli on the basis of phonetically relevant information.

Infants and adults were tested in a variation of the Head Turn procedure (for fuller details, see Kuhl, 1979; 1987). The basic logic of this procedure is that the infants are conditioned to turn their heads when they detect a change in the speech stimulus. Correct (but not incorrect) head turns are reinforced with the activation of single or multiple mechanical toy animals. Adults and older children indicate detection of a change by pushing a button. The procedure can be easily modified to become a categorisation task (see Kuhl, 1979). In our implementation of this procedure, correct performance required that the subjects treat the several exemplars from one phonetic category (e.g. the several retroflex /Ta/'s) as equivalent, and only turn their head when a stimulus from the contrasting category (/ta/) was presented. This task, in contrast to some other infant procedures, requires the infant to categorise the stimuli.

The results indicated that although the Hindi adults and most of the young English-learning infants could reach criterion on the two Hindi contrasts, the majority of the English-speaking adults could not, showing particular difficulty on the retroflex/dental distinction. Indeed, when a second group of English-speaking adults was given 25 training trials on each of the Hindi contrasts, their performance improved on the voicing distinction, but training did not affect performance of the more difficult retroflex/dental contrast. These results confirmed that although young infants are equally sensitive to both native and non-native phonetic contrasts, adult perception is modified by language experience, and the impact of experience is more profound for some non-native contrasts than it is for others (Werker, Gilbert, Humphrey, & Tees, 1981).

The developmental change between infancy and adulthood was subsequently replicated using a non-English contrast from Nthlakampx (Thompson), an Interior Salish Northwest Indian language. The contrast tested was that between a glottalised uvular vs a glottalised velar consonant /k̓i/-/q̓i/. English-learning infants aged 6–8 months and native Nthlakampx-speaking adults were sensitive to this distinction, but the majority of English-speaking adults were not (Werker & Tees, 1984a).

A series of experiments was run to try to identify the age at which the developmental change in sensitivity is first apparent. After first finding that children aged 12-, 8- and even as young as 4-years of age have difficulty with some non-native contrasts (Werker & Tees, 1983), we eventually discovered evidence of a developmental change by 10–12 months of age. Briefly, English-learning infants of 6–8, 8–10, and 10–12 months of age were compared on their ability to discriminate two non-English phonetic contrasts as well as the English bilabial/alveolar contrast, /ba/-/da/. The non-English contrasts were the Hindi retroflex/dental contrast /Ta/-/ta/ and an Interior Salish, Nthlakampx glottalised velar *vs* glottalised uvular contrast /k̓i/-/q̓i/. The youngest English-learning infants could discriminate all three sets of contrasts, but the infants aged 10–12 months could only discriminate the native language /ba/-/da/ distinction. To ensure that the performance of the older infants was not simply a general age-related performance decline, we tested a few Hindi- and Nthlakampx-learning infants aged 11–12 months and found they could quickly reach a 9 out of 10 discrimination criterion on their native contrast (Werker & Tees, 1984a).

This finding of developmental change between 6–12 months of age for the Nthlakampx contrasts has been replicated by Best and McRoberts using a different procedure (reported in Best, in press). They have also recently reported data showing a similar age-related reorganisation for three other click contrasts. There is one very interesting study by Best, McRoberts, and Sithole (1988) that did not replicate our results. In this study, English-learning infants of 6–8, 8–10, 10–12, and 12–14 months of age were compared to both Zulu- and English-speaking adults on their ability to discriminate a Zulu click contrast that does not occur in English. Interestingly, the English adults and the infants of all four ages were able to discriminate this non-native contrast, although the contrast involved two phones that are quite similar acoustically and do not occur in English. Best and colleagues suggested that the developmental change in speech perception did not occur for this contrast because the click sounds were not at all assimilable to English phones. Thus the infants did not process these sounds in terms of their relevance to native-language phonological categories, and therefore retained the ability to discriminate them on the basis of general acoustic cues. This has led to the suggestion that the change from broad-based to language-specific phonetic perception relies on the establishment of a phonological system (Best et al., 1988; Werker, 1991; Werker & Pegg, 1992).

What does this infant data tell us, that may be important for evaluating different cognitive models of speech processing? First, it provides unequivocal evidence that by 10–12 months of age, perceptual sensitivities reflect the distribution of phonetic variability in the ambient language, thus confirming the impact of linguistic experience by this age. Thus any model must include some mechanism for explaining the appearance of language-specific influences by this age. The implications of the results from the infants aged 6–8 months are more ambiguous. The results confirm that infants do have a sensitivity very early in life to many, if not all, of the featural distinctions that specify the phonetic contrasts used across the world's languages. This fact, however, does not disambiguate whether these discriminatory abilities stem from general auditory or specifically linguistic processes.

One way to help disambiguate this issue would be to assess whether infants aged 6–8 months 'categorise' non-native stimuli according to phonetic identity. The initial research did not actually provide direct evidence that infants this young can 'categorise' native stimuli according to phonetic membership. As mentioned earlier the head turn task becomes a categorisation procedure when multiple varying exemplars from both the background and contrasting phonetic categories are used. In our early work, the multiple varying exemplars from each phonetic category were naturally produced by native speakers. This assures that the stimuli have the richness of naturally produced speech, but it does not necessarily control for the acoustic variability within and between categories. Indeed, in the stimuli used in our early work, the variability within each phonetic category was much lower than that between categories. For example, the several retroflex stimuli were much more similar to one another with respect to phonetically informative cues such as the starting frequency of F2 and F3, the characteristics of the burst, etc. than they were to any of the dental stimuli. For this reason, the infants of 6–8 months of age may have grouped the stimuli on the basis of acoustic similarity, and only fortuitously exhibited phonetically relevant categorisation.

To directly assess infants' abilities to categorise CV stimuli according to phonetic category, an equal interval /ba/-/da/-/Da/ continuum was synthesized. The equal steps varied according to the starting frequency of the first and second formant transitions. Infants were tested in the Head Turn procedure using sets of six consecutive stimuli from the continuum. In one condition, the background stimuli comprised the first three stimuli along the continuum, and the test stimuli comprised the next three stimuli. To perform correctly in the Head Turn procedure, the infant had to refrain from turning her head to the presentations of the different stimuli from within the set of background stimuli (the first three adjacent stimuli, being presented in random order), and only turn her head toward the visual reinforcer when one of the next three stimuli was presented. Thus this task required infants to respond selectively to only some changes.[3]

Infants of both 6–8 and 11–13 months of age were tested in three conditions (see Fig. 4.1 for stimulus selections). In the first condition, the two adjacent sets of stimuli were drawn from a section of the continuum such that they were identified as /ba/ and /da/ respectively by adult (English

---

[3] Studies with adults have confirmed that adjacent stimuli from along the continuum are discriminable under at least some testing conditions. Thus it is correct to label this a categorisation task.

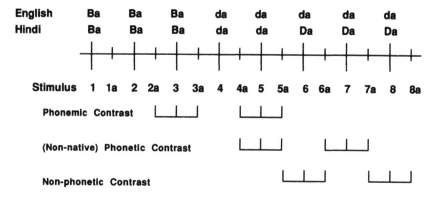

FIG. 4.1. The top part of this figure shows the way English- *vs* Hindi-speaking adults divide the synthetic /ba/-/Da/-/da/ continuum. The bottom half of the figure indicates the stimuli that were used as phonemic, phonetic, and non-phonetic contrasts in Werker and Lalonde, 1988 (Adapted from Werker & Tees, 1992).

and Hindi) listeners. This condition is phonemic to both Hindi- and English-speaking adults. In the second condition the two sets of stimuli were identified as dental /da/ and retroflex /Da/ by adult Hindi listeners, but were all identified as alveolar /da/ by English listeners. This condition is 'phonemic' to a Hindi but not an English listener, but would correspond to a 'universal' phonetic category to an English-speaking adult. In the third condition the two sets of stimuli were identified as primarily all retroflex by Hindi listeners (and as all alveolar by English listeners). This condition, therefore, does not correspond to any phonetic category, and is only defined by equivalent acoustic variability (for further details, see Werker & Lalonde, 1988).

It was reasoned that if perception is phonetically relevant in early infancy, the infants of 6–8 months of age should be able to perform successfully in the first two, but not the third condition. That is, they should be able to categorise sets of varying stimuli according to native or 'universal' phonetic boundaries, but should be unable to categorise stimuli according to an arbitrary point along the continuum that does not conform to a phonetic boundary. This is precisely the pattern of data that was obtained, and confirms the phonetic relevance of speech categorisation in infants as young as 6-months of age. This parallels the research by Kuhl showing that infants of 6-months of age can perceptually categorise vocalic stimuli, differing in speaker and intonation, on the basis of vowel colour (Kuhl, 1979; 1983), and the more recent work showing that vowel categories are organised around phonetic prototypes in human infants (Grieser & Kuhl, 1989) but not in monkeys (Kuhl, 1991). Our cross-language research complements this pattern of data by showing that young infants discriminate stimuli—even stimuli that they have not heard before—in terms of phonetic categories.[4] This pattern of results argues against the generalist's hypothesis that phonetic categories are only gradually constructed by mapping the distribution of variability on to categories, and suggests instead that the young human infant is endowed with a propensity to categorise speech into linguistically significant categories.

The results for the 11–13 month-old infants replicated the findings of Werker and Tees (1984a). These older infants were only able to categorise stimuli according to a phonetic boundary that has functional, phonemic status in their own language, but not according to a phonetic boundary that is ignored by adult speakers of their language. This reconfirms the influence of language experience on the categorisation of speech by the end of the first year of life.[5]

A number of recent studies have shown there to be other native language influences on infant perceptual biases. Mehler et al., (1988) have demonstrated that neonates can discriminate native from non-native speech samples (but not two sets of non-native speech samples) indicating an early sensitivity to the global sound patterning of the native language. Further, it has been shown that infants can detect violations of natural clausal boundaries, by 4 months of age (Hirsh-Pasek et al., 1987), and phrasal boundaries by 9 months of age, but that they cannot detect violations of word boundaries until approximately 11 months of age (Jusczyk, 1992), suggesting that the developmental progression in sensitivity to language-specific sound patterning proceeds from larger to smaller units. Indeed, although infants can detect prosodic differences between native and non-native low-frequency words by as early as 6 months of age, they show no evidence of preferring native words on the basis of phonotactic information until about 9 months of age (Jusczyk, Friedirici, Wessels, Svenkerud, & Jusczyk, in press). These data are all consistent with the finding that sensitivity to language-specific sound patterning at the level of segmental consonantal information is not evident until at least 9 months of age. This only marginally precedes the age at which infants first show a decline in sensitivity to non-native phonetic contrasts. Perhaps recognition of native-language phonotactic patterning is the necessary final step preceding the reorganisation of non-native consonant boundaries.

---

[4] However, our work does not address the question of whether the initial representation is phonetic or syllabic. It would thus be of interest to pursue the question of level of representation using both native and non-native contrasts.

[5] Recent research both in our lab (Polka & Werker, submitted; Werker & Polka, 1993) and by P. Kuhl and her colleagues, (Kuhl, et al., 1991; submitted) suggests that language-specific influences on vowel perception may be apparent by as early as 6-months of age.

RESEARCH IN ADULT CROSS-LANGUAGE
SPEECH PERCEPTION

Research in adult cross-language speech perception makes it clear that although there is a profound impact of experience on cross-language speech perception, developmental changes in sensitivity do not apply to all non-native distinctions (Best et al., 1988; MacKain, 1982; Werker, et al., 1981), and do not indicate an absolute loss of the ability to discriminate non-native distinctions (Werker & Logan, 1985). For example, as mentioned earlier, some Zulu click contrasts are immediately discriminable to adult English speakers (Best, et al., 1988). Similarly, there are many other non-native contrasts that seem quite easy for adult listeners to discriminate (for reviews see Best, in press; Strange, 1986; Werker, in press). In a recent study, Polka (1992) has even shown that there are differences in the ease of discrimination of the Hindi retroflex/dental contrast in different voicing contexts. Furthermore, even in cases where it is clear that adults do have initial difficulty with a non-native distinction, training studies indicate that they can typically improve after being given practice or feedback (Jamieson & Morosan, 1989; Logan, Lively, & Pisoni, 1991; Pisoni, Aslin, Perey, & Hennessy, 1982; Tees & Werker, 1984). It is important to note, however, that in many cases the performance levels they obtain still fall far short of those obtained by native speakers (Polka, 1989; 1991).

Of perhaps even greater interest, is the evidence that adults may show a latent capacity for discriminating even apparently quite difficult contrasts, if the testing procedure is adequately sensitive (Werker & Tees, 1984b). For example, we have shown that although adults most readily discriminate CV speech stimuli in terms of native language phonemic categories, sensitivity to non-native phonetic contrasts is maintained throughout adulthood *even without training* (Werker & Logan, 1985; Werker & Tees, 1984b). This sensitivity to non-native phonetic category differences exists in addition to the already known latent sensitivity to within-phonetic-category acoustic differences (for a review of 2-factor models of speech perception, see Repp, 1983).

To capture the different processing capabilities available to adult listeners, in 1985 Logan and I presented a 3-factor model of adult speech perception including *phonemic, phonetic,* and *acoustic* factors (Werker & Logan, 1985; see also Mann, 1986). Phonemic refers to the privileged sensitivity to phonetic contrasts that have functional phonemic status in one's native language. Phonetic refers to the continued sensitivity to non-native phonetic contrasts. Acoustic refers to the sensitivity to acoustic differences even within a phonetic category.

Our first demonstration of three independent processing factors rested on differential patterns of performance at varying inter-stimulus-intervals

(ISI). At a 1500msec ISI, (and with no practice) adult English subjects could only discriminate pairs of stimuli differing in phonemic status. At a 250msec ISI they demonstrated sensitivity to non-native phonetic differences. Surprisingly, it was at the intermediate ISI of 500msec that subjects demonstrated a sensitivity to within-category, non-phonetic differences.

Recently, we have completed another set of experiments replicating the finding of three separate processing factors, using a new contextual manipulation, and using synthetic rather than naturally produced retroflex and dental tokens (Morosan & Werker, in preparation). The synthetic tokens were the same as those used in the infant study presented at the end of the preceding section: briefly, a continuum was constructed by varying the starting frequency of the second and third formants in equal steps (for stimulus descriptions, see Werker and Lalonde, 1988). A labelling experiment was conducted to ascertain the most common boundaries between /ba/, /da/, and /Da/ (Werker & Lalonde, 1988). In the current study, adult English-speaking subjects were tested in a Same/ Different task on their ability to discriminate pairs of stimuli from along this continuum (refer to Fig. 4.1). The physically identical pairings included a particular stimuli, e.g. step 2 on the continuum, paired with itself. The other three pairings types all included equal numbers of 1- and 2-step pairings taken from the synthetic continuum. The 'phonemic' pairings were selected at points along the continuum to include a /ba/ and a /da/ token (e.g. stimulus 3 vs stimulus 4). The 'phonetically different' pairings included a retroflex /Da/ paired with a dental /da/ (e.g. stimulus 5 vs stimulus 6). The 'acoustically different' pairings included two exemplars from within the same phonetic category (e.g. stimulus 1 vs stimulus 2), with an equal number of pairings from each phonetic category.

The contextual manipulation in this study involved varying the kinds of pairings used in the stimulus set. There were three contextual conditions, with 10 subjects tested in each condition. In the first contextual condition, all four kinds of pairings were present: phonemically different (bilabial/ dental), phonetically different (retroflex/dental), acoustically different (two different bilabial, dental, or retroflex stimuli), and physically identical (the same token paired with itself). In the second contextual condition, the phonemically different pairings were eliminated, leaving only phonetically different, acoustically different, and physically identical pairings. In the third contextual condition, only acoustically different and physically identical pairings were presented.

As expected, in the first contextual condition, subjects could easily discriminate the phonemically different (English bilabial/dental) pairings (over 90% correct). Of greater interest was the relative performance on the phonetically different and acoustically different pairings across the three contextual conditions. Because we feared that an overall improvement in performance on these two pairing types across the three conditions might simply reflect a change in bias, discrimination scores in the phonetically and acoustically different conditions were converted to A^1 scores using the proportion Different responses to physically identical pairings as an index of false alarm rate.

The results from this study revealed that in the first contextual condition in which phonemically different (English bilabial/dental) pairings were part of the stimulus set, subjects showed significantly higher A^1 scores on the phonetically different (Hindi retroflex/dental) pairngs (A^1 = 0.673) than on the acoustically different pairings (A^1 = 0.58). In the second contextual condition, English listeners performed identically on both the phonetically different (A^1 = 0.608) and acoustically different pairings (A^1 = 0.593). Finally, in the third contextual condition, subjects' performance on the acoustically different pairings (A^1 = 0.623) was comparable to their performance on the acoustically different pairings in the other two conditions. These results indicate that phonemic processing is by far the most available and robust processing style, but that phonetic processing is also invoked when linguistically relevant, phonological contrasts are present in the stimulus set. Under such conditions, the phonetic factor appears to take priority over general sensitivity to equally distinct acoustic differences. In the second contextual condition, without the presence of linguistically relevant (phonemic) contrasts, there was no evidence for phonetic processing. Rather, performance on the phonetically different pairings was identical to that on the acoustically different pairings, indicating that in this contextual condition, stimuli were differentiated on the basis of absolute acoustic differences irrespective of phonetic status.

What do these results from cross-language studies with adults tell us about universal capabilities? First, they tell us that although there are clear experientially based changes in the ease with which non-native contrasts can be discriminated, the underlying sensitivity to both universal phonetic and to non-phonetic acoustic differences remains. Thus it would be incorrect to conclude that lack of listening experience leads to some permanent 'loss' in either ability. The results of the final set of studies with adults indicates, however, that the latent sensitivity to features distinguishing non-native phonetic contrasts should not be considered isomorphic to the latent sensitivity to non-phonetic, acoustic differences. The phonetic sensitivites are triggered and heightened in a context that invokes linguistic processing, whereas the non-phonetic auditory sensitivities seem to remain constant across contexts. Thus, although linguistic experience exerts an enormous influence on the ease with which listeners can discriminate minimal pair distinctions, these results leave no doubt that an enhanced sensitivity to universal phonetic distinctions is maintained, even in the absence of supportive linguistic experience. This would argue against a model of speech processing that equates perception of non-native phonetic contrasts (even in adults) to general auditory processing (see for example, Jusczyk, this volume), and would be more consistent with a model in which the perception of information specifying phonetic contrasts is seen to have a special status.

NEW WAYS OF EXAMINING WHETHER SPEECH IS SPECIAL

The hypothesis that is most consistent with a strong 'speech is special' theoretical orientation is that, from very early infancy, speech is perceived by a perceptual module that is explicitly designed to perform phonetic analysis. In considering this possibility, it is important to remember that speech perception is not the only perceptual domain for which domain specificity has been posited. Indeed, one of the most important developments within cognitive science during the last decade has been the increasingly strong influence of modularity (e.g. Fodor, 1983). The general position that has been suggested is that there are specialised computational routines (thought to be accompanied by specialised neural architecture) to perform many perceptual and cognitive functions. Modular processing is described as rapid, mandatory, and impenetrable to higher cognitive operations (Fodor, 1983; Marr, 1982).

In order to evaluate the 'speech is special' proposition in the light of a more generic modular approach, it is thus of interest to examine whether a modular view can adequately account for the findings reviewed here. Three factors will be explored in the remaining pages of this chapter. First, although it is easy to understand how a modular view might account for the abilities shown by a young infant, it is less easy to see how the functioning of a module might be influenced by experience. Thus some consideration will be given to experiential influences on modular functioning. Second, the notion of modularity carries with it the demand that input systems be classified according to functional rather than traditional (e.g. separate sensory systems) divisions. Thus, if the specialised module is one designed to compute phonetic analyses, it could be argued that the sensory modality used is irrelevant, and it should not matter whether the phonetic information received is acoustic or visual in form. An example of research conducted from this perspective will be presented. Finally, the claim that modular phonetic processes are impenetrable to the influence of higher cognitive operations will be considered, and an initial attempt to address this question will also be discussed.

Until recently there has been almost no discussion of how experiential influences might affect the functioning of specialised input modules. One general prediction from learnability theory is that several possible settings exist for each parameter within the Universal Grammar, and language-specific influences simply trigger which value is selected. Consistent with this approach, Liberman and Mattingly, (1991) suggest that age-related changes in cross-language speech perception can be explained by a direct resetting of the parameters in the phonetic module. They argue that the broad-based phonetic sensitivities that are evident in the young infant represent the default settings in the phonetic module. The settings in this module are recalibrated in accordance with the specifications of the phonetic input in the child's language environment. It is this process that leads to a change in sensitivity to non-native contrasts.

Can this explanation account for the set of data reviewed earlier detailing age-related changes in cross-language speech perception? It can adequately account for initial abilities, and would be consistent with a scenario in which perceptual sensitivities increasingly reflect the properties of the native language phonology across the first year(s) of life. It is not as easy, however, to understand how such a view can account for the maintenance of both 'universal' and language-specific capabilities in adulthood. Modular functioning is described as being mandatory. Thus one would predict that if the phonetic module is engaged, adults listeners should only be able to analyse speech signals according to a single value for the parametric settings, and would not simultaneously also show a sensitivity to non-native phonetic variability.[6] However, the research by Werker and Logan (1985), and that by Morosan and Werker (in preparation) suggests that adult listeners can process the same information according to language-specific phonemic, broad-based phonetic, and non-phonetic (acoustic) criteria. Thus, in its present form, it is difficult to understand how the modular explanation can account for the full set of findings in adult cross-language speech perception.

The second prediction resulting from a modular approach is that other sources of information about phonetics—in addition to acoustic signals—should be processed by the phonetic module. One candidate capability is bimodal speech perception. To clarify briefly, in 1976, McGurk and MacDonald published a study showing that visual and auditory information both contribute to the speech percept (see also Summerfield, 1990).

---

[6] It should be noted that it is already recognised that the same signal can be simultaneously analysed by the phonetic module as well as by general purpose auditory perception mechanisms (Whalen & Liberman, 1987). The data pattern presented in the current chapter requires that in addition to this, the phonetic module be capable of having two possible settings simultaneously.

Many researchers (but not all; e.g. Massaro, 1987) interpret this data as support for the proposition that there is an input module designed for phonetic analysis, and that it accepts visual as well as auditory information. The reports that infants as young as a few days old recognise the equivalence between visual and acoustic speech information (Kuhl & Meltzhoff, 1982; MacKain et al., 1983) can be interpreted as evidence that a phonetic module is functioning from a very early age.

A logical extension of this line of reasoning would be to predict that if visual and acoustic information are interchangeable to the phonetic module, then language-specific influences should also lead to a reorganisation in the visual aspects of speech perception. We recently conducted an experiment to test this hypothesis.

In this study French- and English-speaking Canadians were compared on their perception of the interdental fricative viseme /ða/ (Werker, McGurk, & Frost, 1992). This viseme has functional status in English, but not in the French spoken in Quebec, Canada. Five groups of subjects varying in their English proficiency were tested. The first four groups were native French speakers, with beginning, intermediate, advanced, and fully bilingual knowledge of English. The fifth group was composed of English monolinguals. All subjects were tested with presentations of a male speaker articulating the syllables /ba/, /va/, /ða/, /da/, /za/ and /ga/. These stimuli were presented alone in the lip-reading condition. In the auditory-visual condition, the visible articulations were all paired with the spoken syllable /ba/. In addition, there were two auditory-only conditions: /ba/'s alone, and all the above phonemes—/ba/, /va/, /ða/, /da/, /za/, and /ga/.

On the basis of the existing studies of cross-language speech perception, one would predict that the French-speaking Canadians would be less likely to report having perceived /ða/ in the auditory-alone conditions. This data pattern was found. Of more interest, the results showed a clear effect of experience on the visual aspects of speech perception. In the auditory-visual condition there was a linear increase in the percent visual capture responses to /ða/ (reporting /ða/ in the 'ða'-lips 'ba'–voice condition) as a function of English experience (see Fig. 4.2). The French-speaking subjects with little experience with language input in which an interdental fricative is used (in other words, with little experience with English), predominantly perceived the visual articulation in this condition as being a dental French /ta/ or /da/. This is consistent with the possibility that the same processes which lead to a reorganisation in the auditory aspects of speech perception, affect the visual aspects as well. Although other potential explanations could also be posited to explain these data, these findings are compatable with a modular recalibration explanation.

The third line of evidence to be considered, which is relevant to the modularity claim, concerns the issue of whether phonetic processing can

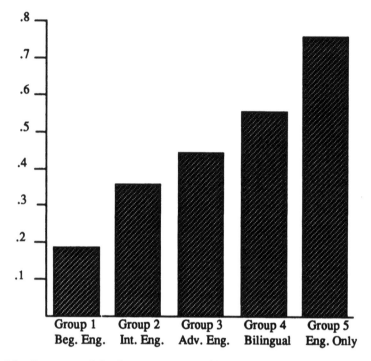

FIG. 4.2. Percentage of visual capture responses (/ð/ responses) to the interdental articulation paired with the acoustic 'ba' as a function of experience with English. Adapted from Werker, Frost, and McGurk, 1992. Canadian Psychological Association. Reprinted with permission.

be influenced by higher cognitive processes. According to the proposition that specialised modules are impenetrable to more general cognitive operations, such influences should not be possible. Recently, Lalonde and I (Lalonde, 1989; Lalonde & Werker, submitted) reported on an initial experiment testing the notion that the developmental reorganisation in cross-language speech perception involves the availability and application of general cognitive abilities to the phonetic domain. In other words, we attempt to falsify one of the tenets of modularity, by testing whether the age-related change in non-native speech perception could be related to other developing cognitive abilities. We reasoned that a tight relationship between age-related changes in speech perception and other cognitive tasks would argue against claims of domain specificity, and might even challenge the notion of the impenetrability of a phonetic module.

The first challenge was to find a fairly basic cognitive skill that first becomes apparent around 9–10 months of age, and then select several tasks that are all thought to rely on this same underlying ability. A conclusion reached by many different researchers working in the area of infant cognition is that between around 8–10 months of age, infants first become able to simultaneously coordinate or relate separate sources of information (Fischer & Pipp, 1984; Piaget, 1952). This is based both on observations (Piaget, 1952), and on empirical evidence in many different task domains including: the delayed-response object-search task (Diamond, 1985); the emergence of coordinated hand movements (Ramsay, 1984); the coordination of patterns of looking behaviour (Bertenthal, Campos, & Haith, 1980); and, perhaps most convincingly, the infant's emerging ability to form perceptual categories on the basis of the correlation between three or four different attributes (Cohen, 1991; Younger & Cohen, 1983). In a series of studies comparing infant monkeys, infant humans, and brain-damaged adults of both species, Diamond has provided some very convincing evidence that this ability to simultaneously relate several sources of information may rely on the development and intact functioning of collosal connections between the hemispheres, as well as measurable changes in prefrontal cortex (Diamond, 1991).

If the developmental reorganisation in cross-language speech perception is made possible by this emerging general cognitive ability, one would expect to see a high interdependency between the developmental change in cross-language speech perception and developmental changes in other tasks that also rely on this same ability. In an initial test of this hypothesis, Lalonde (1989; Lalonde & Werker, under review) compared the developmental emergence of three tasks. The three tasks were chosen to have very different surface characteristics, but to be amenable to explanation on the basis of the same underlying cognitive skill. The three tasks were: (1) delayed-response object search; (2) visual categorisation on the basis of the correlational structure of the attributes, and; (3) non-native speech perception.

In the object search (AB) task, the infant is required to search for an object hidden at a new location, after successfully searching at the first location (Piaget, 1952). In our implementation of this task, a three-second delay precedes the second search (Diamond, 1985). The visual categorisation task required the infant to recognise perceptual categories based on the correlation of visual features in two dimensional drawings (Younger & Cohen, 1983). The speech perception task involved asking infants to discriminate the Hindi (non-English) retroflex-dental contrast as in our previous work (For more details on the task analysis, see Lalonde 1989; Lalonde & Werker, submitted).

Forty infants (19 male and 21 female) aged approximately 9 months (range 8.25–10.09) were tested. The majority of the infants who passed the object search task also passed both the visual categorisation and the speech perception tasks, whereas the majority of the infants who failed the object search task also failed both the other tasks. The infants who showed the AB error were intermediate (and inconsistent) in performance on the other two tasks. Of most importance, this pattern of results held, even when the effect of age was entered as a covariate in an analysis of variance of performance on the different tasks. The results of a prediction analysis also indicated that the 'best' model for accounting for this data is one in which all three tasks are linked developmentally.

Do these data represent a serious challenge to a modular view of speech perception, or can they, in fact, be accommodated by such a view? They are consistent with the possibility that the reorganisation in cross-language speech perception is at least related to, if not dependent on, the emerging cognitive ability to coordinate separate sources of information. On first consideration this could suggest that higher cognitive operations can influence speech perception, thus invalidating both the value of considering this a domain-specific reorganisation as well as invalidating the modularity claim of 'impenetrability'. However, the modularity position with respect to impenetrability turns out to be impossible to falsify. That is, it is argued that although the functioning of the module cannot be affected by more abstract cognitive operations, the 'outputs' from the module can be acted on by general cognitive processes. Thus the evidence of an interdependence between developmental changes in cognitive functioning and age-related changes in non-native speech perception could be explained simply by suggesting that when cognitive abilities emerge, they can be applied to the outputs from any modular system—including the outputs resulting from domain-specific computations within the phonetic module. This lack of falsifiability is very troublesome, and underscores the necessity for further theoretical clarification.

In summary, in this chapter recent research in the area of infant speech perception and cross-language speech perception has been reviewed with the aim of shedding light on the question of whether speech perception involves specialised phonetic or more general perceptual/cognitive abilities. Although no clear conclusions are drawn in the present chapter, areas of interest to this controversy are identified, and areas are highlighted in which further theoretical development is required.

REFERENCES

Bertenthal, B.I., Campos, J.J., & Haith, M.M. (1980). Development of visual organization: The perception of subjective contours. *Child Development, 51*, 1072–1080.

Bertoncini, J., Bijeljac-Babic, R., Jusczyk, P.W., Kennedy, L., & Mehler, J. (1988). An investigation of young infants' perceptual represention of speech sounds. *Journal of Experimental Psychology: General, 117*: 21–33.

Bertoncini, J., Morais, J., Bijeljac-Babic, R., McAdams, S., Peretz, I., & Mehler, J. (1989). Dichotic perception and laterality in neonates. *Brain and Language, 37*, 591–605.

Best, C.T. (in press). The emergence of language-specific phonemic influences in infant speech perception. In J. Goodman & H. Nusbaum (Eds.), *The transition from speech sounds to spoken words: The development of speech perception.* Cambridge, MA: MIT Press.

Best, C.T., Hoffman, H., & Glanville, B.B. (1982). Development of infant ear asymmetries for speech and music. *Perception and Psychophysics, 31,* 75–85.

Best, C.T., McRoberts, G.W., & Sithole, N.N. (1988). The phonological basis of perceptual loss for non-native contrasts: Maintenance of discrimination among Zulu clicks by English-speaking adults and infants. *Journal of Experimental Psychology: Human perception and Performance, 14,* 345–360.

Carey, D., & Gelman, S. (Eds.), (1991). *The epigenesis of mind: Essays on biology and cognition.* Hillsdale, NJ: Lawrence Erlbaum Associates Inc.

Cohen, L.B. (1991). An information processing approach to infant cognitive development. In L. Weiskrantz (Ed.), *Thought without language.* Cambridge, MA: Oxford University Press.

Diamond, A. (1985). The development of the ability to use recall to guide action, as indicated by infants' performance on AB. *Child Development, 56,* 868–883.

Diamond, A. (1991). Neuropsychological insights into the meaning of object concept development. In S. Carey & R. Gelman (Eds.), *The epigenesis of mind: Essays on biology and cognition.* Hillsdale, NJ: Lawrence Erlbaum Associates Inc.

Eimas, P.D. (1975). Developmental studies in speech perception. In L.B. Cohen & P. Salapatek (Eds.), *Infant perception: From sensation to perception, Volume 2.* New York: Academic Press.

Eimas, P.D., Siqueland, E.R., Jusczyk, P., & Vigorito, J. (1971). Speech perception in infants. *Science, 171,* 303–306.

Fischer, K.W. & Pipp, S.L. (1984). Processes of cognitive development: Optimal level and skill acquisition. In R.J. Sternberg (Ed.), *Mechanisms of cognitive development.* San Francisco: W.H. Freeman.

Fodor, J.A. (1983). *The modularity of mind.* Cambridge, MA: MIT Press.

Grieser, D., & Kuhl, P.J. (1989). Categorization of speech by infants: Support for speech-sound prototypes. *Developmental Psychology, 25,* 577–588.

Hirsh-Pasek, K., Kemler-Nelson, D.G., Jusczyk, P.W., Wright-Cassidy, K., Druss, B., & Kennedy, L. (1987). Clauses are perceptual units for young infants. *Cognition, 26,* 268–286.

Jamieson, D.G., & Morosan, D.E. (1989). Training new non-native speech contrasts: A comparison of the prototype and perceptual fading techniques. *Canadian Journal of Psychology, 43,* 88–96.

Jusczyk, P.W. (1989 April). *Perception of cues to clausal units in native and non-native languages.* Paper presented at Society for Research in Child Development. Kansas City, Missouri.

Jusczyk, P.W. (in press). Developing phonological categories from the speech signal. In C. Ferguson, L. Menn, & C. Stoel-Gammon (Eds.), *Phonological development: Models, research and implications.* Parkton Maryland: York Press.

Jusczyk, P.W., & Derrah, C. (1987). Representation of speech sounds by young infants. *Developmental Psychology, 23,* 648–654.

Jusczyk, P.W., Friederici, A.D., Wessels, J., Svenkerud, V.Y., & Jusczyk, A.M. (in press). Infant's sensitivity to the sound patterns of native language words. *Journal of Memory and Language.*

Jusczyk, P.W., Pisoni, D.P., Walley, A., & Murray, J. (1980). Discrimination of relative onset time of two-component tones by infants. *Journal of the Acoustical Society of America, 67,* 262–270.

Kuhl, P.J. (1979). Speech perception in early infancy: Perceptual constancy for spectrally dissimilar vowel categories. *Journal of Acoustic Society of America, 66,* 1168–1179.

Kuhl, P.J. (1983). Perception of auditory equivalence classes for speech in early infancy. *Infant Behavior and Development, 6,* 263–285.

Kuhl, P.J. (1987). Perception of speech and sound in early infancy. In P. Salapatek & L. Cohen (Eds.), *Handbook of infant perception: Volume 2*, New York: Academic Press.

Kuhl, P.J. (1988). Auditory perception and the evolution of speech. *Human Evolution, 3*, 19–43.

Kuhl, P.J. (1991). Human adults and human infants show a 'perceptual magnet effect' for the prototypes of speech categories: Monkeys do not. *Perception and Psychophysics, 50*, 93–107.

Kuhl, P.J., & Meltzhoff, A.N. (1982). The bimodal perception of speech in infancy. *Science, 218*, 1138–1144.

Kuhl, P.K., & Miller, J.D. (1975). Speech perception by the chinchilla: Voice-voiceless distinction in alveolar plosive consonants. *Science, 190*, 69–72.

Kuhl, P.J., & Miller, J.D. (1982). Discrimination of auditory target dimensions in the presence of absence of variation in a second dimension by infants. *Perception & Psychophysics, 31*, 279–292.

Kuhl, P.K., Williams, K.A., Lacerda, F., Stevens, K.N., & Lindblom, B. (1992). Linguistic experience alters phonetic perception in infants by 6 months of age. *Science, 255*, 606–608.

Lalonde, C.E. (1989). *An investigation of the relations among object search skills, cross-language speech perception, and visual categorization in infancy*. Masters Thesis, University of British Columbia.

Lalonde, C.E., & Werker, J.F. (submitted). *Cognitive influences on cross-language speech perception in infancy*.

Liberman, A.M., & Mattingly, I.G. (1985). The motor theory of speech perception revised. *Cognition, 21*, 1–36.

Liberman, A.M. & Mattingley, I.G. (1991). Modularity and the effects of experience. New Haven, CT: *Haskins Laboratories Status Report on Speech Research, SR 105/106*, 65–68.

Logan, J.S., Lively, S.E., & Pisoni, D.B. (1991). Training Japanese listeners to identify /r/ and /l/: A first report. *Journal of the Acoustical Society of America, 89*, 874–886.

MacKain, K.S. (1982). Assessing the role of experience on infants' speech discrimination. *Journal of Child Language, 9*, 527–542.

MacKain, K.S., Studdert-Kennedy, M., Spieker, S., & Stern, D. (1983). Infant intermodal speech perception is a left-hemisphere function. *Science, 219*, 1347–1349.

Mann, V.A. (1986). Distinguishing universal and language-dependent levels of speech perception: Evidence from Japanese listeners' perception of English 'l' and 'r'. *Cognition, 24*, 169–196.

Marr, D. (1982). *Vision*. San Francisco, CA: Freeman.

Massaro, D.W. (1987). *Speech perception by ear and eye: A paradigm for psychological inquiry*. Hillsdale, NJ: Lawrence Erlbaum Associates Inc.

McGurk, H. & MacDonald, J. (1976). Hearing lips and seeing voices. *Nature, 264*, 229–239.

Mehler, J., Jusczyk, P.W., Lambertz, G., Halstead, N., Bertoncini, J., & Amiel-Tison, C. (1988). A precursor of language acquisition in young infants. *Cognition, 29*, 143–178.

Miller, J.L. (1981). Some effects of speaking rate on phonetic perception. *Phonetica, 38*, 159–180.

Miller, J.L., & Eimas, P.D. (1983). Studies on the categorization of speech by infants. *Cognition, 13*, 135–165.

Molfese, D.L., & Molfese, V.J. (1979). Hemisphere and stimulus differences as reflected in the cortical responses of newborn infants to speech stimuli. *Developmental Psychology, 15*, 505–511.

Morosan, D., & Werker, J.F. (in preparation). *Further evidence for three factors in adult speech perception*.

Piaget, J. (1952). *The origins of intelligence in children*. New York: Norton.

Pisoni, D.B., Aslin, R.N., Perey, A.J., & Henenssy, B.L. (1982). Some effects of laboratory training on identification and discrimination of voicing contrasts in stop consonants. *Journal of Experimental Psychology: Human perception and Performance*, *8*, 297–314.

Polka, L. (1991). Cross-language speech perception in adults: Phonemic, phonetic, and acoustic contributions. *Journal of the Acoustical Society of America*, *89*, 2961–1977.

Polka, L. (1992). Characterizing the influence of native language experience on adult speech perception. *Perception & Psychophysics*, *52*, 37–52.

Polka, L., & Werker, J.F. (submitted). Developmental changes in perception of non-native contrasts. *Journal of Experimental Psychology: Human perception and performance*.

Ramsay, D.S. (1984). Onset of duplicated syllable babbling and unimanual handedness in infancy: Evidence for developmental change in hemispheric specialization? *Developmental Psychology*, *20*, 64–71.

Repp, B.H. (1983). Categorical perception: Issues, methods, and findings. In N.L. Lass (Ed.), *Speech and languages: Advances in basic research and practice, Volume 10*. New York: Academic Press.

Strange, W. (1986). Speech input and the development of speech perception. In J.F. Kavanagh (Ed.), *Otitis media and child development*. Parkton, MD: Yorkton Press.

Streeter, L.A. (1976). Language perception of two-month old infants shows effects of both innate mechanisms and experience. *Nature*, *259*, 39–41.

Summerfield, Q. (1990). Visual perception of phonetic gestures. In I.G. Mattingly & M. Studdert-Kennedy (Eds.), *Modularity and the motor theory of speech perception*. Hillsdale, NJ: Lawrence Erlbaum Associates Inc.

Tees, R.C., & Werker, J.F. (1984). Perceptual flexibility: Maintenance of recovery of the ability to discriminate non-native speech sounds. *Canadian Journal of Psychology*, *38*, 579–590.

Trehub, S.E. (1976). The discrimination of foreign speech contrasts by infants and adults. *Child Development*, *47*, 466–472.

Werker, J.F. (1989). Becoming a native listener. *American Scientist*, *77*, 54–59.

Werker, J.F. (1991). Ontogeny of Speech Perception. In I.G. Mattingly & M. Studdert-Kennedy (Eds.), *Modularity and the motor theory of speech perception*. Hillsdale, NJ.: Lawrence Erlbaum Associates Inc.

Werker, J.F. (in press). Cross-language speech perception: Developmental changes does not involve loss. In J.C. Goodman & H.C. Nusbaum (Eds.), The transition from speech sounds to spoken words: The development of speech perception, Cambridge, MA: MIT Press.

Werker, J.F., & Lalonde, C.E. (1988). Cross-language speech perception: Initial capabilities and developmental change. *Developmental Psychology*, *24(5)*, 672–683.

Werker, J.F., & Logan, J.S. (1985). Cross-language evidence for three factors in speech perception. *Perception & Psychophysics*, *37*, 35–44.

Werker, J.F., McGurk, H., & Frost, P.E. (1992). La langue et les levres: Cross-language influences on bimodal speech perception. *Canadian Journal of Psychology*, *46*, 551–568.

Werker, J.F., & Pegg, J.E. (in press). Infant speech perception and phonological acquisition. In C. Ferguson, L. Menn, & C. Stoel-Gammon (Eds.), *Phonological Development: Models, Research, and Implications*, Parkton Maryland: York Press.

Werker, J.F., & Polka, L. (1993). Developmental changes in speech perception: New challenges and new directions. *Journal of Phonetics*, *21*, 83–101

Werker, J.F., & Tees, R.C., (1983). Developmental changes across childhood in the perception of non-native speech sounds. *Canadian Journal of Psychology, 37(2)*, 278–286.

Werker, J.F., & Tees, R.C. (1984a). Cross-language speech perception: Evidence for perceptual reorganisation during the first year of life. *Infant Behaviour and Development*, *7*, 49–63.

Werker, J.F., & Tees, R.C. (1984b). Phonemic and phonetic factors in adult cross-language speech perception. *Journal of the Acoustical Society of America, 75*, 1866–1878.

Werker, J.F., & Tees, R.C. (1992). The organization and reorganization of human speech perception. *Annual Review of Neuroscience, 15*, 377–402.

Werker, J.F., Gilbert, J.H.V., Humphrey, K., & Tees, R.C. (1981). Developmental aspects of cross-language speech perception. *Child Development, 52*, 349–353.

Whalen, D.H., & Liberman, A.M. (1987). Speech perception takes precedence over non-speech perception. *Science, 237*, 169–171.

Younger, B.A., & Cohen, L. (1983). Infant perception of correlations among attributes. *Child Development, 54*, 858–867.

II

Pre-lexical Processing and
Lexical Representation

5

The Time Course of Prelexical Processing: The Syllabic Hypothesis Revisited

Emmanuel Dupoux
University of Arizona, CNRS & ENST, France.

INTRODUCTION

There are two main problems in spoken word recognition. The first one is to understand how speech sounds are categorised, for example, how various utterances of 'dog' are perceived as the same speech object. The second is to model how these categorised sounds, or *prelexical representations*, are mapped onto lexical and phonological representations. In this chapter, I will address mainly the second issue, and examine how recent data using segment detection tasks can tease apart the various hypotheses about prelexical processing.

One of the early approaches was to take phonological theory seriously, and to propose that speech sounds are first represented in terms of distinctive features. These features are then combined to form phonemes, and phonemes are concatenated to build words. Although the notion that the first level of speech processing is composed of feature detectors has lost some impetus during the 1970s (see Diehl, 1976; Eimas & Corbit, 1973; Samuel & Newport, 1979; among many others), this hierarchical picture, where smaller elements are concatenated from left to right to build larger ones, is still the unmarked view in spoken word recognition.

This view has been challenged, however, on various grounds. For instance, machine oriented approaches to speech perception have questioned the view that there are prelexical representations at all. The idea is that having features or phonemes as basic units is undesirable, since it forces the system to lose information at a very early stage, and hence provokes unrecoverable errors (Klatt, 1977, 1980, 1989). In Klatt's model, words are extracted directly from low level spectral templates, without any prior segmentation.

Another challenge, coming from a more psychologically motivated approach, has been directed against the hierarchical picture. It has been denied that syllable identification depends on the prior processing of phonemic segments. On the contrary, it has been proposed that phonemes are derived from larger Gestalt-like units such as the syllable (Mehler, 1981; Segui & Frauenfelder, 1981; Savin & Bever, 1970; Segui, 1984; Segui et al., 1990). For instance, when the word PAL-MIER is presented, the first syllable *pal* is extracted and categorised. This information is in turn used to activate lexical candidates (all words starting with the syllable *pal*) and to extract the phonemic structure of the utterance (/p/ /a/ /l/ . . .).

In the following sections, the empirical evidence that bears on the phoneme *vs* syllable issue will be reviewed. The focus will be on tasks where subjects have to detect individual phonemes or syllabic elements that occur in isolated words. My hope is that the detailed study of how these tasks are performed will shed new light on the levels of processing that are involved in speech perception.

THE PERCEPTUAL REALITY ISSUE

Years of acoustic–phonetic research have shown that the speech stream does not presents itself as a nice string of phonemes. There is no segment of acoustic waveform that uniquely corresponds to a phonetic segment. Nonetheless, even if phonemic segments do not have an *acoustic reality*, it has long been held that they have *perceptual reality*, that is, that phonemes are the units in which the phonological structure of the utterance is represented, and later used to recognise words. It is this contention that we will examine next.

Phoneme *vs* Syllable Monitoring: Who Wins?

In a seminal study, Savin and Bever (1970) found that latencies for detecting a syllable like [ba] were shorter than for detecting a single phoneme /b/. Such a result was unexpected on the view that large segments are the result of the concatenation of smaller ones. Savin and Bever argued that their results were congruent with the opposite view that phonemes are extracted from larger syllable-like units, which are the real perceptual units. This interpretation, to say the least, did not generate universal approval (Healy & Cutting, 1976; McNeil & Linding, 1973; Mills, 1980; Norris & Cutler, 1988). The disagreement concerned: (1) the reality of the effect itself, and; (2) the interpretation of the effect. Let us deal first with arguments about the reality of the effect reported by Savin and Bever.

The superiority of syllables over phonemes was questioned on various grounds; the most serious attack was launched by Norris and Cutler (1988) who argued that the effect is not real, but is an artifact of the experimental conditions. They noticed that in most experiments of the Savin and Bever sort, there were no *catch trials* that would force the subject to perform an exhaustive match between the specified target and the presented utterance. Thus they argued that, in the case of syllabic targets, subjects could base their response, not on the first syllable, but on the first *phoneme* of the utterance. As pointed out by Norris and Cutler, this very observation makes the comparison of reaction times across different target types rather debatable. They also show that when catch trials are included in the experimental lists, the reaction time to syllabic targets becomes slower than the reaction time to single phonemes, reversing Savin and Bever's result. The point here is that if one wants to compare reaction times across different target types, one must be sure that the various parameters that influence decision (bias, number of catch trials, payoff matrix, etc) are held constant across these types. The point is well made, but Norris and Cutler's conclusion may seem a little bit too extreme.

First, simply adding a fixed number of catch trials across the different targets is not really fair, because it is difficult to quantify, if not equate, the *amount* of interference caused by the catch trials across target conditions. What counts as a difficult catch trial in the case of phoneme detection is not the same in syllable detection. In fact, in Norris and Cutler's experiment, syllabic catch trials produced a much larger amount of interference (between 43ms and 133ms) than phonemic catch trials (29ms).

Moreover, in the absence of any catch trials, the pattern of reaction time across different target types is still informative. Even if subjects are partly guessing, they are doing so on the basis of some type of minimal acoustic information. In fact, there is a way of designing the target detection experiment which sidesteps the problem of catch trials. In this technique, the target is always a single phoneme, but in the experimental lists this phoneme may covary with adjacent phonemes (see Day & Wood, 1972; Swinney & Prather, 1980; Wood & Day, 1975). It is thus possible to measure the amount of facilitation or interference on detection times caused by this pattern of correlation. Indeed, Day and Wood (1972) found that the classification of one dimension (for instance place of articulation) was slower when the irrelevant dimension (vowel quality) was varied than when it was kept constant; that is, [ba],[bae] *vs* [da],[dae] was responded to slower than [ba] *vs* [da]. This is comparable to Savin and Bever's syllable superiority effect. Swinney and Prather reported similar results using a different methodology and found that the more varied the vowel was, the longer was the reaction time.[1]

Finally, the syllable versus phoneme debate has to be placed in the more general context of 'metalinguistic performance'. In fact, when one looks across different populations, the superiority of syllables over phonemes is not an accident due to some specific experimental condition, but appears to be the unmarked case. Hence illiterates find it extremely difficult to perform metalinguistic games that involve the manipulation (deletion, insertion, counting) of individual phonemes. In contrast, they perform at quite a good level when it comes to manipulating syllables (see Bertelson, 1986 for a review). This pattern is also found in literates of non alphabetic writing systems (Mann, 1986; Read et al., 1986). So it appears that, whereas syllables are naturally salient units, one needs some kind of formal training to be aware of phonemes. Hence it is not surprising that this difficulty with phonemes is also found in adult reader's reaction times.

In brief, the fact that large units like syllables are more easily detected than single phonemes appears to be experimentally secure. However, as we shall see, there remains considerable controversy about how to interpret this effect in the right way. The controversy concerns not only particular theoretical claims about the role of syllables and other units in speech perception, but, more profoundly, the way in which reaction times studies can be used to infer processing architecture. In Savin and Bever's logic, RTs directly reflect processing complexity: the longer it takes to detect a given segment, the later this segment is supposed to have been computed. However, such an inference is not inevitable. In psycholinguistic tasks, one does not study hard-wired reflexes. Even though the input signal is analysed by an encapsulated, fast, speech specific, processing system that looks like a reflex, the decision to push a button or not is eventually made by a slow, penetrable, general purpose cognitive system (Pylyshyn, 1984; Posner & Snyder, 1975). This system can inspect several representations of the input and use varying response criteria (see Forster, 1979; Dupoux & Mehler, 1992). In this view, response latencies may not necessarily reflect the speed with which the

---

[1] Tomiak, Mullenix and Sawusch (1987) did a Day and Wood type experiment with sine wave speech. Interestingly, they found an interference of the variation of the irrelevant segment only when the stimuli were perceived as speech sounds. When the same physical stimuli were perceived as nonspeech noises, they did not find any difference according to the amount of covariation. This shows that the syllable superiority effect is not just a general 'the bigger the better' type of effect, but is closely related to a speech specific mode of processing.

perceptual system analyses the input signal, but could reflect some attention bias towards one level of representation or another.

Having acknowledged this much, one has then to be very careful when it comes to interpreting results like Savin and Bever's. Some researchers took a rather extreme stance, arguing that reaction time studies of this sort say absolutely nothing about the processing architecture. As McNeil and Linding (1973, p. 930) put it: 'What is "perceptually real" is what one pays attention to. [. . .] There is no clear sense in which one can ask what the "unit" of speech perception is. There is rather a series (or a network) of processing stages and each can in principle be the focus of attention.' To support this line of argument, it was claimed that there is no direct relationship between reaction time and processing priority, and that there may even be an *inverse* relationship: disyllabic words were reported to be detected faster than isolated syllables (Foss & Swinney, 1973) and whole sentences were claimed to be detected faster than single words (Healy & Cutting, 1976; McNeil & Linding 1973). The larger the segment, the faster the reaction time. But obviously one would not say that sentences are computed before single phonemes. The solution to this apparent paradox is to say that the cognitive system is naturally biased to pay attention to the highest levels of structure, irrespective of the order in which these representations are computed. A consequence of this rather extreme view is that differences in RT to different target types say virtually nothing about processing priority, although they say something about decision biases. I will argue that such a conclusion is too extreme.

To start with, there is no convincing experimental proof that target sentences are detected faster than target words.[2] In fact, such an outcome is extremely unlikely, given that, in these tasks, subjects base their response on a small initial portion of the utterance (about the first syllable of the initial word, since their reaction time is around 400 to 300ms). So the claimed inverse correlation between length of the target or level of integration and reaction time cannot hold across the board. Indeed, if pushed too far, this generic argument ends up with absurd predictions: if one were to focus the subject's attention to the discourse level rather than to the sentence level, the integral text of the Bible would be detected more rapidly than the first sentence of this text. This seems rather unlikely. The moral, then, is that even if attentional biases can have an impact on reaction time, this impact is constrained by the amount of information available at the time the response is made.

---

[2] In the only published experiment (McNeil & Linding, 1973), the results cannot be interpreted, since the word detection condition was made artificially more difficult than the sentence condition. The target word could appear anywhere in the experimental utterance, whereas the target sentence would only appear at the onset.

The superiority of word detection *vs* syllable detection seems more secure (Foss & Swinney 1973) than the previous effect, although it would need experimental confirmation. But even if this result is true, it would not necessarily dismiss Savin and Bever's interpretation. In fact, when subjects respond to, say, a disyllabic target, they do so mainly on the basis of the first syllable of the word. Mills (1980) argued that the first syllable of a disyllabic word has some unique coarticulatory characteristics that make it different from an isolated syllable.[3] The author claims that the difference between monitoring syllables and words may be due to the fact that when the target is a word, subjects can form a more precise perceptual image of the first syllable. In brief, one could use the word over syllable superiority effect in favour of Savin and Bever's interpretation rather than against it.

To conclude this section, the fact that syllables are perceived/detected faster than single phonemes seems rather secure. This effect cannot be simply dismissed on the basis of other effects such as a whole word versus syllable differences. However, there remain two possible interpretations of this effect. The first is Savin and Bever's, namely that syllables are bona fide *processing units* that are available first to the perceptual system, and that phonemes or features have later to be extracted from such large units. The second view states that syllables are only *representational* units that are used by subjects in order to specify and memorise target segments. Phonemes or features are the real processing units, but they are encapsulated from the viewpoint of the cognitive system; that is, subjects have a difficult spontaneous access to these units. Here, the syllable superiority effect is a by-product of the fact that the more precise the syllabic representation of the target is, the faster the reaction times are. At this stage, there is no way to distinguish between these two proposals.

More generally, this discussion has shown that there are basically two ways to interpret reaction time differences: the first one invokes processing differences, the second ones only invokes attentional biases or response strategies. I hope to have demonstrated that one cannot decide once and for all between the two alternatives by appealing to generic principles, but that one has to solve the question empirically case by case. For Savin and Bever's syllabic superiority effect, the point has still to be settled, presumably by using other types of data or tasks. But before pursuing this issue, let us note that these two proposals agree on one point: speech is more than just a sequence of phonemes. There must be larger Gestalt-like units that come into play ether at the decision level or at an earlier

---

[3] In contrast, Mills does not find any difference between the first syllable from a disyllabic item versus a trisyllabic item (see also Segui, 1984).

processing stage. But what are these Gestalt-like units? Are they acoustic chunks, diphones, triphones, or more linguistically motivated units like syllables? Experiments using multi-segment monitoring suggest that the latter is correct.

SYLLABLES OR NOT SYLLABLES

Mehler, Dommergues, Frauenfelder, and Segui (1981) showed that monitoring latencies for a sequence of phonemes are strongly influenced by the phonological structure of the word being heard. So, in French, latencies are shorter when the target corresponds to the first syllable of a word than when it does not correspond. For instance, the target *pa* is detected faster in the word PA–LACE than in the word PAL–MIER; it is the opposite when the target is *pal* (Cutler, Mehler, Norris, & Segui, 1983, 1986; Mehler, Dommergues, Frauenfelder, & Segui, 1981). A similar result was reported by Morais et al., (1989) with illiterate Portuguese subjects, showing that syllables are available before any formal teaching. This emphasises once again that there seem to be *coarse grained units* (see Mehler et al., 1990) in terms of which speed sounds are naturally represented and consciously accessed. In contrast, small units like phonemes are rather difficult to represent, and in fact they might not be accessible at all unless we learn to read an orthographic system for our language. What these experiments suggest is that these coarse grained units are similar to the phonological syllable.

However, other data suggest that the syllable is probably not a universal unit of processing/representation. In fact, Cutler et al., (1983; 1986), using material similar to the French study, did not find any evidence for syllabic effects with English speakers.[4] This result seems to depend on the speaker's language rather than on the language of the stimuli. Thus, the French speakers tend to syllabify English, and English speakers tend not to syllabify French (see also Cutler, Mehler, Norris, & Segui, 1989). In Catalan, only words with unstressed first syllables show French-like results (Sebastian et al., 1992). In Spanish, there is some disagreement as to whether there are syllable effects comparable to the French case or not (Sanchez-Casas, 1988; Sebastian et al., 1992). In Japanese, Otake et al. (in press) found evidence for a unit smaller than the syllable, the *mora*.

To summarise, these findings indicate that subjects tend to spontaneously use *coarse grained* representations for speech sounds, in a situation where they could only use very fine grained information (like phonemes).

---

[4] They used words like [balance] and [balcony] which in some phonological descriptions have the same syllabic structure as their French counterparts.

The detailed nature of this representation may depend on the specific properties of the language, although the extent of this variation is not currently known. In the following, we will assume that some syllable-like unit is at play in any language, and we will concentrate mostly on French and English, where most of the investigations have been carried out. Notice, however, that none of the results mentioned earlier allows us to ascertain whether coarse grained units play an early processing role or are only involved at a late response stage. What we know from the previous section is that comparing reaction times to a fixed stimulus across different targets cannot be used to solve this issue. What we need to do is the converse, that is, to keep the representation constant and vary the properties of the stimulus. This will enable us to see what aspect of the stimulus structure is used or not used to effect a given response. So let us again take a step back, and examine in more detail how such an apparently simple task as phoneme monitoring is actually performed.

SYLLABIC COMPLEXITY AND PHONEME MONITORING

Psychophysical studies have shown that the perception of a phonemic segment depends on the nature of adjacent ones. Classical experiments have shown that a given piece of acoustic information such as a consonantal burst or a fricative noise gives rise to the perception of different consonants according to the nature of the following vowel. Other experiments indicate that the acoustic duration of the vowel is taken into account and can reliably shift the perceptual boundary between voiced and unvoiced stop consonants (see Miller & Liberman, 1979; Summerfield, 1981, among others). These studies suggest that the perceptual system, whatever the nature of the processing units, integrates speech information from portions of the signal that are much larger than individual segments (see Fowler, 1984).

These psychophysical studies, however, stay neutral with respect to the time course of information flow between the different units in terms of which speech sounds are categorised and represented during the early stages of processing. The interesting fact is that a number of psychophysical effects seem to have a counterpart in studies of on-line segment classification. Foss and Gernsbacher (1983) showed that phoneme monitoring times depend on the quality of the following vowel, and, more specifically, are correlated to the vowel length (see also Diehl et al., 1987), a result very similar to that which has been observed using psychophysical methods. Moreover, there is some evidence that in order to extract phonemic information, the perceptual system takes into account not only the following vowel, but also the whole syllable. For instance, Segui,

Frauenfelder, and Mehler (1981) found a positive correlation between syllable detection times and initial phoneme detection times. Such a correlation would not be expected if syllables were derived from the concatenation of phonemes. In contrast, it makes a lot of sense if the initial phoneme has first to be extracted from the syllable. Other studies found that phoneme monitoring latencies depend on the structure of the syllable that bears the target (see Fig. 5.1). Thus CVs give rise to faster reaction times than CVCs, which are in turn faster than CCVs (Cutler, Mehler, Norris, & Segui, 1987; Treiman, Salasoo, Slowiaczek & Pisoni, 1982). Segui et al., (1990) analysed this effect in terms of two parameters: (1) the presence or absence of an initial cluster, and; (2) the presence or absence of a final consonant. They found a significant effect of both parameters, suggesting a strong connection between initial phoneme monitoring and the complexity of the target-bearing syllable. The simpler the syllable, the quicker the reaction times. This complexity effect seems pretty robust since it has been reported on both words and nonwords, and on the first syllable of disyllabic items and monosyllabic items.

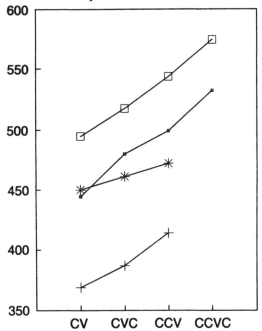

FIG. 5.1.   Initial phoneme monitoring as a function of syllable complexity across different studies using French materials.
- ● Segui et al. (1990); experiment 1.
- + Segui et al (1990); experiment 2.
- * Cutler et al (1987); experiment 1.
- □ Dupoux (1989); experiment 7.

Such a complexity effect can be accounted for by positing that syllables are first extracted from the signal, and phonemes are recovered thereafter; this is a processing-style explanation, in the line of Savin and Bever's original proposal. However, Cutler, Butterfield, and Williams (1987) argued that this is not the only one, and that a representation-style explanation could also do the job. They proposed that subjects use syllabic templates to represent the target, but that phonemes are extracted first from the signal without any reference to syllables. They noticed that in many experiments, a syllabic example (henceforth a 'model') was given to subjects in order to specify a target phoneme (e.g. /p/ as in POO). They proposed that subjects are very likely to use a template whatever syllable model was given as a specification for the target. So when the target appears in a complex syllable, there will be a mismatch between the structure of the target and the structure of the internal model; hence reaction times will be slower. Cutler, Mehler, Norris, and Segui. (1987) showed indeed that the model shown to subjects has a significant effect on reaction time, even inverting the complexity effect. The effect of the model has been reproduced by Segui et al. (1990), although it was not sufficient to account for the complexity effect. Even when there was a total match between the model and the test syllable, the complexity effect was still significant (CV<CVC<CCV). Moreover, Segui et al. found that when the effect of the model was neutralised, (by averaging across different model types, or by presenting a variety of models), the complexity effect was again present.

Of course these results may not allow us to dismiss the idea that complexity effects are due to the decision stage instead of some processing differences. For instance, in the absence of any explicit model, subjects may choose by default a CV syllabic frame. Another version of this account would say that subjects memorise all possible syllabic frames by order of complexity or frequency in the language (CV, CVC, CCV, CCVC) and scan them serially when they perform phoneme monitoring. Such a hypothesis may seem rather ad hoc and stipulatory, but it makes strong predictions: for instance, one should get rid of the complexity effect in lists where the complexity of the test syllables is blocked.

In this section we have seen at work the two possible styles of interpreting reaction time results. The first one tries to infer the processing architecture from the obtained pattern, and the second view tries to negate it by appealing to some property of the decision or response level. For the first view, there exists a *syllable-size processing unit* that mediates the extraction of individual phonemes. The longer it takes to extract a syllable from the signal, the longer it takes to detect one of its constituent phonemes. For the second view, syllables play a role only in memory and affect the late decision component.

Other research is clearly needed to tease apart these two models, but the striking parallelism obtained between phoneme detection studies and psychoacoustical investigations suggests that syllable-like units may play a much earlier role than suggested by high level explanations of the syllabic effects. As mentioned earlier, the vowel length has been found both to modify the classification criterion in a categorical perception paradigm, and to modulate phoneme detection times. It would be strange to try to account for such effects with a model-type explanation. Similarly, it has been noted that the open/closed nature of the test syllable reliably shifts the perceptual boundary between voiced and unvoiced segments (Miller & Liberman, 1979; Summerfield, 1981), an effect quite reminiscent of the impact of closeness on phoneme monitoring. Such parallel results can of course be accounted for in terms of two totally different mechanisms. But a model that related both results to a single source (i.e. a syllabic processing unit) is *prima facie* more appealing.

If syllables are extracted at a prelexical stage, one should be able to demonstrate consequences of the syllabic structure at some other levels, for instance, in lexical access. In contrast, if syllables are restricted to memorisation and late decision, there should be no such effects. The next section will examine this issue.

THE LOCUS OF LEXICAL EFFECTS IN PHONEME MONITORING

Most researchers agree that lexical access in the auditory mode is composed of two separate stages. In the first stage, some initial portion of signal is taken to activate the initial cohort of lexical candidates. The second stage consists of cohort reduction (Marslen-Wilson, 1984; Marslen-Wilson & Tyler, 1980; Marslen-Wilson & Welsh, 1978; Tyler & Marslen-Wilson, 1982).

We will focus here on the nature of the minimal portion of signal that can activate lexical representations (henceforth, the *contract code*). It has already been claimed that no lexical candidates can be activated unless about 150ms of signal has been processed (see Tyler & Wessels, 1983). Interestingly, such a duration corresponds roughly to the duration of the first syllable of a word (at least, it corresponds more closely to the length of a syllable than to the length of a phoneme). Other research suggests that the initial phoneme is not sufficient to activate an initial cohort, but the initial syllable is. Segui (1984) reports an experiment where the first syllable of the word [bibelot] could be shown to activate the word [biberon]; in contrast, the first phoneme of [bonbon] could not generate such an activation. It still remains to be seen whether such an access code is defined in terms of acoustic duration, syllables, phonemes, or whatever.

Some studies have tried to handle this question using the *lexical superiority effect* in initial phoneme monitoring. It has been noted that under certain circumstances, phonemes are detected faster if they occur at the initial position of words than in nonwords (Cutler, Mehler, Norris, & Segui, 1987, Rubin, Turvey, & Van Gelder, 1976 among others). The idea here is that phoneme detection can either be based on pre-lexical representations, or can be derived from lexical information; the race model (Cutler, Mehler, Norris, & Segui, 1987; Cutler & Norris, 1979; Foss & Blank, 1980; Newman & Dell, 1978) postulates that the fastest process will determine the nature of the response. In fact, one of the major variables that determines the presence or absence of lexical effects in this task is the length of the target bearing item. With short words, word superiority effects have been measured, as well as frequency effects (Dupoux & Mehler, 1990) and semantic priming effects (Dupoux, 1989).[5] In contrast, no such effects have ever been observed in polysyllabic items.

The interaction of length with lexical effects in phoneme monitoring connects nicely with the notion of a contact code for lexical access. In a nutshell, a very short word might directly contact a lexical representation, without needing any process of cohort reduction. In that case, stored information can be retrieved and will speed up the process of phoneme detection. In contrast, the initial portion of a long word is generally not sufficient to uniquely specify its identity. Further processing is needed to reduce the cohort of candidates substantially, thus lexical access is delayed and cannot influence target detection.

Under these premises, it becomes possible to study the nature of the contact code, by looking at the locus of lexical effects in phoneme monitoring. Dupoux and Mehler (1990) have thus argued that the access code is defined in terms of structure rather than acoustic duration. They showed that in French no frequency effect is found on disyllabic items, even when such items are artificially compressed and have an acoustic duration less than natural monosyllabic items. Dupoux and Mehler (in preparation) also compared the lexical superiority effect on items of various phonological structures in French. Three categories of items were used: simple monosyllabic items (CV, CVC and CCV items), complex monosyllabic items CCVC and 'simple' disyllabic items CVCV. The results show a significant lexical superiority effect for monosyllables, and no effect

---

[5] However, lexical effects are not *always* observed in monosyllabic items. Attentional factors seem to influence greatly the likelihood of observing such an effect (see Cutler, Mehler, Norris, & Segui, 1987; Dupoux & Mehler, in preparation; Eimas, Markovitz Hornstein, & Payton, 1990; Foss & Gernsbacher, 1983)

for disyllables.[6] This result shows that items that have the same number of phonemes (four phonemes in CCVC and in CVCV) appear nonetheless to be treated in a qualitatively different fashion with respect to lexical access.

These studies indicate that the presence or absence of lexical effects in phoneme monitoring is related to the number of syllables of the target bearing item, rather than to the number of phonemes or acoustic duration. Such a result is evidence in favour of the view that the minimal unit that is used to contact lexical representation is defined in terms of syllables.[7] Such data need to be extended to other techniques and languages, but if true, it flies in the face of models that reduce the syllable to high level representations or top down perceptual strategies.

THE STANDARD SYLLABIC MODEL

To sum up the discussion so far, I have presented two rather extreme models of prelexical processing: one model states that only small sized units (phonemes or features) play a role in prelexical processing. Any amount of higher order structural effect is assimilated to the influence of general knowledge on response-making. That is, the knowledge that subjects have of their language, for instance, as being composed of syllables, will influence the way in which they memorise a particular target, exactly in the same fashion that knowing about baseball rules will help to remember a particular game. In this model, the syllable over phoneme superiority effect, and the paradoxical correlation between phoneme detection time and syllable detection time, are accounted for as memory-related effects at the response level. In each particular experimental setup, subjects will develop an ad hoc kind of response strategy that will account for the observed results.

Although the available data do not allow us to dismiss any of these specific accounts, the framework in general does not appear to give a very coherent picture of prelexical syllabic effects on segment detection. In addition, in order to account for the interaction of syllabic structure on

---

[6] No lexical superiority effect was found for a fourth category of items: CVCCs. The authors suggest that, following phonological theory, these items are not truly monosyllabic, and that the last consonant is an appendix that does not belong to the syllable. Thus this structure is represented and processed like disyllabic items.

[7] Of course, it could be the case that the second stage of lexical access, namely cohort reduction is based on phonemes instead of syllables. However, a model that construes a single type of unit for contact code and cohort reduction is more restrictive (and more falsifiable) than a model that allows the two codes to differ. Although more research is needed to determine which alternative is correct, the first one is clearly to be preferred as a default.

lexical access reported earlier, this model would have to say that syllables are computed prior to lexical access, and are not restricted to memory and/ or decision components. So, by and large, I consider that this model in its extreme form can be discarded.

In the remainder of this chapter I will favour another extreme type of model—one that proposes that high order structures such as syllables play an on-line role during speech processing. In this view, knowledge of language phonology is not just like another ordinary piece of knowledge, but is incorporated or pre-compiled into the processing architecture. In particular, such a model states that syllable-like structures are computed before lexical access and even before individual segments are extracted. One can turn this proposal into a more concrete form of imagining that the prelexical level is constituted by a dictionary of syllables (see Mehler, Dupoux, & Segui, 1990). Thus, for each syllable in the language, there would be a corresponding specific detector, which would contain something like a spectral prototype of the syllable, and which would fire during signal analysis whenever a given syllable occurs.[8] It is at the level of input files of this syllabary that temporal normalisation and categorisation would occur. As soon as a syllable is detected in the acoustic signal, the corresponding detector would fire, giving rise to lexical activation. Such a detector could also activate a phonemic representation giving the phonological structure of the syllable.

This roughly sketched model has the following characteristics: (1) the information flows in a strictly ascendant fashion (the process of selection of the best syllabic candidate is not guided by context, but only by the incoming signal); (2) the treatment is passive (the selection is done with a pattern matching type of mechanism), and; (3) this process operates in a discontinuous manner—in the model, nothing can happen either in the lexicon, or in the phonemic extraction process before a unique syllabic candidate has been isolated.

In this radical form the model is useful, because its predictions are rather clear and can be evaluated. In the following sections, I will review some experimental results that challenge the syllabic model. More specifically, the third claim of the model is questioned: it seems that under particular circumstances, a segment detection task can be performed before a unique syllabic candidate has been isolated. So let us return to the phoneme monitoring data once again.

---

[8] Such a proposition is not absurd from the computational viewpoint, as 6000 syllables are sufficient to cover a lexicon of 200,000 words (inflected forms, Cerf et al., 1989)

A TRUNCATION EFFECT IN PHONEME DETECTION

As previously described, phoneme detection latencies depend both on the presence or absence of an initial cluster, and on the open/closed nature of the syllable. According to Segui et al. (1990), this result suggested the existence of a strong relation between initial phoneme monitoring and syllabic complexity of the target bearing syllable. As mentioned earlier, this finding is compatible with the view that syllables function as an information processing bottleneck: nothing happens before the syllable has been fully processed, from onset to coda. The complexity effect itself can be accounted for either at the syllabic level (more complex syllables take longer to be detected) or in the syllable to phoneme transduction process (more complex syllables take longer to decompose). In any case, onsets and codas contribute to syllabic complexity in a rather symmetrical fashion.

There is some indication, however, that onsets and codas do not play a symmetrical role in prelexical processing. For one thing, Norris and Cutler (1988) reported that introducing different types of catch trials in the distractors of a syllable monitoring experiment changed the overall syllable detection latencies. That is, if during the test list subjects have to detect targets like [dev] and they hear words like *definite*, they tend to make mistakes, and their overall reaction time to other targets is increased by more than 110ms. In contrast, if the target is [tef] and the word *definite*, then subjects make less errors and their reaction times increase only by 30ms or so. Such a difference between catch conditions is not to be expected if one assumes that syllables are processed as undecomposable units. This result suggests that at the very least subjects assign more weight to onset than to coda in a detection task. Such a differential weight is hard to explain in a model where syllables are basic atomic units.

The aim of the next section is to re-examine in rather more detail the nature of the link between phoneme detection and syllabic complexity. I will then turn to structural effects in syllable detection.

Syllabic Complexity Re-examined

In this section, I will re-examine some of the findings reported in Segui et al. (1990), taking a closer look at the potential differences between the role of onsets and codas. In the original experiments both factors had a significant influence on phoneme detection times. It turned out, however, that some of the effects were not homogeneous across subjects, and that fast and slow subjects showed markedly different results. In Dupoux (1989), and Dupoux and Mehler (in preparation) we re-analysed the data, taking into account the speed of the subjects. Subjects' data were distributed into three groups of twenty subjects according to their average speed (from slow to fast, 616, 490, and 360ms). Table 5.1 lists the reaction times for the four syllabic structures in the three groups of subjects.

As can be seen in Table 5.1, the effect of *Coda* (that is, the difference in latencies between closed and open syllables) has an uneven amplitude across the different groups of subjects. In fact, there is a powerful interaction between *Coda* and *Speed* ($F_{2,37} = 5.27, p < 0.001$). This interaction is due to the fact that although the effect of *Coda* was significant for the medium and slow group of subjects ($F_{1,12} = 15.1, p < 0.005$ and $F_{1,13} = 5.58, p < 0.05$, respectively), it was not significant for the fast group of subject (-5ms, F<1). In contrast, the effect of *Onset* is significant for the three groups and does not interact with speed.

Thus the presence of an *initial cluster* does affect the performance of both fast and slow subjects. In contrast, the presence of a *final consonant* has a significant effect only for the slow subjects. The two structural factors studied by Segui et al. (1990) do not have the same status with respect to syllabic complexity. Although the onset of a syllable seems to be obligatorily taken into account, the coda seems to be only optional. Such a result would indicate that contrary to the syllabic hypothesis, prelexical processing involves several stages. In an early stage, the open part of the syllable (onset and nucleus) is extracted and available for phonemic extraction. At a later stage the whole syllabic structure is taken into account. In other words, it seems that fast subjects can *truncate* closed syllables and only take into account their initial portion.

Of course, it could be the case that these two stages are purely contingent on the particular experiment described earlier. The fastest subjects had an average latency of around 360ms (and some of them were below 300ms). It should be emphasised that monosyllabic items in isolation

TABLE 5.1
Phoneme Monitoring Time as a Function of Syllabic Structure and Average Speed of Response

Groups	CV	CVC	CCV	CCVC	Onset	Coda
Slow	535	630	629	672	68**	69**
Medium	455	473	486	547	52**	39*
Fast	342	337	383	378	41**	−5
Overall	444	480	499	532	53***	34***

Reanalysis of Segui et al., (1990).
* $p < 0.05$
** $p < 0.01$
** $p < 0.001$

have a duration of around 500ms. Given a motor response of around 100ms, and fast responses have presumably been issued well before the information concerning the nature of the final consonant is available in the signal (see Warren & Marslen-Wilson, 1987; 1988). Thus it is not surprising that for fast subjects no difference is found between the reaction times of open and closed syllables.[9] This simple account predicts that a truncation effect should be found only in cases where the syllable bearing target spans a long acoustic duration. But when the initial syllable is very short, such as the initial syllable of a polysyllabic item, no such effect should be measured.

The data needed to test the generality of the truncation effect is already available in Segui et al.'s (1990) second experiment. In this experiment, subjects monitored for phonemic targets in lists of disyllabic items. The first syllable of the target bearing items was either CV, CVC or CCV.[10]

As in the previous analysis, the 30 subjects were divided into three groups according to their average speed (respectively 488ms, 405ms, and 277ms). The results are displayed in Table 5.2.

Initial phoneme monitoring in bisyllabic items is sensitive to the presence or absence of an initial cluster. This effect is robust and is found across the whole range of reaction time (see Fig. 5.2). In contrast, the presence or absence of a final consonant only produces a significant effect in the slowest subjects. Thus, what was called the truncation effect can be observed in the first syllable of disyllabic items. Such a result obtains even though the first syllable of a disyllabic item is around twice as short as a syllable spoken in isolation, and so it is probable that even fast subjects

TABLE 5.2
Phoneme Monitoring Time as a Function of Syllable Structure and Average Speed of Response

Groups	CV	CVC	CCV	Onset	Coda
Slow	465	498	502	37*	32*
Medium	388	401	425	36*	13
Fast	255	260	315	61**	6
Overall	370	387	414	45	17

Reanalysis of Segui et al. (1990).
* $p < 0.05$
** $p < 0.001$

---

[9] What *is* surprising for the syllabic hypothesis is that subjects can respond so fast.

[10] The aim of this experiment was to challenge the claim made by Cutler, Butterfield, and Williams (1987) that the model with which the target was given was responsible for the syllabic complexity effect. In the following discussion, I will ignore this aspect of the experiment, and average across model types.

could make their responses on the basis of the entire syllable. Nonetheless they do not seem to be sensitive to the information concerning the coda of the syllable. Thus the truncation effect is quite a strong one, and can be observed in a variety of situations, at least for isolated words. Of course, the lability of the complexity effect in closed syllables is insufficient to conclude anything about the nature of the prelexical segment. Along the lines of Cutler, Butterfield, and Williams, (1987), one could argue that such an effect is purely due to a matching process between the internal model with which subjects represent the phonemic target and the incoming acoustic information. Thus, fast subjects would weight the initial portion of syllables more heavily, whereas slow subjects would wait until they have resolved every phoneme in the syllable.

Fortunately, the complexity effect is just one test among many others to investigate the properties of the processing units. In fact, other studies indicate that what has been called the truncation effect reflects more than high level attentional factors. Miller and Dexter (1988), using psychophysical methods reported a very similar finding to that presented earlier. They found that when subjects are asked to respond as quickly as possible, the previously observed effect of vowel length on the perceptual boundary between voiced and unvoiced consonants vanishes. In speeded decision, subjects' perceptual boundaries correspond to those of short syllables. In other words, there seems to be an early stage where only an initial fraction of the syllable is processed by the perceptual system as if it were a short syllable. This suggests that the truncation effect reported earlier may have a perceptual basis. I will turn now to the implications of such an effect for the first stages of lexical access.

Truncating the Lexical Superiority Effect

Dupoux et al. (in preparation) explored what would happen to the lexical superiority effect if subjects were to respond much faster. If at an early stage of processing, the coda of the syllable can be ignored, then we would expect to see the lexical superiority effect disappearing for CVC items. If, on the other hand, the truncation effect is only a high level attentional effect, this should not have any impact on lexical access, and we should obtain an intact lexical superiority effect for the three structures.

We chose to replicate an experiment that was quite successful in obtaining the lexical superiority effect, namely the first experiment reported by Cutler, Mehler, Norris, and Segui. (1987). We took the same experimental materials as in this experiment, which included CV, CVC and CVC words and nonwords, and ran another 30 French subjects in

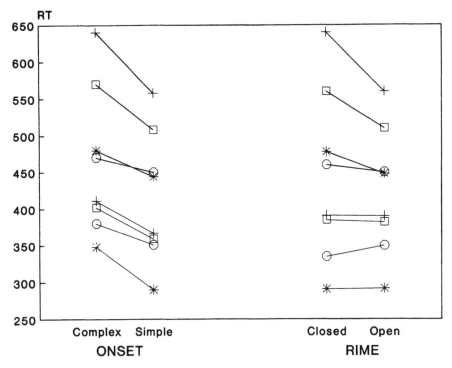

FIG. 5.2.   Effect of complex onset and coda on phoneme detection across a wide range of reaction times in French. From top to bottom:
- + Segui et al. (1990); experiment 1, slow Ss.
- □ Dupoux (1989); experiment 7.
- ∗ Segui et al. (1990); experiment 2, slow Ss.
- ○ Cutler et al. (1987); experiment 1.
- + Segui et al. (1990); experiment 1, fast Ss.
- □ Dupoux (1989); replication of experiment 7 with fast Ss.
- ○ Dupoux (1989); replication of Cutler et al. (1987).
- ∗ Segui et al. (1990); experiment 2, fast Ss.

We can see that below 400ms, no effect of the last consonant is visible, although an effect of the initial cluster is still significant.

TABLE 5.3
Phoneme Monitoring Times in Monosyllabic Words and Nonwords of Different Syllabic Complexity

Syllabic Structure	Nonword	Word	Lexical Superiority Effect
CV	370 (1%)	332 (1%)	38**
CVC	341 (1%)	333 (4%)	8
CCV	387 (4%)	367 (2%)	20*

Speeded replication of Cutler, Mehler, Norris, and Segui's (1987) experiment 1.
* $p < 0.03$
** $p < 0.005$

exactly the same conditions, except that they were really urged to respond as fast as materially possible.

The reaction times according to lexical status and syllabic structure are shown in Table 5.3. First of all, the mean reaction times were 100ms faster than in the original experiment, showing that a minor change in the experimental requirements may result in substantial changes in the level of performance. But this was not the only change: (1) with respect to the lexical superiority effect, the experimental items fall neatly into two categories. Open syllables (CV and CCV) show a lexical superiority effect, whereas CVC do not; (2) with respect to syllabic complexity, results show an influence of the presence/absence of an initial cluster, but not of the open/closed nature of the syllable. Here again, CVC are off the track compared to the Cutler et al. results.

These results fit nicely with the hypothesis that there is a stage in prelexical processing where the information relevant to the end of the syllable is not yet available. Still subjects can use the initial portion of the syllable either to access the lexicon or to extract phonemic targets. Note that such results do not undermine the claim that syllables play an important role in prelexical processing. It is plainly impossible to account for the pattern of results obtained in slow responses without postulating a syllabic level of processing.

THE TIME COURSE OF SYLLABLE DETECTION

If the phenomenon of truncation were true, then one ought to find some similar effects of speed on syllable monitoring. Recall that Mehler et al. (1981) found that syllable monitoring times were faster when the target matched the first syllable of the word than when it didn't match. Such results could be only due to slow subjects who would use the whole syllabic representation, whereas fast subjects would not show any interaction at all.

There is already some indication that syllable monitoring may tap different processing stages according to the experimental conditions, as illustrated by the various discrepancies in the syllable monitoring literature. For instance, some researchers have found that syllable detection is sensitive to syllabic structure in Spanish (Sanchez-Casas, 1988), whereas others (Sebastian et al., submitted) have found the contrary result. In English, too, there are some discrepancies between the results reported by various investigators (see Sanchez-Casas, 1988, and Cutler Mehler, Norris, & Segui, 1987). In fact, as we will see, these studies have obtained markedly different ranges of reaction times.

Mehler, Dommergues, Frauenfelder, and Segui (1981) Revisited

We took the data obtained by Mehler et al. (1981), and distributed the 42 subjects in three groups of 14 subjects according to their average speed (278ms, 339ms, 474ms). As in Mehler et al., an interaction between target type and word type was found ($F_{1,39}$ = 8.96; $p < 0.005$). This interaction (henceforth *syllabic effect*) was due to the fact that CV targets were detected faster in CV_words than in CVC_words (25ms; $F_{1,39}$ = 11.29; $p < 0.01$).[11] In contrast, CVC target were not detected faster in CV than in CVC_words; in fact, there was a non significant trend in the opposite direction (F = 1.6; ns). The reaction times across the three groups and according to target type and word type are shown in Table 5.4.

As Table 5.4 shows, the amplitude of the syllabic effect seems to decrease with mean reaction time, although the interaction between syllabic effect and speed did not reach significance ($F_{2,39}$ = 1.52, ns). However, the syllabic effect was only significant in the slowest group of subjects (slow: $F_{1,13}$ = 5.22, $p < 0.04$; medium: $F_{1,13}$ = 2.37, ns; and fast: $F_{1,13}$ = 1.46, ns). Similarly, the word type effect for CV targets (the fact that CV targets were detected faster in CV than in CVC_words) was only significant for the slowest group (slow: 45ms $F_{1,13}$ = 8.33, $p < 0.02$;

TABLE 5.4
Syllabic Effect as a Function of Average Response Time

	CV targets	CVC targets
Slow Group		
CV_words	445	492
CVC_words	490	470
Word Type Effect	45*	−22
Medium Group		
CV_words	334	337
CVC_words	357	328
Word Type Effect	22	−10
Fast Group		
CV_words	278	276
CVC_words	287	271
Word Type Effect	9	−6

Reanalysis of Mehler et al. (1981)
*$p < 0.05$

---

[11] This word type effect is similar to what was observed in phoneme monitoring, namely, CV_words give rise to faster latencies than CVC_words, see previous sections.

medium: 22ms $F_{1,13}$ = 3.18, ns; fast: 9ms F < 1). The detection of CVC targets in CV and CVC_words, in contrast, only showed a small decrease in amplitude across groups, and never reached significance. To confirm this analysis, a set of correlations were run between the following variables:

$$MeanRT \qquad = (CV_{/CV\_} + CVC_{/CV\_} + CV_{/CVC\_} + CVC_{/CVC\_})/4$$
$$WordEffectForCV \quad = CV_{/CV\_} - CVC/_{CV\_}$$
$$WordEffectForCVC = CV_{/CVC\_} + CVC_{/CVC\_}$$
$$SyllabicEffect \qquad = WordEffectForCV - WordEffectForCVC$$

First, the correlation between the variables *SyllabicEffect* and *MeanRT* was significant (r = 0.422, t_{41} = 2.94, p < 0.01), confirming the fact that the syllabic effect is mainly due to slow subjects' responses. Similarly, *WordTypeEffectForCV* and *MeanRT* were significantly correlated (r = 0.36, t_{41} = 2.43, p < 0.05). The correlation between *WordTypeEffectfor-CVC* and *MeanRT* was not significant (r = 0.27, t_{41} = 1.79, ns).

The main result of this analysis concerns the subjects' responses to CV targets. The detection times of CV targets closely mirror the detection times of C targets in the previously described phoneme detection experiments: slow subjects show an effect of word type, namely, CVC_words give rise to longer reaction times than CV_words. This effect, however vanishes when responses are faster, indicating that subjects can extract the phonemic target before having fully identified the syllable. The net result is a considerable weakening of the interaction between word type and target type for fast subjects' responses. The response pattern to CVC, however, show a less dramatic change with mean reaction time, and there is no significant word type effect in any group of subjects.[12]

In any event, it seems clear that syllable detection is as sensitive to absolute speed as phoneme detection, and that the same kind of truncation effect can affect both techniques. At fast response times, subjects tend to use the information relevant only to the first part of the syllable. It is only by looking at longer response time that we can see a substantial effect of the syllable as a whole.

---

[12] This weak effect could be due to two opposing strategies with CVC targets. The first one is to make sure that every single phoneme in the target is present. Hence, in CV_CV words, subjects would have to wait until the second syllable in order to check the third phoneme. Another possible strategy would be simply to forget about the last phoneme, and to concentrate on matching the first two. The absence of catch trials allows such a strategy, which would make CVC detection times similar to CV detection times. If subjects use a mixture of these two strategies, it becomes hard to interpret the results on CVC targets.

The Case of Spanish

As mentioned earlier, there is some empirical disagreement about the role of the syllable in Spanish. Sanchez-Casas (1988) reproduced the interaction between word type and target type found by Mehler et al. (1981) in French. They concluded that in Spanish, the syllable is a basic processing unit, as it is in French. However, Sebastian et al. (1992) found mixed results. In one experiment they found no interaction whatsoever, only a bias for detecting CV targets faster than CVC targets, irrespective of the type of word.

At first sight, these results seem flatly contradictory. However, in the context of the previous observations, it might be possible that the two different results simply reflect two different stages in prelexical processing. This hypothesis is all the more probable given that the two studies show very different mean reaction times. The mean reaction times observed by Sanchez-Casas (1988) were rather slow (500–600ms), but those obtained by Sebastian et al. in experiment 2 were much shorter (350–375ms). In fact, these mean latencies in Sebastian et al.'s study are similar to those of the fast group of subjects analysed in the previous section. The results are quite parallel too, namely, no interaction between word type and target type, and no effect of word type with CV targets. In contrast, the reaction times obtained by Sanchez Casas are more comparable to the slow group of subjects in the Mehler et al. (1981) experiment. Both also show a strong interaction between target and word type, and a significant word type effect for CV targets. This interpretation is corroborated by the fact that Sebastian et al. obtained a syllabic interaction with the same stimuli as in their previous experiment just by slowing down the subjects. Also Sanchez Casas (personal communication) ran other experiments with Spanish subjects. The range of reaction times obtained in this study is around 450ms, which is intermediate between the two other studies. Interestingly enough, the results are also intermediate. The interaction between word and target type is now severely reduced and there is no significant effect of word type for CV targets.

Figure 5.3 summarises the results of the three studies. We can see a general trend towards the disappearance of a word type effect for both CV and CVC targets. This picture is quite similar to the one obtained in French subjects.[13]

---

[13] There are, however, differences between fast subjects in Spanish and in French. Spanish subjects are significantly faster to detect CV targets than CVC targets. No such effect is found in fast French subjects, and if anything, the trend would be in the opposite direction (see Table 5.4). As mentioned earlier, the comparison of reaction times across different targets is always difficult, and sensitive to the nature of the distractors—needing their interpretation independent evidence about the stages involved in prelexical processing.

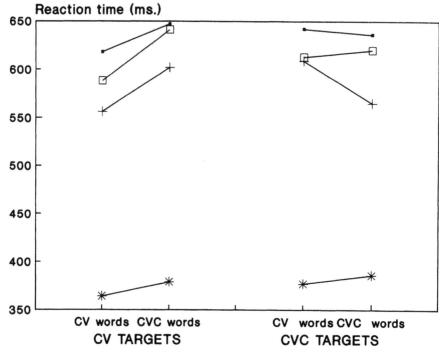

FIG. 5.3   Detection of CV and CVC targets in CV_ and CVC_ words in Spanish.
- Sanchez Casas (1988); experiment 1.
+ Sanchez Casas (1988); experiment 2.
* Sebastian et al. (1992); experiment 2.
□ Sebastian et al. (1992); experiment 3.

The same kind of argument could be explored to account for the discrepancy between Cutler, Mehler, Norris, and Segui (1987) and Bradley et al.'s (1988) results in English. Cutler et al. found that words like *balance* gave rise to faster reaction times than words like *balcony* (irrespective of the target). In contrast, Bradley et al. did not find any such effect (but they found that CVC *targets* were detected faster than CV targets). Here again, subjects' mean reaction times were different in the two studies, and the word type effect was only found in the slowest response times (around 480ms in Cutler et al. experiment, and 395ms in Bradley et al.). It should be emphasised, however, that such results do not undermine the potential processing differences between languages that have been highlighted in these studies. There is no way in which the truncation effect could account for the different reaction times observed between English and French (Cutler et al., 1986; 1989), or Catalan and Spanish (Sebastian et al., submitted). But such cross linguistic differences are not likely to be well understood unless the role of such a powerful variable as the speed of response is taken into consideration.

To sum up, the analysis of performances in simple target monitoring tasks uncovers quite intricate processes. We have shown that detecting a phonemic target may be done in two different ways: (1) by extracting the target from a syllabic representation of the signal; and (2) by using some early 'presyllabic' information that spans only a fraction of a syllable. The last point suggests that there is an early stage where the whole syllable has not been completely recovered from the signal. Such information can nonetheless be used to activate higher levels of processing, and trigger both phonological extraction and lexical access. However, this information is not available for a long time period, and as later-occurring information gets integrated, larger representations such as full syllables phase in. I will turn to the implication of this finding for the syllabic hypothesis in the next section.

TWO STAGES IN PRELEXICAL PROCESSING: CRACKING THE SYLLABLE?

The standard syllabic hypothesis (as previously described) postulates: (1) that there exists a unique level of prelexical representation which serves to segment and categorise speech sounds and contact lexical representations; (2) that this level implies a coarse grained unit that gives rise to a discontinuity in the flow of bottom up information. This hypothesis proposes that there exists an unbreakable atom of processing, i.e. that the syllable needs to be treated in its totality before the information can contact higher levels of representation. Another way to put this is that syllables function as an information bottleneck. Detecting phonemes or accessing the lexicon should be blocked until the syllable has been identified.

By and large, we have shown that although the syllabic hypothesis accounts for most of the results obtained in segment detection tasks (see the first sections) it only accounts for them *on the average*. A closer analysis of the results has shown that the pattern of results is markedly different as a function of the speed of subjects' responses. Onsets and codas play an asymmetrical role in an early stage of prelexical processing and subjects can clearly detect phonemes before a syllables has been fully processed.[14]

---

[14] Of course, this asymmetry has only been established for the processing of isolated speech. It remains to be seen whether truncation effects obtain with target detection in continuous speech. Isolated words differ in many respects from words in natural connected speech: they are almost twice as long, they show much less coarticulation, and their boundaries are very clear. It could be that these special circumstances allow subjects to have access to a very peripheral processing level that is otherwise not accessible for connected speech.

The standard syllabic hypothesis cannot account for this pattern of results, but it can accommodate them. The idea is to keep the bulk of the syllabic hypothesis, but to relax one of the specific conditions mentioned earlier: *processing discontinuity*, or *uniqueness of the prelexical level*.

Rounding off Discontinuities: The Cascade Syllabic Model

The syllabic hypothesis that I have presented postulates that the acoustic signal is segmented in terms of syllable-like prelexical units. The signal is compared to an access file in the syllabery that contains something like a spectral template for each syllable in a language. A discontinuous version of such a model is comparable to a logogen model. Each syllabic detector gradually accumulates information, and when some threshold is attained the relevant syllabic detector fires. The output of the syllabic level is thus all or none. In particular, higher levels cannot have access to the information unless the appropriate syllabic detector has fired. Such a model, as I have already pointed out, is incompatible with the data mentioned earlier. However, it is possible to imagine another version that would fit better. Suppose that the activation levels of the various syllabic detectors were in fact continuously available to higher levels of processing, as they accumulate sensory information. Such a model would resemble a cohort model (Marslen-Wilson, 1984) for syllables. In such a model, both lexical and phonemic levels of processing could integrate the prelexical information distributed across the different syllables detectors, even though a single syllable has not been identified.

In such a framework, there are two effects to account for: (1) the complexity effect, and; (2) the truncation effect, that is, the disappearance of components of the complexity effect for fast responses. The conjunction of these two requirements turns out to be extremely constraining when it comes to precise modelling. It is not the aim of this paper to solve this issue. Rather, what we want here is to give a flavour of cascade-like models in order to determine the major predictions they make. Let us assume, then, that the complexity effect arises at the syllabic level. That is, more complex syllables take longer to identify than less complex ones.[15] Now, if subjects wait until a single syllable has been identified, then of course more complex syllables will give rise to slower phoneme detection RTs

---

[15] This could be modelled either by appealing to acoustic duration distribution (more complex syllables are usually longer), or by competition among syllabic candidates, or by syllabic frequency effect. Note that each of these possibilities makes very different predictions.

[16] Which would be defined as for words, see Warren and Marslen-Wilson, 1987; 1988.

than less complex ones. However, when pressed to go as fast as possible, subjects could lower their response threshold and respond on the basis of partial activation of the syllables. Such a response is possible because at the early portion of the syllable [pal], many syllable candidates like [par], [pat], [pak], etc. are still activated. Hence, all the syllables could *conspire* and activate the /p/ phoneme unit.

Whatever the exact details, such a model makes two major claims: (1) it is essentially the duration of the syllable that will determine the possibility of a truncation effect. In fact, *truncation should only occur when subjects respond before the 'identification point' of the syllable.*[16] No truncation effect should be found for very short syllables (such as in initial position of polysyllabic items or in artificially compressed words). (2) The truncation effect is explained in the model by proposing that there is some initial activity of the open syllable detectors. This activity is supposed to be sufficient to trigger a phoneme monitoring response. It should also be sufficient to trigger lexical access. In other words, we should measure *an early effect of the lexical status of the initial CV of a CVC syllable.*

With respect to the first claim, the analysis of Segui et al.'s second experiment already showed that a truncation effect obtains for the first syllable of disyllabic items—that is, for very short syllables. Notice, however, that subjects were much faster in this experiment than in Experiment 1, where they were presented with nonwords. Indeed, the fastest group of subjects responded with a speed of 280ms, and it is still possible that their response was made prior to the identification point of the syllable. Thus the first claim still needs some empirical examination. The second claim is related to the cascade nature of the model. A tentative post-hoc analysis of the available data proved to be inconclusive.[17] Of course, a proper experiment is needed to evaluate this claim empirically, but there is some indication that cascade effects in speech perception are rather limited. For instance, Segui (1984) presented an experiment where a lexical superiority effect is found in monosyllables (cri *vs* cra), but not when this syllable is part of a disyllabic item (cri/tere *vs* cra/tere). These results suggest that the lexical status of the first syllable of polysyllabic items does not count.

The syllabic model just outlined makes challenging predictions, but has

---

[17] In the replication of Cutler et al.'s experiment, we rearranged the data of the CVC items according to the lexical status of their CV portions. The reaction time to the 10 CVC items that yield frequency words was 348ms and the reaction time of the 10 other pairs (8 non words and 2 very low frequency words) was 333ms. In this reanalysis, there is no trace of lexical influence on the truncated part of the CVC items.

still a number of loose ends. For instance, what is the size of this putative syllabary? It has been claimed that around 6000 syllables are sufficient to cover nearly all lexical forms in French (Cerf et al., 1989). Although this number is large, it is not unreasonably so. Moreover, if one restricts the syllabary to syllables with simple codas (one consonant at most), then this number reduces to 3300 syllables. However, notice that these syllables represent only a fraction of the total number of *potential syllables* in French, i.e. syllables that could exist (according to phonotactic constraints) but just happen not to occur in any word. If we take the notion of a syllabary seriously, we ought to predict that actual *vs* potential syllables should be processed very differently. For instance, phonemic sequences should take much longer to detect if they occur in potential *vs* actual syllables. Moreover, if the syllabary is really a speech categorisation device, the psychophysical properties of non-actual syllables should be radically different than for actual ones. In fact, these potential items should show the same kind of perceptual boundaries as is observed in very young infants. Such predictions are extremely strong, and a positive outcome may seem unlikely. However, some studies have already demonstrated that there is a range of speech sounds where these predictions are true. Best and her colleagues (1988) showed that Zulu clicks have these properties, namely that English speaking adults show exactly the same perceptual boundaries as young infants. It remains to be seen whether or not such a phenomena can be found in sequences of phonemes that belong to the speaker's native language.

Dissociating Categorisation and Access: Half Syllables and More

It has been assumed so far that there exists a unique prelexical level whose job is to simultaneously categorise and represent speech sounds, and contact lexical entries. However, these several tasks could in principle be handled by different levels of processing.

In fact, it could be argued that syllables are not very good candidates for carrying out categorisation. As mentioned earlier, around 3000–4000 syllabic templates are sufficient to cover a language like French. However, such a hypothesis is committed to the claim that the processing of items like *bive*, and *plabe* is radically different than for *bine* and *plade*, because the latter are actual syllables in French whereas the former are not. Such an outcome is possible but seems *prima facie* rather implausible. Of course, it could be proposed that the syllabery contains not only actual but also any potential syllable in the language. The problem is that we end up with about 33000 syllabic templates, a number that could seem excessive in comparison with the size of the mental lexicon.[18] Similar problems recur if the same type of proposal is made for other languages. For instance, in English it could be claimed that the *foot* is an important unit for speech segmentation and lexical access (see Cutler 1990; Cutler & Norris, 1988). However, if the unit of lexical access and the unit of categorisation are the same, we end up with an enormous number of templates.

Let us admit that lexical access and categorisation may be carried out by two different mechanisms. The natural proposition would be to postulate that categorisation is made possible by something like *semi-syllables*. Semi syllables are good candidates for categorisation, because much of the variability and coarticulation occurs at the transition between consonants and vowels.[19] The other advantage of semi-syllables is that they are much less numerous than syllables (over 2000 to cover all phonotactically legal syllables). Thus it could be proposed that there exists a repertoire of 2000 templates that represent the possible minimal articulatory gestures—that is, alternation between onset and nucleus, or nucleus and coda. In such a model, the syllable plays a role at a later stage, where the information spanning over two semi-syllables is integrated. The role of this later syllabic stage is to transform the perceptual output into a format compatible for lexical retrieval.

In such a model, one would expect that subjects could use either level of representation to perform target detection tasks. In fact, it is not obligatory to wait for the complete identification of a syllable in order to detect a phonemic target. It is possible to recover this information from the semi-syllabic level. Fast subjects have a strong tendency to attend to this early level, whereas slow subjects rely primarily on the syllabic level, which is probably perceptually more stable. The claim is then that the truncation effect will be found on any type of material, whatever the acoustic duration of the syllable. In particular, one should find such an effect even in heavily compressed or very short syllables. However, this model is a non cascade model, so that no effect of the lexical status of the 'truncated' part of closed syllables is expected. Finally, this model claims that no perceptual differences should be found between actual *vs* nonactual albeit legal, syllables. Note that it still claims that phonemic sequences with impossible onsets such as /dla/ should be processed in different ways than legal onset sequences such as /dra/.

---

[18] Such a count was based on the computerised French database BDLEX (which has 20000 lexical items). The database revealed 145 different onsets, 15 different nuclei, and 20 different simple codas. The product of these three quantities (and removing some constraints on the combinations of semi consonants and vowels) is about 33600.

[19] This meshes well with some of the psychoacoustical studies that show that there is no cross adaptation between /pa/ and /ap/. The present proposal predicts some cross adaptation between /pa/ and /pat/, whereas the syllabic model predicts the opposite result.

An interesting feature about this proposal is that the locus of cross linguistic variation is made more explicit. For instance, English, French, and Chinese would use the same type of semi-syllabic templates for speech categorisation, but the organisation of lexical entries would be very different, and would depend on the specific phonological properties of these languages (syllable time, vocalic reduction, contrastive stress, presence of tone, etc). For example, French would organise the perceptual units in terms of syllables, English would organise them in terms of feet, and Japanese in *morae*. Of course, the present proposal is much less detailed than syllabic model previously described. However it has the advantage of presenting the problem in a broader perspective where results in a diversity of languages could be stated. Yet the two models make rather clear-cut predictions that can be put to the test.

CONCLUSION

In brief, we end up with a rather puzzling state of affairs. On the one hand, there are a number of arguments suggesting that syllable-sized structural effects are not just byproducts of late response biases, but reflect properties of the on-line speech processing apparatus. On the other hand, there are also data showing that some of the structural effects are not as early as they should be if they really reflected on-line processing.

At this stage, there are two alternatives: one is to say that structural effects are decision effects after all. Although this is certainly a possibility one has to take into account, it does not seem very promising. A more inspiring avenue is to stop considering prelexical processing as a monolithic bloc, and suggest that it is composed of several different stages. Each stage may have its own time-scale and integrate different types of information. Indeed, I suggest that there are two such stages, one infra-syllabic which deals with information spanning portions of syllables, and a syllabic stage which relates to structural information of the size of a syllable. This theoretical move makes it possible to give a coherent account of structural effects in speech processing while acknowledging the differing time courses that these effects seem to show. The *cascade model* and the *semi-syllables* model are just two among a number of possibilities that could be developed along these lines. Further research is needed to explore these issues more thoroughly, but one can feel confident that the different variants of the segment monitoring technique will still be with us for some time. Despite the fact that these methods are complex to use and give results that are even more complex to interpret, I believe that they have given us valuable data. They show that both structural effects and a complex time course are at work when we listen to speech.

ACKNOWLEDGEMENTS

I would like to thank Kerry Green, Jacques Mehler, and Juan Segui for their help, comments, and fruitful discussion. This research was carried out with the help of CNET (Convention 837BD28 00790 9245 LAA/TSS/ CMC), CNRS (ATP 'Aspects Cognitifs et Neurobiologiques du Langage'), INRIA, the Fyssen Foundation, and the Human Frontier Science Program.

REFERENCES

Bertelsan, P. (1986). *The onset of literacy*, Cambridge, MA: MIT Press.

Best, C.T., McRoberts, G.W., & Nomathemba, M.S. (1988). Examination of perceptual reorganization for non-native speech contrasts: Zulu click discrimination by English-speaking adults and infants. *Journal of Experimental Psychology: Human Perception and Performance, 14*, 345–360.

Cerf, H., Danon, T., Derouault, A.M., El Beze, M., and Merialdo, B. (1989). Speech recognition in French with a very large dictionary. *Proceedings of Eurospeech 89*, 150–153, Paris: La Vilette.

Cutler, A. (1990). Exploiting prosodic probabilities in speech segmentation. In G. Altmann (Ed.), *Cognitive models of speech processing*, Cambridge, MA: MIT Press.

Cutler, A., Butterfield, S., & Williams, J.N. (1987). The perceptual integrity of syllabic onsets. *Journal of Memory and Language, 26*, 406–418.

Cutler, A., Mehler, J., Norris, D., & Segui, J. (1983). A language specific comprehension strategy. *Nature, 304*, 159–160.

Cutler, A., Mehler, J., Norris, D., & Segui, J. (1986). The syllable's differing role in the segmentation of French and English. *Journal of Memory and Language, 25*, 385–400.

Cutler, A., Mehler, J., Norris, D., & Segui, J. (1987). Phoneme identification and the lexicon. *Cognitive Psychology, 19*, 141–177.

Cutler, A., Mehler, J., Norris, D., & Segui, J. (1989). Limits on bilinguism. *Nature, 320*, 229–230.

Cutler, A., & Norris, D. (1979). Monitoring sentence comprehension. In W.E. Cooper, & E.T.C. Walker (Eds.), *Sentence processing: Psycholinguistic studies presented to Merrill Garrett*, Hillsdale, NJ: Lawrence Erlbaum Associates Inc.

Cutler, A., & Norris, D. (1988). The role of strong syllables in segmentation for lexical access. *Journal of Experimental Psychology: Human Perception and Performance, 14*, 113–121.

Day, R.S., & Wood, C.C. (1972) Mutual interference between two linguistic dimensions of the same stimuli. *Journal of the Acoustical Society of America, 52*, 175.

Diehl, R.L. (1976). Feature analyzers for the phonetic dimension stop *vs* continuant. *Perception & Psychophysics, 19*, 267–272.

Diehl, R.L., Kluender, K.R., Foss, D.J., Parker, E.M., & Gernsbacher, M.A. (1987). Vowels as islands of reliability. *Journal of Memory and Language, 26*, 564–573.

Dupoux, E. (1989). *Identification des mots parlés: détection de phonèmes et unité prélexicale*. PhD dissertation, EHESS, Paris, France.

Dupoux, E., & Mehler, J. (1990). Monitoring the lexicon with normal and compressed speech: Frequency effects and the prelexical code. *Journal of Memory and Language, 29*, 316–335.

Dupoux, E., & Mehler, J. (1992). Unifying awareness and on line studies of speech: A tentative framework. In J. Alegria, D. Holender, J. Morais, & M. Padeau (Eds.), *Analytic approaches to human cognition.* (pp. 59–76). The Netherlands: Elsevier.

Dupoux, E., & Mehler, J. (in preparation) *More on attentional effects in phoneme monitoring.*

Eimas, P.D., & Corbit, J.D. (1973). Selective adaptation of linguistic feature detectors. *Cognitive Psychology, 4,* 99–109.

Eimas, P.D., Marcovitz Hornstein, S.B., & Payton, P. (1990). Attention and the role of dual codes in phoneme monitoring. *Journal of Memory and Language, 29,* 160–180.

Forster, K.I. (1979). Levels of processing and the structure of the language processor. In W.E. Cooper & E.C. Walker (Eds.), *Sentence processing: Psycholinguistic studies presented to Merrill Garrett.* Hillsdale, NJ: Lawrence Erlbaum Associates Inc.

Foss, D.J., & Blank, M.A. (1980). Identifying the speech codes. *Cognitive Psychology, 12,* 1–31.

Foss, D.J., & Gernsbacher, M.A. (1983). Cracking the dual code: Toward a unitary model of phoneme identification. *Journal of Verbal Learning & Verbal Behavior, 22,* 609–632.

Foss, D.J., & Swinney, D.A. (1973). On the psychological reality of the phoneme: Perception, identification and consciousness. *Journal of Verbal Learning & Verbal Behavior, 12,* 246–257.

Fowler, C.A. (1984). Segmentation of coarticulated speech in perception. *Perception & Psychophysics, 36,* 359–368.

Healy, A.F., & Cutting, J.E. (1976). Units of speech perception: Phoneme and syllable. *Journal of Verbal Learning & Verbal Behavior, 15,* 73–84.

Klatt, D.H. (1977). Review of the ARPA Speech Understanding Project. *Journal of the Acoustical Society of America, 62,* (6). 1345–1366.

Klatt, D.H. (1980). Speech perception: A model of acoustic-phonetic analysis and lexical access. In R.A. Cole (Ed.), *Perception & production of fluent speech.* Hillsdale, NJ: Lawrence Erlbaum Associates Inc.

Klatt, D.H. (1989). Review of selected models in speech perception. In W.D. Marslen-Wilson (Ed.), *Lexical representation and process.* Cambridge, MA: MIT Press.

Mann, V.A. (1986). Phonological awareness: The role of reading experience. *Cognition, 24,* 31–45.

Marslen-Wilson, W.D. (1984). Functions and process in spoken word recognition. In H. Bouma, & D.G. Bouwhuis (Eds.), *Attention & performance X: Control of language process,* Hillsdale, NJ: Lawrence Erlbaum Associates Inc.

Marslen-Wilson, W.D., & Tyler, L.K. (1980). The temporal structure of spoken language understanding. *Cognition, 8,* 1–71.

Marslen-Wilson, W.D., & Welsh, A. (1978). Processing interaction & lexical access during word recognition in continuous speech. *Cognitive Psychology, 10,* 29–63.

McNeill, D., & Linding, K. (1973). The perceptual reality of phonemes, syllables, words and sentences. *Journal of Verbal Learning & Verbal Behavior, 12,* 419–430.

Mehler, J. (1981). The role of syllables in speech processing: Infant & adult data. *Philosophical Transactions of the Royal Society, B 295,* 333–352.

Mehler, J., Dommergues, J.Y., Frauenfelder, U., & Segui, J. (1981). The syllable's role in speech segmentation. *Journal of Verbal Learning and Verbal Behavior, 20,* 298–305.

Mehler, J., Dupoux, E., & Segui, J. (1990). Learning constraints on models of speech perception. In G. Altmann (Ed.), *Cognitive models of speech processing,* Cambridge, MA: MIT Press.

Mehler, J., Segui, J., & Frauenfelder, U. (1981). The role of the syllable in language acquisition and perception. In T. Myers, J. Laver, & J. Anderson (Eds.), *The Cognitive representation of speech,* Amsterdam: North Holland.

Miller, J.L., & Dexter, E.R. (1988). Effects of speaking rate and lexical status on phonetic perception. *Journal of Experimental Psychology: Human Perception and Performance*, *14*, 3, 369–378.

Miller, J.L., & Liberman, A.M. (1979). Some effects of later-occurring information on the perception of stop consonants and semivowels. *Perception & Psychophysics*, *25* (6), 457–465.

Mills, C.B. (1980). Effects of the match between listener expectancies and coarticulatory cues on the perception of speech. *Journal of Experimental Psychology: Human Perception and Performance*, *6*, 528–535.

Morais, J., Cary, L., Alegria, J., & Bertelson, P. (1979). Does awareness of speech as a sequence of phones arise spontaneously? *Cognition*, *7*, 323–331.

Newman, J.E., & Dell, G.S. (1978). The phonological nature of phoneme monitoring: A critique of some ambiguity studies. *Journal of Verbal Learning & Verbal Behavior*, *17*, 359–374.

Norris, D.G., & Cutler, A. (1988). The relative accessibility of phonemes and syllables. *Perception & Psychophysics*, *43*, 6, 541–550.

Otake, T., Hatano, G., Cutler, A., & Mehler, J. (submitted). Mora or syllable? Speech segmentation in Japanese *Journal of Memory and Language*.

Posner, M.I., & Snyder, C.R.R. (1975). Facilitation and inhibition in the processing of signals. In P.M.A. Rabbit & S. Dornic (Eds.), *Attention and performance V* (pp. 669–682). London: Academic Press.

Pylyshyn, Z.W. (1984). *Computation and cognition*. Cambridge, MA: Bradford.

Read, C., Yun-Fei, Z., Hong-Yin, & Bao-Qing, D. (1986). The ability to manipulate speech sounds depends on knowing alphabetic writing *Cognition*, *24*, 31–45.

Rubin, P. Turvey, M.T., & Van Gelder, P. (1976). Initial phonemes are detected faster in spoken words than in nonwords. *Perception & Psychophysics*, *19*, 394–398.

Samuel, A.G., & Newport, E.L. (1979). Adaptation of speech by nonspeech: Evidence for complex acoustic cue detectors. *Journal of Experimental Psychology: Human Perception and Performance*, *5*, 563–578.

Sanchez-Casas, R.M. (1988). *Access representation in visual word recognition*. PhD dissertation, Monash University, Australia.

Savin, H., & Bever, T. (1970). The nonperceptual reality of the phoneme. *Journal of Verbal Learning & Verbal Behavior*, *9*, 295–302.

Sebastian, N., Dupoux, E., Sergui, J. & Mehler, J. (1992). Contrasting syllabic effects in Catalan and Spanish. *Journal of Memory and Language*, *31*, 18–32.

Segui, J. (1984). The syllable: A basic perceptual unit in speech perception? In H. Bouma, & D.G. Bouwhuis (Eds.), *Attention and performance X, Control of language processes*, Hillsdale, NJ: Lawrence Erlbaum Associates Inc.

Segui, J., Dupoux, E., & Mehler, J. (1990). The role of the syllable in speech segmentation and lexical access. In G. Altmann (Ed.), *Cognitive models of speech processing*, Cambridge, MA: MIT Press.

Segui, J., Frauenfelder, U., & Mehler, J. (1981). Phoneme monitoring, syllable monitoring & lexical access, *British Journal of Psychology*, *72*, 471–477.

Summerfield, Q. (1981). Articulatory rate and perceptual constancy in phonetic perception. *Journal of Experimental Psychology: Human Perception and Performance*, *7*, 1074–1095.

Swinney, D.A., & Prather, P. (1980). Phonemic identification in a phoneme monitoring experiment: The variable role of uncertainty about vowel contexts. *Perception & Psychophysics*, *27*, 2, 104–110.

Tomiak, G.R., Mullenix, J.W., & Sawusch, J.R. (1987). Integral perception of phonemics: Evidence for a phonetic mode of perception. *Journal of the Acoustical Society of America*, *81*, 3, 755–764.

Treiman, R., Salasoo, A., Slowiaczek, L.M., & Pisoni, D.B. (1982). *Effects of syllable structure on adults' phoneme monitoring performance.* Progress Report No. 8, Indiana University, Speech Research Laboratory.

Tyler, L.K., & Marslen-Wilson, W. (1982). Speech comprehension process. In J. Mehler, E.T.C. Walker, & M. Garrett (Eds.), *Perspectives on mental representation.* Hillsdale, NJ: Lawrence Erlbaum Associates Inc.

Tyler, L.K., & Wessels, J. (1983). Quantifying contextual contributions to word-recognition processes. *Perception & Psychophysics, 34,* 409–420.

Warren, P., & Marslen-Wilson, W. (1987). Continuous uptake of acoustic cues in spoken word recognition. *Perception & Psychophysics, 41,* 3, 262–275.

Warren, P., & Marslen-Wilson, W. (1988). Cues to lexical choice: Discriminating place and voice. *Perception & Psychophysics, 43,* 21–30.

Wood, C.C., & Day, R.S. (1975). Failure of selective attention to phonetic segments in constant-vowel syllables. *Perception & Psychophysics, 17,* 346–350.

6 Language-specific Processing: Does the Evidence Converge?

Anne Cutler
MRC Applied Psychology Unit, Cambridge, UK.

Language-specific processing is not a concept that psycholinguists leap to embrace. If all language processing were specific to the language being processed, psycholinguistics would be a very different discipline; among other things, it would forfeit much of its interest in the eyes of its superordinate field, cognitive psychology. Cognitive psychologists study the structures and processes involved in human cognition, and therefore, when they study language processing, they are interested in human language processing in general rather than processing in the individual case. By extension, language-specific processing simply seems not to be an interesting phenomenon.

Nevertheless, there is an increasing body of evidence in favour of language-specificity in certain aspects of language processing. Dupoux's chapter, and the wider conference discussion to which this chapter is also addressed, have both reviewed and extended this evidence. The conclusion that emerges is an encouraging one: not only is language-specific processing an extremely interesting phenomenon, it also poses no problem to psycholinguistics as a sub-discipline of cognitive psychology, because it can in fact be tractably interpreted within a language-universal framework.

The evidence that first put language-specific processing in the spotlight came mostly from experiments with a single technique, syllable-monitoring; studies in French, English, Spanish, and Catalan produced unexpectedly disparate results. The experiments measured listeners' response time to detect a match between a target CV (e.g. BA-) or CVC (e.g. BAL-) sequence and the initial sounds of a word. In French, RT was crucially determined by whether or not the target corresponded exactly to a syllable of the word (Mehler, Dommergues, Frauenfelder, & Segui, 1981); thus RT to BA- was faster in *balance*, which has an open initial syllable, than in *balcon*, which has a closed initial syllable, while RT to BAL- was faster in *balcon* than in *balance*. In English, in contrast, there was no effect of syllabicity, but a strong effect of whether the target-bearing word began CVCV (*balance*) or CVCC (*balcony*; Cutler, Mehler, Norris, & Segui, 1986); this latter finding perhaps reflects the relative frequency of these patterns in the English vocabulary (Cutler, Norris, & Williams, 1987). The English result was partially replicated by Bradley, Sánchez-Casas, and García-Albea (1993): they also found no effect of syllabicity, but also no effect of word structure. In Spanish, however, they found exactly the effect of syllabicity that Mehler et al. (1981) had observed in French; but this result in turn was not replicated by Sebastián-Gallés, Dupoux, Segui, and Mehler (1992), who conducted further such experiments in Spanish and Catalan. In Spanish, there was only an effect of target size, whereas in Catalan there was a syllabicity effect which appeared only in words with non-initial stress, and a target size effect which appeared only in words with initial stress. Varying word stress in English, however, had no analogous effect—whatever the stress pattern, no syllabicity effect appeared (T. Mintz, personal communication; Rhodes-Morrison, 1992).

Given the psycholinguistic aim to study the human language processing system in general, it was somewhat disturbing to obtain such a variety of results from the same experimental paradigm in languages that are, historically, quite closely related. Some of the disparities—notably the disparities between two experiments on the same language—could be explained in terms of methodological artefacts. The odd study out is that of Bradley et al. (1993), which produced results on English that differed from those of Cutler et al. (1986), Mintz (personal communication), and Rhodes-Morrison (1992); and results on Spanish that differed from those of Sebastián et al. (1992). The way in which Bradley et al.'s study differed methodologically from the others is that it included foils, i.e. words containing a syllable that is highly similar but not identical to the target syllable (for instance, *badger* in a list with the target BAL-). When foils are included, subjects in syllable-monitoring experiments adopt a cautious response criterion (Norris & Cutler, 1988) and hence respond more slowly (indeed, the RTs reported by Bradley et al. are slower than the RTs in all the other experiments). As Dupoux (this volume) has demonstrated, response patterns are crucially dependent on subjects' response criterion; in particular, syllabicity effects are more likely when subjects respond slowly than when they respond rapidly.

The disparities between the results with different languages, however, could not be explained in such terms. Irrespective of experimental detail, no experiment found a syllabicity effect for English; but such effects did appear, under appropriate conditions, for French, for Spanish, and for Catalan. Instead, the researchers invoked as explanation phonological differences between the four languages. Cutler et al. (1986) invoked rhythmic structure in explaining the French-English differences; whereas French has a basically syllabic rhythm, they argued, English is characterised by stress rhythm, involving especially the opposition of strong and weak syllables (i.e. syllables with full *vs* reduced vowels). Importantly, syllabic rhythm is also characteristic of Spanish and Catalan. Similarly, Sebastián et al. (1992) pointed to the difference in the size of the vowel inventory (large in French, small in Spanish) in accounting for the French-Spanish difference, and to the presence of reduced vowels in Catalan in explaining the Spanish-Catalan difference. According to their account, the larger the vocalic inventory, the more likely a syllabicity effect is to be observed. Putting these explanations together, the results converge on a consistent and plausible model. Firstly, it appears that an absolute prerequisite for the appearance of syllabically based responding in a syllable-monitoring task is that the language has syllabic rhythm. Given this, however, syllabic responding is most likely if the language has a large vowel inventory (French), somewhat less likely if the vowel inventory is intermediate (Catalan), and least likely if the vowel inventory is small (Spanish). In the latter case, syllabic responding will only appear when experimental conditions encourage subjects to adopt a cautious response criterion.

Subsequently, this series of studies was extended to a language that is *not* related to the four already discussed. Japanese does not have syllable rhythm, but it does have a clear and simple phonological structure, and very simple syllable structure. Exactly analogous experiments to those conducted in the four European languages produced no trace of syllabic effects with Japanese listeners (Otake, Hatano, Cutler, & Mehler, 1993). Instead, the Japanese listeners appeared to be basing their responses on mora units; the mora, a sub-syllabic unit which can be of the form V, CV, CCV, or syllabic coda, is the unit of rhythm in Japanese.

The balance of evidence therefore suggests that certain characteristics of a language's phonological repertoire exercise constraints on processing by native speakers of the language; in other words, some part of language processing is language-specific. One of the most important aspects of this series of studies is the fact that they included fully cross-linguistic investigations of listeners' processing: not only native-language processing, but also listeners' performance with foreign-language input. These cross-linguistic comparisons showed that if a syllabic response pattern appeared in a listener's native language, the listener could also produce that response pattern with input in a foreign language (for instance, French listeners produced a syllabic response pattern with English and with Japanese); but no listener could produce a response pattern with foreign language input if that pattern was not characteristic of the native language (thus English listeners did not respond syllabically with French input or Spanish input, and neither English nor French listeners produced a mora-based response pattern with Japanese input). These findings made it quite clear that language-specific processing was a property of the listener, not of the input being presented to the system.

This aspect of the earlier results led Cutler, Mehler, Norris, and Segui (1989; 1992) to extend their investigations with syllable-monitoring to French–English bilinguals; interestingly, they found processing differences even in bilinguals whose command of both languages was, to all intents and purposes, equivalent and perfect. Specifically, a measure of language dominance predicted whether or not a syllabic response pattern would be observed with French-language materials: if on this measure the subjects were classified as French-dominant, they produced a syllabic response pattern; if they were classified as English-dominant, they did not. The same measure predicted whether or not a stress-based response pattern could be observed with English-language materials. Evidence from a number of paradigms suggests that English listeners' response patterns in speech recognition are stress-based: for instance, segmentation errors show a consistent pattern, whereby word boundaries are inserted before strong syllables, but overlooked before weak syllables (Cutler & Butterfield, 1992). Similarly, segmentation at strong syllables predicts the interference patterns observed in a task in which real words are detected in nonsense bisyllables (Cutler & Norris, 1988). Testing the French–English bilinguals on this latter task, Cutler et al. (1992) found that only subjects who were classified as English-dominant gave evidence of stress-based responding. Cutler et al. concluded that both syllabic and stress-based response patterns reflect language-specific segmentation procedures, of which only one may be available to a language user's processing system; in bilinguals, the available procedure would be determined by some (as yet unspecified) critical period or experience in language development. The choice, however, was determined by rhythmic characteristics of the language: syllabic rhythm encouraged a syllabic segmentation procedure, stress-based rhythm a stress-based segmentation procedure.

The suggestion that language-specificity occurs at the level of *segmentation processes* clearly offers a way in which the language-specific evidence might be integrated within a universal model of processing. The model tentatively proposed by Cutler et al. (1992) and Otake et al. (1993) assumes the existence of specific processes which act to postulate likely word boundaries in continuous speech input. The continuity of spoken language poses a significant problem for the perceiver, since language can only be understood by accessing lexical representations, and these representations are discrete. Only rarely does speech provide reliable and robust cues to where one word ends and the next begins. Procedures that exist specifically to deal with this problem by exploiting language experience to segment speech with maximum efficiency are logically independent of perceptual units (see Norris & Cutler, 1985, and Cutler & Norris, 1988, for further arguments on this point). As Cutler et al. (1992) point out, there is a remarkable similarity in the syllabic effects shown by French listeners and the stress-based effects shown by English listeners, in that both patterns reflect the basic *rhythmic structure* of the language in question—syllabic rhythm in the case of French, stress rhythm in the case of English. The mora-based response pattern shown by Japanese listeners admits of exactly the same interpretation. This offers the opportunity for restitution of the universal dimension (and, incidentally, severe restriction of the possible range of language-specificity): the child is born with the capacity to develop aids to segmentation which exploit linguistic rhythm. That these procedures turn out to be language-specific derives from the fact that rhythmic structure differs across languages.

Since this proposal, if true, would appear to have some considerable importance for psycholinguistic theory, it is perhaps unfortunate that the majority of the body of research summarised earlier comes from studies with a single task: monitoring for CV and CVC sequences in spoken words. It would seem to be desirable to assemble converging evidence, not only from many experiments (this is surely already available) but from many experimental paradigms. To what extent is this possible?

In a sense, studies that are essentially monolingual can provide relevant evidence. For instance, the studies of stress-based processing in English, mentioned earlier, provide crucial evidence for the involvement of rhythmic factors in processing in English. Although such studies are obviously useful in the bilingual case, they do not allow fully cross-linguistic comparisons, since they cannot be replicated in, say, French. This is because French does not have English-like stress; only in other stress languages is replication of stress studies possible. Of course, it is possible to test alternative hypotheses monolingually; thus Cutler and Norris (1988) were able to show that a syllabic hypothesis would have predicted a completely different pattern of data in their word-spotting experiment. In addition, it is possible to construct similar monolingual experiments, testing language-specific hypotheses, within a particular experimental paradigm; thus word-spotting in French shows clear syllabic response patterns (J. Segui, personal communication).

Some exploratory work presented at the conference by Sebastián and by Altmann used a completely different technique: the presentation to listeners of time-compressed speech. Such a technique is extremely attractive because it appears to be quite language-independent—no language-specific phonological constructs are involved. In principle, speech in any language can be presented with any degree of compression. Previous work with this methodology has indeed suggested that there may be language-specific effects in how compression affects intelligibility (Wingfield, Buttet, & Sandoval, 1979). Sebastián's and Altmann's preliminary findings suggest possible effects both at this level, and at the level of perceptual adaptation to speech compression within *vs* across languages. If such effects prove reliable, this technique would allow fully cross-linguistic investigations.

A different technique was used by Mack (personal communication; Mack, Tierney, & Boyle, 1990), who studied the recognition of natural and synthetically produced sentences by native speakers of English and by highly proficient bilinguals. The materials were presented without any noise-masking, time-compression or other distortion, in American English. Unsurprisingly, recognition by native speakers of American English was at a very high level indeed for both the natural and the synthetic speech; native speakers of another dialect of English (British) performed as well. Bilinguals, however, performed less well, despite the fact that Mack's bilingual subject population was exclusively composed of individuals who had been living and performing at a high academic level in an English-language environment for many years. Moreover, how well the bilinguals performed was apparently determined by their first language: bilinguals whose first language was German performed well (over 90% correct) with naturally produced speech, and less well (70% correct) with synthesised speech, but bilinguals whose first language was French scored only 73% correct for natural speech and 49% correct for synthesised speech—i.e. they performed significantly less well than the German–English bilinguals. Rhythmically, German resembles English to a far greater degree than French does, and it is clearly possible that Mack's studies have tapped into a difference in segmentation performance in a manner analogous to the syllable-monitoring studies. Thus Mack's results provide converging evidence with the Cutler et al. (1989; 1992) finding of unexpected processing limitations in bilingual speakers.

Yet another technique, and one that is particularly suited to the investigation of units of speech segmentation, is the illusory word detection task devised by Kolinsky and Morais (Kolinsky, 1992; Kolinsky & Morais, 1992). With this technique listeners are presented dichotically with competing signals and asked to judge whether one or other of them was a specified target word. The crucial experimental conditions occur when a subject's detection report would involve combination of parts of each of the two signals. For instance, with a target word *bijou*, a detection report from the simultaneous input of two nonwords *cojou* and *biton* would involve migration between the two input words at the syllabic level, whereas a detection report from an input *kijou/boton* would involve migration of the initial phoneme. Preliminary investigations with French suggest that syllabic migrations are common in that language (Kolinsky, 1992; Kolinsky & Morais, 1992).

It may be said, then, that language-specific processing is already fairly well supported by converging evidence from diverse studies and tasks, and that the amount of available evidence is likely to increase. On one view, furthermore, the current evidence would seem to present a coherent picture, within which language-specificity does not conflict with the necessity of universality in a model of human language processing. Dupoux (this volume), however, offers a more radical interpretation, which seeks to restore universality at the perceptual unit level. The universal unit in terms of which speech is categorised is postulated to be the demisyllable. Demisyllables are combined at a later stage of processing into a second universal unit, the syllable. Language-specific differences are localised at the lexical level, in that it is only in some languages that the universal perceptual units also serve as the units of lexical access.

In postulating perceptual units that are not necessarily units of lexical access, Dupoux's proposal would seem not to have advantages of parsimony on its side. It would also seem to predict that the effects of response criterion on response patterns in the syllable-monitoring experiments ought to be constant across languages. Dupoux shows an impressive correlation in the French experiments between the size of the syllabic effect and the subjects' mean response times. However, post-hoc analysis of the three experiments reported by Cutler et al. (1986) with English listeners—experiments with English words, French words, and 'English' nonwords—does not support the constancy prediction. None of the three experiments shows a correlation between mean RT and syllabic effect; nor is there a correlation between mean RT and word effect (CV), as found by Dupoux for the French data. The correlation of mean RT with word effect (CVC), which Dupoux found to be insignificant for French listeners with French words, is also insignificant for English listeners with English words, but is significant for these listeners with both French words and 'English' nonwords; however, the two significant correlations are in the opposite direction to one another. It is unclear what one can make of this latter contradiction; what *is* clear, however, is that the results of these correlations for English listeners do not mimic the results produced by French listeners. If there is indeed universality across languages at the perceptual unit level, then its failure to manifest itself in the syllable-monitoring comparison of French and English requires independent explanation.

Although the detailed implications of Dupoux's proposal are not spelt out, his proposal is evidence that language-specific processing effects may be explained within a universal model of language processing in more than one way. The rhythm-based segmentation proposal of Cutler et al. (1992) and Otake et al. (1993) also stands in need of fuller specification. Nevertheless, the existence of alternative proposals with the same basic aim is highly encouraging. The evidence is indeed converging: part of human language processing *is* language-specific, but in no way does this language-specificity serve to counter the essential universality of the human language processing system.

ACKNOWLEDGEMENT

Financial support is acknowledged from the Human Frontier Science Program.

REFERENCES

Bradley, D.C., Sánchez-Casas, R., & García-Albea, J. (1993). The status of the syllable in the perception of Spanish and English. *Language & Cognitive Processes, 8*, 197–234.

Cutler, A., & Butterfield, S. (1992). Rhythmic cues to speech segmentation: Evidence from juncture misperception. *Journal of Memory and Language, 31*, 218–236.

Cutler, A., Mehler, J., Norris, D.G., & Segui, J. (1986). The syllable's differing role in the segmentation of French and English. *Journal of Memory and Language, 25*, 385–400.

Cutler, A., Mehler, J., Norris, D.G., & Segui, J. (1989). Limits on bilingualism. *Nature, 340*, 229–230.

Cutler, A., Mehler, J., Norris, D.G., & Segui, J. (1992). The monolingual nature of speech segmentation by bilinguals. *Cognitive Psychology, 24*, 381–410.

Cutler, A., & Norris, D.G. (1988). The role of strong syllables in segmentation for lexical access. *Journal of Experimental Psychology: Human Perception & Performance, 14*, 113–121.

Cutler, A., Norris, D.G., & Williams, J.N. (1987). A note on the role of phonological expectations in speech segmentation. *Journal of Memory and Language, 26*, 480–487.

Kolinsky, R. (1992). Conjunction errors as a tool for the study of perceptual processing. In J. Alegria, D. Holender, J. Morais, & M. Radeau (Eds.), *Analytic approaches to human cognition*, pp. 133–149. Amsterdam: North Holland.

Kolinsky, R., & Morais, J. (1992). Représentations intermédiares dans la reconnaissance de la parole: Apports de la technique de création de mots illusoires. *Actes des 19èmes Journées d'Etudes sur la Parole*, pp. 129–133, Brussels.

Mack, M., Tierney, J., & Boyle, M.E.T. (1990). *The intelligibility of natural and LPC-vocoded words and sentences presented to native and non-native speakers of English.* (Technical Report No. 869). Cambridge, MA: Lincoln Laboratory.

Mehler, J., Dommergues, J.-Y., Frauenfelder, U., & Segui, J. (1981). The syllable's role in speech segmentation. *Journal of Verbal Learning and Verbal Behaviour, 20*, 298–305.

Norris, D.G., & Cutler, A. (1985). Juncture detection. *Linguistics, 23*, 689–705.

Norris, D.G., & Cutler, A. (1988). The relative accessibility of phonemes and syllables. *Perception & Psychophysics, 43*, 541–550.

Otake, T., Hatano, G., Cutler, A., & Mehler, J. (1993). Mora or syllable? Speech segmentation in Japanese. *Journal of Memory and Language, 32*, 358–378.

Rhodes-Morrison, F. (1992). *The role of sublexical units in speech segmentation.* Undergraduate project, Hatfield Polytechnic, UK.

Sebastián-Gallés, N., Dupoux, E., Segui, J., & Mehler, J. (1992). Contrasting syllabic effects in Catalan and Spanish. *Journal of Memory and Language, 31*, 18–32.

Wingfield, A., Buttet, J., & Sandoval, A.W. (1979). Intonation and intelligibility of time-compressed speech. Supplementary report: English *vs.* French. *Journal of Speech and Hearing Research, 22*, 708–716.

7 Representation and Access of Derived Words in English

L.K. Tyler
Department of Psychology, Birkbeck College, University of London, UK.

R. Waksler
Department of Linguistics, San Francisco State University, San Francisco, USA.

W.D. Marslen-Wilson
Department of Psychology, Birkbeck College, University of London, UK.

ISSUES

To comprehend a spoken utterance, listeners need to map the speech input onto representations of lexical form and content in their mental lexicon. When the word they are hearing is morphologically complex, what are the properties of these representations? Is the word represented as a *full form*, or in terms of some type of *morphologically decomposed* representation (Butterworth, 1983; Henderson, 1989)? In answering this question we need to distinguish between what we can call the *access representation* and the *lexical entry*. We take the lexical entry to be the modality-independent core representation of a word's syntactic and semantic attributes, as well as its abstract phonological properties. The access representation, in contrast, is modality-specific and constitutes the perceptual target for lexical access either in the visual or in the auditory domain.

This distinction, between access representations, and lexical entries, is not a new one in theories of the mental lexicon, and can be found in a variety of models, such as Forster's (1976) early search model, and Morton's (1969) logogen model. Despite this, psycholinguistic research into morphologically complex words has frequently failed to maintain this distinction, making it difficult to sort out whether claims and evidence for full-listing or decomposition apply to the access representation, the lexical entry, or both.

The research described here is concerned with the lexical entry. It addresses the issue of how this is organised; whether lexical representations are word-based or morpheme-based. To answer these

125

questions, we need to study the access and representation of morphologically complex words—words that are made up of two or more constituent morphemes. These allow us to dissociate word- and morpheme-based theories of representation, as well as their associated theories of lexical access. We can determine, for example, whether the word *management* is represented in the lexicon as a single unit or as the morphemes {manage} + {ment}, where the stem {manage} may also participate in the representation of othe words, such as *manager, managing*, etc.[1]

In evaluating these possibilities, we need to take seriously the modality-specific nature of the access representation. What holds for the access of lexical representations from written words may not hold for access from the speech signal (and vice-versa). One difference is the sequential delivery and interpretation of stimulus information in the auditory domain, with the consequences this has for the processing of prefixed as opposed to suffixed words (with their different ordering of stem and affix). Another important difference is in the presence of cues to morphological structure in one modality but not in the other. For example, the prefix in *return* and in *rebuild* is spelt in the same way but pronounced differently. The pronunciation of *re-* with a full vowel in words like *rebuild* but not in words like *return* is a cue to morphological structure that is available to the listener but not to the reader. Thus, although the lexical entry itself may be modality-independent, different access routes can give different pictures of its properties, as well as themselves having different properties.

Derivational Suffixes in English

We will focus here on the representation of derived suffixed words in English. Derivational morphological processes in English can cause changes to the semantic, syntactic, and phonological properties of the base-forms to which derivational affixes are applied. For example, derivational suffixes can alter the syntactic form-class of base-forms, as in *write/writer*; *trouble/troublesome*. In addition, these forms may become semantically opaque over time (as in *department*), and some classes of derivational suffixes change the phonological form of their stems (as in *chaste/chastity*; *decide/decision*).

These variations in transparency and opacity have potential consequences for both the access representation and the lexical entry. Let us consider first the factor of semantic transparency, and the role it plays in determining whether a derived word will be independently represented at

---

[1] We will use the convention of curly brackets {} to indicate reference to abstract morphemes at the level of the lexical entry.

the level of the lexical entry. A derived word is semantically transparent if its meaning is synchronically compositional. Words like *happiness* or *happily* are semantically transparent because their meaning is primarily derivable from the meaning of their stem {happy} together with their respective affixes {-ness}, {-ly}. It is unlikely that the lexical entries for words like this would not be related to the lexical entry for the word *happy*.

In contrast, words like *department* are no longer semantically transparent, although historically they once would have been. At the level of the lexical entry, these words are likely to be represented differently from semantically transparent words. If *department* is represented as {depart} + {ment}, this would have to be a different {depart} than the phonologically identical stem in words like *departure*. One possibility, then, is that semantically opaque words are no longer represented in the lexical entry in terms of their original morphological structure [stem+affix], but as morphologically undecomposed forms, rather like the morphologically simple words *table* or *mouse*. This would mean that the lexical entry for words like *department* would not be related to words containing phonologically identical but semantically unrelated stems (as in *departure* or *departed*).

The alternative possibility is that semantically opaque forms can, nonetheless, be represented in a morphologically decomposed manner. Aronoff (1976), for example, argues that morphological relations can be identified, which involve morphemes that have no clear semantic interpretation.[2] If this view is correct, then the listener may indeed analyse *department* into {depart} + {ment} and represent it in this way. This, in turn, would imply that the lexicon contained two homophonic morphemes {depart}.

These claims about independent or shared representations in the lexical entry will have consequences for how access representations are organised. For example, if *happiness* and *happily* share the lexical entry for *happy*, it is possible that access is *via* a representation of the stem rather than the full derived form. In contrast, the access of derived words like *department* is more likely to be *via* the full-form of the word.

Similarly, the phonological transparency of a derived form also has consequences for both the access representation and the lexical entry. What we mean by phonological transparency is the degree to which there is a change in the phonetic realisation of the stem (and possibly the affix) when it occurs in a morphologically complex form. Pairs like *vain/vanity* and *deceive/deception* are examples of this.

---

[2] For example, words like *permit, transmit,* and *submit* do not share a common meaning, but they are linked by a common phonological rule, which is specific to verbs containing the root [-*mit*].

It is cases like these, where the stem+affix relation is semantically transparent but phonologically opaque, that provide the best argument for distinguishing the access representation from the lexical entry. Consider the derived word *deception*, which has, as its stem, the word *deceive*. Assuming a sequential access process of the type proposed in the cohort model (Marslen-Wilson, 1987; Marslen-Wilson & Welsh, 1978) the stored phonological representation of the stem *deceive* may not be directly accessible by the phonetic input corresponding to *deception*. This suggests that there must be separate access representations to allow both words to be available as targets for the perceptual access process.

Phonological alternation in the surface form of a stem raises questions about the properties of the form representation in the lexical entry. We assume that this includes a specification of the abstract phonological properties of the word (cf Lahiri & Marslen-Wilson, 1991). This implies that, in the case of derived words where the stem undergoes some form of phonological alternation, the representation will be in terms of the underlying rather than the surface form of the stem. Take, for example, the pair *vain/vanity*. On recent linguistic analyses (e.g. Myers, 1987), the underlying phonological representation of the stem *vain*, which surfaces as [veyn] when heard in isolation but as [væn] in the context of [-ity], is assumed to be [vÆn].[3] This suggests a highly abstract relationship between the form of the stem in the lexical entry and its phonetic form in the derived word.

In the experiments described in the next section, we ask whether the lexical entry is structured along morphological lines. In doing so, we take into account the possible role of phonological and semantic transparency in determining the answer to this question.

EXPERIMENTAL STUDIES

Task

All our experiments used the cross-modal repetition priming task, where subjects hear a prime word and, at its acoustic offset, they see a target word. They make a lexical decision to the word that they see. The important contrast is between decision latencies to the visual target word when it occurs after a related prime word, as opposed to an unrelated control prime. We predicted that if the stem of a word is accessed when listeners hear a derived word (e.g. *happiness*), then when they see the stem

---

[3] The capitalised vowel symbol (Æ) denotes a vowel segment unspecified for tenseness (Myers, 1987).

(*happy*) after hearing the derived word, their latencies to make a lexical decision will be facilitated, relative to the control condition, where they see the stem after they have heard an unrelated word (e.g. *table*).

We used this task because we assume: (1) that it taps selectively into activation-effects at the level of the lexical entry; and (2) that because prime and target are presented in different modalities, it is not sensitive to purely phonological or orthographic overlap between prime and target at lower levels of the system.

Experiment 1

Is the lexical entry for derived words in English structured morphologically, irrespective of whether the morphological relation between stem and derived word is phonologically transparent or opaque?

Relatively few studies have looked at this issue for derived words in English. One study by Bradley (1980) used frequency effects to determine whether suffixed words are accessed as full forms or by means of some sort of stem-based representation. She attempted to determine, for a variety of different kinds of suffixed words, whether the frequency effect associated with a given derived form reflected the frequency of the form itself, or the frequency of the underlying stem. For example, the words *sharpness* and *briskness* are equally common forms in the language. However, the stem *sharp* (including the other morphologically complex forms in which it participates) is much more frequent than the stem *brisk*. If access to the two derived words, as measured in a visual lexical decision task, involved access to their stems, then response times should differ, with the word containing the most frequent stem (*sharpness*) eliciting the fastest response.

Bradley looked at four types of suffixed word: those with the affixes [-*ness*], [-*er*], [-*ment*] and [-*ion*]. She only found an effect of the frequency of the stem for those words containing affixes that did not induce phonological changes in the stem ([-*ness*], [-*ment*] and [*er*]). When the affix did cause phonological changes in the stem ([-*ion*], as in *dictate/dictation*), then there was no longer a bias in favour of stem frequency. Thus, she argued that it was only phonologically transparent derived words that were accessed via their stems. Bradley's results are not completely clear-cut, and they are in the visual domain and therefore might not generalise to spoken words. Nonetheless, they suggest that morphological structure does affect the access and representation of derived suffixed words in English, and that this interacts with phonological transparency.

Later research by Napps (1989) used the repetition priming task with visually presented words and found that morphologically related words primed each other, even when the relationship between them was phonologically opaque. There are, however, a number of problems with the experiments. First, the stimulus items did not form a homogeneous set. Napps used a mixture of inflected and derived words, and within the derivational set there were both prefixed and suffixed forms. It is possible that the effects she found applied only to specific subsets of items. Second, the degree of phonological change varied considerably between members of the sound-and-spelling change set. In addition, she found less priming from suppletive pairs (*bear/bore*) than for non-suppletive pairs which involved sound-and-spelling changes, even though some of the suppletive pairs had the same amount of phonological variation as some of the sound-and-spelling change pairs. These experiments, therefore, do not give a straightforward picture of the relationship between phonological variation and morphological structure.

To investigate this issue in the spoken domain, we used pairs of words consisting of a derived word and its stem (such as *friendly/friend*) and varied the phonological relationship between members of the pair.[4] Our main criteria for deciding whether words were morphologically related were the following: first, the derived form had to have its affixes listed in authorities such as Marchand (1969) or Quirk, Greenbaum, Leech, and Svartvik (1985); second, when the suffix was removed, the pairs of words should have the same underlying stem; and third, the pair of words should share the same historical source word (or etymon) as determined by the Oxford Dictionary of English Etymology (1983) or the Longmans Dictionary of the English Language (1991). This was to exclude pairs that had coincidentally homophonic stems

The major variable in this study was the phonological relationship between the stem and the derived word. This required us to construct groups of word-pairs varying in the phonological transparency of the relationship between the derived–stem pairs. If the lexical entry is morphologically structured, such that the representation of the derived form in the lexical entry shares the same stem as the stem in isolation, then the stem should always be primed by the derived word, irrespective of the surface phonological relationship between them.

The first set consisted of phonologically transparent words (see Table 7.1).[5] These were cases where the stem had the same phonetic form, both when it appeared without a suffix, and when it was part of the derived word (e.g. *friendly/friend*). These contrasted with two further sets of words where the relationship between prime and target was phonologically

---

[4] All pairs were judged to be semantically transparent.

[5] In this table, and all others, we use the following labels to refer to the various conditions: +Morph = morphologically related; −Morph = morpholigically unrelated; +Phon = phonologically transparent; −Phon = phonologically opaque.

TABLE 7.1
Experiment 1: Test Conditions

Conditions	Examples
1. [+Morph, +Phon]	friendly–friend
2. [+Morph, −Phon]	elusive–elude
3. [+Morph, −Phon]*	serenity–serene
4. [−Morph, +Phon]	tinsel–tin

* In condition 3 the surface form of the stem in isolation does not correspond to its underlying representation.

opaque. In condition 2, we used cases like *tension/tense* or *elusive/elude*, where the stem had a different phonetic form in isolation than when it appeared in the derived word. In condition 3, we went a step further, using pairs like *vanity/vain* or *gradual/grade*, where not only does the stem have a different phonetic form in isolation, but also the underlying representation of the stem (as determined by standard linguistic analysis) is not identical to its surface form. This had the effect of increasing the abstractness of the relationship between the stem and the phonetic form of the derived word. To the extent that priming in this task is morphemic—mediated by shared morphemes in the lexical entries for prime and target—then the amount of priming should not be affected by these variations in the surface phonetic transparency of the relationship between derived word and stem.

As a final condition we used word-pairs that were not morphologically related, but which overlapped phonologically (from word-onset). An example of such a pair is *forty/fort*. The shorter of the two words (e.g. *fort*) was transparently contained in the longer word. This condition acted as an additional control. If *forty* primed *fort*, we would be unable to argue that any priming we found for the morphologically related pairs was due to their morphological relationship. It could be caused simply by the phonological relationship between them.

The derived word (and the longer of the two morphologically unrelated words) was always the word that subjects heard. They then saw the stem, and were asked to make a lexical decision to it. For each prime–target pair there was also an unrelated control prime, which was matched in frequency to the test prime.[6] No subject encountered the test target-prime and control target-prime for the same pair of words.[7] Table 7.2 shows the mean

---

[6] Pairs were matched across conditions for frequency, number of syllables, and grammatical category. For each stem and derived form, we calculated the aggregate frequency of the appropriate inflected forms. So, for example, if the test word was *departure*, we summed the frequency of *departure* and *departures*.

[7] In this and all the other studies reported here, we included a large number of filler items of various types, which were designed to obscure the regularities in the test set.

TABLE 7.2
Experiment 1: Lexical Decision Latencies (msec.)

Condition	RT/test	RT/control	Difference
1. [+Morph, +Phon]	539	583	−44*
2. [+Morph, −Phon]	563	623	−60*
3. [+Morph, −Phon]	572	608	−36*
4. [−Morph, +Phon]	647	638	9

*p<0.05

lexical decision latencies to the target word when it follows a test prime and when it follows a control prime.

To determine whether lexical decision latencies were facilitated by the presence of a related prime word, we subtracted RTs to the target when it followed the test prime from RTs to the target when it followed the control prime. These difference scores are shown in the final column of Table 7.2.[8]

First, we find that phonological overlap *per se* does not produce facilitation. When the prime and target are similar phonologically, but are not related morphologically (condition 4), RTs to the target are no faster than when it is preceded by a phonologically unrelated control word.[9] Second, we obtain significant facilitation when the prime and target are morphologically related. Given the absence of priming in condition 4, we can be confident that this is not due simply to phonological overlap between prime and target. Moreover, derived words prime their stems even when the relationship between them is phonologically opaque (conditions 2 and 3). This is evidence for the abstractness of the underlying phonological specification of the stem. It is also, along with the results for the other conditions, evidence that the task we are using here does indeed tap into the system at the level of the lexical entry. Otherwise, we would have expected phonological factors to have played a more important role, with decision latencies being affected by the surface phonetic relationship between prime and target.

---

[8] For all of the experiments reported here, we analysed the data in the following way. Errors and extreme values were removed from the data set. We then computed midmeans for each subject and each item. Midmeans were entered into two ANOVAs and MinF' values were then computed.

[9] In an additional analysis, we looked more closely at the stimuli in condition 4 to ensure that they did not differ from the stimuli in condition 1 in terms of resyllabification. This is defined as a change in the prosodic status of the final segment of the stem when it is followed by a derivational suffix. Most of the stems in condition 1 did resyllabify (22/30) as did most of the pseudo-stems in condition 4 (23/29). Looking at the resyllabification cases on their own, the priming results were unchanged, at +13msec in condition 4 ⌐nd −41msec in condition 1.

The results of Experiment 1 support, therefore, the hypothesis that a derived word's lexical entry is morphologically structured [stem+affix] and this morphological structure is made available when the word is identified. On this account, the stem morpheme in the derived word is the same morpheme that is accessed when the subject sees the stem in isolation. This is why lexical decision latencies to the stem are faster when it follows a derived word than when it follows a control word.

There is, however, an alternative account of the results so far. It is possible that the effects we have ascribed to morphological factors are, in fact, due to *semantic* relatedness. Although we did not explicitly test for the degree of semantic relatedness between the morphologically related words in this study, all of the derived–stem pairs were judged to be semantically transparent, so that the meaning of the stem and the meaning of the derived form were closely related. It is possible that the priming we observed was due to this semantic relation rather than to morphological factors. The next experiment investigates this issue.

Experiment 2

The aim of this study was to investigate the role of semantic factors in priming between morphologically related prime/target pairs. Earlier research that has addressed this issue suggests that the priming of morphologically related words is not merely due to semantic relatedness (Emmorey, 1989; Henderson, Wallis, & Knight, 1984; Napps, 1989). Emmorey (1989) found priming for prefixed morphologically related words (e.g. *submit/permit*) that were not semantically related, using an intra-modal auditory repetition task. However, she also found priming for words that were not related phonologically (e.g. *balloon/saloon*), suggesting that the priming she found between prefixed bound stems was phonological rather than morphological in nature.

Napps (1989) also argues that priming for morphologically related words is not due to semantic relatedness. However, this conclusion is not based on direct experimental evidence. Rather, she infers this from the fact that although she does not find priming for synonyms in a delayed repetition priming task, she does find priming for morphologically related words.

In our experiment we test directly for priming of words that are morphologically but not semantically related, by varying the degree of semantic relatedness between word-pairs (see Table 7.3). We tested this for two types of morphologically related primes and targets. Conditions 1 and 2, paralleling the stimuli in Experiment 1, used stem–derived pairs that were morphologically related (following the same criteria as in Experiment 1) but which were semantically opaque in one condition (e.g. *casual/casualty; emerge/emergency*) and semantically transparent in the

TABLE 7.3
Experiment 2: Conditions

Conditions	Morphological Type	Examples
1. [+Morph, −Sem]	Derived–stem	casualty–casual
2. [+Morph, +Sem]	Derived–stem	punishment–punish
3. [+Morph, −Sem]	Derived–derived	successful–succession
4. [+Morph, +Sem]	Derived–derived	confessor–confession
5. [−Morph, +Sem, −Phon]	n/a	idea–notion
6. [−Morph, −Sem, +Phon]	n/a	fortify–forty

other (e.g. *punish/punishment*). Conditions 3 and 4 consisted of word-pairs where both members of the pair were derived words sharing the same stem (on the same linguistic and historical criteria of morphological relatedness). Again, in one condition, the two words were semantically transparent (e.g. *confessor/confession*) and in the other way they were opaque (e.g. *successful/succession*).

Derived words sharing the same stem should prime each other for the same reason that derived words prime their stems. A pair like *confessor/confession*, for example, should be represented as sharing the stem {confess}. When the subject hears the prime *confessor*, {confess} would be accessed. This same stem will be accessed when the subject subsequently sees the target *confession*, and residual activation of the stem should lead to faster lexical decision latencies, in the same way that free stems showed facilitation in Experiment 1. If semantically unrelated derived words, such as *successful/succession*, also share a common stem at the appropriate level of lexical representation, then they should prime each other as well. If they do not, then they should not prime, despite the high degree of phonetic overlap between prime and target.

We also included two additional control conditions. The first (condition 5), contained synonym prime/target pairs (e.g. *idea/notion*), which were semantically but not morphologically related. We ensured that these pairs were not associates (cf Fischler, 1977; Moss, Ostrin, Tyler, & Marslen-Wilson, 1992), by conducting a pre-test where subjects were asked to provide associates to the synonym prime words. This was to maintain comparability with the morphologically related pairs, which in general were not associatively related.

The final condition consisted of pairs of words that were phonologically, but not morphologically, related. This was included, as in Experiment 1, as a control for phonological priming. Since the morphologically related pairs overlapped by an average of two syllables, we selected word-pairs for this control condition in which the pairs also shared a two-syllable overlap (e.g. *fortify/forty*).

The definition of semantic transparency is crucial for this experiment. Derived forms are normally transparent when they come into the language, in that the meaning of the form can be directly established from the composition of the stem with its affix. The issue for these experiments is to determine whether this still holds synchronically; for current users of the language. To establish this, we carried out extensive pre-tests, asking groups of subjects to rank the semantic relatedness of potential prime/ target word-pairs on a 9-point scale, where 1 was very unrelated and 9 was very related. The list of pairs included candidates for all the categories of pairs described earlier, as well as some completely unrelated pairs. The mean rating for the morphologically related and semantically transparent pairs selected for the experiment was 7.8, whereas the rating for the opaque pairs was 2.3. The mean ratings for the synonyms and for the unrelated word-pairs were 8.5 and 1.3, respectively. The results are shown in Table 7.4. This presents the mean lexical decision latencies to the target word when it follows a test prime and when it follows a control prime, together with the difference scores.

First, words that are only semantically (and not associatively) related, prime each other (condition 5). This is additional evidence that the cross-modal task taps into the lexical entry, since it is presumably only at this level that semantic information is represented in the lexicon and can form the basis for a priming effect.

In the other control condition (6) we found, once again, that words which are only related phonologically do not prime. In this condition, the amount of overlap was closely matched to the amount of overlap in the morphological conditions. This means that priming in the other conditions is not attributable to surface phonological similarities between prime and target.

TABLE 7.4
Experiment 2: Lexical Decision Latencies (msec.)

Condition	RT/test	RT/control	Difference
1. [+Morph, −Sem] (derived–stem)	544	559	−15
2. [+Morph, +Sem] (derived–stem)	504	539	−35*
3. [+Morph, −Sem] (derived–derived)	578	582	−4
4. [+Morph, + Sem] (derived-derived)	540	542	−2
5. [−Morph, +Sem, −Phon]	558	585	−27*
6. [−Morph, −Sem, +Phon]	593	595	−2

* $p < 0.05$

For the morphologically related pairs, we only find priming for derived–stem pairs that are semantically transparent (condition 2). The derived–stem pairs that are semantically opaque (condition 1) do not show significant priming. Not only is the effect much smaller than for the semantically transparent pairs, but it is also more variable across items.[10] In addition, there is no priming in either of the derived–derived conditions (3 and 4). Even when the pairs are semantically related, there is only a 2msec difference between test and control. When subjects hear *excitable*, this does not facilitate responses to *excitement*. The derived–derived semantically transparent pairs are just as strongly semantically related as the derived–stem pairs, and yet they do not prime each other.

These results have potentially far reaching implications for the model we are trying to develop. If semantically unrelated pairs do not prime, then this implies that morphologically related words will only be linked in the mental lexicon if there is a synchronically transparent semantic relationship between a derived form and its stem. If derived–derived pairs do not prime even when they are semantically related, then this implies that semantic relatedness is not the only factor controlling responses in this task, and that morphological factors have to be taken into account.

The next experiment was designed as a replication of these two main results. We felt that the effects for derived–derived pairs and for semantically unrelated stem–derived pairs should be re-tested for a larger and more homogeneous stimulus set. The derived–derived pairs contained a number of bound morph pairs (e.g. *dentist/dental*), and it is possible that these do not play the same role in lexical representations as free stems. For the stem–derived pairs, there was a numerical trend towards priming for the semantically unrelated pairs, and we felt it was important to establish whether this trend held up in subsequent tests.

Experiment 3

There were five conditions in this study. Four were the same as in the previous experiment—semantically opaque, and transparent derived–derived and derived–stem pairs (see Table 7.5), but each now contained a larger and more homogeneous set of stimuli than in experiment 2. The number of items per condition now averaged 20, and the derived–derived sets only contained pairs with free stems (as in *confessor/confession*). Once again, these materials were pre-tested for their semantic relatedness; mean relatedness for the semantically related pairs was 7.5, and for the unrelated

---

[10] Only 8 out of 14 items show priming in condition 1, whereas 16 out of 18 items show priming in condition 2.

TABLE 7.5
Experiment 3: Conditions

Condition	Morphological Type	Example
1. [−Sem, +Morph]	(derived–stem)	casualty–casual
2. [+Sem, +Morph]	(derived–stem)	punishment–punish
3. [−Sem, +Morph]	(derived–derived)	successful–successor
4. [+Sem, +Morph]	(derived–derived)	confession–confessor
5. [+Sem, +Morph]	(stem–derived)	friend–friendly

pairs 2.3. We also included a fifth condition, consisting of semantically transparent forms where the stem was the prime and the target was a derived form (e.g. *harm/harmless, predict/predictable*). This was to check whether, as the shared morpheme account also predicted, derived forms could be primed when preceded by their stem rather than by another derived form. Priming for these stem–derived cases should be obtainable for the same reasons as priming in the derived–stem conditions in experiments 1 and 2.

The results (see Table 7.6) were very similar to those observed previously. There were no priming effects in either of the derived–derived conditions, and a clear difference between the semantically transparent and opaque derived–stem pairs. There is now no hint of priming for the opaque pairs, but a large and significant priming effect (41msec) for the transparent pairs. This confirms the effects found in Experiment 2. Suffixed derived–derived pairs do not prime each other, even when they are strongly semantically related. Suffixed derived–stem pairs do prime each other, but only when they are semantically related.

Finally, in the new condition included here, semantically related stem–derived pairs show solid priming effects. This rules out the possibility that

TABLE 7.6
Experiment 3: Lexical Decision Latencies (msec.)

Condition	RT/test	RT/control	Difference
1. [−Sem, +Morph] (derived–stem)	575	574	1
2. [+Sem, +Morph] (derived–stem)	554	595	−41*
3. [−Sem, +Morph] (derived–derived)	611	614	−4
4. [+Sem, +Morph] (derived–derived)	580	591	−11
5. [+Sem, +Morph] (stem–derived)	578	630	−52*

* $p < 0.05$

derived–derived pairs fail to prime because derived forms are in some way unsuitable as probes.

CONCLUSIONS

We can draw three main conclusions from the studies reported here. First, the task taps into an abstract representation of lexical form. We can infer this from the fact that phonetic overlap *per se* between primes and targets does not produce priming. Moreover, the amount of priming for morphologically related words is not affected by variations in the phonological transparency of the relationship between prime and target.

Second, semantic relatedness between a prime and its target is a necessary but not sufficient condition for priming to occur. Semantically unrelated pairs do not prime reliably. Third, the type of morphological relation between a prime and target affects whether or not priming is obtained. Derived forms prime their stems, and stems prime related derived forms. Derived suffixed forms, however, do not prime, even if they are semantically related and share the same stem.

On the basis of these results, we can begin to sketch a model of how morphological structure is represented in the mental lexicon. In the model, we need to postulate two different types of representation—one for semantically transparent and another for opaque forms. The lexical entry for transparent forms, like *government*, consists of the stem morpheme [*govern*] and a link to the suffix [*-ment*]. The same stem morpheme also functions as the lexical entry for the morphologically simple form *govern*. Recognition of the word *government* involves the access of the stem morpheme and the associated affix. This changes the state of the stem morpheme such that when the visual probe *govern* is immediately presented—mapping onto the same morpheme via a different perceptual route—the lexical decision response to this probe is facilitated.

In contrast, a word like *department* will be represented at the level of the lexical entry as if it were a morphologically simple word. It can enter into combination with other morphemes (as in *departmental* or *interdepartmental*) but itself has no internal structure. In particular, it does not share a stem morpheme with words like *departure*. This has a separate representation consisting of the free stem {depart}, linked to the affix {-ure}.

The different patterns of priming for semantically opaque and semantically transparent derived forms reflect, on this account, the fact that listeners do not represent words as sharing the same stem, and therefore as morphologically related, unless there are semantic grounds for doing so. This, in turn, is a claim about language acquisition. The structure of the adult lexicon reflects individuals' experience with the language as they learn it. A word like *department*, although it has a phonetically transparent morphological structure on the surface, will not be analysed during language acquisition into [depart]+[ment] at the level of the lexical entry, because this gives the wrong semantics.

How does this model accommodate the absence of priming between derived–derived suffixed pairs? This result argues against a purely semantic explanation of the morphological priming effects that we have obtained. However, at first glance, it also seems to pose problems for an account of semantically transparent words in terms of a shared stem. If hearing the word *government* activates {govern}, and it is this residual activation that facilitates responses to the visual probe *govern*, then why does *government* not facilitate responses to *governor*, with which it shares a stem? We suggest that hearing a semantically transparent form like *government* activates *govern* and at the same time inhibits other suffixed forms sharing the same stem. This is because words like *government* and *governor* are mutually exclusive competitors within the same lexical paradigm [*govern*]. This inhibitory relationship is best captured by inhibitory links between the two suffixes [-*ment*] and [-*or*], rather than between the two lexical items *governor* and *government*. This avoids a situation in which the stem is both activated (by being part of *government*) and inhibited (by being part of *governor*).

The consequence of these inhibitory connections is that when a suffixed word is heard it will momentarily inhibit the combination of the stem with other suffixes. This will have the effect of slowing recognition to a subsequently presented suffixed word, even though the same stem is activated. In contrast, when the stem is presented following a suffixed word, there will be no inhibition, and so recognition of the stem will be facilitated. Similarly, when the stem functions as the prime, this will change the state of the shared stem morpheme, but it will not affect the state of any of its links to suffixes. Thus, when a suffixed form follows as a probe, the effects of stem activation will facilitate recognition without any counterbalancing inhibitory effects.

This morphologically structured model, with inhibitory links between suffixes, can accommodate all of our experimental findings. It accounts for why semantically transparent suffixed forms prime their stems, and why derived forms can be primed by their stems but not by other related derived forms. It constitutes the beginning of our attempt to provide a comprehensive account of the representation of morphologically complex words in English.

ACKNOWLEDGEMENT

This research was supported by grants from the SERC and MRC to W.D. Marslen-Wilson and L.K. Tyler.

REFERENCES

Aronoff, M. (1976). *Word formation in generative grammar*. Cambridge, MA: MIT Press.

Bradley, D. (1980). Lexical representation of derivational relation. In M. Aronoff & M-L Kean (Eds.), *Juncture*. Cambridge, MA: MIT Press.

Butterworth, B. (1983). Lexical representation. In B. Butterworth (Ed.), *Language production*, Vol. 1. London & San Diego: Academic Press.

Emmorey, K. (1989). Auditory morphological priming in the lexicon. *Language and Cognitive Processes, 4*, 73–92.

Fischler, I. (1977). Semantic facilitation without association in a lexical decision task. *Memory & Cognition, 5*, 335–339.

Forster, K. (1976). Accessing the mental lexicon. In E. Walker, & R. Wales (Eds.), *New approaches to language mechanisms*. Amsterdam: North Holland.

Henderson, L. (1989). In W.D. Marslen-Wilson (Ed.), *Lexical representation and process*. Cambridge, MA: MIT Press.

Henderson, L., Wallis, J., & Knight, D. (1984). Morphemic structure and lexical access. In H. Bouma, & D. Bouwhuis (Eds.), *Attention and performance X: Control of language processes*. Hillsdale, NJ: Lawrence Erlbaum Associates Inc.

Lahiri, A., & Marslen-Wilson, W.D. (1991). The mental representation of lexical form: A phonological approach to the recognition lexicon. *Cognition, 38*, 243–294.

Longmans Dictionary of the English Language (19xx). London: Longman.

Marchand, H. (1969). *The categories and types of present-day English word-formation*. Munich: Beck.

Marslen-Wilson, W.D. (1987). Functional parallelism in spoken word recognition. *Cognition, 25*, 71–102.

Marslen-Wilson, W.D., & Welsh, A. (1978). Processing interactions and lexical access during word recognition in continuous speech. *Cognitive Psychology, 10*, 29–63.

Morton, J. (1969). Interaction of information in word recognition. *Psychological Review, 76*, 165–178.

Moss, H., Ostrin, R.K., Tyler, L.K., & Marslen-Wilson, W.D. (April, 1992). *Auditory associative and semantic priming*. Paper presented at the Experimental Psychology Society meeting, Oxford.

Myers, S. (1987). Vowel shortening in English. *Natural Language and Linguistic Theory, 5*, 485–518.

Napps, S. (1989). Morphemic relationships in the lexicon: Are they distinct from semantic and formal relationships? *Memory and Cognition, 17*, 729–739.

Oxford Dictionary of English Etymology. (1983). Oxford, UK: OUP.

Quirk, R., Greenbaum, S., Leech, G., & Svartvik, J. (1985). *A comprehensive grammar of the English language*. London: Longman.

What Determines Morphological Relatedness in the Lexicon? Comments on the Chapter by Tyler, Waksler, and Marslen-Wilson.

Cristina Burani
Institute of Psychology of the National Research Council, Rome, Italy.

INTRODUCTION

In the last years, many experimental studies have shown that morpho-logical relationships among words affect subjects' performance in tasks, such as lexical decision or tachistoschopic recognition, which are con-sidered to require lexical access. A variety of models have proposed that morphological relationships are represented within some component of the lexical processing system. More specifically, some models assume that morphological relatedness acts as a principle of organisation among lexical entries, that is, within the component in which lexical representations are permanently stored (e.g. Burani & Caramazza, 1987; C.˙ ˌamazza, Laudanna, & Romani, 1988; Jarvella & Meijers, 1983; Lukatela, Gligorijevic, & Kostic, 1980; Taft & Forster, 1975; Tyler, Behrens, Cobb, & Marslen-Wilson, 1990).

However, two morphologically related words are generally very similar in (orthographic and/or phonological) form and have close meanings. Thus one can raise the following question: are morphological effects distinct from semantic and formal (orthographic or phonological) effects, or should they be interpreted as the combined effects of semantic and formal relationships between words? To put it differently: can morphological relationships between entries be represented in the lexicon independently of semantic and formal representations, or does the representation of morphology merely reflect the convergence of representations of meaning and form?

Tyler, Waksler, and Marslen-Wilson's chapter (Chapter 7, this volume) addresses this latter issue directly, and provides rich evidence drawn from cross-modal priming in lexical decision tasks, which in part converges and in part is at variance with recent data obtained in research on access to printed (Bentin & Feldman, 1990; Napps, 1989) or spoken (Emmorey, 1989) words. In synthesis, current experimental evidence argues in favour of a lexical component in which morphological relationships are represented, possibly independently of (or in a way not reducible to) both semantic and phonological relationships.

In this chapter I shall not directly discuss the possibility of having morphological relationships represented in the lexicon independently of semantic and formal relationships. This suggestion is in fact convincingly supported by an increasing set of data. Rather, I shall concentrate on some theoretical/methodological problems that are still open in this area of research, and do not specifically characterise Tyler et al.'s study. Thus Tyler et al.'s paper will be discussed in a more general framework.

I shall discuss two main issues. First, like most data on morphological effects, Tyler et al.'s evidence seems compatible with a variety of theoretical accounts. This state of affairs does not seem to be due to the fact that current data are not adequate to distinguish between existing models. On the contrary, it seems to reflect the fact that current models of lexical processing are too vague and underspecified for a number of relevant dimensions, so that empirical data, although rich, cannot easily discriminate among them. The form of lexical morphological organisation suggested by the authors is one of various possible solutions. More specifically, the data seem to be accounted for not only by a 'decom-positional' hypothesis (like that adopted by Tyler et al.), which assumes that lexical entries for morphologically complex words are represented in morphologically decomposed form, with stems[1] connected to the affixes they can be combined with. Data on morphological effects can also

---

[1] In this chapter, I shall use the term 'stem' adopted by Tyler et al., as well as by many authors in the psycholinguistic literature, to refer to the morphemic constituent that corresponds to that part of a word which remains when all affixes have been removed. I am aware that there are proposals, in linguistics, for designating that same morpheme with the term 'root', and for reserving the term 'stem' to the part of the word-form that remains when only the inflectional affixes have been removed. In the latter sense, a stem may or may not contain derivational affixes, whereas a root never contains any affixes (see e.g. Bauer, 1983). Although I am more sympathetic with the latter proposal, which has also been adopted in the experimental studies on Italian (see e.g. Burani & Caramazza, 1987; Burani & Laudanna, 1992; Burani et al., 1984; Laudanna et al., 1992), I am also aware that in the psycholinguistic literature, which deals mainly with the English language, there is a preference for using the term 'stem' for the word's constituent that remains after removing *all* the affixes. Therefore, hereafter I shall adopt the terminology that is more currently used in psycholinguistics when referring to English, so as not to introduce too many terminological distinctions (see also Footnote 5, p. 155).

be accounted for by assuming that morphologically related words are represented in the lexicon as whole forms interconnected along morphological lines.[2]

I do not propose that the interpretation based on undecomposed entries is necessarily the best one, although there may be reasons to consider it as particularly adequate for words with derivational affixes (which differ from inflections in a number of respects, e.g. in that they do not constitute a paradigm, while inflections do—see e.g. Scalise, 1984). I really think that data are compatible with a variety of accounts, and at the moment there are no crucial elements to give one preference over the other. However, I shall discuss the account provided by one version of the 'undecompositional' model as exemplification of this general statement.

A second related issue deals with the consideration of some linguistic and empirical dimensions, such as affix productivity or frequency, the difference between stem and base, and the nature of the relation between base and derived forms, which are underevaluated in most studies on processing and representation of morphology. A closer inspection of these dimensions can contribute to specifying principles of morphological organisation, providing hypotheses on the factors responsible for the establishment of a morphological relationship in the inner lexicon. Furthermore, the consideration of these factors can suggest different representation modalities, according to differences among types of affixes, and among languages.

The chapter is organised in the following way. In the next section, I shall discuss how an interpretation based on undecomposed lexical representations interconnected through morphological links can explain both Tyler et al.'s and other authors' results. The role of productivity, frequency and other distributional properties of affixes in determining morphological relatedness will be examined. Experimental evidence, including some recent results obtained in my laboratory, will be discussed with reference to the possibility of characterising morphological relationships as purely structural. In the final section, data by Tyler et al., as well as by other authors, will be discussed with reference to the differences between 'stem' and 'base', and to the type of relationship linking the base to its derived forms. Possible differences in representations reflecting differences among language types will be considered.

---

[2] There seems to be a confusion, in the experimental literature, between 'word-based' and 'independent' lexical representations, which are sometimes considered as synonymous. To say that lexical representations are word-based does not, however, imply that they are also independent from one another: whole-word representations corresponding to morphologically related words can be interconnected through morphological or purely structural links.

MORPHOLOGICAL DECOMPOSITION OR MORPHOLOGICAL CONNECTIVITY? LINGUISTIC AND EMPIRICAL ASPECTS AFFECTING MORPHOLOGICAL RELATEDNESS

Research on visual lexical access has suggested morphological organisation for derived words that have productive suffixes and no ortho-phonological variations with respect to their bases (Bradley, 1979; Burani & Caramazza, 1987), or for suffixed derived words considered as a whole set with no particular distinctions among them (Napps & Feldman, 1985; Napps, 1989; Stanners, Neiser, Hernon, & Hall, 1979a). Tyler et al.'s paper systematically explores how far the lexicon's morphological organisation extends to the variety of suffixed derived words.

By means of a cross-modal repetition priming task, Tyler et al. investigate morphological relationships between a suffixed derived word and the word corresponding to its base, as well as between two suffixed words derived from the same base, having different degrees of phonological and semantic overlap. They find that a suffixed derived word primes lexical decisions to its base in a number of cases. Priming occurs when the suffixed derived word prime is both phonologically and semantically transparent with respect to its base (e.g. *friendly–friend*) as well as when it is only semantically (e.g. *judicial–judge*) transparent. By contrast, no reliable priming is found when the suffixed derived word prime is only phonologically, and not semantically, transparent (e.g. *department–depart*).

Tyler et al. give the following interpretation of their results. Facilitation on lexical decisions to the target occurs because both the prime and the target access the same lexical entry. Suffixed derived words that are both phonologically and semantically transparent, as well as suffixed derived words that are only semantically transparent, are stored in the lexicon in decomposed form as stem plus affixes. Priming of the target base form is caused by the activation, subsequent to presentation of the prime, of the derivative's stem, which is represented in abstract phonological form and is the same for both the derived and the base surface forms. By contrast, a derived word that is semantically opaque (e.g. *department*) is represented as a whole form independently of its etymological base's lexical entry (e.g. *depart*). Thus activation of a semantically opaque derived word's lexical entry would not lead to any activation of the lexical entry corresponding to the word that was its base etymologically. Consequently, no priming occurs. (We might also predict that no priming would occur when the suffixed derived word prime is both phonologically *and* semantically opaque (e.g. *courteous—court*)).

Tyler et al. introduce inhibitory links between affixes that are connected to the same stem, in order to explain why no priming is found when both the prime and the target are suffixed derived words sharing the same stem, independently of their being semantically transparent or opaque. In this case, according to Tyler et al., although the same stem is activated by both the prime and the target, no priming occurs, because of the inhibitory link existing between the two suffixes. In other words, when a derived word is accessed, the stem and its affix are activated, but the other derivational affixes are inhibited.

I shall now consider how a non-decompositional hypothesis might explain the same pattern of results. I shall not discuss the general lines of an interpretation of this type (for similar proposals, see Dell, 1986; Fowler et al., 1985; Lukatela et al., 1980), but I shall concentrate on the aspects that are relevant to the issues under discussion. Let us assume that all entries in the lexicon correspond to whole words, but they are not independent from one another; rather, lexical entries are interconnected through a variety of links, some of which are morphological links. Thus the lexical entry corresponding to a derived word would be connected to the lexical entry of its base word. After an input recognition stage in which words are processed as whole forms, each suffixed derived word would activate its corresponding undecomposed lexical entry, which in turn would activate the lexical entry corresponding to the word that is the derivative's base. The activation of the latter lexical entry would be caused by activation spreading along the connection linking the derived word's entry to its base word's entry.

Tyler et al.'s data seem to indicate that not all representations of suffixed derived words are connected to the representations of their bases. Morphological connections would exist between a suffixed derived word's lexical representation and its base's representation only when there is a semantic relationship between the derived word and its base word. By contrast, no such morphological connection would typically exist in the lexicon between a semantically opaque derived word's representation and the representation of the word that historically constituted its base.

If morphological connections exist in the lexicon only between *some* lexical entries, then the central question to be addressed in a framework which assumes undecomposed lexical entries is: what are the principles by which a morphological connection becomes established and consolidated in the lexicon? The issue of assessing whether phonological and/or semantic relationships are necessary in order to establish a morphological connection between two entries, can be considered from a slightly different perspective, by taking into account factors like the number and the frequency of words constituting a morphological 'family', or the productivity or frequency of the affixes involved.

Let us consider English phonologically transparent derivatives, and semantically transparent derivatives. There seems to be a tendency for both types of derived words to include a part that is recurrent in other words in the language. This is more obvious for a phonologically transparent word: in English, a derivative of this kind is constituted by a sub-part (the stem) which has exactly the same form of the word corresponding to its base, and is also contained in the base's inflected forms. However, there is also a sense in which a semantically transparent derivative (independently from having a phonologically transparent stem) tends to contain a recurrent sub-part: a semantically transparent word usually includes a sub-lexical portion (corresponding to the affix) which is recurrent in other words of the language. In fact, quite often a suffixed derived word is semantically transparent with respect to its base by virtue of including a so-called *productive* suffix, that is, a suffix that is used to form new words and tends to have a predictable meaning (Aronoff, 1976; Bauer, 1983). Of course there are exceptions: not all semantically transparent derivatives include productive affixes, and not all derivatives including productive affixes are semantically transparent with respect to their bases. However, there seems to be some correlation between semantic transparency and affix productivity, as well as betv `∴n affix productivity and number of word–types in which the affix occurs (see e.g. Baayen & Lieber, 1991).

By contrast, derived words that are both phonologically and semantically opaque tend to be constituted by sub-lexical units which appear in few other words in the language. No recurrent sub-parts possibly corresponding to morphemes are easily evident in these words: neither the stem (which is phonologically different from the base word and its inflected forms), nor the suffix. It might in fact be the case that completely opaque derived words (like English *courteous*) include suffixes that do not appear in enough words in the language to act as potential sub-lexical units. There are obviously some exceptions in this case too.

The hypothesis of a correlation between semantic transparency and the productivity or frequency of the derivational affix should be verified empirically, and taken into consideration when attributing a role to a derivative's semantic transparency. This latter factor might in fact be led back to differences among derivational affixes. Here, I wish to stress the methodological issue: when studying derivatives, the role of the derivational affix should be taken more seriously into consideration. This means that when suffixed derived words are investigated experimentally, the types of suffixes included should be better controlled for, and taken into account as a possible factor of explanation of results. (I will come back to this issue when I will discuss the variability across items of the effects found by Tyler et al. with phonological transparent but semantically opaque derived words).

Within linguistically based interpretations, morphological productivity is considered a determining factor of whether a word is more likely to be listed independently in the lexicon, or as morphologically related to other words (see e.g. Bybee, 1985). Since the distribution of non-productive suffixes can be accounted for only in terms of the specific bases with which they occur, in a sense it can be argued that these suffixes are lexicalised within the word forms in which they occur, with each form independent of the other. Thus, linguistics provides a principle of morphological organisation. However, it is not obvious that the linguistic dimension of morphological productivity corresponds to a processing/representation principle as well. Affix productivity might be one of the factors contributing to morphological relatedness among words. Other factors might play a role as well, or might interact with productivity (see Burani & Laudanna, 1992; Frauenfelder & Schroeder, 1991).

For instance, morphological relatedness among words might be more likely to emerge when the recurrent sub-lexical units corresponding to stems and affixes appear in a large set of words in the language, or when the words in which they occur are relatively frequent in the language. In other words, both the number of word-types sharing a given sub-lexical unit, and the frequency of these recurrent sub-lexical units (that is the number of tokens in which they are realised), could constitute additional (or interacting) factors for morphological relatedness among words. These factors, which reflect characteristics of the input language and are generally not so much considered by linguists, do not necessarily identify with productivity. For instance, there can be productive affixes that give rise to comparatively few existing words, or to words that are not used frequently in the language. In these latter cases, although corresponding to a productive affix, the sub-lexical unit would not be likely to emerge as a structural configuration stable enough to act as a principle of relatedness.

In addition to productivity and frequency of the sub-lexical units possibly corresponding to morphemes, and to the number of word-types in which they occur, other relevant dimensions can be identified. A sub-lexical unit's length (in phonemes or graphemes) might be one of these dimensions, with longer units being more likely to emerge as a factor of relatedness. A second dimension might be the ratio between the number of words (like *replay, remark*) in which a given sub-lexical unit (e.g. *re*) occurs in combination with sub-lexical units which in turn recur in other words (e.g. *play, mark*), and the number of words (like *religion*) in which that same unit (*re*) occurs randomly combined with a variety of strings. In other words, what might be relevant is the proportion of cases in which, in the words of a given language, a string of phonemes/graphemes corresponds to a morpheme combinable with other morphemes, and not to a pseudo-morpheme (see Burani & Laudanna, 1992).

Laudanna, Burani, and Cermele (submitted) have investigated whether this latter dimension plays a role in the recognition of a string of letters as a potentially morphological sub-part (see also Burani & Laudanna, 1992). The authors studied lexical decision times to non-words constituted by a sequence of letters corresponding to an Italian prefix followed by a real word of the Italian language not combinable with it. The hypothesis was that non-words should take longer to be rejected when the potential prefix appears as an actual prefix in a high proportion of words beginning with that sequence of letters, than when it appears as a prefix in a low proportion of words. A second factor that was hypothesised to affect the probability of recognising a unit as a morphemic unit was the absolute number of word-types in which a prefix occurs: decisions on non-words might be delayed when the potential prefix appears as an actual prefix in many words of the Italian language. The results showed that the most important factor in determining the probability for a sequence of letters to be identified as a morphological sub-lexical structure, is the proportion of cases in which it appears as such in the language's words. The absolute number of word-types in which a prefix occurs was also shown to have an effect in delaying the rejection of non-words, although weaker than the effect of the first factor.

In synthesis, in the view I am suggesting here, the principle by which a morphological connection becomes established in a lexicon which stores whole-word representations can be provided by generalisation of a structural configuration recurrent within many words of the language in combination with other recurrent forms. These recurrent structures would correspond to stems (in phonologically transparent words) and also to affixes when they are productive or when they occur in many word-types or in a high proportion of potentially affixed words. There are obvious differences between affix types. Within derivational affixes, prefixes are certainly different from suffixes in a number of respects, which may interact differentially with factors like productivity, frequency, or word-types' numerosity. However, the factors mentioned here are potentially relevant, although perhaps in different degrees, for both derivational prefixes and suffixes.

As already mentioned, for phonologically transparent derivatives, a recurrent structural configuration can also be provided by the stem as it is present in other words. By contrast, no organisational principle would be available for word pairs constituted by a base word and a derivative when the latter does not include an affix with the characteristics suggested earlier and when its stem is different in (orthographic or phonological) form from the base word.

This principle of *purely structural* 'schema generalisation' is a different formulation of Tyler et al.'s acquisitional account for the establishment of a morphological relationship. According to Tyler et al., a morphological relationship is established in the lexicon as a consequence of learning, during language acquisition, that two structurally similar words are not only similar in structure, but are also related in meaning. There is also, however, an unreliable trend in Tyler et al.'s Experiment 2 for phonologically transparent, semantically opaque relationships (e.g. *casualty—casual*) to mediate priming. (This was true for 8 out of the 14 items, but was not replicated in Experiment 3 in which a 'larger and more homogeneous set of stimuli' were used; the precise differences between these stimuli is of some importance here.) I am suggesting here that the establishment of a morphological relationship, in this apparent minority of cases, can rely on purely structural grounds, through a process that can be roughly described as follows.

After being exposed to many occurrences of (spoken or written) words in the course of time, a person may become sensitive to the recurrence of some forms (or parts of words) within many words of the language, if they tend to occur in combination with particular types of other forms. For instance, a configuration corresponding to a stem is recurrently associated, within a word, to a limited set of forms (corresponding to the affixes). By generalisation of structural recurrent configurations, some associations between lexical representations sharing these configurations would become established in the lexicon. These connections between entries sharing structural aspects can give rise to purely structural (i.e. not necessarily semantic) morphological relations.

This seems to imply a revised notion of the 'morpheme', which is traditionally considered to be a unit to which a unitary meaning is associated. In this account, as well as in the traditional view of the morpheme, a morphological relationship would emerge because some forms occur in complementary distribution with one another. However, differently from the traditional account, it is not required that these recurrent and complementary forms have a stable meaning.[3]

The proposed interpretation implies that morphological relationships are represented in a component that is independent of, although related to, the component where semantic representations are stored. Morphological effects would thus be able to arise within the component in which

---

[3] The notion of the morpheme as a unit to which a stable meaning is not necessarily associated, has been suggested by Aronoff (1976) with reference to derived words with bound stems (like *reject, inject, object*). Aronoff states that the principle by which two words including the same morpheme with different meanings are morphologically related, is that the two words undergo the same morpho-phonological rule (e.g. *rejection, injection, objection*). However, when considering word processing, the principle providing morphological organisation among lexical entries can differ from that suggested by Aronoff. Other factors, such as the number or frequency of the word forms sharing a given sub-lexical unit, might be more important in determining morphological relatedness among lexical representations.

whole-word lexical entries are interconnected through structural links, and would be relatively independent of the activation of the semantic component.

With regard to the latter issue, the undecompositional account seems to provide a potential explanation of the priming effects found in a minority of semantically opaque (and phonologically transparent) derivatives. By contrast, a decompositional hypothesis, if applied to these cases, would not easily find a solution to the following problem: if the stem is represented independently, and it is unique for the various morphologically related forms, then all the forms containing that stem would have access to the same semantics via activation of the semantic node corresponding to the stem. At the same time, when accessing a derivative, the meaning of its affix would also be activated. But, since the meaning of a semantically opaque derivative does not identify with the combination of the two morphemes' meanings, how could the derivative's specific meaning be accessed (and used for integration of semantic properties in the interpretation process) if the only route to meaning is through compositionality of the stem's meaning and the affix meaning?

By contrast, in a lexicon including undecomposed representations, each lexical entry points to its specific semantic node in the semantic component. This organisation, although not causing any problem to higher-order processes of semantic integration, still assigns the locus of morphological effects to the component where structural relations are represented. In this latter component a semantically opaque (but phonologically transparent) derivative might be connected to its base word by virtue of the following properties: it shares with the base word a structural pattern corresponding to the stem, and it includes another structural pattern corresponding to the suffix, in the case this is shared by many other words in the language. With reference to Tyler et al.'s results, it might be the case that the items which in Experiment 2 showed priming although rated as semantically opaque, included suffixes that are frequently used, or are shared by many other words in the language. This property of the suffixes included in the derivatives, in addition to their phonological transparency with respect to the base, might have provided a principle of morphological relatedness between the derived and the base words.

The suggested interpretation seems also to explain some data, like Emmorey's (1989) (see next section for a more detailed discussion), which indicate the existence of relationships between affixed words composed by the same 'bound' stem, that is, a stem not free to appear alone as a word, but which appears only in combination with a limited set of derivational affixes (e.g. *gress* in *ingress, progress, regress*). (For a discussion of 'bound' stems, see also Selkirk, 1982, p. 98.) This is a clear case in which a relationship can emerge by identification of a structural configuration (corresponding to the bound stem) which is recurrent in a number of words in combination with a set of affixes, although these words do not necessarily share aspects of meaning. It might be disputed whether these 'structural' relationships between words should be any longer characterised as 'morphological'. However, increasing experimental data, as well as some recent theoretical suggestions, point to the necessity of enlarging the domain of morphological relatedness towards including relationships among words of this type.

Some studies on visual lexical access have shown that prefixed words with bound stems behave like prefixed words with free stems. Using morphemic repetition priming, Stanners, Neiser, and Painton (1979b) found facilitation effects on lexical decisions to prefixed words with bound stems by primes including the same stem; the facilitation effect was not different in size from the facilitation produced by prefixed word primes with free stems on prefixed word targets sharing the same stem. In other lexical decision experiments, Bergman, Hudson, & Eling (1988) found longer decision times and higher error rates for pseudo-prefixed words than for truly prefixed words. Truly prefixed words with bound stems did not behave differently from truly prefixed words with free stems. Finally, Lima (1987) monitored eye-movements on prefixed and pseudo-prefixed words, and found longer fixations on pseudo-prefixed words than on prefixed words. The latter included both words with free stems and words with bound stems.

These data, along with the already cited results by Emmorey (1989) seem in accordance with the theoretical proposal made by Aronoff (1976) for including bound stems with no stable meanings into the class of morphemes (see again Footnote 3, p. 149). However, Aronoff's view still relies on the notion of morphemes as lexical items. More recent and more radical suggestions within linguistics (Anderson, 1988; 1992) provide an alternative ('a-morphous') view of morphology, not based on morphemes as minimal signs. According to this view, morphological material would be represented in the lexicon by relations between word forms, or by processes through which one word can be constructed from another. In a sense, in this view morphological form is represented as the application of rules for mapping words onto other words.

STEMS, BASES, DERIVATIVES: WHICH RELATIONSHIPS AMONG THEM IN THE LEXICON?

In the preceding section, I stressed that morphological relations exist between a derived word and its *base* word (or form). By stressing *base word* instead of *stem*, as used by Tyler et al. as well as by many authors in the literature, I wish to point out a characteristic of the English language that makes it a good candidate for a non decomposed representation of lexical entries. In English, a word's (free) stem always corresponds to an existing real word, namely the base word with no affixes. Furthermore, the inflected words that can be formed from a stem/base are relatively few. Thus, in English, a 'morphological family' of words is composed of few members. These two aspects (the fact that the stem identifies with a real word, and the existence of few inflected forms), converge to suggest the undecomposed form of representation as appropriate for a language like English. For other languages, in which there are no real words that work as base forms, but in which stems function as the bases for word formation rules, and a very rich set of inflectional affixes give rise to a lot of inflected forms, a morphologically decomposed form of representation may be more appropriate.

In what follows, I shall discuss how an interpretation based on whole-word lexical entries would provide an explanation of Tyler et al.'s finding of no priming between two suffixed derived words. The hypothesis of different representational modalities according to types of affixed words considered (whether suffixed, prefixed, or infixed), to types of stems (whether free or bound) and to the language-type under investigation might explain the apparent inconsistency of Tyler et al.'s finding with other results in the experimental literature (e.g. Stanners et al., 1979b); Emmorey, 1989; Bentin & Feldman, 1990).

In a lexical organisation in which lexical entries correspond to whole words, morphological relationships among word forms are not uniformly represented, but some asymmetries show up. The lexical entry corresponding to the base word would function as the nucleus (of a morphological family) around which the lexical entries corresponding to derived words cluster, in a way similar to what proposed by Lukatela et al. (1980) for Serbo-Croatian nouns inflected for case.

Morphological connections may also vary in strength (or closeness). It can be argued (Bybee 1985; 1988) that the derived forms, which are generally the weaker forms (in that they are less frequent and more complex than the base), are learned and stored in the lexicon in relation to stronger forms, namely their bases (by 'stronger forms', Bybee means the more frequent, morphologically simpler forms, which act as the bases for innovation). According to Bybee, the continued frequency imbalance between the weaker and the stronger forms will maintain the dependent relation of the more complex form on the simpler one. This would cause a strong connection between the derived and the base form, while no analogous connection would relate a derived form to the other derivatives sharing the same stem. In a sense the base-word representation would act as 'attractor' of the weaker form (the derivative), which would be represented in terms of the base form, but not in terms of the other derivatives.

A similar proposal has been made by Feldman & Fowler (1987) for the representation of 'oblique' cases in Serbo-Croatian, which would cluster around the nominative. The authors suggested this interpretation on the basis of results from repetition priming, in which they found that the nominative singular can prime and be primed by its oblique cases, while an oblique case (e.g. dative) preceded by a different oblique case (e.g. instrumental) does not prime as effectively. According to the authors, these data reveal inhomogeneities in the coherence of the satellite system. The connections between two satellite entries corresponding to two different inflected-case forms are weaker than the connection linking a satellite entry to its nucleus.

A similar account can be proposed for derivatives that share the same stem. They might have not developed relationships one with the other, or these relationships might be weak, because of the strength of the relationship linking each derivative to its 'attractor' (the base form). Connections among derivatives sharing the same stem might even be weaker than connections among nouns with the same stem but differently inflected for case, because derivatives may belong to different grammatical categories.

In this interpretation, no inhibitory link is assumed between two derived forms' representations. Access to one of the forms derived from a base would not lead to any activation of the representation of another form derived from the same base because no direct (or a weak) structural connection would exist between the two derived forms' lexical entries.

An organisation of this kind predicts no priming of a derived word by another word derived from the same base, as found by Tyler et al. However, at least three pieces of evidence in the literature are apparently not consistent with Tyler et al.'s results. The data I will discuss now showed priming effects between two derivatives sharing the same stem.

A first set of results (Emmorey, 1989; Stanners et al., 1979b) relate to English prefixed forms with bound stems, that is, stems not corresponding to existing words. Stanners et al. (1979b) showed repetition effects on visually presented prefixed targets when they were preceded at lags of 8–12 items by another prefixed word sharing the same bound stem. In this study, prime and target were not contiguous. Therefore I shall discuss only a second set of data (Emmorey, 1989) in which facilitatory effects were found between prefixed words with bound stems, when prime and target were presented contiguously at the SOA of 50msec. By auditory presentation of both prime and target, Emmorey (1989) found that a prefixed verb (e.g. *object*) primed another prefixed verb (e.g. *inject*) which had the same stem but was not associated for meaning to the prime. Each prime was phonologically similar to its target (prime and target included the same bound stem, with no formal variation). However, priming did not seem to be caused by phonological similarity. Control pairs of words that were phonologically related, but did not share any morpheme, (e.g. *balloon–saloon*) either did not show priming (Experiment 1), or showed some priming, but reduced in size with respect to morphological priming (Experiments 2 & 3). Emmorey concluded that morphological relationships among derived words are represented in the lexicon even in the absence of semantic relatedness—that is even when they are purely structural.[4]

Let us now consider possible reasons for the differences between Emmorey's and Tyler et al.'s results. The discrepancy between these results might indicate that morphological relations among prefixed words derived from the same stem are represented differently from morphological relations among suffixed derived words. A number of characteristics differentiate the prefixed word pairs studied by Emmorey (1989) from the suffixed word pairs investigated by Tyler et al. First, Emmorey's prefixed word pairs were constituted by words belonging to the same grammatical class (that of verbs), whereas Tyler et al.'s suffixed word pairs included words of different grammatical classes. Moreover, in Emmorey's study all prime-target pairs included the same stem with no phonological variations, while Tyler et al.'s suffixed word pairs showed phonological differences between prime and target's stems (e.g. *successful–succession; confessor–confession*). These factors might contribute to a higher degree of morphological relatedness between prefixed than between suffixed words derived from the same base.

---

[4] The fact that in two other experiments Emmorey (1989) found some phonological priming for morphologically unrelated word pairs that shared the final syllables, might suggest that intramodality priming induced phonological low-level effects. This might attenuate Emmorey's conclusions, according to which the priming effects found in her study arise in the lexicon. However, it should be noted that previous studies which investigated auditory priming did not consistently find phonological effects. When facilitatory effects were reported, they were generally weak and were found only under particular experimental conditions (see e.g. Goldinger, Luce, & Pisoni, 1989; Slowiaczek, Nusbaum, & Pisoni, 1987; Slowiaczek & Pisoni, 1986).

Emmorey's findings could rather be interpreted as effects of syllabic priming. This would suggest a role of syllables as representational units, an hypothesis currently under debate. However, morphological effects do not seem to be reducible to syllabic effects, as supported by two types of considerations. First, morphological priming is consistently found under many experimental conditions. Second, the amount of priming produced by morphologically related primes is consistently much larger, if compared to other types of priming effects. This is true also of Emmorey's results: although the size of syllabic priming effects varied between 74 and 77msec, the amplitude of morphological priming, caused by a prime sharing the bound stem with the target, was 143msec.

However, the aspect that might play a more important role is that affixed words considered by Emmorey had bound stems, whereas Tyler et al.'s derived words had free stems (in Experiment 3). The hypothesis that derived words with non free-standing stems are more related than derived words sharing a free-standing stem, can sound rather counterintuitive. However, if we adopt the hypothesis advanced in the preceding section, according to which morphologically related words may be represented as whole forms interconnected through structural links, and structural/morphological relations among entries may emerge as consequence of sharing a recurrent structural pattern, a difference between the two cases becomes apparent.

As with derived words with free stems, derived words that share a bound stem can be connected through structural links when they include affixes that occur in many other words in the language, and when the derivatives belong to a rather numerous morphological 'family', that is when the bound stem occurs in various words in combination with different affixes (evidence for this comes from a study by Burani, Laudanna, and Cermele, in press, on experimentally induced prefix–substitution errors). But, unlike affixed words with free stems, no base forms' representations exist for affixed words with bound stems. Thus, in the lexical representation of derived words of the latter type, there will be no entry with a special status in terms of 'basic-ness' or structural simplicity, able to work as attractor of other forms. No asymmetrical relationship between entries will be set up, and all the affixed entries constituting a set will be equally interconnected. This form of organisation might favour a high degree of relatedness among affixed words with bound stems (see again Burani et al., in press).

The second set of results that seem to contradict Tyler's finding of no priming between two words derived from the same stem is reported by Bentin and Feldman (1990). In a visual lexical decision task, these authors did find priming effects between words derived from the same root[5], both when they were, and when they were not, semantically related. The priming effect was found both when prime and target were contiguous, and when they were separated by a lag of 15 intervening items. The language investigated was modern Hebrew: in this language, words are derived by embedding the root (which is not a word, but an abstract structure usually formed of three consonants in a given sequence) into one of several 'word-

---

[5] Hereafter I shall use the term 'root' with reference to the abstract structure not realised as an existing word in a number of languages, among which are Hebrew and Italian. In so doing, I follow the terminology adopted by the authors who have studied the latter languages (Burani & Caramazza, 1987; Bentin & Feldman, 1990; Burani & Laudanna, 1992; Laudanna et al., 1992).

patterns', which are also abstract structures that specify what kind of material (vowels, Ø, reduplication) can fill the blanks between the consonants in the root, and at the root's edges. To form a word, the vowels and the consonants constituting a word pattern are added to the root by (sometimes simultaneous) infixation, prefixation, and suffixation. Thus both roots and 'word patterns' can be characterised as 'discontinuous morphemes': related words do not share a continuous string of segments forming a root or an affix, but are related by non-concatenative processes. Both the word patterns and the roots are generally productive, and derivatives usually do not derive directly from other words, but the process of derivation is mediated by the abstract root.

The discrepancy between Bentin and Feldman's, and Tyler et al.'s results does not seem to be related to differences between intramodality (visual/visual) priming, as adopted by the first authors, and the intermodality priming used by the latter. One might think that some formal (orthographic) priming between words that are orthographically similar (as it was the case for the pairs of Hebrew derivatives) is responsible for the observed facilitation. However, the facilitatory effect of orthographic repetition tends to be small, and is not consistently observed. It tends to occur under particular conditions, such as when the prime is masked, and prime and target are contiguous, and it may even be inhibitory (see Colombo, 1986; Forster, Davis, Schoknecht, & Carter, 1987; Humphreys, Evett, Quinlan, & Besner, 1987; Napps & Fowler, 1987). Moreover, when morphological and orthographic repetition were compared directly, it was found that the orthographic repetition inhibited or had no effects on lexical decision for words (Henderson, Wallis, & Knight, 1984).

Alternatively, these different results might reflect differences in the representation of morphological relationships that have their source in structural differences among languages. For morphologically complex words, no base words exist in Hebrew. Thus, for Hebrew, as in the case (as discussed earlier) of English affixed words with bound stems, if lexical representations consist of interconnected whole-word lexical entries, there would not be one lexical entry with a special status that would function as attractor of other forms. Thus, no asymmetrical relations between derived and base words would emerge to prevent relationships between derivatives from playing a role.

For a language like Hebrew, a decompositional account might also be appropriate. Hebrew words do not usually derive directly from other words. They are constructed from a common root, but not one from the other. Moreover, along with derived words, various inflected words are constructed by combination of the same root pattern with other word patterns. These aspects suggest a 'combinatorial' form of representation for this language, in which roots and affixal word patterns are represented independently, and words are recognised (and possibly produced) by accessing both the root's and the affix's lexical entries. In a framework like this, the facilitatory effect of a derivative on another word derived from the same root would have its source in the activation of the root's lexical entry by both the prime and the target words.

More generally, the morphologically decomposed form of representation seems particularly adequate for languages with a rich system of inflectional affixes, and in which the root, instead of the word, is the base for derivation. Increasing experimental evidence has led, for instance, to proposals of a morphologically decomposed representation for Italian, a language with a very rich inflectional morphology, and in which roots do not correspond to existing words, but are realised as words only in combination with an inflectional suffix (see e.g. Burani & Caramazza, 1987; Burani & Laudanna, 1992; Burani, Salmaso, & Caramazza, 1984; Caramazza et al., 1988; Jarvella, Job, Sandstrom, & Schreuder, 1987; Job & Sartori, 1984; Laudanna, Badecker, & Caramazza, 1992; Laudanna & Burani, 1985).

In conclusion, experimental studies on morphological processing provide rich evidence for the representation of morphological/structural relationships in the lexicon. However, current models of lexical access and representation seem insufficiently developed to account for morphological phenomena in a detailed way. More specifically, the component in which morphological relationships among lexical entries are permanently represented and stored should be further developed in its internal organisation, and its relations with the other components of lexical processing should be better defined. In this chapter, I have tried to show how, in detailing aspects of representation of morphological/structural relatedness, it would be worthwhile to assign a more central role to both linguistic properties and distributional characteristics of morphologically complex words. This might help in clarifying what contributes to morphological relatedness among lexical entries, and what the principles of organisation among them are. Furthermore, the consideration of differences in morphology among languages may serve to distinguish which representational modalities are specific to a given language, and which are possibly more general.

ACKNOWLEDGMENTS

I would like to thank Alessandro Laudanna and Anna Maria Thornton who both helped me during various discussions to clarify some of the points made in the paper. Of course, the interpretation of these points is entirely my responsibility.

REFERENCES

Anderson, S.A. (1988). Morphological theory. In F.J. Newmeyer (Ed.), *Linguistics: The Cambridge Survey* (Vol. 1, pp. 146–191). Cambridge, UK: Cambridge University Press.

Anderson, S.R. (1992). *A-Morphous Morphology*. Cambridge, UK: Cambridge University Press.

Aronoff, M. (1976). *Word formation in generative grammar*. Cambridge, MA: MIT Press.

Baayen, H., & Lieber, R. (1991). Productivity and English derivation; A Corpus based study. *Linguistics, 29*, 801–843.

Bauer, L. (1983). *English word-formation*. Cambridge, UK: Cambridge University Press.

Bentin, S., & Feldman, L.B. (1990). The contribution of morphological and semantic relatedness to repetition priming at short and long lags: Evidence from Hebrew. *Quarterly Journal of Experimental Psychology, 42A*, 693–711.

Bergman, M.W., Hudson, P.T.W., & Eling, P.A.T.M. (1988). How simple complex words can be: Morphological processing and word representations. *Quarterly Journal of Experimental Psychology, 40A*, 41–72.

Bradley, D. (1979). Lexical representation of derivational relation. In M. Aronoff & M.L. Kean (Eds.), *Juncture*, (pp. 37–55). Cambridge, MA: MIT Press.

Burani, C., & Caramazza, A. (1987). Representation and processing of derived words. *Language and Cognitive Processes, 2*, 217–227.

Burani, C., & Laudanna, A. (1992). Units of representation for derived words in the lexicon. In R. Frost & L. Katz (Eds.), *Orthography, phonology, morphology and meaning*, pp. 361–372. North Holland: Elsevier.

Burani, C., Laudanna, A., & Cermele, A. (in press). Errors on prefixed verbal forms: Effects of root type and number of prefixed related forms. *Rivista di Linguistica, 2*.

Burani, C., Salmaso, D., & Caramazza, A. (1984). Morphological structure and lexical access. *Visible Language, 4*, 348–358.

Bybee, J.L. (1985). *Morphology: A study of the relation between meaning and form*. Amsterdam: J. Benjamins.

Bybee, J.L. (1988). Morphology as lexical organization. In M. Hammond & M. Noonan (Eds.), *Theoretical morphology*, (pp. 119–141). San Diego: Academic Press.

Caramazza, A., Laudanna, A., & Romani, C. (1988). Lexical access and inflectional morphology. *Cognition, 28*, 297–332.

Colombo, L. (1986). Activation and inhibition with orthographically similar words. *Journal of Experimental Psychology: Human Perception and Performance, 12*, 226–234.

Dell, G.S. (1986). A spreading-activation theory of retrieval in sentence production. *Psychological Review, 93*, 283–321.

Emmorey, K.D. (1989). Auditory morphological priming in the lexicon. *Language and Cognitive Processes, 4*, 73–92.

Feldman, L.B., & Fowler, C.A. (1987). The inflected noun system in Serbo-Croatian: Lexical representation of morphological structure. *Memory & Cognition, 15*, 1–12.

Forster, K.I., Davis, C., Schoknecht, C., & Carter, R. (1987). Masked priming with graphemically related forms: Repetition or partial activation? *Quarterly Journal of Experimental Psychology, 39A*, 211–251.

Fowler, C.A., Napps, S.E., & Feldman, L.B. (1985). Relations among regularly and irregularly morphologically related words in the lexicon as revealed by repetition priming. *Memory & Cognition, 13*, 241–255.

Frauenfelder, U.H., & Schroeder, R. (1991). Constraining psycholinguistic models of morphological processing and representation: the role of productivity. In G.E. Booij & J. van Marle (Eds.), *Yearbook of morphology*, (pp. 165–183). Dordrecht: Foris.

Goldinger, S.D., Luce, P.A., & Pisoni, D.B. (1989). Priming lexical neighbors of spoken words: Effects of competition and inhibition. *Journal of Memory and Language, 28,* 501–518.

Henderson, L., Wallis, J., & Knight, D. (1984). Morphemic structure and lexical access. In H. Bouma & D. Bouhuis (Eds.), *Attention and Performance X,* (pp. 211–226). Hove, UK: Lawrence Erlbaum Associates Ltd.

Humphreys, G.W., Evett, L.J., Quinlan, P.T., & Besner, D. (1987). Orthographic priming: qualitative differences between priming from identified and unidentified primes. In M. Coltheart (Ed.), *The psychology of reading,* (pp. 105–125). London: Lawrence Erlbaum Associates Ltd.

Jarvella, R.J., Job, R., Sandstrom, G., & Schreuder, R. (1987). Morphological constraints on word recognition. In A. Allport, D. MacKay, W. Prinz, & E. Scheerer (Eds.), *Language perception and production,* (pp. 245–262). London: Academic Press.

Jarvella, R.J., & Meijers, G. (1983). Recognizing morphemes in spoken words: Some evidence for a stem-organized mental lexicon. In G.B. Flores D'Arcais & R.J. Jarvella (Eds.), *The process of language understanding,* (pp. 81–112). New York: Wiley.

Job, R., & Sartori, G. (1984). Morphological decomposition: Evidence from crossed phonological dyslexia. *Quarterly Journal of Experimental Psychology, 36A,* 435–458.

Laudanna, A., Badecker, W., & Caramazza, A. (1992). Processing inflectional and derivational morphology. *Journal of Memory and Language, 31,* 333–348.

Laudanna, A., & Burani, C. (1985). Address mechanisms to decomposed lexical entries. *Linguistics, 23,* 775–792.

Laudanna, A., Burani, C., & Cermele, A. (submitted). *Prefixes as processing units.*

Lima, S.D. (1987). Morphological analysis in sentence reading. *Journal of Memory and Language, 26,* 84–99.

Lukatela, G., Gligorijević, B., Kostić, A., & Turvey, M.T. (1980). Representation of inflected nouns in the internal lexicon. *Memory & Cognition, 8,* 415–423.

Napps, S.E. (1989). Morphemic relationships in the lexicon: Are they distinct from semantic and formal relationships? *Memory & Cognition, 17,* 729–739.

Napps, S.E., & Fowler, C.A. (1987). Formal relationships among words and the organisation of the mental lexicon. *Journal of Psycholinguistic Research, 16,* 257–272.

Scalise, S. (1984). *Generative Morphology.* Dordrecht, The Netherlands: Foris Publications.

Selkirk, E.O. (1982). *The Syntax of Words.* Cambridge, MA: MIT Press.

Slowiaczek, L.M., Nusbaum, H.C., & Pisoni, D.B. (1987). Phonological priming in auditory word recognition. *Journal of Experimental Psychology: Learning, Memory and Cognition, 13,* 64–75.

Slowiaczek, L.M., & Pisoni, D.B. (1986). Effects of phonological similarity on priming in auditory lexical decision. *Memory & Cognition, 14,* 230–237.

Stanners, R.F., Neiser, J.J., Hernon, W.P., & Hall, R. (1979a). Memory representation for morphologically related words. *Journal of Verbal Learning and Verbal Behavior, 18,* 399–412.

Stanners, R.F., Neiser, J.J., & Painton, S. (1979b). Memory representation for prefixed words. *Journal of Verbal Learning and Verbal Behavior, 18,* 733–743.

Taft, M., & Forster, K.I. (1975). Lexical storage and retrieval of prefixed words. *Journal of Verbal Learning and Verbal Behavior, 14,* 638–647.

Tyler, L.K., Behrens, S., Cobb, H., & Marslen-Wilson, W. (1990). Processing distinctions between stems and affixes: Evidence from a non-fluent aphasic patient. *Cognition, 36,* 129–153.

III
Interaction and Variation in Lexical Processing

9 Modularity and the Processing of Closed-class Words

Richard C. Shillcock
Centre for Cognitive Science
University of Edinburgh

Ellen G. Bard
Centre for Cognitive Science; Human Communication Research
Centre; and Department of Linguistics, University of Edinburgh

INTRODUCTION: MODULARITY AND THE LEXICON

In recent years, much psycholinguistic research has been aimed at discovering the degree to which the various components of human language processing ability are modular (Fodor, 1983; Tanenhaus, Dell, & Carlson, 1987; Tanenhaus, Leiman, & Seidenberg, 1979; Tanenhaus & Lucas, 1987). In this chapter we present new data concerning the processing of closed-class words, and we investigate some of the claims concerning modularity in the light of these data.

In the investigation of the architecture of the human speech processing mechanism, one of the more experimentally tractable characteristics of modular processing has been informational encapsulation. An informationally encapsulated module accepts only a designated type of information as input, and is impervious to information from other modules. The classic finding in this area (Swinney, 1979; Tanenhaus et al., 1979) is that stretches of speech sound are initially mapped onto all lexical items which provide a phonological match, regardless of the syntactic acceptability of any of those options in their sentential contexts. Thus, on hearing 'they all rose', the listener accesses stored representations of both meanings of *rose* ('stood up' and 'flower'), and lexical decisions for associates of both are facilitated. Tanenhaus et al. account for this result in terms of a lexical access module which is insulated from the output of a second module responsible for syntactic processing.

Even as this account became generally accepted, models of the processing of closed-class words were being developed which tacitly contradicted it. The claim was made in these models that open-class words (nouns, verbs, adjectives, etc.) and closed-class words (pronouns, auxiliary verbs, prepositions, etc.) are accessed by different, and dissociable, mechanisms and may even belong to separate sub-lexicons. Any claim involving a choice of access routes has serious implications for the nature of a model of word recognition. If only the appropriate route or sub-lexicon permits successful recognition, a correct choice has to be made by the lexical access module. Of course, an informationally encapsulated lexical access module which works only from speech sound lacks the information about the syntactic context which would enable it to choose the correct route. To avoid frequent and predictable mistakes, either pre-lexical analysis of the speech input must distinguish the routes, or the lexical access component will have to be non-modular.

In the next section we deal with the three assumptions involved in that last statement. We will examine the view that open- and closed-class words are stored and processed differently, and we discuss the evidence that the speech signal itself contains information which could enable an a-syntactic lexical access module to discriminate closed- from open-class words. We will then deal with the possibility that lexical access may sometimes be non-modular with respect to syntactic information.

In particular, we will propose that closed-class words constitute a principled exception to the general encapsulation of lexical access from syntactic information. This hypothesis is motivated by the computational interpretation of modularity advanced by Tanenhaus and Lucas (1987), and Tanenhaus, Dell, and Carlson (1987), who point out that providing lexical access with syntactic information is not computationally attractive. If syntactic information is delivered as activation of appropriate lexical items, then the information that the incoming word is a verb would activate the tens of thousands of verbs in the lexicon, most of which would not be competitors on acoustic/phonetic grounds. A more attractive option is to allow the processor initially to contact all senses of a word like *rose*, irrespective of syntactic considerations, and then use syntactic information to select the most appropriate one. For the much smaller closed classes, however, this argument may not apply. Thus, although 'they all rose' primes *flower*, 'they all would' may not prime *timber*. We will present a series of experiments on the processing of homophones like *would/wood* and *can* (modal)/*can* (noun). Finally, we will offer a revised account of modularity in human speech processing, because our experiments will give evidence for the non-modular access of closed-class words.

LEXICAL ACCESS AND CLOSED-CLASS WORDS

Evidence for Different Processing of Closed-class Words

Closed- and open-class words are distinguished by their ability to accrue new members. Closed-class words are generally function or grammatical words (auxiliary verbs, pronouns, prepositions, conjunctions, determiners, quantifiers, etc.) and they belong to small classes to which new members are rarely, if ever, added. Open-classes, on the other hand, contain the very numerous lexical words (nouns, verbs, adjectives, most adverbs), and are constantly being augmented by the addition of new words.

The difference in grammatical function between open and closed classes is reflected in differences in frequency of occurrence of the two types of words; although there are only about 150 different closed-class words in English, they account for about 40% of spoken English word tokens. When the 33,000 words with unique phonological transcriptions in the MRC Psycholinguistic Database (Coltheart, 1981)) are grouped into word-initial cohorts (see Bard & Shillcock, Chapter 12, this volume), only 67 of the 808 cohorts have closed-class words as their most frequent member, but these are more frequent on average than their open-class counterparts in the other 741 cohorts.

It is the substantial distributional differences between typical open- and closed-class words which have prompted investigators to look for processing differences between the two sets of words, and indeed there do seem to be psychological differences in both production and perception. For instance, Joshi (1985) notes differences between the classes when bilinguals switch between languages within a sentence; the closed-class words in a constituent tend to belong to the language which provides the constituent's syntax. Similarly, there are differences in word formation and in speech errors. Sound exchanges tend to involve open-class words but not closed-class words, whereas the latter are uniquely affected by stranding errors and morpheme shifts (Garrett, 1976; 1980). When the two classes are involved in movement errors, the prosodic consequences are different (Cutler & Isard, 1980): if a closed-class word carrying sentence accent moves position in a speech error, accent appears to travel with it, whereas an accented open-class word leaves its accent behind when it changes position. Open- and closed-class words have different acquisition profiles (Bloom, 1970; Radford, 1990), with closed-class categories typically being deployed later than open-class categories. Several models of language production have proposed separate treatments of one form or another for closed- and open-class elements (Dell, 1989; Garrett, 1976, 1980; Levelt, 1989; Shattuck-Hufnagel, 1982; Sternberg, Monsell, Knoll,

& Wright, 1978). Closed-class words also appear to be the more difficult to monitor closely when reading (Greenberg & Koriat, 1990).

Perhaps the most influential results are due to Bradley and her colleagues. In their studies, normal adults showed a frequency effect in lexical decision for open-class words, responding more quickly to more frequent words. This effect did not obtain for closed-class words (see Bradley, Garrett, & Zurif, 1980). In contrast, Broca's aphasic patients, whose syntactic processing is characteristically impaired, showed a significant frequency effect for both kinds of words. The implication was that the dysphasics lacked the normal processing route.

A second finding concerns interference in lexical decision by words embedded within non-words. Normal subjects took longer to reject visually presented non-words containing an open-class word, like '*thin*age', compared with a baseline non-word, but did not show the same effect for non-words containing closed-class words, like '*than*age' (Bradley, 1978). The finding held even when open-class words which do not participate in word-formation processes were contrasted with closed-class words, which are typically barred from such processes. There was, however, no disparity between the word classes when the non-words were given to dysphasics (Bradley & Garrett, 1979). Once again, there was a difference between normals and Broca's aphasics, which could be interpreted as a failure on the part of the aphasics to engage special close-class processing routines.

To explain the differences, Bradley and her colleagues proposed a special frequency-independent access route for closed-class words in addition to a common route shared by both classes (Bradley, 1978; Bradley & Garrett, 1983; Bradley, Garrett, & Zuriff, 1980; Rosenberg, Zuriff, Brownell, Garrett, & Bradley, 1985). In dysphasia, the frequency-independent route is said to be disrupted, so that only the frequency-dependent common route is left for both classes of word.

These claims are controversial. First of all, Bradley's results have been contested in a number of different studies of normals. (Besner, 1988; Cutler & Foss, 1977; Friederici & Heeschen, 1983; Gordon & Caramazza, 1982, 1983, 1985; Matthei & Kean, 1989; Segui, Mehler, Frauenfelder, & Morton, 1982) and dysphasics (Gordon & Caramazza, 1983). Although the foregoing failed to demonstrate differential frequency sensitivity of open- and closed-class words, the interference effect with non-words has been replicated (Kolk & Blomert, 1985; Matthei & Kean, 1989).

Second, it is unclear what the relationship between the access routes should be in normals. If normals operate frequency-dependent and frequency-independent routes to closed-class words in their mental lexicons, and if the routes operate in parallel, then it is difficult to see why only the independent route should affect lexical decision. The selection of this route implies not two systems operating in parallel but some mechanism for making an early choice between routes. To summarise: researchers have been concerned for more than a decade to test the notion that closed- and open-class words are housed separately in the mental lexicon and accessed via different routes. Although the issue is far from resolved in detail, pervasive behavioural distinctions between open- and closed-class words require explanation. Among a range of architectures which might model the distinctions is the application of differential processing early in perception. Bradley et al. (1980) argue that the dysphasics are unlikely to have developed novel processing routes postictally: their abnormal responses to closed-class words must therefore be due to a mechanism that is present but selectively suppressed in normal subjects. Their analysis, however, begs the question of the information on which selection is based.

Discriminability of Closed-class Words

Separate lexical access routes for closed- and open-class words would present no architectural difficulty within a modular system if the sublexical characteristics of open- and closed-class items were clearly distinct. In this section we review the evidence for the claim that the two classes of words have different phonological characteristics in English, and we examine lexical access models that depend on this distinction.

The principal phonological difference between English open- and closed-class words is set out by Cutler and Carter (1987). Open-class words tend to begin with, or consist solely of, a strong or metrically stressed syllable, that is, a syllable containing a full vowel. Closed-class words tend to consist of a single weak, unstressed syllable, that is, a syllable with a nucleus consisting of *schwa*, or of an abbreviated or centralised version of some other vowel. Cutler and Carter estimate, on the basis of dictionary transcriptions, that in the 188,000 words of the London-Lund Corpus of English Conversation (Svartvik & Quirk, 1980), 90% of the lexical (open-class) words should have been pronounced with strong initial syllables. On the other hand, only 9.5% of the closed-class items would necessarily have contained a strong initial syllable. The basis of pre-lexical categorisation appears to be available here, and at least two models of lexical access make use of the metrical contrast.

Cutler and her colleagues (Cutler & Carter, 1987; Culter & Norris, 1988) propose a Metrical Segmentation Strategy (MSS) for English, which assumes that there are separate lists, or sub-lexicons, for open- and closed-class words. The processor imposes a hypothetical word onset before every strong syllable, and consults the open-class list for words starting with that syllable. When a word has been completely accounted for, but the following syllable is weak, the closed-class list is consulted for the new syllable. The closed-class list can also be revisited should the operations with the open-class list break down.

Building on earlier suggestions by Cutler (1976) and Bradley (1980), Grosjean and Gee (1987) also propose that syllables perceived as metrically strong initiate a lexical search, but in this case, the strong syllable may be assumed to be anywhere within a word. Weak syllables are identified by means of a pattern-recognition-like analysis and with the help of the listener's knowledge of phonotactic and morphophonemic rules, for weak syllables include the unstressed syllables of polysyllables as well as free-standing closed-class words. Nonetheless, in Grosjean and Gee's model, closed-class words can also be found in the lexicon, so that they can be recognised when they contain a stressed syllable.

By exploiting the association of form class with metrical stress, and by giving different treatment to stretches of speech which are likely to be open- and closed-class words, these models offer both pre-lexical form class selection and protection against a potential hazard to which more uniform systems are prone. Machine speech recognition systems which allow weak syllables to spawn closed-class word hypotheses without syntactic and morphological constraints suffer an explosion of lexical hypotheses. This happens because portions of most polysyllabic words can be parsed as closed-class words: *international* contains sequences which resemble *in*, *to*, *a*, *an*, for instance. The fact that tokens of closed-class words are often subject to considerable phonological reduction may encourage consideration of even relatively poor matches with the input. If word frequency is allowed to influence processing, the typically high frequency of the closed-class candidates will make them all the more damaging to the chances of recognizing open-class words. The Metrical Segmentation Strategy, as set out by Cutler and Carter (1987), precludes this kind of confusion by blocking closed-class hypotheses in stretches of input initially assigned to an open-class word. Grosjean and Gee's model achieves the same goal by allowing weak syllables to give rise only to those lexical hypotheses which parse in some construction containing the strong-syllable-bearing word.

However useful such mechanisms might be, the question remains as to whether speech really displays sufficient association between the strong/weak and open/closed distinctions to permit accurate recognition by this means. Cutler and Carter's figures were estimates based on a number of assumptions about the behaviour of closed-class words. Shillcock, Bard, and Spensley (1988), however, examined 288 randomly sampled utterances representing the unscripted conversations of 24 British adults. In these materials, 66% of the 911 closed-class word tokens contained only weak syllables, leaving the other third of these items to be mis-classified by the metrical criterion. Among the 617 open-class items, 87% contained a strong initial syllable and a further 2% contained only non-initial strong syllables, with 11% containing no strong syllable at all. Overall, then, models relying on a metrical distinction would initially misclassify one in four words in this sample.

Although these figures promise less accurate metrical classifications of words than Cutler and Carter estimate, both strategies outlined here contain failsafe mechanisms for recognising atypical closed-class words containing strong syllables, and, less gracefully, for recovering weak-only open-class words. In both cases the failsafe mechanisms appear to be secondary, back-tracking mechanisms, and should be associated with inefficient recognition. In Shillcock et al.'s data, this prediction is not supported in the case of atypical closed-class words containing strong syllables.

The materials examined by Shillcock et al. had earlier been used for a word-level gating experiment in which subjects heard an utterance augmented by one word at a time, and were required, after each presentation, to record their perceptions of the words heard so far. Overall, some 20% of attempts at recognising words were successful only when subjects had heard one or more words of the subsequent context. While 'late' recognition of this kind extended to all syntactic categories, it was more common for closed-class words. It was not, however, the case that the late-recognised closed-class items were atypical in being metrically strong. Both open- and closed-class words were more efficiently recognised if they contained at least one strong syllable.

To summarise: although there is a general tendency for closed- and open-class items to be distinguishable on grounds of metrical stress, the distinction is not complete. In one sample of spontaneous speech from several speakers, about a third of closed-class words not only had atypical strong syllables, but also proved easier to recognise than more typical weak-only closed-class words. The strategy used by the subjects in Bard et al.'s gating experiments seemed to treat open- and closed-class items alike in this respect. Whether listeners always process both classes alike, or whether identical treatment is restricted to words containing strong syllables, remains to be seen. At the very least, a sizeable minority of closed-class word tokens have to be distinguished from open-class items on non-phonological grounds.

Restrictions on Modularity

Are there any grounds for believing that lexical access might not be completely impervious to syntactic information? The seminal cross-modal priming experiments quoted earlier (Tanenhaus et al., 1979) certainly displayed effects which would be difficult to explain if syntactic information were freely available during the early stages of lexical access. Although in the phrase 'they all rose' the word 'rose' is constrained to be a verb, a subject hearing 'they all rose' is able to respond more quickly to the visual word 'flower' presented at the acoustic offset of 'rose' than to a matched control word. Syntactic constraints do not prevent access to the noun reading of *rose*, with the result that both readings are briefly available.

Although lexical access is therefore said to be informationally encapsulated from syntax, Tanenhaus notes that genuine feedback apparently operates between the lexical level of description and the prelexical/phonemic level. When a phoneme in a spoken word is replaced with noise, listeners perceptually restore the phoneme appropriately and hear an intact word (Samuel, 1981a,b; Warren, 1971). Moreover, such restored phonemes generate the same contextual effects as genuine phonemes: they influence the listener's judgements of the identity of the following segment (Elman & McClelland, 1989).[1]

Thus there appear to be both situations in which there is genuine feedback, and situations in which there is informational encapsulation. Tanenhaus and his colleagues (Tanenhaus, Dell, & Carlson, 1987; Tanenhaus & Lucas, 1987) have more recently made the provocative suggestion that there is a principled computational distinction to be made between the two situations. The intriguing thing about their suggestion is that it is the computational principle, rather than the individual components of the system, which determines the nature of the relationship.

The available evidence suggests, they argue, that there is genuine feedback from the lexical level to the phonemic level, because the phonemes are related to lexemes by a *part-whole* relationship: the phoneme /p/ is part of the phonemic representation of the lexical item *pen*. In contrast, there is no such feedback from the syntactic level to the lexical level, because lexemes are related by *set-membership* to the form classes whose distribution syntax controls: *pen* belongs to the set of nouns.

Tanenhaus et al. suggest that these differing relationships underlie the computational distinction. Assuming that strong interactions work by activating suitable items rather than by inhibiting unsuitable items, Tanenhaus et al. focus their arguments on the additional elements activated top-down by the interaction. When 'pen' is heard, part of it, /p/, can be assumed to be present and confirmatory activation may be passed as genuine feedback downwards to some phoneme-level representation of /p/, one out of 40 or so different phonemic representations. When a

---

[1] However, see Norris (this volume) for a radical reassessment of such 'top-down' effects from a connectionist perspective. Within a similar bottom-up framework, Shillcock, Lindsey, Levy and Chater (1992) have advanced an alternative account for some of Elman et al's data.

developing interpretation allows the syntactic prediction that the next word is probably a verb, however, the situation is very different. Although it might seem desirable to pass activation from the syntactic level to the lexical level, feedback operations which activate a set of lexical entries are computationally unattractive here. First, predictions of the next syntactic category are not totally reliable, given that modifiers can always be added, even if parenthetically: 'they all rose', 'they all just rose', 'they almost all just sort of rose'. Second, knowing definitely that the next constituent is a verb would still activate thousands of verbs in the lexicon, most of which bear no phonological resemblance to the input. If the listener must resolve the competition among activated lexical hypotheses in order to recognise a word, the additional candidates will only protract the process of identification.

Modularity is seen as reflecting the computational aspects of the problem of language processing. From this perspective, closed-class words differ from open-class words, despite the fact that both are related by set-membership to their syntactic categories. First, closed-class words tend to be the more predictable from context, and second, there are fewer words in any closed class than in any open class. Knowing that the next word is a verb only restricts the candidate set to an intractably large number of verbs, but knowing that the next word is a preposition leaves a candidate set small enough to make genuine feedback a computationally useful option. Even within the lexical-syntactic relationship, then, there may be sub-domains where an absence of modularity would optimise computa-tional—and perceptual—efficiency. Accordingly, there is reason to doubt that informational encapuslation obtains between the syntactic level and the lexical level for the closed-class sub-domain, however secure encapsu-lation may be for open-class words. This architectural distinction may be what caused Bradley's findings.

EXPERIMENTS ON OPEN- AND CLOSED-CLASS WORDS

Alternative Models and Alternative Predictions

We have now seen that closed- and open-class words may be subject to separate storage and access, that their phonological characteristics may allow for separate treatment in lexical access, and that a non-modular treatment of lexical access for closed-class words has computational advantages. In fact, several different architectures might survive among the findings.

The first is a *common modular architecture*, with open- and closed-class words stored in a single lexicon, lexical access informationally encapsulated with respect to syntactic information, and all words accruing activation in proportion to their frequency. This proposal essentially generalises to closed-class words the sort of mechanisms often thought to be used for open-class words. To make this proposal, we would have to side with Bradley's critics and reject her claims for the frequency independence of closed-class processing. With these assumptions, the behaviour of Broca's aphasics is taken as evidence for loss of syntactic rather than lexical processes.

Of course, even if the lexicon is not partitioned into open- and closed-class sectors, the presence or absence of a strong syllable (Cutler & Norris, 1988; Grosjean & Gee, 1987) can be used to achieve a functional partitioning. Rather than shunting input to one or other partition of the lexicon, the metrical characteristics of the word might serve to activate lexical competitors of similar metrical structure more highly than others in the lexicon as a whole (see, however, Cutler & Clifton 1988). Insofar as open- and closed-class words have typically different metrical structures, the resulting set of candidate identities for a word will be similar to that which a partitioned lexicon would give. Thus, over something like 90% of open-class words and two-thirds of closed-class words, a common lexicon and a partitioned lexicon might produce similar results. In the remaining cases, where open- and closed-class words compete, the closed-class words should be the stronger competitors, given their greater frequency.

A second plausible approach is a *class-dependent modular architecture*. This differs from the *common modular architecture* in only one way: open-class words accrue activation in proportion to their frequency, whereas, as Bradley suggests, closed-class words do not. Again, only where words are metrically atypical of their class should cross-class competition occur. If only open-class words show noticeable effects of frequency, then open-class competitors will not be overwhelmed by closed-class competitors, because the latter will not have high levels of frequency-related activation. Both open- and closed-class competitors should remain active. Later in processing, higher level information could help select suitable lexical hypotheses.

Third, the human speech processing mechanism might have a *non-modular architecture*, in the sense that local syntactic clues to the occurrence of closed classes would increase the activation of closed-class hypotheses. Lexical access for open-class words would remain modular with respect to syntax. This model directly challenges the claim that lexical access is completely encapsulated against strong, or instructive, interactions with parsing or interpretation. It does, however, have advantages. As we have seen, there are computational reasons to favour the early use of syntax in the recognition of closed-class words. Instructional interactions with syntax could account for correct form-class assignment when phonological clues are lacking or misleading. Furthermore, if syntactic information ensured the dominance of closed-class words in suitable contexts, it would be less important whether or not these were stored in a separate lexicon of showed different sensitivity to frequency. The varied results on frequency sensitivity in the recognition of closed-class words could then be attributed to the unnatural task of recognising closed-class words in a list rather than in the syntactic contexts which usually control their recognition.

To distinguish among these models, consider their predictions for a cross-modal priming experiment in which the auditory primes are closed-class/open-class homophones like *would/wood* or *can/can*, each of which is produced as a strong syllable in a syntactically appropriate sentence context. Of the architectures proposed earlier, only one predicts that /wʊd/ will prime the associates of *wood* (*e.g. timber*) regardless of context—the *class-dependent modular* model. In this model, context is unimportant because lexical access is informationally encapsulated against syntax. Open-class *wood* will remain active whatever the input, because the closed-class word *would* will not quickly dominate the open class competitors on grounds of frequency. Consequently, /wʊd/ whatever its form class in context, should always prime *timber*.

In the *common modular architecture*, the default model where all words are activated in proportion to frequency, the much more frequent closed-class homophone (*would*) should tend to dominate the set of lexical competitors whenever a sequence like /wʊd/ is heard.[2] If this is so, however, the open-class homophone *wood* may be a weak contender at the end of the word. If this architecture makes any prediction at all here, it is the counterintuitive prediction that the open-class homophone (*wood*) will not be strong enough to prime its associates at the acoustic offset of /wʊd/. Since lexical access is not supposed to show any significant effects of syntax at this point, priming of an associate of the open-class homophone (*timber*) is in danger of being suppressed in all cases: whatever the syntactic context, /wʊd/ should prime *timber* weakly, if at all.

Under the *non-modular architecture* a third prediction is made. A syntactic context demanding an auxiliary verb should make *would*, the closed-class homophone, dominant, so that the representation of *wood* will be unable to prime *timber*. In a syntactic context suitable for a noun, no impediment is imposed: /wʊd/ should prime *timber* only in a context suitable for *wood*. Table 9.1 summarises the three models.

---

[2] Compare with the results from a pronunciation task reported by Dell (1989), which he interprets as showing that homonymns like *wee* and *we* share various partial representations that are facilitated in proportion to their total frequency of use. In effect, the retrieval of the phonological form associated with *wee* and *we* is dominated by the contribution of the more frequent item.

TABLE 9.1.
Summary of the Priming Predictions of the Three Models

	Predictions		
	Homophone priming open-class class associate (*timber*)		
Model	Open-class (*wood*)	Closed-class (*would*)	Negative correlations with priming
Common modular	little or none	little or none	frequency advantage of closed-class word
Class-dependent modular	yes	yes	—
Non-modular	yes	no	predictability of closed-class syntactic context

The latter two models can also be distinguished on the basis of their predictions about the factors affecting the degree of priming. In a *common modular architecture*, priming should be related to the relative frequencies of the open- and closed-class homophones. Since the frequency advantage of the closed-class word should allow little or no priming of the associates of the open-class word, any priming will tend to be in homophone pairs with a smaller frequency advantage for the closed-class word. In a *non-modular architecture*, on the other hand, priming should depend on contextual constraints. The more firmly the word's context selects the closed-class homophone, therefore, the more dominant the closed-class item should be at the point when priming is measured. The more the context demands *would*, the less /wʊd/ should prime *timber*.

Experiment 1: Does *Would* Prime *Timber*?

We tested these predictions with a cross-modal priming experiment using quartets of sentences based on 24 different closed-/open-class homophone pairs like *would/wood*, *might/might*, *in/inn*, and *can/can*.

(1a). CLOSED-CLASS HOMOPHONE
John said that he didn't want to do the job, but his brother *would*, as I later found out.

(1b). CLOSED-CLASS UNRELATED
John said that he didn't want to do the job, but his brother *might*, as I later found out.

(1c). OPEN-CLASS HOMOPHONE
John said that he didn't want to do the job with his brother's *wood*, as I later found out.

(1d). OPEN-CLASS UNRELATED
John said that he didn't want to do the job with his brother's *car* as I later found out.

For each homophone pair, a sentence like (1a) was devised containing a closed-class homophone (*would*) in clause-final, but not sentence-final position, thus allowing the word to be spoken in an unreduced form. The sentence was constructed to select as strongly as possible for the closed-class represented by the critical item, though it is not feasible to construct a context in which all other classes are ungrammatical at that point. A matched sentence, like (1b), contained an unrelated closed-class item ('might'). A third sentence, (1c), altered the basic carrier form so as to allow the critical open-class homophone ('wood') to appear phrase-finally, and a fourth sentence, (1d), replaced the homophone with an unrelated open-class word ('car'). In all four sentences, a synonym of the open-class homophone, here 'timber', was presented visually at the acoustic offset of the critical word. Priming from the ambiguous open-class homophone to this target (measured as the difference between lexical decision times to 'timber' after 'wood' and after 'car') can be compared with priming from the closed-class homophone to the same target ('timber' after 'would' and 'might'). The members of each quartet were distributed over four groups of materials, balanced for condition, and each was presented to a separate group of subjects. (For further details, see Shillcock & Bard, submitted.)

To review (see Table 9.1), there are three outcomes relevant to the predictions from the models discussed here. First, both homophones ('would' and 'wood') may prime the associate of the open-class word ('timber'). This is the prediction of the *class-dependent* model, in which open-class competitors are always strong. Second, neither homophone may prime the associate of the open-class word significantly. This would be predicted by the *common modular* model, in which closed-class competitors dominate on grounds of frequency. Third, there may be priming in the open-class context ('wood') but not in the closed-class context ('would'). This is congruent with a *non-modular* model, in which context is critical.

Figure 9.1 shows that the results were congruent with the *non-modular* prediction. The open-class homophone in an open-class context ('with his brother's *wood*') primed its associate ('timber'), producing faster lexical decision times than were found after the unrelated open-class word in the same context ('with his brother's *car*'): 658msec *vs* 694msec. In contrast, closed-class homophones in closed-class contexts ('but his brother *would*') failed to produce lexical decision times faster than those after the unrelated closed-class word ('but his brother *might*'): 688msec *vs* 685msec.

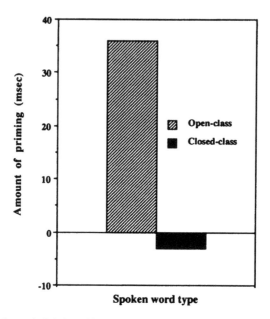

FIG. 9.1. Experiment 1. Priming effects in lexical decision to an associate of the open-class homophone in open- and closed-class contexts (priming = *rt* after a control word minus *rt* after a homophone)

The interaction was significant ($F_1 = 4.68$, $df = 1, 40$, $p = 0.037$, Newman-Keuls test at $p < 0.05$; $F_2 = 7.02$, $df = 1, 23$, $p = 0.014$, Newman-Keuls test at $p < 0.01$).

It might possibly be argued that listeners consciously or unconsciously adopted an unnatural strategy in this experiment because it included so many open-class homophones of closed-class words. This flaw was not present in a similar experiment where the open-class homophones were not used; only sentences resembling (1a) were presented in a two-condition experiment where priming was the difference between lexical decision times for a related ('timber') and a matched unrelated ('temper') visual target. As in Experiment 1, there was no priming in closed-class contexts: lexical decision times for related and unrelated words were, 670.4msec and 665.2msec ($F_1 < 1$; $F_2 < 1$) respectively.

Experiment 2: Is There Priming of *Timber* Halfway Through *Would?*

The results of Experiment 1 are distinctly uncomfortable for some of the accepted views of lexical access. Experiments 2 and 3 eliminate two simple artefacts which might be responsible.

Experiment 2 deals with the possibility that priming was absent in the closed-class contexts in Experiment 1 because recognition of the closed-class item (*would*) was so efficient as to be complete well within the critical word. By the time that the visual target was presented at word offset, the expected activation of the contextually inappropriate homophone (*wood*) might already have returned to its resting level. To test the hypothesis that modular processes had operated, but earlier than the test point, Experiment 2 was run using the same auditory materials as Experiment 1, but testing earlier: the presentation of the visual target was aligned with the midpoint of the vowel in the prime, as determined by ear and by examination of the time-amplitude waveform.

If Experiment 1 probed too late in the lexical access process, the predictions made for word offsets (see Table 9.1) should now apply to mid-vowel test points. On the other hand, if word-offsets actually did coincide with the full functioning of the process of interest, then earlier test points may simply produce no priming. The design was the same as in Experiment 1.

With mid-vowel test points, there was indeed no priming at all. There was no overall difference between reaction times after homophones and after controls ($F_1 = 1.07$, $df = 1, 28$, *n.s.*; $F_2 < 1$). Nor was reaction time after the open-class homophones different from reaction time in any other condition (for the interaction, $F_1 = 1.01$, $df = 1, 28$, *n.s.*; $F_2 = 2.56$, $df = 1, 23$, *n.s.*).

The *class-dependent* model receives no support: there is no evidence for priming of the open-class associate throughout. Which of the other two models is supported depends on whether we believe the mid-vowel test point was too early, or the word-offset test point was too late. If the mid-vowel test point was too early to find such priming as there was, the results of Experiment 1 stand: in suitable contexts, closed-class words fail to prime associates of open-class homophones, as would be the case if non-modular effects of syntactic processing were controlling activation. If we suppose instead, that the word-offset test point was too late to tap lexical access itself, priming here may be only a by-product of the integration of the contextually appropriate sense of the word into the interpretation. In which case, the results of Experiment 2 stand: frequency-based competition between homophones in a *common modular* system always ensures the dominance of the closed-class word.

The present stimulus materials have the expected frequency imbalance, but the imbalance does not account for subjects' behaviour. The closed-class homophones are a good deal more frequent (occurring in an average of 330 out of the 500 samples of 2000 words in the Kučera Francis (1967) corpus, *s.d.* 159) than their open-class counterparts (occurring in an

average of 62 samples, *s.d.* 96; $t = 6.85$, $df = 23$, $p < 0.0005$, 1-tailed).[3]
If this asymmetry were responsible for the mid-vowel priming results,
however, the greater the frequency advantage of the closed-class homophones, the less priming should be found: there should be a negative
correlation between priming and the frequency advantage of the closed-
class homophone. In fact, there is no such negative correlation: $r = 0.26$
for closed-class contexts and 0.21 for open-class contexts (*n.s.* in
both cases).[4] The most attractive conclusion, therefore, is that the
mid-vowel test points did not tap frequency-driven processes in lexical
access. Instead, these test points simply seem to have been premature.
For these monosyllables, the effects of interest were to be found at word
offset.

Experiment 3: Were *Would* and *Wood* Pronounced Differently?

Experiment 3 deals with an even more elementary source of artefact, the
possibility that the acoustic forms of the homophones still signalled their
form class in some way. Even though both homophones were read with
full vowels, the stressed particle *by*, for instance, may be shorter than the
stressed verb *buy*. To test for any such differences, we asked four
phoneticians to listen to an audiotape containing closed-class and open-
class tokens of the critical homophone pairs digitally excised from the tapes
used in the previous experiments and presented in random order. The
subjects were informed that all of the words were closed-/open-class
homophones, which had been produced phrase-finally with full vowels,
and they were asked to judge on a 5-point scale whether each token had
been produced as a closed-class or an open-class word.

The phoneticians could not reliably distinguish closed- from open-class
homophones. The mean scores for open- and closed-class tokens did not
differ significantly on a matched *t*-test (a mean of 12 for open-class
tokens and 10.75 for closed-class, where 20 represented complete con-
fidence in an open-class judgment by all subjects). Moreover, there was
no significant correlation between the judgments of any pair of phoneticians. On the grounds of acoustic shape, the words were not systematically
distinguishable.

---

[3] In 14 of the 24 pairs, the closed-class item is a high-frequency outlier for its word-initial
cohort (see Bard and Shillcock, this volume), whereas open-class items have this role for
only two pairs.

[4] The corresponding correlations for priming at word-offset were 0.27 for closed-class
contexts and −0.03 for open-class contexts; again, neither correlation was significant.

Experiment 4: Were the Contexts Sufficiently Constrained?

It would appear that the failure of closed-class words to prime associates of their open-class homophones cannot be attributed to an unsuitable test point, to frequency effects, or to different pronunciations of the critical words. This leaves effects of context to consider. To attribute the results of Experiments 1 and 2 to non-modular effects of syntactic processes, it is necessary to establish that the contexts of the critical homophones were as different as we supposed. Closed-class contexts must select for closed-class items, whereas open-class contexts must select for open-class items, and neither should allow responses of the other class.

A cloze test was employed to determine whether our intuitions about the experimental materials were matched by those of our subject population. The left context of each of the 48 critical prime words from Experiments 1 and 2 was presented to a new group of 35 subjects. The left context of each pair of homophones were divided between the two parts of the experiment, with the parts balanced for form class and for order. In the blank following each left context, subjects were to write what they believed the next word might be, in the understanding that the word to be supplied might not be the last in the sentence.

All responses were categorised as: (1) the original word; (2) another word belonging to the original word's form class loosely defined (e.g. other nouns, like *toys* or *water* for the noun *down*); (3) another word belonging to a different class which was syntactically acceptable in the context (e.g. '. . . filled the box with *some*' instead of '. . . filled the box with *down*'), or; (4) another word belonging to a syntactically unacceptable class (e.g. '. . . filled the box with *on*'). In addition, (5) the type/token ratio (the number of different lexical items per number of responses) was calculated, and (6) those unacceptable words belonging to the form class of the item's homophone were separately tallied. Table 9.2 summarises the results.

TABLE 9.2.
Experiment 3. Distribution of Responses to Cloze Test on Closed- and Open-class Context
Sentences used in Experiment 1 (for all *t*-tests, *df* = 22)

	Omitted word			
Response	Closed-class	Open-class	t	p
(i) Original word	34.4%	1.3%	5.22	<0.0001
(ii) Form class (loose)	39.9%	83.3%	−5.19	<0.0001
(iii) Other acceptable	23.4%	14.7%	1.33	n.s.
(iv) Unacceptable	2.4%	0.7%	1.56	n.s.
(v) Type/token ratio	0.30	0.47	−4.33	<0.0005
(vi) Class of homophone	0.24%	0.62%	−0.93	n.s.

The paired contexts created distinct sets of constraints. The bulk of responses in each case (74% in total for closed-class contexts, 85% for open-) belong to the class of the omitted critical word. Less than 1% of the responses in either case belonged to the category of the omitted word's homophone. More finely categorised, the two distributions were distinct ($\chi^2 = 49.26$, $df = 3$, $p < 0.001$), but as the t-tests in the table show, open- and closed-class contexts differed principally in which members of the appropriate class they elicited. As might be expected from the relative sizes of closed and open classes, the original word was produced much more often for closed-class contexts than for open-, whereas the latter more often elicited other words of the same class as the original word. It would appear that the sentence contexts used for Experiment 1 were sufficiently distinct to support a non-modular explanation, which depends on the bias due to sentence contexts.

Not only do the materials present distinct contexts for open- and closed-class words, but the distinction is reflected in subjects' behaviour. If priming is affected by context, then the more strongly the context demands the closed-class homophone, the more likely the closed-class item is to dominate lexical competition, and the less priming of the open-class associate we should find: there should be a negative correlation between priming and the proportion of closed-class responses in the cloze test. This predicted negative correlation is found both at the end of the word ($r = -0.32$, $df = 22$, $p < 0.05$) and at mid-vowel ($r = -0.51$, $d.f. = 22$, $p < 0.05$). Even if frequency measures are included among the predictor variables in a multiple regression equation, they make no contribution to predicting priming ($\beta = 0.12$, $t = 0.61$, n.s.), whereas contextual constraints continued to contribute ($\beta -0.47$, $t = -2.44$, $p < 0.025$; $R^2 = 0.27$; $F = 3.91$, $df = 2,21$, $p < 0.04$). The more restrictive the closed-class context, the less priming for the contextually inappropriate sense. Note that the analogous prediction is not made for open-class contexts; non-modular processing is excluded for open-class words on grounds of computational efficiency. Correlations in open-class contexts are not significant ($r = -0.11$, $df = 22$, n.s., at word offset; $r = -0.04$, $df = 22$, n.s. at mid-vowel). Closed- and open-class contexts differ in precisely the way suggested.

SUMMARY AND CONCLUSIONS

Prior to this study, cross-modal priming experiments had reliably demonstrated that syntactically inappropriate senses of open-class words are accessed during the processing of spoken sentences. We have found no evidence, however, of analogous priming for closed/open-class homophones.

Both of the modular architectures consonant with the literature on closed-class words fail to account for the data from our experiments, for both predict context-independent effects. Under the class-dependent modular architecture, the associates of the open-class homophones should be primed regardless of the homophone's immediate syntactic context. Yet we found no priming with closed-class contexts either at word offset (Experiment 1) or at mid-vowel (Experiment 2).

Under the common modular architecture, the more frequency-dominant the closed-class homophones, the less likely the priming of the open-class associate, whatever the context. At word-offset (Experiment 1), however, we found significant priming in open-class contexts. At mid-vowel (Experiment 2), although there was no priming in either context, the frequency advantage of the closed-class homophones was not correlated with the attention of priming.

Only a non-modular architecture can account for an effect of syntactic context on priming. The cloze test experiment (Experiment 4) demonstrated that the contexts in which the homophones were presented created distinct and appropriate constraints on the form classes of the critical words. For these contexts, the prediction of the non-modular model is confirmed: priming of open-class associates was least where closed-class contexts most constrained the homophone's form class. Since the homophones were not distinguishable on grounds of pronunciation (Experiment 3), we cannot attribute the results to bottom-up effects. We are left with the conclusion that associates of the open-class homophones are not primed in contexts demanding a close-class word, because lexical access is sensitive to syntactic context in the recognition of closed-class words.

This conclusion helps to explain Bradley's results, in two senses. First, it prescribes specific syntactic effects which will differentiate lexical access processes for closed- and open-class words. Second, and consequently, it predicts that the ability to apply syntactic regularities will determine how closed-class words are processed.

Our conclusion joins the accumulating evidence that the informational encapsulation of lexical access from higher-levels is not complete. Tabossi (1988), Blütner and Sommer (1988), and Colombo and Williams (1990) have demonstrated that lexical access may be subject, in certain circumstances, to interference from at least semantic and pragmatic factors. More important, the conclusion accords with the computational account of modularity advanced by Tanenhaus et al., described earlier. This holds that informational encapsulation obtains in set-membership relationships where strong, instructional interaction is not an attractive computational option. In contrast, in part-whole relationships, strong interaction is appropriate.

As we commented earlier, the set-membership/part-whole distinction can also be made on grounds of efficiency. As the word *pen* is being heard, a phonological representation containing /p/ is presumably active. Increasing that activation will further the process of recognising *pen* without spawning further lexical competitors not already activated by the input: any word containing /p/ should already be active to some degree. In contrast, activating all the nouns in the lexicon would generate extraneous lexical competitors (*house, people, man, decalcification, syzygy* . . .), which would complicate the process of achieving a single percept.

For closed-class words, the part-whole/set-membership criterion and the computational efficiency criterion make different predictions. If sets are not activated, then the set of closed-class words should not be selected by suitable syntactic contexts. On grounds of efficiency, however, closed-class words are excellent candidates for non-modular processing. As closed-class words are often pronounced as weak syllables, they are distinct, likely to have shortened, centralised vowels or no vowels at all, as well as reduced, imperfectly articulated consonants. The set of lexical competitors activated by such poor input could be quite large, and yet, because the acoustic evidence is so poor, have no clear front-runners. Moreover, the large, low-grade set of competitors could be activated whenever and wherever a weak syllable is uttered. Syntactic information selecting a particular closed class could be very useful in creating a smaller set of likelier word candidates where there actually is a closed-class word. Where the syllable in question is part of a longer, usually open-class, item, there should be no syntactically-based encouragement to recognise a closed-class word. Because present findings suggest a non-modular relationship between lexical access and syntax in the recognition of closed-class words, they can be used to argue for the efficiency criterion rather than the part-whole/set membership criterion.

We would suggest, then, that both the modular relationship between lexical access and syntax for open-class words, and the non-modular relationship for closed-class words, hold because they promote perceptual and computational efficiency. If cognitive architectures are organised in ways which maximise the efficiency of perceptual computation, they should impose modular constraints on unhelpful strong interactions, but permit those strong interactions which facilitate processing. In this view, modularity is an adaptation to the nature of language.

The interesting feature of adaptive behaviour is that it can be acquired, either by a species or an individual. A system which is modular only where modularity is perceptually efficient is a system which might have acquired modularity in the course of attempts at perception. Several models of learning, including connectionist models, tune the associations between components in response to the utility of those associations. To view modularity as the outcome of such a process, we must, however, make the assumption that modularisation of components is not the original state of the cognitive system. If initially, there are connections between domains of processing they can be strengthened, so that the relationship is ultimately non-modular, or they can be weakened to produce informational encapsulation. The final state of the perceptual system should be composed of a number of locally adaptive arrangements, like the one which appears to hold between syntactic information and the recognition of closed-class words.

ACKNOWLEDGEMENT

This work was carried out under ESRC grant R 000 23 1396.

REFERENCES

Bard, E.G., & Shillcock, R.C. (this volume). *Competitor effects during lexical access: Chasing Zipf's tail.*

Besner, D. (1988). Visual word recognition: Special-purpose mechanisms for the identification of open and closed class items? *Bulletin of the Psychonomic Society*, 26(2), 91–93.

Bloom, L. (1970). *One word at a time.* The Hague: Mouton.

Blütner, R., & Sommer, R. (1988). Sentence processing and lexical access: The influence of the focus-identifying task. *Journal of Memory and Language*, 27(4), 359–367.

Bradley, D. (1978). *Computational distinctions of vocabulary type.* PhD dissertation. Cambridge, MA: MIT Press.

Bradley, D. (1980). Lexical representation of derivational relation. In M. Aronoff & M.-L. Kean (Eds.), *Juncture.* Saratoga, CA: Anma Libri.

Bradley, D.C., & Garrett, M.F. (1983). Hemisphere differences in the recognition of closed and open class words. *Neuropsychologia*, 21(2), 155–159.

Bradley, D.C., Garrett, M.F., & Zuriff, E.B. (1980). Syntactic deficits in Broca's aphasia. In D. Caplan (Ed.), *Biological studies of mental processes.* Cambridge, MA.: MIT Press.

Colombo, L., & Williams, J. (1990). Effects of word- and sentence-level contexts upon word recognition. *Memory and Cognition*, 18(2), 153–163.

Coltheart, M. (1981). The MRC psycholinguistic database. *Quarterly Journal of Experimental Psychology*, 33A, 497–505.

Cutler, A. (1976). Phoneme monitoring reaction time as a function of preceding intonation contour. *Perception and Psychophysics*, 20, 55–60.

Cutler, A., & Carter, D.M. (1987). The predominance of strong initial syllables in the English vocabulary. *Computer Speech and Language*, 2, 133–142.

Cutler, A., & Clifton, C. (1984). The use of prosodic information in word recognition. In H. Bouma & D.G. Bouwhuis (Eds.), *Attention and Performance, X.* (pp. 183–196). Hillsdale, NJ: Lawrence Erlbaum Associates Inc.

Cutler, A., & Foss, D.J. (1977). On the role of sentence stress in sentence processing. *Language and Speech*, 20, 1–10.

Cutler, A., & Isard, S. (1980). The production of prosody. In B. Butterworth (Ed.), *Language production: Vol. 2.* Cambridge, MA: MIT Press.

Cutler, A., & Norris, D.G. (1988). The role of strong syllables in segmentation for lexical access. *Journal of Experimental Psychology: Human Perception and Performance, 14,* 113–121.

Dell, G.S. (1989). The retrieval of phonological forms in production: Tests of predictions from a connectionist model. In W. Marslen-Wilson (Ed.), *Lexical representation and process*. Cambridge MA: MIT Press.

Elman, J.L., & McClelland, J.L. (1989). Cognitive penetration of the mechanisms of perception: Compensation for coarticulation of lexically restored phonemes. *Journal of Memory and Language, 27*, 143–165.

Fodor, J. (1983). *The modularity of Mind: An essay on Faculty Psychology*. Cambridge, MA: Bradford.

Friederici, A., & Heeschen, C. (1983, October). *Lexical decision of inflected open class items and inflected closed class words*. Paper presented at the 21st Annual Meeting of the Academy of Aphasia, Minneapolis, MN.

Garrett, M. (1976). Syntactic processes in sentence production. In R. Wales & E. Walker (Eds.), *New approaches to language mechanisms*. Amsterdam: North Holland.

Garrett, M. (1980). Levels of processing in sentence production. In B. Butterworth (Ed.), *Language production* (Vol. 1). London: Academic Press.

Gordon, B., & Caramazza, A. (1982). Lexical decision for open- and closed-class words: Failure to replicate differential frequency sensitivity. *Brain and Language, 15*, 143–60.

Gordon, B., & Caramazza, A. (1983). Closed- and open-class lexical access in agrammatic and fluent aphasics. *Brain and Language, 19*, 335–345.

Gordon, B., & Caramazza, A. (1985). Lexical access and frequency sensitivity: Frequency saturation and open/closed class equivalence. *Cognition, 21*, 95–115.

Greenberg, S., & Koriat, A. (1990). The missing-letter effect in Hebrew—word frequency or word function. *Bulletin of the Psychonomic Society, 28*, No. 6, 506.

Grosjean, F., & Gee, J.P. (1987). Prosodic structure and spoken word recognition. In U. Frauenfelder & L. Tyler (Eds.), Spoken Word Recognition. *Cognition* special issue. Cambridge, MA: MIT Press.

Joshi, A.J. (1985). Processing of sentences with intrasentential code switching. In D.R. Dowty, L. Karttunen, & A.M. Zwicky. (Eds.), *Natural language parsing*. London: Cambridge University Press.

Kolk, H., & Blomert, L. (1985). On the Bradley hypothesis concerning agrammatism: The nonword-interference effect. *Brain and Language, 26*, 94–105.

Kučera, H., & Francis, W.N. (1967). *Computational Analysis of Present-day American English*. Providence: Brown University Press.

Levelt, W.J.M. (1989). *Speaking: From intention to articulation*, Cambridge, MA: MIT Press.

Matthei, E.H., & Kean, M.-L. (1989). Postaccess processes in the open vs. closed class distinction. *Brain and Language, 36*, 163–180.

Radford, A. (1990). *Syntactic theory and the acquisition of English syntax*. Oxford: Basil Blackwell.

Rosenberg, B., Zurif, E., Brownell, H., Garrett, M., & Bradley, D. (1985). Grammatical class effects in relation to normal and aphasic sentence processing. *Brain and Language, 26*, 287–303.

Samuel, A.G. (1981a). Phonemic restoration: Insights from a new methodology. *Journal of Experimental Psychology: General, 110*, 474–494.

Samuel, A.G. (1981b). The role of bottom-up confirmation in the phonemic restoration illusion. *Journal of Experimental Psychology: Human Perception and Performance, 7*, 1124–1131.

Segui, J., Mehler, J., Frauenfelder, U., & Morton, J. (1982). The word frequency effect and lexical access. *Neuropsychologia, 20*, 615–627.

Shattuck-Hufnagel, S. (1982). Three kinds of speech error evidence for the sole of grammatical elements in processing. In L.K. Obler & L. Menn (Eds.), *Exceptional language and linguistics*. New York: Academic Press.

Shillcock, R., & Bard, E.G. (submitted). Restricting modularity in the lexical access of closed-class words: "Would" does not prime "timber".

Shillcock, R., Bard, E.G., & Spensley, F. (1988). Some prosodic effects on human word recognition in continuous speech. In R. Lawrence (Ed.), *Proceedings of Speech '88, 7th FASE Symposium*, 827–834. Edinburgh, UK: Institute of Acoustics.

Shillcock, R.C., Lindsey, G., Levy, J., & Chater, N. (1992). A phonologically motivated input representation for the modelling of auditory word perception in continuous speech. *Proceedings of the 14th Annual Cognitive Science Society Conference, 1992*, Bloomington, pp. 408–413.

Sternberg, S., Monsell, S., Knoll, R.L., & Wright, C.E. (1978). The latency and duration of rapid eye-movement sequences: Comparison of speech and typewriting. In G.E. Stelmach (Ed.), *Information processing in motor control and learning*. New York: Academic Press.

Svartvik, J., & Quirk, R. (1980). A Corpus of English Conversation *Lund Studies in English, 56*. Lund: Lund University Press.

Swinney, D. (1979). Lexical access during sentence comprehension: (Re)consideration of context effects. *Journal of Verbal Learning and Verbal Behavior, 15*, 545–69.

Tabossi, P. (1988). Accessing lexical ambiguity in different types of sentential contexts. *Journal of Memory and Language, 27*,(3) 324–340.

Tanenhaus, M.K., Dell, G.S., & Carlson, G. (1987). Context effects and lexical processing: A connectionist approach to modularity. In J.L. Garfield (Ed.), *Modularity in knowledge representation and natural language understanding*. Cambridge, MA: MIT Press.

Tanenhaus, M.K., Leiman, J.M., & Seidenberg, M.S. (1979). Evidence for multiple stages in the processing of ambiguous words in syntactic contexts. *Journal of Verbal Learning and Verbal Behavior, 18*, 427–440.

Tanenhaus, M.K., & Lucas, M.M. (1987). Context effects in lexical processing. In U. Frauenfelder & L. Tyler (Eds)., Spoken Word Recognition. *Cognition* special issue. Cambridge, MA: MIT Press.

Warren, R.M. (1971). Perceptual restoration of missing speech sounds. *Science, 167*, 392–393.

10 Issues of Process and Representation in Lexical Access

William Marslen-Wilson
Birkbeck College, University of London, UK.

INTRODUCTION

A psycholinguistic theory of lexical access is a theory about how the human listener projects from the speech input onto stored mental representations of lexical form. This means that a complete account of lexical access will have to answer three different kinds of questions.

These are questions, first, about the mental representation of lexical form. Listeners know what the words in their language sound like. This knowledge, constituting what we can call the *recognition lexicon*, defines the perceptual targets of the access process. What are the properties of these target representations?

Second, the theory must define the properties of the *input representation*. Information derived from the speech input is projected onto the lexical level. Under what description is this information made available for lexical access? What is the output of pre-lexical analyses of the speech input?

Third, the theory must specify the processing environment for lexical access. Some set of computational processes relates information in the speech signal to target representations in the mental recognition lexicon. What is the overall structure of these processes (their *functional macrostructure*), and what are their detailed properties (their *functional microstructure*)?

These three sets of questions are highly interdependent. In the research I will present here, I will concentrate on two of them (the properties of the recognition lexicon and the processing microstructure of the system), and show how each depends on the other. The first part of this chapter describes a series of experiments that lead to a picture of lexical processing as intolerant of even minor (single feature) mismatches between input and lexical target. This result seems inconsistent, however, with the prevalent noise and variation in the speech input. In the second part of the chapter I argue that this apparent inconsistency can only be evaluated relative to an explicit theory of the target representation in the mental lexicon. When the appropriate theory is adapted, variation does not, in fact, create mismatch. More generally, a processing theory of lexical access cannot be properly evaluated except in the context of an adequate theory of lexical representations, specifying the perceptual targets of the access process.

THE PROCESSING ENVIRONMENT FOR LEXICAL ACCESS

There are two levels at which one can construct a processing theory of lexical access. The first, the macrostructural, is concerned with the overall properties of the system—what is the general class of processing systems that one is dealing with? I will assume here an answer of the following sort, consistent with current versions of the cohort model (Marslen-Wilson, 1987; 1989; 1990) and with certain aspects of interactive activation approaches to lexical access (e.g. McClelland & Elman, 1986).

Specifically, I will assume: (1) that perceptual processing is based on a process of competition between simultaneously active candidates; (2) that the activation metaphor is the appropriate one for representing the goodness of fit between sensory inputs and lexical form representations; and (3) that perceptual choice is based on the relationship between levels of activation. Thus, for an event in the auditory modality, there will be an initial joint activation of multiple candidates, the emergence over time of the best fitting candidate, with the discrimination decision becoming possible as the level of activation (reflecting the computed goodness of fit) for the correct candidate reaches a criterial level of difference from the levels of activation of its competitors. Whether we represent these operations in terms of the behaviour of single points over time, or as the differentiation of more distributed patterns of activation, the basic metaphor remains the same.

Given these macrostructural assumptions about the general properties of the process, a host of more specific questions then emerge about its microstructure; questions that have to be answered if we are to develop a precise account of the access process. In the context of a theory based around the notion of a 'cohort', where perceptual outcomes depend on the relationship between the item being heard and its ensemble of potential competitors, the most urgent questions are about the basic processing determinants of this relationship.

The currently most complete answer to this kind of question is provided by models of the interactive activation type, of which the most prominent in the speech domain is McClelland and Elman's (1986) TRACE model of lexical access. Here, activation-level is primarily determined by the amount of overlap between the input and target form-representations. The better and more complete the match, the higher the level of activation. Mismatch between inputs and representations, in contrast, has no direct effects on activation level. The negative effects of mismatch are mediated instead by lateral connections between units within levels—a highly activated (best-fitting) element will inhibit the activation-level of its close competitors.

In earlier research (Marslen-Wilson & Zwitserlood, 1989) we contrasted this set of assumptions with those developed within the cohort framework. These differed in two main ways. First, the cohort model had always placed more emphasis on the sequential nature of the access process, with membership of the set of competitors requiring a match between input and target from word-onset, irrespective of the amount of subsequent overlap. Secondly, the cohort approach handled mismatch quite differently, allowing for direct bottom-up inhibition, so that mismatch between input and representation directly affected the status of the relevant recognition unit (Marslen-Wilson & Welsh, 1978). This meant that lateral effects between competitors played little or no role in the operations of the system, contrary to TRACE-type assumptions (c.f. Bard, 1990).

Neither of these sets of assumptions, however, were based on any direct empirical data about the functional microstructure of the processing system. Research had instead been addressed at macrostructural questions, trying to determine the global characteristics of the system. To remedy this, I and my colleagues have conducted a series of experiments over the past few years investigating the detailed structure of lexical processing.

Issues in Processing Microstructure

In research I will review here, we were interested in the following questions about the local processing characteristics of lexical access: (1) What does it mean for an input to *match* a target representation? How closely does the input need to correspond to the internal target for this to be counted as match rather than mismatch? (2) What are the consequences of *mismatch* between an input and a representation? Is there direct bottom-up inhibition, or simply an absence of continued facilitation? (3) What does *competition* mean? Does it mean lateral inhibition between candidates, where the best-fitting item directly inhibits the activation level of its close competitors? Or are competition effects simply decision-stage effects, with no direct consequences for activation-level?

Our investigation of these questions emerged from a preliminary experiment (Marslen-Wilson & Zwitserlood, 1989), which had looked at an apparent major difference between the TRACE approach and the cohort approach. We asked whether perceptual choice was determined just by the total amount of overlap between input and target representation, or whether strict sequentiality (matching from word-onset) was important as well. I will begin by reviewing this experiment, since it provides the empirical and methodological starting-point for the later research.

We had shown earlier (Marslen-Wilson, 1984; 1987; Zwitserlood, 1989) that word fragments matching from word-onset were effective primes of associates of the word in question. Using a cross-modal priming task where the associate was presented visually at the offset of the auditory prime, we found that a fragment such as [kæpt], from the word *captain*, was almost as effective as the complete word (kæptən) in priming lexical decisions to an associate SHIP. In Marslen-Wilson and Zwitserlood (1989), we used the same cross-modal priming task to ask whether fragmentary primes that did not match from word-onset were similarly effective in priming associates to the word. To do this we constructed *rhyme* primes, which overlapped with the original word at least as much as fragmentary primes like (kæpt] overlapped with their target representations. Table 10.1 gives a sample stimulus set.

Here we define the Original Word as the word to which the rhyme primes are partially matched. What we look for across conditions is any evidence that the associate of the Original Word has been activated by these partially matching primes. To the extent that it has, then we take this as an indication that the rhyme prime has activated the Original Word. In Table 10.1, the Original Word is *battle* and its associate is WAR. Lexical decisions to the associate, presented visually at the offset of the auditory prime, are compared to responses to the same prime presented at the offset of a control word, designed to be phonologically and semantically unrelated to the Original Word. The test-control difference score, given in Table 10.1, shows that responses were significantly faster in the Original

TABLE 10.1
Rhyme Priming Stimuli and Results

Prime Type	Example Prime	Example Probe	Test-Control Difference (ms)
Original Word	battle	WAR	−32*
Word Rhyme	cattle	WAR	−11
Nonword Rhyme	yattle	WAR	−10
Control Word	packet	WAR	

* $p < 0.05$

Word condition, indicating facilitation of the lexical decision response by the related prime.

The crucial comparison is with the effects of rhyme primes on responses to WAR. We used two types of rhyme prime—Real word primes, such as *cattle*, and Nonword primes such as *yattle*.[1] If amount of overlap between input and target representation was the sole determinant of activation level, then both types of rhyme prime should activate *battle*, and therefore facilitate lexical decision reponses to WAR.

On a TRACE-type account, the two types of rhyme prime should differ in their effects. The Real Word rhyme prime (*cattle*) should not result in effective activation of the Original Word (*battle*) or its associates. This is because of lateral inhibition at the lexical level between the node representing *cattle* and the node representing *battle*. Even though the spoken input [kætəl] will strongly activate the node for *battle*, because of rhyme overlap, this activation will be inhibited by lateral links with the competitor item *cattle*, which is even more strongly activated by the speech input. In contrast, for the Nonword rhyme primes like *yattle*, where there is just as much bottom-up overlap, there is no better-fitting lexical node to damp down this activation via lateral inhibitory links.

In fact, we found that neither type of rhyme prime was effective in activating the words they rhymed with. Lexical decision to WAR following *cattle* or *yattle* was not significantly different from the baseline condition.[2] Furthermore, this held true irrespective of the amount of overlap. A word like *mobility*, with several syllables' overlap with its rhyme target (*nobility*), is just as ineffective as a prime like *cattle*, with only one or two syllables of overlap.

It was this failure of rhyme primes to generate significant priming that led us to focus on the kinds of microstructural questions raised earlier. Did the rhyme primes fail to prime (in contrast to partial primes matching from word-onset) because of the effects of mismatch? Would rhyme primes be more effective if the initial segment of the prime was phonologically more similar[3] to the initial segment of the Original Word? Was the competitor

---

[1] The original experiment was carried out in Dutch. These English examples of the stimulus materials are for illustration only.

[2] The experiment also contained a second control, or baseline condition, using nonwords as primes (e.g. *dacket*). This was to allow for the possibility that hearing a non-word as a prime had additional effects on response time. However, there were no differences in response times following real-word and non-word controls. To simplify the analysis, therefore, we used only the real-word controls in reporting the results.

[3] The rhyme primes in Marslen-Wilson and Zwitserlood (1989) were constructed so that their initial segments were as distinct as possible from the initial segments of the Original Words.

environment appropriately varied in this study—would competitor effects show up under more stringently controlled conditions? To answer these questions we needed to look much more systematically at match, mismatch, and competition in the early stages of lexical access.

Perceptual Distance and Competition

The next series of experiments continued with the rhyme priming paradigm, and used it to ask more focused questions about the perceptual criteria for matching a target representation, and about the effects of the lexical competitor environment. In the first of these experiments—carried out in Dutch with the collaboration of Stef van Halen—we covaried the phonological closeness of the initial segment of a Nonword Rhyme Prime, of the target Original Word, and of the Original Word's closest Rhyme Competitor. The *rhyme competitor* was defined as another word in the language that rhymes with the Original Word, and which is therefore also a potential match with the Nonword Rhyme Prime.

This meant the construction of stimulus triplets of the type illustrated in Table 10.2. In Group 1, the Nonword Rhyme prime was phonologically very close to the Original Word, whereas the distance of the potential Rhyme Competitor was varied. Closeness and distance were defined here in terms of phonological features.[4] Thus, in Group 1, the initial segment of the rhyme prime and the original word differed only in one phonological feature (usually place)—for example *tonijn* (Original Word) and *ponijn* (Nonword Rhyme prime). We co-varied this factor with the closeness of the initial segment of the potential Rhyme Competitor. Thus, in condition 1A, the Rhyme Competitor *konijn* also differed by only one phonological feature from the Nonword Rhyme prime. Note that we are talking here about two real lexical items (*tonijn* and *konijn*) and a non-word prime *ponijn* that may or may not succeed in activating one of them, as measured by lexical decisions to a probe word that is an associate of the Original Word.

In Group 1B, holding the Nonword Rhyme Prime/Original Word distance constant, the Rhyme Competitor was now made more distant— i.e. with its initial segment differing from the initial segment of the Nonword Rhyme Prime by at least two distinctive features. For example,

---

[4] We define perceptual distance in terms of phonological features, since we assume that lexical representations are specified featurally, so that this is the appropriate vocabulary for talking not only about lexical form representations themselves but also about the 'input representation' that maps onto these representations. In the experiments reported here, however, we are not invoking any specific phonological feature set. The term *feature* is being used to cover broad traditional categories such as voice, place, and manner.

TABLE 10.2
Perceptual Distance and Competition

Rhyme Competitor	Original Word	Nonword Rhyme	Probe
Group 1: Close Original Word (1 feature)			
1A: Close (konijn 'rabbit')[1]	tonijn 'tuna'	ponijn	VIS 'fish'
1B: Distant (hostie 'host')	tostie 'toast'	postie	KAAS 'cheese'
1C: Absent (—)	tomaat 'tomato'	pomaat	ROOD 'red'
Group 2: Distant Original Word (2+ features)			
2A: Close (kervel 'chervil')	wervel 'vertebra'	pervel	KOLOM 'column'
2B: Distant (gaffel 'fork')	waffel 'waffle'	paffel	MOND 'mouth'
2C: Absent (—)	woestijn 'desert'	poestijn	ZAND 'sand'

[1] Words in brackets are lexical competitors (where present)

as in Table 10.2, the Rhyme Competitor (*hostie*) differs from the Nonword Rhyme Prime (*postie*) in both place and manner. Here, therefore, the Nonword Rhyme Prime is phonologically closer to the Original Word than to the Rhyme Competitor—as opposed to condition 1A, where it was equidistant between the two. Group 1C makes this contrast even stronger, by selecting stimuli where there is no Rhyme Competitor at all—that is, cases where the Original Word (such as *tomaat*) has no rhymes in the lexicon.[5]

These three conditions in Group 1 were matched by a parallel set of conditions in Group 2, where the initial segment of the Nonword Rhyme Prime was held constant at two or more distinctive features distance from the Original Word. Across conditions 2A—2C, the Rhyme Competitor again varied in its distance from the Nonword Rhyme. Thus, in 2A, the Nonword Rhyme (*pervel*) is two or more features distant from the Original Word (*wervel*)[6] but only one feature distant from the Rhyme Competitor (*kervel*). In 2B the NonWord Rhyme (*paffel*) is now two or more features distant from the Rhyme Competitor (*gaffel*) as well, whereas in 2C there is again no Rhyme Competitor lexically available.

This combination allowed us to evaluate the consequences of perceptual distance between an input and a target representation as a function of the presence or absence of close or distant lexical competitors. Under which of these conditions, if any, would the nonword rhyme prime start to be

---

[5] Note that subjects never hear the Rhyme Competitor itself. The prime word is always either the Original Word or the Nonword Rhyme (or a control prime). The Rhyme Competitor is not a stimulus, but part of the listener's assumed stimulus environment.

[6] Note that Dutch orthographic <w> corresponds (approximately) to phonetic [v], and orthographic <g> to phonetic [x].

treated as a sufficient match with the original word to generate priming of associates to that word? Clearly, on a TRACE-type account, we should expect some sort of gradient of activation, with the strongest effects in Condition 1C—that is, where the rhyme prime is phonologically very close to the original word, and where there is no rhyme competitor. This is a situation directly parallel to the *pleasant/bleasant* effect reported in McClelland and Elman (1986), where the input *bleasant* is 'recognised' by TRACE as a token of *pleasant*, and where the input not only rhymes with the target word, but also has no rhyme competitor.

We ran this experiment using an intra- rather than cross-modal priming task, where the auditory prime is followed at a 250msec delay by an auditory probe. The subjects' task is to make a lexical decision response to the second stimulus in each pair, and what we are looking for, as before, is signs of facilitation in any of the rhyme prime conditions. The results, plotted as test–control difference scores, are given in Fig. 10.1. We found consistent and strong priming by the Original Word across all conditions,

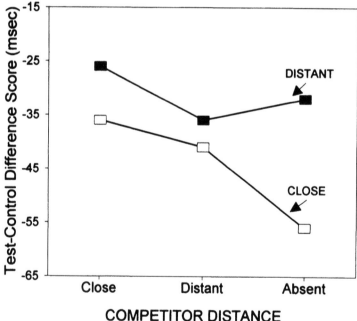

FIG. 10.1.   Test-Control Difference Score as a function of Competitor Distance and Prime Distance. Competitor Distance is the distance in features between the initial segment of the Rhyme Competitor and the initial segment of the Nonword Rhyme Prime. Prime Distance is the distance between the NonWord Rhyme and the Original Word. Close Rhyme Primes (i.e. those whose initial segment is close to the initial segment of the Original Word) are indicated by the unfilled squares, and Distant Primes (distant from the Original Word) by the filled squares. Negative difference scores indicate facilitation—responses are faster following the prime than following the control word.

and much weaker priming by the Nonword Rhyme Primes. But there are only weak effects of the manipulations of the phonological distance between the initial segments of the Nonword Rhyme, the Original Word, and the Rhyme Competitor.

For Group 1 (unfilled squares in Fig. 10.1), where the NonWord Rhyme is only one phonological feature different from the Original Word, priming of the associate of the Original Word increases from 36msec in 1A, where the Rhyme Competitor is also one feature distant from the Original Word, to 56msec in 1C, where there is no Rhyme Competitor. For Group 2, where the Nonword Rhyme prime is perceptually more distant from the Original Word, priming is uniformly weak, averaging 31msec across all three competitor conditions. But these are only trends, and do not approach significance.

It is clear from these results that, even under the apparently most favourable conditions, an input mismatching by just one distinctive feature is not treated by the system as a token of the target original word—priming is always significantly less to the Rhyme Prime than to the Original Word. This suggests two things: first, that mismatch between input and representation may not be functioning in the way postulated in TRACE. As we argued in Marslen-Wilson and Zwitserlood (1989), the failure of rhyme primes may reflect the direct bottom-up effects of mismatch on the state of the Original Word representation; second, that since a one-feature difference counts as a sufficient difference for the access process, any effects of the competitor environment, inhibitory or otherwise, may be overridden or obscured by the effects of mismatch.

To explore this second possibility in more detail, we resolved to carry out a further experiment where the mismatch at word-onset was even weaker—that is, by constructing stimuli with perceptually ambiguous onsets. In contrast to the previous experiments, this was carried out in English (Marslen-Wilson, van Halen, & Moss, 1988; Moss, Marslen-Wilson, & Spence, 1989). A sample stimulus set is given in Table 10.3.

The goal of this experiment was to determine the limits on the system's sensitivity to mismatch. We therefore took pairs of words that differed only in a single distinctive feature, and constructed ambiguous stimuli that were intermediate between them. The feature we chose was *voice*—differentiating, for example, [p] and [t] from [b] and [d] in English. Thus, as in the first stimulus group in Table 10.3, the Original Word is *plank*, the Rhyme Prime is the real word *blank*, and the Ambiguous Prime is *pl blank*.[7] This contrasts with a second stimulus group, where the Rhyme

---

[7] The Ambiguous primes were constructed by manipulating the VOT of naturally produced tokens of the stimuli and then pre-testing them for ambiguity. In the pre-test, subjects were given the initial segment, followed by 50msec of the vowel, and asked to make a forced choice phoneme identification judgement.

TABLE 10.3
Perceptual Ambiguity and Competition

Prime Type	Prime	Probe
Group 1: Word Competitor		
Original Word	plank	WOOD
Rhyme Prime	blank	WOOD
Ambiguous Prime	b/plank	WOOD
Control	faint	WOOD
Group 2: No Competitor		
Original Word	task	JOB
Rhyme Prime	dask	JOB
Ambiguous Prime	d/task	JOB
Control	crisp	JOB

Prime is a nonword, so that the Ambiguous Prime is now intermediate between a real word and a nonword—*d/task* is midway between *task* and the non-word *dask*.

We expected to find no priming effects, as in Experiment One, for the real word and nonword rhyme primes—*blank* should not prime WOOD, nor should *dask* prime JOB. For the Ambiguous primes, there were two questions. First, would this degree of disruption, where the input does not fully match but does not clearly mismatch either, still prevent sufficient activation of the Original Word to create priming of an associate? Secondly, would an effect of competitor environment now emerge—if the input is ambiguous, would it make a difference if there were two lexical items with which it was compatible, as opposed to just one?

The results, given in Fig. 10.2, confirm that single-feature (i.e. phonologically minimal) mismatches at word-onset are sufficient to prevent rhyme priming, irrespective of competitor environment. There is strong priming of the associate of the Original Word, but both real word and nonword Rhyme primes had no effect—listeners obstinately refused, for example, to hear *dask* as a token of *task*.[8] Where we do see a change in

---

[8] The absence of rhyme-priming here contrasts with the previous experiment, where rhyme primes do show an across-the-board effect of about 40msec. This difference is likely to be a time-course effect. Response-times in the first experiment, using auditory presentation of the target, averaged 720msec, which is much slower than the 500msec average in the current, cross-modal experiment, using visual probes. Recent research by Connine, Blasko, & Titone (1992) is also consistent with a time-course account, since they find priming by non-word rhyme primes in a cross-modal task where response times are also relatively long, falling into the range 650–700msec. There is little doubt that listeners can eventually identify strings like *dask* as mispronunciations of *task*, especially in the context of the probe word *job*, and this linkage may be picked up at longer response latencies. At shorter response latencies, the absence of priming effects suggests that mismatch at word-onset does disrupt initial, first-pass access to the Original Word, irrespective of amount of subsequent overlap.

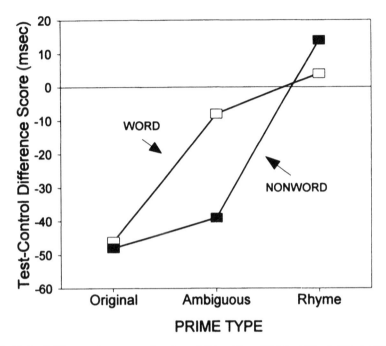

FIG. 10.2. Difference Scores as a function of Prime Type (Original Word, Rhyme Prime, Ambiguous Prime) and of Competitor Type (Word, Nonword).

the pattern, and an interaction with competitor environment, is for the Ambiguous Primes. In the Nonword condition, where there is no rhyme competitor, the Ambiguous prime is nearly as effective as the Original Word (48 *vs* 39msec facilitation). But in the Word condition, where the Ambiguous Prime is compatible with two possible words, the priming effect disappears. Whether this competitor effect is evidence for lateral inhibition is an issue I will return to later.

These first three experiments suggest a system that is more sensitive to bottom-up mismatch—and less sensitive to amount of overlap—than an interactive activation framework would suggest, and where lateral inhibition does not seem to play the major role assigned to it in the workings of models like TRACE. All three experiments however, focus on word-beginnings: it may be that word-beginnings have a special processing status in lexical access, and that mismatches later in the word are treated in a different way—possibly in ways more consistent with the interactive-activation approach. This possibility was explored in a further series of experiments looking at mismatch and competitor effects at word-offset.

Mismatch, Competition, and Recognition-point

In the original cohort model of spoken word-recognition (Marslen-Wilson & Welsh, 1978), word-onsets had a special informational status, since it was the initial one or two segments of a word that defined the lexical search space (or 'cohort') within which subsequent analysis of the input took place. If word-onsets do have this special function, then the processing system may be especially sensitive to mismatches early in a word. In a new experiment, therefore, I decided to look at mismatch effects paralleling those of the *task/dask* type, but now placed at the end of a monosyllabic word rather than its beginning (see Table 10.4). This not only allows a test of effects of mismatch later in a word, when a cohort of candidates has already been activated, but also allows a different and better controlled test of competitor effects than was possible for word-onset mismatches.

When a mismatch occurs at the end of a word, as in the *street/streak*, *fleet/fleak* examples given in Table 10.4, the on-line lexical competitor environment is restricted to the subset of words in the language that begin with the initial sequence [stri] or [fli]. Thus, when the final segment [k] is heard, we know that if it follows [stri] it will match the lexical item *streak*, and that if it follows [fli] there is not only no lexical item *fleak* which is active, but also no other likely lexical competitors which share the same initial sequence, and which have the same general phonetic properties as the final segment of the Original Word *fleet* (i.e., there are no words *fleeg*, *fleep*, *fleed*, *fleeb*, etc.). This is in contrast to word-initial mismatches, where, for example, the string [dɑsk] will mismatch *task*, but will nonetheless match all of the words in the language beginning with [dɑ].[9] These other candidates (such as *dark*, *dart*, *darn*, etc.) will drop out as more of the word is heard, but their presence complicates the competitor environment in a way that can be avoided for word-offset mismatches.

TABLE 10.4
Word Offset Mismatch: Monosyllables

Prime Type	Prime	Probe
Group 1: Word Mismatch		
Original Word	street	ROAD
Word Mismatch	streak	ROAD
Control	plain	ROAD
Group 2: Nonword Mismatch		
Orignal Word	fleet	SHIP
Nonword Mismatch	fleak	SHIP
Control	grace	SHIP

---

[9] The word *task* is pronounced here as Southern British [tɑsk].

In the first experiment in this new series, again asking the subjects to make lexical decision responses to visual probes presented at the offset of auditory primes, we examined essentially the same contrasts as in the earlier word-onset studies.[10] In the Word group, activation of the Original Word (such as *street*) is measured by looking for facilitation of an associate (ROAD) by a Word Mismatch (*streak*), differing from the Original Word by a single feature (place of articulation).[11] In the Nonword group, activation of the Original Word (such as *fleet*) is assessed following a Nonword Mismatch (*fleak*), also differing from the Original Word by a single feature.

The predictions of a TRACE-type account seem very clear here. When the string [fli] is heard, this will activate the lexical representation corresponding to *fleet*, and there will be no inhibition of this activation when a final [k] follows, since the system does not permit bottom-up inhibition, and there is no basis for lateral inhibition by a better-matching lexical competitor. There is no reason, therefore, why SHIP (the associate of *fleet*) should not show at least some priming when *fleak* is heard.

The results, summarised in Fig. 10.3, exactly follow those of the preceding word-onset mismatch experiments. The Original Words (*street, fleet*) strongly prime their associates (ROAD, SHIP), but neither Mismatch prime is in the least effective. Not only does a single feature mismatch still knock out activation of the Original Word, but also there is no interaction with lexical status. Mismatch is just as effective in the Nonword case, where there is no source of lateral inhibition at the lexical level, as it is in the Word case, where the mismatch does involve a lexical competitor.

There is still the possibility, however, that the mismatches are occurring in informationally special situations. The stimuli in this experiment were monosyllabic, and for most monosyllables all of the word is critical for its correct identification. The listener needs to know the end of the word, just as much as the beginning, in order to discriminate it from other possible words. Thus, by using monosyllables as the stimuli, we may not have significantly changed the degree of processing attention paid to the segments in which the mismatch occurred. To test for this, and to set up still more favourable conditions for TRACE-type predictions to succeed, we constructed a further set of stimuli, which allowed us to place mismatching segments at points in a word which varied in their informational significance, relative to the *recognition-point* of the word (Marslen-Wilson, Gaskell, & Older, 1991).

---

[10] I thank Rachel Spence and Helen Moss for their help with this experiment.

[11] In fact, the experiment contained an additional variable of Competitor distance, with half the competitors mismatching by a single feature, and half by several features. Since this factor had no effect—single feature mismatches were just as effective as multiple feature mismatches—we will not describe it further here.

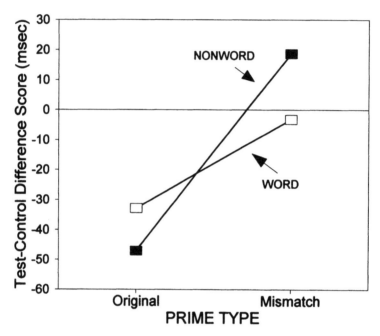

FIG. 10.3. Difference Scores for word-offset mismatch as a function of Prime Type (Original Word, Mismatch) and Lexical Status (Mismatch forms a Word or a Nonword).

The concept of recognition-point is central to the cohort approach (Marslen-Wilson, 1987; Marslen-Wilson & Welsh, 1978), and is definable as the sequential point in a word at which it becomes uniquely and securely identifiable—that is, as the point where the word diverges from the other members of its word-initial cohort. For the monosyllables we used in the previous experiment, the recognition-point always fell on the last segment— it was only when the final [t] was heard, for example, that *street* or *fleet* could be correctly identified. In the new experiment (see Table 10.5), we contrasted three types of disyllabic stimuli. This allowed us to keep the position of the mismatch constant at the end of the word, but to vary the informational conditions under which it occurred.

In the first two types (Groups 1 and 2: Late Recognition-Point), recognition-point again fell at the end of the word. In Group 1 the mismatch prime was a word and in Group 2 a nonword. This is analogous to the previous experiment, with the exception that more stimulus information has been heard at the point where the mismatch occurs, and only two word-candidates will normally still be active. The critical contrast is with Group 3 (Early Recognition-Point), where recognition-point falls earlier

TABLE 10.5
Word Offset Mismatch: Disyllables

Prime Type	Prime	Probe
Group 1: Late Recognition Point/Word Mismatch		
Original Word	cabbage	PATCH
Word Mismatch	cabin	PATCH
Control	vital	PATCH
Group 2: Late Recognition Point/Nonword Mismatch		
Original Word	bandage	WOUND
Nonword Mismatch	bandin	WOUND
Control	salad	WOUND
Group 3: Early Recognition Point/Nonword Mismatch		
Original Word	sausage	MEAT
Nonword Mismatch	sausin	MEAT
Control	tulip	MEAT

in the word (on average at the first consonant of the second syllable), and where the mismatch prime is always a nonword.

For cases like this, the mismatch not only falls at the end of word, under conditions where there are no other lexical competitors active, but also it occurs at a point that is no longer informationally critical for the identification of the word. Here, if anywhere, we should be able to detect activation of the Original Word. There should be at least some priming of the associate of the Original Word, especially in comparison to the other conditions, where the mismatch occurs at the recognition-point, and where the mismatching prime may itself be a word.

We can reinforce the strength of the test here by also looking at performance in conditions where listeners are given word-fragments as primes. The same words presented as primes in one half of the experiment can be presented in the other half with their last segment spliced off, so that primes like *sausin* ([sosɪn]) become *sausi* ([sosɪ]), *cabin* ([cæbɪn]) become *cabi* ([cæbɪ]), etc.[12] The crucial contrast here, for the TRACE-type account of processing microstructure, is between the *presence* of mismatching input and the *absence* of matching input. In Nonword Competitor cases, such as *sausage/sausin*, the TRACE acount treats these two as the same. It provides no basis for discriminating the presence of the mismatching [n] in *sausin* from the absence of the final segment of

---

[12] The stimuli were constructed by splicing off the final segment, setting the splice-point at the offset of the medial vowel of the second syllable. Depending on the nature of the final segment, some partial cues to its identity will be present in the vowel preceding the splice point (Warren & Marslen-Wilson, 1988).

sausage in the prime *sausi*. In each case the final segment does not increase activation of *sausage*, and since there is no lexical item *sausin*, the presence of the [n] in the complete prime should have no additional effects on the state of the lexical node corresponding to *sausage*.[13]

Looking first at the results for Whole Word primes (Fig. 10.4), we find as before that none of the Nonword Competitors are effective primes (the 16msec effect for the Late/Word Competitor is also not significant). Again, there is no comfort for the view that the inhibitory effects of mismatch between input and lexical form representation are mediated *via* lateral inhibition from more activated lexical nodes. Listeners behave as if mismatch directly affects activation of the lexical node in question, and that this effect is independent of the lexical status of the mis-matching segment. It is also, apparently, independent of the informational status of the mismatch. There is no sign here that the nonword mismatch

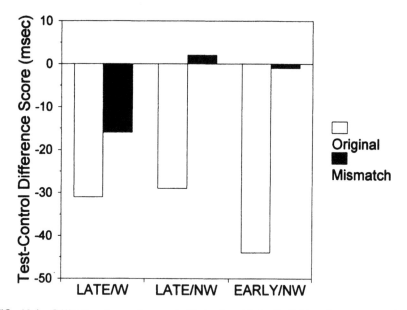

FIG. 10.4.   Difference Scores for word-offset mismatch in disyllabic primes presented as complete words. Plotted as a function of Prime Type (Original Word, Mismatch) and of Word Condition (Late recognition-point with Word Mismatch; Late recognition-point with Nonword Mismatch; and Early recognition-point with Nonword Mismatch).

---

[13] These claims about the behaviour of TRACE are confirmed by simulations that we have run using the TRACE programme, where the system was indeed unable to distinguish [sosɪn] from [sosɪ], even though it could exploit lexical effects to discriminate [cæbɪn] from [cæbɪ] (as a prime of *cabbage*).

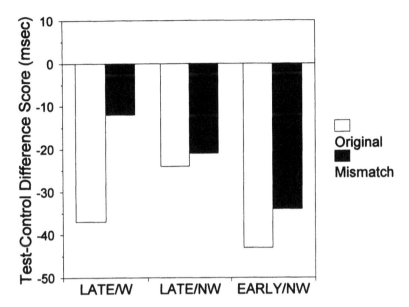

FIG. 10.5. Difference Scores for word-offset mismatch in disyllabic primes presented as word fragments (release of final consonant spliced off). Plotted as a function of Prime Type (Original Word, Mismatch) and of Word Condition (Late recognition-point with Word Mismatch; Late recognition-point with Nonword Mismatch; and Early recognition-point with Nonword Mismatch).

in the Early Recognition-Point conditions is any less effective in disrupting activation of the Original Word than in the corresponding Late Recognition-Point condition.

Turning to the results for Fragment primes in Fig. 10.5, we find a very different pattern. The absence of match is treated entirely differently from the presence of mismatch. Consistent with other work using fragmentary primes (Marslen-Wilson, 1987; Moss, 1991; Zwitserlood, 1989), Nonword Competitor primes like *sausi* and *bandi* are as effective as the Original Words in priming their associates.[14] It is hard to see how interactive-activation assumptions of the type realised in TRACE can accommodate this marked difference, in human performance, between absence of match and presence of mismatch. In our work using TRACE, the only way we could simulate these results was by introducing bottom-up inhibition into the model, so that mismatch could now have a direct effect on activation

---

[14] The Word Competitor fragment (e.g. [cæbɪ]), in contrast, does not prime. This is because a token of [cæbɪ] excised from [cæbɪn] is a better match for *cabin* than for *cabbage*, so that there is relatively less activation of the Original Word than in the conditions where the Competitor fragment derives from a Nonword.

at the lexical level, irrespective of the lexical status of the mismatching segment (Marslen-Wilson et al., 1991).

Processing Microstructure: Conclusions and Implications

This sequence of experiments suggests the following answers to the question we asked about processing microstructure earlier in the paper.

• What counts as a *match* between an input and target representation? The results suggest that we are working with a processing system that is engaged in a very precise matching of inputs to target representations. A deviation by even a single feature is sufficient to disrupt the activation of the item in question. This seems to hold true independent of the position of the mismatch in the word, suggesting that word-onsets do not have special processing properties.[15]

In fact, given the organisation of lexical space, this degree of sensitivity is not surprising. Most monosyllabic words (and 70% of the words a listener hears are monosyllabic) only differ from some other word by a single distinctive feature. The lexicon could only have evolved like this in the context of a processing system that was able to pick up this kind of fine-grained information. Unless listeners could reliably distinguish between words differing, for example, only in a single place or voice feature, it seems implausible that the recognition lexicon could be built around differences of this order. Distinctive features, in effect, do have to be genuinely perceptually distinguishable if they are to do the work of keeping lexical items distinct from each other—not only in the recognition lexicon, but also in the process of accessing different items stored in this lexicon.

• What are the consequences of *mismatch* between input and target representation? The effects of mismatch (by a single feature or by several) were consistent throughout the series of experiments described here. The effects are immediate, and independent of lexical status. Mismatch between input and target disrupts activation of the target directly, without mediation through lexical competitors.

Mismatch does not, however, completely rule out identification of the mispronounced word-form, especially when the mismatch creates a

---

[15] The absence of word-position effects, found here for words in isolation, does not necessarily hold for words heard in normal utterance contexts. In earlier research (Marslen-Wilson & Welsh, 1978) we found strong position effects, with mismatches having much less effect on shadowing performance when they occurred late in a three-syllable word. This position effect interacted strongly with contextual predictability, suggesting that these are decision-stage effects, possibly amplified by the processing demands of the shadowing task.

non-word rather than another word in the lexicon. The significant rhyme priming effects in our auditory-auditory priming experiment (see Fig. 10.1) and the signs of rhyme effects in Marslen-Wilson & Zwitserlood (1989),[16] show that even stimuli with word-onset mismatch can be related to the words they rhyme with. This suggests that the strongest cohort-type claims about word-onsets are not correct. Inputs can still be mapped onto lexical representations, even if they mismatch at the first segment. However, this does not mean that the lexical items in question enter into the lexical search space in the same way as items matching from word onset. Mispronounced *pomato* is not perceived as *tomato* in first-pass processing. Presence of mismatch always disrupts perceptual processing. Nonetheless, *tomato* is sufficiently activated for the listener to be able to recover, in second-pass processing, what the intended word should be.

This pattern of effects can be modelled in an interactive activation framework that allows bottom-up inhibition, so that mismatch directly reduces the activation level of lexical items. It does not, however, operate in an all-or-none manner, to obliterate a given item from the candidate set. The item retains some level of activation, reflecting the matching input it has received, and this allows recovery from the mismatch under the appropriate conditions—in particular, when the competitor environment is favourable.

• What does *competition* mean at the lexical level? We find no evidence to support the view that competition takes the form of lateral inhibition between simultaneously active lexical candidates. The effects of mismatch do not diminish when the mismatch creates a nonword rather than activating a lexical competitor. In the one case where there is an effect of lexical environment, there is no mismatch, but rather an ambiguous input (see Table 10.3 and Fig. 10.2). Ambiguous primes like *b/plank* are consistent with two possible words, and the system cannot directly discriminate them. There seems no need to postulate lateral effects here.

Instead, competition should be viewed in more cohort-like terms. Items are indeed in competition with each other, as long as they remain consistent with the current input. But this has no consequences for the relative levels of activation of the competing items. This activation level reflects the computed goodness-of-fit between input and internal target, and its level is determined only by degree of bottom-up match or mismatch. Competition has its effects, instead, in determining when a given item can be identified. Recognition depends on the differentiation

---

[16] The effects of rhyme primes were detectable to two ways in the Marslen-Wilson & Zwitserlood (1989) study. First, there was a significant correlation between responses to Original Words and responses to Rhyme Primes, and, second, we found significant facilitatory effects for rhyme primes when there was only one lexical rhyme competitor.

of the activation level of the item from the activation level of its competitors. The more similar the item is to its closest competitors, the longer the relative delay until it can be securely identified. Competition, therefore, is a decision-stage phenomenon, reflecting the effects of competitor environment on the system's ability to discriminate the activation levels of candidate words.

The Problem of Variation

In the preceding section I summarised a view of the processing environment for lexical access as apparently intolerant of even minor deviations between input and target representation, where correct identification in first pass processing depends on the complete absence of detectable mismatch. This is a claim that seems markedly inconsistently with what we know about the properties of natural conversational speech. The research I described earlier was carried out using isolated words, carefully pronounced under studio conditions, and listened to through headphones in quiet testing rooms. This is not what ordinary speech is reputed to be like. Ordinary speech is noisy and, above all, variable.

There are two major sources for this variability—variations in the physical properties of speakers, and variations in the phonological conditions under which a given form is realised. Speakers differ, first, in the properties of their vocal tracts. This leads to wide variations in the acoustic–phonetic realisation of the same forms by different speakers. More importantly, speakers also differ in the properties of their phonological systems. Different dialects of English vary in the kinds of phonological rules that they apply. American English, for example, flaps intervocalic alveolar stops under certain conditions, whereas British English does not.

Phonologically based variation is not, however, just a matter of dialect variation between speakers. In the output of any individual speaker, the phonetic realisation of a given form can vary quite radically, according to the phonological conditions under which it is produced. These conditions include not only the properties of the immediate phonological environment (what precedes and follows the form in the speech stream), but also factors such as register and speech rate. This means that word-forms will regularly be produced with their segmental—even syllabic—properties changed in different ways. Segments may be deleted; they may appear as allophonic variants; they may change their form due to assimilation with neighbouring items, and so on.

This highly prevalent variation—one of the great stumbling blocks for automatic speech recognition—appears to rule out the view of the processing environment that I sketched earlier. A system that was intolerant of minor deviation could not function under these conditions. If lexical candidates were de-activated when minor mismatches were encountered, and if minor mismatches were the rule rather than the exception, then the system would consistently fail to access the lexical items that were in fact intended by the speaker.

However, to determine whether this argument actually applies as an argument against the view of processing that I have outlined here, we have to evaluate it relative to a theory of representation. Whether or not variation in the surface realisation of a lexical items is treated as deviation —that is, as mismatching the target representation in the lexicon—will depend on what the properties of these representations are; on the exact *content* of the representation. It is only in terms of what is actually specified in the recognition lexicon that we can determine whether or not some property of the speech input is deviant.

The argument I want to make here is that a major class of variation —phonologically regular variation in the realisation of word-forms in continuous speech—does not constitute deviation as far as the on-line goodness-of-fit computation is concerned. This is because lexical form representations in the recognition lexicon are highly *abstract*, in ways that mean that permissible variation does not create a mismatch with the perceptually relevant representations in the mental recognition lexicon.

A PHONOLOGICAL APPROACH TO THE RECOGNITION LEXICON

Together with Aditi Lahiri (Lahiri & Marslen-Wilson, 1991; 1992), I have developed an approach to the mental recognition lexicon which assumes that phonological principles determine the properties of the lexical form representations that are the perceptual targets for lexical access. In order to deal with variation in the surface realisation of words as phonetic forms, the underlying representation of these must be highly abstract. Phonological theory provides us with a principled way of defining what abstractness means here. We assume the following:

1. Only *distinctive* information is coded in the lexicon, where distinctiveness is defined in linguistic terms, according to the set of distinctive features in the language. This means that regular phonetic properties of a word-form which do not involve distinctive features in the language—for example, syllable-initial aspiration of unvoiced stops—will not be specified in the lexical form representation.
2. The representation is *non-redundant* so that properties of the word-form that are redundant are not specified underlyingly. For example, all nasal consonants in English are also voiced. Thus, if a consonant is specified as [nasal], there is no need to also specify that it is [+voice].

3. The representation is *underspecified*—only the marked (or non-default) values of distinctive features are specified. For example, for the oral/nasal parameter, being nasal is the marked case. If, therefore, a vowel or a consonant is underlyingly nasal (English, for example, has underlyingly nasal consonants, but no underlyingly nasal vowels), this is *specified* in the lexical representation. But if the segment is oral, then it is unspecified along this parameter—it is not listed as [oral] or as [−nasal]; it simply has no specification along this feature dimension.

Given a lexicon that contains only the marked values of non-redundant distinctive features, this allows us, in principle, to give a precise account of what will and what will not count as a mismatch between information in the recognition lexicon and information in the speech signal. Where phonologically regular variation is concerned, it should be the case that no mismatch is ever created between information in the signal and information directly specified in the recognition lexicon.

Variation, on this account, is not treated as deviation: it will not, therefore, create a mismatch between inputs and lexical representations. One kind of variation that we have studied in detail (Lahiri & Marslen-Wilson, 1991; 1992) is the nasalisation of underlying oral vowels when they precede a nasal consonant (for example, the vowel in English *ban* is normally nasalised, in contrast to the same vowel in *bad*). On the kind of account we have suggested, the lexical representation does not specify the properties of English vowels along the oral-nasal dimension. This means that the presence or absence of vowel nasalisation should simply be irrelevant to the listener's goodness-of-fit computation as the vowel is heard.

Our data, in a gating task, support this. Listeners are willing to give *ban* as a response when they hear the phonetically oral vowel in *bad*. This is because the vowel in *ban* is not underlyingly nasal, and is therefore left unspecified in the lexical representation. Conversely, listeners are also willing to give *bad* as a response when they hear the nasalised vowel in *ban*. This is because the vowel in *bad* is also underlyingly unspecified along the oral/nasal dimension, so that the presence (or, indeed, absence) of nasalisation on the vowel does not enter into the goodness-of-fit computation.

This contrasts with listeners' behaviour in languages like French or Bengali, which do have underlying nasal vowels. Here, as we found in parallel gating studies, listeners never give words containing nasal vowels as responses to phonetically oral vowels. This is because there is a mismatch here between information in the signal and information specified in the recognition lexicon.

We predict that similar phenomena should be observable for other featural dimensions where the marked and unmarked cases can be securely identified. One possibility, for example, is the place dimension in English, where the major distinctions are between labial, coronal, and velar place. It is widely agreed that coronal place is unmarked, and therefore unspecified (c.f. Paradis & Prunet, 1991). If so, this would explain why English permits assimilation of place for words ending in coronals, but not for words ending in labials and velars. If the word *sweet* is articulated as [swip] preceding *boy* but as [swik] preceding *girl* this does not create any problems in lexical access, since the place of articulation of the final consonant in /swit/ is unspecified. Variation in surface place is permissible here because it does not create a mismatch between speech information and lexical representation. In contrast, for words ending in labials or velars, where place of articulation is, *ex hypothesi*, directly specified in the recognition lexicon, variation in surface place cannot be permitted, since it would lead to mismatch, and hence to recognition failure.

CONCLUDING REMARKS

I have argued here for a highly precise processing environment for lexical access, which is intolerant of even small deviations. This becomes a feasible basis for a lexical access system in the context of a set of claims about the contents of lexical form representations. The consequence of this set of claims is that phonologically legal variation will not be treated as deviation. The system is only sensitive to informative deviation, and this is defined in terms of the featural information that is or is not specified in the recognition lexicon.

The wider moral of the story is that claims about processing need to be evaluated in the context of claims about representation. In fact, without a good theory of representation, it is doubtful that we will ever make much progress in developing adequately precise theories of processing—and *vice versa*, of course.

REFERENCES

Bard, E.G. (1990). Competition, lateral inhibition, and frequency. In G.T.M. Altmann (Ed.), *Cognitive models of speech processing*. Cambridge, MA.: MIT Press.

Connine, C.M., Blasko, D.G., & Titone, D. (1992). *Do the beginnings of words have a special status in auditory word recognition?* Manuscript, SUNY Binghampton.

Lahiri, A., & Marslen-Wilson, W.D. (1991). The mental representation of lexical form: A phonological approach to the recognition lexicon. *Cognition, 38,* 245–294.

Lahiri, A., & Marslen-Wilson, W.D. (1992). Lexical processing and phonological representation. In D.R. Ladd & G.J. Docherty (Eds.), *Second conference on laboratory phonology*. Cambridge, UK: Cambridge University Press.

Marslen-Wilson, W.D. (1984). Function and process in spoken word-recognition. In H. Bouma & D.G. Bouwhuis (Eds.), *Attention and performance X: Control of language processes*. Hilldale, NJ: Lawrence Erlbaum Associates Inc.

Marslen-Wilson, W.D. (1987). Functional parallelism in spoken word-recognition. *Cognition, 25*, 71–102.

Marslen-Wilson, W.D. (1989). Access and integration: Projecting sound onto meaning. In W.D. Marslen-Wilson (Ed.), *Lexical representation and process*. Cambridge, MA: MIT Press.

Marslen-Wilson, W.D. (1990). Activation, competition, and frequency in lexical access. In G.T.M. Altmann (Ed.), *Cognitive models of speech processing*. Cambridge, MA: MIT Press.

Marslen-Wilson, W.D., Gaskell, M.G., & Older, L. (1991). *Match and mismatch in lexical access*. Paper presented at the Experimental Psychology Society meeting, Cambridge, UK.

Marslen-Wilson, W.D., van Halen, S., & Moss, H. (1988). *Distance and competition in lexical access*. Paper presented at the Psychonomics Society Meeting, Chicago.

Marslen-Wilson, W.D., & Welsh, A. (1978). Processing interactions and lexical access during word recognition in continuous speech. *Cognitive Psychology, 10*, 29–63.

Marslen-Wilson, W.D., & Zwitserlood, P. (1989). Accessing spoken words: The importance of word onsets. *Journal of Experimental Psychology: Human Perception and Performance, 15*, 576–585.

McClelland, J.L., & Elman, J.L. (1986). The TRACE model of speech perception. *Cognitive Psychology, 18*, 1–86.

Moss, H.E. (1991). *Context effects on the access of lexical semantic information*. Paper presented at the Experimental Psychology Society meeting, Cambridge, UK.

Moss, H.E., Marslen-Wilson, W.D., & Spence, R. (1989). *Perceptual distance and competition in lexical access*. Paper presented at the Experimental Psychology Society meeting, London.

Paradis, C., & Prunet, J-F. (1991). *Phonetics and phonology volume 2: The special status of coronals*. San Diego: Academic Press.

Warren, P., & Marslen-Wilson, W.D. (1988). Cues to lexical choice: Discriminating place and voice. *Perception and Psychophysics, 43*, 21–30.

Zwitserlood, P. (1989). The locus of effects of sentential-semantic context in spoken-word processing. *Cognition, 32*, 25–64.

11

Bottom-Up Connectionist Models of 'Interaction'

Dennis Norris
Medical Research Council Applied Psychology Unit, Cambridge, UK.

MUST CONNECTIONIST MODELS BE INTERACTIVE?

One of the longest running debates in psycholinguistics centres around the question of whether processes such as syntax semantics, word recognition, and phoneme identification interact or not. Connectionism has given this old debate a new lease of life. Once it was easy to criticise interactive theories on the grounds that they never presented a clear specification of how interaction between processes might actually take place. Connectionism provides a clear answer to such criticism. A connectionist model such as TRACE (McClelland & Elman, 1986) gives us an explicit computational account of the mechanism whereby phoneme and word recognition interact. No longer is there any room for debate over what that theory can explain, or exactly what its predictions should be.

Connectionism seems to provide just the right set of tools we need to construct highly interactive models of language processing. Almost all of the most frequently cited connectionist models in psychology are interactive. However, we should remember that just because connectionism can supply the computational nuts and bolts for building interactive theories, this doesn't in itself lend any support to those theories. Those same computational nuts and bolts can equally well be used to construct highly modular bottom-up theories. Connectionism just provides the tools; it doesn't tell us what we should build with them. If a connectionist theory is interactive it is because the theorist wants it that way, not because of the dictates of connectionism.

Although connectionism is neutral with respect to interaction, most early connectionist models of language processing were interactive. Theories such as Rumelhart and McClelland's (1982) model of visual word recognition, McClelland and Elman's (1986) TRACE model of speech recognition, and Dell's (1985; 1986) theory of speech production were all interactive-activation models. The interactive-activation models are hard-wired networks with no ability to learn. Most new connectionist models incorporate a learning mechanism. The current modal model in connectionism is the three layer back-propagation network. Although it is possible to construct interactive models using back-propagation, most models use simple feed-forward (bottom-up) networks with a single layer of hidden units. Even a relatively complex model such as the Seidenberg and McClelland (1989) model of reading aloud has this simple structure.

Although Seidenberg and McClelland draw their model as though it had a feedback loop from the hidden units back to the input nodes (see Fig. 2 of their 1989 paper), in fact there is no feedback loop in the model at all. So, rather strangely, as the technology has moved on from interactive-activation models to back-propagation, connectionist models have lost their interaction. The same people who were once proposing interactive models are now endorsing bottom-up models instead. Presumably this doesn't represent a complete conversion to modularity by one-time interactionists.

A proponent of interaction might well want to say that these are early days yet in our understanding of connectionist learning algorithms, and we will soon be in a position to put interaction back in our models. However, back-propagation is a very powerful learning mechanism, and it turns out that very simple feed-forward networks can exhibit behaviour that we would once have thought characteristic of interactive systems, rather than bottom-up ones. If feed-forward networks can produce the kind of behaviour we expect from interactive models, then perhaps there is no need to build any more interaction into them. Perhaps feed-forward networks are 'interactive' enough as it is. In the rest of this chapter I want to present a number of simulations using very simple bottom-up back-propagation networks, all of which can account for results that were once taken as evidence for interaction. I will try to shed some light on the features of connectionist learning models which can produce 'interaction' from bottom-up systems.

SIMULATING A 'TOP-DOWN' EFFECT IN
VISUAL WORD RECOGNITION

We can illustrate the ability of back-propagation networks to simulate 'interactive' behaviour by considering a very simple network for visual word recognition (Norris 1990c; 1992). The network shown in Fig. 11.1

WORDS   LETTERS

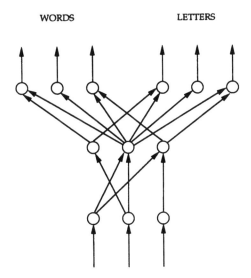

FIG. 11.1.   Simple feed-forward network to identify words and letters.

was designed to simulate one of the classic 'top-down' effects in visual word recognition, the word superiority effect (WSE) (Reicher, 1969; Wheeler, 1970). In the WSE, tachistoscopically displayed letters can be identified more readily when they form part of a word than when they form part of a non-word or are presented in isolation. The Interactive Activation Model of Rumelhart and McClelland successfully simulates the WSE. Letters in a word receive more top-down activation from the word-level than do letters in non-words. Although letters in non-words may partially activate a number of words, the inhibitory links between words will cause these partially activated words to inhibit each other. Therefore the total top-down activation will be much less than in the case of a word where a single lexical node is activated.

The network shown in Fig. 11.1 has a completely bottom-up architecture. As a psychological model, this network has a rather unusual structure. Instead of having the normal hierarchial feature-letter-word organisation of the interactive-activation model, letters and words are both represented by nodes in the output layers. Letters are nothing more than short words. I wouldn't want to be forced to defend the psychological plausibility of this model too strongly—however, its behaviour is rather interesting.

The network shown in Fig. 11.1 was trained on a set of 50 words and 50 non-words. In fact all 100 items were real English words, but the net was only trained to classify 50 of these items as 'words'. Letters were coded in terms of the same feature set used in Rumelhart and McClelland's Interactive Activation Model. Like the Interactive Activation Model the network also used position-specific letter representations. The net received two kinds of training, which alternated with each other on successive training cycles. In one kind of training, the net was presented with only the words, and was trained to activate the corresponding word node in response to each input word. The letter nodes were treated as a 'don't care' condition—that is, whatever output the net produced at the letter nodes, it was told that it had produced the correct output, or to put it another way, it was never told that it had made an error. This condition was designed to represent teaching a child to recognise words while not giving any feedback about the identities of the letters within those words. In the second kind of training, the net was presented with both the word and the non-word inputs. This time the word nodes were treated as a don't care condition while the net was taught to identify the letters in the input. This condition was designed to represent training on identifying letters of the alphabet. Overall, therefore, the net was taught how to classify half of the stimuli as words, and was given equal training on identifying the letters in both words and non-words.

At the end of the training procedure the net was found to be able to identify letters in words better than it could identify letters in non-words. This word-superiority-effect still held even when the experiment was repeated with assignment of stimuli to the word and non-word categories reversed. Whatever the basis of this result, it is clearly not due to the nature of the particular stimuli employed in the word and non-word conditions.

A similar experiment was performed using a set of word stimuli and a set of 'letter' stimuli. In this stimulation the net was trained to identify words, and to identify letters appearing 'in isolation'. (Because the net has position sensitive input slots, the net was trained on position-specific letters with empty slots set to zero.) Subsequent testing revealed that the net was able to identify letters in stimuli it had learned to classify as words better than in a new set of 'non-word' stimuli that the net had never been exposed to. In this experiment the word superiority effect still held despite the fact that the net had never been taught to identify letters in either the words or the non-words used in testing. As with the previous simulation, the same results were obtained with the assignment of stimuli to the 'word' and 'non-word' conditions reversed.

Once a network like this has been trained, and the learning mechanism has been turned off, the flow of information is completely bottom-up. The network's performance is based on a single forward pass of information through the network. Yet the network's behaviour looks suspiciously interactive! The interaction between words and letters can't be due to any exchange of information between word and letter nodes in the output layer, because there is no path of communication between them. Instead, the 'interaction' is a consequence of the network's training experience.

Basically, the network looks interactive because it fails to generalise properly. It fails to learn to identify letters independently of the context in which they appear. When those letters appear in a new context (nonwords), performance drops. In part this is because we are stretching the capacity of the network somewhat. With more hidden units, or with letter that are easier to discriminate, the size of the WSE diminishes. With enough hidden units and training, the network can learn to assign some hidden units to letter identification and some to word recognition. The two tasks can then be performed independently and there is no WSE. So, when we do get a WSE, it is not because of any top-down flow of lexical information, but simply because the network is making use of contextual information to recognise the letters. It is the nature of the letter identification process that gives rise to the WSE, not the relation between letter identification and word identification. The crucial lesson to be learned from this simple simulation is that behaviour that looks like interaction between processes can arise from learning, rather than from any genuine on-line interaction between processes.

SIMULATING TOP-DOWN EFFECTS IN SPEECH RECOGNITION

A second example of the problems that arise in trying to relate the behaviour of connectionist models to conventional notions of interaction is a simulation of the results of an ingenious experiment by Elman and McClelland (1988). Although the WSE looks as through it requires a top-down explanation, it does have some bottom-up non-connectionist explanations too. For example, one can argue that letter information can be read out from either a letter or a word level of representation. That is, the lexical representations contain a specification of their constituent letters. When both letter and word representations are available, letter identification is therefore more accurate than when only a letter level representation is available. Similar bottom-up accounts can be given for lexical effects in spoken word recognition. For example Cutler and Norris (1979) account for lexicality effects in phoneme monitoring by assuming a race between access to a phonological representation derived from perceptual analysis and a lexically derived phonological representation.

In the Ganong effect (Ganong, 1980), for example, a string such as /?aIp/, where /?/ is half way between /t/ and /d/, will tend to be heard as the word /taIp/ rather than the non-word /daIp/. Once again we can argue that this is simply due to subjects reading information out from the lexical level, rather than any interaction between the lexical and phoneme levels.

This kind of explanation for the Ganong effect stands in contrast to the account offered by a highly interactive model like TRACE. In TRACE, phonemes can only be identified by determining the level of activation in the phoneme nodes. The lexical nodes do not contain any phonemic representations themselves. The Ganong effect must therefore be explained by assuming that activation from lexical nodes is fed back to the phoneme nodes. In this kind of interactive model, activation of a phoneme node caused by top-down information will be indistinguishable from activation from bottom-up information. So, if we could find some way of tapping into the phoneme level we could construct a strong test of interactive versus bottom-up theories by looking to see whether 'top-down' effects really do alter the phoneme level itself. Elman and McClelland's solution to this problem was to combine the Ganong effect with an effect of compensation for coarticulation described by Mann and Repp (Mann & Repp, 1981; Repp & Mann, 1981).

The phonemes /s/ and /S/ influence both the production and the perception of following stop consonants. A /t/ produced after an /S/ tends to be rather more like a /k/, and a /d/ is more like a /g/. Conversely, after /s/, a /k/ is more like /t/, and a /g/ is more like /d/. However, listeners compensate for these effects of coarticulation so that phonemes are categorised the same way in different contexts. Because a /t/ will tend to be more like a /k/ and /S/, listeners shift the boundaries between the phonetic categories towards the /k/ end of the continuum. This ensures that the coarticulated /t/ following /S/ will still be correctly categorised as a /t/. The consequence of this boundary shift is that an ambiguous sound half way between /t/ and /k/ is more likely to be perceived as /t/ after /S/, but as /k/ after /s/.

TRACE accounts for these coarticulatory effects by allowing phoneme nodes to vary the strength of connections between the feature level and the phoneme level in adjacent time slices. Therefore, if the activation of a phoneme node is altered by activation from the lexical level, this will induce the compensation for coarticulation in exactly the same way as if the activation of the phoneme node had been entirely determined by bottom-up perceptual evidence. This predicts that if the identification of a phoneme half way between /s/ and /S/ could be biased towards /S/ by lexical information, that phoneme should cause compensation for coarticulation just the same as if there were a real /S/ present.

It is very difficult to see how compensation for coarticulation could be a lexical level effect. The compensation effect, therefore, provides an index of events happening at the phoneme level which is unlikely to be influenced by events at the lexical level. Elman and McClelland's experiment, therefore, employed an effect of compensation for coarticulation to determine whether the Ganong effect was genuinely top-down or not by presenting subjects with the following kinds of stimuli:

christma?*apes
fooli?*apes

where /?/ is half way between /s/ and /S/ and /*/ is half way between /t/ and /k/.

The Ganong effect should result in /?/ being perceived as /s/ in the context of /christma/ and /S/ in the context of /fooli/. If this has no top down effect on the phoneme level, then any compensatory effects between /?/ and /*/ should be identical in both cases. However, if the phoneme level has been altered, then there should be different compensation for coarticulation in the two cases. /*/ should be more likely to be perceived as /k/ in the case of /christma?/ and /t/ in the case of /fooli?/. Indeed, this is exactly what Elman and McClelland found. This looks like very convincing evidence that the top-down lexical influence has altered the phoneme level, which has then resulted in compensation for coarticulation.[1]

It is interesting to ask whether a simple bottom-up network could explain this result as well as the WSE. However, the problem with a simple network like that shown in Fig. 11.1 is that it has no way of representing the temporal nature of speech. In the previous Sperlonga conference (Norris, 1990a) I described how the addition of connections with a time delay enables quite simple networks to recognise patterns which, like speech, unfold over time. Examples of such networks are shown in Figs. 11.2a and 11.2b. The networks in Figs. 11.2a and 11.2b are in fact functionally identical. However, the operation of the networks is perhaps easier to grasp from Fig. 11.2a. Figure 11.2b simply shows that the delay connections are not really 'top-down' connections, they are just connections between the hidden units.

The delay connections serve to give the net a memory for its previous states. Figure 11.2a shows that the network can be thought of as presenting the hidden unit activations of the network as new input at the next time slice. So, if the network is presented with a sequence of inputs (say, successive phonemes of a word) its analysis of any one input is always performed in the context of its operations on previous inputs. But note that the input units receiving input from the hidden units in Fig. 11.2a aren't really dealing with the same information as the other input units. Ordinary input units are receiving input from the outside world (or an earlier stage in the system); the 'state' units are simply recirculating information between the hidden units themselves. For that reason, Fig. 11.2b is a more useful representation of the network if we are concerned

---

[1] We should bear in mind that interpretation of Elman and McClelland's results has to be tempered by recent findings that the Ganong effect may only be obtained when the speech signal is in some way degraded (Burton, Baum, & Blumstein, 1989; McQueen 1991).

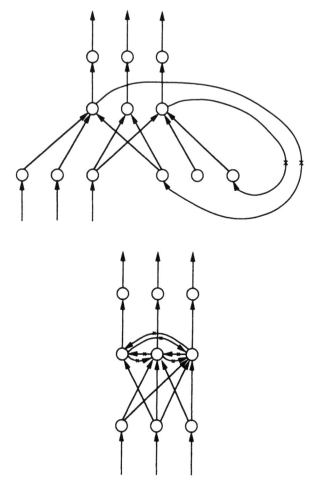

FIG. 11.2a & b.   Recurrent network with delayed weights. Fig. 11.2a shows fixed weight delayed connections feeding into a set of 'state units'. Fig. 11.2b is a functionally equivalent network where the delayed connections have variable (trainable) weights interconnecting the hidden units. Connections marked with an 'x' are delayed connections. Not all connections are showing.

with distinctions between top-down and bottom-up information processing systems. Figure 11.2a gives the impression that the network has a top-down feedback loop, but Fig. 11.2b demonstrates that the network should properly be thought of as a bottom-up system with delay connections between the hidden units. No information is passed back down to the input units representing the featural description of the input. There is no way that the state units represent some 'earlier' stage of processing.

To make this network recognise words from a sequence of phonemes, the net is presented with the featural representations of each of the phonemes in series. In the simulations described in Norris (1990a) the network was trained to recognise a set of 50 words. The network had 11 input units, 20 hidden units, and 50 output units. Input to the net consisted of phonemes coded as a set of 11 features. One phoneme was presented to the net at each time slice. The training words were presented to the net in a continuous sequence with no gaps or silences between the words. The net was trained to activate one of the 50 output units for each of the 50 words in its lexicon. The output pattern for a word was present during the presentation of each phoneme in the word.

Trained in this way, the network does a good job a recognising words from a continuous stream of input words, and gives an accurate simulation of the left-to-right, or 'cohort'-like nature of human speech recognition. For example, the network learns to recognise words at the earliest point at which they become unique. Note that, unlike TRACE, the network has only a single output node for each word. TRACE has to have a complete lexical network at all positions where a word might start in the input.

Because the dynamic net scans through the input in a left to right fashion it only has to have a single output node for each word. That output node indicates which word the net has recognised in the input at that point in time.

We can make a network like this recognise phonemes as well as words by adding a set of phoneme nodes to the output nodes, as shown in Fig. 11.3. The network can then be trained to identify both the current word

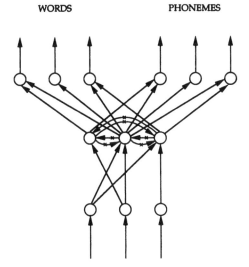

FIG. 11.3. Simple recurrent network for recognising words and phonemes. Connections marked with an 'x' are delayed connections.

and the current phoneme. Because the network always takes previous context into account in processing the current input, the network naturally learns to perform compensation for coarticulation. In TRACE, compensation for coarticulation has to be performed by special hand-wired connections between the feature and the phoneme levels, whose sole purpose is to perform compensation. In this network, compensation for coarticulation happens as an automatic consequence of the way the network uses prior context. It would actually be very difficult to prevent a network like this showing compensation for coarticulation by somehow making it ignore the context.

So, bottom-up networks can show compensation for coarticulation and they can simulate 'top-down' lexical effects. But can these two effects be combined to simulate Elman and McClelland's results?

With a model like this we can do exactly the same thing as with the simple feed-forward net that we used to simulate the word-superiority effect. We can add phoneme nodes to the output layer, and train it to identify both words and phonemes. It should be very easy to get such a net to show the coarticulation effect; because it is always identifying each phoneme in the context of the preceding input, it should easily learn that in one context a given stimulus should be identified as a /k/, and in another context it should be identified as a /t/. Additionally, if the simple feed-forward network can demonstrate a lexical effect like the WSE, then this network should also be able to simulate the Ganong effect.

So, what happens when we put these two effects together and present the network with Elman and McClelland style stimuli? In order to simulate Elman and McClelland's experiments, I used a lexicon of 12 CVC words constructed from a set of eight phonemes. The network had 14 input units, 10 hidden units, and 20 output units. There were 12 output units representing the 12 words in the net's vocabulary, and eight output units representing the eight phonemes. The net was trained on pairs of words, and the activation in the hidden units was zeroed after each pair. In the featural coding of the phonemes, /t/ and /k/ differed only in terms of the value of the feature representing place of articulation. During training, noise was added to the input by flipping the value of a randomly selected subset of the input features.

Normally the place feature for /k/ was coded as 0.25, and the feature for /t/ was coded as 0.75. Coarticulation would make the /t/ more like a /k/ after an /S/, and the /k/ more like a /t/ after an /s/. Therefore the input features for /k/ and /t/ following /S/ and /s/ were modified so that after /S/ the place feature for /k/ was set to 0.0, and the feature for /t/ set to 0.5. After /s/ the place feature for /k/ was set to 0.5, and the feature for /t/ set to 1.0. In the test phase /t/ and /k/ both had the place feature set to 0.5 in the input after the phonemes /s/ or /S/. During training the net never experienced the test pair in the order they were to appear in the test phase, so there is no possibility that the net could learn any associations between the test words. In addition, the probability of the phonemes /t/ or /k/ appearing after any of the words in position 1 of the test pair during training was equated. After training, the net was tested by presenting it with the word pairs shown in Table 11.1. The final phoneme in the first word of the pair was ambiguous between /s/ and /S/. In the initial phoneme of the second word the value of the feature distinguishing /k/ from /t/ was varied through the range 0–1.0. The crucial test is when the initial phoneme in the second word is ambiguous between /k/ and /t/. As in Elman and McClelland's experiments, any bias in the net's response to the initial phoneme of word 2 cannot simply be due to the identity of the preceding phoneme. The results of the simulation are shown in Fig. 11.4. The top panel shows the identification function for words, and the bottom panel shows the identification function for phonemes.

In these figures, the horizontal axis indicates the value of the feature that distinguishes /t/ from /k/. The vertical axis represents the networks response to that input, and the value of the vertical axis is given by the activation of the /k/ node divided by the sum of the activation of the /k/ and /t/ nodes.

Elman and McClelland's task required subjects to report the identity of the word they heard, not its phoneme. Both the word and phoneme identification functions clearly show that the identity of word 1 influences the identification of word 2 in precisely the manner exhibited by the subjects in Elman and McClelland's experiment.

The stimuli 'Sos' and 'sos' are both words in the network's lexicon but 'SoS' and 'soS' are not. Therefore, the ambiguous stimuli 'So?' and 'so?' both have a lexical bias towards /s/. After /s/, an ambiguous phoneme half way between /t/ and /k/ tends to be perceived more like a /k/ than a /t/. This means that the /t/, /k/ boundary shifts towards the /t/ end of the continuum because more responses are /k/ responses. The converse applies to 'to?' and 'ko?' which have a lexical bias towards 'toS' and 'koS'. In that

TABLE 11.1
Word Pairs Presented After Training

Critical words in net's vocabulary	Non-words	Test pairs
Sos	SoS	So? *oS
sos	soS	so? *oS
koS	kos	ko? *oS
toS	tos	to? *oS

? is ambiguous between /S/ and /s/.
* is ambiguous between /t/ and /k/.

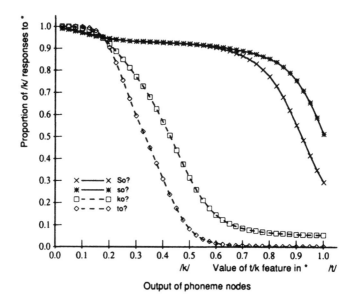

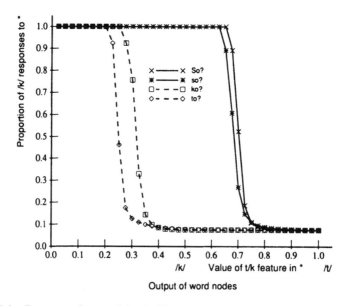

FIG. 11.4.   Response of network in the Elman and McClelland simulation. Upper panel shows output óf phoneme nodes following ambiguous final phoneme, lower panel shows output of word nodes.

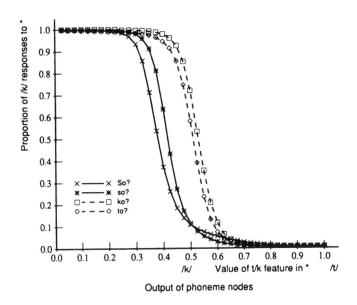

Output of phoneme nodes

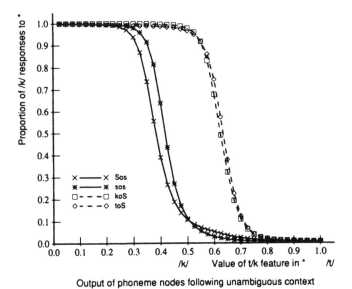

Output of phoneme nodes following unambiguous context

FIG. 11.5. Response of network trained with word nodes always set to zero and with coarticulation the opposite of that in Fig. 11.4. Upper panel shows output with ambiguous final phoneme, lower panel shows output following unambiguous phoneme.

case, the /t/, /k/ boundary shifts towards the /k/ end of the continuum because more responses are /t/ responses.

For comparison, Fig. 11.5 shows the phoneme identification function when the simulation is re-run with the direction of the coarticulation effect reversed. After /S/, the place feature for /k/ was set to 0.5, and the feature for /t/ set to 1.0; after /s/, the place feature for /k/ was set to 0.0, and the feature for /t/ set to 0.5. The lower panel of Fig. 11.5 also shows the results of testing this network with unambiguous context. As is to be expected, reversing the coarticulation reverses the direction of the effect, and the effect with unambiguous context is simply somewhat stronger.

How Does This Bottom-Up Network Produce 'Top-down' Behaviour?

When we examine the performance of this network in more detail, it becomes apparent that its ability to simulate the Elman and McClelland data does not really depend on simply combining the WSE simulation with a network capable of simulating compensation for coarticulation. Because the recurrent network is designed to simulate the fact that speech recognition is a process that unfolds over time, it actually simulates the lexical effect in a very different way from the way the simple bottom-up network simulates the WSE. The recurrent network is able to simulate the 'cohort'-like behaviour of the human listener; it will learn to recognise words at the earliest point where they become uniquely distinguishable from other words. So, /SoS/ can actually be identified after the net has only been presented with /So/, because there is no other word in the training set starting /So/.

The same applies to all the other critical words in the simulation. All these CVC words can be recognised as soon as the net is presented with the vowel. This fact has important implications for the way the net explains the Ganong effect. By the time the final phoneme in the word is presented the network has already identified the word. Furthermore, the network continues to activate the correct lexical output node when the final phoneme is presented. Clearly there is no way that information from the lexical output nodes can be passed back down the network to influence the phoneme nodes. However, the information that the output nodes use is present in the hidden unit activations when the vowel is presented. Because of the way information is passed around the network by delay links, exactly the same information must be available to the network at the next cycle, when the final phoneme in the word is presented. Indeed, the network continues to activate the correct lexical node, even when all the features in the final phoneme have a value of 0.5. Under these circumstances the network manages to identify the expected output phoneme even when there is no bottom-up evidence at all.

If we think about the network in terms of Fig. 11.2a, it is as if the hidden unit activation pattern present when the word is recognised at the second phoneme (vowel), is presented as input to the network at the third phoneme (final consonant). So, information that could be used to identify the word is present in the hidden units when the final phoneme is being presented as input. The network therefore has two sources of information that can be used to identify the final phoneme in the word. The phoneme can either be identified purely on the basis of bottom-up information, or it can be identified on the basis of the preceding context.

The possibility that preceding context may contribute to phoneme identification greatly complicates the analysis of this network. Usually we think that the input to a phoneme identification process will be restricted to the current acoustic/phonetic input along with sufficient phonetic context to take advantage of cues supplied by coarticulation. However, in this kind of network there is no way to constrain the information used in phoneme indentification. So, for example, identification of /s/ could well take advantage of the knowledge that the only phoneme to appear in the context /krIsm@/ is /s/. (Or the only phoneme to appear in the context of /so/ is /s/.) In most models this possibility gets ruled out on the grounds of parsimony. There is no point having the phoneme identification process to learn about such contextual constraints because the same information is available from the lexicon. If the lexicon already knows that /s/ is the last phoneme in /krIsm@s/, then it is surely more economical for phonemic processing to get that information from the lexicon rather than learn the same information itself. Of course, if you stipulate that such information can only be stored in the lexicon, then the only way phoneme identification can access that information is by means of an interaction between the phonemic and lexical processes. That is, the lexical information must be passed down to the phoneme level. But duplication of processing capacity allows us to sidestep the need for interaction.

If one allows unlimited duplication of information and processing capacity in different processors, the prospect of distinguishing between serial and interactive theories becomes rather remote. Whenever there is a need for information to be passed from some later process B to an earlier process A, then we can avoid any need for interaction by duplicating some part of process B inside process A. Process A will then have access to its own internal source of the necessary information, and there will be no need for interaction. The plausibility of such a move obviously depends on how much of process B needs to be duplicated. Duplication of some small and fairly general-purpose part of B might make good sense; duplicating B in its entirety just to avoid interaction would border on the ridiculous.

What Representations are the Hidden Units Computing?

In the network shown in Fig. 11.2 the option of direct interaction between the lexical and phoneme nodes is ruled out by the choice of architecture. There are no direct connections between lexical and phoneme nodes, so, if the phoneme nodes need information present in the lexical nodes they must either compute it themselves or get it from elsewhere. In this case, elsewhere could be the hidden units. In fact, it is possible that both lexical and phonemic representations are computed by the hidden units. The output layer might simply translate the hidden unit representations into the particular localist representations that the network is trained to produce. If this were the case, we would have to place a rather different interpretation on the operation of the network. The underlying lexical and phonemic representations and processes would be located in the hidden units. The output layers would be nothing more than a read-out process. The lexical and phoneme representations would now be interconnected by the delayed weights (Fig. 11.2a) in a way that would allow information to be passed between them. Lexical and phonemic processes would therefore be interactive, although still bottom up!

It is also possible that the hidden units could compute some intermediate representations encoding statistical properties of the input that could be used by both the phonemic and lexical processes. For example, they might form representations corresponding to frequently occurring strings of phonemes in the language, which could then be used both for word recognition and to provide contextual constraints for phoneme recognition.

We can see from this that the physical architecture of a connectionist network does not necessarily give us an adequate description of its functional architecture. The learning algorithm has considerable freedom to distribute processing operations around the network in a manner that is not immediately apparent solely from a physical description of the network. Ultimately, the only way to understand completely how the network functions is to take a look inside it and discover the kind of representations it computes—something that is easier said than done!

Taking a look inside the network in Fig. 11.2 reveals a state of affairs that seems to correspond most closely to the hidden units actually representing both words and phonemes. The network has only 10 hidden units. These hidden units must be able to encode eight phonemes and 12 words. So there is no way that the network can use a simple localist representation where a single hidden unit is assigned to each word or phoneme. However, the network could use some simple code such as a binary representation. For example, it might be possible for one half of the units to encode words, and the other half to encode phonemes. Using five hidden units each for words and phonemes, the network could encode

TABLE 11.2
Hidden Unit Activations for Phonemes

	Hidden unit number									
	1	2	3	4	5	6	7	8	9	10
a	1	2		0			7	8	9	10
e	0	0		4		0		8		
o	1	0			5	0	7	8		
i						6	7	8		
k			3	0		6	7	0		10
t		2		0			0	8		10
S	1				5		0	0	9	
s	1	2	0				7	0		

Activation patterns over the 10 hidden units in response to each phoneme. 0 indicates activation always 0(<0.2) for all occurrences of that phoneme. Number indicates always 1(>0.8). Blank indicates activation varies with different instances of the phoneme.

32 phonemes and 32 words. In fact the network uses a rather more complex representation, in which some units play a role in representing both words and phonemes. Table 11.2 shows the hidden unit activations for both phonemes and words. For phonemes, the Table shows the hidden units which are always on when a given phoneme is presented—this procedure averages out variation in the pattern due to the different words in which the phonemes appear. However, this procedure is more successful with consonants than with vowels at partialling out activation due to words. All of the consonants sometimes appear in word initial position, where the word output nodes never have an activation level greater than about 0.4. The vowels are all in word medial positions, when the correct word output node has an activation of 0.7 or higher.

All phonemes appear in a number of different words, so it is fairly easy to discover a pattern of activation that is common to a particular phoneme in all lexical environments. But words always contain the same set of phonemes, so it is harder to determine which parts of the representation are due to the words, and which to their constituent phonemes. After all, the representation of the final phoneme in a word may actually constitute part of the representation for the word itself. Fortunately, the fact that these words are all recognised at their vowel means that we can look at the lexical representations with two different phoneme representations— the vowel and the final consonant. Table 11.3 shows the hidden unit activations at both the vowel and the final consonant, and for each word shows the part of the pattern common to both patterns.

Note for example that 'o' and 'S' both always have units 1 and 5 active, and that 1 and 5 are the only two units common to the two 'toS' patterns.

TABLE 11.3
Hidden Unit Activations at Vowel and Final Consonant

	Hidden unit number									
	1	2	3	4	5	6	7	8	9	10
toS 'o'	1	0	0	0	5	0	7	8	0	0
toS 'S'	1	0	0	0	5	0	0	0	9	0
	1	0	0	0	5	0				0
koS 'o'	1	0	0	0	5	0	7	8	0	10
koS 'S'	1	2	0	4	5	0	0	0	9	10
	1		0		5	0				10
Sos 'o'	1	0	0	0	5	0	7	8	9	10
Sos 's'	1	2	0	0	5	0	7	0	9	10
	1		0	0	5	0	7		9	10
sos 'o'	1	0	0	4	5	0	7	8	9	10
sos 's'	1	2	0	4	5	0	7	0	9	10
	1		0	4	5	0	7		9	10
keS 'e'	0	0	3	0	5	0	0	8	0	10
keS 'S'	1	2	3	0	5	6	0	0	9	10
			3	0	5		0			10
teS 'e'	0	0	3	0	5	0	0	8	0	0
teS 'S'	1	2	3	0	5	6	0	0	9	0
			3	0	5		0			0
tis 'i'	0	0	0	0	5	6	7	8	0	0
tis 's'	1	2	0	0	5	6	7	0	0	0
			0	0	5	6	7		0	0
kis 'i'	0	0	0	0	0	6	7	8	0	10
kis 's'	1	2	0	0	5	6	7	0	0	10
			0	0		6	7		0	10

Hidden unit activations at the vowel and final consonant for a subset of the words. First row for each word indicates the pattern of activation on presentation of the vowel—the first point at which the word is identified. The second row indicates the pattern on presentation of the final consonant in the word. Bottom row shows pattern common to both positions. 0 indicates always 0. Number indicates always 1.

So the lexical representation for 'toS' just seems to be part of the representation for the phonemes 'o' and 'S'. However, looking at the weights, rather than just the activation levels, gives us a better clue as to which units are important. The weight between a hidden unit and an output unit tells us how large a contribution the activation of a particular hidden unit makes to the activation of that output unit—the larger the weight, the more important its contribution. The output nodes of 'o' and 'S' have very small weights connecting them to hidden unit 10, showing that they are quite indifferent to the activation of that unit. However, the output node for 'toS' has a large negative weight from hidden unit 10, and the node for 'koS' a large positive weight. Therefore 'toS' can only be recognised when unit 10 has low activation. Low activation of 10 is obviously not sufficient to recognise 'toS' though, because 'teS' and 'tis' also have low activation on 10. So the representation for 'toS' seems to consist of a pattern of high activation for 1 and 5, with low activation on unit 10. Units 1, 5, and 10 are therefore involved in both word representations and phoneme representations.

Several conclusions can be drawn about the behaviour of this network. First, although it is trained to produce a localist output representation of words and phonemes, it does so by constructing overlapping distributed representations at the level of the hidden units. So, although the output nodes and the weights to the output nodes deal solely with either word recognition or phoneme recognition, the hidden units, and the weights feeding the hidden units, are involved in processing both words and phonemes. Like human listeners, the network is able to recognise words at the earliest point where they become distinct from other words in its vocabulary. The test words can therefore be recognised by their penultimate phoneme, and a representation of the word's identity is available at the hidden units. This information can then be passed between the hidden unit representations by means of the delayed weights, so that knowledge of the prior context can influence recognition of the final phoneme in a word. There can be no top-down flow of information because the network architecture simply does not permit it.

Do the Hidden Units Represent Lexical or Just Contextual Information?

One question that does remain concerns how we want to classify the 'lexical' representations at the hidden units. Certainly there are distinct representations for each of the lexical items in the vocabulary, but a system that was simply constructing representations based on the statistical properties of the phoneme strings in the input might show the same behaviour. Perhaps the network has simply learned that /S/ is the most probable phoneme to occur after /So/. That is to say, the fact that the network has actually been trained to identify words may have no role in determining its ability to simulate the Elman and McClelland data. Perhaps we would get the same results even if the network had never been trained to identify words?

To investigate this possibility, I repeated the simulation with all word output nodes set to zero. With no words to learn, the network clearly needs less capacity, so I ran the simulation a number of times using between 6 and 10 hidden units. Under these circumstances the network still shows the basic compensation for coarticulation effect, but it no longer produces the Elman and McClelland effect. That is, it shows no sign of taking account of context further back than the preceding phoneme.

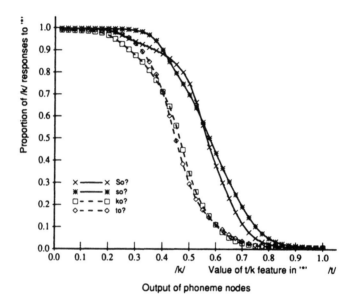

Output of phoneme nodes

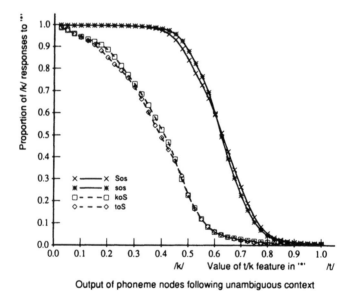

Output of phoneme nodes following unambiguous context

FIG. 11.6. Response of network trained with word nodes always set to zero and final phoneme in first word (?) replaced with noise. Upper panel shows output with ambiguous final phoneme, lower panel shows output following unambiguous phoneme. Data here averaged over 10 runs of simulation.

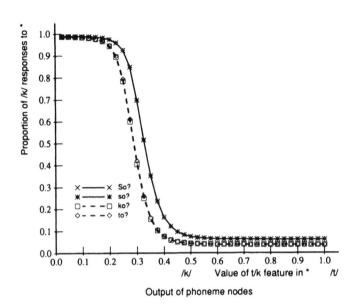

Output of phoneme nodes

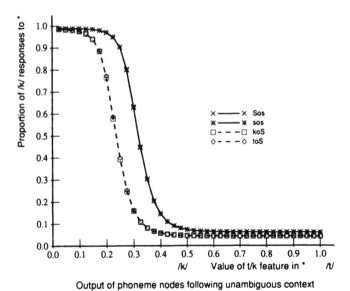

Output of phoneme nodes following unambiguous context

FIG. 11.7. Response of network trained to predict next phoneme. Word nodes always set to zero. Upper panel shows output with ambiguous final phoneme, lower panel shows output following unambiguous phoneme.

This means one of two things: either lexical representations are essential to produce the effect, or the need to identify words forces the network to construct representations of the context, which can be used to aid phoneme recognition. There are two ways we can encourage a network without words to construct representations of the context. One is simply to add large amounts of noise to the final phoneme of the first word, but to leave all other phonemes clear. The network will then have to use context to identify the noisy phoneme, and the necessary context will always be clear. A second possibility is to train the network to predict the next phoneme in the input; in order to do this, the network must take account of more than just the single phoneme of context needed to produce compensation for coarticulation. Such a task should therefore force the network to construct a more complete representation of the context.

The results of these two simulations (tested under noise-free conditions) are shown in Figs. 11.6 and 11.7. Figure 11.6 shows that data from the simulation blocking out the third phoneme with noise, and Fig. 11.7 shows the results from the prediction network. Because there was a fair degree of variability between different runs, the data shown in Fig. 11.6 are the means of 10 runs of the simulation. As both of these Figures show, we can now simulate the Elman and McClelland results even with networks that are never trained to identify words!

The behaviour of these networks can't possibly be due to any interaction between lexical and phonemic processes—There just aren't any lexical processes to interact with. Once we have a network that can take prior context into account, we can simulate the Elman and McClelland result with or without lexical representations. If lexical and phonemic processing took place in separate networks, they would both need to construct similar representations of the context; there would be some degree of process duplication. However, when lexical and phonemic processing are performed in the same network, the two processes can use a common representation of the context. So this leaves us with two alternative interpretations of our first simulation of the Elman and McClelland results: either there are both lexical and phonemic representations at the hidden unit which interact by means of the delay weights, or the representations at the hidden units should just be thought of as representations of the context, which are common to both phoneme and word recognition.

LEARNING GIVES LOW-LEVEL PROCESSES THE POWER TO AVOID INTERACTION

Elman and McClelland's results look like very convincing evidence of an interaction between phoneme identification and lexical knowledge. The effect they observed was predicted by a highly interactive connectionist model (TRACE), but contrary to the predictions of any existing bottom-up theory. However, neither TRACE nor any of its bottom-up competitors considers the learning process. The ability of the simulations described here to produce 'interactive' behaviour from bottom-up models stems entirely from the use of the models that are capable of learning for themselves. Models using connectionist algorithms such as back-propagation force us to focus our attention on the learning process. Normally theorists have complete control over the specification of the functional architecture of any model they devise. However, by using a learning mechanism that allows a model to construct its own internal representations, the theorist loses some control over the details of the model's behaviour. In the present simulations, the networks learned to perform phoneme identification by using information that was not strictly necessary for the task in hand. The networks managed to make use of contextual information (knowledge about the sequence of preceding phonemes), which gave the impression of an interaction between lexical knowledge and phoneme identification. As the final simulations demonstrated, a similar result can be obtained even when the network has no access to lexical information.

Connectionist networks that learn actually seem to be capable of giving bottom-up theories a new lease of life. As I have demonstrated here, connectionist networks with a bottom-up architecture can learn to perform in ways that we might once have thought to typify highly interactive theories. The simulations described here do this by departing from the convention that low level processes, like phoneme and letter identification, should be prevented from processing contextual information themselves. Such information is usually considered to lie entirely within the realm of lexical processing. If the empirical evidence suggests that phoneme or letter recognition is sensitive to contextual information, then the only permitted move is to assume that the lower level processes get that information by interacting with the lexicon. However, if each process has its own capacity to learn, it may be difficult to prevent lower level processes making use of the contextual information that we normally think of as the prerogative of higher level processes.

REFERENCES

Burton, M.W., Baum, S.R., & Blumstein, S.E. (1989). Lexical effects on the phonetic categorization of speech: The role of acoustic structure. *Journal of Experimental Psychology: Human Perception and Performance*, 15, 567–575.

Cutler, A., & Norris, D. (1979). Monitoring sentence comprehension. In W.E. Cooper & E.C.T. Walker (Eds.), *Sentence processing: Psycholinguistic studies presented to Merrill Garrett*. Hillsdale, NJ: Lawrence Erlbaum Associates Inc.

Dell, G. (1985). Positive feedback in hierarchical connectionist models: Applications to language production. *Cognitive Science*, 9 2–23.

Dell, G. (1986). A spreading-activation theory of retrieval in sentence production. *Psychological Review*, *93*, 283–321.

Elman, J., & McClelland, J. (1988). Cognitive penetration of the mechanisms of perception: Compensation for coarticulation of lexically restored phonemes. *Journal of Memory and Language*, *27*, 143–165.

Ganong, W.F.III (1980). Phonetic categorization in auditory word perception. *Journal of Experimental Psychology: Human Perception and Performance*, *6*, 110–125.

McClelland, J., & Elman, J. (1986). The TRACE model of speech perception. *Cognitive Psychology*, *18*, 1–86.

McQueen, J.M. (1991). The influence of the lexicon on phonetic categorisation: Stimulus quality and word-final ambiguity. *Journal of Experimental Psychology: Human Perception and Performance*, *17*, 2, 433–443.

Mann, V.A., & Repp, B.H. (1981). Influence of preceding fricative on stop consonant perception. *Journal of the Acoustical Society of America*, *69*, 548–558.

Norris, D. (1990a). A dynamic net model of human speech recognition. In G.E. Altmann (Ed.), *Cognitive models of speech processing*. Cambridge, MA: MIT Press.

Norris, D. (1990b). How to build a connectionist idiot (savant). *Cognition*, *35*, 277–291.

Norris, D. (1990c). Connectionism: A case for modularity. In D.A. Balota, G.B. Flores d'Arcais, & K. Rayner (Eds.), *Comprehension processes in reading*. Hillsdale, NJ: Lawrence Erlbaum Associates Inc.

Norris, D. (1992) . Connectionism: A new breed of bottom-up model? In R.G. Reilly & N.E. Sharkey (Eds.), *Connectionist Approaches to Natural Language Processing*. Hove, UK: Lawrence Erlbaum Associates Ltd.

Reicher, G.M. (1969). Perceptual recognition as a function of the meaningfulness of stimulus material. *Journal of Experimental Psychology*, *81*, 275–180.

Repp, B.H., & Mann, V.A. (1981). Perceptual assessment of fricative-stop coarticulation. *Journal of the Acoustical Society of America*, *69*, 1154–1163.

Rumelhart, D., & McClelland, J. (1982). An interactive activation model of context effects in letter perception: Part 2. The contextual enhancement effect and some tests and extensions of the model. *Psychological Review*, *89*, 60–94.

Seidenberg, M., & McClelland, J. (1989). A distributed, developmental model of word recognition and naming. *Psychological Review*, *96*, 523–568.

Wheeler, D.D. (1970). Processes in word recognition. *Cognition*, *1*, 59–85.

12 Competitor Effects during Lexical Access: Chasing Zipf's Tail

Ellen Gurman Bard
Centre for Cognitive Science; Human Communication Research Centre; and Department of Linguistics, University of Edinburgh.

Richard C. Shillcock
Centre for Cognitive Science, University of Edinburgh

INTRODUCTION

Background

Discussions of lexical access, whether for heard or read words, now generally accept that a number of lexical candidates compete for recognition during a process which ultimately yields a single word percept. There is some doubt, however, about which words compete, and what the basis for competition is. This paper shows that a single mechanism may account for apparently contradictory results which have been used to support a number of different models of lexical access.

The apparent conflicts have to do with three major accounts of how the words resembling a stimulus effectively compete with it for recognition. Each account is supported by experimental evidence, although none can present a solid case for rejecting the others. The first, which amounts to Universal Franchise, holds that at some stage in the recognition of a word, all the words resembling it compete for recognition. The second account could be called Universal Frequency Franchise: the same words compete with the stimulus, but now each competitor is weighted according to its frequency of occurrence in the language. The third, a sort of Frequency Dictatorship, holds that only the most frequent of the similar words competes with the target.

The Universal Franchise position, which allows equal competition to all similar words, appears with several definitions of similarity—psychoacoustic, phonological, or orthographic. Supporting studies show that the size of some rationally defined set of candidate words determines the difficulty or

235

latency of recognition of the target. For instance, Jakimik (1979) found slower monitoring for spoken words belonging to larger word-initial cohorts (*complain* vs *shampoo*). In various experiments, Luce (1986) examined the role of the auditory lexical 'neighbourhood', where neighbourhood is defined in a number of different ways, ranging from the set of words differing by only one phone from the target word, to the set of words with the same number of syllables as the target, weighted for phonetic similarity. The larger the lexical neighbourhood, the slower auditory word naming and lexical decision were and the poorer the recognition of the target in noise. Interestingly, though auditory word naming was less accurate in large neighbourhoods, it was not affected by neighbourhood frequency. Goldinger, Luce, and Pisoni (1989) found that the recognition of words presented in noise was less accurate when words came from larger neighbourhoods. In this case, however, neighbourhood size covaried with neighbourhood frequency, so that it is unclear which characteristic of the competitor set should be held responsible for the result. When lexical neighbourhood ('N') is defined as number of words of the same length as the stimulus but differing from it in a single letter, non-words belonging to larger neighbourhoods produce longer visual lexical decision times (Andrews, 1989; Coltheart, Davelaar, Jonasson, & Besner, 1977).

In contrast to results associating size of competitor set and difficulty of recognition are others in which the role of size is neutral or facilitatory. Visual lexical decision time for real words is usually found to be unaffected by size of orthographic neighbourhood (Coltheart et al., 1977; Grainger, O'Regan, Jacobs, & Segui, 1989). Luce (1986, pp. 53–4), reported that although the number of auditory competitors (*neighbourhood density*) tended to increase lexical decision *times* for auditorily presented high frequency words, density had no effect on lexical decision *accuracy* for those words, and actually tended to increase the accuracy of decisions for low frequency words. As Luce's lexical decision measure could not have distinguished 'yes' decisions due to correct recognition of the intended words from those in which the stimulus was mistaken for some similar higher frequency item, these data might have been only an artefact of increased opportunities for mis-recognition in a large neighbourhood. Andrews' (1989) similar results in the visual modality, appear less subject to this criticism, because she achieved parallel effects with the same set of materials in both lexical decision and naming tasks. Here only low frequency words showed any effect of neighbourhood size, and again neighbourhood size facilitated responding in both tasks.[1] In fact (see Segui

---

[1] The words do not appear to have been matched for initial segment across the four cells of the design, though this would have been a desirable control to employ in a study where

& Grainger, this volume), words from larger neighbourhoods tend in general to allow quicker visual naming (Grainger, 1990; Gunther & Greese, 1985; Scheerer, 1987).

It is awkward for the Universal Franchise position that auditory and, to a greater extent, visual effects of competitor set size may be facilitatory or inhibitory. Two views of the mechanisms which might be responsible are available. One applies to the auditory domain, and ascribes the uncertainty to the lexical level. In simulations using a version of TRACE (McClelland & Elman, 1986) with lateral inhibition but without frequency effects. Frauenfelder and Peeters (1990) have shown how the recognition of a word which forms one syllable of a polysyllabic word (*cat* or *log* in *catalog*) can be impeded by competition from the polysyllabic carrier which represents its 'worst enemy' in a lexicon containing only two or three words. When competitor set size was increased by including more words in the lexicon, however, mutual competition might further suppress the smaller word, or it might actually enhance its chances of being recognised, as the poly-syllabic competitor was itself suppressed by cumulative lateral inhibition from the additional words. Thus, since TRACE permits competition in proportion to the summed activation of all overlapping competitors, it is the particular topography of a set of partially overlapping word candidates that determines the outcome.

Another explanation for the presence of both facilitatory and inhibitory effects is that competitor set size affects two levels of processing, lexical and sub-lexical. A result attributable to competition at both levels was reported by Shillcock (1990) for the recognition of spoken words within words: for words presented in spoken sentences, the cross-modal priming of an associate of an embedded word (e.g. of *arrears* by the second syllable of *cadet*) was inversely proportional to the number of different second-syllable onsets among the words in the cohort generated by the first syllable of the carrier (*cavort, collide, careen, catastrophe, connect, capricious, . . .*). The greater the variety of second syllable onsets among the lexical competitors of the carrier, the less the actual second syllable primed its contextually irrelevant sense. If, like TRACE, human lexical access included a sub-lexical segmental level with bottom-up input from the representation of the speech signal, and top-down input from the lexical representations which it in turn feeds, then this might be the site of the competition effects. At the onset of the embedded word *debt*, the *ca*-cohort includes the lexical competitors listed earlier. These should feed

---

activation down to the segmental level where /v/, /l/, /r/, /t/, /n/, etc. compete in the process of recognising the /d/ in *debt*. Since many of the segment candidates do not very closely resemble the sound actually present in the spoken word *cadet*, their activation would be due not to bottom-up routes from the stimulus, but largely to top-down activation from its lexical competitors. Thus, Shillcock's results may support a model in which lexical competitor effects are realised by proxy competition at a sublexical level, which in turn, modifies competition at the lexical level itself (see also Taraban & McClelland, 1987).

The involvement of a sub-lexical level offers some account of the facilitatory effects of increased neighbourhood size, particularly for visual naming. Facilitation will arise in an activation model only where neighbours function as allies rather than competitors. Although different definitions of competitor set or neighbourhood are available, the usual definition of orthographic neighbourhoods, Coltheart's N, includes only words which differ minimally from a stimulus. So although the competitors of *tale* might include longer words like *talent* and *stalemate*, its neighbours are usually defined as words of the same length differing in a single letter (*sale, pale, gale, . . . , tape, take, tame, tare, tile, tall, talc* etc.). At a sublexical orthographic level, each neighbour of this kind is an ally of the visual stimulus in three of its letters and a competitor in one. Because any longer or less closely matching competitors will probably not be such good sublexical allies as these, Coltheart's N may be a sensitive measure of sublexical facilitation.

A third explanation of the occasional utility of increased numbers of lexical competitors also deals with their dual identity. This time, the lexical competitors operate as 'friends', that is, items with the same grapheme-phoneme correspondences as the target word. In general, words with more *consistent* spellings, that is, words with orthographic neighbours which exclusively or preponderantly rhyme with the stimulus, are read aloud at shorter latencies (Glushko, 1979). Where more neighbours provide more friends, they may facilitate visual recognition. Where they provide more enemies, they may inhibit it. Why the facilitatory effect of neighbourhood size should be found only for rare stimuli (Andrews, 1989) cannot, however, be explained by a model which depends only on number of lexical competitors.

In contrast, the second view of competition in lexical access, which we have called Universal Frequency Franchise, holds that competitor frequency is critical: competitors are effective in proportion to their frequency of occurrence in the language. In defence of this view, Zwitserlood (1989) showed that before the uniqueness point of a word, cross-modal priming to associates of the competitors (for *kap-, kapitaan, kapitaal*) reflected the competitors' frequency.

Two versions of the mechanisms have been put forward. In one, absolute frequency is important: competitor sets of the same size should interfere with the recognition of a word differently when they have different aggregate frequencies. Some such interpretation is suggested by Luce's (1986) experiments in which lexical decision times, and word recognition in noise, were both worse for words in neighbourhoods of higher mean frequency, whether the neighbourhood was large or small. Jared, McRae, and Seidenberg (1990) have shown that consistency effects are based on frequency: words which are themselves of low frequency, but which have a high total frequency of friends and a low total frequency of enemies, were identified more quickly than matched low frequency words with low total frequency of friends and high total frequency of enemies. Merely having more neighbours had no effect on naming times.

In the other version of frequency-based competition, it is frequency of competitors relative to the target word which determines the effects of the neighbourhood. Grainger (1990), and Segui and Grainger (1990) found that unmasked priming with less frequent words at an ISI of 350ms increased visual lexical decision times for their more frequent neighbours. Grainger and Segui propose that the recognition of any word requires the suppression of all its more frequent competitors. Again, however, facilitation was found in naming: in Grainger's (1990) experiment, low frequency words which were *not* the most frequent in their neighbourhoods were named faster as the number of higher frequency neighbours rose.

The third view of competition attributes a critical role, not to all more frequent competitors, but only to the most frequent, a single Frequency Dictator. Although they found no effects of orthographic neighbourhood size on visual lexical decision or on eye fixation times, Grainger et al. (1989) found instead that words which were the most frequent in their neighbourhoods yielded faster lexical decisions, fewer decision errors, and shorter eye fixations than words with one or more higher frequency neighbours. The number of higher frequency neighbours had no effect in this study: stimuli which are the most frequent in their neighbourhood are easier or faster to recognise than any other similar word (see also Grainger, 1990). Using membership in the target's word-initial cohort as the definition of lexical competitor, Marslen-Wilson (1990) reported an effect of the frequency of the most frequent competitor of an auditory prime on cross-modal lexical decision time for visual stimuli which were wholly or partly identical to the primes. Among both common and rare stimuli, responses were slower for words whose highest frequency competitor was a common word, and faster for those whose highest frequency competitor was rare. A similar result is also cited for a purely auditory gating task. Brown (1987), in fact, suggests a model of competition carried on via lateral inhibition, in which only the most frequent item in a set of visual competitors contributes lateral inhibition to the others. As this item inhibits in proportion to its own frequency, Brown's model should approximate both the Grainger et al. and the Marslen-Wilson results.

Although all three proposals outlined here have empirical support, each appears to be distinct from the other two and unable to account for the data on which the others are based. If the size of the competitor set determines the amount of competition, then either the number of competitors, or the *unweighted* total of their activation levels as derived from similarity to the stimulus, defines the competition to a stimulus word. But if individual competitors are active in proportion to their frequency of occurrence, then competition is suitably measured by some function of activation *weighted for frequency*.[2]

Whereas all words resembling the stimulus are its competitors under the first two views, the third seems to mean that only one competitor is effective. To achieve this, it is probably necessary either to posit a special mechanism which singles out the most frequent word in the competitor set (Brown, 1987) or to adopt a perceptual decision rule tantamount to a race model (Marslen-Wilson, 1990) in which the most frequent member of the stimulus word's cohort is the only item which can compete with it in activation level. In either case, the mechanisms of lexical competition which depend on cohort size or aggregate frequency ought to be without effect if only the frequency of the most frequent item is critical to the effective competition with the target word.

What we wish to argue in this paper is that the three proposals discussed earlier are *not* distinct. In fact, the effects predicted by the other two models are subsumed by the Universal Frequency Franchise model, in which all words resembling the target are its competitors to a degree dependent on both similarity to target and frequency of occurrence. Under this system, the highest frequency competitor nonetheless plays a major role. Simple size of competitor set has only artefactual effects.

---

[2] To reconcile the two kinds of results, Luce (1986) and Goldinger et al. (1989) have resorted to a bipartite mechanism in which speech quality affects 'sound patterns' and so determines neighbourhood size, while frequency serves to bias decisions about the lexical elements that correspond to only some sound patterns. Tasks sensitive to number, but not frequency, of competitors have then to be shown to be achieved by a mechanism invulnerable to bias. Though this solution suits Luce's data, it may ultimately prove unparsimonious, particularly in view of the evidence for the perceptual nature of frequency effects (Gardner, Rothkopf, Lapan, & Lafferty, 1987; McRae, Jared, & Seidenberg, 1990; Monsell, Doyle, & Haggard, 1989).

Partitioning the Lexicon into Sets of Lexical Competitors

The three views outlined earlier seem to conflict only because we assume, probably on no other grounds than our near total immersion in parametric statistics, that sets of lexical competitors have normal distributions of frequency of occurrence. We assume, therefore, that each set's modal frequency approximately equals its mean and its median frequencies, and that these measures of central tendency should adequately characterise the set as being of high, low, or intermediate frequency. Compared to the set's mean frequency, its most frequent item should be relatively uninformative about the set as a whole, perhaps as uninformative as its least frequent member. Nor should the size of the set of competitors necessarily determine either the set's mean or its maximum frequency: normal distributions centred anywhere in the frequency dimension could have any kind of range. Under the assumption of normality, competitor set size, mean frequency[3] and maximum frequency are independent. Accordingly, the finding that one and not the others is associated with difficulties in word recognition is not surprising, but it is surprising that there is experimental evidence for all three.

Is there any empirical support for the claim that sets of lexical competitors, cohorts, or neighbourhoods have normal frequency-of-occurrence distributions? We have not been able to find any. There are, however, long-standing accounts of word frequency in the population of words that competitor sets partition, and they are found in studies of large corpora.

Figure 12.1 is a graphical representation of data which appeared in Zipf's *Psychobiology of Language* (1935/1965, pp. 26–28), summarising a study of American newspapers by Eldridge (1911). Not reproduced here are data from studies of Zipf himself (1932) on the Latin of Plautus and on spoken Peking Chinese, which produce frequency polygons of the same general shape. On the horizontal axis of Fig. 12.1 is what we normally think of as word frequency, the number of tokens of a word form in a large sample of text. We will call this variable *text frequency* to distinguish it from the variable on the vertical axis, which we will call *lexicon frequency*, the number of different unique word forms in the sample or items in a dictionary which have a particular text frequency.

---

[3] It might legitimately be argued that the proper measure of frequency-weighted activation should be the sum of the frequencies of the competitors, and not their mean. We have chosen the mean frequency for two reasons. First, this was the measure associated with Luce's (1986) results. Second, the total frequency of words in a competitor set should rise with set size, for more items contribute more frequency-weighted activation. The mean frequency for a competitor set should not always be subject to this relationship. In general, our comments about mean frequency will apply to total frequency as well.

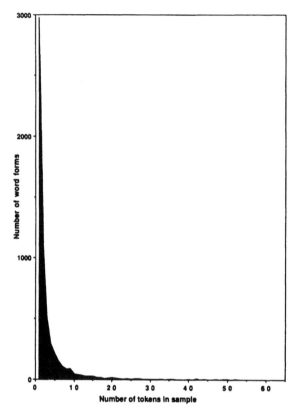

FIG. 12.1.   The frequency distribution of a sample of American English (after Eldridge, 1911).

Although we usually remember Zipf for the related observation that words with higher text frequency are shorter, Zipf, like Eldridge, and everyone else who has ever done the exercise, found that over a large list of different word forms, most are rare in texts and a few are very frequent. In our terminology, low text frequency is associated with high lexicon frequency, while high text frequency is associated with low lexicon frequency. This has to be the case: given that some word types occur frequently in a text of fixed length, fewer word tokens are available in the text to correspond to other word types (Miller, 1965). The population of text frequencies should, therefore, not be normally distributed.

This fact is relevant to the problem in hand if we ask how sets of lexical competitors might partition an extensive word list like the ones which Zipf composed, or like the one which comprises an individual's mental lexicon. Consider two ways in which the partitioning might work: First, sets of words which are similar enough to be lexical competitors may simply be random samples from the lexicon, in the sense that they reflect the characteristics of the lexical population. In this case, frequency distributions for lexical competitor sets would resemble those in Fig. 12.2. Here all the sets of competitors tend to have the same positive skew as the distribution in Fig. 12.1. The peak low in the frequency range in Fig. 12.1 is the sum of numbers of similar peaks in individual sets of competitors. Although the distributions in Fig. 12.2 have an unfamiliar shape, they behave only as we would expect random samples from the population in Fig. 12.1 to do: they approximate its shape to varying degrees, the larger sets more closely than the smaller.

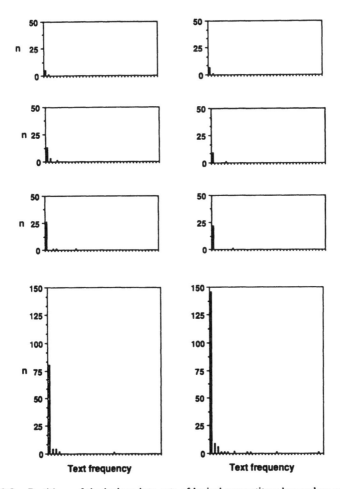

FIG. 12.2.   Partitions of the lexicon into sets of lexical competitors by random sampling.

Moreover, if lexical competitor sets comprise random selections from a highly skewed mental lexicon, then the apparently inconsistent definitions of competition in word recognition can be reconciled (Bard, 1990). If text-frequent words are rare in the lexicon, individual randomly selected sets of lexical competitors will have very little chance of accruing such items. Since higher text frequency is associated with lower lexicon frequency, the higher ranges of the samples will be very sparsely populated indeed. In fact, the competitor with the highest text frequency is likely to be an outlier in its set, far from the low frequency peak and widely separated from other competitors along the text frequency continuum.

Now, if lexical candidates compete with strength proportional to their text frequency, the outlier, which is so much more frequent than other words in its set, will be the dominant competitor for all the other members. Moreover, given the sensitivity of means to outliers, the mean text frequency for this sort of distribution will depend to a disproportionate degree on the eccentricity of the outlier. Thus, effects of maximum frequency should be associated with analogous effects of mean frequency for a given set of competitors. In distributions like those in Fig. 12.2, the two measures are not independent.

With this model it is only slightly more complicated to account for apparent effects of the size of competitor sets. In such positively skewed distributions, frequency-weighted competition should show little true effect of the number of competitors in the set. Because almost all of the items in the set have very low text frequency, their weighting will be very low, and the number of such items may be of negligible importance compared to the frequency (or weighting) of the single frequent outlier. What there can be under these circumstances is an artefactual effect of the size of the set of competitors. To understand this, we need to examine Figs. 12.1 and 12.2 together.

If Fig. 12.1 were to cover all the words in the mental lexicon, rather than just those in Eldridge's sample, then the higher the text frequency, the lower the probability of selecting a text-frequent word from the lexicon in a single random choice. Large competitor sets, like those in row 4 of Fig. 12.2, can be thought of as providing more opportunities to 'select' text-frequent but lexicon-rare words. And although a competitor set of any size may, quite by chance, have a very frequent item as its outlier, on average ever larger samples will be needed to capture words of ever higher text frequency. In effect, the size of the competitor set (or cohort or neighbourhood) should correlate positively with the text frequency of the high frequency outlier. If the frequency-based activation of that outlier dominates the activation of the whole set of competitors, the apparent effects of cohort size, or of neighbourhood density, may be nothing more than the effect of the frequency of the outlier.

To summarise this whole argument, if the population of words in the mental lexicon has the positively skewed frequency distribution illustrated in Zipf's and Eldridge's data (Fig. 12.1), then random samples from it should also tend to be positively skewed, like those in Fig. 12.2, and the population tail will be represented in random samples by outliers of high text frequency. In distributions of this shape, the mean frequency of a sample will be much affected by, and so correlated with, the frequency of its high frequency outlier. Furthermore, if sets of lexical competitors are random samples, then larger sets will have more chance of including higher frequency outliers, having higher mean frequencies, and therefore providing stronger competition during the recognition of any but the most frequent member of that set.

Thus, the three views of the basis of competition in lexical access could well collapse into a single view, if the lexicon has the characteristics which Zipf identified, and if it is partitioned into sets of lexical competitors by random sampling on the basis of sub-word phonological or orthographic units. We will call the proposal that sets of lexical competitors are formed in this way the *Generalised Competitor Set Hypothesis*. We describe the hypothesis as 'generalised' because it is supposed to apply to all ways of forming lexical competitor sets, and so to provide a general resolution of the three conflicting views on lexical competition.

It is easy enough to see that if one kind of basis for partitioning the lexicon has certain characteristics, the others should largely share them. For example, partitioning the lexicon into word-initial cohorts, which are phonologically similar up to the mid-point of the first vowel, is tantamount to classifying words in terms of the onsets and nuclei of word-initial syllables. Since these are likely to include the majority of all possible syllable onsets and all possible syllable nuclei in the language, other onset-plus-nucleus-based classifications (e.g. strong syllables) should also offer random partitions of the lexicon if word-initial cohorts do. Since the set of syllable onsets also forms a large part of the set of syllable-final segments, the argument can be extended to segments in general, or to rhymes, whole syllables, their phonological features, etc., and to any orthographic symbols which regularly represent these. In effect, all ways of grouping perceptually similar words into competitor sets correlate to some degree: despite the differences in modality, domain, and representation, both the cohort and the orthographic neighbourhood for *mile* contain *mice*, *mine*, *mire*, *mite*, and *mike*. The generality of the *Generalised Competitor Set Hypothesis* depends on this overlap.

The inviting aspects of the Generalised Competitor Set Hypothesis notwithstanding, it is still instructive to consider a second hypothesis about sets of lexical competitors: that the usual tacit assumption is true, and that despite the very skewed shape of the population distribution of text frequency, individual sets of lexical competitors are normally distributed. The peak of text-rare items, like the tail of text-frequent items should, therefore, be subdivided into small sets of words, each of which has a lexicon-frequency distribution which is symmetrical about its mean. The peak might be composed of many such normal distributions, and the tail of few, or there might be a tendency for larger sets to have lower mean frequencies.

If this partitioning now seems bizarre, it is because it requires *non-random* selection of competitor sets from the lexicon's population of words. To partition a lexicon with a skewed distribution like that in Fig. 12.1 into sets of words with normal distributions, a non-random association is needed between the partitioning 'key' and a 'typical' text frequency for words containing the key: each feature shared by a set of words would need to be associated with a particular region on the text frequency continuum. With such an association, it would be possible, for example, to describe particular segments or their orthographies as typical of high, medium, or low frequency words.

Evidence for such an association is assumed to be of three sorts: differences in overall frequency of phonological and orthographic units; Zipf's comments on language change; and experimental findings by Landauer and Streeter (1973). All appear to be weak.

First, although phonological or orthographic units certainly have different *total* frequencies of occurrence, the units do not necessarily occur in words with different *characteristic* text frequencies. High total frequencies of phonemes, syllables, or letters, can be achieved by occurrence in a few very frequent words, or in numerous rarer words or both. High characteristic frequencies would be achieved only by occurrence in words with a mode high in the frequency range, and not by any of the other ways of producing a high total frequency. Known differences in total frequencies of letters or phonemes, therefore, provide no direct evidence for the form-frequency association which would make it possible to partition the lexicon into normally distributed sets of competitors.

Second, we have Zipf's (1935/1965, Chapter III) suggestions that some segments require less effort than others and should, by the principle of least effort, occur more often. But Zipf proposed that this arrangement comes about diachronically. Words themselves, he noted, have a frequency of occurrence dependent on their semantic and syntactic roles. Sounds occurring frequently, because they occur either in frequent words or in many words, are so predictable that they cease to carry information. At this point, they become vulnerable to historical change, and are replaced with a similar sound requiring less effort. Whatever the diachronic truth of Zipf's claims, the important fact is that predictable, frequent sounds do not have to occur only in frequent words—for total, not characteristic frequency indicates predictability. Accordingly, Zipf's claims are irrelevant to any possible association between sound and characteristic word frequency.

Finally, work by Landauer and Streeter (1973) is often cited as evidence for the association. Landauer and Streeter's first study found that the orthographic neighbourhoods for 50 common four-letter words contained words of higher average frequency, even excluding the original item, than the neighbourhoods of 50 rare words. From this they concluded that there must be something essentially 'high-frequency-ish' about the phonological contents of high frequency words. Yet the Generalised Competitor Set Hypothesis, which contradicts their conclusion, exactly predicts their result.

Because words which are frequent in texts are rare in the lexicon, larger competitor sets have a greater chance of containing any number of high frequency words than do small competitor sets. When Landauer and Streeter looked for the neighbours of common words, they should usually have found larger neighbourhoods, which also contained other high frequency words. Thus, mean neighbourhood frequency, even excluding the original items, ought to be high, as they found it was. But because they had started with extremely common words, these original items may well have been high frequency outliers in their neighbourhoods, and mean frequency for the rest of the neighbourhood, regressing towards the population mean, should have been very much lower than mean original item frequency. This they also observed: original common items had mean frequency of 577 (Kučera & Francis, 1967), whereas their same-length neighbours, of which there were on average 8.64, had a mean frequency of only 116. On the other hand, rare words, because there are so many of them, can turn up in competitor sets of all sizes and maxima. Their neighbourhoods should, on average, be smaller than the neighbourhoods of the common words, and the mean frequencies of the rare words' neighbours should be lower than the mean of the common words' neighbours (because the neighbourhoods need not contain a very high frequency outlier), but higher than the mean for the original rare items themselves. Again, this was the finding: all the original rare items had a frequency of 1, whereas their neighbours had a mean frequency of 100, and mean neighbourhood size was now only 4.85. There is nothing in this result to conflict with the Generalised Competitor Set Hypothesis.

In their second study, Landauer and Streeter phonemically transcribed 450 rare and 450 frequent words matched in length, and then determined what proportion of all the phones in each frequency group was accounted for by each of an exhaustive set of 38 phonemes. They then split each frequency group randomly into two subsamples, and compared within-group differences to between-group differences. A similar procedure was followed for letters of the conventional spellings of the same 900 words.

For each of these data matrices of 38 phonemes (or 26 letters) by two levels of frequency by two subsamples, they found a significant segment (or letter) by frequency interaction, with some segments being more common in rare, and others in frequent, words. Landauer and Streeter concluded that frequent and rare words were distinguishable on phonological grounds, as they should be if phonological partitions of the lexicon display normal distributions around characteristic frequencies.

The difficulty here is that a significant interaction might have been achieved if 37 of the 38 phonemes occupied equal proportions of the rare and frequent items, while only one phoneme showed an uncharacteristic imbalance. No *post hoc* tests are reported: the authors appear to have drawn their conclusion without determining which of the phonemes or letters occupied significantly different proportions of rare and frequent words, or whether such phonemes actually accounted for a sizeable proportion of the sampled material.

To see how general the imbalance was we examined Landauer and Streeter's Tables 2 (p. 125) and 3 (p. 126) for phonemes and letters, which cover markedly different proportions of the sampled rare and frequent words. Although there are marked differences in both directions, they appear to represent a minority phenomenon. Out of 38 phonemes, only six (/θ, ð, tʃ, ŋ, ɒ, ɚ/) account individually for a percentage of transcribed phones in frequent words at least 1.5 times as great as the percentage of rare word phones which they cover. But the percentage in each case is small: together these six phonemes account for only 8.8% of the phones transcribed from frequent words. Out of the remaining 32 phonemes, only another six (/g, p, z, dʒ, æ, ɑ/) show the opposite effect, and account for a percentage of transcribed phones in rare words at least 1.5 times the percentage of frequent words which they cover. Together this set of six phonemes cover 17.2% of the rare word segments. In each frequency group, then, the majority of transcribed segments belong to phonemes which show no strong association with words of that frequency. With ratios close to 1, moreover, 26 of the 38 phonemes appear to exhibit no strong association with text frequency.

A similar situation holds for the orthographic analysis. Only 3.9% of the letters in frequent words are covered by the single 'frequent word letter' (H), and only 7.7% of the letters in rare words are covered by the six 'rare word letters' (J, Q, X, Z, B, P). Again, the letters which are typical of either frequency group are in a minority, and account for a small minority of the group with which they are associated. It seems, then, that Landauer and Streeter's strongest arguments in favour of typical text frequencies for segments are not especially compelling.

With no strong evidence for associating typical text frequencies with phonological partitions of the lexicon, there is little reason to believe that sets of lexical competitors have normal distributions of frequency. It may well be that the Generalised Competitor Set Hypothesis is correct, that sets of lexical competitors are random samples from the skewed population of the text frequencies available in the whole lexicon and that, therefore, the predictions of the Universal Franchise, Universal Frequency Franchise, and Frequency Dictatorship models actually coincide. The credibility of our hypothesis depends, of course, on the true shape of the distribution of token frequencies in the lexicon, and on whether the sets of lexical competitors partition the lexicon into random samples. Consequently the bulk of this chapter will deal with the extent to which lexical facts meet our predictions. In the two studies which follow, we test these predictions, first on an exhaustive partitioning of a phonemic lexicon into word-initial cohorts, and second, on a small sample of orthographic neighbourhoods.

STUDY 1: WORD-INITIAL COHORTS

Predictions

Considerable experimental evidence (see Marslen-Wilson, 1990, for a summary) indicates that words sharing the onset of an auditorily presented stimulus word are among its lexical competitors. Because it is straightforward to achieve a complete partitioning of a phonemically transcribed lexicon into word-initial cohorts, these allow a thorough test of the predictions of the Generalised Competitor Set Hypothesis:

1. If Zipf's and Eldridge's observations apply to some representation of the words in a mental lexicon, then a lexicon should also have the positively skewed distribution of word frequencies found in Fig. 12.1.[4]
2. Sets of lexical competitors should have the characteristics of random samples from such a population:
   a. Sets should have text frequency distributions which are positively skewed.
   b. The larger the set, the more accurately it should estimate the critical features of the population distribution.
3. For our argument to provide any explanation of experimental results, the most frequent word in each set should be capable of major

---

[4] Because this study treats the *lexicon* as the population, and *sets of lexical competitors* as the samples, it is distinct from studies in the tradition of Carroll (1967), which took *all English texts* as a population and attempted to make predictions about *particular texts* as samples.

influence on the competition that the set can provide. Although the functions relating frequency to competition can be many and various, we would expect at least the following:

    a. The word of highest text frequency will be a real outlier in the distribution of set members.

    b. That word will be separated from other high frequency items to the extent that it can have a significant effect on the skew and mean of its distribution.

4. For the effect of set size to be an artefact of outlier frequency, the competitor sets should have another characteristic of random samples: the larger sets should tend to contain the rarer events in the population, the words with high text frequency.

Method and Materials

Lexicon

The basis for this study was the MRC Psycholinguistic Database (Coltheart, 1981). Of the 98,538 entries in its dictionary, 33,504 corresponded to unique transcriptions supplied from Daniel Jones' *Pronouncing Dictionary of the English Language* (Guierre, 1966) and represented free forms. To measure the text frequency of each word, we used the number of 2000-word samples in the Brown Corpus within which the word had appeared. Not only does this measure offer an account of the breadth of use of each word, but it seems to correlate rather better with lexical access task results than other measures. Note, however, that because its range (1–500) is smaller than the range of raw frequencies, it will tend to compress the frequency ranges of individual cohorts and so offers a conservative test of the tendency towards a long, high text frequency tail.

Sets of Lexical Competitors

The lexicon was partitioned into sets of lexical competitors corresponding to word-initial cohorts. Each of the diphthongs was replaced by a unique vowel symbol in the phonemic transcription, and all the different transcription onsets up to and including the first vowel were found. There were 808 different onsets: 17 defined by a single segment (V); 352 defined by two segments (CV); 382 by three (CCV); and 57 by four (CCCV).

The distribution of cohort sizes appears in Fig. 12.3. Average cohort membership was 49 words. Of the 808 cohorts, 76 (9%) contained only a single word. Although all 808 cohorts can be examined in terms of size and maximum frequency, only the 732 multiword cohorts will be investigated in much of what follows. In some Figures, problems of scale

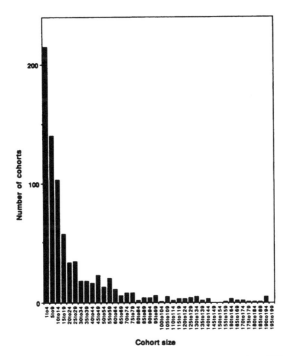

FIG. 12.3.   The distribution of cohort sizes for cohorts with less than 200 members (N = 784).

dictate that the 24 cohorts which contained more than 200 members be omitted.

Each cohort was assessed in terms of the raw text frequencies of its members, and in terms of a log transform of those frequencies [ln $(x + 1)$]. Because the latter reduces the range of text frequency measurements still further, it facilitates graphical presentation of results. More important, the log transform would tend to make a skewed distribution more nearly normal in shape and provide an even more conservative measure of text frequency skew than the raw measure.

For each cohort, measures of central tendency (mean, mode), dispersion (standard deviation), maximum frequency, and skew were taken. Of the measures available to assess skew, we used the one which is least likely to magnify effects of outliers: (mean–mode)/(standard deviation). The measure is convenient because it has the value 0 when the distribution is symmetrical, and positive values when high outliers pull the mean above the mode.

Results

The Frequency Distribution of the Lexicon has Positive Skew

Figure 12.4 shows that our lexicon as a whole resembles Zipf's samples in having positive skew. The Figure contains the distribution of raw frequencies over all words for comparison with Fig. 12.1. This distribution has a positive skew (0.2223) ($\mu_{\text{text-freq}}$ = 7.035, σ = 31.637, mode = 0). For the log-transformed frequencies, the skew is still positive (0.6534) ($\mu_{\ln(\text{text-freq} + 1)}$ = 0.775, σ = 1.186, mode = 0).[5]

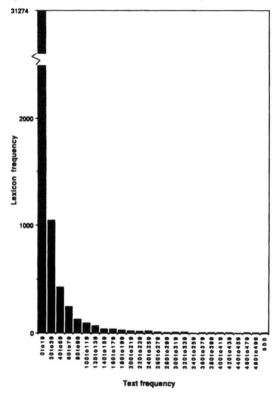

FIG. 12.4. The distribution of text frequencies in the transcribed words of the MRC Psycholinguistic Database (N = 33,504).

---

[5] It may be confusing that the log-transformed values, which are supposed to yield the more conservative measures of skew, produce the higher skew measure. The outcome has to do with the fact that the log transform expands the lower part of the range, where the mean and the mode lie, relative to the whole, while severely contracting the full numerical range (0 to about 6 rather than 0 to 500). As a result, the standard deviation, the denominator of the skew measure, reduces more than the numerator, the deviation of the mode from the mean.

Sets of Competitors are Random Samples from the Lexicon Population

The Skew of Individual Cohorts is Positive.   Our second prediction was that individual sets of lexical competitors, in this case word-initial cohorts, should resemble random samples from the lexicon population in approximating the shape of the parent distribution. We asked whether, like the examples in Fig. 12.2, the word-initial cohorts were positively skewed.

Some 67 of the 732 multi-member cohorts have no modes, and so fail to meet our prediction. The remaining 665 cohorts (90% of the multi-member cohorts or 82% of all cohorts) have modes, and allowed the calculation of our chosen measure of skew. The distribution of these skew measures done on log-transformed frequencies appears in Fig. 12.5. The distributions of log-transformed text frequency in individual cohorts are almost all positively skewed. The average of the skew measures for 665 cohorts is 0.6554, and the standard deviation 0.2297. This mean is significantly different from a skew of 0 which a symmetrical distribution would yield ($z = 73.58$, $p < 0.0005$). Thus, the positively skewed distributions illustrated in Fig. 12.2 are actually typical of the distributions created by partitioning of the lexicon into word-initial cohorts. In fact, Fig. 12.2 portrays a number of real cohorts.

Larger Cohorts Approximate the Population Distribution.   As random samples from the lexicon, the cohorts ought to approximate the population distribution better as they get larger. Figure 12.6 shows that the law of

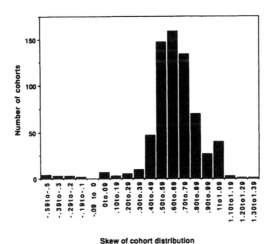

FIG. 12.5. Skew values for distributions of log-transformed text frequencies within individual cohorts (skew = [mode-mean]/s; $N = 665$).

large numbers operates nicely for cohorts. Figure 12.6a displays mean transformed text frequency of items within a cohort plotted against the number of items in the cohort. Figure 12.6b plots the modal transformed text frequency of each cohort against its size, and Fig. 12.6c plots skew against cohort size. In each case, the value of the parameter for the whole population appears as a solid line. In Fig. 12.6a and 12.6c, smaller cohorts produce sample estimates that vary considerably around the population parameter, whereas larger cohorts show less variance. In Fig. 12.6b, all the variance is above the population mean, because the latter is equal to a raw frequency of 0, the lowest value available in the frequency scale. The highest cohort mode, however, is equivalent to a raw frequency of only 3.

Cohorts were classified into size intervals containing roughly equal numbers of cohorts. Table 12.1 gives the intervals used and number of cohorts in each. For the cohorts in each interval, the mean and standard deviations were calculated over the cohort estimates of mean, skew, and mode of log-transformed text frequencies. Table 12.1 displays the outcomes. For each measure, larger cohorts provide, on average, better estimates of the population value: not only do the means for the intervals tend to approach the population measure, but also the standard deviation of sample measures reduces as the cohort size increases. Kruskal-Wallis tests for the relationship of all measures to cohort size were significant. Figure 12.2 illustrates this characteristic of the data as well. It portrays two cohort frequency distributions with typical mean, skew, and mode for the last four intervals used in Table 12.1.

TABLE 12.1
Means and Standard Deviations of Cohort-based Estimates of Population Text-Frequency Parameters for Cohorts of Different Sizes

Cohort Sizes	[n]	Text-frequency Parameters			
		Mean	Mode	Skew	Maximum
2–4	139	0.43 (0.42)	0.15 (0.32)	0.59 (0.43)	1.64 (1.46)
5–9	140	0.78 (0.45)	0.09 (0.29)	0.61 (0.27)	2.71 (1.28)
10–19	160	0.89 (0.41)	0.04 (0.16)	0.70 (0.19)	3.65 (1.23)
20–49	143	0.81 (0.31)	0.0 (0)	0.68 (0.13)	4.23 (1.14)
50+	151	0.79 (0.22)	0.0 (0)	0.66 (0.10)	5.07 (0.89)
Lexicon	33,504	0.77	0	0.65	6.22
Kruskal-Wallis H-test ($df = 4$)		71.91	49.87	10.71	334.18
p		<0.0001	<0.0001	<0.03	<0.0001

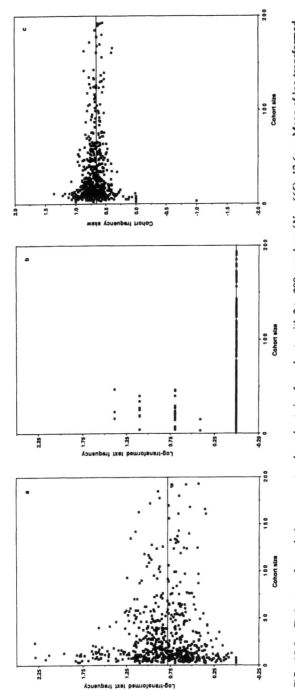

FIG. 12.6. Estimates of population parameters by cohort size for cohorts with 2 to 200 members ($N = 665$): 12.6a. Mean of log-transformed text frequencies; 12.6b. Modal text frequency; 12.6c. Skew values for distribution of text frequencies.

The Most Frequent Word is an Outlier

The Most Frequent Word Lies Beyond the Largest Frequency Difference. Our third prediction dealt with a characteristic of positively skewed distributions which would allow the most frequent member of a cohort to dominate competition during lexical processing: the maximum of the range must be a considerable outlier, rather than a part of a cluster of very frequent words.

We reasoned that an outlier with the required properties should be separated from the next most text-frequent member of the cohort by a large interval. Because of the reduction of lexicon frequency with the increase in text frequency, bigger gaps should separate more frequent cohort members, with the biggest difference separating the most frequent and the next most frequent word. Accordingly, for each cohort, we arranged all the members in order of text frequency, subtracted the log-transformed frequency of each from log-transformed frequency of the next in rank, and determined whether the largest difference in the set separated the two most frequent words.

Figure 12.7 shows the results of that investigation. Starting with cohorts of three items, the smallest that offer a choice of position for the largest gap, and working through the cohort size intervals used in Table 12.1, the dark columns show the number of cohorts where the largest text frequency difference separates the two most frequent items. The light columns display what the outcome would have been under a null hypothesis. They show the number of cohorts in the interval where the largest frequency difference should have separated the two most frequent words if all successive pairs of words had an equal probability of being separated by this difference. In 488 of the 674 cohorts (72%) which contained three or more members, the difference separating the most frequent item from the next was the largest.[6] Last differences should have been largest in only 12% of these cohorts if all differences had an equal probability of being the largest. Over these intervals of cohort size, the number of times when last differences are largest differs significantly from the numbers expected under the null hypothesis ($\chi = 6629.67$, $df = 3$, $p < 0.001$).

The Most Frequent Word Significantly Affects the Mean and Skew of its Distribution. Of course, if all the differences which we rank ordered were

---

[6] In a further 16%, the largest difference was one rank down, separating the second and the third most frequent items. In the remaining 8% of the cases the largest difference was from the third to the eighth from last.

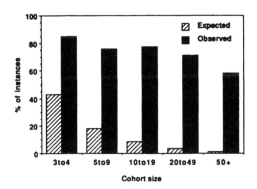

FIG. 12.7. Cohorts with the most frequent item following largest difference in text frequency between adjacent frequency-ordered members: expected and observed values by cohort size for all cohorts with more than three members ($N = 674$).

quite small, then several high frequency items might still be clustered in absolute, if not in relative, terms. If numbers of items are clustered at the end of the distribution, the elimination of one of them should make little difference to the skew or the mean of the distribution. To see whether the outliers were clustered in this way or spaced as we had predicted, we eliminated the highest frequency item from each cohort and calculated the skews and means for the cohort trimmed of its most frequent member. If removal of the outlier reliably affects the mean and skew of the distribution, then this item is unlikely to be one of a cluster. Figure 12.8a contains the distributions of skews for full and trimmed cohorts, while Fig. 12.8b shows the distributions of mean frequencies. The 'untrimmed' values in Fig. 12.8 differ from those in Fig. 12.5, which was based on 665 cohorts, because comparisons were made here only for the 586 cohorts with five or more members. The distributions of the smaller cohorts become awkward to characterise when trimming reduces their size further. A comparison of Fig. 12.8a and Fig. 12.5 shows that the distributions of skew measures for the two sample sizes of full cohorts are very similar.

The mean skew for full cohorts (Fig. 12.8a) is 0.6645, whereas for cohorts trimmed of their highest frequency item (Fig. 12.8b), it is 0.6272. The difference is highly significant ($F = 80.17$; $df = 1,582$; $p < 0.00001$). This difference is not due to changes in only a few cohorts: 337 of the 586 cohorts involved showed some decrease in skew when trimmed.

Unsurprisingly, the means of the cohorts are similarly affected by loss of the most frequent item. The mean log-transformed text frequency for full

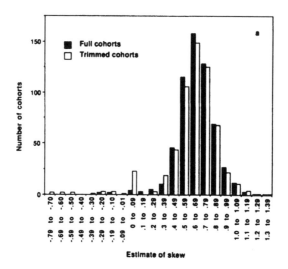

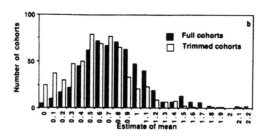

FIG. 12.8.   Comparisons between statistics for full cohorts and cohorts trimmed of their most frequent member for all cohorts with more than four members ($N = 586$): 12.8a. Skew values for distributions of log-transformed text frequencies; 12.8b.   Mean log-transformed text frequency.

cohorts, 0.8199, falls by about 20% to 0.6449 for trimmed cohorts. Again the difference is highly significant ($F = 1840.56$; $df = 1,582$; $p < 0.00001$).

Cohort Size Correlates with Frequency of the Most Frequent Member

Our final prediction concerned the relationship which would make cohort size effects an artefact of frequency effects: a positive correlation between cohort size and maximum frequency. Figure 12.9 plots log-transformed text frequency of most frequent cohort member against cohort size. The mean and standard deviation for each of the cohort-size intervals is found in Table 12.1

The frequency of the most frequent item correlates positively with cohort size (for all 808 cohorts, including those with a single member, $r = 0.32$, $p < 0.001$; for all 732 multi-member cohorts, $r = 0.40$, $p < 0.001$; for the 665 cohorts with modes, $r = 0.32$, $p < 0.001$). Like the scattergrams for mean, skew, and mode, Fig. 12.9 shows that the sample estimates converge on the population parameter, again portrayed as a solid line.

As ought to happen if cohorts are randomly selected from the lexicon, the range of maxima differs with cohort size. As a short series of random selections from the lexicon, a small cohort may include only the low text frequency items which have high lexicon frequency and will rarely include a lexicon-improbable high text frequency item. As Figure 12.9 shows, the smaller cohorts include many low maxima and an ever lighter sprinkling of higher maxima. When cohort size and number of random selections increase, however, the chances increase that at least one high text

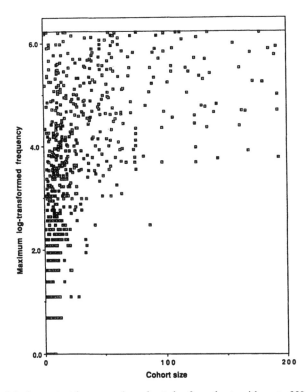

FIG. 12.9.   Maximum text frequency by cohort size for cohorts with up to 200 members ($N = 784$.)

frequency item will be selected. Appropriately, among the large cohorts in Fig. 12.9, high frequency maxima predominate. For cohorts with over 100 members, none have low frequency maxima.

The relationship can be seen even more clearly in the representation of averaged maxima over intervals of cohort size (Table 12.1). As with the other parameters, the larger the cohort size, the closer to the population parameter [here $\ln(500 + 1)$ or 6.22] the estimates are and the lower the standard deviation. (Kruskall-Wallis One-Way Analysis of Variance statistic = 334.18, $df = 4$, $p < 0.0001$).

Discussion

Word-initial cohorts fulfilled all our predictions. Like Zipf's and Eldridge's samples, the transcribed words in the MRC Psycholinguistic Database suggest a lexicon with a positively skewed frequency distribution. Cohorts behave like random samples from that distribution. They provide estimates of population parameters,—mean, mode, skew,—which are more and more accurate, in the sense of being less and less variable, as the sample size increases.

Furthermore, the distribution which the cohorts share has the shape which conflates the three different sorts of competition phenomena we discussed earlier. The modal frequency of most cohorts is extremely low. The maximum of most is an outlier which significantly affects the skew and mean of the frequency distribution.

These facts stitch together a set of relationships (summarised in Fig. 12.10) under which all the supposedly different experimental results could indeed derive from a single source. The first candidate for a measure of competition, the number of words in the cohort or competitor set, correlates with the second candidate measure, the text frequency of the most frequent item ($r = 0.315$, $n = 665$, $p < 0.0001$). The text frequency of that outlying competitor, in its turn, correlates with the mean text frequency of the cohort ($r = 0.631$, $n = 665$, $p < 0.0001$).[7] The relationship between the number and mean text frequency of words in a cohort is less straightforward.

---

[7] Tabossi (this volume) comments that the figures for a mental, as opposed to a physical, lexicon might well be less convincing, because listeners may know fewer low frequency words than the lexicon contains. If all the words in the lexicon with 0 frequency are removed, the correlations change very little. Over all cohorts with more than one member of frequency higher than 0, the correlation between cohort size and text frequency of the most frequent item is still 0.374 ($df = 607$, $p < 0.0001$), and the correlation between mean text frequency of a cohort and its size is 0.567 ($n = 609$, $p < 0.0001$).

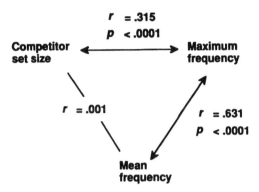

FIG. 12.10. Correlations among mean frequency, maximum frequency, and size of word-initial cohorts (for cohorts with 2 to 200 members).

Although both are associated with the frequency of the cohort outlier, size and mean frequency are not correlated overall ($r = 0.001$, $n = 665$, n.s.) because larger cohorts with higher frequency outliers also contain more low frequency words: larger cohorts extend further along both axes (see Fig. 12.2). In a rough way, however, there is a relationship between cohort size and mean frequency. Cohorts below the median cohort size of about 14 have lower mean text frequencies [averaging $\ln(x + 1) = 0.702$] than those above the median size [averaging $\ln(x + 1) = 0.813$; $t = 2.89$, $df = 739$, p, < 0.005]. For the smaller cohorts, there is a significant correlation between cohort size and mean text frequency of cohort members ($r = 0.218$, $n = 368$, $p < 0.01$), while the larger cohorts show no correlation ($r = -0.08$, $n = 381$, $p > 0.10$). Again the two halves of the size range differ significantly (for the difference between two simple regression equations, $F = 19.75$, $df = 2,737$, $p < 0.00001$). Thus size/frequency relations depend on location of the cohort's size in the size range.

In general, experimental manipulations of any one of the three variables studied should have consequences for each of the others, as much because of combinations which are not available as because of those which are. For example, as Table 12.1 and Fig. 12.6a and 12.9 show, smaller cohorts have a tendency towards lower means and lower maxima, but overall a wider range of mean and maximum frequencies than larger cohorts do. Large cohorts with extreme means or low maxima are lacking.

Before considering the implications of these facts for our interpretation of the literature, we need to know how general the findings are. To contrast with an exhaustive analysis of the phonologically based word-initial cohorts partitioning a lexicon, Study 2 tests the predictions of the Generalised Competitor Set Hypothesis on a number of orthographic neighbourhoods.

STUDY 2: A SAMPLE OF ORTHOGRAPHIC
NEIGHBOURHOODS

Introduction

This study differs from Study 1 not only in the modality used, but also in the definition of competitor set and the completeness of the computational exercise. Unlike a cohort, which includes words sharing segments only at word-onset and which may include words of very different lengths, orthographic neighbourhoods (Coltheart et al., 1977) share a letter length and all but one of the letters of a target word, with the dissimilar letter occurring in different places for different neighbours. If such sets of lexical competitors behave like random samples from the lexicon, then special characteristics of word onsets cannot be held responsible. Moreover, instead of exhaustively partitioning the lexicon into orthographic neighbourhoods, we have examined only a small sample of neighbourhoods, those based on the list of four-letter words used by Andrews (1989). If the Generalised Competitor Set Hypothesis is true, then even the materials chosen for individual experiments ought to display the characteristics which would encourage us to reinterpret their results.

Andrews' neighbourhoods are by no means a random sample of English orthographic neighbourhoods. Rather, they were selected to include stimulus words of contrasting text frequency, and to offer two distinct neighbourhood sizes. Clearly no attempt was made to sample neighbourhoods for words of different letter lengths: it would make little sense to do so if a single eye fixation is liable to include only four or five letters. For these reasons we will test only those generalisations from the cohort study which are pertinent to the explanation of artefacts in neighbourhood-based results:

1. If orthographic partitions of the lexicon are random with respect to text frequencies, orthographic neighbourhoods should resemble word-initial cohorts in having the low mode and positive skew of the population which is portrayed in Fig. 12.4.
2. Like the most frequent cohort member, the most frequent member of each orthographic neighbourhood should be capable of major influence on the competition which the set can provide:
   a. The word of highest text frequency should be an outlier in its neighbourhood's distribution.
   b. The outlier should have a significant effect on the mean and skew of the neighbourhood's distribution.
3. It must be possible for the effect of competitor set size to be an artefact of outlier frequency: the larger neighbourhoods must contain outliers of higher frequency.

Method and Materials

Sets of Lexical Competitors

Sixty sets of lexical competitors were used, one for each of the four-letter words listed by Andrews (1989). Thirty of her stimuli were rare words, with maximum frequency of 36 in the Carroll, Davies, and Richman (1971) count. The other thirty were frequent words, whose minimum frequency of occurrence was 85. Andrews formed neighbourhoods for all of these items by finding all other four-letter words which differed from the stimulus word by a single letter, giving for *mite* neighbours like *mire*, *mile*, *mine*, *mime*, *mice*, *mate*, *mote*, *mute*, *bite*, *rite*, *site*. . . . She chose her stimuli so that the neighbourhoods for half of each group included no more than five additional words in each case, whereas those for the other half included no less than nine.

Lexicon and Text Frequency Measures

As Andrews did not list the neighbours, neighbourhoods were re-formed, selecting by Andrews' criterion from the MRC Psycholinguistic Database, and using the same raw frequency measure as in Study 1. Andrews' distinctions, though blurred, still remained significant. The low frequency stimulus words occurred in an average of 4.7 2000-word Brown corpus samples (range from 0 to 39), and the high frequency words occurred in an average of 112.2 samples (range 0 to 460) ($t = 4.44$, $df = 58$, $p < 0.0005$, one-tailed). The small neighbourhoods contained from 1 to 10 words with an average of 5.1, the large neighbourhoods from 8 to 24 words with an average of 15.1 ($t = 12.8$, $df = 58$, $p < 0.0005$, one-tailed). Further measures used were the same as in Study 1.

Results

The Distribution of Text Frequencies in Orthographic Neighbourhoods Resembles the Distribution in the Lexicon Population

The Modes of the Text Frequency Distributions for Individual Neighbourhoods are low. Of the 60 neighbourhoods generated from Andrews' materials, 59 had more than one member. In raw frequency measures, 35 of these had identifiable modes, 27 of which were at a frequency of 0, 6 at 1, and 2 at 2. If viewed in 10-point intervals of text frequency, as fine a scale as can be used to portray the results graphically, 51 neighbourhoods (86% of the multi-member neighbourhoods or 85% of all) had identifiable modes. All modes were in the lowest interval (0–9).

The Skew of Individual Neighbourhoods is Positive. To simplify calculations of skew, all text frequency measures were classed in 10-point intervals, and replaced by the frequency at the middle of the interval. The alteration of any score by as much as half an interval is almost certainly well within the error of measurement at most text frequencies. The mid-interval scores were log-transformed, and the skew calculated for each neighbourhood. The solid bars in Fig. 12.12a show the distribution of resulting skew measures. Like word-initial cohorts, these neighbourhoods have positively skewed distributions of text frequency. The mean skew of 0.6803 with standard deviation 0.1672 is significantly different from symmetrical ($t = 29.06$, $df = 49$, $p < 0.0005$, one-tailed).

The Most Frequent Word is an Outlier

In all but one neighbourhood, the maximum text frequency belonged to only a single item. As in Study 1, the characteristics of these items were examined in two ways, via the separation of the most frequent item from its nearest neighbour, and via its effects on the mean and skew of the distribution.

The Most Frequent Word Lies Beyond the Largest Frequency Difference. The gaps in text frequency were examined to determine whether the most frequent item in the neighbourhood was separated from the next item by a large interval. For each of the four cells of Andrews' design, Fig. 12.11 shows in dark bars the numbers of neighbourhoods whose most frequent member followed the neighbourhood's largest difference in log-transformed frequency between items adjacent in rank order. In 45% of

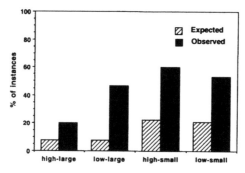

FIG. 12.11. Orthographic neighbourhoods with the most frequent item following largest difference in text frequency between adjacent frequency-ordered neighbours: expected and observed values by cells of Andrews' (1989) design for all neighbourhoods with more than three members ($N = 59$).

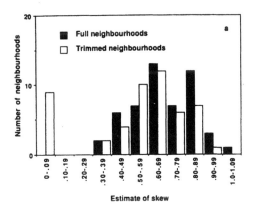

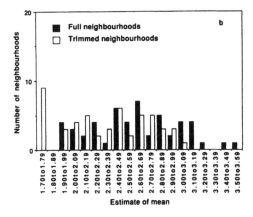

FIG. 12.12. Comparisons between statistics for full orthographic neighbourhoods and neighbourhoods trimmed of their most frequent member ($N = 59$): 12.12a. Skew values for distributions of log-transformed text frequencies; 12.12b. Mean log-transformed text frequency.

the neighbourhoods, the largest difference separated the two most frequent items.[8] As in Fig. 12.7, the light bars show how many times the largest difference should have been last if it was equally likely to separate any adjacent pair of words. As was the case in cohorts, the most frequent neighbours follow the largest gap significantly more often than might be

---

[8] In a further 12% of neighbourhoods it separated the second and third most frequent items, and in 15% the third and fourth.

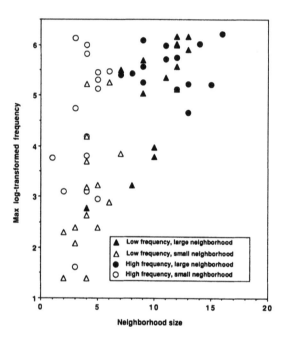

FIG. 12.13.   Maximum text frequency by orthographic neighbourhood size for small and large neighbourhoods built around low and high frequency stimuli in Andrews (1989), ($N = 60$).

expected if largest gaps were equiprobable throughout the distribution ($\chi = 49.60$, $df = 3$, $p < 0.001$).

The Most Frequent Word Significantly Affects the Mean and Skew of its Distribution.   The most frequent neighbour was removed from each neighbourhood, and the mean and skew for log-transformed text frequencies recalculated. Figure 12.12a displays skew measures for full and trimmed neighbourhoods. Positive skew reduces significantly with the loss of the most frequent neighbour (from 0.6803 to 0.5357, $t = 4.72$, $df = 50$, p, < 0.0005, one-tailed). Figure 12.12b shows the mean neighbourhood frequencies for full neighbourhoods (solid bars), and for the same neighbourhoods trimmed of their most frequent members (light bars). With trimming, the mean frequency reduces significantly from 2.633 to 2.346 ($t = 5.56$, $df = 50$, $p < 0.0005$, one-tailed). As was the case with word-initial cohorts (see Fig. 12.8), neighbourhoods have outliers extreme enough to affect their mean and skew values.

Neighbourhood Size Correlates with Frequency of Most Frequent Member

Once more, the apparent effects of the size of a set of lexical competitors might be artefacts of the frequency of the set's most frequent member. Over the 60 neighbourhoods, set size correlates positively with outlier frequency ($r = 0.58$, $t = 5.38$, $df = 58$, $p < 0.0005$). The scattergram for neighbourhood size and log-transformed text frequency of most frequent neighbour is found in Fig. 12.13.

Discussion

Although the sample of orthographic neighbourhoods which we have examined covers only a small fraction of the lexicon, it appears to indicate that sets of lexical competitors formed on orthographic criteria have the same critical characteristics as word-initial cohorts. Both are random samples from the distribution of text frequencies in the lexicon as a whole. Both have modes at very low text frequencies, as well as a long low tail extending further into the high text frequencies for larger sets of competitors. Consequently the same correlations among measures are present, and the same artefacts are available: orthographic neighbourhood size correlates with frequency of most frequent neighbour ($r = 0.58$, $t = 5.38$, $df = 58$, $p < 0.0005$); frequency of most frequent neighbour in turn correlates with mean neighbourhood frequency ($r = 0.59$, $t = 5.63$, $df = 58$, $p < 0.0005$). Again, the direct correlation between size of competitor set and mean frequency is not significant ($r = 0.18$). Since Andrews' materials were designed to control neighbourhood size across target frequency, they did not permit random sampling of sizes, item frequencies, or mean frequencies. Nonetheless, the mean frequencies of small neighbourhoods for low (2.15) and high frequency words (2.91) differ more than the corresponding means in large neighbourhoods (2.54 v. 2.82; $F = 4.98$, $df = 1,56$; $p < 0.05$). This is to be expected if small competitor sets offer a wider range of mean frequencies than their larger counterparts.

GENERAL DISCUSSION

Whether sets of lexical competitors are defined orthographically or phonologically, the shape of their frequency distributions allows the possibility that some experimental results are not quite what they seem. Variations in size, or in mean frequency of competitor set, are likely to entail corresponding variation in frequency of most frequent competitor and vice versa. Some changes in size of competitor set (either gross variations in size, or small variations low in the size range) will probably produce variations in the set's mean frequency. With critical measures linked, many of the results in the literature are difficult to attribute uniquely. Far from being mutually exclusive, any of the models outlined earlier might account for effects ascribed to any other.

The simplest and most easily generalisable of the possibilities seems to be *Universal Frequency Franchise*, a model with a long and honourable history in accounts of lexical access (Forster, 1976; Marslen-Wilson, 1987, 1990; Morton, 1969, 1970; see also Goldinger et al., 1989). In this model all lexical competitors resembling the stimulus word have an activation level, or probability of being chosen as the percept, which is a function of their similarity to the stimulus word, and of their text frequency. For largely overlapping alternatives, the pedictions of the model are the same, whether or not the active elements laterally inhibit one another (see Bard, 1990), because lateral inhibition can only affect the speed with which activation-based competition resolves, and not the relative availability of the final percept. In fact, the predictions hold whether the perceptual decision rule is a Luce (1959) rule, in which the target word must be responsible for a criterial proportion of all activation, or a race rule, which depends on the difference between target activation and activation of most frequent lexical competitor (Marslen-Wilson, 1990).

This model has the advantage of parsimony over the other possible models. It requires no special mechanism to determine the most active competitor or to suppress more active competitors. Nor does it demand separate mechanisms to account for the effects of the frequency of the stimulus word itself, and the effects of the set of competitors. With few embellishments, this model will account for the standard results, including some attributed to other mechanisms.

Among the standard results, the effects of stimulus frequency are the original motivation for this model: rare words will take longer to recognise than frequent words, because they rise in activation more slowly and because their competitors may be a good deal more frequent and a good deal more active (Marslen-Wilson, 1990). Effects of the frequency of competitors to the stimulus derive from the same mechanism.

Because of the distribution of text frequencies in sets of lexical competitors, the Universal Frequency Franchise model will account for the effects which gave rise to various versions of the Frequency Dictatorship model. It accommodates the demonstration by Grainger et al. (1989) and Grainger (1990) that the most frequent item in a neighbourhood is more easily recognised than any less frequent neighbour, while the ranking of the stimulus among less frequent neighbours is unimportant. The most frequent neighbour is, as we have shown, likely to have the maximum advantage in frequency-based activation over any other word in its orthographic neighbourhood. The frequency advantage available to any other neighbour over any third will be small in comparison. For these same reasons, the present model also predicts Marslen-Wilson's (1990) finding that the detrimental effect of the most frequent competitor will depend on its absolute frequency.

The Universal Frequency Franchise model can also account for those effects of cohort size or neighbourhood density which are usually attributed to the model we have called Universal Franchise. Whatever the shape of frequency distributions, larger competitor sets should on average produce greater total frequency-based activation. In the positively skewed distributions we have examined, the larger sets are associated with more potent individual competitors because they contain more high frequency words and outliers of higher frequency. In some cases, mean frequency will also be greater for larger sets. As a result, whenever special care is not taken to separate these variables, effects of size may turn out to be attributable to frequency. Even when it is an experimenter's express intention to manipulate frequency and density independently, artefacts may persist. Both Fig. 12.9 and Fig. 12.13 suggest that it will be extremely difficult to find any large competitor set with such a low maximum frequency than it provides no strong competitor under Universal Frequency Franchise. Smaller cohorts, while allowing a great range of maxima and means, tend towards lower means and lower maxima (Fig. 12.6a). They will therefore tend to provide weaker competition.

Luce's (1986; Goldinger et al., 1989) fastidious attempts at separating set size (density) and mean frequency show how difficult it is to outsmart the lexical statistics. First, Luce split phonologically based neighbourhoods into dense and sparse groups at the median of all neighbourhood sizes, while also splitting them into rare and frequent groups at the median of all average neighbourhood frequencies. If neighbourhoods resemble cohorts in their division of sizes (see Fig. 12.3), then there are likely to be more small neighbourhoods than large, so that division at the median size offers a smaller size range for sparse than for dense competitor sets (median cohort size is about 14, whereas the top of the size range is over 1000). But very small cohorts have lower mean frequencies in general than do larger cohorts (see Table 12.1). As a result, the sparse neighbourhoods should be low frequency neighbourhoods, and sparse neighbourhoods which are also below the grand median of neighbourhood frequencies ought to have lower means than the dense neighbourhoods which are also categorised as low frequency. Indeed, in Luce's materials, neighbourhood density and frequency correlate highly (Luce, 1986, p. 13).

In a later study, Luce tried to select neighbourhoods which would match density across frequency categories, and match frequency across density categories, while not selecting from those which were close to the median in either ranking. Again, if neighbourhoods resemble cohorts (Fig. 12.6a), the larger ones have a restricted range of mean frequencies, so that only competitor sets near the frequency median are likely to be matchable across the size range. Room for experimental manoeuvre is limited. More recent treatment of the density issue (Goldinger et al., 1989) has succumbed to the nature of the lexicon: only the dense-frequent *vs* sparse-rare contrast is used. If density and frequency are related, and both measures are examined, then either may show a statistical effect properly belonging to the other. The varied outcomes on density and frequency may all turn out to be due to Universal Frequency Franchise.

The version of Universal Frequency Franchise put forward here is intentionally simple and lexically based. The most serious challenges to it are due to evidence for more complex mechanisms and non-lexical bases of responding. Universal Frequency Franchise seems able to survive these.

One more complex mechanism is post-recognition 'damping' of strong lexical competitors (Segui & Grainger, 1990). Segui and Grainger (1990) found that visually presented rare words inhibit visual lexical decision for their more frequent orthographic neighbours presented 350ms later, whereas frequent primes have no effect at the same ISI. The experimenters attribute this effect to a mechanism which suppresses the important higher frequency competitors, so that a lower frequency word can be recognised, for with premasking and at an ISI of 60ms, subjects do not recognise primes, and rare primes do not delay lexical decision for frequent neighbours. Under a simple assumption about decay of activation, Universal Frequency Franchise can account for these results. Even without damping, competition at the lexical level can account for inhibition by primes which are still active while the target is being recognised, so long as recognition requires achieving dominant activation. So long as decay rates are either constant or proportional to rise rates, the reported inhibition may simply be delay in resolution of the competition in favour of the target in the presence of a still-active competitor. Rare primes should be recognised more slowly than frequent for reasons rehearsed earlier (see Goldinger et al. for a variant). At a short ISI, only frequent prime words should compete with related targets, and so delay their recognition, because only frequent words have had a chance to become highly activated. At a longer ISI, a frequent prime may have returned to its resting level, whereas a rare prime may still be sufficiently active to delay the recognition of the competitor represented by the ensuing target.

This, in summary, is what Segui and Grainger (1990) and Grainger (1990) found in a number of visual experiments comparing high frequency words with words of low and medium frequency.[9] Goldinger et al. (1989)

---

[9] In the experiments cited, rare prime words have been paired at 350ms ISI with only frequent probes, because the damping model deals with the suppression of the frequent probes. Our account predicts that rarer probes would also be inhibited, because it is the

have reported a similar result in the auditory modality: poorer recognition for words presented in noise when rare neighbours preceded targets at 50ms ISI, than when unrelated words did. Frequent primes did not have this effect. In an auditory experiment, if the probe word was presented 50ms after the offset of the prime, itself probably some 150–200ms long, the total onset-to-onset delay was not far from the longer, 350ms, visual ISI.

The second complication is one which we have already mentioned: the facilitation of recognition rather than its inhibition with increased size or frequency of competitor sets. With the exception of one visual lexical decision experiment (Andrews, 1989), these effects are all found when stimuli are presented visually for naming. All models of these effects attribute them to some kind of phonological or orthographic/phonological conspiracy: larger sets of visually similar words may include more words which are spelled similarly ('allies' in our terminology) and more which are both spelled and pronounced similarly ('friends'). There is no reason why Universal Frequency Franchise should preclude phonological effects. It should predict that the frequency of the target word, and of its friends and allies, will affect facilitation. This is certainly the case. Typically (Andrews, 1989; Jared et al., 1990) the stimuli subject to neighbourhood facilitation in naming are rare words, words which should on average be recognised at well below ceiling speeds and which should feed little frequency-based activation downwards from a lexical to an orthographic or phonological level. Moreover, Jared et al. have shown that it is the relative frequency of friends and enemies which determines the effects of neighbourhoods.

The third challenge comes from the proposal that sensory representations of words are not projected to active perceptual elements corresponding to individual words or morphs, but are distributed among a number of sites. In Seidenberg and McClelland's model (1989), a large set of orthographic words are presented during the training phase, each with a frequency derived from text frequency norms. The distributed representation of spelling-sound correspondences which the model develops inherits frequency effects, becoming more proficient at pairing spellings and sounds which co-occur in many words, in frequent words, or in both, and less proficient at pairings which are rare overall. Jared et al. argue against a discrete representation of individual lexical items in a lexical 'level', because in their experiments on consistency effects, only total frequency

---

prime frequency, not the probe frequency, which is critical. Experiments on different frequency combinations, summarised in Segui and Grainger (this volume), are gradually filling in the gaps in the paradigm, though not necessarily for any one language or orthographic system.

of friends and enemies was important in determining naming time: additional manipulation of number of neighbours had no effect. Of course, their argument bites only if lexical items are assumed to have an effect independent of their frequency-related activation. But under Universal Frequency Franchise, as set out in this chapter, there should be no effects for size of competitor set *per se*. Rather, as we have shown, the effects of lexical competitors can all be traced to their frequencies.

The work of Seidenberg and his colleagues on word reading may leave open the issue of whether lexical items should have individual representation in a mental lexicon. The presence of both facilitatory and inhibitory effects in lexical tasks suggests that there ought to be two kinds of mechanism. As we noted earlier, facilitation proportional to lexical competition indicates some kind of collusion among units corresponding to parts of words. Interference where more, or more common, alternate lexical percepts could be available points to competition among discrete word representations.[10] Universal Frequency Franchise allows for the effects of frequency of occurrence to be felt at a number of levels, and of all the lexical models, it is most free of the special mechanisms which distinguish lexical from distributed representation models of word recognition. For this reason, Universal Frequency Franchise shares with Seidenberg and McClelland's model an ability to reflect faithfully the characteristics of the mental lexicon which are captured by the Generalised Competitor Set Hypothesis.

Experimental comparison of the two models lies in the future, if it is possible at all. At present, what is important is the contribution made by accurate accounts of the text frequencies of sets of lexical competitors. The examples set out here indicate the kinds of simplifications available to

---

[10] A system in which there are both lexical and sub-lexical representations of words should produce inhibitory and facilitatory effects for the same word in different tasks. A *post hoc* analysis of Andrews' (1989) data comes close to showing this pattern: multiple regression analyses were run using target frequency, frequency of most frequent orthographic neighbour, and neighbourhood size, to predict both visual lexical decision times (for all 60 words, Multiple-$R^2 = 0.321$, $F = 8.82$, $df = 3, 56$, $p < 0.0001$; for the 30 rare words, Multiple-$R^2 = 0.268$, $F = 3.17$, $df = 3, 26$, $p < 0.05$) and immediate naming times (for all 60 words, Multiple-$R^2 = 0.260$, $F = 6.57$, $df = 3, 56$, $p < 0.0007$; for the 30 rare words, Multiple-$R^2 = 0.258$, $F = 3.02$, $df = 3, 26$, $p < 0.05$). Two predictor variables had consistent facilitatory effects across tasks: reaction time fell as stimulus frequency rose (even with neighbourhood size and maximum frequency in neighbourhood partialled out), and as neighbourhood size rose (even with stimulus and maximum frequency partialled out). The role of the most frequent competitor differed across response measures, however. In the naming task, stimuli with more frequent outliers produced faster responses, just as we would expect if the outlier functioned as an ally with a strength proportional to its frequency. In the lexical decision task, stimuli with more extreme outliers yielded slower responses. The outlier now appears to be a competitor.

models of lexical access which make use of the nature of the lexicon. The distribution of word frequencies in that lexicon, and the random partitioning of the lexicon into sets of lexical competitors, allow us to avoid many of the special mechanisms which might otherwise seem necessary to explain how listeners and readers recognise words. What other behaviours may also be explained more simply in the light of the distributions explored here remains to be seen.

ACKNOWLEDGEMENTS

This work was supported to an ESRC IRC grant to the University of Edinburgh and by ESRC Project Grant ROOOO 23 1396 to the authors. The authors are grateful to J.B.L. Bard, S.D. Isard, and D. Rutovitz for advice and assistance and to K. Forster, K. Stenning, and S. Garrod for helpful criticism. Any remaining errors are our own. Reprint requests should be sent to the first author at the Human Communication Research Centre, University of Edinburgh, 2 Buccleuch Place, Edinburgh EH8 9LW, U.K.

REFERENCES

Andrews, S. (1989). Frequency and neighbourhood effects on lexical access: Activation or search? *Journal of Experimental Psychology: Learning, Memory, and Cognition, 15*, 802–814.

Bard, E.G. (1990). Competition, lateral inhibition, and frequency: Comments on the papers of Frauenfelder and Peeters, Marslen-Wilson, and others. In G.T.M. Altmann (Ed.), *Cognitive models of speech processing: Psycholinguistic and computational perspectives.* Cambridge, MA: MIT Press.

Brown, G.D.A. (1987). Constraining interactivity: Evidence from acquired dyslexia. *Proceedings of the Ninth Annual Conference of the Cognitive Science Society.* (pp. 779–793). Hillsdale, NJ: Lawrence Erlbaum Associates Inc.

Carroll, J.B. (1967). On sampling from a lognormal model of word frequency distribution. In H. Kučera & W.N. Francis, (Eds.), *Computational analysis of present day American English,* (pp. 406–24). Providence, RI: Brown University Press.

Carroll, J.B., Davies, P., & Richman, B. (1971). *The American heritage word frequency book.* New York: American Heritage.

Coltheart, M. (1981). The MRC psycholinguistic database. *Quarterly Journal of Experimental Psychology, 33A*, 497–505.

Coltheart, M., Davelaar, E., Jonasson, J.T., & Besner, D. (1977). Access to the internal lexicon. In S. Dornic (Ed.), *Attention and performance VI* (pp. 535–555). New York: Academic Press.

Eldridge, R.C. (1911). *Six thousand common English words.* Buffalo: The Clement Press.

Forster, K.I. (1976). Accessing the mental lexicon. In R.J. Wales & E.W. Walker (Eds.), *New approaches to language mechanisms.* Amsterdam: North-Holland.

Frauenfelder, U., & Peeters, G. (1990). On lexical segmentation in TRACE: An exercise in simulation. In G.T.M. Altmann (Ed.), *Cognitive models of speech processing: Psycholinguistic and computational perspectives.* Cambridge, MA: MIT Press.

Gardner, M.K., Rothkopf, E.Z., Lapan, R., & Lafferty, T. (1987). The word frequency effect in lexical decision: finding a frequency-based component. *Memory and Cognition,* *15*(1), 24–28.

Glushko, R.J. (1979). The organization and activation of orthographic knowledge in reading aloud. *Journal of Experimental Psychology: Human Perception and Performance, 5,* 674–691.

Goldinger, S., Luce, P., & Pisoni, D. (1989). Priming lexical neighbours of spoken words effects of competition and inhibition. *Journal of Memory and Language. 28,* 501–518.

Grainger, J. (1990). Word frequency and neighbourhood frequency effects in lexical decision and naming. *Journal of Memory and Language, 29,* 228–244.

Grainger, J., O'Regan, J., Jacobs, A.M., & Segui, J. (1989). On the role of competing word units in visual word recognition: The neighbourhood frequency effect. *Perception and Psychophysics, 45*(3), 189–195.

Guierre, L. (1966). Un codage des mots anglais en vue de l'analyse automatique de leur structure phonetique. *Etudes de Linguistique Appliquee, 4,* 48–64.

Gunther, H., & Greese, B. (1985). Lexical hermits and the pronunciation of visually presented words. *Forschungsberichte des Instituts für Phonetik und Sprachliche Kommunikation des Universität München, 21,* 25–52.

Jakimik, J. (1979). *The interaction of sound and knowledge in word recognition from fluent speech.* Unpublished doctoral dissertation, Carnegie-Mellon University.

Jared, D., McRae, K., & Seidenberg, M. (1990). The basis of consistency effects in word naming. *Journal of Memory and Language, 29,* 687–715.

Kučera, H., & Francis, W.N. (1967). *A computational analysis of present-day American English.* Providence, RI: Brown University Press.

Landauer, T., & Streeter, L. (1973). Structural differences between common and rare words: failure of equivalence assumptions for theories of word recognition. *Journal of Verbal Learning and Verbal Behavior, 12,* 119–131.

Luce, P. (1986). Neighbourhoods in the mental lexicon. *Research on Speech Perception Technical Report No. 6.* Bloomington, Indiana: Dept. of Psychology, Speech Research Laboratory, Indiana University.

Luce, R.D. (1959). *Individual choice behaviour.* New York: Wiley.

McClelland, J., & Elman, J. (1986). The TRACE model of speech perception. *Cognitive Psychology, 18,* 1–86.

McRae, K., Jared, D., & Seidenberg, M. (1990). On the roles of frequency and lexical access in word naming. *Journal of Memory and Language, 29,* 43–65.

Marslen-Wilson, W. (1987). Functional parallelism in spoken word-recognition. *Cognition,* *25,* 71–102.

Marslen-Wilson, W. (1990). Activation, competition, and frequency in lexical access. In G.T.M. Altmann (Ed.), *Cognitive models of speech processing: Psycholinguistic and computational perspectives.* Cambridge, MA: MIT Press.

Miller, G. (1965). Introduction to G.K. Zipf, *The psycho-biology of language: An introduction to dynamic philology* (pp. v–x). Cambridge, MA: MIT Press.

Monsell, S., Doyle, M., & Haggard, P. (1989). Effects of frequency on visual word recognition tasks—where are they. *Journal of Experimental Psychology: General, 118*(1), 43–71.

Morton, J. (1969). Interaction of information in word recognition. *Psychological Review,* *76,* 165–78.

Morton, J. (1970). A functional model for memory. In D.S. Norman (Ed.), *Models of human memory.* New York: Academic Press.

Scheerer, E. (1987). Visual word recognition in German. In D.A. Allport, D. Mackay, W. Prinz, & E. Scheerer (Eds.), *Language perception and production: Shared mechanisms in listening, speaking, reading and writing* (pp. 227–244). London: Academic Press.

Segui, J., & Grainger, J. (1990). Priming word recognition with orthographic neighbours: Effects of relative prime-target frequency. *Journal of Experimental Psychology: Human Perception and Performance, 16*(1), 65–76.

Segui, J., & Grainger, J. (this volume). *An overview of neighbourhood effects in word recognition.*

Seidenberg, M., & McClelland, J. (1989). A distributed, developmental model of word recognition and naming. *Psychological Review, 96*, 523–568.

Shillcock, R. (1990). Lexical hypotheses in continuous speech. In G.T.M. Altmann (Ed.), *Cognitive models of speech processing: Psycholinguistic and computational perspectives.* Cambridge, MA: MIT Press.

Tabossi, P. (this volume). *Connections, competitions, and cohorts: Comments on the chapters by Norris, Bard and Shillcock, and Marslen-Wilson.*

Taraban, R., & McClelland, J.L. (1987). Conspiracy effects in word pronunciation. *Journal of Memory and Language, 26*, 608–631.

Zipf, G.K. (1932). *Selected studies of the principle of relative frequency in language.* Cambridge, MA: Harvard University Press.

Zipf, G.K. (1965). *The psycho-biology of language: An introduction to dynamic philology.* Boston: Houghton-Mifflin. Cambridge, MA: MIT Press. (Original work published 1935).

Zwitserlood, P. (1989). The locus of effects of sentential semantic context in spoken word processing. *Cognition, 32*, 25–64.

13

Connections, Competitions, and Cohorts: Comments on the Chapters by Marslen-Wilson; Norris; and Bard and Shillcock

Patrizia Tabossi
Universita' di Ferrara, Italy.

INTRODUCTION

The chapters by Norris, by Bard and Shillcock, and by Marslen-Wilson all deal with the processing of lexical information in continuous speech. They address, therefore, issues that are tightly interrelated and share much of the theoretical vocabulary currently employed in the field. The three chapters focus, however, on different aspects of this complex topic, and have rather different methodological approaches to it.

The chapter by Norris (Chapter 11) concerns notions such as interactivity, top-down, bottom-up, feedforward, and feedback, and aims to show that phenomena typically considered to require interactive processing can be handled by a model where the flow of information is strictly bottom-up, provided that the model is connectionist rather than of the traditional box-type. Far more specific is the chapter by Bard and Shillcock (Chapter 12), whose goal is to elucidate the notion of set of competitors. Roughly speaking, this refers to the lexical candidates that compete for recognition during the process of word identification. But which words do actually enter into a competitor set? Bard and Shillcock carry out a statistical investigation of the distribution of words and word frequencies, and suggest a hypothesis that appears to reconcile current and seemingly contradictory views on the issue. Finally, somewhat in between Norris' general claims on the flow of information in the cognitive system and Bard and Shillcock's specific discussion of an individual notion, is the chapter by Marslen-Wilson (Chapter 10), who presents his theory of spoken word recognition along with various pieces of empirical evidence in its support.

Given the relative heterogenity of these chapters, and their emphasis on different aspects of lexical processing, I will consider each of them separately. Needless to say, my comments are not intended as a review of the papers, but as a brief discussion of only a few issues, selected on entirely idiosyncratic grounds from the many raised in the chapters.

BOTTOM-UP CONNECTIONIST MODELS

In recent years, one of the liveliest debates in cognitive science has centred around two views of the functional architecture of the mind. According to the modular view, the cognitive system is made up of several largely autonomous modules, which operate as input systems, and a central processor, which integrates the outputs of those modules. Modular processes have several characteristics: they are assumed to function in a bottom-up fashion, are domain specific, mandatory, fast, informationally encapsulated, automatic, and associated with a fixed neural architecture (Fodor, 1983).

The opposite view emphasises, in contrast, the inherently interactive nature of the cognitive system, where top-down and bottom-up processes may operate together at all levels. Here, behaviour is not considered to be the result of a single component of the cognitive system, but as the product of many components, interacting with each other and together determining the behaviour of the system (Rumelhart, 1989).

Often intertwined with this dispute is the debate on connectionism and its relation to more traditional approaches to cognitive science (Broadbent, 1985; Fodor & Pylyshyn, 1988; Rumelhart & McClelland, 1985). On the one hand, there are those—typically in favour of modularity—who see connectionism as nothing more than a new way of implementing old theories. On the other hand, there are those—typically in favour of the interactive nature of the mind—who believe that connectionist theories are a genuinely new approach to cognition. Obviously this clearcut distinction oversimplifies matters in several ways, finessing the fact, for instance, that modularity and interactivity are no longer considered a dichotomy, but rather the two extremes of a continuum along which different processes may vary on their degree of autonomy, automacity, etc. (Tanenhaus, Dell, & Carlson, 1987). In addition, claims concerning the modularity/interactivity issue, and claims concerning connectionism, mix variously among researchers, giving place to almost all possible combinations. Roughly speaking, however, connectionism does hold an interactive view of the cognitive system, and indeed its debate with the modular approach has prompted much research.

So far, this work has not been very successful in discriminating between the two hypotheses, since scholars in both camps face the almost insoluble problem of demonstrating two negative claims. Modularists need to show that perceptual processes are not affected by other cognitive processes, whereas connectionists need to show that seemingly cognitive effects on perception do not take place within the perceptual system (Umilta', 1988).

There are data on word recognition, however, that have proven particularly challenging for the modular approach. Potentially troublesome for this view is the so called word superiority effect, i.e. a letter is easier to identify when it occurs in the context of a word (Johnston & McClelland, 1974; McClelland & Rumelhart, 1981). Similarly, an ambiguous phoneme in a spoken string is more likely to be perceived as one that makes it part of a word than of a nonword (Ganong, 1980). In both cases, letter/phoneme identification seems to be influenced by higher level lexical knowledge.

Even more difficult to reconcile with the modular hypothesis of lexical processing are the results of a study by Elman and McClelland (1988). They presented their subjects with stimulus pairs such as 'Christma* ?apes' and 'fooli* ?apes', where * indicates a phoneme ambiguous between /s/ (as in Christmas) or /ʃ/ (as in foolish), and ? indicates a stop consonant that is ambiguous between /k/ (as in capes) and /t/ (as in tapes). On presentation of a pair, the subjects had to decide whether the initial sound of the second word was a /k/ or a /t/. The results showed that the subjects reported 'capes' more often after 'Christma*' than after 'fooli*', whereas the reverse was true for 'tapes'. Again, these findings strongly suggest that lexical information influences phoneme identification, providing evidence for top-down, interactive effects in language processing.

In contrast with this interpretation, Norris's chapter shows that both word superiority and compensation for coarticulation can be dealt with by connectionist networks in which the flow of information is entirely bottom-up. The simpler network considered is a feedforward network with a single layer of hidden units, trained by back-propagation. Connections in the net are between input and hidden units, and between these and output nodes, with no flow of information from top-down.

Norris reports an experiment in which this simple feedforward net was trained in two steps. First it learnt to identify word inputs, and then to associate correct letter outputs to both word and nonword inputs. After training, when tested for letter identification, the network showed a better performance with word than with nonword inputs, thus exhibiting the word superiority effect, in spite of the absence of any top-down flow of information in its processing.

A recurrent, or dynamic, net is then presented in order to cope with Elman and McClelland's compensation for coarticulation (1988). This net is analogous to the network initially proposed by Jordan (1986) for the production of sequences, and subsequently modified by Elman (1988) for comprehension. Compared to the simple feedforward network, the new recurrent net still has only one layer of hidden units that receive activation from the input units and send activation to the output units. In addition, however, hidden units are also connected to one another with links that have a time delay.

After training, during which pairs of words were never given in the same order as in the test phase, the ability of the recurrent net to recognise pairs similar to those used by Elman and McClelland (1988) was tested. Again, it produced results comparable to Elman and McClelland's subjects: the identification of the first word influenced the net's recognition of the second one, in spite of the fact that in this model the flow of information is always bottom-up.

According to Norris, these models prove two points. First, they show that connectionism is more than another system for computational description. In fact, if it were just a new way of implementing 'classical' theories, the connectionist and the box-type frameworks should lead to similar theoretical conclusions. Instead, the dynamic net shows that phenomena like compensation for coarticulation, while calling for an interactive explanation in the framework of box-models, do not necessarily require such an explanation in the connectionist framework, which indeed changes our theoretical approach to the mind.

Second, on the modularity/interactivity issue, which in the area of word recognition is instantiated as the problem of deciding whether lexical and nonlexical processes interact or not, the dynamic net shows that Elman and McClelland's results are not definitive evidence for interaction between lexical and phonemic processing. In the net's structure, in fact, the phoneme and word nodes don't interact, and the processing is bottom-up.

Although I agree entirely with Norris's conclusion on the first point, I find the second more questionable. In particular, the nets considered here demonstrate that the connectionist framework is powerful enough to allow phenomena such as word superiority or compensation for coarticulation to be obtained in models where the flow of information is both bottom-up and top-down, as well as in models in which the flow of information is only bottom-up. But whether, in addition, the dynamic net also provides a plausible feedforward model of spoken word recognition is less clear.

Norris does compare the nets considered here with their most obvious interactive alternatives, IAM (McClelland & Rumelhart, 1981) and TRACE (McClelland & Elman, 1986), pointing out the advantages of his models. One advantage is that unlike the other models, the dynamic net does not have a hierarchical structure. TRACE, for instance, has three distinct levels: features, phonemes, and words. The phoneme level, however, neither has a direct output—a further component must be added to the model in order to read out the phonemic information—nor is it necessary for TRACE to perform word and phoneme identification. Compared to

TRACE, the internal structure of the dynamic net is easier: it has only a single layer of hidden units that learn to mediate correctly between input and output, no matter what kind of representations they develop during training. Also, it does not need an extra output component for phonemes, which are treated by the dynamic net in the same way as word units. Furthermore, unlike its interactive alternatives, the dynamic net is a learning system, so that behaviours do not need to be built into it, but are 'spontaneously' exhibited by it after the training phase.

These considerations would render the dynamic net not only comparable, but indeed preferable, to the interactive models, provided that they were equally plausible as theories of word recognition. But how plausible is the dynamic net in this respect? In its simple version, for example, it is not clear how it could avoid producing outputs in which a nonword input is at the same time spelt correctly and misidentified as a real word, or conversely a word input is identified correctly and spelt wrongly. These effects would correspond to behaviours where a person presented with DAR reports seeing the word CAR spelled D A R, or presented with CAR recognises it, but reads it out as D A R or C O R.

Moreover, Norris draws several comparisons between training procedures in his model and learning. Thus, in the first simulation of the simple net, he claims that the first part of the training was designed to represent teaching a child to recognise words, while not giving any feedback about identities of the letters within those words. Likewise, the second part of the learning procedure was designed to represent training on identifying letters of the alphabet. But if training is to be considered for the implications it has for human learning, one might wonder what processes the training of the sequential net could be compared with. Here, the net had to learn how to identify words from a continuous input. This was achieved by training the net to associate for each input phoneme the word it belonged to: if the word to be presented was CORNER, for instance, during training the net was made to associate each of its phonemes starting from the initial /k/ to the target only, regardless of the fact that items such as CORONER or CORONET were also words in the model. But what learning processes could this training correspond to?

Although on several occasions in this chapter and elsewhere (Norris, 1990) Norris argues for the psychological plausibility of the dynamic net, probably his main concern is to show that it is not impossible for a bottom-up, non-interactive model to deal with phenomena such as word superiority and compensation for coarticulation.

His argument for the non interactivity of the dynamic net is as follows. Typically, in order for a system to be interactive, there must be two or more identifiable processes at different stages that may interact under some conditions. As in other PDP models, however, it is not possible to identify a series of separate, discrete processes in the dynamic net, to which, therefore, the issue of interactivity does not apply.

However, whether a stimulating aspect of PDP models, or a severe limitation to the relevance of these systems for our comprehension of the mind, these processing characteristics, in my view, do not justify the conclusion that the dynamic net is not interactive. As Norris points out, in fact, the absence of discrete stages in the dynamic net can simply indicate that the whole system is interactive. Moreover, he also correctly notes that whether a system is interactive or not depends on the level of granularity at which we describe it, i.e. how many modules we posit. The level Norris chooses, however, is that of lexical and sublexical processing, and we know that the dynamic net operates on objects—units and connections—which incorporate simultaneously knowledge pertaining to both the phoneme/letter and word domain. Hence, lexical and sublexical information is not 'encapsulated', but rather locked together in the dynamic net, which thus fails—it seems to me—a crucial test for modularity.

But even assuming that the dynamic net were able to cope with the intended phenomena non interactively, the possibility of the system working in a non-modular way must still be permitted. During the learning phase, in fact, the error term must be propagated down the network, and, as Norris notes, that back-propagation, by its nature, involves top-down flow of information. Hence, the relevant question is not so much whether the cognitive system can produce certain phenomena non interactively and in a strictly bottom-up fashion, but whether or when this way is preferable.

In the same vein, Norris interestingly observes that to date back-propagation networks operate in a feedforward manner. In Seidenberg and McClelland's model of word recognition and naming (1989), for example, the orthographic output is computed on the basis of the activation of the hidden units, whose activation, in turn, is determined by the activation of the input units, and nowhere in the system does information from a higher level enter into the computation of the activation of a lower one. Thus, although the figures in Seidenberg and McClelland's paper give the impression that in their model the orthographic output is fed back to the input, a careful reading of the text reveals that this is not the case. But does this fact change the interactive nature of the theory implemented in that model? In my view, if one has to take seriously Seidenberg and McClelland's claim on the interaction between phonology and orthography, or between these and the semantic level, none of which is actually implemented in the model, their theory is indeed both feed-back and interactive. There are, no doubt, many and well-known problems related to the theoretical interpretation of computational models, and the increasing complexity of connectionist nets is not going to facilitate matters. It seems to me, however, that these difficulties should not induce either proponents or recipients of theories and computational models to overlook the fact that they are different objects, and relations among them are not usually as straightforward as one might wish.

The view I am advocating here is one that does not consider interactivity and modularity as alternatives, but as approaches that both capture important aspects of the cognitive system. Consequently, my preferences are for those studies that try to specify under what circumstances one or the other of these possibilities is actually exploited by the system, whereas Norris's paper, aimed at defending bottom-up non interactive models against the challenge of new pieces of evidence, appears to me more an exercise in computing than an attempt at elucidating psychological mechanisms.

Admittedly, however, my biases would easily lead me to take phenomena like word superiority and compensation of coarticulation at their face value, whereas it is a merit of work such as Norris's to remind me—and perhaps others—that, in psychology at least, data never speak for themselves.

DEFINING COMPETITORS AND GENERALISING FROM DICTIONARIES TO THE MENTAL LEXICON

Bard and Shillcock call our attention to a well known and yet usually ignored property of the vocabulary of a language: frequency is not normally distributed across the lexicon, so that most words are low frequency and only few are high frequency (Zipf, 1932). Thus, the probability of randomly picking up a low frequency word from a dictionary is much higher than the probability of picking up a high frequency word.

Bard and Shillcock show that this fact holds not only for the vocabulary at large, but also for the sets of lexical competitors that are activated during the process of recognition of a word. The typical frequency distribution of these sets, in fact, is not normal. Rather they tend to be positively skewed, containing many low frequency words and only one or two very frequent items, which are clearly outliers in the distribution. In addition, frequency distribution correlates positively with the size of sets, so that the larger the set, the higher is its probability of exhibiting that distribution.

In the light of this analysis, Bard and Shillcock discuss what constitutes a set of competitors, and argue that their hypothesis, according to which all competitors are effective in proportion to their frequency, can in fact be reconciled with two otherwise conflicting claims (and related data).

One of these views holds that only the most frequent word in the set competes with the target for identification (Brown, 1987; Grainger, O'Regan, Jacobs, & Segui, 1989). The second hypothesis states, in contrast, that all words similar to the target compete with it, and hence a crucial factor in word identification is the size of the competitor set (Frauenfelder & Peeters, 1990; Luce, 1986a).

But as Bard and Shillcock point out, the former alternative is mutually exclusive with their own only insofar as the frequency distribution of the competitors in a set is normal. If, however, the frequency distribution is skewed with one very frequent outlier, both hypotheses will converge on attributing to this element the largest effect on the identification of the target. As for the second hypothesis, since there is a correlation between size of a set and frequency of its most frequent members, apparent size effects are probably artifactual and reflect the fact that high frequency words are more likely to be found in larger sets than in smaller ones.

This argument, which, if correct, will reconcile a rather heterogeneous set of data, rests on two crucial assumptions. First, although Bard and Shillcock's investigation concentrates on sets that include words with the same initial part up to the first vowel, the distributional characteristics of these sets can be generalised to others built with different criteria. Second, the distributional characteristics of the dictionary reflect those of the mental lexicon.

In support of the former assumption, Bard and Shillcock argue that the set of word onsets in English closely resembles the set of all syllable onsets in the language, and the set of initial-syllable nuclei is more or less the set of syllable nuclei. Accordingly, the consequence ought to be that using the onsets or nuclei of other syllables as additional keys to partitioning the lexicon should give the same results.

In addition, they analyse the sets used by Andrews (1989) in a study on visual word recognition, where competitors were defined as those words that shared with the target all but one letter. Though built in a completely different way, Andrews' competitor sets had the same distributional characteristics as those based on word initials.

Although, in my view, it is still an open empirical question whether the properties of word-initial competitor sets will hold for sets where similarity is assessed in terms of individual phonemes (Luce, 1986a), I think Bard and Shillcock's arguments do support the generalisation from the sets they have considered to a large class of other possible sets, in particular those based on various types of syllabic, subsyllabic, or morphemic segmentation.

More problematic, in my opinion, is the second assumption, according to which properties of the dictionary reflect properties of the mental lexicon. It is well known, in fact, that people do not know all the words of their language, but only some subset of them. Seashore and Eckerson (1940), for example, found that American college students knew an average 150,000 of the 450,000 entries in the *New Standard Dictionary of the English Language.* Although this corresponds approximately to only one third of the words listed in that dictionary, it is now generally agreed that Seashore and Eckerson's estimate was largely in excess, and an educated English speaker knows on average something between 50,000 to 100,000 words.

Regardless of the accuracy of those figures, it is a fact that speakers normally know far fewer words than there are in their language. Hence, in the mental lexicon, sets of competitors will be smaller, and small sets will be more numerous, than in a dictionary. Bard and Shillcock show, however, that whereas larger sets approximate nicely to the dictionary distribution, smaller sets are very variable. Thus, if the number of small sets turns out to be high—in the corpus analysed by Bard and Shillcock, sets with less than ten competitors are 43.9%—this might severely limit the possibility of generalising from the lexicon at large to sets of competitors.

In addition, compared to a dictionary, one's mental lexicon is likely to include a higher percentage of high frequency words and a lower percentage of low frequency ones. Eliminating extreme low frequency items from the lexicon, however, might also affect skewedness, which is determined as the ratio between (mean–mode) and standard deviation, possibly reducing it on occasions.

These considerations need not be particularly troublesome for Bard and Shillcock, who carried out their investigation on the MRC Psycholinguistic Database (Coltheart, 1981). This corpus contains 98,538 entries, 33,504 of which correspond to the unique transcriptions actually considered by Bard and Shillcock. This number of word forms is well within the range of lexical knowledge of an educated English speaker, and might be a reasonable approximation of the lexical repertoire available to people. Dictionaries, however, are often based on principles that do not necessarily match psychological criteria. The *Oxford Advanced Learner's Dictionary of Current English* (Hornby, 1974), for instance, contains only 60,000 entries including homographs and homophones—but no derivatives or compounds —yet it includes items such as 'kookaburra', 'wadi', 'eon', and many others that are unlikely to be familiar to most English speakers. Thus, it is an open empirical matter to what extent Bard and Shillcock's claims do apply to the mental lexicon.[1]

With this proviso, however, I think that Bard and Shillcock give us an interesting way of reconciling various pieces of evidence. Moreover, we all

---

[1] Bard and Shillcock (personal communication) report that if all the words in the lexicon with 0 frequency are removed, the correlations change very little. Over all sets of competitors which then have more than one member, the correlation between set size and text frequency of the most frequent item is still 0.374 ($df = 607$, $p < 0.0001$), and the correlation between mean text frequency of a set and its size is 0.567 ($n = 609$, $p < 0.0001$).

know how crucial the selection of materials is in determining results in most areas of psycholinguistic research. One of the problems is assessing the generality of findings obtained with one specific set of materials. With respect to precisely this difficulty, Bard and Shillcock develop a tool that is potentially very useful in helping us to evaluate how well the fast increasing evidence on neighbourhood effects may generalise to words other than the necessarily small samples considered in specific studies.

THE PSYCHOLOGICAL STATUS OF WORD ONSETS

The most popular set of competitors in the field of spoken word recognition is the cohort. In fact, the idea itself of set of competitors is largely modelled after the notion of the cohort, first proposed and then modified in various ways by Marslen-Wilson and his colleagues. In this section I discuss one particular aspect—the status of word onsets—of the processing theory that forms the backdrop of Marslen-Wilson's chapter.

The cohort theory has undergone numerous and sometimes substantial changes (Lahiri & Marslen-Wilson, 1991; Marslen-Wilson, 1987; Marslen-Wilson & Welsh, 1978). The hypotheses concerning the representation of information in the mental lexicon have changed, and so has the way in which the theory envisages context effects. However, one aspect that has not changed is that spoken word recognition is conceived as a fast process that starts as soon as the processor receives the acoustic/phonetic information corresponding to the beginning of the word. According to the cohort theory, the onset of a word plays a fundamental role in its recognition. In fact, the cohort of lexical candidates against which the target word will eventually win the competition for identification is formed on the basis of the perceptual information provided by the initial part of the word. Moreover, a necessary presupposition implicit in this view, it seems to me, is the idea that the processor uses perceptual information chiefly in a sequential, left to right fashion. In fact, since the onset of a word is so critical in initiating its recognition, it is fundamental that the listener routinely has that information available on-line. That is to say, on most occasions at the onset of a new word the listener has already correctly segmented the preceding stream of speech, and used that information to identify the prior lexical item (Frauenfelder & Peeters, 1990; but see Shillcock, 1990).

Marslen-Wilson and Zwitserlood (1989) address the role of word onsets in a study in which their subjects listened to an item and then performed a lexical decision task on a string presented at the offset of the auditory prime. In the critical cases the string was always a word (e.g. BIJ, Dutch for BEE). The auditory prime was either an associate of the target (e.g.

'honing', Dutch for 'honey'), or a semantically unrelated word rhyming with the associate prime (e.g. 'woning', Dutch for 'dwelling'), or a rhyming nonword (e.g. 'foning'), or a control word (e.g. 'pakket', Dutch for 'parcel') or nonword (e.g. 'dakket'). The results showed that the target was responded to significantly faster after the associate prime than after any of the other conditions, which did not differ from one another in speed of response.

According to the authors, these results suggest that word onsets do indeed have a special status in the process of word recognition, in activating a lexical hypothesis. If the criterion to enter a cohort, and hence to become a candidate for recognition, is similarity, at least the semantically unrelated word rhyming with the associate prime should facilitate the target. As Marslen-Wilson and Zwitserlood point out (1989, p. 578): 'if the simple amount of matching input is the critical variable in determining amount of activation, then the rhyming stimulus like "woning" should facilitate responses to BIJ at least as much as a stimulus like "kapi" should facilitate responses to GELD and BOOT'. 'Kapi' is an example of the initial fragment of the priming words 'kapitaal' and 'kapitein' (Dutch for 'capital' and 'captain') that, in a crossmodal priming study (Zwitserlood, 1989), have been found to facilitate lexical decision on targets associated to either completion (e.g. GELD and BOOT, Dutch for GOLD and BOAT). Because 'honing' and 'woning' share, like 'kapitaal' and 'kapitein', about 4.5 segments, and what changes is whether these segments are at the beginning or at the end of the words, if position is irrelevant, one should find, as in Zwitserlood (1989), an equal facilitation of BIJ by 'woning' and 'foning'.

Unlike 'kapi', however, in Marslen-Wilson and Zwitserlood (1989) the rhyming primes are not shared fragments of different words. They are perfect, complete words of Dutch, which are semantically unrelated to the target. To keep the parallel, Marslen-Wilson and Zwitserlood's condition is probably more similar to the situation in Zwitserlood's study in which the target word was presented after the prime's uniqueness point. There, however, as in Marslen-Wilson and Zwitserlood (1989) and the bulk of the semantic priming literature, primes, while still facilitating their associated targets, no longer facilitated the targets associated with their competitors.

A further problem with Marslen-Wilson and Zwitserlood's (1989) study is that the acoustic primes are presented in isolation. This might obscure the fact that in continuous speech there may be no clear cues to the location of word onsets and offsets. In a list of isolated words, for instance, subjects never have to entertain the hypothesis that 'terrain' could be 'to rain' (Bard, 1990), which allows them the possibility of relying on strategies that would not be safe during comprehension of continuous speech.

The notion that onset plays a unique role in spoken word recognition has recently been challenged by various pieces of evidence, suggesting that parts other than word onsets are relevant to what gets activated in the lexicon (Nooteboom, 1981; Salasoo & Pisoni, 1985; Slowiaczek & Pisoni, 1986). Slowiaczek, Nusbaum, and Pisoni (1987) asked their subjects to identify target words embedded in noise. Targets could be preceded by primes that shared with their targets a number of phonemes ranging from none to all of them. The results showed an effect of phonological priming regardless of whether phonemes were shared from the beginning (e.g. target: STILL; prime: dream, sand, stamp, stiff, still) or from the end of the words (e.g. target: HAND, prime: fret, dried, send, sand, hand). Although these results would not be particularly relevant to Marslen-Wilson's assumption if they only reflected phonological priming, Slowiaczek et al. (1987) showed that the priming effect was largely, though not exclusively, lexical.

Also at odds with Marslen-Wilson's assumption are the results of a study by Shillcock (1990) who showed that in speech lexical activation is produced not only by word onsets, but also word endings. 'Trombone', for example, was found to facilitate the target RIB, which is semantically associated to its final part 'bone'.

As already noted, the Cohort Theory seems to assume that the process of word recognition operates sequentially from the word beginning. Related to this view is the assumption that more often than not listeners must be able to establish, as soon as they receive acoustic-phonetic information, when it corresponds to the onset of an upcoming word. The tenet, however, is not uncontroversial.

Luce (1986b) analysed a corpus of phonetic transcriptions of about 20,000 English words and found that a high percentage of short words—indeed, most frequent words in English are short—are not uniquely identifiable until some time after their offset. Though overlooking the importance of syntactic, semantic, and prosodic cues, Luce's analysis of isolated words is more likely to under- rather than overestimate the problem of segmentation, entirely finessing all the temporary ambiguities that arise from embedding words in fluent speech. Moreover, the difficulty of establishing word offsets on-line persists in sentential contexts and is observed even in studies that use the gating technique and tend, therefore, to encourage guessing strategies in the subjects (Grosjean, 1985; Grosjean & Gee, 1987).

The major difficulty that this evidence poses to the Cohort Theory is not related, in my view, to the notion of earliness of word recognition. In fact, as Marslen-Wilson (1987, p. 76) points out, '"late selection" does not constitute a problem for theories, like the Cohort Model, which emphasise the real-time nature of the word-recognition process . . . Activation-based versions of the Cohort Model . . . function equally well independent of whether the critical sensory information arrives before or after the word boundary . . .'

If, however, the processor operates sequentially and receives the acoustic-phonetic information relative to an upcoming word while still engaged in the 'selection' of the preceding one, how can it identify that information on-line as word initial and use it to build the cohort that is so crucial to recognising the new word?

Since it is usually acknowledged that early recognition is more problematic with function and short content words, Donia Scott, Cristina Burani and I (Tabossi, Scott, & Burani, 1991) have recently made an attempt to explore the scope of the problem by looking at polysyllabic content words. To this end, we selected Italian trisyllabic words (e.g. 'visite', Italian for 'visits') with embedded bisyllabic words (e.g. 'visi', Italian for 'faces') to use as primes in a cross-modal priming study. For each of these words we also selected a semantically associated or related target (e.g. PARENTI, Italian for RELATIVES). Three sentences were then constructed: one sentence contained the longer word (Appropriate condition); another sentence contained the shorter word followed by a word whose first syllable matched the last syllable of the longer word (Inappropriate condition); the third sentence was an unrelated control (Control condition). The following Italian example along with its verbatim English translation illustrates the three experimental conditions:

Appropriate condition   Le circostanze rendevano inevitabili visite* di altri membri della commissione.
(The circumstances rendered inevitable visits of other members of the committee.)

Inappropriate condition   Le circostanze rendevano inevitabili visi te*diati e stanchi.
(The circumstances rendered inevitable faces bored and tired.)

Control condition   Le circostanze rendevano inevitabili vendite* di altri immobili.
(The circumstances rendered inevitable sales of other real estate.)

At the point in time marked by *, the subjects were presented with the visual target PARENTI, on which they performed a lexical decision task. The predictions were as follows. The appropriate condition should facilitate the target and hence give faster reaction times than the control condition where no word in the sentence primes the target. In the inappropriate condition, there is a potential lexical hypothesis which includes all of 'visi' and the first syllable of 'tediati'. If the processor activates this 'visite' lexical hypothesis, then the materials in the appropriate condition should effectively prime the target PARENTI, just the same as the appropriate one.

The results supported this prediction, suggesting that even following two-syllable words the processor may still be considering lexical hypotheses that span the two-syllable word and some part of the next word.

As Marslen-Wilson (personal communication) has pointed out, however, there is an alternative explanation of these results: the facilitation of the target in the inappropriate condition could reflect the residual activation of 'visite' that only gradually disappears after the recognition of 'visi' has already taken place and the processing of 'tediati' has started. 'Visite' is in the cohort initiated by 'visi'. The second experiment in the study deals with this possibility. Here, in the inappropriate condition the word following the bisyllable prime did not maintain the ambiguity with the trisyllabic one, as illustrated in the following example:

Inappropriate condition   Le circostanze rendevano inevitabili visi se*ri e stanchi.
(The circumstances rendered inevitable faces serious and tired.)

If in Experiment 1 the priming effect in the inappropriate condition is due to the residual activation of 'visite', i.e. a member of the cohort activated during the process of recognition of 'visi', the same activation should be observed here in the inappropriate condition. If, in contrast, the results in Experiment 1 reflect the continued processing of the input matching the lexical hypothesis 'visite', then in Experiment 2 the inappropriate condition, which no longer maintains the strong corresponding to 'visite', should not prime the target. Reaction times to PARENTI in this condition should therefore be significantly slower than in the appropriate condition.

This is in fact what we found. Here, the control and inappropriate conditions did not differ significantly from each other, but were both reliably slower than the appropriate condition. The priming found in the first experiment was not residual priming from 'visite' being in the 'visi' cohort. Instead, subjects in the first experiment seem to have been continuing with at least one lexical hypothesis after the end of the intended word.

These results are problematic for the Cohort Model only insofar as it embraces a sequential view of speech recognition. Nothing in the present evidence, in fact, rules out the possibility that if the processor receives the acoustic-phonetic information from the onset of the next word while there is still a viable hypothesis involving the preceding one, it can activate the new cohort while still assessing the viability of the hypothesis that spans the two words. Admittedly, this view of speech processing is not incompatible, in principle, with the Cohort Theory. However, the immediate availability of word onsets is always taken for granted in the model, and no reference is ever made to the possibility that pieces of speech other than word onsets can generate cohorts. This suggests a sequential, left to right view of speech processing, and the present data may pose problems for this view.

Even so, we do misunderstand every now and then, and showing that the processing system may go wrong under some very peculiar circumstances, as in the study just described, is neither surprising nor challenging for any model of word recognition. What is of interest, instead, is to know how common the phenomenon demonstrated here with artificially created stimulus materials is in natural language, and whether or not there are reliable acoustic cues to segmentation.

Indeed, various studies suggest that detecting word onsets on the basis of purely sequential information may be problematic on many occasions; there are unlikely to be any completely reliable cues to segmentation. First, some evidence indicates that segmenting spoken English in a left to right fashion is a rather challenging task (Bond & Garnes, 1979; Browman, 1980; Pollack & Pickett, 1964). Second, it has been shown that in spontaneous speech subsequent context is involvd in the recognition of preceding words in a substantial number of cases (Bard, Shillcock, & Altmann, 1988). Third, languages are likely to differ in the cues they provide to listeners. Thus, in a so-called stress-timed language like English, it is possible that people learn to take advantage of the dichotomy between strong and weak syllables to develop a strategy that allows them to detect word junctures reasonably successfully on the basis of sequential acoustic/ phonetic cues (Cutler & Norris, 1988). (For a discussion of the reliability of this strategy, cf. Bard, 1990.)

In Italian, the ability of listeners to correctly detect junctures between syllables or words on the basis of the perceptual input seems to be much poorer than that of listeners of English (Agard & Di Pietro, 1965). Successful detection is so low as to justify the suggestion (Bertinetto, 1981, p. 218) that 'the acoustic input provides so little cues to segmentation, that under normal circumstances, recognition relies mostly on semantic redundancy (both linguistic and situational) of the message, rather than on the presence of particular junctural cues. In the absence of such hints the utterance tends to show a high degree of ambiguity.'

Admittedly, psycholinguistic evidence on segmentation in Italian is still very limited, and to claim that in this, and presumably other languages with similar characteristics, listeners do not have sufficient cues to develop on-line perceptual strategies to detect word boundaries would be premature. However, in my view there are reasons to indicate that the problem of speech segmentation is far from settled and whether word onsets are available on-line for lexical processing is still an open question.

ACKNOWLEDGEMENTS

The present research was supported by Fondi Ministeriali 40% and 60%. I would like to thank Ellen Bard, Pier Marco Bertinetto, Cristina Burani, Corrado Cavallero, Dennis Norris, William Marslen-Wilson, Sergio Scalise, and Arianna Uguzzoni for discussing some of the topics in this paper with me on several occasions.

REFERENCES

Agard, F.B., & Di Pietro, R.J. (1965). *The sounds of English and Italian.* Chicago: Chicago University Press.

Andrews, S. (1989). Frequency and neighbourhood effects on lexical access: Activation or search? *Journal of Experimental Psychology: Learning, Memory, and Cognition, 15,* 802–814.

Bard, E.G. (1990). Competition, lateral inhibition, and frequency: comments on the papers of Frauenfelder and Peeters, Marslen-Wilson, and others. In G.T.M. Altmann (Ed.), *Cognitive models of speech processing: Psycholinguistic and computational perspectives.* Cambridge, MA: MIT Press.

Bard, E.G., Shillcock, R.C., & Altmann, G.T.M. (1988). The recognition of words after their acoustic offsets in spontaneous speech: Effects of subsequent context. *Perception and Psychophysics, 44,* 395–408.

Bertinetto, P.M. (1981). *Structure prosodiche dell'Italiano.* Firenze: Accademia della Crusca.

Bond, Z., & Garnes, S. (1979). Misperceptions of fluent speech. In R.A. Cole (Ed.), *Perception and production of fluent speech.* Hillsdale, NJ: Lawrence Erlbaum Associates Inc.

Broadbent, D. (1985). A question of levels: Comments on McClelland and Rumelhart. *Journal of Experimental Psychology: General, 114,* 189–192.

Browman, C.P. (1980). Perceptual processing: Evidence from slip of the ear. In V.A. Fromkin (Ed.), *Errors in linguistic performance: Slips of the tongue, ear, pen, and hand.* New York: Academic Press.

Brown, G. (1987). Constraining interactivity: Evidence from acquired dyslexia. *Proceedings of the ninth annual conference of the cognitive science society.* Hillsdale, NJ: Lawrence Erlbaum Associates Inc.

Coltheart, M. (1981). The MRC psycholinguistic database. *Quarterly Journal of Experimental Psychology, 33A,* 497–505.

Cutler, A., & Norris, D. (1988). The role of strong syllables in segmentation for lexical access. *Journal of Experimental Psychology: Human Perception and Performance, 14,* 113–121.

Elman, J.F. (1988). *Finding structure in time.* Center for Research in Language Technology. Report 8801. University of California, San Diego.

Elman, J.F., & McClelland, J.L. (1988). Cognitive penetration of the mechanism of perception: Compensation of coarticulation of lexically restored phonemes. *Journal of Memory and Language, 27,* 143–165.

Fodor, J.A. (1983). *The modularity of mind.* Cambridge, MA: MIT Press.

Fodor, J.A., & Pylyshyn, Z.W. (1988). Connectionism and cognitive architecture: A critical analysis. *Cognition, 28,* 146–165.

Frauenfelder, U., & Peeters, G. (1990). On lexical segmentation in TRACE: An exercise in simulation. In G.T.M. Altmann (Ed.), *Cognitive models of speech processing: Psycholinguistic and computational perspectives.* Cambridge, MA: MIT Press.

Ganong, W.F. III (1980). Phonetic categorization in auditory word perception. *Journal of Experimental Psychology: Human Perception and Performance, 6,* 110–125.

Grainger, J., O'Regan, J., Jacobs, A.M., & Segui, J. (1989). On the role of competing word units in visual word recognition: the neighbourhood frequency effect. *Perception and Psychophysics, 45,* 189–195.

Grosjean, F. (1985). The recognition of words after their acoustic offset: Evidence and implications. *Perception and Psychophysics, 28,* 299–310.

Grosjean, F., & Gee, J.P. (1987). Another view of spoken word recognition. *Cognition, 25,* 135–155.

Hornby, A.S. (1974). *Oxford advanced learner's dictionary of current English.* Oxford: Oxford University Press.

Johnston, J.C., & McClelland, J.L. (1974). Perception of letters in words: Seek not and yet shall find. *Science, 184,* 1192–1194.

Jordan, M. (1986). *Serial order: A parallel distributed processing approach.* ICS Report 8604. La Jolla: University of California, San Diego.

Lahiri, A., & Marslen-Wilson, W.D. (1991). The mental representation of lexical form: A phonological approach to the recognition lexicon. *Cognition, 38,* 245–294.

Luce, P. (1986a). *Neighborhoods in the mental lexicon.* Doctoral Dissertation, Indiana University, Bloomington, Indiana.

Luce, P. (1986b). A computational analysis of uniqueness points in auditory word recognition. *Perception and Psychophysics, 39,* 155–158.

Marslen-Wilson, W.D. (1987). Functional parallelism in spoken word-recognition. In U. Frauenfelder & L.K. Tyler (Eds.), *Spoken word recognition.* Cambridge, MA: MIT Press.

Marslen-Wilson, W.D., & Welsh, A. (1978). Processing interactions during word recognition in continuous speech. *Cognitive Psychology, 10,* 29–63.

Marslen-Wilson, W.D., & Zwitserlood, P. (1989). Accessing spoken words: The importance of word onsets. *Journal of Experimental Psychology: Human Perception and Performance, 15,* 576–585.

McClelland, J.L., & Elman, J.F. (1986). The TRACE model of speech perception. *Cognitive Psychology, 18,* 1–86.

McClelland, J.L., & Rumelhart, D.E. (1981). An interactive activation model of context effects in letter perception: Part 1. An account of the basic findings. *Psychological Review, 88,* 375–407.

Norris, D. (1990). A dynamic net model of human speech recognition. In G.T.M. Altmann (Ed.), *Cognitive models of speech processing: Psycholinguistic and computational perspectives.* Cambridge, MA: MIT Press.

Nooteboom, S.D. (1981). Lexical retrieval form fragments of spoken words: Beginnings versus endings. *Journal of Phonetics, 9,* 407–424.

Pollack, I., & Pickett, J. (1964). Intelligibility of excerpts from fluent speech: Auditory vs. structural context. *Journal of Verbal Learning and Verbal Behavior, 3,* 79–84.

Rumelhart, D.E. (1989). The architecture of mind: A connectionist approach. In M.I. Posner (Ed.), *Foundations of cognitive science.* London: Bradford Books.

Rumelhart, D.E., & McClelland, J.L. (1985). Levels indeed! A response to Broadbent. *Journal of Experimental Psychology: General, 114,* 193–197.

Salasoo, A., & Pisoni, D.B. (1985). Sources of knowledge in spoken word identification. *Journal of Memory and Language, 24,* 210–231.

Seashore, R.H., & Eckerson, L.D. (1940). The measurements of individual differences in general English vocabularies. *Journal of Educational Psychology, 31,* 14–38.

Seidenberg, M.S., & McClelland, J.L. (1989). A distributed, developmental model of word recognition and naming. *Psychological Review, 96*, 523–568.

Shillcock, R. (1990). Speech segmentation and the generation of lexical hypotheses. In G.T.M. Altmann (Ed.), *Cognitive models of speech processing: Psycholinguistic and computational perspectives*. Cambridge, MA: MIT Press.

Slowiaczek, L.M., Nusbaum, H.C., & Pisoni, D.B. (1987). Phonological priming in auditory word recognition. *Journal of Experimental Psychology: Learning, Memory, and Cognition, 13*, 64–75.

Slowiaczek, L.M., & Pisoni, D.B. (1986). Effects of phonological similarity on priming in auditory lexical decision. *Memory and Cognition, 14*, 230–237.

Tabossi, P., Scott, D., & Burani, C. (1991). *Word recognition in continuous speech*. Paper presented at the 32nd Annual Meeting of the Psychonomic Society, San Francisco.

Tanenhaus, M.K., Dell, G.S., & Carlson, G. (1987). Context effects in lexical processing: A connectionist approach to modularity. In J. Garfield (Ed.), *Modularity in knowledge representation and natural language processing*. Cambridge, MA: Bradford Books.

Umilta', C. (1988). Attenzione e penetrabilita' dei processi cognitivi. In G. Kanizsa & N. Caramelli (Eds.), *L'eredita' della psicologia della Gestalt*. Bologna: Il Mulino.

Zipf, G.K. (1932). *Selected studies of the principle of relative frequency in language*. Cambridge, MA: Harvard University Press.

Zwitserlood, P. (1989). The locus of the effects of sentential–semantic context in spoken-word processing. *Cognition, 32*, 25–64.

IV Sentence-level Processing

14 More on Combinatory Lexical Information: Thematic Structure in Parsing and Interpretation

Michael K. Tanenhaus, Julie E. Boland, Gail A. Mauner, and Greg N. Carlson
Department of Psychology, University of Rochester, Rochester, NY, USA.

INTRODUCTION

The seminal work of Marlsen-Wilson and colleagues in the early 1970s highlighted the fact that language comprehension takes place rapidly, with readers and listeners making commitments to at least partial interpretations soon after receiving the linguistic input (e.g. Marslen-Wilson, 1973). Because comprehension takes place on-line, it is essential to know what information is available to the processing system as a sentence unfolds in time, and how different types of information are coordinated in real-time processing. One of the richest sources of information available to the processing system is 'combinatory' lexical information, or lexically-based information about how a word combines syntactically and semantically with other words in a sentence. Combinatory lexical information would be especially useful to the processing system if it provided (1) information that would allow the system to rapidly integrate the word with prior input and (2) information about—i.e. constraints on—the nature of the incoming input. In much of our recent work, we have been developing and exploring the hypothesis that information associated with the argument structure of verbs, especially thematic information, has just these properties (Boland & Tanenhaus, 1991; Boland, Tanenhaus & Garnsey, 1990; Carlson & Tanenhaus, 1988; Tanenhaus & Carlson, 1989; Tanenhaus, Garnsey, & Boland, 1990).

Verbs occur with a range of arguments, and individual verbs differ both in the number and types of arguments with which they can occur. The 'argument-taking' properties of verbs can be described both syntactically and semantically. The syntactic subcategorisation of a verb describes the syntactic properties of its possible arguments or complements. The lexical conceptual structure of the verb, conceptualised here in terms of 'thematic structure', includes a description of the semantic roles that the entities described in these complements play in the type of event that the verb denotes.

If immediately accessed and used by the processing system, verb-argument structure is among the richest sources of information available to the system to guide syntactic processing. And, when coupled with some simple processing assumptions (see Carlson & Tanenhaus, 1988; Tanenhaus & Carlson, 1989), this information could also be used for making provisional semantic commitments and for coordinating semantic, syntactic, and discourse-based information. As an example, consider, the verb 'donate', focusing primarily on thematic structure and syntactic-thematic mapping. Its sense or 'core meaning' is a certain type of event. Associated with the event are three entities, one participating as an agent, another as a theme, and another as a recipient. The verb requires a subject, as do all English verbs, and most typically takes an object NP and a dative PP afterwards (e.g. 'John donated fifty dollars to the charity'). In the case where the subject plays the role of agent, the object NP is the theme, and the PP is the recipient. These roles may be implicit even when they are not realised by a complement, as in the sentence 'John donated $50', where the money must have been donated to someone or something. Let's assume that the comprehension system accesses and uses all of this information whenever the verb 'donate' is encountered. Immediate access to the thematic structure of 'donate' would allow the reader or listener to assign a provisional interpretation to much of the sentence either by leaving the particular identities of the theme and recipient temporarily unspecified (John donated something to someone) or by inferring one or more of these roles from the context.

In this chapter, we review experimental evidence in support of two hypotheses about the use of verb-based thematic structure in language comprehension. The first hypothesis is that recognition of a verb provides immediate access to the verb's thematic structure, and that the accessed thematic structure can be used to make provisional semantic commitments during sentence processing. Evidence for this comes from a line or research we have been conducting on the use of argument structure in processing sentences with long-distance dependencies. Our previous research, presented at Sperlonga several years ago, and summarised in Tanenhaus, Garnsey, and Boland (1990), provided some initial support for the thematic filling hypothesis that we first presented in Carlson and Tanenhaus (1988). In this chapter, we review some newer experiments that provide additional support. These experiments use indirect object questions to demonstrate that fillers are semantically interpreted prior to the syntactic location of the gap.

Given that many arguments in English are optional, immediate access to thematic structure means that the processing system will frequently access thematic roles that are not associated with a syntactic complement. The second hypothesis under examination here is that thematic roles that are not assigned to a syntactic complement are sometimes present as unspecified entities in the semantic or conceptual representation of a sentence. We review evidence that in certain cases the identities of these unspecified or 'open' thematic roles are inferred from the context, with the thematic role serving an anaphoric function. Thus, thematic structure not only allows the system to make provisional semantic commitments, but it also functions anaphorically to integrate sentences in local discourse. For other cases, we demonstrate that the entity associated with an open thematic role remains unspecified, but is still present in the representation of the sentence.

THEMATIC FILLING

Much of our evidence for the immediate access and use of thematic structure comes from a line of research in which we examine the processing of sentences with wh–constructions, such as those illustrated in:

1.a. Which charity$_i$ did Bill give a donation to__$_i$?
   b. What donation$_i$ did Bill give__$_i$ the charity?

In these sentences a wh–phrase or 'filler' must be linked to an empty category or 'gap'. In the terminology of current grammatical theory within the GB framework, filler–gap constructions like these are treated as a type of referential dependency in which the antecedent phrase is co-indexed with a type of empty syntactic category, 'wh–trace' (cf. Fodor, this volume; Nicol, this volume). The filler inherits its thematic role from a trace that is left behind when the filler is moved from its canonical position. Other types of grammatical frameworks use different devices to account for the filler–gap dependency (cf. Fodor, this volume). We will not review alternative approaches, because the research we are conducting is not intended to adjudicate among alternative treatments of empty categories (see Fodor, 1989; this volume, for discussion of these issues).

Processing accounts of gap-filling typically assume that interpreting a filler involves identifying the syntactic location of the gap, and then associating the filler with the gap (but cf. Pickering and Barry, 1991, for arguments against empty category treatment of long-distance dependencies). Thus, interpretation of the filler depends on identifying the location of the gap. In sentence (1a) the filler 'which charity' is interpreted as the indirect object of the verb 'give'. The gap follows the preposition 'to'. In (1b), the filler 'what donation' is interpreted as the direct object of the verb 'give' and the gap immediately follows the verb.

Research using a variety of experimental paradigms has converged on the conclusion that filler–gap interpretation for wh–trace takes place immediately on encountering a verb that is typically used transitively.[1] There are three lines of evidence that support this conclusion. The first comes from the 'filled-gap effect' initially reported by Crain and Fodor (1985) and explored in depth by Stowe (1986). For example using sentences such as:

2.a. We wondered which guest the hostess introduced us to__$_i$ at the party?
   b. We wondered if the hostess introduced us to a guest at the party?

Stowe found longer reading times at 'us' in sentence (2a) compared to sentence (2b), a non-wh control sentence. This result suggests that readers had assumed that there was a gap after the verb 'introduce'. When readers encountered a noun phrase 'us' in direct object position, the initial gap analysis had to be revised, resulting in longer reading times.

The second line of evidence comes from 'embedded anomaly' studies conducted in our laboratory. In these studies, we varied the plausibility of a filler with respect to a particular gap position, typically a gap immediately following the first main verb after the filler. For example, we contrasted the two fillers illustrated by:

3.a. Which book$_i$ did the boy read__$_i$ in class?
   b. Which food$_i$ did the boy read__$_i$ class?

Here 'book' is a plausible object of 'read', whereas 'food' is not. Since sentence (3b) does not become implausible until the filler 'food' has been interpreted as the direct object of the verb 'read', the point at which subjects first 'notice' the implausibility indicates where in the sentence the gap has been posited and filled. Note that sentence (3b), like all the implausible sentences that we have used in our studies, has a possible completion in which the filler would be plausible, e.g. 'Which food did the boy read about?'.

---

[1] Whether or not gaps are initially posited after verbs that are typically used intransitively remains more controversial. For discussion see Kurtzman, 1989; Clifton and Frazier, 1989; and Garnsey, Tanenhaus, and Chapman (1991).

Using both event-related potentials in which the magnitude of the N400 response was taken as an index of plausibility (Garnsey, Tanenhaus, & Chapman, 1989; Tanenhaus et al., 1990) as well as word-by-word reading, in which plausibility effects are indexed by either increased reading times or judgments that a sentence has stopped making sense, we found that plausibility effects began at the verb (Tanenhaus, Stowe, & Carlson, 1985; Tanenhaus, Boland, Garnsey, & Carlson, 1989a; Stowe, Tanenhaus, & Carlson, 1992), indicating that the filler is linked to the verb as soon as the verb is encountered.

The third source of evidence comes from studies using cross-modal lexical priming paradigms (for review see Fodor, 1989; Nicol, this volume; Nicol & Swinney, 1989). In these studies, faster lexical decision or naming times are found to a target word that is an associate of the filler (compared to an unrelated control word) beginning at the verb. This demonstrates that the filler becomes more salient at this point as a consequence of having been co-indexed with the gap. These facilitation effects are interpreted by the authors as evidence that the gap reactivates its antecedent.

All of these results are consistent with a syntactically based account of gap-filling in which the location of gap must be identified before the filler is interpreted. However, they are also consistent with an account in which the filler is initially interpreted using semantic information that is made available as soon as the verb is recognised. Carlson and Tanenhaus (1988) argued for an account like this in which fillers are initially interpreted using thematic structure on the basis of admittedly shaky evidence. In discussing the Tanenhaus et al. (1985) evidence for interpretation at the verb, and some (weak) evidence that readers have more difficulty recovering from missed gaps than from incorrectly assigned gaps, Carlson & Tanenhaus (1988, p. 287) suggested that:

> . . . if thematic roles become available upon opening a verb's lexical entry, and if thematic assignments are made on-line as soon as possible to potential fillers as well as to other arguments [assumptions that we had argued for earlier on in the article] then we would expect effects of assignment at the verb, instead of after. On this view, then, a preliminary semantic interpretation is defined on an incomplete syntactic representation and is maintained unless inconsistent information arrives; thus syntax acts more like a filter for proposed interpretations than as the input. A filler is assigned to a remaining available role once the subject NP has received its role and before subsequent structure has been identified.

Subsequent research using the embedded anomaly logic has provided stronger support for the thematic hypothesis. These results are presented in Tanenhaus et al. (1990) and Tanenhaus et al. (1989a), so we will discuss them only briefly.

The key finding is that the place in a sentence where anomaly effects occur depends on the argument structure of the verb. In particular, we do not find anomaly effects at the verb even when the filler would be implausible as the object of the verb, as long as the argument structure of the verb provides another argument position in which the filler would be plausible. We have examined two cases like this: (1) dative verbs where the filler would be an implausible direct object but a plausible indirect object; and (2) object control verbs, in which the filler would be an implausible object, but could plausibly fill a role associated with a subcategorised infinitive complement. We used materials in which the word after the verb provided clear syntactic evidence that the filler had to be the object of the verb, as illustrated for the dative verb 'read' in (4), and the object control verb 'remind' in (5). The plausible fillers are presented in parentheses.

4. Which baby (poem) did the babysitter read in a funny voice.
5. Which movie (girl) did the woman remind to watch the show.
6. Which stone (star) did the assistant watch all through the night.

For the object control verbs and the dative verbs, plausibility effects did NOT begin at the verb, but rather they began one word later when the next word, taken in conjunction with the verb's subcategorisation properties, made it clear that there had to be a gap after the verb. In contrast, sentences using verbs that subcategorise for only a single argument showed plausibility effects beginning immediately at the verb. An example of such a sentence with the verb 'watch' is presented in (6). Note that (6), like all the sentences that we used in our experiments, could be continued plausibly, e.g. 'Which stone did the assistant watch us carve . . .'

Using the object control verbs, we also found filled gap effects with sentences such as those illustrated in (7) when the filler was a plausible object (7a) but NOT when the filler was an implausible object, (7b).

7.a. Which girl did the woman remind us to watch?
   b. Which movie did the woman remind us to watch?

These results demonstrate that readers assigned the filler to the role that would be associated with the object of the verb 'remind', immediately at the verb, when the filler could plausibly fill this role. This finding is important, because it rules out the possibility that delayed plausibility effects are seen with verbs with complex argument structures because readers delay making a filler–gap assignment when the verb contains a complex argument structure.

These results cannot easily be accounted for without assuming that the processing system has immediate, or nearly immediate, access to information about the argument structure of the verb. In particular, the processing system must have access to the set of possible arguments associated with the verb, and the semantic restrictions on these arguments. The results for dative sentences can be accounted for simply by assuming that recognition of the verb makes available the set of thematic roles associated with the verb. The filler is evaluated in parallel against the set of roles, with the bias towards the direct object role. A filler that is plausible as the direct object of the verb will be provisionally assigned the Theme role, whereas a filler that could be a plausible indirect object, but not a plausible direct object, would be interpreted as the Recipient. Thus both sentences will initially be plausible at the verb.[2] The sentence for which the filler was implausible as the direct object becomes implausible only when subsequent information makes it clear that the filler must, in fact, be assigned the Theme role. On this account, then, fillers are immediately assigned to a role, i.e. interpreted, at the verb. Plausibility effects will be seen at the verb only when the filler is implausible in all of the available roles (Boland & Tanenhaus, 1991; Tanenhaus et al., 1989b, 1990).

A simple thematic account is not, however, sufficient to explain the results with the object control verbs. The reason for this is that the actual role to which the filler must ultimately be assigned is made available by the verb in the infinitive complement rather than the matrix verb. For example, in the sentence 'Which movie did Bill remind us to watch__?', 'movie' receives a thematic role from 'watch' and not from 'remind'. One possibility is that the processing system assumes that the filler will be a general 'Theme' and then this interpretation is elaborated when the complement is encountered. This account assumes that a partial semantic interpretation is built on the basis of an incomplete syntactic commitment (Weinberg, 1992, develops a more detailed account of how such a system might work).

Although a thematic filling hypothesis nicely accommodates the effects of verb argument structure that we have reported, the strongest predictions made by the hypothesis are not directly tested in our prior experiments. The thematic hypothesis predicts that a filler is semantically interpreted

---

[2] Note that this account of gap filling would predict 'priming' effects for targets related to the antecedents of gaps following verbs like 'remind', even when the filler was not a plausible object of the verb. Hickock, Conseco-Gonzalez, Zurif, and Grimshaw (1991) find just this result, though they interpret it as counter-evidence to our claims.

prior to encountering the empty category. In contrast, syntactic accounts of gap filling typically assume that interpretation of the filler depends on the parser having first identified the gap on the basis of bottom-up syntactic evidence.

Consider the dative example illustrated in (4). The filler is an implausible object, but a plausible indirect object. On the basis of the results described earlier, we can infer that the filler is assigned the role associated with the indirect object (Recipient) immediately at the verb. The logic is as follows: If only the role associated with the direct object (Theme) was available, or if the filler was implausible in both roles, then plausibility effects would have been seen at the verb. Therefore the sentence was plausible up through the verb because the filler was immediately assigned to the Recipient role. Note, however, that the results do not provide direct evidence that the filler has, in fact, been assigned the Recipient role prior to the actual location of the gap. Nor do they provide direct evidence that the interpretation of the filler has taken place prior to when the empty category is encountered, as the thematic hypothesis clearly predicts. We would have more direct evidence for both of these hypotheses if we could: (1) create an implausibility that is contingent on the filler having been assigned a particular role; and (2) have the implausibility precede the syntactic location of the empty category.

In order to do this, we used indirect object questions with dative verbs such as 'contribute' and 'donate'. These verbs take both a direct and an indirect object, but they do not subcategorise for double object constructions (e.g. one can 'contribute money to a charity', but not 'contribute a charity money'). Sample test sentences are illustrated in (8):

8.a. Which campus party$_i$ did John contribute some cheap liquor to__$_i$ last week.
   b. Which public library$_i$ did John contribute some cheap liquor to__$_i$ last week.

Both the filler phrases in (8a) and (8b) are implausible themes but plausible recipients of a contribution. One can plausibly contribute to, but not contribute, either a campus party or a public library. The direct object of the verb was chosen so that it would be plausible in one of the sentences, but not the other. Thus, one can plausibly contribute cheap liquor to a campus party but not to a library. Consequently, 'cheap liquor' becomes implausible in the sentence only when 'public library' has filled the Recipient role. This manipulation allows us to determine at what point in the sentence readers interpret the filler in the Recipient role. The thematic filling hypothesis predicts that interpretation can take place as soon as the verb 'contribute' is encountered. In contrast, a syntactic filling hypothesis, in which fillers cannot be interpreted until an empty category is en-countered, predicts that the filler will not be interpreted as the Recipient until after the preposition 'to', which marks the syntactic location of the gap. There is no way to determine directly whether the filler is assigned the Recipient role at the verb. The earliest point that we could observe an effect is at the direct object, 'cheap liquor'. Note that because the verbs we used do not allow double object constructions in American English, the questioned indirect object could not be associated with a gap following the verb (i.e. one cannot say 'Which campus party did John contribute the cheap liquor?').

Subjects saw the sentences one word at a time in an accumulating display. They were instructed to read each sentence as rapidly as they could while maintaining 'good comprehension'. Subjects pressed a 'Continue' button to see the next word in the display. They were also told that some of the sentences might not make sense, and if the sentence they were reading stopped making sense, they should press a 'No' button (see Boland et al., 1990 for details of this procedure). Word by word reading times using this procedure are about 100 to 200msec per word slower than the reading times that we find with comparable sentences using a moving window presentation. Figure 14.1a presents the cumulative percentage of sentences judged to stop making sense for critical word positions in the sentence. Figure 14.2a presents reading times at each position to those words that were judged to make sense.

Subjects clearly noticed the oddity in the implausible condition prior to the syntactic position of the gap. There is a plausibility difference between the two conditions beginning at the adjective (some of the direct objects were actually compound nouns) and clearly established at the noun. Since the plausibility of the object depends on the filler having been interpreted as the indirect object of the verb, the results demonstrate that readers had assigned the filler to the indirect object role prior to the syntactic position of the gap. We should note that these results do not distinguish between two alternative hypotheses. The first is that assignment of the filler to the Recipient role actually takes place at the verb. The alternative is that assignment of the filler to the Recipient role is delayed until the noun phrase 'cheap liquor' is assigned to the Theme role. The filled gap logic might be used to rule out a delay hypothesis, as we did with object control verbs, if suitable materials could be developed with datives. Nicol (this volume) reports complementary findings using a cross-modal lexical decision task that support the early thematic assignment hypothesis. She also used dative verbs and indirect object questions to examine thematic effects at the verb. Nicol finds facilitation to targets related to the filler several words prior to the place in the sentence where the trace is located.

(a)

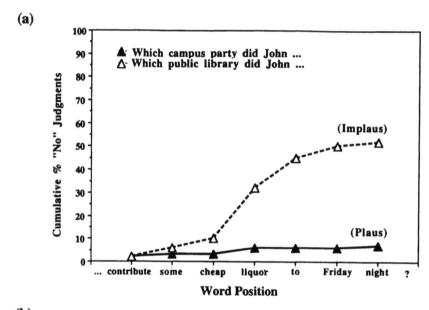

(b)

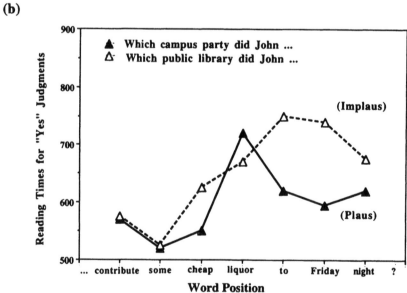

FIG. 14.1.   1a presents the cumulative percentage of 'No' responses for plausible and implausible direct object questions across selected words positions. 1b presents reading times for the 'Yes' judgements.

However, it is possible to reconcile the results of our preceding experiment with a syntactic account, if we assume that a gap is posited after the verb, even though the verb would not allow an indirect object to be extracted from object position. (See Mitchell, 1989, and Ferreira & Henderson, 1990 for arguments in support of this hypothesis, but cf. Trueswell, Tanenhaus, & Kello, in press.) This analysis would then be revised when subcategorisation information was consulted. Because both the plausible and implausible sentences would be revised in this way, the effects would not be detectable in our data. Thus, we also conducted an experiment using the same type of plausibility manipulation, but this time using verbs that can be used in a double object construction, such as 'send', 'grant', and 'read' (Boland et al., 1990). These verbs allow an indirect object gap immediately after the verb, as in:

9.a. We wondered which secretary$_i$ Ann granted the maternity leave to__$_i$ this morning?
   b. We wondered which bachelor$_i$ Ann granted the maternity leave to__$_i$ this morning?

With verbs like these, indirect object questions in which the gap follows the verb are grammatical in most dialects of American English, though they are somewhat awkward for many speakers, and clearly ungrammatical for speakers of British English. Thus, a gap posited after the verb would not have to be revised when subcategorisation information was accessed. The results from this experiment were virtually identical to those presented in Fig. 14.1, that is, plausibility effects began at the noun. Thus, the results of this experiment demonstrate that the filler has been assigned the indirect object role at, or shortly after, the verb. On the syntactic account that we sketched earlier, there is a trace after the verb to which the filler has been co-indexed. We also know from the plausibility effects that the filler has been assigned to the Recipient role. Therefore, the processing system should not be anticipating a gap after the direct object 'maternity leave' in (10) since the filler has already been co-indexed with a gap. Encountering clear evidence for such a gap would require syntactic reanalysis, which would be reflected in processing difficulty.

10. Which secretary did Ann grant the maternity leave . . .

Thus, the proposition marking the gap in (11a) should force the parser to revise its analysis, whereas no such revision should be necessary in sentence (11b).

11.a. Which secretary$_i$ did Ann grant a maternity leave to __$_i$ last week?
  b. Which secretary$_i$ did Ann grant __$_i$ a maternity leave last week.

We compared sentences like (11a) and (11b), again using self-paced reading with the stop-making-sense task. Judgment data are presented in Fig. 14.2a and reading times for only those trials judged to make sense are presented in Fig. 14.2b. Both the judgment and the reading time data show longer reading times to the sentences in which the gap immediately followed the verb. Thus the results clearly do not support the predictions made by the syntactic hypothesis.

The studies that we have reviewed with indirect object questions, and the research reported in Tanenhaus et al., 1990 combine to make a strong case for some form of a thematic filling hypothesis. Because most of these studies used the stop-making-sense task, it is important to consider whether the results might have been an artefact of the task. During the last five years our group has used most of the standard psycholinguistic tasks that are currently used to study on-line comprehension during reading, including self-paced reading with a variety of display types, secondary tasks, and presentation units, eye-tracking, probe recognition 'priming', and monitoring ERPs. Each of these tasks has advantages and disadvantages. We generally use the stop-making-sense task for exploratory studies and when the logic of the experiments depends on effects that rely on fairly subtle plausibility manipulations. The data obtained with this task typically show the same pattern as other self-paced reading tasks (there are currently not enough direct comparisons available to compare the task with eye-tracking), however, the effects are typically more robust. There are several concerns about the task that can be raised. First of all, word-by-word self-paced reading, regardless of task, may encourage early commitments because readers cannot see parafoveal information, especially short function words. In Stowe et al., (in press), see also Tanenhaus et al., (1990), we attempted to address some of these concerns by using whole-sentence presentation. The early plausibility effects that we observe with monotransitive verbs also occur with whole sentence presentation. A second concern is that the task is unlike 'normal reading' because reading is slower, and because subjects are required to make a sensicality judgment for each word. Consequently, subjects adopt special purpose strategies. All on-line tasks present difficulties of one sort or another. The only way to put a set of results on really secure footing is to replicate them across several different types of tasks. As we indicated earlier, the basic early filling results with monotransitive verbs have now been replicated in experiments using a wide variety of tasks. Recently, Boland (1991; 1992) has reported results using a cross-model lexical decision task and naming, which separate the effects of thematic structure

(a)

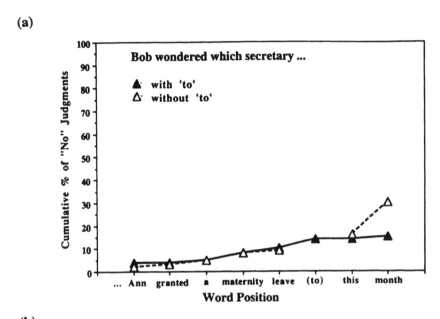

(b)

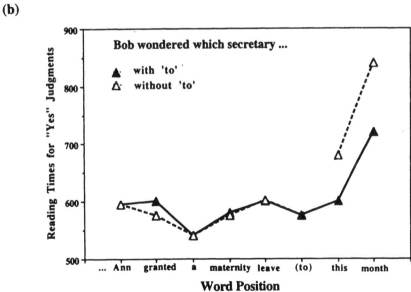

FIG. 14.2. 2(a) presents cumulative percentage of 'No' responses for indirect object questions. 2(b) presents readings times for 'Yes' judgements.

and subcategorisation. Boland's results support the early thematic interpretation hypothesis. We are also in the process of replicating our argument structure studies using the filled gap logic with eye-tracking.

A crucial aspect of the account we have offered is that recognition of the verb makes available representations for arguments of a verb that are often not expressed, that is syntactically realised. Thus, the semantic/conceptual representation of a sentence will, at least temporarily, contain representations associated with complements that are not realised syntactically. We now turn to a brief description of some recent research that demonstrates that semantic representations associated with unrealised complements are in fact part of the representation that is constructed during comprehension.

IMPLICIT ARGUMENTS

Most English verbs have multiple subcategorisations. In some cases, the thematic structures associated with the different subcategorisations are clearly different. For example, in the transitive (causative) use of 'hurry' there are two participants in the situation, an agent and a theme ('John hurried his kids out the door'; whereas in the intransitive (ergative) use of 'hurry', there is only one participant, a theme. However, in many other cases the same set of entities appear to be associated with several subcategorisations, with the subcategorisations differing in which participants (or events, in the case of optional infinitival complements) are explicitly mentioned (Fillmore, 1986; Carlson & Tanenhaus, 1988). Consider these examples:

12.a. Bill reminded Tom to go to the bank.
  b. Bill reminded Tom.
13.a. Bill donated fifteen dollars to the Red Cross.
  b. Bill dontated fifteen dollars.
14.a. The ship was sunk by the captain to collect the insurance money.
  b. The ship was sunk to collect the insurance money.
15.a. Bill unloaded the suitcases from the car.
  b. Bill unloaded the car.

In each pair of sentences, the subcategorisation used in the first sentence contains a syntactic complement that is missing in the second sentence. However, the syntactically unrealised argument still seems to be implicit in our understanding of the sentence. So, (12b) implies that Tom was reminded to do something; (13b) implies that there was a recipient of the donation; (14b) implies that someone sank the ship; and (15b) implies that something was unloaded from the car.

As we have seen, one consequence of the verb-based access of thematic structure is that roles that are initially accessed when the verb is encountered will often not be realised syntactically in the sentence. The examples in (12–15) suggest that these unexpressed verbal arguments may nonetheless still be represented in the comprehender's mental model of the situation invoked by the sentence.

Whether or not an argument is expressed syntactically is a question that interacts with discourse in fairly subtle ways that we will have little to say about here. However, at one extreme there appear to be arguments that typically need to be expressed unless relevant information is provided by the local discourse context. For example, sentence (12b) is quite awkward unless it is preceded by a context that provides information about what Tom was reminded to do, or reminded about. However, it is completely felicitous in such a context, as is illustrated by (16):

16. Tom nearly forgot to go to the bank before it closed. Fortunately, Bill reminded him.

In context, the unexpressed verbal complement appears to function anaphorically, picking up its reference from an entity already present in the context, much like a pronoun (Fillmore, 1986; Grimshaw, 1977; Hankamer & Sag, 1976). At the other extreme, there are implicit arguments such as the implicit agent associated with short verbal passive constructions, for example (14b), 'The ship was sunk . . .' that are clearly not anaphoric. In fact a discourse like the one in (17) is extremely awkward, if not completely infelicitous.

17. The captain wanted to collect some insurance money on his old ship. The ship was sunk.

The implicit argument associated with the unrealised theme in spray/load verbs such as 'unload', exemplified in (15b) is somewhat intermediate between those implicit roles that are clearly anaphoric and those that are not.

In previous work, we explored cases such as those in (15) (Carlson & Tanenhaus, 1988; Tanenhaus, Burgess, Hudson-d'Zmura & Carlson, 1987). We contrasted context sentences containing a verb with an implicit argument (or 'open thematic role'), such as (18a), with a sentence that did not contain an implicit argument (18b). We then followed the context with a target sentence that began with a definite noun phrase that did not have an explicit antecedent in the context (19).

18.a. Bill unloaded the truck.
  b. Bill hurried through the airport.
19. The suitcases were very heavy.

Definite noun phrases without explicit antecedents slow comprehension, presumably because the reader must make an inference to relate the anaphoric noun phrase to the context (Haviland & Clark, 1974). The definite noun phrases that we used were chosen to be plausible in the situation described by both context sentences. In addition, they specified the identity of the role that was left implicit in the open role contexts. We reasoned that if the open role was represented in the reader's discourse model and thus provided an 'address' for the definite noun phrase, then comprehension would be easier for the target in the open role contexts. This prediction was confirmed. Response times, to judge that the target sentences made sense in the context, were significantly faster in the open role contexts. In addition, more of the sentences in these contexts were judged to make sense.

Recently, we have begun to explore clear cases of implicit arguments that have apparent anaphoric properties, as well as clear cases of implicit arguments that do not appear to be anaphoric. In conjunction with Aaron Halpern (Halpern, 1991; Halpern, Mauner, & Tanenhaus, in press) we have conducted a series of experiments using the probe recognition task that has been widely used in studies of explicit anaphors (Cloitre & Bever, 1988; Dell, McKoon, & Ratcliff, 1983; Gernsbacher, 1989) and empty syntactic categories (MacDonald, 1989; McElree & Bever, 1989). In these studies, recognition time to decide that a word occurred in the preceding sentence or short discourse is faster when the word is the antecedent for a subsequent anaphor.

Our first experiment was designed to see whether similar effects would occur for probe words that were the antecedents of a verb phrase anaphor. We created two sentence discourses containing a context sentence (20) followed by three types of target sentences, exemplified in (21 a–c).

20. I don't know who should sweep the crumbs off the floor.
21.a. However, I bet Carol was the one who made the mess.
  b. However, I bet Carol will volunteer to, reluctantly.
  c. However, I bet Carol will volunteer (to do it), reluctantly.

We included a control sentence (21a) that made sense in the context but did not contain a verb phrase anaphor, as well as a verb phrase ellipsis condition (21b), and a sentence that either contained an explicit VP anaphor, usually 'do-it' anaphora, or an unexpressed verbal complement (null complement anaphora).

The procedure was modelled after MacDonald (1989). Subjects read the context sentence followed by the target sentence, and then judged whether or not a probe word had occurred in either sentence. On test trials, the probe word was the verb from the context sentence, e.g. 'sweep'. The verb was the head phrase that was the antecedent for the verb phrase anaphor in the target sentences. Recognition times to the verb were significantly faster for the verb phrase ellipsis condition (1201msec) and the 'do it' anaphora/null complement anaphora condition (1176msec), compared to the non-anaphor control condition (1283msec). In addition, there were no differences between the implicit (null complement) and the explicit ('do it') anaphors. Thus this experiment demonstrates 'priming' effects for verb phrase anaphors that are similar to those that have been demonstrated previously for noun phrase anaphors. In addition, the results suggest that null complements can, in fact, function like other anaphors.

In a second experiment, we directly compared null complement anaphora with verb phrase ellipsis. We also constructed contexts that allowed us to probe with either a verb that was the antecedent for a verb phrase anaphor in the subsequent sentence, or a verb that was not part of the antecedent, as in:

22.a. The teachers union decided to *demand* that the school board *develop* a better retirement plan.
   b. The school board agreed to, to avoid a strike.
   c. The school board agreed, to avoid a strike.

The antecedent probe 'develop' was responded to significantly faster than the non-antecedent probe 'sweep' for the verb phrase ellipsis condition (1238msec *vs* 1438msec), and for the null complement anaphora condition (1249msec *vs* 1412msec), with the magnitude of the difference being similar for both types of anaphors. Taken together, then, these experiments provide clear evidence that unexpressed verbal complements can function as anaphors.

As we mentioned earlier, not all implicit arguments have anaphoric properties. Other unexpressed arguments are more like indefinites (Fillmore, 1986). A classic example of such a structure is an agentless verbal passive, exemplified by:

23. The ship was sunk last night.

These sentences are often analysed as containing an unexpressed agent so that sentence (23) is understood to mean 'The ship was sunk by someone or something'. This intuition can be highlighted by contrasting a verbal passive with an 'ergative' construction, in which the same verb is used intransitively, but there does not appear to be an implicit agent:

24. The ship sank.

Because the identity of an implicit agent is unspecified and because the implicit argument does not have anaphoric properties, priming or probing methodologies are unlikely to be fruitful. In fact, MacDonald (1989) failed to find priming effects following verbal passives when the probe was a plausible agent that has been mentioned in the preceding sentence.

The logic that we adopted makes use of the fact that sentences with 'purpose' clauses require there to be an agent that functions as the 'understood' subject of the clause (PRO in the GB grammatical framework). We constructed sets of materials in which a sentence that ended with a purpose clause began with one of four constructions: (a) an intransitive; (b) a full passive; (c) an active; and (d) a short passive. A sample set of materials is:

25.a. The ship sank to collect the insurance money.
  b. The ship was sunk by the owner to collect the insurance money.
  c. The owner sank the ship to collect the insurance money.
  d. the ship was sunk to collect the insurance money.

The ergative does not provide an agent that could serve as the understood subject of the purpose clause. Therefore, subjects should find the sentence incongruous at the point where the understood subject is interpreted. In contrast, both the full passives and the actives provide explicit agents and should be fully felicitous. The short passives should pattern with actives and full passives rather than with the intransitives, if they do in fact contain an agent in their representation.

We presented the sentences one word at a time in a self-paced reading task using the stop-making-sense task described earlier (for details, see Mauner, Tanenhaus, & Carlson, 1992). Figure 14.3 presents the cumulative percentage of 'No' responses beginning with the word before the purpose clause.

All of the conditions pattern together until the verb, at which point subjects begin to respond 'No' significantly more often to the intransitives. Both types of passives and the actives pattern together, with very few 'No' responses. Thus, the results indicate that short passives do, in fact, contain implicit agents. In addition, the results demonstrate that subjects interpret

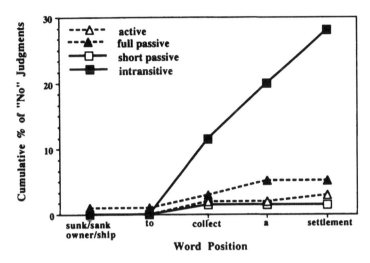

FIG. 14.3. Cumulative percentage of 'No' responses for actives, full passives, short passives, and ergatives across word positions.

the understood subject of an infinitive (Pro) immediately, as argued by Boland et al. (1990), rather than after a delay, as has been suggested by Nicol and others (e.g. Nicol & Swinney, 1989).

However, the judgment data do not by themselves provide clear evidence about when readers created an implicit agent in the sentences with short passives. The agent could have been introduced into the representation as soon as the verb was encountered, as would be expected if thematic roles are accessed as soon as a verb is recognised. Alternatively, subjects might have made an inference to create an agent only after they encountered the purpose clause. On this view, the short passive allows an agent to be inferred more easily than an intransitive, but it is the requirements of the purpose clause that drive the inference. If we make the plausible assumption that an inference should be reflected in increased reading times in this task, we can choose between these alternatives by examining the reading time data to just those trials on which subjects continued on to the next word without responding 'No'. If readers had to make an inference for the short passives when they encountered the verb in the purpose clause, we should see longer reading times beginning at the verb for the short passives than for the actives and full passives. If, however, the agent was already present in the reader's representation, then reading time should be similar for these conditions. The reading time data are presented in Fig. 14.4.

There are baseline differences at the first word that are completely due to differences in length and frequency among the conditions. Reading

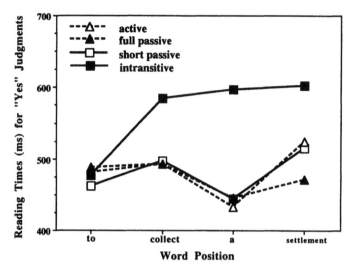

FIG. 14.4.   Reading times (msecs) for actives, full passives, short passives, and ergatives for 'Yes' judgements.

times to the ergatives are significantly different from the other three conditions beginning at the verb, and most strikingly at the next word.[3] This is the data pattern typically found with this task: the reading time data nearly always show the same effects as the judgment data, but the effects are delayed by one word. Crucially, there is not an inference effect in the reading time data for the short passives compared to the explicit agent conditions. Reading times do increase slightly from the preposition to the verb for the short passives, but not for the full passives or for the actives. However, this is because reading times to 'to' were faster in the short-passive condition than in the other two conditions. Moreover, the interaction between position and sentence type (excluding the ergatives) does not approach significance, and the reading times at the embedded verb are virtually identical for the three conditions. Thus the results indicate both that a unspecified agent is part of the representation of a short verbal passive, and that readers create a representation for the agent as soon as they encounter the verb.

CONCLUSION

Our goal in this article has been to provide support for two related claims. The first claim is that recognition of a verb provides immediate access to semantic information about the potential arguments of the verb. We conceptualised this information in terms of thematic structure, and reviewed results that indicate that the initial interpretation of fillers in wh–construction make use of thematic information. Central to our argument was a variety of evidence that indicated that the interpretation of the fillers takes place prior to the gap or empty category. A natural consequence of a model claiming that semantic information about arguments can be used to construct provisional interpretations, is that interpretation will make use of semantic representations for arguments that are not syntactically realised. Our second claim was that a variety of implicit arguments or unspecified thematic roles are in fact used during comprehension. We presented a handful of results in support of this claim, including new evidence that unexpressed verbal complements can function as anaphors, and new evidence that comprehension of a verbal passive introduces an unspecified agent into the comprehender's model. Our results indicate that further explorations of semantically-based implicit arguments are likely to be fruitful.

We should note in closing, however, that we did not address several difficult issues. We had little to say about how the semantic and syntactic aspects of argument structure are coordinated during comprehension (but see Boland, 1991, and Tanenhaus, Boland, Garnsey, & Carlson, in preparation, for some proposals; also Nicol, this volume). This issue clearly needs to be addressed in more detail in future work. A second important issue has to do with our assumption that the semantic representations that we were investigating are best characterised in terms of thematic structure. Although we have found thematic structure to be a useful heuristic, it is possible that the results that we have described might be equally well accounted for by theories of lexical representation that do not make use of thematic roles (e.g. Dowty, 1991). These caveats aside, the results that we have reviewed add to the growing body of evidence indicating that the semantic aspects of combinatory lexical information, verb-argument structure in particular, play a crucial role in real-time language comprehension.

ACKNOWLEDGEMENT

This research was supported by NSF grant BNS-8617738 and NIH grant HD-27206.

REFERENCES

Boland, J.E. (1991). *The use of lexical knowledge in sentence processing.* Unpublished doctoral thesis, Rochester University, NY.
Boland, J.E. (in press). The role of verb argument structure in sentence processing: Distinguishing between syntactic and semantic effects, *Journal of Psycholinguistic Research.*

Boland, J.E., & Tanenhaus, M.K. (1991). The role of lexical representations in sentence processing. In G. Simpson (Ed.), *Understanding word and sentence* (pp. 331–366). New York: North-Holland.

Boland, J.E., Tanenhaus, M.K., Carlson, G., & Garnsey, S.M. (1989). Lexical projection and the interaction of syntax and semantics in parsing. *Journal of Psycholinguistic Research, 18,*(6), 563–576.

Boland, J., Tanenhaus, M.K., & Garnsey, S.M. (1990). Evidence for the immediate use of verb control information in sentence processing. *Journal of Memory and Language, 29,* 413–432.

Carlson, G.N., & Tanenhaus, M.K. (1988). Thematic roles and language comprehension. In W. Wilkins (Ed.), *Thematic relations.* New York, NY: Academic Press.

Clifton, C., & Frazier, L. (1989). Comprehending sentences with long-distance dependencies. In G. Carlson & M. Tanenhaus (Eds.), *Linguistic structure in language-processing.* Dordrecht: Reidel.

Cloitre, M., & Bever, T.G. (1988). Linguistic anaphors and levels of representation. *Language and Cognitive Processes, 3*(4), 293–322.

Crain, S., & Fodor, J.D. (1985). How can grammars help parsers? In D. Dowty, L. Kartunnen, & A. Zwicky, (Eds.), *Natural language parsing.* Cambridge: Cambridge University Press.

Dell, G.S., McKoon, G., & Ratcliff, R. (1983). The activation of antecedent information during the processing of anaphoric reference in reading. *Journal of Verbal Learning and Verbal Behavior, 22,* 121–132.

Dowty, D.R. (1991). Thematic proto-roles and argument selection *Language, 67,* 547–619.

Ferriera, F., & Henderson, J. (1990). The use of verb information in syntactic parsing: A comparison of evidence from eye-movements and word-by-word self-paced reading. *Journal of Experimental Psychology: Learning, Memory & Cognition, 16,* 555–568.

Fillmore, C.J. (1986). Pragmatically controlled zero anaphora. *Proceedings of the Twelfth Annual meeting of the Berkeley Linguistics Society,* 95–107.

Fodor, J.D. (1989). Empty categories in sentence processing. *Language and Cognitive Processes, 4,* 155–209.

Garnsey, S.M., Tanenhaus, M.K., & Chapman, R.M. (1989). Evoked potentials and the study of sentence comprehension. *Journal of Psycholinguistic Research, 18,* 51–60.

Garnsey, S.M., Tanenhaus, M.K., & Chapman, R.M. (1991). *An ERP study of preferred argument structure in parsing.* Manuscript submitted for publication.

Gernsbacher, M.A. (1989). Mechanisms that improve referential access. *Cognition, 32,* 99–156.

Grimshaw, J. (1977). *English Wh–constructions and the theory of grammar.* Unpublished dissertation, University of Massachusetts.

Halpern, A. (1991). *Priming in VP anaphora.* Poster presented at the 1991 CUNY Sentence Processing Conference, Rochester, New York.

Halpern, A., Mauner, G.A., & Tanenhaus, M.K. (in press). Priming of structural and conceptual verb phrase anaphors. In *Proceedings of the twenty-third annual meeting of the Northeastern Linguistics Society.* Amherst, MA: GLSA publications.

Hankamer, J., & Sag, I. (1976). Deep and surface anaphora. *Linguistic Inquiry, 7,* 391–426.

Haviland, S.E., & Clark, H.H. (1974). What's new? Acquiring new information as a process in comprehension. *Journal of Verbal Learning and Verbal Behavior, 13,* 512–521.

Hickok, G., Canseco-Gonzalez, E., Zurif, E., & Grimshaw, J. (1991). *Modularity in locating Wh–gaps.* Poster presented at 1991 CUNY Sentence Processing Conference, Rochester, New York.

Kurtzman, H.S. (1989). Locating Wh–traces. In C. Tenny (Ed.), *The MIT parsing volume*. Cambridge, MA: MIT Press.

MacDonald, M.C. (1989). Priming effects from gaps to antecedents. *Language and Cognitive Processes, 4*(1), 35–56.

Marslen-Wilson, W.D. (1973). Linguistic structure and speech shadowing at very short latencies. *Nature, 244*, 522–523.

Mauner, G.A., Tanenhaus, M.K., & Carlson, G.N. (1992). Implicit argument inferences in on-line comprehension. *Proceedings of the Fourteenth Annual Conference of the Cognitive Science Society*, 480–485. Hillsdale, NJ: Lawrence Erlbaum Associates Inc.

McElree, B., & Bever, T.G. (1989). The psychological reality of linguistically defined gaps. *Journal of Psycholinguistic Research, 18*, 21–35.

Mitchell, D.C. (1989). Verb guidance and other lexical effects in parsing. *Language and Cognitive Processes, 4*, 123–154.

Nicol, J., & Swinney, D. (1989). The role of structure in coreference assignment during sentence comprehension. *Journal of Psycholinguistic Research, 18*, 5–20.

Pickering, M., & Barry, G. (1991). Sentence processing without empty categories. *Language and Cognitive Processes, 6*, 169–264.

Stowe, L.A. (1986). Parsing wh–constructions: Evidence for on-line gap location. *Language and cognitive processes, 2*, 227–246.

Stowe, L.A., Tanenhaus, M.K., & Carlson, G.N. (in press). Filling gaps on-line: Use of lexical and semantic information in sentence processing. *Language and Speech*.

Tanenhaus, M.K., Boland, J., Garnsey, S.M., & Carlson, G.N. (1989a). Lexical structure in parsing long-distance dependencies. *Journal of Psycholinguistic Research: Special Issue on Sentence Processing. 18*(1), 37–50.

Tanenhaus, M.K., Boland, J.E., Garnsey, S.M., & Carlson, G.N. (in preparation). *Argument structure and the parsing of sentences with long-distance dependencies*.

Tanenhaus, M.K., Burgess, C., Hudson-d'Zmura, S., & Carlson, G. (1987). Thematic roles in language processing. In *Proceedings of the Ninth Annual Meeting of the Cognitive Science Society* (pp. 587–596). Hillsdale, NJ: Lawrence Erlbaum Associates Inc.

Tanenhaus, M.K., & Carlson, G.N. (1989). Lexical structure and language comprehension. In W. Marslen-Wilson (Ed.), *Lexical representation and process*. Cambridge, MA: MIT Press.

Tanenhaus, M.K., Carlson, G.N., & Trueswell, J.C. (1989b). The role of thematic structures in interpretation and parsing. *Language and Cognitive Processes, 4*, 211–234.

Tanenhaus, M.K., Garnsey, S.M., & Boland, J. (1990). Combinatory lexical information and language comprehension. In G.T.M. Altmann (Ed.), *Cognitive models of speech processing: Psycholinguistic and computational perspectives*. Cambridge, MA: MIT Press.

Tanenhaus, M.K., Stowe, L.A., & Carlson, G.N. (1985). The interaction of lexical expectation and pragmatics in parsing filler-gap constructions. In *Proceedings of the Seventh Annual Cognitive Science Society Meetings*.

Trueswell, J.C., Tanenhaus, M.K., & Kello, C. (in press). Verb-specific constraints and sentence processing: Separating effects of lexical preference from garden-paths. *Journal of Experimental Psychology: Learning, Memory & Cognition*.

Tyler, L.K., & Marslen-Wilson, W.D. (1977). The on-line effects of semantic context on syntactic processing. *Journal of Verbal Learning and Verbal Behavior, 16*, 683–692.

Weinberg, A. (in press). Minimal commitment: A parsing theory for the nineties. *Language and Cognitive Processes*.

15 Reconsidering Reactivation

J.L. Nicol
University of Arizona, USA

INTRODUCTION

In order to correctly understand a sentence such as *That's the man that Susan admired*, the noun phrase *the man* must be understood as the object of the verb *admired*. One way to represent this fact is to posit a place holder—a phonologically empty noun phrase—in the object position of this sentence, and a link between the empty noun phrase (NP) and its antecedent, *the man*. This is the standard analysis given to such cases in syntactic theory. A central tenet of Government-Binding (GB) theory (Chomsky, 1981), for example, is that the internal constituency of a phrase remains invariant under movement: the transitive verb *admire* is transitive in all its manifestations, including constructions in which the direct object appears to be located at a distance. This allows a maximally simple theory of complement structure. The verb *admire* is lexically specified as having an NP complement immediately to its right, and this complement must always be present in the syntactic representation in which the verb occurs.

It is quite plausible to suppose that these two aspects of the sentence given earlier (the existence of a phonetically null direct object, and the referential dependency between this element and the relative clause head) are recovered in a direct fashion by the processing system. In Nicol (1988), it is argued that the processing system has (at least) two distinct sub-systems: the parser proper, which is responsible for the assignment of a phrase structure to the input string; and a coreference processor, which establishes referential dependency between a dependent element (e.g. the trace above) and its antecedent. The operations of the coreference processor must, necessarily, follow those of the constituent parser, since referential dependencies are greatly constrained by syntactic configuration. Thus, the output of the parser is the constituent structure in (1) (the trace is represented by t):

1. [$_S$That [$_{VP}$ is [$_{NP}$ [$_{NP}$ the man [$_{S'}$ that [$_S$ Susan [$_{VP}$ admired [$_{NP}$ t]]]]]]]

The coreference processor establishes the referential dependency between the empty NP (or *trace*) and its antecedent *the man*, giving the articulated structure (2), in which coindexing (by subscripts) represents the dependency:[1]

2. [$_S$ That [$_{VP}$ is [$_{NP}$ [$_{NP}$ the man$_i$ [$_{S'}$ that [$_S$ Susan [$_{VP}$ admired [$_{NP}$ t]$_i$]]]]]]]

A number of interesting processing questions arise when one considers these structures. First, since the trace is (by definition) phonetically empty, its presence in the string must be deduced from other aspects of the syntactic representation, such as the subcategorisation properties of the verb. Second, the antecedent of the trace must be properly identified. The question of how, when, and with what accuracy these processes take place is a topic that has been extensively examined and discussed.

EXPERIMENTAL STUDIES

Recent studies that have examined these questions fall into two general methodological categories: studies that examine points of processing difficulty or disruption (e.g. Boland & Tanenhaus, 1990; Boland, Tanenhaus, Carlson, & Garnsey, 1989; Boland, Tanenhaus, & Garnsey, 1990; Clifton & Frazier, 1989; Crain & Fodor, 1985; Frazier & Clifton, 1989; Kurtzman, Crawford, & Nychis–Florence, 1991; Stowe, 1986; Tanenhaus, Boland, Mauner, & Carlson, this volume; Tanenhaus & Carlson, 1989; Tanenhaus, Garnsey, & Boland, 1990), and priming studies (Bever & McElree, 1988; Bever et al., 1990; Byma, 1991; Fodor, 1990; Garnsey, Tanenhaus, & Chapman, 1989; MacDonald, 1989; MacDonald & Clark, 1989; McElree

---

[1] I have simplified here for exposition. It is standardly assumed that the relative clause head *the man* is generated in its surface position, and that the trace is immediately bound by the relative pronoun *that*, or an empty operator moved to a position adjacent to *that*. On this type of analysis there are two distinct dependencies in a relative clause: the dependency between the trace and the relative operator, and another between this operator and the relative clause head.

& Bever, 1989; Nakayama, 1990; Nicol, 1988; Nicol & Pickering, in press; Nicol & Swinney, 1989; Swinney, Ford, & Bresnan, 1989; Swinney & Osterhout, 1990.)

The processing-disruption studies typically use reading paradigms in which processing difficulty is registered in longer reading latencies and, in some experiments, a greater incidence of judgments of implausibility. Taken together, such studies strongly suggest that gap-filling is immediate: antecedents (or fillers) are readily identified and linked to a trace position.

For example, a number of studies (Clifton & Frazier, 1989; Crain & Fodor, 1985; Stowe, 1986; Tanenhaus, Boland, Garnsey, & Carlson, 1989) have shown a 'filled gap effect'; that is, reading times (in self-paced word-by-word or phrase-by-phrase presentations) increase for a word in direct object position, in constructions where a gap is expected. For example, Stowe compared reading times at the word *us* in sentences such as (3), where a gap is expected following the verb *bring*, and (4), where no such gap is expected. Note that gap-expectation must be the result of having identified a filler—(e.g. *who* in (3))—which needs to be linked to a trace, and *not* the result of failing to find a NP after a verb which subcategorises for one.

3. My brother wanted to know who Ruth will bring *us* home to at Christmas.
4. My brother wanted to know if Ruth will bring *us* home to Mom at Christmas.

These findings suggest, on one analysis, that at the verb, a trace is projected, and a connection between the antecedent and the projected trace is made. The appearance of *us* in direct object position in (3) indicates that this position is not the correct gap site after all; this produces longer reading latencies.

Another set of studies used a self-paced word-by-word sensibility judgment task. In this task, subjects decide with each new word whether the sentence continues to make sense or not. Processing difficulty, or the detection of implausibility, will be registered in longer reading times and/ or increased number of implausibility judgments, compared to a plausible control sentence. Like the self-paced reading tasks, these experiments also suggest that gap-filling is immediate. For example, Tanenhaus et al. (1989), examined the processing of sentence pairs such as the following, in which one sentence contained a semantic anomaly, whereas its counterpart did not.

5. The businessman knew which article the secretary called *t* at home.
6. The businessman knew which customer the secretary called *t* at home.

One would expect the implausibility of 'calling an article' to be apparent only once the connection is made between the filler and gap. This study showed that subjects were able to make this connection as soon as possible; at the point of the verb *called* in (5), reading times increased and subjects judged the sentence to be nonsensical. This finding is supported by results of experiments using Event-Related Brain Potentials (ERP) as the dependent measure. Garnsey et al. (1989) had subjects read sentences presented word by word on a computer screen. Subjects were asked to make a sensibility judgment at the end of the sentence. During presentation, ERPs, which were timelocked to the sentence presentation, were recorded. Once again, an anomaly effect was found at the verb *called* in sentences such as (5). This effect was manifested by the appearance of a relatively negative peak—in (5) compared to (6)—400msec. after the appearance of the verb *called*. To sum up, the reading studies suggest that both the postulation and filling of gaps is immediate.

What the *priming studies* suggest is that this process of immediate 'gap-filling' involves a *re-activation* of the antecedent of the WH-trace. For example, Swinney et al. (1989) report that there is significant priming of the NP associated with the trace just at the point where the trace would appear in the string. In a sentence such as (7), for instance, *boy* was significantly primed at a point just following the verb *accuse*, but *not* at a point just before the verb.

7. The policeman noticed the *boy* that the crowd at the party accused *t* of the crime.

Findings such as these (and others such as Byma, 1991; Clifton & Frazier, 1989; Hickok, 1991; Nicol, 1988; Swinney & Osterhout, 1990; Swinney et al., 1989) support the results of the processing-difficulty studies described here; both the postulation of the empty category, and the establishment of a referential link to the correct antecedent, occur very rapidly.

VERB-DRIVEN VS. TRACE-DRIVEN EFFECTS

Although it has been argued that the priming results provide evidence for the validity of a syntactic theory that postulates the presence of traces (see, e.g. Bever et al., 1990; Bever & McElree, 1988; Fodor, this volume; McElree & Bever, 1989), there are opposing views, which hold that the locus of both the reading latency effects and the priming effects in not the *trace*, but the verb itself.

On one such view, proposed by Tanenhaus and colleagues (e.g. 1989;

1990; this volume) the assignment of thematic (or *theta*) roles (such as *agent*, *theme*, *goal*) occurs as soon as the verb is encountered. Hence all the arguments of the verb that have already appeared by the time the verb appears will be evaluated with respect to the possible theta roles associated with a given verb, and these roles will be assigned to these arguments. For example, given an input such as (5), *Which food did the boy read t in class?*, when the verb *read* appears, its argument structure will be accessed, and the leftward arguments *which food*, and *the boy* will be assigned the *theme* and *agent* roles, respectively.

Pickering (1991), and Pickering and Barry (1990), argue that priming may be a result of the formation of a dependency, that is, the establishment of a link between two constituents. This notion is expressed within the framework of a *dependency grammar*, in which the arguments of a verb are all *dependent* on the verb. Hence, the predictions that follow from such grammars are in keeping with the predictions made by Tanenhaus and his colleagues.

Note that the priming effect obtained with constructions such as that reported in the Swinney et al. experiment is compatible with either a verb-driven or trace-driven explanation. In the sentences they used, the WH-trace immediately follows the verb; hence, any effect at the verb could be due to the projection of a trace, or it could be due to processes that relate directly to the structural or thematic properties of the verb.

Clearly, the possible effects of the trace need to be deconfounded with the possible effects taking place at the verb. Boland et al. (1989) conducted just such an experiment, using the sensibility judgment task described earlier. They examined sentences such as the following:[2]

8. Which bachelor did Ann grant the maternity leave to *t*?

The question they asked was: at what point does this sentence become implausible? Boland et al. consider two possibilities. If assignment of theta-roles to leftward arguments occurs at the verb, then *which bachelor* will be construed as the *recipient* (or *goal*) of the subsequent direct object. *As soon* as that direct object (*the maternity leave*) is processed, then the plausibility of *a bachelor* as a recipient of *the maternity leave* may be evaluated; there should be a plausibility effect at just this point. But if the process is trace-driven, then the role of the argument *which bachelor* will only be assigned once the trace is encountered; i.e. at the preposition *to*. Hence, the critical question is whether or not the plausibility effect appears

---

[2] See also Fodor (1978) for discussion of the processing of this type of construction.

before or after the appearance of the preposition *to*. Their findings indicate that the implausibility is detected *prior* to the appearance of the preposition *to*, during processing of *the maternity leave*. Hence, they argue, theta-role assignment may occur even before it is licensed by the syntax.

If we assume that the verb-driven accounts of priming are correct, then two predictions follow: (1) There should be evidence of priming *at the verb* in sentences such as (8) above, in which the indirect object is preposed; (2) The *subject* of a sentence should also be primed at the verb, since the subject argument receives a theta-role from the verb, or, on the *dependency grammar* version of this account, has a dependency relation with the verb. These predictions are tested in Experiments 1 and 2 described here.

Experiment 1

The first prediction was tested, in a study conducted in collaboration with Martin Pickering, using sentences in which a prepositional phrase (or *PP*) is questioned, as in the following (the complements of the verb are bracketed):

9. [To which butcher] did the woman who had just inherited a large sum of money give [the very expensive gift] [*t*] the other day?

Here, the verb is separated from the trace by an NP in object position. If the priming observed in the earlier experiments is due to the argument structure of the verb, and not due to the trace, then one would expect priming of *butcher* only at the verb, and not at the trace position. If, however, it is the trace that triggers priming, then there should be priming only at the trace position, and not at the verb.

Although such 'pied piping' constructions (in which the preposition is moved along with the WH-phrase) are less common in informal American English than 'preposition stranding', as in (8) and (10), it was necessary to test just such constructions rather than those used in the Boland et al. 1989 study. If we had used constructions like (8), which contains a stranded preposition, any effect at the verb could be due to the postulation of a false gap. For example, suppose the sentence were as follows:

10. [Which butcher] did the woman who had just inherited a large sum of money give [the very expensive gift] [to *t*] the other day?

If we were to find priming for *butcher* at the verb, this could be due to the fact that the verb *give* subcategorises for a NP, hence a trace would be projected at this point. Recall the 'filled gap' effect discussed earlier; once the phrase *which butcher* has been identified as a filler, a gap may be postulated at the first possible point in the sentence—just after the verb. The implausibility of *butcher* as a direct object of the verb may not matter; it is possible that the implausibility can only be established once *butcher* has been reactivated (see Hickok, Canseco-Gonzalez, Zurif, & Grimshaw, 1991; Nicol, 1989; and Swinney & Osterhout, 1990, for similar arguments). To offset this possibility, we used constructions in which the entire prepositional phrase was fronted.

Method

The methodology employed in this experiment (and in Experiment 2) is the cross-modal priming technique. This is a dual-task paradigm, which, in this experiment, involves having subjects listen to sentences and make lexical decisions to visually-presented word/nonword targets. This technique has been shown to be reliably sensitive to the activation of word meanings (e.g. Shillcock, 1982; Swinney, 1979; Swinney et al., 1989; Tanenhaus, Carlson, & Seidenberg, 1985; Tanenhaus, Leiman, & Seidenberg, 1979). Further, it has the advantage of providing *on-line* measures of activation: this permits one to probe for activation at relevant points within the sentence. Ideally, referential and thematic dependencies of the type discussed earlier can be tracked, as their representation is postulated by the processor.

In this experiment, subjects listened to sentences while monitoring a computer screen. Visual targets appeared at two sentence positions: at the offset of the verb (probe point 1), and at the offset of the last lexical item in the NP in direct object position (probe point 2), as shown by # in the following (and throughout).

11. To which *butcher* did the woman who had just inherited a large sum of money give # the very expensive gift # *t* the other day?

Subjects. Forty-seven University of Arizona undergraduate or graduate students participated in this experiment (which was run simultaneously with Experiment 2) either for course credit, or for $6 per session.

Materials and Procedure. (See Appendix A.) Eighteen sentences of the form in (11) were constructed. Each of these was paired with a probe, which was either related to the preposed NP, or was an unrelated control word, matched in length and frequency to the related target (different target types were counterbalanced across subject groups; see discussion). For contrast, another six sentences of exactly the same form were created, and paired with a probe which was related to the *subject* NP. In addition, eighteen sentences with this structure (the *pseudo-experimental sentences*) were paired with nonword targets, in order to avoid a correlation between sentence type and response type. These were combined with 62 filler sentences, of which half were paired with real word targets and half with non-word targets. Ten of these fillers were used as practice items. In all, there were 104 sentences. Of these 104 sentences, 55 were paired with real words, and 49 with nonwords.

Two counterbalanced presentation lists were created. These contained probe words that were either related to a critical item in the sentence, or were unrelated control words. These items were balanced across lists, so that there were equal numbers of related and unrelated targets in each list. To ensure that related and unrelated targets produced equivalent reaction times in isolation, these items were tested using a simple lexical decision task. They produced roughly equal response times; averaging across 22 subjects, the mean response time to the associates was 3.7msec. faster than to the control items ($F < 0.47$).

Sentences were recorded on a Technics cassette tape recorder. The sentences were recorded by a female speaker reading at a normal rate of speech. All sentences (experimental and filler) were digitised at a sampling frequency of 16K. A wave-form editing system was used to identify and label the point in each sentence at which a probe was to appear. (These labels were then converted to pulses.) In the experimental and pseudo-experimental sentences, the probe point was either at the offset of the main verb, or at the offset of the last word in the noun phrase.[3] The sentences and pulses were then recorded simultaneously onto audio tape; the sentences were recorded onto the right channel, the pulses onto the left. Two separate tapes were made: in one, the experimental sentences contained a trigger for the probe word to appear at probe point 1; in the other, the sentences contained a trigger for a word to appear at probe point 2.

Sentences were presented auditorily through headphones. Subjects heard only the right track of the audio tape, which was presented in stereo. The left track, which contained only pulses, was connected to a voice trigger, which signalled an IBM computer to: (1) display the appropriate target (for 400ms) on a computer screen that was positioned in front of each subject; and (2) to start a timer. Subjects made a lexical decision to

---

[3] In fact, due to the initial misplacement of the probes, four points were probed; those already mentioned, and one 100msec prior to each point. Hence, we tested at the verb offset, and at a point 100msec prior to this point, and at the trace position and at a point 100msec prior. The patterns of priming turned out to be essentially identical at the correct probe point and its minus-100ms counterpart, and so were collapsed for analysis.

the target item, and pressed the appropriately labelled button. The press of the button stopped the timer. To prevent subjects from attending only to the lexical decision task, subjects were tested on a proportion of the sentences. Subjects were told that they would hear a bell after some portion of the sentences, and that at the sound of the bell, they were to write down the immediately prior sentence. They were told that they did not have to report the sentences verbatim, but that they were to report enough of the sentence so as to make it clear that they had understood each sentence. Since this task was included only to encourage subjects to attend to the sentences, paraphrases obtained from the subjects were not scored or analysed.

Results

Any subject's data was excluded from further analysis if that subject's overall error score was greater than 20%, or their mean RT was greater than 1500ms. Data from five subjects were thus excluded. Two other subjects were excluded in order to balance the number of subjects across conditions. (In these cases, for a given condition, it was the last subject tested who was excluded.) In addition, all reaction times greater than 4000ms. and less than 200ms. were treated as errors, and all scores greater than or equal to two standard deviations from the subject's mean were converted to the cutoff value.

Two analyses of variance were performed on the data from each probe position: the first treated subjects as a random factor (F1); the second treated items as a random factor (F2). At both probe positions, there was a significant main effect of target type, i.e. response times to related targets were significantly faster than to unrelated targets. For probe point 1: $F_1(1,36) = 33.98, p < 0.00001; F_2(1,32) = 9.17, p < 0.005$. At probe point 2: $F_1(1,36) = 28.27, p < 0.00001; F_2(1,32) = 9.82, p < 0.005$. These data were also analysed all together to determine whether or not priming differed significantly in the two cases. The interaction of probe point with target did not approach significance ($p_1 > 0.29; p_2 > 0.77$).

The mean reaction times to targets (collapsed across subjects and items) are presented in Table 15.1.

Discussion

At first glance, these results suggest that *both* verb argument structure and trace trigger reactivation of the antecedent. It may seem odd that the sentence processor should work this way: if priming arises from theta-role assignment, why should there be reactivation *again* downstream? I will suggest in the General Discussion that priming at the two probe points

TABLE 15.1
Mean Reaction Times in the Different Treatment Conditions, and Magnitude of Priming
(in Milliseconds)

	Mean RT's		
	Related to antecedent	*Unrelated to antecedent*	*Magnitude Priming*
Probe point 1	674	727	53**
Probe point 2	632	676	44**

** p < 0.005 for both subjects and items analyses

could represent two aspects of theta-role assignment: at the verb, the moved argument is evaluated with respect to the theta roles associated with the verb, and there may be provisional theta-role assignment; at the trace, theta assignment is confirmed. First, however, we will consider alternative explanations.

1. Erroneous Reactivation at the Verb. Reactivation could be triggered by a trace in *both* cases: correctly at the actual trace position, *incorrectly* at the verb. That is, a trace is erroneously posited at the verb, and reactivation results. This would mean that, despite the fact that the typical sequence of post-verbal arguments is NP–PP (the verb is immediately followed by the direct object, and the direct object is immediately followed by an indirect object), the processor would posit a trace of the moved PP just after the verb. Why would the processor make this error? One reason is that there do exist verbs that take only a PP complement; hence, a moved PP may be correctly associated with the immediately post-verbal trace (as in, for example, *To which police officer did John lie t?*). We should point out that none of the verbs we used carried this option; therefore, we would expect such an error to occur *only* if the parser does not have immediate access to the specific argument structure of the verb. There is experimental evidence that the argument structure of the verb is indeed available immediately. The view put forward by Tanenhaus et al. is, in fact, predicated on this notion, and their experiments support it. A number of other experiments also suggest that a verb's argument structure and/or subcategorisation possibilities are available as soon as the verb is encountered (see Chodorow, 1979; Clifton, Frazier, & Connine, 1984; Fodor, 1979; Gorrell, 1987; Kurtzman, 1985, 1989; Nicol, 1989; Shapiro, Zurif, & Grimshaw, 1987), though there is also some evidence to the contrary (see Ferreira & Henderson, 1990; Mitchell, 1987).

Even if the argument structure of the verb *is* immediately accessible, the existence of two types of phenomena could tempt the parser to posit a trace post-verbally, despite the possibility of error. One is *complement ellipsis*, the other is *heavy-NP shift*. Note that ellipsis could produce *To which charity did you give, this year?* Hence, despite the fact that in non-elliptical cases, a PP never directly follows *give*, the possibility of ellipsis is always present. But in the current experiment, only a small number of sentences (3/18) allow such ellipsis; although ellipsis may occur with *give*, it cannot readily occur with verbs such as *introduce, show, send*, or *tell*.

A second way in which a trace-based analysis could be reconciled with our findings would be to suggest that sentences like (9) have undergone *Heavy NP Shift (HNPS)*; that is, shifting of a lengthy (or 'heavy') NP to the right of the indirect object. An example of such movement is shown in (12).[4]

12. Mary gave t_i [to Susan] [the old desk that she'd kept for years but hadn't ever really liked]$_i$.

If our experimental sentences are assumed to have undergone HNPS, they would have the structure in (13):

13. [To which butcher]$_j$ did the woman who had just inherited a large sum of money give [t_i] [t_j] [the very expensive gift]$_i$ the other day?

It has been argued, however, that when HNPS has occurred, the VP becomes 'frozen' for further syntactic movement (Ross, 1967; Wexler & Culicover, 1980). This would account for the ungrammaticality of (14):

14. *Who$_i$ did Mary give t_j [to t_i] [the old desk that she'd kept for years but hadn't ever really liked]$_j$?

It is *not* the case that movement out of a prepositional phrase is prohibited, since questions such as (15) are perfectly acceptable.

15. Who$_i$ did you give [a really nice big present] [to t_i]?

Therefore, it is unlikely that it is movement out of a prepositional phrase *per se* that is prohibited, but rather, movement out of the particular syntactic environment created by HNPS. If HNPS bars further movement of *either* a NP or PP, then there cannot be a trace of the PP just following the verb. Hence, in the HNPS cases, the syntactic position of the WH-t would have to be *after* the heavy NP.

---

[4] Note that such constructions could also be said to violate a constraint against *non-nested* or *intersecting* dependencies (see e.g. Fodor, 1979).

However, there are alternative analyses of constructions such as (14) that are relevant here. Janet Fodor (personal communication) has pointed out to me that in sentences like (16), extraction from a PP is prohibited, yet such constructions cannot have undergone HNPS, since there is no NP complement to shift.

16. *Who$_i$ did you say [to t$_i$] [that you were hungry]?

Fodor's point about these constructions is that there seems to be an independent constraint against extraction out of a PP in certain syntactic positions—she cites Kuno's (1973) constraint against extracting from specific types of constituent in non-final position in the sentence.[5] Given the independent constraint, it is difficult to make the argument that it is HNPS that creates the special environment from which extraction is prohibited. And if the constraint is independent of HNPS, then there may be no constraint against extraction of the *entire PP* from its post-verbal position in HNPS sentences, since Kuno's constraint bars only extraction *out of* a non-final PP, not extraction of the entire PP. It then follows that if extraction of the *entire PP* is allowed, there could be a trace just after the verb, and this trace is giving rise to priming.

There is a counterargument, however, in favour of the original HNPS-related freezing principle, and that is that sentences like (16) *do* in fact involve movement of a heavy constituent; that is, movement of the clause *[that you were hungry]* to a rightward position, as shown in (16').[6]

16'. *Who$_i$ did you say t$_j$ [to t$_i$] [that you were hungry]$_j$?

This would mean that sentences such as (16) represent another example of shifting of a heavy constituent. Any such shifting could create a syntactic environment that is *frozen* for further movement. In all, although the possibility of erroneous trace postulation cannot be dismissed, it appears to be extremely unlikely.

2. Incidental Reactivation at the Trace. Notice that the trace coincides with the end of a *theta domain*, the domain in which all theta-roles have been discharged. Despite the fact that the sentences were deliberately made to continue after the probe, the continuation consisted of an adverbial phrase (e.g. *yesterday afternoon*), which was not a complement,

---

[5] The constraint alluded to here is *The Clause Nonfinal Incomplete Constituent Constraint*, p. 381.

[6] See Stowell (1981) for extensive discussion.

and so was not critical to the well-formedness of the sentence. At the second probe point—the trace position—the arguments of the verb have all been processed. It is conceivable that at the end of a verb phrase, there is a re-consideration of all the verb's arguments, as listeners integrate the constituents of the sentence into a core proposition. Although this is certainly a plausible explanation for the priming effect at the trace, at this time, we have no external evidence to support this view.

3. Maintained Activation. This type of account suggests that priming is not due to *re*-activation, but to *maintained activation*. This alternative will be addressed by testing at additional probe points (this work is in progress). One variant of this account is that only the verb reactivates the antecedent, and that the priming observed at the trace point is due merely to residual priming. A second variant is that priming at *both* points is due to residual activation. Until we have the results of testing at the critical positions—(1) at a point prior to the verb, and (2) within the region between the verb and the trace—we cannot rule out this type of explanation.

Experiment 2

This experiment examines whether or not the *subject* of a verb is reactivated at the verb in sentence such as (17). Recall that the verb-driven priming account predicts that theta-role assignment to an argument of the verb will trigger priming. On the other hand, if priming is trace-driven, then there should be no priming effect for the subject argument.

Method

The methodology and design are identical to that described for Experiment 1,[7] with the following differences in materials. Fourteen experimental sentences (see Appendix B), of the type shown in (17) were constructed (# indicates probe point):

17. The *actress* who had caused such a sensation among the critics is #
    a failure with the general public.

The construction of materials was constrained as follows. The item being probed needed to be sufficiently distant from the probe point (the offset

---

[7] Note that the sentences in this experiment were tested in the same experimental session as Experimental 1. Hence, these were subject to the double-probe error as in Experiment 1; the results were dealt with in identical fashion.

of the verb) that any priming effect is likely *not* to be due simply to residual activation. Such materials are difficult to construct, since even in sentences like (17), in which the NP *the actress* is separated from the verb *is* by a number of lexical items, the subject of the verb is actually the entire complex NP *The actress who had caused such a sensation among the critics*, and this complex NP subject is *adjacent* to the verb. Despite this complication, it is clear that if verbs prime their subjects, the NP *the actress* will need to be refreshed at the verb.

For each such sentence, a variant was created which contained a 'raising verb', such as the verb *seems*, as in *The actress who had caused such a sensation among the critics seems to be a failure with the general public.* This was done to examine a separate question, which will not be discussed in detail here, and since this particular manipulation turned out to have no apparent effect on patterns of priming, in further discussion, no distinction will be made between one variant and the other.

Each of these sentences was paired with a real word target, which was either semantically related to the head of relative clause within the complex subject—e.g. *actress* in (17)—or was an unrelated control word. In addition, 32 sentences of similar construction were created and paired with non-word targets. These were mixed with the 42 experimental and pseudoexperimental sentences described in Experiment 1, and with 30 fillers.

Results

Subjects' data were excluded on the same grounds as described in Experiment 1. Further, two items were excluded due to improper placement of probes.

Again, two analyses of variance were performed on the data. There was a significant main effect of target type; i.e. response times to related targets were significantly faster than to unrelated targets. These means (collapsed across subjects and items) are displayed in Table 15.2.

TABLE 15.2
Mean Reaction Times and Magnitude of Priming (in Milliseconds)

	Mean RTs		
	Related to antecedent	*Unrelated to antecedent*	*Magnitude Priming*
Sentential Subjects	663	704	41*

* p < 0.005 for both subjects and items analyses

Discussion

As indicated in Table 15.2, there is significant priming of the subject. This result is compatible with the notion that reactivation occurs with theta-role assignment.[8] However, as was the case for Experiment 1, there are alternative explanations that must also be considered.

1. Maintained Activation. Despite the fact that the head of the relative clause in subject position was separated from the verb by approximately nine words, it is possible that the priming observed in this experiment reflects not *re*-activation, but residual activation. One reason that activation of the head might be maintained is that the relative clause following the head *modifies*, or provides further information about, the head. By contrast, in the sentences tested in Experiment 1, what intervened between the fronted constituent and the verb was *another argument of the verb*. If the processing system is designed to focus attention on verbal arguments, one can imagine that in the sentences in Experiment 1, there is a shifting of attention away from the moved PP to the subject NP, and then back to the moved PP during theta-role assignment. In the sentences used here, there were no intervening arguments; therefore, the head of the relative clause could simply remain active.

Just as for Experiment 1, the possibility of residual priming can only be rejected if one finds no priming at a point *before* the verb.

2. Trace Postulation. Although it is standardly assumed that subjects are base-generated, there are, in fact, several accounts of syntactic structure in which subjects of clauses originate inside the VP and are moved to clausal subject position (in the mapping from D-Structure to S-Structure), leaving behind a NP-trace (Diesing, 1990, 1992; Kitagawa, 1986; Koopman & Sportiche, 1988; Kuroda, 1986; Sportiche, 1988). The basic idea is that all the arguments of a verb are generated inside the VP, including the subject; this allows a maximally simple theory of the structural conditions necessary for theta-marking.[9] Given the

---

[8] It should be pointed out that in roughly half of the experimental sentences used in Experiment 2, it is not the verb (*is/seems to be*) that assigns theta-roles, but the *predicate nominal*, e.g. *a failure*. That is, in the sentence *The actress is a failure*, *the actress* receives a theta role from *a failure*. With respect to the priming effect, this raises a question as to why priming was obtained as *early* as the verb. If it is the predicate nominal that triggers reactivation, then we should not expect priming until the nominal is processed. However, copular verbs are special cases, and clearly recognisable as such. Hence it is likely that the predicate NP does not need to be fully processed to give rise to activation of the subject NP.

[9] A verb (and all other theta-assigning heads) will simply theta-mark within its maximal projection, i.e. theta-marking will be constrained by the relation of government.

structure *[The actress]ᵢ is [vp tᵢ . . .]*, the priming observed here could be due to the postulation of a trace.

This possibility is difficult to eliminate, since one cannot de-couple the trace from the verb position (as was possible for the movement cases examined in Experiment 1). If one accepts the analysis that subjects move out of the VP, then the proper construal of the results of Experiment 2 awaits further research examining the priming of subjects (specific research questions will be raised later).

General Discussion

The results of the two studies presented here are compatible with the notion that priming may be linked to theta-role assignment, or the establishment of a dependency.[10] A number of alternative explanations were raised: maintained activation; erroneous trace postulation (in the fronted PP sentences); proper trace postulation (in the subject-priming sentences). These are still viable, and can only be ruled out with additional empirical study.

Even so, it may be worthwhile at this point to consider more closely how the verb-driven priming account works. Although the priming results obtained in Experiment 2 may be straightforwardly assumed to be due to assignment of a theta-role to the subject, there remains the problem noted in the discussion of Experiment 1: if priming is due to the processes involved in theta-role assignment, why should there be priming of the PP at *two* different points within the sentence? Here is a tentative answer. Suppose that the two priming effects in Experiment 1 represent two parts of a single process: at the verb, the preposed constituent is reactivated in order to determine which theta role it best fits, and this constituent is provisionally assigned one of the theta-roles; then, at a point following the direct object, it is activated again so that theta role assignment may be confirmed.

Let us consider the stages of processing that this would involve. Assume, as a number of studies have shown, that the thematic grid of a verb is accessed immediately on encountering the verb (Pritchett, 1988; Shapiro et al., 1987; Trueswell, Tanenhaus, & Garnsey, 1990). Let us further assume that when an NP is encountered, its local syntactic environment is assessed to determine whether or not that NP is assigned a theta role in its surface position (i.e. whether it is in a theta-marked argument position). Finally, let us assume that this information is taken into account during

---

[10] See Pickering, 1991, for a discussion of priming effects as a reflection of dependency formation.

theta-role assignment. Information concerning argument position is relevant to theta-role assignment because it may help the processor match theta-roles with arguments. For example, in the sequence $NP_{non-arg}$ + NP_{arg} + VP, (where *non-arg* refers to a *non-argument*, [or A'] position, and *arg* refers to an *argument* [or A] position), it is very likely that the first NP is a complement, and the second NP is the subject.

Consider a simplified version of sentence (9): *To which butcher did the woman give the gift t.* Theta role assignment would proceed as follows (parentheses indicate theta-roles that have been provisionally assigned).

The verb *give* has three theta roles to assign, one of which (the agent role) is to be assigned directly to the subject *the woman*, as indicated.

18. [pp To [which butcher]]$_{A'}$ did [the woman)$_A$ *GIVE* . . .

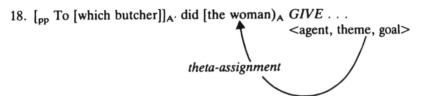

This leaves one leftward NP (*the butcher*) lacking a theta role, and two theta roles (the *theme* and *goal* theta-roles of *give*) unassigned. The preposed constituent—which lacks a theta-role—is then *retrieved* and evaluated as a potential recipient of one of these theta-roles.[11] Since a PP argument is more likely to be a goal than a theme, this role is provisionally assigned to the PP.

19. [pp To [which butcher]]$_{A'}$ did [the woman]$_A$ *GIVE* . . .

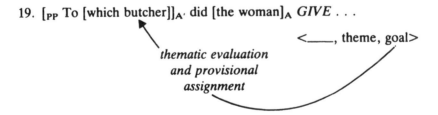

At the next stage, the NP following the verb is processed. This NP is assigned the *theme* role.

---

[11] No claims are made here about the nature of the information used to evaluate arguments as appropriate recipients of particular theta roles. Clearly, there is likely to be some reference to syntactic position (such as *A-positions*), and syntactic category information (e.g. PPs are likely to be recipients). Tanenhaus and his colleagues imply that real-world information may also be appealed to during this process.

20. . . . did [the woman]$_A$ *GIVE*   [$_{NP}$ the gift] . . .

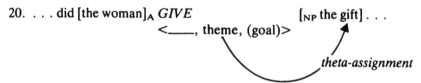

Next, the trace is posited. The subcategorisation frame for *give* indicates that it takes a NP and a PP complement, but there is no PP complement present at that point in the string. Hence, the trace is postulated. This gives rise to reactivation of the moved PP. The assignment of the *goal* theta-role may then be confirmed.

21. . . . did [the woman]$_A$ *GIVE*   [$_{NP}$ the gift] [$_{PP}$ *trace*] . . .

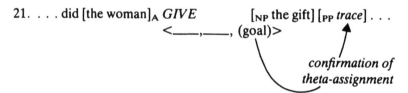

On this model, the reactivation of an argument would be associated with the processes involved in theta-role assignment (including provisional theta-role assignment). Of course, arguments may not need to be *re*-activated if they have not had a chance to *de*-activate; this would be true of adjacent arguments, especially if the argument is to the immediate right of the verb (e.g. *the gift*).

This model is compatible with the priming effects observed in both studies reported here, and in Swinney et al. (1989). Furthermore, it makes clear predictions about intersentential priming in other types of structures: *whenever there is theta-role assignment (or provisional assignment), the theta-role recipient should show priming.* Are there other priming results that support this prediction? There are other results, and some of them do support the prediction. Others do not. Let us examine these findings.

1. Priming of the Subject of the Verb in Passive Sentences.   The verb-driven priming theory predicts priming for the subject of the verb in any construction, including passive constructions such as (22) (priming should be observed at the #):

22. The *actor* who'd just moved into the neighbourhood was hired # by the baker to speak to the staff.

A number of studies have examined priming in such constructions. Unfortunately, the results so far are mixed. Whereas the results of several *probe recognition* studies suggest that the subject of a passive is reactivated, these findings indicate that the reactivation is not immediate (McElree &

Bever, 1989), unless the probe appears sentence-finally (Bever & McElree, 1988; MacDonald, 1989; McElree & Bever, (1989)). A delayed effect was also found by Osterhout and Swinney (1992), using the cross-modal priming methodology. They found non-significant priming of the subject of the verb at a point just after the appearance of the verb (there was a significant effect only after a substantial delay after the verb). Replication of this result with the cross-modal methodology is clearly needed.

2. Priming of the Understood Subject of the Infinitive. If subjects are reactivated, then they should prime in infinitival constructions such as (23):

23. The *actor* was hired by the baker who'd just moved into the neighbourhood [to speak # to the staff].

Again, there are mixed results. The probe recognition task shows some facilitation, though it is not always significant, for the understood subject of the infinitive (McElree & Bever, 1989). Using the cross-modal technique, Nicol and Osterhout (reported in Nicol & Swinney, 1989) found no such priming in constructions such as *The actress was invited by the dentist* to go *to the party*. However, the experiment lacked power, and the data were quite variable. Again, constructions of this type need to be tested further.

3. Priming of the Subject in Conjoined Verb Phrase Constructions. The subject of a verb should also show priming in constructions such as the following:

24. The *actor* called up some old friends, and then left # the theater.

To date, such constructions have not been examined; they are clearly important to test.

It is important to point out that although the observation of priming in each of these cases would support a verb-driven account of priming, such results would not *disprove* trace theory, nor a processing theory that tied priming to trace postulation. In each of the three cases discussed here, an empty category in the vicinity of the verb could produce a priming effect: within a Government-Binding framework, there is a NP-trace following the verb in passive sentences such as (22), a PRO as the subject of an infinitive, as in (23), and, on the view that subjects originate in the VP and move leftward into subject position, there could be a trace of *the actor* in the verb phrase containing the verb *left*.

How can one decide, then, between the two accounts of priming? It seems to be the case that wherever there is a verb, there is an empty category in the vicinity of the verb. And in the one construction where the verb and trace are separated—the moved-PP sentences tested in Experiment 1—the lurking possibility of Heavy Constituent Shift, and the possible (erroneous) postulation of a trace after the verb makes even *this* case difficult to interpret.

In a certain respect, it may not matter which account is right. After all, the syntactic arguments for the existence of empty categories are intimately linked to the thematic structure of verbs. One argument for postulating an empty category at surface structure is to preserve a constant mapping between a verb's argument structure and the syntactic structure of a sentence (Chomsky's 1981 *Projection Principle*). The *agent* argument, for example, is always assigned to a position outside the VP (Travis & Williams, 1982), and to the left of the VP in languages like English.[12] Given the link between empty categories and theta-role assignment, it is not surprising that it may be difficult to disentangle to two accounts.

CONCLUDING REMARKS

In this paper, I have attempted to integrate the results of a number of filler-gap experiments. More specifically, I have tried to recast the priming results in terms of a model of sentence processing which supposes that *at the verb*, the verb's arguments are evaluated with respect to a verb's theta roles, and theta-role assignment immediately follows.

This interpretation is offered tentatively; the current body of data is compatible with a number of explanations (some of which were raised in the discussion of results of Experiment 1), and although the verb-driven account is compatible with the processing account offered by Tanenhaus et al., a good deal of further experimentation is required to settle a number of questions that have been left unanswered.

I think that there is merit in continuing this line of inquiry. There is much to be learned from discovering at which points in a sentence an argument of the verb is active. In determining how the different arguments of a verb relate to one another it seems plausible that the sentence processor will need to refresh the first mentioned arguments at various

---

[12] This generalisation would seem to be a problem for passive constructions, in which (on typical analyses, e.g. Jackendoff, 1972) the agent is typically expressed by the *by-phrase* following the verb, or is simply inferred, in the case of short passives. Jaeggli (1986) argues extensively that the generalisation noted in the text holds even for passives; the *agent* role is assigned to a VP-external clitic morpheme (the passive morpheme–EN), which for morphological reasons becomes associated with the verb stem as an affix. This clitic constitutes the actual agent argument; the by-phrase constitutes a 'doubling' phrase, on a par with the clitic-doubling constructions that occur in several dialects of Spanish.

points throughout the sentence. It would illuminate the operation of this processor to learn just when this happens.

ACKNOWLEDGEMENTS

This research was supported in part by a grant from the McDonnell-Pew Cognitive Neurosciences Program, and in part by funding from the Child Language Laboratory at the University of Arizona (US Department of Education Grant H029D90109). I would like to thank Gerry Altmann, Andrew Barss, Janet Fodor, Mike Tanenhaus, and an anonymous reviewer for extremely helpful comments on an earlier draft of this chapter. In addition, I have benefited greatly from discussion of these issues with Gerry Altmann, Andrew Barss, Janet Fodor, Ken Forster, Martin Pickering, Richard Shillcock, Mike Tanenhaus, and the participants of the workshop on Cognitive Models of Speech Processing, Sperlonga, Italy, June, 1990.

REFERENCES

Barss, A. (this volume). *Transparency and visibility: Sentence processing and the grammar of anaphora.*

Bever, T.G. & McElree, B. (1988). Empty categories access their antecedents during comprehension. *Linguistic Inquiry 19*, 35–43.

Bever, T.G., Straub, K., Shenkman, K., Kim, J.J., & Carrithers, C. (1990). The psychological reality of NP-trace. *Proceedings of NELS 20*. GLSA, University of Massachusetts.

Boland, J.E., & Tanenhaus, M.K. (1990). The role of lexical representations in sentence processing. In G.B. Simpson (Ed.), *Understanding word and sentence*. Amsterdam: North-Holland.

Boland, J.E., Tanenhaus, M.K., Carlson, G., & Garnsey, S.M. (1989). Lexical projection and the interaction of syntax and semantics in parsing. *Journal of Psycholinguistic Research, 18*, 563–576.

Boland, J.E., Tanenhaus, M.K., & Garnsey, S.M. (1990). Lexical structure and parsing: Evidence for the immediate use of verbal argument and control information in parsing. *Journal of Memory and Language, 29*, 413–432.

Bresnan, J. (1982). *The mental representations of grammatical relations*. Cambridge, MA: MIT Press.

Byma, G. (1991). *Processing WH-filler-gap constructions: A consideration of the reactivation hypothesis using cross-modal and intra-modal designs*. Unpublished ms., Brown University, Providence, RI.

Chodorow, M. (1979). Time-compressed speech and the study of lexical and syntactic processing. In W.E. Cooper, & E.C.T. Walker (Eds.), *Sentence processing: Psycholinguistic studies presented to Merrill Garrett*. Hillsdale, NJ: Lawrence Erlbaum Associates Inc.

Chomsky, N. (1981). *Lectures on government and binding*. Dordrecht: Foris.

Clifton, C., & Frazier, L. (1989). Comprehending sentences with long-distance dependencies. In G.N. Carlson, & M.K. Tanenhaus (Eds.), *Linguistic structure in language processing*, (pp. 273–317). Dordrecht/Boston/London: Kluwer Academic Publishers.

Clifton, C., Frazier, L., & Connine, C. (1984). Lexical expectations in sentence comprehension. *Journal of Verbal Learning and Verbal Behavior, 23*, 696–708.

Crain, S., & Fodor, J.D. (1985). How can grammars help parsers? In D.P. Dowty, L. Karttunen, & A.M. Zwicky (Eds.), *Natural language parsing: Psychological, computational and theoretical perspectives*. Cambridge: Cambridge University Press.

Diesing, M. (1990). *The syntactic roots of semantic partition*. Unpublished doctoral dissertation, UMASS, Amherst.

Diesing, M. (1992). *Indefinites*. Cambridge, MA: MIT Press.

Ferreira, F., & Henderson, J.M. (1990). The use of verb information in syntactic parsing: Evidence from eye movements and word-by-word self-paced reading. *Journal of Experimental Psychology: Learning, Memory, and Cognition, 16*, 555–568.

Fodor, J. (1979). Superstrategy. In W.E. Cooper & E.C.T. Walker (Eds.), *Sentence processing: Psycholinguistics studies presented to Merrill Garrett*. Hillsdale, NJ: Lawrence Erlbaum Associates Inc.

Fodor, J. (1990). Processing empty categories: Distinguishing syntactic and semantic reactivation effects. In G. Altmann (Ed.), *Cognitive models of speech processing: Psycholinguistic and computational perspectives*. Cambridge, MA: MIT Press.

Fodor, J. (this volume). *Empty categories in sentence processing: A question of visibility*.

Frazier, L., & Clifton, C. (1989). Successive cyclicity in the grammar and the parser. *Language and Cognitive Processes, 4*, 93–126.

Garnsey, S.M., Tanenhaus, M.K., & Chapman, R.M. (1989). Evoked potentials and the study of sentence comprehension. *Journal of Psycholinguistic Research: Special Issue on Sentence Processing, 18*, 51–60.

Gorrell, P. (1987). *Studies in human sentence processing: Ranked-parallel versus serial models*. Unpublished doctoral dissertation, University of Connecticut.

Hickok, G. (1991). *Gaps and garden-paths: Studies on the architecture and computational machinery of the human sentence processor*. Unpublished doctoral dissertation, Brandeis University, Waltham, MA.

Jackendoff, R. (1972). *Semantics in generative grammar*. Cambridge, MA: MIT Press.

Jaeggli, O. (1986). Passive. *Linguistic Inquiry, 17*, 587–622.

Kitagawa, Y. (1986). *Subjects in Japanese and English*, Unpublished doctoral dissertation, UMASS, Amherst.

Koopman, H., & Sportiche, D. (1988). *Subjects*. Unpublished ms., UCLA.

Kuno, S. (1973). Constraints on Internal Clauses and Sentential Subjects, *Linguistics Inquiry, 4*, 363–386.

Kuroda, S.-Y. (1986). *Whether we agree or not*. Unpublished ms., UCSD.

Kurtzman, H. (1985). *Studies in syntactic ambiguity resolution*. Unpublished doctoral dissertation, MIT, Cambridge, MA.

Kurtzman, H., Crawford, L.F., & Nychis–Florence, C. (1991). 'Locating WH–traces,' in R.C. Berwick, S.P. Abney, & C. Tenny (Eds.). *Principle–based parsing: Computation and psycholinguistics*. Dordrecht: Kluwer Academic Publishers.

MacDonald, M.C. (1989). Priming effects from gaps to antecedents. *Language and Cognitive Processes, 4*, 35–56.

MacDonald, M.C., & Clark, R. (1989). Empty categories, implicit arguments, and processing. *Proceedings of Northeastern Linguistics Society, 18*, 300–314. Graduate Linguistics Student Association, University of Massachusetts, Amherst.

McElree, B., & Bever, T.G. (1989). The psychological reality of linguistically defined gaps. *Journal of Psycholinguistic Research, 18*, 21–35.

Mitchell, D.C. (1987). Lexical guidance in human parsing: Locus and processing characteristics. In M. Coltheart (Ed.), *Attention and performance, Volume 12, The psychology of reading*. Hillsdale, NJ: Lawrence Erlbaum Associates Inc.

Nakayama, M. (1990). *Priming and anaphoric expressions in Japanese*. Unpublished ms., The Ohio State University.

Nicol, J. (1988). *Coreference processing during sentence comprehension.* Unpublished doctoral dissertation, MIT, Cambridge, MA.

Nicol, J. (1989). What the parser knows about the grammer: Psycholinguistic evidence. In E.G. Fee & K. Hunt (Eds.) *Proceedings of the West Coast Conference on Formal linguistics.* VIII, 289–302. Centre for the Study of Language and Information, Stanford University, CA.

Nicol, J.L., & Pickering, M.J. (in press). Processing syntactically ambiguous sentences: Evidence from semantic priming. *Journal of Psycholinguistic Research.*

Nicol, J., & Swinney, D. (1989). The role of structure in coreference assignment during sentence comprehension. *Journal of Psycholinguistic Research, 18,* (1), 5–19.

Osterhout, L., & Swinney, D. (1992, March) . Timecourse of antecedent availability following NP-trace. Poster presented at the 1992 CUNY Conference on Sentence Processing, New York, NY.

Pickering, M.J. (1991). *Processing dependencies.* Unpublished doctoral dissertation, University of Edinburgh, UK.

Pickering, M., & Barry, G. (1990). *Sentence processing without empty categories.* Unpublished ms., Centre for Cognitive Science, University of Edinburgh, UK.

Pritchett, B.L. (1988). Garden path phenomena and the grammatical basis of language processing. *Language, 64,* 539–576.

Ross, J.R. (1967). *Constraints on variables in syntax.* Doctoral dissertation, MIT, Cambridge, MA.

Shapiro, L., Zurif, E., & Grimshaw, J. (1987). Sentence processing and the mental representation of verbs. *Cognition, 27,* 219–246.

Shillcock, R. (1982). The on-line resolution of pronominal anaphora. *Language and Speech, 25,* 385–401.

Sportiche, D. (1988). A theory of floating quantifiers and its corollaries for constituent structure, *Linguistic Inquiry, 19,* 425–499.

Stowe, L.A. (1986). Parsing WH-constructions: Evidence for on-line gap location. *Language and Cognitive Processes, 1*(3), 227–245.

Stowell, T. (1981). *Origins of Phrase Structure.* Doctoral dissertation, MIT, Cambridge, MA.

Swinney, D. (1979). Lexical Access during sentence comprehension: (Re)consideration of context effects. *Journal of Verbal Learning and Verbal Behavior, 18,* 645–659.

Swinney, D., Ford, M., & Bresnan, J. (1989). On the temporal course of gap-filling and antecedent assignment during sentence comprehension. In B. Grosz, R. Kaplan, M. Macken, & I. Sag (Eds.), *Language structure and processing,* Stanford, CA: CSLI.

Swinney, D.A., & Osterhout, L. (1990). Inference generation during auditory language comprehension. *The Psychology of Learning and Motivation, 25,* 17–33.

Tanenhaus, M.K., Boland, J.E., Garnsey, S.M., & Carlson, G.N. (1989). Lexical structure in parsing long-distance dependencies. *Journal of Psycholinguistic Research, 18,* 37–50.

Tanenhaus, M.K., Boland, J.E., Mauner, G.A., & Carlson, G. (this volume). *More on combinatory lexical information: Thematic structure in parsing and interpretation.*

Tanenhaus, M., & Carlson, G. (1989). Lexical structure and language comprehension. In W.D. Marslen-Wilson (Ed.), *Lexical representation and process.* Cambridge, MA: MIT Press.

Tanenhaus, M., Carlson, G., & Seidenberg, M. (1985). Do listeners compute linguistic representations? In A Zwicky, L. Kartunnen, & D. Dowty (Eds.), *Natural language parsing: Psycholinguistic, theoretical, and computational perspectives.* London & New York: Cambridge University Press.

Tanenhaus, M.K., Garnsey, S.M., & Boland, J. (1990). Combinatory lexical information and language comprehension. In G.T.M. Altmann (Ed.), *Cognitive models of speech processing: Psycholinguistic and computational perspectives.* Cambridge MA, & London, UK: MIT Press.

Tanenhaus, M.K., Leiman, J.M., & Seidenberg, M.S. (1979). Evidence for multiple stages in the processing of ambiguous words in syntactic contexts. *Journal of Verbal Learning and Verbal Behavior, 18*, 427–440.

Tanenhaus, M.K., Stowe, L.A., & Carlson, G. (1985). The interactions of lexical expectation and pragmatics in parsing filler-gap constructions. In *Proceedings of the Seventh Annual Cognitive Science Society Meeting*, Hillsdale, NJ: Lawrence Erlbaum Associates Inc.

Travis, L., & Williams, E. (1982). Externalization of arguments in Malayo-Polynesian languages. *The Linguistic Review, 2*, 57–77.

Trueswell, J.C., Tanenhaus, M.K., & Garnsey, S.M. (1990). *Semantic influences on parsing: Use of thematic role information in syntactic disambiguation.* Unpublished ms.

Wexler, K., & Culicover, P. (1980). *Formal principles of language acquisition.* Cambridge, MA: MIT Press.

APPENDIX A

Experimental Materials for Experiment 1

The antecedent that was probed is indicated in italics. Probe points are shown by # (probe point 1), and ## (probe point 2). Related targets (R) and unrelated targets (U) are shown for each sentence. Targets were counterbalanced across presentation lists; although several targets appear to have been repeated (these are indicated by *), these appeared in different lists.

1. To which *pilot* did the soldier who was recovering from an illness in San Francisco send # some new popular cassettes ## on Wednesday morning?
   R: plane   U: scene

2. To which *dentist* did the janitor who had recently moved into the area tell # the rather complicated story ## during the evening?
   R: tooth   U: flood

3. To which *cyclist* did the grocer who owned the shop which was on the outskirts of town send # the long apologetic letter ## in the late afternoon?
   R: bicycle   U: vitamin

4. To which *duke* did the violinist who was starting to drink very heavily bring # some extremely welcome news ## yesterday at lunch time?
   R: duchess   U: buffoon

5. With which *astronomer* did the reporter working free-lance for the new agency discuss # an important sought-after job # # a month ago?
   R: star   U: stem

6. To which *boxer* did the swimmer who was meeting some friends in the coffee house show # the extremely impressive collection of trophies ## sometime before lunch?
   R: punch   U: stem

7. To which *writer* did the athlete who was hoping to become famous in the next few years show # the not particularly impressive award ## after the dinner?
   R: book   U: plan

8. To which *uncle* did the researcher wearing a large grey overcoat and carrying an umbrella give # the small green book ## yesterday after work?

    R: aunt   U: sand

9. To which *architect* did the colonel who would retire at the end of the year give # an enormous wrapped-up gift ## immediately after breakfast?

    R: building   U: picture

10. To which *doctor* did the bricklayer from a small community in North Dakota give # a long thick winter coat ## a few weeks ago?

    R: nurse   U: lodge

11. To which *waitress* did the botanist who hoped to earn a lot of money offer # the important well-paid job ## almost a month ago?

    R: tip   U: bus

12. To which *playwright* did the scientist who used to be a collector of antique furniture tell # the slightly confusing account of this hobby ## one early evening?

    R: play   U: town

13. To which *actress* did the shopkeeper who was going to leave the country in a few weeks bring # a valuable old leather-bound book ## late one evening?

    R: stage   U: space

14.* To which *astronomer* did the geologist who had recently been appointed as chair of the important committee send # the very detailed plans ## sometime last week?

    R: star   U: stem

15.* To which *boxer* did the sportsman who had developed quite a reputation in recent months bring # some enthusiastic young admirers ## after lunch on Thursday?

    R: punch   U: barge

16.* To which *writer* did the explorer who had just returned from a long and dangerous journey offer # the extremely warm sleeping bag ## on Monday last week?

    R: book   U: plan

17.* To which *uncle* did the wrestler who was going to retire in a month's time explain # the highly complicated reasons ## sometime last week?

    R: aunt   U: sand

18.* To which *cyclist* did the repairman carrying some overalls and a rolled-up newspaper show # the very badly drawn plans ## early in the morning?

    R: bicycle   U: vitamin

APPENDIX B

Experimental Materials for Experiment 2

There are two different versions of each sentence. These different versions showed the same pattern of priming, and are listed separately here for expository clarity and completeness. Related (R) and unrelated (U) targets are shown with each sentence pair. The probe point is indicated by the symbol #.

1a. The salesman who won the company's annual contest had seemed to # be an unlikely candidate for first place.

1b. The salesman who won the company's annual contest was # an unlikely candidate for first place.
R: sale   U: path

2a. The policeman who was shot in the leg during the chase actually happened to be # off-duty at the time.

2b. The policeman who was shot in the leg during the chase was # actually off-duty at the time.
R: badge   U: straw

3a. The stewardess who needs a date for the big New Year's party only happens to # be in town because her flight was cancelled.

3b. The stewardess who needs a date for the big New Year's party is # only in town because her flight was cancelled.
R: pilot   U: minor

4a. The countess whose jewels were stolen from the hotel safe doesn't need to # be concerned about the theft.

4b. The countess whose jewels were stolen from the hotel safe isn't # concerned about the theft.
R: count   U: guard

5a. The actress who had caused such a sensation among all the critics continues to # be a failure with the general public.

5b. The actress who had caused such a sensation among all the critics is # a failure with the general public.
R: movie   U: panel

6a. The king that met the press in his flowing crimson robes certainly appears to # be fit for the duties of royal office.

6b. The king that met the press in his flowing crimson robes is # certainly fit for the duties of royal office.
R: throne   U: thrift

7a. The baker who specialises in European bread and holiday confections seems to # enjoy producing dark and crusty country-style loaves.

7b. The baker who specialises in European bread and holiday confections enjoys # producing dark and crusty country-style loaves.
R: oven   U: pony

8a. The paperboy who has worked in this neighbourhood for several years usually seems to # know what he's doing.

8b. The paperboy who has worked in this neighbourhood for several years usually knows # what he's doing.
R: news   U: mass

9a. The businessman who caused the automobile accident on the freeway the other day ridiculously continues to # believe that the other driver was at fault.

9b. The businessman who caused the automobile accident on the freeway the other day ridiculously still believes # that the other driver was at fault.

     R: office   U: result

10a. The mechanic who never wears anything but blue coveralls tends to # work more slowly on antique cars than on modern ones.

10b. The mechanic who never wears anything but blue coveralls works # more slowly on antique cars than on modern ones.

     R: wrench   U: breath11a. That quarterback who does all of the   boring   television   commercials   doesn't   appear   to # like very many advertisements.

11b. That quarterback who does all of the boring television commercials doesn't appear # in very many advertisements.

     R: football   U: backlash

12a. The professor who received a long-awaited and much-deserved promotion last year continues to # publish yearly despite her new job security.

12b. The professor who received a long-awaited and much-deserved promotion last year publishes # yearly despite her new job security.

     R: college   U: service

13a. The waitress who was so popular with all the customers in fact tended to # resent the demands of the patrons.

13b. The waitress who was so popular with all the customers in fact resented the demands of the patrons.

     R: restaurant   U: laboratory

14a. The detective who works part-time for the small private company needs to # improve his relationship with the local police.

14b. The detective who works part-time for the small private company has improved # his relationship with the local police.

     R: crime   U: bread

V Issues of Process in Formal Linguistics

16 Processing Empty Categories: A Question of Visibility

Janet Dean Fodor
Graduate Center, CUNY, New York, USA

BACKGROUND

Methodological Assumptions

The results have been coming in from experiments on empty categories in sentence processing, and there seems to be a general willingness to regard them as bearing on the truth of theoretical linguistic claims. Though I have disagreed (Fodor, 1989) with some of the interpretations that have been proposed, I applaud the general research strategy of trying to use psycholinguistic findings to answer linguistic questions. Not all psycholinguistic findings are suitable for this purpose, of course, and nor are all linguistic issues, but the empty category project seems to have just the right properties to succeed.

An experiment to find out, for instance, which reading of an ambiguous sentence the processing routines prefer to compute, may have nothing to offer theoretical linguistics. But any experiment that reveals how a sentence is mentally represented by language users could in principle show something about its derivation that linguistics would like to know. For this to be so, we must assume that the structural representations assigned by the processing routines reflect the structural representations defined by the mental (competence) grammar. Without denying the possibility of a mismatch between the two (e.g. because of on-line parsing errors), many psycholinguists these days are prepared to accept this transparency principle as at least a working hypothesis, to be given up only when there is specific reason to.

Not just any experiment on mental representations of sentences will be informative. To be useful to linguistics, it must address some aspect of sentence structure that linguists don't already know about. To be worth the trouble and expense of running an experiment, it must address an aspect of sentence structure that linguists couldn't easily find out about by conventional linguistic methods. The most efficient way to determine whether Latvian is a pro-drop language, for example, is probably not to put 60 Latvian speakers through a self-paced reading task.

I have argued elsewhere (Fodor, 1991) that the linguistic issues that stand to benefit most from psycholinguistic investigation are the central points that distinguish one general theory of language from another. These issues have just the profile we are looking for. (1) Competing theories of grammar typically entail different structural representations for certain sentences; to find out which theory is right, we can try to find out which structure is right; (2) The issue, almost by definition, is one that linguists don't yet know the answer to, in the sense that two (or more) different answers have been argued for on linguistic grounds and there is no agreement as to which is correct; (3) The disagreement typically cannot be quickly resolved by the usual linguistic methods, because whatever new linguistic facts are brought into the debate are accommodated somehow by each theory, with suitable adjustments of its rules or principles if necessary. The theories present quite different pictures of how the various facts group, what kinds of formal mechanisms grammars employ, what levels of representation there are, and so on; but (at least ideally) they cover the same range of linguistic data.

The questions about empty categories that have been addressed in recent experiments meet all three of these criteria. (1) The issue is how certain sentences (passives, questions, etc.) are mentally represented. An empty category is a syntactic constituent of a sentence that has no phonological form. Since it has no physical realisation, it is superficially indistinguishable from the absence of a constituent, but it plays an important role in the syntactic derivation and semantic interpretation of a sentence, and interacts in an orderly way with grammatical principles. If it could be shown that there is *NO* constituent, where some linguistic theory says there is an *EMPTY* constituent, or vice versa, then the principles of that theory must be wrong. (2) The questions haven't all been answered yet. A decade of linguistic research on empty categories has uncovered some extremely interesting patterns and universal trends. But there are two or three differing, but each more or less stable, theoretical positions that cover the facts and yet disagree about exactly which sentences contain empty categories. (3) The theories have not settled their differences, at least so far, on the basis of linguistic arguments. So this looks like just the kind of area in which discoveries about sentence processing, of interest in themselves, may also have linguistic relevance.

To proceed, we need an experimental method that will allow us to tell whether the human sentence processor, given a word string whose phrase marker is claimed by some theory to contain an empty category, constructs a mental representation that does contain an empty category, or represents nothing there at all. Such methods have been developed and refined over the last few years, and I will discuss them later. The results they are producing are interesting but also complicated, and I believe there is still a lot of thinking to be done about exactly how the connections between experimental data and linguistic conclusions should be drawn. In many cases, also, it turns out that we need to clarify or extend current linguistic analyses in order to establish exactly what some theory does or does not predict about certain sentence constructions, or to decide which constructions it would be profitable to put to experimental test.

This chapter illustrates what I believe is a very general truth: that it takes a lot of linguistics to design and interpret one psycholinguistic experiment. Perhaps the present example is an extreme one, but I argue here that the import of the empty category results depends crucially on what level of linguistic representation they relate to, and in addressing this I have found it necessary to explore the relations between syntax and semantics, and between syntax and phonetic form. The discussion will move from linguistics to psychology and back again, as I believe it must, and I have done my best to make it intelligible to readers from both disciplines.

Interpreting Previous Results

We may begin with Government Binding theory (GB), which recognises more types of empty category than other theories do. These are illustrated in (1).[1]

(1)a. Who$_i$ did John speak to *WH-trace$_i$*?
   b. John$_i$ was arrested *NP-trace$_i$* by the police.
   c. John$_i$ seemed *NP-trace$_i$* to tremble.
   d. John$_i$ tried *PRO$_i$* to climb the hill.
   e. (Ecco *Gianni$_i$*.) *pro$_i$* Sta mangiando.

---

[1] Government Binding theory (Chomsky, 1981 and since; e.g. 1986a) is a development out of earlier transformational theories. The last few years have seen further significant changes stemming largely from Chomsky's *Barriers* (1986b), but there will be no need here to distinguish between the Barriers theory and the earlier GB theory.

In (1a), the question word *who* is the object of the preposition *to*, but has been moved to pre-sentence position; left behind in the underlying position of the *who* is what is called a *trace* of movement, i.e. an empty category co-indexed with the moved phrase. In (1b) and (1c) there is also a trace of movement, but the movement here is different; what has moved is not a WH-phrase but an ordinary noun phrase (NP), and it has moved not to pre-sentence position but into the subject position of the sentence. In (1b) the NP has moved from object position, creating a passive sentence; in (1c) the NP has moved from the subject position of the lower clause (subject of *to tremble*), creating what is often called a 'raising' construction. In (1d) the empty category PRO is not created by movement but is generated as empty; it functions as the subject of an infinitival subordinate clause, and is coreferential with (controlled by) the subject of the main clause. In (1e) the empty category *pro* (small pro or little pro, to contrast with big PRO) is also generated in place; it functions as the subject of a finite clause, and refers to an individual in the discourse context; *pro* does not occur in English.

I will not present the reasons within GB for distinguishing these four types of empty category, and I will not say anything more at all about *pro*. What matters for present purposes is that, of the other three empty categories, other linguistic theories postulate only one or none. Generalised Phrase Structure Grammar (GPSG) and its more recent descendant Head-driven Phrase Structure Grammar (HPSG) assume only WH-trace.[2] Lexical Functional Grammar (LFG) also for many years acknowledged only WH-trace (see Bresnan & Kaplan, 1982). But the most recent work in LFG denies that any of these phenomena, even WH-movement, involve empty categories at the level of constituent structure, and treats them instead at the level of functional structure at which predicate-argument relations are represented (see Kaplan & Zaenen, 1989).

These non-transformational theories do not disagree with GB about what sentences mean. At the semantic level, all theories make essentially the same claims about which predicates have which arguments.[3] It is the

---

[2] See Sells (1985) for a summary of GPSG, and Gazdar, Klein, Pullum, and Sag (1985) for details. See Pollard and Sag (1987; 1993) on HPSG. The differences between the two theories will not be relevant to my arguments here.

[3] This is only very roughly true. Comparison of the theories with respect to their treatment of semantics is a quagmire that I shall determinedly skirt in this paper. GB assumes that semantic interpretation is mediated by a level of Logical Form (LF) that represents the scope of quantifiers and related items. LFG assumes that semantic interpretation is mediated by a level of functional structure (f-structure) that represents predicate-argument relations. In both theories there may also be, though this is not entirely clear, a level of semantic representation that captures everything that an ideal speaker/hearer knows about the meaning of a sentence (though possibly this is not a purely linguistic representation). GPSG admits no level more abstract than (surface) syntactic structure, and assumes that semantic rules relate sentences directly to the situations in the world that they describe. GPSG is not intended to model psychological reality; a psychological theory based on it might posit some sort of mental representation of sentence meaning. HPSG takes a more explicitly representational approach to sentence meaning.

mechanism by which this interpretation is assigned that differs from one theory to another. If the syntax contains an empty category, the interpretive rules can assign it a role in the meaning of the sentence just as they would for any other sentence constituent. Where there is no empty category in the syntax, there must be special interpretive processes that supply predicates with their missing arguments. For example, in theories without NP-trace, the lexical entry for a raising predicate, such as *seem* in (1c), specifies that the subject of *seem* will fill the semantic role that would be associated with the subject of the complement verb (in this case *tremble*) if that verb had an overt subject.[4]

The experiments that look for signs of empty categories during sentence processing are based on the idea that when the processor identifies an empty category in a sentence, it will assign its antecedent to it. This implies that the antecedent phrase should be activated at the position in the sentence at which the empty category appears. It is assumed that the meaning of each overt word of a sentence is activated temporarily as that word is processed. So in a sentence like (2), the meaning of *boy* will be activated when the word *boy* is processed.

(2) [Which boy]$_i$ should the girl from the orphanage have spoken to *WH-trace*$_i$ at the party?

That activation will gradually decline over the next few words, but then the meaning of *boy* should be *RE*activated at the position of the WH-trace since *which boy* is the antecedent of the trace.

Recent experiments have utilised two different tasks to reveal the predicted reactivation of antecedents. One is a probe recognition task (see Bever & McElree, 1988; MacDonald, 1989; McElree & Bever, 1989), in which a visually presented sentence (or sequence of sentences) is followed by presentation of a single word, and the subject's task is to say as quickly as possible whether the word occurred in the sentence. In all cases of interest, the probe is a word that appears in the phrase which is the antecedent of the postulated empty category. The other experimental paradigm involves cross-modal priming (see Nicol, 1988; Swinney, Ford, Bresnan, & Frauenfelder, 1988; and other references in Fodor, 1989). At some point during the presentation of a spoken sentence, a string of letters appears briefly on a screen and the subject's task is either to decide

---

[4] I am ignoring another distinction here, though it may hold insights for the interpretation of the experimental data. It is possible that 'missing' arguments remain absent even at the level of semantic representation, and are filled in (perhaps optionally) by inference rules. See Fodor and Fodor (1980); Chierchia (1984); Dowty (1985) and references therein. A psychological adaptation of GPSG (but not HPSG) would have this character. As I will construe them, the results of the probe experiments discussed here indicate that missing arguments are identified by the processor, but they do not clarify whether this identification involves semantic representation or inference.

whether the letters constitute a word (lexical decision task) or to read the word aloud (naming task). In either case, the target in cases of interest is a word that is a semantic associate of the head noun of the antecedent phrase. Reactivation by an empty category of its antecedent should show up as a decrease in reaction time (relative to a suitable baseline) for a probe, lexical decision, or naming target associated with the antecedent.

Apparently conflicting results have been obtained from the probe recognition task and the cross-modal priming tasks. Probe studies have been claimed to show reactivation of antecedents for all the GB empty categories (WH-trace, NP-trace, and PRO) though to somewhat different degrees; in particular, the effect for the two traces appears stronger than that for PRO.[5] Cross-modal priming tasks have shown a sharp contrast between immediate reactivation of the correct antecedent in the case of WH-trace, and delayed reactivation (sometimes of a wrong antecedent) for NP-trace and PRO. In Fodor (1989) I proposed to reconcile these findings by assuming that the two tasks are sensitive to different levels of representation. Specifically, I suggested that the probe task taps semantic representations, and hence is responsive to all aspects of sentence meaning, whereas cross-modal priming effects are driven primarily by the (surface) syntactic structure and are only marginally sensitive to semantics. It should be emphasised that an empty category is a *SYNTACTIC* entity, and that its existence can be demonstrated *ONLY* by a task that (to the best of our knowledge) taps syntactic representations and not semantic representations. My suggestion about tasks and levels would thus entail that the only real empty category (aside perhaps from *pro*) is WH-trace.

The grounds for sorting the tasks by linguistic levels in this way are fairly flimsy. The evidence is largely internal; that is, drawing this distinction between the tasks makes sense of the results. Linguistic considerations

---

[5] In Fodor (1989) I argued that the probe recognition studies conducted so far do not in fact provide reliable *COMPARISONS* between WH-trace and other types of empty category, because of other uncontrolled differences between the sentence types tested. Even the probe recognition evidence for the *EXISTENCE* of some empty categories is weak, because it relies on comparison with baseline sentences without an empty category, and these comparisons are also vulnerable to lexical and other mismatches. At present, the evidence of probe recognition priming seems most secure for NP-trace. For the purposes of argument, in this paper I will follow the standard interpretation in the literature and assume probe recognition priming for all three empty categories. But I note for the record that in the case of WH-trace, the mismatch with baseline sentences works against it (see Fodor, 1989, p. 195); so we might surmise that the probe effect for WH-trace is even stronger in reality than the data superficially indicate, significantly stronger than for NP-trace or PRO. If so, this opens the possibility that the pattern of results does not, after all, differ across the two tasks. In that case, the explanation I offer in this section for why they do differ would be beside the point. Remaining sections of the paper would be unaffected, however, since it could be assumed that *BOTH* tasks are primarily sensitive to syntax or phonetic form.

suggest that in all three kinds of construction there should be an implicit argument at the semantic level (whether or not there is an empty category at the syntactic level); and the probe recognition task shows reactivation effects for all three. Linguistic considerations allow that there might be fewer empty categories in syntax than implicit arguments in semantics, but not vice versa. In particular there is a linguistic theory which says that WH-trace exists at the syntactic level, but NP-trace and PRO do not; and the cross-modal priming paradigm shows just this split between them.

Such external considerations as can be called on are at least consonant with this interpretation of the data. The cross-modal priming effects are fairly rapid. Mean RTs in these experiments range from approximately 550 to 750msec. And the effect for WH-trace is obtained even when the target word is presented immediately following the trace position. So it is reasonable to suppose that this task catches the processor in the course of computing syntactic structure as a basis for subsequent semantic interpretation. By contrast, responses in the probe task are typically slower (mean RTs approximately 850 to 1050msec). And it appears that an effect is obtained for empty categories only if the task is post-sentential, not if it is on-line.[6] This suggests that it taps completed sentence representations, which are presumably semantic.[7] (For more detailed discussion see Fodor, 1989.) Finally, Bever et al. (in press) have shown that the probe task is sensitive to the semantic/pragmatic distinction between abstract and concrete adjectives (e.g. *nice* / *tall*), while Nicol and Swinney (1989) have argued that the cross-modal priming task is not sensitive to pragmatic information about potential antecedents but only to structural properties. This is compatible with the idea that cross-modal priming operates at a shallower (more syntactic, less semantic) level than the visual probe task.

---

[6] A probe recognition effect is obtained after a sentence fragment for overt coreferential items such as full lexical NPs (Dell, McKoon, & Ratcliff, 1983) and overt reflexives (in preliminary results of a comparative study of NP-trace and WH-trace by Re, Taber, Fodor, and Swinney, 1991), though Greene, McKoon, and Ratcliff (in press) have found no effect for overt pronouns. For empty categories, the only significant result to date for a probe following a sentence fragment is for null pronouns in American Sign Language (Emmorey & Lillo-Martin, 1991).

[7] I don't think it is necessary to claim that if a task is insensitive to a given linguistic representation, it follows that that representation is not mentally present at the moment that the task is performed. In particular, I don't mean to imply that syntactic structure must have been discarded by the time the probe task is performed, or that no semantic analysis has been computed by the time the cross-modal priming task is performed. Also, it might be supposed that the cross modal priming paradigm *SHOULD* show semantic sensitivity because the relation between the antecedent noun and the target word is a semantic association. However, that wouldn't be a relevant consideration if what elicits the interpretive processes that feed priming is all and only constituents that exist at the syntactic level.

An experiment whose results might or might not corroborate this speculation would compare implicit reflexives as in (3a) with explicit reflexives as in (3b). Simple intransitives such as (3c) would serve as control.

(3)a. The boy washed in the pond.
 b. The boy washed himself in the pond.
 c. The boy played in the pond.

A reflexive object is understood in (3a), and we may assume it is present at the semantic level; but it can be argued that there is no syntactic empty category in (3a) on *ANY* linguistic theory. An implicit object in English does not function like an overt object (as it does in Italian; see Rizzi, 1986); it cannot, for example, serve as the antecedent for PRO as in (4d).

(4)a. The boy surrendered himself to the pleasure of the music.
 b. The boy surrendered to the pleasure of the music.
 c. The boy surrendered himself to PRO enjoying the music.
 d. * The boy surrendered to PRO enjoying the music.

Priming of the antecedent would be expected for the reflexive in (3b) since it is an overt element at the syntactic level. Nicol (1988) has shown that overt anaphors and pronouns do reactivate their antecedents. The linguistic levels explanation of the task difference predicts that there will be no cross-modal priming effect for the implicit reflexive in (3a), but that there will be antecedent reactivation in the probe recognition task for the implicit as well as the explicit reflexive. Note that the size of the effect for an implicit argument can be compared with that for NP-trace by testing such pairs as *The boy has washed*, with an implicit reflexive after *washed*, and *The boy was washed*, with an NP-trace (according to GB) after *washed*; in both cases the antecedent is *the boy*.

The results of an experiment such as this would reflect back on the proper interpretation of the empty category studies. But we do not yet have these results, or others like them that could pin down unambiguously which tasks relate to which linguistic levels. In the meantime we may be able to explore these matters in a more indirect fashion. For example, the persuasiveness of the linguistic levels hypothesis depends in part on whether there is any *OTHER* plausible explanation for the weak showing of NP-trace and PRO in the cross-modal task. Two possibilities in particular warrant serious attention. According to the linguistic levels hypothesis, WH-trace shows significantly more cross-modal priming than NP-trace and PRO because the former exists at the syntactic level but the latter do not; if so, GPSG/HPSG is supported over GB (which assumes they are all syntactic) and over LFG (which assumes none are). But alternative explanations include: (1) a processing based account, due to Nicol (1988); and (2) an account based on GB's level of Phonetic Form (PF). I will discuss these in turn. I have some data to contribute regarding (1). With regard to (2), further experiments suggest themselves, but how much illumination they can shed depends on finding answers for some linguistic questions about PF.

PROCESSING FACTORS

Nicol (1988) observed that a WH-trace may be easier for the processor to anticipate or interpret than an NP-trace or a PRO, and that this could be why WH-trace gives sturdier effects in an on-line task than NP-trace or PRO.[8] For example, passive verbs are often ambiguous with adjectives, and passive *by* with locative or temporal *by*. Hence the processor may need to wait until the end of the clause, and perhaps consult semantic or pragmatic information, to determine whether a passive NP-trace is present or not. This is clearly important. NP-trace could hardly be expected to show reactivation of its antecedent within 500msec or so, if the processor takes more than 500 msec to decide that an NP-trace is present and what its antecedent is. This could also explain why cross-modal priming is weak or inaccurate when it does eventually occur. By the time the parser had identified the NP-trace, other parts of the sentence would be being processed, so any late effect of the NP-trace would be attenuated.

There is actually a fine distinction to be made here. One might imagine that on unexpectedly encountering an NP-trace the processor has so much computation to do that the extra workload offsets the facilitative effect of reactivation on the target word; then the NP-trace would not show priming, even if it were genuinely there in the syntactic structure. However, this argument is not sound. In the cross-modal studies, RT to

---

[8] For simplicity, from now on I shall drop the disjunction 'NP-trace or PRO' and will restrict discussion to NP-trace. NP-trace is the more interesting of the two to study, since it is linguistically better matched to WH-trace. GB assumes that both kinds of trace are co-indexed with their antecedents in the syntactic component; but PRO, though it exists in the syntax, is usually assumed to be co-indexed with its antecedent (its controller) only at the level of Logical Form (LF). Also, in an early version of the experiment reported later, in which we used PRO rather than NP-trace to mediate the pronoun/anaphor interpretation, we found signs of just the sort of ambiguity that Nicol warned of. In a sentence like *The fireman persuaded the duke PRO to save himself from the blaze*, the infinitival clause was apparently construed as ambiguous between a complement clause with PRO and *himself* co-indexed with the object of the main clause (*duke*), and a purpose clause with PRO and *himself* co-indexed with the subject of the main clause (*fireman*). This ambiguity typically does not arise in NP-trace constructions.

the target word associated with the antecedent is always compared with RT to a control target that is unassociated with the antecedent but is matched with the associated target with respect to length and frequency. Any variations in processing load should affect response to both targets, whereas reactivation should affect only the associated target. Therefore priming should still be detectable in the comparison between the associated and unassociated targets.[9] If processing problems are to explain a lack of priming by NP-trace, they must therefore be problems of a kind that would prevent the NP-trace or its antecedent from being *IDENTIFIED* as such. Then any increase in load would slow responses to both, and there would no reactivation to speed responses to either. Only in such a case is it possible to appeal to a processing problem as a means of reconciling a claim of syntactic reality for NP-trace with a lack of detectable priming.

So let us group together all and sundry complications (unpredictability, ambiguity, etc.)[10] that might result in the parser not realising until too late (for priming) that it has in fact encountered an NP-trace. What we need to know is whether any such complication in fact occurs. If it does, it may warrant reinstating NP-trace as a syntactic entity. Unfortunately, as noted in my earlier paper, quantifying potential processing complications is extremely tricky. How *MUCH* harder is it to identify an NP-trace on-line than a WH-trace? Enough to account for their reactivation differences, or not?

Instead of attempting to answer these conundrums, we have taken a different tack. If the processing difficulty account is true, it implies that NP-trace is slow to be interpreted. But if the processing difficulty account is false, and the linguistic levels account is true, then it is possible that NP-trace (or rather, its semantic counterpart) is in fact identified and interpreted quite rapidly, despite the fact that it shows only late reactivation of its antecedent. What we need to find out, then, is whether or not the *INTERPRETATION* of NP-trace is significantly delayed. This was the purpose of a recent experiment by Fodor, McKinnon, and Swinney. The sentences tested are exemplified in (5); they contained an NP-trace followed by an anaphor (reflexive) or a pronoun. (Note that here, as

---

[9] Note that for the reasons just discussed, it is quite possible that response to an associated target will be *SLOWER* at an empty category position than at some other position in the sentence. This might show only that the processing load is greater, for whatever reason, at the empty category position than at the other position. In that case, antecedent reactivation could show up as a smaller increase in RT at the empty category position for the associated target than for the unassociated target, or as identity of RT for the associated target across the two positions while RT for the control target increases. Such patterns of results present no special problems of interpretation.

[10] Or the occurrence of NP-trace in non-canonical position; see discussion of Pesetsky's proposal in the next section, but especially footnote 22.

elsewhere in this chapter, I represent all possible empty categories in the examples, without intending to beg the question of whether they really exist. According to LFG and GPSG/HPSG there is no NP-trace in [5a,b].)

(5)a. [The boxer]$_i$ knew that [the doctor for the team]$_j$ was sure *NP-trace*$_j$ to blame himself$_j$ for the injury.

  b. [The boxer]$_i$ knew that [the doctor for the team]$_j$ was sure *NP-trace*$_j$ to blame him$_i$ for the injury.

These sentences are based on materials constructed by Nicol (1988) for a cross-modal priming study of lexical pronouns and anaphors. Nicol's materials included (6).

(6)a. [The boxer]$_i$ told [the skier]$_j$ that [the doctor for the team]$_k$ would blame himself$_k$ for the injury.

  b. [The boxer]$_i$ told [the skier]$_j$ that [the doctor for the team]$_k$ would blame him$_{i,j}$ for the injury.

To keep things simple, we omitted one of the potential antecedent NPs from Nicol's sentences. Crucially, we added an extra clause in between the potential antecedents and the pronoun or anaphor. This clause contained a 'raising' predicate such as *was sure to*, *seemed to*, *was believed to*, etc., which is followed (according to GB) by an NP-trace. Nicol found a significant antecedent reactivation effect for both *him* and *himself* in contexts as in (6). Our question was whether a similarly strong effect would occur when the determination of the correct antecedent for *him* or *himself* is mediated by an NP-trace, as it is in (5). If so, it would indicate that the NP-trace (or equivalent in non-GB analyses) was being accurately interpreted on-line.

Note that interpretation of the NP-trace in (5) is crucial to interpretation of the lexical pronoun or anaphor. An anaphor in object position, such as in (5a), is required to be coreferential with the subject of its clause. In (5a) the subject is the NP-trace. The NP-trace is coreferential with the noun phrase *the doctor for the team* (since the trace was created by movement of that noun phrase from its deep position as subject of *blame*). So the trace refers to the doctor. Hence the anaphor *himself* must also refer to the doctor. By contrast, an object pronoun as in (5b) is required to be disjoint in reference from the subject of its clause. So in (5b) *him* must be disjoint in reference from the trace. Just as in (5a), the trace in (5b) refers to the doctor. Hence *him* must *NOT* refer to the doctor. Since the only other candidate in this sentence is the boxer, *him* must refer to the boxer. (The pronoun could in principle refer to someone not mentioned in the sentence, but this is not a likely interpretation when no context is provided.)

To summarise: *himself* must refer to the doctor, and *him* must refer to the boxer; and both of these facts depend crucially on the fact that the NP-trace refers to the doctor. Thus if the processor interprets *him* and *himself* accurately in these sentences, we know that it has already, at that point, interpreted the NP-trace.[11] (I should emphasise, though I won't keep repeating the point, that if this is all true, it would add support to the theory which claims that there *IS* no NP-trace. So where I talk of the NP-trace in these sentences having been interpreted, this should be translated into talk of the implicit agent of the lower clause having been established by the semantic processor.) Note especially that if the point at which we can demonstrate that NP-trace has been interpreted is prior to the point at which the NP-trace shows a reactivation effect, then we could conclude that NP-trace is still not an optimal reactivator even when it has been identified and interpreted. That would not be compatible with the processing complexity explanation but would be compatible with the linguistic levels explanation. That is, in the absence of any more plausible suggestion, it would support the idea that antecedent reactivation in the cross-modal paradigm is triggered only by syntactic constituents, and that NP-trace is not a syntactic constituent. The results are given in (7).[12]

(7) Priming in msec (N=40):

Target:	FIRST NOUN (*boxer* in (5))	SECOND NOUN (*doctor* in (5))
HIMSELF	8	26*
HIM	46*	11

There was significant priming of the correct antecedent for both *him* and *himself* (for *him* $t(39) = 2.61$, $p < 0.005$; for *himself* $t(39) = 3.00$, $p <$

---

[11] Janet Pierrehumbert (personal communication) has observed that the processing routines might bypass the NP-trace and nevertheless interpret *him/himself* correctly on the basis of a simple strategy: assign the closest overt NP as antecedent to a reflexive, and all but the closest overt NP as potential antecedents to a pronoun. This could account for Nicol's results as well as those we report here, and it would obviously invalidate our attempt to show rapid interpretation of NP-trace in these constructions. To exclude this possibility we can test sentences such as *The skier was believed by the doctor for the team to blame him/himself for the injury* in which the closest NP to the *him/himself* is the wrong antecedent for the anaphor, and the furthest NP is the wrong antecedent for the pronoun. Or we could compare (6a) with *The boxer thinks the skier introduced the doctor for the team to himself*—the second NP here is a possible antecedent for the anaphor, but the second NP in (6a) is not.

[12] Response times for related and unrelated (control) targets are shown in (i).

(i) Target:	FIRST NOUN			SECOND NOUN		
	Control	Related	Difference	Control	Related	Difference
HIMSELF	584	576	8	590	564	26*
HIM	602	556	46*	573	562	11

0.002). There was no significant priming of the incorrect antecedent for either *him* or *himself* (for *him* $t(39) = 0.68$, $p < 0.25$; for *himself* $t(39) = 0.26$, $p < 0.5$). The interaction between first/second noun and *him/himself* is also significant ($F(1,39) = 4.32$, $p < 0.05$). Note also that there is no evidence of reactivation by the NP-trace of its antecedent, by the point in the sentence at which *him/himself* occurs. With *himself*, this would be difficult to discern, since the second NP is the correct antecedent both for the trace and for the anaphor; an effect of the trace would show only as an increase over the reactivation effect due to the anaphor. But with *him*, the first NP is the antecedent for the pronoun, whereas the second NP is the antecedent for the trace. So reactivation by NP-trace would be apparent as priming for the second NP in the *him* sentence. Although there is 11msec of priming in that condition, it is not significant.[13]

Additional points need to be checked to clarify the import of these data.[14] But at least as far as they go, the results of this mediating NP-trace

---

[13] It is important to our argument to exclude the possibility that antecedent reactivation by the NP-trace has already occurred and died away again before the pronoun/anaphor position. Testing at a point between the NP-trace and the pronoun/anaphor would permit evaluation of this. It seems most unlikely, however, in view of the finding that prompted this whole line of reasoning—that cross modal reactivation effects are slow for NP-trace. Osterhout and Swinney (in preparation) report reactivation for a target presented 1000msec after NP-trace, but none for a target 500msec after the trace. The sentences in the present experiment were designed so that the pronoun/anaphor occurred as soon as possible after the NP-trace, but this was not easy to achieve, and we succeeded only in bringing the interval between them (i.e. between the offset of *to*, which reveals presence of the trace, and the offset of the pronoun/anaphor, where the target word was presented) down to approximately 800msec for *him* and approximately 1200msec for *himself*. We could wish that the pronoun/anaphor fell more safely within the known window of inertness for NP-trace (= something less than 1,000msec). On past evidence the likeliest explanation of the absence of reactivation by NP-trace at the anaphor/pronoun position is that this was too *EARLY* to find NP-trace effects, not because it was too *LATE*. However, this certainly needs to be checked, especially because (as Janet Nicol has reminded me, personal communication) the timing in the Osterhout and Swinney experiment may not be exactly extrapolable to the present experiment, because the former examined NP-trace in within-clause passive constructions only, whereas the latter tested a mix of passive and raising constructions. There has been no cross-modal priming study of NP-trace in simple raising constructions (i.e. without *him/himself*), so for comparison purposes we will also test our materials with the *him/himself* excised and some sort of non-referential phase in its place.

[14] What follow-up studies would be informative? It is standard to test at a point between the potential antecedents and the empty category, to establish that activation resulting from the overt occurrence of an antecedent has died down and so cannot be confused with REactivation. But had there been any residual effects in our experiment from the original occurrence of the antecedents (or perhaps just the second one), they should have affected the *him* and *himself* sentences alike and so could not have been responsible for the significant differences we observed between them. The most important controls to run are therefore those discussed in footnotes 11 and 13, to ensure that the NP-trace is indeed mediating the interpretation, and to establish a baseline for NP-trace alone.

experiment favour two conclusions. First, the bashfulness of NP-trace is not due to processing problems in locating and interpreting it. Second, given that the syntax and semantics of these constructions apparently harbour no other plausible cause of these results,[15] they enhance the plausibility of the claim that cross-modal priming occurs only for elements present in syntactic structure, and that NP-trace is not among them.[16]

LEVELS OF REPRESENTATION: SYNTAX AND PF

PF-visibility

The conclusion just adumbrated is not favourable to GB. But it is also not warranted by the experimental results, however charitably we interpret them. The reason is that GB has more than one level of sentence representation shallower than semantics at which the cross-modal priming findings might be accounted for.

In all, GB assumes four levels of representation, related to each other as shown in (8).

(8)

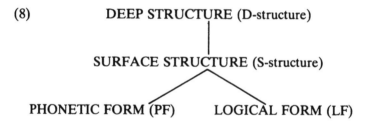

DEEP STRUCTURE (D-structure)

SURFACE STRUCTURE (S-structure)

PHONETIC FORM (PF)   LOGICAL FORM (LF)

---

[15] I will make this assumption, but it deserves to be considered more carefully. Very little is known about semantic representations. It is not known, for example, whether or to what extent they are sequentially ordered. Imaginably, a task that taps semantic representations might fail to pick up a certain semantic element because its position is not fixed, and so the timing of any effect it triggers varies unpredictably across subjects and/or occasions. And possibly NP-trace is more susceptible to variable positioning than WH-trace is; see later discussion of Pesetsky's proposal. However, our experimental results indicate that NP-trace has been interpreted within three or four syllables, and prior to the end of its VP, so there is not a great deal of scope for such an explanation.

[16] Strictly speaking, GB's level of Logical Form (LF; see later comments) also qualifies as syntactic. But it contrasts with surface structure in the sense that I intend here, i.e. LF renders the meaning of the sentence explicit at the expense of its pronunciation. Incidentally, quantified NPs move at LF to positions that reflect their semantic scope, leaving traces. My hypothesis predicts that these traces might be detectable in a probe paradigm, though not in an on-line priming paradigm. However, I don't see any obvious way of trolling for these LF traces experimentally, since they are coincident with the surface positions of the quantified phrases. (Linguists might like to consider the possibility of identifying LF experimentally by exploiting the effects of reconstruction at LF, which returns part but not all of a syntactically moved phrase to its base position.)

We can probably afford to ignore D-structure here. S-structure is derived from D-structure by transformational operations, as in earlier versions of transformational grammar. But now these transformations leave traces marking the positions of phrases before they are moved, so the surface level encodes information about deep structure as well. S-structure thus contains all the information needed to determine the logical form and the phonetic form of the sentence. Unlike early transformational models of sentence processing, it is now generally assumed that a processor need not recover the deep structure of a sentence (see Berwick & Weinberg, 1984).

Of the other three levels, we have so far eliminated only LF (or more generally, semantic representation) as a basis for explaining the cross-modal priming results. The argument has been that LF is tapped by the probe recognition task, that the cross-modal tasks tap some level more superficial (less semantic) than the probe task does, hence the cross-modal tasks tap a level more superficial than LF. But two such levels are still in the running: S-structure and PF. All previous discussions, including my own, have simply overlooked the possibility that these experiments are telling us something about PF rather than S-structure. But this makes an enormous difference, because although GB does postulate the existence of NP-trace and PRO at S-structure, it assumes only WH-trace at PF. So if it were true that cross-modal priming phenomena are driven by PF rather than by syntactic structure, the results to date would be just as compatible with GB as they are with GPSG/HPSG.[17]

Why does GB allow some empty categories, but not all, to disappear between S-structure and PF? The answer is that there is evidence, long known, that WH-trace, but not the other empty categories, interacts with phonetic phenomena. An empty category has no phonetic content, but it can nevertheless have phonetic effects. In particular, it can get in the way of phonetic (or phonological or morphological—I won't distinguish here) processes that require adjacency of other elements. The most celebrated

---

[17] I don't mean to imply that cross-modal priming might be a phonetic phenomenon. The priming that occurs in these tasks is based on a semantic or associative (not phonetic) relation between the target word and the antecedent for which it tests. And it is standardly thought of as triggered by the process of assigning the antecedent to the empty category, a process which is either syntactic or semantic, not phonetic. It is conceivable, nevertheless, that the relative timing of mental computations is such that only items which have been determined to be present at PF will feed into whatever mechanism causes priming. I admit, though, that I can't think why this should be so; and a possible problem for this view is the fact that recognising an empty category at PF will typically require consulting considerable syntactic information. In fact this is one of those cases in which sentence processing cannot simply reverse the linguistic derivation; PF representations as rich as GB posits could not, in general, be constructed until *AFTER* most of the S-structure had been determined.

example is the blocking of '*wanna*-contraction' by a WH-trace, exemplified in (9c).[18]

(9)a. Does John$_i$ want PRO$_i$ to (wanna) go to the movies?
   b. Who$_j$ does John$_i$ want PRO$_i$ to (wanna) go to the movies with WH-trace$_j$?
   c. Who$_j$ does John$_i$ want WH-trace$_j$ to (*wanna) go to the movies?

In (9a), *want* and *to* can contract into *wanna*. The two words are separated by a PRO, but this evidently does not block their fusion. (9b) is exactly similar except that the sentence happens to contain a Wh-phrase and its WH-trace; *wanna*-contraction can still occur. In (9c), on the other hand, the WH-trace intervenes between the *want* and the *to*, and now *wanna*-contraction cannot occur.[19] To the extent that it can be tested, NP-trace behaves like PRO in not blocking the fusion of *to* onto a preceding verb. Example (10a) shows the contraction of *to* with the raising verb *supposed*, across NP-trace; this contrasts with (10b) where a WH-trace intervenes (though unfortunately the verbs are not really identical across the examples; see Jacobson, 1982, for a test of NP-trace that avoids this problem).

(10)a. John$_i$ is supposed NP-trace$_i$ to (sposta) leave before noon.
    b. Who$_j$ do you think John$_i$ supposed WH-trace$_j$ to (*sposta) be the cleverest student?

It seems, then that only WH-trace is active—or as Lightfoot (1976) was the first to say, *VISIBLE*—at the phonetic level.

One refinement is needed in this conclusion. Not all WH-traces present at S-structure in GB are visible at PF. GB assumes that there is a WH-trace not only in the deep structure position of a moved phrase, but also

---

[18] For the history of this discovery, and many references, see Postal and Pullum (1978; 1986). Postal and Pullum (1982) observed that an intervening empty category is not a necessary condition for the blocking of *wanna*-contraction; contraction also fails in a host of contexts in which the structural relation between *want* and *to* in the tree is not appropriate to contraction. (Linear adjacency is insufficient; apparently the *to* must be the infinitival marker of the clause that is the complement of *want*.) I will not discuss this configurational condition on *wanna*-contraction here. Its existence does not preclude the relevance of empty categories as well.

[19] This is apparently not true of all varieties of English; there are speakers who produce and accept *wanna* even in constructions like (9c) (see Postal & Pullum, 1986, for references). This does not invalidate the assumption that the contraction facts follow from innate principles of universal grammar, rather than from parochial rules. It requires, though, that the principles in question be parameterised, or express defaults rather than absolute restrictions so that language-specific rules can override them in the marked case.

in the pre-sentential Complementiser position in each clause on the route between that lowest trace and the final (highest) position of the moved WH-phrase. The WH-phrase does not move in one swoop all the way to its final position but must stop along the way; there are various constraints on movement (most notably Subjacency) which require each movement to be quite local. Long-distance movement results from successive local movements, first from the deep structure position to the Comp(lementiser) position in its clause, then from there to the Comp of the next clause up, and so on. Each movement leaves a trace. Therefore in (9b), there is an intermediate WH-trace (not shown) in the Comp position of the lower clause. This WH-trace is between the verb *want* and the empty subject PRO. Thus the sequence is *want–WH-trace–PRO–to*. The fact that *wanna*-contraction is perfectly acceptable here shows that an intermediate WH-trace, unlike a 'lowest' WH-trace as in (9c), is not PF-visible.

What might explain this rather peculiar array of facts (i.e. phonetic effects of the lowest WH-trace, but not of intermediate WH-trace or any other empty categories)? Jaeggli (1980) noted that the empty categories that show no phonological effects are those that have no (abstract) case: the lowest WH-trace is in argument position and so is case-marked, but (for various reasons within GB theory) NP-trace, PRO, and intermediate WH-trace are not case-marked.[20] Pesetsky (1982) pointed out that a noun phrase without case does not need to appear in a position to which case is assigned. In particular, an NP-trace or PRO subject has no case and so it need not precede the verb phrase, as 'normal' case-marked subjects do in English. It is free to follow the verb phrase, and then it would not intervene between *want* and *to* and block contraction.[21,22] A similar story would not be plausible for intermediate traces, for various reasons, but Lasnik and Saito (1984) showed that intermediate traces can be deleted at S-structure and hence absent from PF. (They can then be restored at LF in time to satisfy the Empty Category Principle, a constraint on LF to which intermediate traces are crucial.)

---

[20] There are other views of the matter even within GB. For example, Bouchard (1986) argues that government of *to* by *want* is the only relevant factor; Aoun, Hornstein, Lightfoot, and Weinberg (1987) agree that case is relevant but disagree with Pesetsky about the mechanism. Also, see Gorrell in Lasnik and Uriagereka (1988).

[21] NP-trace in object position (e.g. in passives) also doesn't receive case, but no phonological phenomena have yet been found that are sensitive to empty objects and could tell us whether object NP-trace is PF-visible. The trace of an adjunct has no case. Rita Manzini (personal communication) has suggested to me that it would be informative to see whether adjunct traces show antecedent reactivation in a cross modal priming task. Unfortunately the locus of an adjunct in a sentence is so fluid that it would be unclear where to test for reactivation, unless we could find enough examples of verbs with an obligatory subcategorised adjunct in the VP, as in *How did she word it?*, *How well did he behave?*. Hornstein (1991) has suggested looking for antecedent reactivation by certain instances of PRO in Icelandic

With NP-trace, PRO, and intermediate WH-trace thus accounted for, GB can comfortably accommodate the differential PF-visibility of the various kinds of empty categories.[23] Indeed it might be maintained that GB actually predicts these differences, to the extent that the mechanisms that account for them are independently motivated in the theory.

GPSG/HPSG can account for these same facts without postulating that empty categories in the syntax become invisible in phonetic form. Exactly those empty categories that the contraction tests indicate are not PF-visible are those that, for independent reasons, GPSG/HPSG does not acknowledge in the syntax: PRO, NP-trace, and intermediate WH-trace in Comp. GPSG/HPSG does not have NP-trace or PRO because the associated phenomena (passive, raising, 'control') are all local and can be analysed as involving just lexical rearrangements of the argument structure of a verb (or other predicate). The arguments here are essentially those of Bresnan (1978). A sharp distinction is drawn between these local constructions, and the (potentially) long-distance extraction of WH-phrases. WH-trace is assumed in long-distance extraction constructions, though only in the 'lowest' position of the WH-phrase. Intermediate WH-traces aren't needed because the restrictions on extraction that are captured by successive cyclic movement in GB follow from other constraints in GPSG/HPSG (e.g. the Head Feature Convention in GPSG). Thus GPSG/HPSG, without assuming any adjustment between syntactic and phonetic structure, can

---

and Russian, which he argues (1989) are case-marked. By the case-marking criterion, *pro* should also be PF-visible, and we are currently working on experiments that compare *pro* with PRO in Spanish.

[22] In the Fodor, McKinnon and Swinney experiment, the NP-trace was apparently interpreted well before the end of the verb phrase. This does not invalidate Pesetsky's observation, since it is only optional for a subject without case to appear non-preverbally. The experimental sentences didn't contain contracted verb forms, so nothing would prevent the NP-trace from being analysed as in preverbal position. However, the results of our experiment do exclude the hypothesis that NP-trace has generally shown only weak priming effects because the experiments have tested for it at the wrong positions: i.e. have tested at the canonical argument positions for case-marked NPs, while NP-trace is free to occur elsewhere. Note that if this were so, our experiment should have shown either (a) failure to interpret the pronoun/anaphor correctly, or (b) correct interpretation of the pronoun/anaphor *AND* a priming effect for NP-trace (if we assume, as Jerry Fodor, personal communication, has suggested, that NP-trace is interpreted earlier than usual *IF* something else in the sentence has need of it, as the pronoun/anaphor in our materials did). In fact our results suggest that the NP-trace *WAS* interpreted in canonical subject position (on enough trials to influence the results for the pronoun/anaphor), yet still did not exhibit priming.

[23] The term 'visibility' suits the notion that an empty category has phonetic effects only if it has case. It is not appropriate if the lack of phonetic effects is attributed to the element being deleted from PF, or to its being there but in an irrelevant position. But I will stay with this terminology, which does no harm as long as too much is not read into it.

accommodate the PF-visibility facts, and it too could justifiably claim to predict them.

We see, then, that the experimental results so far could be explained by GB on the basis of its level of PF, or by GPSG/HPSG on the basis of either its syntactic level or PF.[24] So these experimental results can't tell us which theory is correct. If we are to make further progress in the general project of using psycholinguistic data about empty categories to address linguistic issues, we need to do one of two things. We must either: (a) establish *WHICH* level of representation the cross-modal experiments are sensitive to; or else (b) find some other variety of empty category to test, that the theories make different predictions about at *BOTH* levels (PF and syntax).

If we opt for (a), the most sensible way to begin would probably be to forget empty categories temporarily, and standardise the experimental tasks by applying them to other phenomena whose affiliation with linguistic levels is not in dispute. It's not easy, though, to see how to adapt cross-modal priming to the detection of the kinds of readjustments that occur between syntax and PF (e.g. the flattening of structure noted by Langendoen, 1975, in examples like *[[This is the cat][that chased the rat][that ate the cheese] . . .]*). Finding a way of linguistically calibrating the tasks that we use is an important goal; it would be helpful beyond measure to have secure information about exactly when and how the processing of the task stimulus interacts with the processing of the sentence. But I will take the alternative tack (b), looking for a way to finesse our current methodological ignorance, and proceed with the general project by other means. In particular, it would be handy if there were some variety of empty category that we could test which would allow us to distinguish between theoretical claims *REGARDLESS* of which level of representation the experiments are sensitive to.

It happens that the theories do differ with respect to one species of WH-trace: the trace of a WH-subject extraction. GB assumes that subject WH-traces exist; GPSG/HPSG assumes that they don't. So far all the experiments on WH-trace have studied object traces, but that could easily be remedied. A cross-modal test of antecedent reactivation in subject extraction constructions promises to provide the crucial evidence we are looking for.

---

[24] GPSG/HPSG assumes only one syntactic level, at which elements appear in the positions in which they will be pronounced. PF is not discussed. I think it can be assumed to differ minimally in configurational respects from the GPSG/HPSG syntactic structure, except for whatever re-bracketing principles are needed for the determination of prosody. I will assume that there is no tampering with empty categories between syntax and PF in GPSG/HPSG.

Subject Extraction

What is it about subject extraction that might lead a linguistic theory to accord it special treatment? It has been observed that subject extraction is generally more restricted than object extraction in natural languages. In GB this is attributed to the Empty Category Principle (ECP), a constraint whose details are not important here. The ECP predicts a number of subject/object asymmetries, for example the '*that-trace effect' illustrated in (11). An object may be extracted from a subordinate clause in English, whether or not the clause has an overt complementiser(= *that* in [11]) but a subject may be extracted only in the absence of the complementiser.[25]

(11)a. Who does John think that Mary loves WH-trace?
   b. Who does John think Mary loves WH-trace?
   c. * Who does John think that WH-trace loves Mary?
   d. Who does John think WH-trace loves Mary?

Thus GB permits the extraction of subjects, but imposes tight constraints on it. By contrast, GPSG/HPSG forbids the extraction of subjects (by means of the Head Feature Convention or the Trace Principle, neither of which we need to discuss here). It then provides other means of generating constructions that *LOOK* as if they exhibit subject extraction. I will sketch the relevant derivations briefly, omitting various linguistic details. From the point of view of the empty category experiments, all we need to keep an eye on is which WH-constructions contain a trace according to GPSG/ HPSG.

For subject questions like (12a), where the subject of the highest clause is the WH-phrase, GB assumes that the subject moves into Comp, but GPSG/HPSG assumes that the structure is exactly like that of a declarative: there is no extraction at all, hence no empty category.[26]

(12)	GB	GPSG/HPSG
	a. Who$_i$ WH-trace$_i$ left the room?	a. Who left the room?
	b. Sue left the room.	b. Sue left the room.

---

[25] This is not true for all languages, or even for all speakers of English (see Sobin, 1987). So the ECP is subject to parametric variation, or interacts with something else that is parameterised (e.g. case assignment to subjects, see Koopman & Sportiche, 1988; or agreement in Comp, see Rizzi, 1990).

[26] In *Barriers*, Chomsky allows the possibility that a WH-phrase in highest subject position might not move into Comp, but stay in subject position. Thus the *Barriers* theory would tolerate both the GB structure (12a) and the GPSG/HPSG structure (12a).

Now consider a question such as (13), in which the WH-phrase corresponds to the subject of an infinitival complement.

(13) Who do you believe to have left the room?

GB assumes the structure in (14a), with a trace as subject of the complement clause.

(14) a. GB QUESTION   b. GB DECLARATIVE

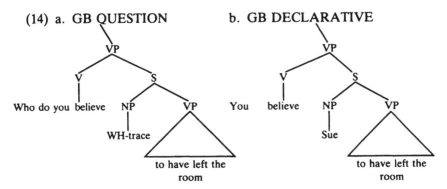

But GPSG/HPSG asumes the structure in (15a). There is no subject in the complement (it is just a verb phrase); there is a trace, but it is in object position in the main clause. (Note: for simplicity I have omitted from (15a) the SLASH features that link the antecedent to the trace in GPSG; see footnote 28.)

(15) a. GPSG/HPSG QUESTION b. GPSG/HPSG DECLARATIVE

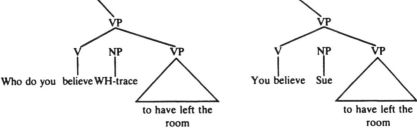

Note that this is not a special fact about WH-extraction constructions. The GPSG structure (15b) for the declarative also has a VP complement with no subject, and an object in the main clause. One reason for assuming that this noun phrase is the object of the higher verb is that it has accusative case, as objects typically do. If *Sue* in (15b) were replaced by a pronoun it would be *her* rather than *she*; and for those who make a *who/whom* distinction, (15a) requires *whom*.

Thus when a WH-trace associated with a following infinitive is accusative, the two theories adopt quite different analyses. GB treats it as an accusative subject in the complement clause, and GPSG treats it as an object in the matrix clause. On both theories, though, there is an empty category associated with the fronted WH-phrase.

Now consider the declarative example (16). Here the complement has a finite verb, and GPSG/HPSG assumes it is a full clause with a subject, just as GB does. This is because the relevant NP here is nominative, as subjects typically are; note that a pronoun in place of *Sue* would be *she*, not *her*.

(16) GB, GPSG/HPSG   You believe $_s$[Sue left the room].

For the corresponding question, GB assumes movement of the embedded subject to the higher Comp position, as in (17).

(17) GB   Who$_i$ do you believe [WH-trace$_i$ left the room]?

But in GPSG/HPSG some special treatment is necessitated by the ban on subject traces. The *who* obviously can't be left unmoved here, as it could in (12). And it can't be construed as an object, as it could in (13), because it has nominative case. Gazdar (1981) proposed that the grammar contains a metarule, which reflects the superficial similarity between an S missing its subject, and a VP. (The words *left the room*, for example, qualify as either one. Note that an S missing any NP other than its subject, e.g. *Mary was talking to*, is not equivalent to a VP or to any other standard syntactic category.) The Gazdar metarule permits the grammar, in effect, to substitute a VP wherever it would have generated an S with a subject gap.[27] As a result, the structure of the question here need not be (18a), which is illicit in GPSG/HPSG, but can be (18b):

(18) GPSG/HPSG   a.–*Who$_i$ do you believe $_s$[WH-trace$_i$ left the room]?
                   b. Who do you believe $_{VP}$[left the room]?

Note particularly that there is no trace in (18b). In general: wherever GB has a nominative trace, GPSG/HPSG has no trace at all.

---

[27] The metarule does not transform sentence structures directly. A metarule derives rules from rules. Thus more precisely: constituent structure rules that introduce VP are derived from constituent structure rules that introduce S with a subject gap.

There is a variety of evidence that supports this apparently eccentric analysis of subject extraction.[28] Gazdar (1981) observed that the comple- ment in (18b) behaves like a VP, in that it can be conjoined with another VP, but not with a clause containing a trace (i.e. an S[SLASH NP] in the terms of footnote 28). Chung and McCloskey (1983) pointed out that extrac- tion from a WH-island is more acceptable if the WH-phrase is the highest subject, which would be explicable if highest subjects, as in (12a), don't undergo extraction. Engdahl (1983) noted that extraction of the subject of a finite complement is the only kind of WH-extraction that does not license a parasitic gap (i.e. a second empty category with the same antecedent), and Sag (1983) observed that this would follow from the assumption that this is the only kind of WH-extraction that creates no trace.

To sum up: GPSG/HPSG recognises accusative WH-traces (including those that GB treats as the subject of an infinitive) but not nominative traces. The latter have exactly the same status as NP-trace, PRO, and intermediate WH-trace. That is, they are all predicted to be invisible at PF because they do no work in the theory at all; they do not exist at any level.

So here we have a clear empirical difference between the two theories. GB says that at the syntactic level there are WH-traces that are the subjects of embedded finite clauses, and GPSG says that there are not. Furthermore, each theory must apparently say the same of PF as it does of syntax. For GB: since the subject of a finite clause necessarily has case

---

[28] It may seem that (18b) couldn't be correct because, in the absence of a trace, there is no way to relate the WH-phrase at the front to the 'deep' position which determines its semantic role in the sentence. But this is not so. GPSG/HPSG relates a filler to its gap by means of a special feature [SLASH] on the nodes in the tree between the two. These features are not shown in (18). The tree diagrams corresponding to the strings in (18) are (a) and (b); only (b) is well-formed.

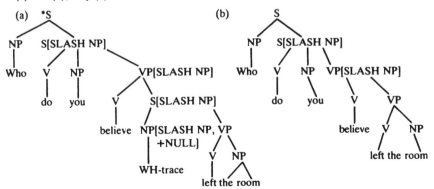

Structure (b) *IS* unusual in having a WH-antecedent but no trace associated with it; but the trail of [SLASH NP] markings provides sufficient information to the semantic component to determine that the fronted WH-phrase is functionally the subject of the lower VP.

(nominative), it seems to follow that it must be visible at PF. For GPSG/ HPSG: assuming that traces which don't exist in the syntax can't pop up out of the blue at PF, there can be no nominative traces at PF. So it appears that finally we have identified contrasting linguistic claims, which permit a clear experimental test. According to GB, nominative traces exist in syntax and at PF; according to GPSG/HPSG they exist at neither level. Therefore, regardless of which level our experiments tap, we should be able to determine which theory is correct about empty categories.

Unfortunately, there is one more complication to be grappled with before the theoretical motivation for an experiment on nominative traces is in the clear. There is a tension within GB theory concerning nominative traces at PF, and until it is resolved we can't be confident that GB does— or should—predict their existence. GB principles seem to entail it, but there is empirical evidence that appears to contradict it.

As Schachter (1984) pointed out, auxiliary reduction occurs in examples like (19) where, according to GB, there is a nominative trace in subject position between *think* and *is*.[29] (Note: I have omitted the intermediate trace in Comp from the representations in (19) because, as noted earlier, even in GB it is not visible at PF.)

(19)a. What$_i$ do you think [WH-trace$_i$ is (think's) happening]?

   b. What$_i$ do you think [WH-trace$_i$ has (think's) been happening]?

The phonological reduction here is perfectly clear cut; there need be no more of a vowel between *think* and *s* in (19) than there is when the *s* is the third person present inflection (e.g. in *John thinks slowly*). Also, as Schachter notes, there is voicing assimilation with the final segment of the verb, just as in the inflectional case; compare (19) with (20), where the *s* is voiced.

(20) What do you imagine's happening?

This pattern of reduction is also evident with other auxiliaries and other matrix predicates; a small sample is shown in (21).[30]

---

[29] Bresnan (1971) had presented comparable examples (e.g. *Do whatever you think's necessary*) several years earlier, before there were traces and before there was a theory like GPSG/HPSG drawing a distinction between subject extractions in finite and non-finite clauses. Bresnan's analysis of these examples is discussed later.

[30] The reduction is more complete in some cases than in others. In (21c), for example, many speakers can delete the vowel entirely, whereas in (i) it can only reduce to ə.

   (i) Who did you hope WH-trace would (hope'əd, *hoped) be there?

It turns out that such details are important, but I will postpone discussion of them for a few pages, until the general outline of the argument has become clear.

(21)a. Who$_i$ do you think [WH-trace$_i$ will (think'll) win it]?
   b. What$_i$ is John afraid [WH-trace$_i$ is (afraid's) going to happen]?
   c. I wonder [how many of them]$_i$ she knew [WH-trace$_i$ would (knew'əd) be leaving?

Note the contrast between the examples in (19)–(21) and the *wanna* example (9c), repeated here, where the complement clause is infinitival and the intervening trace does block the contraction.

(9c) Who$_j$ does John$_i$ want WH-trace$_j$ to (*wanna) go to the movies?

In (19)–(21), the trace is nominative, and has no effect; in (9c) the trace is accusative, and does have an effect. The comparison can be drawn more closely still with a verb like *mean*, which can occur not too unnaturally with both a finite and an infinitive complement, though unfortunately it does not show such a striking contraction effect as *want* does. (Again, I have represented the GB empty categories here; in GPSG/HPSG the WH-trace in (22a) and the PRO in (22c) don't exist.)

(22)a. Who$_i$ do you mean WH-trace$_i$ is (mean's) giving out the prizes?
   b. Who$_i$ do you mean WH-trace$_i$ to (*meanta) give out the prizes?
   c. Who$_i$ do you$_j$ mean PRO$_j$ to (meanta) give out the prizes to WH-trace$_i$?

The nominative WH-trace in (22a) has no effect, and nor does the PRO in (22c); but the accusative WH-trace in (22b) does block contraction. This pattern of facts is exactly as GPSG/HPSG would predict, since GPSG/HPSG holds that nominative WH-trace and PRO do not exist, but accusative WH-trace does. But the contraction facts are not as GB would predict, if GB principles require that all case-marked empty categories, nominative as well as accusative, are PF-visible.

Thus there is a linguistic question here for GB, and we need to know what the answer is before we can tell whether it would be interesting to look for on-line antecedent reactivation by nominative traces. The question is: what should be done to adapt GB's theory of PF-visibility, which works so well for *wanna*-contraction, so that it can cope with *think's*-contraction too? One possibility is that GB will find a principled reason for claiming that accusative traces are PF-visible but nominative WH-traces are not. Alternatively, it might be argued that the Schachter phenomenon is not a suitable test of PF-visibility, so that it can be maintained that nominative as well as accusative traces do exist at PF. In the first case, the GB prediction about nominative traces at PF would converge with that of GPSG/HPSG, and a nominative trace experiment would be uninformative (in the absence of independent evidence about which level is relevant to these experiments). In the second case, the linguistic predictions would remain distinct, and experimental data on nominative trace could be expected to decide between them.

So now we must consider the GB solution to the problem of *wanna*-contraction vs *think's*-contraction. In fact, several different and mutually conflicting proposals have been made. I will review these in the next section. Readers who are not interested in the linguistic details may safely skip to the last section, which summarises what is common to all of these approaches and considers the implications for the proposed experiment.

NOMINATIVE TRACE AND AUXILIARY REDUCTION IN GB

Chomsky: Rule Ordering

Chomsky (1986a) suggests that though case-marked empty categories enter the phonetic component, there is a subsequent process of 'elimination of any category that is not required by presence of lexical material within it' (p. 163). This occurs partway through PF derivations. Those processes that are sensitive to empty categories, such as *wanna*-contraction (also the auxiliary reductions noted by King, 1970, to be discussed later) apply before the empty categories have been eliminated. The *think's*-contraction rule, which is not sensitive to empty categories, applies after they have been eliminated.[31] Chomsky (1986a, p. 164) observes that 'the ordering is presumably determined on more general grounds', but does not pursue the matter. I think it is true that the relevant principles have not so far been identified.

Bresnan: Direction of Cliticisation

An unpublished paper by Bresnan (1971) long ago offered a comprehensive account of auxiliary reduction and its relation to movement and deletion processes. Bresnan had already noted what I have been calling the Schachter phenomenon or *think's*-contraction, and she compared it with another reduction phenomenon that had been noted by King (1970). King observed that there are restrictions on the reduction of auxiliaries when they *PRECEDE* (rather than *SPAN*) an empty category. His examples include those in (23). Note that the 'gaps' in King's examples include not only what we would now call WH-trace, but also the results of what was traditionally regarded as deletion, as in (23a,b). (I will assume that there are empty categories in [23a,b] because then Bresnan's account can be updated into GB terms to provide a uniform explanation of all the King examples. A common assumption nowadays is that these 'deletion'

---

[31] Chomsky actually proposes to factor the King phenomenon into a destressing rule before empty category elimination, and the reduction of destressed auxiliaries after empty category elimination. The latter process would be involved in both the King effect and *think's*-contraction. This changes the details but not the essence of the proposed solution.

empty categories are base generated and that at LF the antecedent is copied into the empty category position; see May, 1985.)

(23)a. Joan's taken more from you than Bill has (*Bill's) $_V[\phi]$ from me.
   cf. . . . than Bill's taken from me.
   b. Who's hungry? John is (*John's) $_{AP}[\phi]$ most of the time.
   cf. John's hungry most of the time.
   c. I wonder where Gerard is (*Gerard's) WH-trace today.
   cf. I wonder if Gerard's there today.
   d. We told him what a big boy you are (*you're) WH-trace.
   cf. We told him you're a big boy.

To explain this curious sensitivity of contraction to following material, Bresnan suggested that the reduced auxiliary actually attaches to the item on its right. We may suppose that when the rightward constituent is empty, the auxiliary cannot contract for lack of a host to contract onto.[32] Bresnan also observed that this same assumption—that auxiliary reduction is pro-cliticisation—will account for *think's*-contraction as well. The sequence here is matrix verb–WH-trace–reduced auxiliary. Reduction of the auxiliary will be indifferent to the WH-trace subject between it and the matrix verb, because the auxiliary attaches to what is on its right; the trace is on its left and hence does not get in the way of the contraction.

In short: though English orthography suggests the analysis *Who do you [think's] clever?*, Bresnan argued for *Who do you think ['sclever]?* Note that if this is correct, it should be that the *think's* type of contraction does block when there is an empty category to its right. And this is so.

(24) We might go to the beach. Who else do you think WH-trace will (*think'll) $_{VP}[\phi]$?
   cf. Who else do you think'll go to the beach?

This is exactly comparable to examples like King's, where the auxiliary follows an overt subject:[33]

---

[32] My presentation here departs somewhat from Bresnan's, which was given within a 1971 pre-GB framework without any movement traces. Bresnan assumed that auxiliary reduction involves a syntactic adjunction process occurring in the transformational cycle, prior to the movement or deletion operation that would remove the host constituent. The movement or deletion transformation would then be inapplicable to the auxiliary + host combination. For various reasons this analysis would not be tenable in GB. I have tried to retain the essence of Bresnan's explanation while recasting it in terms of empty categories.

[33] King gives only one example involving an item other than an auxiliary immediately following an overt subject. This illustrates the failure of a preposition to reduce immediately before a trace; in (ii) the æ of *at* cannot reduce to ə.

(i) You were looking at (ət) the same one yesterday.
(ii) It's the same one that you were looking at (*ət) WH-trace yesterday.

(25)a. We might go to the beach, but actually I doubt that we will
(*we'll) $_{VP}[\phi]$.
cf. I doubt that we'll go to the beach.
  b. Tom may go to the beach but I doubt that Frank will (*Frank'll)
$_{VP}[\phi]$.
cf. I doubt that Frank'll go to the beach.

Bresnan notes that just the reverse is true of *wanna*-contraction. This *IS* sensitive to a WH-trace to its left, as in (9c), but it does *NOT* show the King effect: *wanna*-contraction is perfectly acceptable even with an empty VP to its right, as in (26).

(26) We might go to the beach but I'm not sure if I want PRO to
(wanna) $_{VP}[\phi]$.

Bresnan therefore proposes that the reduced *to* in *wanna* does associate to its left, and hence is sensitive to what precedes it but not to what follows it. Bresnan's proposal thus renders all the PF-visibility effects explicable within GB. What looked like a contradiction turns out on this approach to be just a minor morphological difference between reduced auxiliary verbs and reduced infinitival *to*: the former lack a word boundary to their right, and the latter lacks a word boundary to its left.

Bresnan thus provides a neat account of the contrast between *wanna*-contraction and *think's*-contraction, which does *NOT* require the assumption that a nominative WH-trace is invisible at PF. Taking *'s* to be proclitic can explain both why it *IS* sensitive to an empty category that follows it and why it is *NOT* sensitive to an empty category—a perfectly *VISIBLE* empty category—that precedes it. But despite its elegance, this account cannot stand as it is. Klavans (1985) notes that the procliticisation proposal was criticised by Lakoff (1972) and by Wood (1979) on the grounds that reduction of *is* and other auxiliary verbs exhibits phonetic sensitivity to the preceding item, not the following one. This is true both when the auxiliary is preceded by its subject and when it is preceded (overtly) by the matrix verb. The subject + auxiliary case is illustrated in (27). Note that in (27a,b) there is voicing assimilation of the *'s* of *has* to the final consonant of the preceding word, and in (27c) an epenthetic vowel has to be inserted, beause of incompatibility of the two consonants.

(27)a. Jack's got brains.
  b. Ray's got brains.
  c. Midge's got brains.

The matrix verb + auxiliary case is illustrated in (28). As noted earlier, there is voicing assimilation between a reduced *is* and the final segment of the preceding verb, and vowel epenthesis is conditioned by that segment also, in (28) just as in (27).

(28)a. Who do you think's clever?
   b. Who do you imagine's clever?
   c. Who do you judge's clever?

So it appears from the phonetic evidence that a reduced *is* (and presumably other auxiliaries likewise) is enclitic not proclitic after all. If so, we lose Bresnan's explanation of why the reduction isn't blocked by a WH-trace.

However, the phonetic facts need not be fatal to the procliticisation proposal. Klavans (1985) argues that the direction of phonetic sensitivity is not necessarily indicative of the direction of syntactic attachment. She presents examples from a number of languages, which show that an item which cliticises to the right syntactically may cliticise to the left phonologically, or vice versa. For example, in Kwakwala (Kwakiutl), every non-nominative NP has a preceding particle that marks its grammatical function, but the particle attaches phonologically to the preceding word, regardless of what that word is.

Once a mismatch of directionality for cliticisation is established as a possibility in natural languages, the phonetic properties of auxiliary reduction in English can no longer disqualify Bresnan's account of its sensitivity to empty categories. The *'s* of *think's* could require a non-empty syntactic host to its right, even though it attaches phonetically to a host on its left. If this assumption is tenable, then GB would be able to accommodate the last remaining oddity about which empty categories are visible at PF. That is, it could be maintained after all that a nominative trace *IS* visible at PF, and we merely lack any test to reveal its presence; the Schachter reduction test is irrelevant because it looks in the wrong place.

The combined Bresnan/Klavans hypothesis covers the facts very cleverly. But a great deal rests on it, as we've seen, and there are some problems, of varying degrees of severity, that need to be faced before GB can rest confident that the visibility of nominative WH-trace is under control.

The simplest, but I think most telling, objection is that the Klavans amendment, which protects the Bresnan hypothesis against the phonetic counterevidence, thereby robs it of its rationale. 'Emptiness' is a phonetic (or phonological) property.[34] If the host to the right were a phonetic host,

---

[34] Phonetic emptiness (sometimes represented as [+NULL] in syntax) *IS* deemed to have certain syntactic consequences, not unrelated to the old notion of 'recoverability of deletion'. An empty category has to be licensed (by proper government) and identified (by coindexation with something from which its interpretation can be recovered). It is an assumption on my part, though I think a reasonable one, that this is *ALL* that emptiness should affect; it should not be relevant to the possibility of syntactic adjunction processes. (Later, I consider the Bresnan/Klavans proposal without this assumpton.)

it would make sense that an empty category on the right should block reduction: an overt morpheme wouldn't be expected to combine with an empty morpheme to form a single phonological word. But if the host to the right is a *SYNTACTIC* host, why should it matter if it's phonetically empty? And if the host to the left is the phonetic host, why *DOESN'T* it matter if it's phonetically empty?

The problem results from trying to carry over the Bresnan (1971) proposal into GB theory (see footnote 32). It worked much better in the pre-GB theory *WITHOUT* empty categories than it does with them. Klavans' subsequent revision of Bresnan's explanation did not consider the impact on it of assuming empty categories. Klavans discussed only examples in which the auxiliary was stranded by VP Deletion, and she took deletion to be the complete elimination of a sentence constituent, leaving no empty category. This would indeed explain why syntactic procliticisation of the auxiliary would be impossible: a clitic can't attach to nothing. However, as King observed, auxiliary reduction is sensitive not only to a following deletion site, but also to a following trace of movement, as in the examples (23c,d), repeated here.

(23)c. I wonder where Gerard is (*Gerard's) WH-trace today?
   d. We told him what a big boy you are (*you're) WH-trace.

Whatever it should say about empty categories resulting from deletion, GB is clearly committed to the syntactic existence of WH-trace. Hence Klavans' explanation of why an auxiliary cannot lean syntactically to the right in the King examples will not cover the full range of cases. It does not say why, in (23c) for instance, a clitic *'s* could not attach syntactically to WH-trace and phonetically to *Gerard*.

To summarise: this first worry about the Bresnan/Klavans (henceforth B/K) hypothesis has been that an empty category ought to inhibit a *PHONOLOGICAL* cliticisation process, but not a *SYNTACTIC* cliticisation process. So the B/K hypothesis should predict that reduction is blocked by an empty category on the left, and not by an empty category on the right. But this is exactly the opposite of the English facts that need to be explained. In order to move on, let us now, for the sake of argument, give up this objection and assume that phonological emptiness *CAN* block syntactic adjunction processes. This wouldn't save the B/K explanation of the Schachter reductions, but it would save the B/K account of the King effect: the reduced auxiliary needs to lean syntactically to the right, but the empty category there will not bear its weight. However, a second problem for this approach now arises: at least for some auxiliaries, there is evidence that they lean syntactically to the left (as standard punctuation suggests), not to the right.

Evidence that a reduced auxiliary leans syntactically (as well as phonetically) to its left would be that there are syntactic constraints on what items can appear to its left. Wood (1979) claimed that this is not so, and cited examples such as (29) which are indeed perfectly acceptable.

(29)a. What I think's not important.
    b. The man who sold you that car's a real snake.
    c. John, I think's, a fool.

But Zwicky (1970) notes that the various auxiliary verbs differ considerably with respect to how context-sensitive they are: *'s* (= *is* or *has*) is completely indifferent to what appears on its left (as in Wood's examples), while *'d* (= *would* or *had*) is syntactically indifferent but will only follow vowels. But the fully contracted forms of *will, have, am,* and *are* may follow only certain pronouns, and only if the pronoun is the subject of the auxiliary or fronted by WH-movement, not if it is conjoined, not if it is part of a relative clause, etc. It should be noted that Zwicky is referring here to full deletion of the vowel of the auxiliary; what he calls Glide Deletion, leaving a reduced vowel, occurs more freely. Even if one doesn't agree with all of his judgements, the kinds of differences he is pointing to do seem to exist.

(30)a. You'll go.
    b. Who'll go? Who'll he go with?
    c. *Sue'll go.   Sue'əll go.
    d. *Grace and you'll go.   Grace and you'əll go.
    e. *The guy next to you'll go. The guy next to you'əll go.

The syntactic nature of the constraints exemplified in (30) is hard to reconcile with the idea that *'ll* is syntactically dependent only on its rightward neighbour.[35]

---

[35] Two points here. First, I will not consider here the possibility that there might be syntactic constraints on an item other than that to which the auxiliary attaches syntactically. Second, though I have some sympathy with it, I won't pursue here the idea that, as full reduction of *will, am,* etc., is compatible with such a small number of preceding items, it should be assumed that such examples are simply lexicalised: *you'll* would be a lexical item, but *Sue'll* wouldn't. (Note that the syntactic category of *you'll* would be something of a problem, except in a categorial grammar.) This lexical analysis does no better than a syntactic approach does at explaining the King effect in (31) and (32). (But see the section on lexicalisation of *wanna*.)

We have evidence, then, that at least some auxiliaries are syntactically left-leaning, even if others may lean to the right.[36] What we need to know, to clarify the PF-visibility issue, is whether an auxiliary that leans leftward syntactically shows the King effect (blocking of reduction before an empty category) and the Schachter effect (reduction across a nominative trace). If so, that will be a second reason for thinking that these effects are *NOT* due to rightward syntactic leaning of the auxiliary, as the B/K account assumes.

The King effect is perfectly clear: *you'll* and *who'll* as in (30a,b), also *you've* and *who've*, can no more precede a deletion site than can any other reduced auxiliary; see (31).

(31)a. *Joan's taken more from you than you've $_V[\phi]$ from me.
   b. Who'll be talking? *I know who'll $_{VP}[\phi]$ most of the time.
      *You'll $_{VP}[\phi]$ most of the time.

The same is true when the empty category is a movement trace, as in (32).

(32)a. How hungry does John think I am (*I'm) WH-trace?
   b. What kind of athlete did you say you are (*you're) WH-trace?

It seems clear, then, that the King effect couldn't be due to a need for the reduced auxiliary to procliticise syntactically onto a phonetically non-null item.[37]

---

[36] There is further evidence that auxiliaries differ in this respect. Bresnan notes that some reduce in sentence-initial positions, which suggests that they lean rightward. This is true of *'s* and of *'əll* when it retains a vowel as in Bresnan's example (i); the phonetic transcription is hers. However, the reductions that Zwicky notes as being restricted seem not to occur initially; (i) without the initial vowel is impossible. Bresnan also gives examples in which an auxiliary reduces after a parenthetical. Again, her examples have *'s* and *'əll*, the syntactically insensitive forms; it doesn't seem possible to construct an example in which *will* reduces fully; consider (ii). The failure of any reduction in (iii) where the auxiliary precedes the parenthetical can be attributed, I believe, to the fact that in that context it must have stress, as Bresnan notes.

   (i) Will one do? —> 'll one do? [əlwʌnduw]
   (ii) These things, dear Sue, 'əll (*Sue'll) amuse you eventually.
   (iii) *These things'əll, dear Sue, amuse you eventually.

[37] I suppose it might be suggested that though *'m* (as in [32a]) leans leftward onto *I*, the whole of *I'm* is proclitic and so needs a non-empty host to its right. The same would have to be true of *I'd've* and *they'd've*, which also cannot appear in the King context. Note that all of these contrast in this respect with *I would've* though they differ from it only in reduction of the *NON*-final auxiliary. See the discussion in the section on prosodic phrasing.

When we try to test the Schachter effect with these syntactically leftward leaning auxiliaries we run into a problem. The relevant examples are as in (33).

(33)a. Who did he say's going to be there?
    b. *Who did he say'll be there? (unlike: We'll be there.)
    c. Who did he say'əll be there. (like: Ray'əll be there.)
    d. Which wine did he say's in the cellar?
    e. *Which wines did he say've been in the cellar? (unlike: They've been in the cellar.)
    f. Which wines did he say'əv been in the cellar? (like: Bert and Ray'əv been in the cellar.)

The judgements are delicate, but it appears that *will* and perfective *have* do not fully reduce here, though the vowel-retaining form is clearly acceptable, and so is full reduction of *is*. If (33b,e) had been acceptable, that would have been informative: it would have told us that syntactic cliticisation to the left is unaffected by an empty category to the left. Unfortunately, the negative outcome of the test leaves matters unresolved. If the left-syntax-sensitive auxiliaries *DID* fully reduce in the Schachter context, that would indicate not only that they don't care about the WH-trace, but also that they find a verb to the left as acceptable a host as a pronoun to the left. But of course there's no particular reason why the latter should be so.[38] Thus the fact that these auxiliaries *DON'T* completely contract onto the main verb could be just another sign that they are left-syntax-sensitive, and dislike the verb on the left; it cannot show that they are repelled by a *TRACE* on the left.

The conclusion of this convolute argument is that we cannot, after all, establish whether syntactic cliticisation (to the left) is blocked by the phonetic emptiness of the prospective host. The B/K account of the King

---

[38] Curiously, even the auxiliaries that Zwicky notes are not normally left-sensitive show some left-sensitivity in the Schachter construction. Even for *'s*, for instance, a preceding verb as in (i) is better than a preceding noun as in (ii). (Note that the word string (ii) is acceptable with auxiliary contraction but only on a different analysis, as in (iii), where the trace is in the main clause, and the auxiliary reduces onto the subject.)

(i) Who did you say WH-trace is (say's) going to be there?
(ii) Who did you convince Ray [WH-trace is (?*Ray's) going to be there]?
(iii) Who did you convince WH-trace [Ray is (Ray's) going to be there]?

With a pronoun such as *him* in place of *Ray* in (ii), the contraction is much improved. I wonder if this odd collection of facts is due to a no-ambiguity constraint requiring (ii) to be pronounced differently from (iii).

effect presupposes such blocking, at least for syntactic cliticisation to the right, and for reduced auxiliaries like '*s*, which demonstrably lean away from a following empty category phonetically and hence must depend on it syntactically if they depend on it at all.

Let us now move on to the third concern about the B/K proposal. I have argued so far that it is not as explanatory as it at first seems, and that for some auxiliaries it cannot account for the King effect. Now I note that even for an auxiliary to which it does apply, it appears to give a wrong explanation of the King effect. Consider the examples in (34) where the second of two auxiliaries has contracted before a deletion site.

(34)a. In the end we didn't go to the beach, but we might have (might'əv) $_{VP}[\phi]$.
  b. He said he went to the beach but he couldn't have (couldn't'əv) $_{VP}[\phi]$.
  c. Sam didn't buy Sadie a birthday present, but he shoulda $_{VP}[\phi]$.
  d. George spent more on Sadie's birthday present than he shoulda $_{VP}[\phi]$.

If the reduced *have* leans rightward here, it ought to be unacceptable before the empty VP but it isn't. Can we find independent evidence of which way the reduced *have* leans? Unfortunately, this isn't easy. For instance, there seems to be no example that permits a test of whether full reduction or only Glide Deletion is acceptable in this context. It's true that full vowel deletion is unacceptable in **may've*, but this is so in any context, not just before an empty category. Furthermore, since *have* is the only contractable auxiliary that can follow another auxiliary, it is the only possible source of examples like (34), and so we cannot be sure that (34) doesn't simply reflect some idiosyncrasy of *have*, as has been suggested by Wood (1979). The last two examples in (34) are Wood's. She presented them as troublesome for Bresnan's procliticisation proposal, but suggested that a way out would be to claim that '*ve* is enclitic though all other reduced auxiliaries are proclitic. In fact that wouldn't work, since '*ve* does show the King effect when it is the first (only) auxiliary.

(35)a. *John hasn't been to the beach but we've $_{VP}[\phi]$.
  b. *Sam's bought Sadie more presents than you and Bill've $_{VP}[\phi]$.

Bresnan herself attributed the contrast between (34) and (35) to a difference between untensed *have* and tensed *have*, but with no explanation of why tense should matter; she simply claimed that 'non-tense-bearing *have* is insensitive to deletion on the right' (p.25). By her principles this must entail, I think, that it cliticises syntactically to the left. But the King effect in (35) clearly requires, by the same principles, that tensed *have* cliticises to the right. This is not impossible, but a shade *ad hoc*. A variant would be an elsewhere analysis: one could claim that *have* associates syntactically to its left if there is another auxiliary available there as its host, but otherwise associates syntactically to its right. Although this isn't absolutely out of the question, an alternative story would be welcome.

Wood: The Empty VP Constraint

Wood herself argued for a quite different explanation of the *shoulda* phenomenon—an explanation that has nothing to do with empty categories as hosts or blockers of contraction, and which makes the difference between the two *have*'s simply a matter of their different positions: to reduce a tensed *have* before a gap is more serious because it leaves no verb in the clause at all. Wood proposed an Empty Verb Phrase Constraint, prohibiting any contraction that would eliminate the whole VP. (One might nowadays refer to Infl': rather than VP, but details of formulation can be overlooked here.) This would distinguish between the examples in (35) where the contracted *have* is all that remains of the VP on the surface, and the examples in (34) where another auxiliary is overt. (Note that Wood assumes that a contracted auxiliary following the subject has moved out of the VP to cliticise to the subject.) A constraint against empty verb phrases has some plausibility, since VP Deletion is in any case subject to the constraint that at least one auxiliary verb be retained; if there is no other, then a '*do*-support' *do* must be introduced as in (36c). (Note that in (36d), infinitival *to* appears to behave like an auxiliary verb with respect to this constraint; I will return to this later.)

(36)a. John won't go even though I will.
　　　*John won't go even though I.
　　b. John could have left if Sam could (have).
　　　*John could have left if Sam.
　　c. John left whether or not Sam did.
　　　*John left whether or not Sam.
　　d. John left and Sam wants to.
　　　*John left and Sam wants.

So for these examples the King phenomenon could be captured by a simple rider on the VP Deletion constraint, to the effect that the auxiliary obligatorily left by VP Deletion must be left within the VP (the Infl'); it must not be moved out to adjoin to the subject. However, this wouldn't work for examples like (23c,d) where the gap is created by WH-extraction rather than by VP Deletion; for these, a separate and more general constraint such as Wood's is required.

But Wood's Empty Verb Phrase Constraint has its own share of problems. Wood notes that it fails to cover cases where reduction is blocked even though there remains an adverb or some other element that would have been thought to be part of the VP. Her hypothesis would account for (37), for instance, only if *in the bottle* were outside the VP, though it is often analysed as inside.

(37) I wonder how much wine there is (*there's) WH-trace in the bottle.
cf. There's wine in the bottle.

Even clearer counterexamples are provided by Gapping, as in (38), where the verb deletes but its direct object remains.

(38) John's washing the car, and Bill is (*Bill's) $_v[\phi]$ the truck.

A more adequate statement of the facts would be, as Wood herself expresses it at one point, that reduction is prohibited if it would eliminate the 'verb complex' (= a string of adjacent auxiliaries and main verb). This is an unattractive constraint, since the verb complex is not a constituent. Yet reference to it may independently be required; for example, in Gapping constructions it is permitted to delete from one end or the other of the verb string, but not both, and not only the middle of it. An 'Empty Verb Complex Constraint' would correctly block reduction in (37) and (38), as well as making the (34)/(35) distinction for untensed/tensed *have*. Nevertheless this constraint also has descriptive troubles. One is that it seems to outlaw standard cases of Gapping as in (39), where the whole verb complex has been deleted.

(39) John is washing the car and Bill $_v[\phi]$ the truck.

However, it is known that Gapping which eliminates the tensed verb is very much more restricted than Gapping which leaves the tense. The latter may occur in a wide range of contexts, including across sentence boundaries and across speakers. But if the tense is deleted, Gapping is restricted to a very specific context: the Gapped verb must be in the highest clause of a clause which is conjoined to a previous clause, whose highest clause contains the antecedent for the Gapped verb. A small part of the evidence is shown in (40); see Fodor (1975; 1985) for further examples and discussion.

(40)a. John must be washing the car if Bill is $_v[\phi]$ the truck.
   b. *John must be washing the car if Bill $_v[\phi]$ the truck.
   c. Speaker A: John isn't washing the car.

Speaker B: So I hear. But Bill is $_V[\phi]$ the truck.
d. Speaker A: John isn't washing the car.
Speaker B: So I hear. *But Bill $_V[\phi]$ the truck.

Perhaps it can be assumed, then, that the elimination of tense in 'full Gapping' examples like (39) is due to some special process that is restricted to directly conjoined clauses and is not subject to the Empty Verb Complex Constraint.[39]

Thus, as Wood proposed, it may be possible to account for the King effect in a way that has nothing to do with empty categories or failed attempts to cliticise onto them. However, other problems remain, which I think will be difficult to cope with and which suggest that some reference to empty categories *IS* needed. First, a constraint on the verb complex won't extend to the prepositional example in footnote 33, which does feel as if it has to do with the need for a host for a reduced preposition. Second, the examples in (41) show that the last remnant of the verb complex *CAN* be reduced or moved in certain circumstances.

(41)a. John's clever.
   b. John's a doctor.
   c. There's wine in the bottle. = (37b)
   d. I've a penny in my pocket. (some dialects)
   e. Is John clever?
   f. How's John?

Examples (41e,f) show that removal of the auxiliary by subject-aux inversion is immune to the constraint; apparently a violation occurs only when an auxiliary is present following the subject, but is reduced. And examples (41a–d) show that there's no penalty for reducing the last remaining auxiliary, as long as it doesn't precede an empty category. Compare these with (42):

(42)a. *Bill's clever and John's $_{AP}[\phi]$ too.
   b. *Bill has hidden a dime and I've $_V[\phi]$ a penny. (meaning: I've hidden a penny)

It must be concluded, then, contrary to Wood, that empty categories *ARE* relevant to the acceptability of auxiliary reduction in some fashion. And if we ask why that should be so (other than because reduction is cliticisation needing a non-empty host), the only answer that comes to

---

[39] The ungrammaticality of examples such as *John is walking if Mary $_V[\phi]$ running* shows that it is indeed the tense that must remain; another verb in the complex is not sufficient.

mind is that it has to do with stress. Auxiliaries that cannot reduce seem to bear more stress than auxiliaries that can. So perhaps there has to be a non-reduced verb before a gap because there has to be stress before a gap.

Prosodic Phrasing[40]

The idea that the influence of empty categories on auxiliary reduction is indirect, mediated by prosodic requirements, has been explored by Jacobson (1982), Zwicky (1982), Selkirk (1984), and others, with various differences of detail that I won't attempt to document here. The general idea is that an empty category forces a preceding item to bear stress, and that it is the stress which prevents the item from reducing. Why does an empty category have this effect? Normally a function word such as an auxiliary, since it lacks full status as an independent phonological word, must be grouped into a phonological phrase with its syntactic sister. Thus an auxiliary is grouped with its sister VP, and the main stress on the predicate as a whole (= the Infl') will typically fall on a word within the VP; hence the auxiliary need not bear stress and is free to reduce. But if the VP sister is missing, then the auxiliary constitutes the whole phonological phrase by itself, hence it must carry the stress for that phrase, and so it cannot reduce.

This prosodic approach explains the basic King effect (e.g. *Tom's shouting louder than Bill's*) where the VP sister to the auxiliary has been deleted or moved. It also explains why reduction in that context is possible for the second of two auxiliaries (untensed *have*) when the first is unreduced, as in (34); and why it is impossible to reduce both, as in the examples in footnote 37. As long as the first auxiliary carries the required stress for the predicate, the second is free to reduce. A prosodic approach will also resolve the problem about Gapping, given the familiar observation that Gapping requires a major stress on *BOTH* remaining fragments of a clause or phrase that has been broken apart by deletion of an item or items in the middle. In an example such as (38), the direct object remains, so the VP is not empty, but the auxiliary is the only item in the lefthand fragment of the predicate, and so it must bear stress and not reduce. Wood's constraint did not distinguish this case from (39), where the auxiliary has been Gapped along with the main verb. On the stress-based account (39) is acceptable because the constituent that is broken up by Gapping in this case is the sentence, and its lefthand fragment is the subject, which bears the requisite stress.

---

[40] My grasp of the matters discussed in this section and the next is due largely to the excellent tuition of Sharon Inkelas and Draga Zec. They are not responsible for errors of content or exposition, but anything I have right I owe to them.

Note that this account escapes the major objection to the Bresnan/ Klavans account. It was not clear why syntactic cliticisation of the auxiliary onto its right sister should be affected by the emptiness of the host category. By contrast, on the phonological phrasing hypothesis it is perfectly clear why the empty category has the effect that it does on the auxiliary—whatever else an empty category can do, it obviously cannot bear stress. It may be possible, then, to rescue the insight behind the B/K proposal by ascribing to prosody the role that B/K attributed to syntactic cliticisation. Of course we mustn't forget the assimilation facts in (28), which suggest that reduced auxiliaries lean leftward phonetically. But this too can be accommodated. Though unreduced auxiliaries, and partially reduced forms such as *əll*, group prosodically to the right (in a suitable context), we may assume that the fully reduced forms without vowels always cliticise to the left. This would also explain why they are impossible at the beginning of a sentence (or phrase preceded by juncture) as in Bresnan's example (see footnote 36): *Will one do?* --> *əlwʌnduw*, not **lwʌnduw*. This cliticisation is also impossible if the auxiliary is needed to carry stress.

Once the role of empty categories in blocking reduction has been demoted in this fashion from direct cause to indirect cause, it is a short step to eliminating it altogether. The claim would be that the blocking of reduction is caused *NOT* by the existence of an empty category, but by the *NON*-existence of other (overt) constituents within a phrase. The consequence would be that the prosodic explanation for the King effect is neutral with respect to whether or not empty categories exist at PF.

The prosodic account of the King effect therefore does not dictate what stance GB should take with respect to the Schachter effect, i.e. contraction *ACROSS* empty categories. the puzzling contrast between (19) and (9c) remains: *think's*-contraction is apparently indifferent to WH-trace, but *wanna*-contraction is apparently sensitive to it. The prosodic approach itself doesn't seem to offer any account of why this difference should exist. However, it might indirectly contribute to solving the Schachter problem, by expanding the descriptive options: it permits GB either to assume, or not to assume, empty categories at PF, for purposes of the King effect.

If GB does assume that WH-trace exists at PF and blocks reduction, then the *wanna*-reduction facts are accounted for, and the *think's*-reduction facts are the problem. If instead GB were to assume there were no (visible) empty categories at PF (as the prosodic account of the King effect permits), then the *think's*-reduction facts would be accounted for, and the *wanna*-reduction facts would be the problem. Seeing *wanna* rather than *think's* as the guilty party could improve the explanatory situation, if some independent account of the behaviour of *wanna* could be found. One approach that is sometimes advocated is to treat *wanna* as a single lexical item.

Lexicalisation of *Wanna*

Lexical treatments of *wanna* have been contemplated by Selkirk (1972; 1984), Bolinger (1981), and even by Chomsky and Lasnik (1978, footnote 4). The details vary; sometimes the idea is mentioned only to be rejected, for example by Aoun and Lightfoot (1984), and Pullum and Postal (1979). Except for the latter, it is generally presumed that if *wanna* were a lexical item it would have to be an auxiliary verb; and since it demonstrably isn't, the lexical approach is deemed unworkable. However, the classification of *wanna* as an auxiliary is by no means necessary (see later discussion), so it would be unwise to dismiss the lexical approach without due consideration.[41]

One reason for suspecting that the contracted form *wanna* might be represented in the lexicon is that the set of verbs which combine with a reduced *to* in this fashion is very small and quite unsystematic: aside from *wanna* there is *gonna* and *hafta* and just a few others, but there is no **meanna* or **planna* or **intenna*.[42] The arbitrariness of this set would be explained if there were no rule but merely a number of exceptional lexical entries; and the smallness of the set means that lexical specification is feasible. Furthermore, the pronunciation of the reduced form is not predictable on the basis of any general phonological rule in English, so it must be registered somewhere in the grammar, as a memo in the lexical entry for *want*—or perhaps in the lexical entry for the word *wanna*. It is interesting to observe that *think's*-contraction, by contrast, does not exhibit these properties that invite a lexical treatment. It is completely general: every main verb in English apparently permits it. And the reduced form shows no variation in the phonetic shape of the main verb (though, as we have seen, the degree of reduction of the auxiliary varies from one auxiliary to another). Thus the information to be stored in the lexicon in this case is a matter of which auxiliaries have which reduced forms, and what conditions they impose on their hosts (see earlier section on Bresnan's analysis); no pre-combined V+Aux forms such as *think's* need to be lexically listed.

---

[41] Pullum and Postal have a different objection to a lexical approach, which is that it would treat *hasta* and *hafta* as two separate lexical items, and the presence of an internal inflection would not be captured. They are certainly right that this constitutes an inelegance in the analysis, but it is a minor one and surely not decisive; it would fit perfectly well into a lexical approach that acknowledged the historical sources of these reduced forms (see later comments).

[42] Reduction to *to* to *tə* is possible following *mean* and all these other verbs. It is a consequence of a quite general rule of unstressed vowel reduction in English, and would not be expected to be lexically governed.

Given a lexical analysis of *wanna*, there would be no such process as '*wanna*-reduction'. There would just be a word *wanna* that could be inserted into certain contexts and not others. What is commonly thought of as 'the blocking of *wanna*-contraction by WH-trace' would be no such thing, but would be just one instance of a presumably quite general constraint on all possible lexical items: no word can contain an internal NP available for extraction. (See discussion of the 'lexical integrity hypothesis' by Sproat & Ward, 1987.) Thus the contrast between *Who do you wanna dance?* (trace inside lexical item) and *Who do you wanna dance with?* (no word-internal trace) would be accounted for.[43]

If *wanna* were a lexical item, what would be its properties? It is presumably a verb, and a main verb (*NOT* an auxiliary) since it doesn't invert (*Do you wanna dance?* not *Wanna you dance?*). It means the same as *want* does. Also like *want*, it takes a complement clause (or complement VP in non-transformational theories), which exhibits subject control of PRO. But *wanna* has three peculiarities. First, its complement lacks infinitival *to* (*I wanna to dance*). Second, it is specified as present tense or tenseless, and as plural or non-third person only (*He wanna dance*). Third, unlike other main verbs, it permits VP deletion without leaving the usual obligatory auxiliary (or *to* in infinitives) in final position (e.g. *John is dancing but I don't wanna* unlike *John is dancing but I don't want*). Are these properties so peculiar that the theory of the lexicon should exclude them? If so, the lexical solution to the *wanna*-reduction problem could not be maintained.

In fact, there are precedents for all of these non-standard properties of *wanna*. The main verbs *let* and *make* (as in *Let him go, I made him cry*) take infinitival complements that lack the marker *to* (though it shows up in the passive *He was made to cry*). The very odd verb *beware* has only uninflected forms (e.g. *Beware of the dog!* but not *John bewares of the dog*, *John was bewaring of the dog*; Fodor, 1972). And the apparent idiosyncrasy with respect to VP Deletion can be seen instead as *wanna* permitting its complement clause to be null. A number of otherwise perfectly normal complement-taking verbs have this property also. For example, *know* and *try* permit their complements to be empty (*I don't know*, *Please try!*). Other verbs, e.g. *intend, assume*, do not (*I certainly*

---

[43] If it is to be maintained that a lexical item cannot contain *ANY* empty category, there must be an analysis of *wanna* where it is legitimate, as in *I wanna dance*, which does not involve PRO. A candidate is outlined later. As far as I can see, it is not incompatible with a theory that assumes there is PRO in the corresponding unreduced forms, as GB does.

do not intend!, **Sorry; I just assumed*).[44] In fact *wanna* is very like the verb *help*, which can take a complement without *to* (e.g. *I helped wash the dishes*) and also a null complement (e.g. *John washed the dishes and I helped*). Thus the apparent contrast between *wanna* and *want* with respect to VP Deletion is not a problem but can be taken to indicate merely that *wanna* falls into the *know/try/help* class, whereas *want* falls within the *intend/assume* class.

Thus it appears that a verb like *wanna*, though clearly exceptional, is not an impossibility. The lexical approach can account for both of the facts that concerned Bresnan: that *wanna* (unlike *think's*) *IS* incompatible with an intervening WH-trace, and is *NOT* incompatible with a following empty category. Obviously the existence of this peculiar verb in the language, and even the specific nature of its peculiarities, are causally related to the existence of *want to* in English and a common tendency to reduce it. But it does not follow that *wanna* must be derived from *want to* synchronically, and we have seen some advantages to assuming that it is not.

Summing up: it may be possible to defend a package consisting of a prosodic explanation of the King effect, a lexical account of *wanna*, and no empty categories (or no blocking of reduction by empty categories) at PF. Of course, this would mean relinquishing *wanna*-contraction as phonetic evidence for the reality of empty categories. That would be a disappointment, since the phonetic confirmation of abstract syntactic hypotheses is reassuring for linguists and quite dramatic for nonspecialists. But setting aside these targets, and the fact that the lexical analysis is decidedly unexciting from a theoretical point of view, there appears to be nothing against this solution. And it would achieve what was needed in GB; that is, it would demolish the problem about the contrasting behaviour of nominative WH-trace and accusative WH-trace at PF. On the prosodic/lexical account there is no contrast between nominative and accusative trace. Possibly neither exists at PF, or possibly both do (but don't block reduction). That would be for other aspects of the theory to decide, since the comparison of *wanna*-contraction with *think's*-contraction no longer bears on the matter.

Other Accounts

The search for the perfect solution to the auxiliary reduction problem is still on. Rothstein and Snyder (1991) have recently proposed an analysis in which it is case *ASSIGNERS* rather than case-marked categories that

---

[44] For all verbs that take infinitival complements, VP Deletion is acceptable if it leaves the *to*. So VP Deletion might perhaps be analysed as involving a null complement for *to*, which would be lexically specified for it just as *know* and *try* and most auxiliaries are (though not, e.g. *being, need*).

must be visible at PF, and that block contraction if they intervene. A nominative WH-trace as in (43a) is assigned case by the Infl (inflection) that follows it; this does not intervene between *think* and *is* and so it does not block contraction.

(43)a. Who do you think WH-trace is (think's) clever?
    b. Who do you want PRO to (wanna) dance with WH-trace?
    c. Who do you want WH-trace to (*wanna) dance?
    d. Who do you believe WH-trace to be a winner?

PRO is required by GB principles to be ungoverned and caseless, so it has no case assigner; thus in (43b) there is no case-assigner that could block the contraction. But WH-trace in (43c) is assigned case by an empty complementiser (similar to the overt complementiser *for*, which shows up in *We wanted very much for Sam to dance*). This empty complementiser precedes the subordinate clause, i.e. it immediately precedes the WH-trace subject, hence it is between *want* and *to*, and blocks the contraction. Thus the visibility requirement on case assigners successfully distinguishes (43c) from (43a,b). However, Rothstein and Snyder note that it also predicts the acceptability of contraction in examples like (43d), where case is assigned neither by Infl in the subordinate clause nor by an empty complementiser; the case-assigner here is the main verb *believe*, which obviously does not intervene between itself and the *to*, and so should not block contraction. To my ear there is no reduced form of *believe to* (except for vowel reduction in the *to*, which is generally acceptable; see earlier comments). Of course this might be just a lexical gap; perhaps it just happens that no special phonological form of *believe* + *to* exists. But no other verbs in the *believe* class reduce convincingly either (e.g. *suppose* doesn't in [10b]). So this approach could be maintained only if it is prepared to claim that every one of these missing forms is an accidental gap.

Goodall (1991) has proposed a novel analysis of *wanna*-reduction as one instance of a more general *restructuring* process which 'converts biclausal structures . . . into monoclausal structures' (p. 244). He argues that the restructured form contains no PRO, and that it is the lexical subcategorisation of the matrix verb that determines whether restructuring occurs.

Barss (this volume) presents another new account. The standard suggestion is that *wanna*-reduction is blocked by the trace of WH-movement, but Barss suggests instead that WH-movement is blocked by the trace of *wanna*-reduction (more precisely: by the trace of the *to* in Comp as *to* moves up to combine with *want*). Note that this account, like Goodall's, is purely syntactic and does not crucially assume empty categories at PF.

It would be frustrating if further experimental work had to wait on a final determination of which of these various approaches to *wanna* and *think's* is correct. Earlier we found a way of bypassing a psychological uncertainty (= which level drives cross-modal priming?). Now we need a way of bypassing a linguistic uncertainty (= are there empty categories at GB's level of PF?). In the next and final section I will explain how this might be done.

NOMINATIVE TRACE AND ANTECEDENT REACTIVATION

In the first section of this chapter, I proposed to argue from the cross-modal priming results that the only genuine empty category is WH-trace. But I admitted a possible loophole in this argument: perhaps other empty categories exist, but only WH-trace is experimentally detectable. In the next section, I considered one variant of this: the possibility that only WH-trace is processed rapidly enough to be observed in an on-line task; but I argued that this is not so. I then considered another variant: the possibility that only empty categories which are phonetically active affect the cross-modal task (for whatever reason). To evaluate this possibility, it was necessary to consider whether WH-trace, and only WH-trace, is phonetically active, as has traditionally been assumed on the basis of the *wanna*-contraction facts. In the last section I considered a broader range of phonological evidence, paying attention to apparent differences between nominative and accusative WH-traces. Unfortunately GB theory is not settled in its treatment of these facts. It is not even settled with respect to the central question of whether or not these facts support the existence of empty categories at PF; some of the analyses proposed require their existence, but others do not (though they tolerate it).

However, one characteristic that is shared by all these analyses is that they do *NOT* solve the empirical problem by assuming that at PF (or any other linguistic level) accusative traces exist and nominative traces do not. Indeed it is not easy to see how such a difference between accusative and nominative traces could be justified on GB principles. Suppose, then, that we take the chance of assuming that GB theory does not, and will not, adopt a level of PF (or any other level) which admits accusative traces but not nominative traces. Then we can skirt all the remaining unknowns and arrive finally at an experimental design that should put GB and GPSG/HPSG to a clear test.

The argument is indirect, but only slightly so. GB has no obvious explanation for the cross-modal priming data based on S-structure (because of the weakness of the effects for NP-trace and PRO). So its explanation must be based on PF. All the strong cross-modal priming effects that have been obtained have involved accusative WH-trace. So to explain the priming facts, GB must postulate the existence of at least accusative WH-trace at PF (whether or not it needs to do so in order to account for the auxiliary reduction facts). Now, if we can assume (see earlier comments) that GB principles don't/won't warrant a distinction between accusative and nominative traces with respect to PF, then we can conclude that a GB explanation of the experimental data also presupposes the existence of nominative WH-traces at PF.[45] But then GB and GPSG/HPSG clearly differ in their predictions about PF, since GPSG/HPSG, as we have seen, does not admit nominative WH-traces at any level.

Now we no longer have to worry about whether the cross-modal task taps syntax or PF. Either way, if nominative traces show antecedent reactivation, GPSG/HPSG must be wrong and GB could be right. And either way, if nominative traces show no reactivation (under experimental conditions in which accusative traces do), then GB would appear to be wrong but GPSG/HPSG could be right. Thus an experimental investigation of nominative traces should be informative whatever its outcome. Of course we know that theories are more often modified than abandoned outright, in the face of recalcitrant data. So it would be silly to suppose that either theory would succumb instantly to the results of one experiment, however sturdy and replicable they might be. But still, the nominative trace experiment seems to speak fairly directly to theoretical linguistic concerns. The sorts of materials that need to be tested are illustrated in (44).

(44) [Which lecture room] does the art teacher at the night school . . .
    a. . . . believe WH-trace(?) might be unsafe while the renovations are in progress?
    b. . . . believe WH-trace to   be unsafe while the renovations are in progress?

Version (44a) contains the nominative WH-trace whose existence is in dispute. Version (44b) is for purposes of comparison: its complement is infinitival and its trace is accusative, but it is otherwise similar to (44a). Other details (e.g. several words between antecedent and trace) are as in previous experiments. Certain difficulties arise in constructing such materials, but none that seems unsuperable. For example, for a left-to-right processor there is a temporary ambiguity in both versions of (44).

---

[45] There may be no WH-trace in the case of a highest subject extraction, if GB permits a derivation without string-vacuous movement from subject position into the adjacent Comp (see footnote 26). But all subordinate subject extractions from finite clauses, as in (17), should leave a nominative trace.

The verb *believe* need not take a clausal complement but may be followed by a noun phrase direct object. The processor might anticipate in (44) that *believe* will have a direct object, and that the direct object will be the trace associated with the fronted WH-phrase (as in *Which lecture room does the art teacher use WH-trace?*, with a simple transitive verb). This would cause a garden path in (44). It would be a short-lived garden path: it is semantically disconfirmed at *believe*, and syntactically disconfirmed at the next word *might* or *to*. There are very few verbs in English that can appear in both the (a) and (b) versions, and that do *NOT* allow a simple direct object; so it is difficult to design materials that exclude this garden path altogether. But even if it does make some contribution to processing time for the sentence, it should not affect the critical comparison between the (a) and (b) versions, since it occurs in both.

The cue to the existence of a trace in (44) is the word *might* or *to*, but the thematic role of the trace is not established until *unsafe* two words later. Nicol (this volume) has suggested that reactivation effects may have to be understood as occurring at those points in a sentence at which thematic roles can be assigned, whether or not these coincide with the positions of empty categories. To explore this, it would be interesting to compare these sentences with similar ones in which thematic role assignment is moved forward by using a main verb (without auxiliaries) immediately after the trace. (However, the need for infinitival *to* in [b] would mean that the match across the versions couldn't then be quite so close.)

Finally, we should consider a potentially confounding factor which, though linguistic, is not relevantly connected with the theoretical issue of interest here. It is arguable that nominative traces are more marked than accusative traces. Keenan and Comrie (1977) observed that, both within and across languages, relativisation of subjects is most common, relativisation of direct objects is less common, and of oblique complements is least common, and they suggested that this *accessibility hierarchy* 'directly reflects the psychological ease of comprehension' (p. 88). However, the subject extractions they surveyed involved only the highest subject. Comrie (1982/1989) later included in the hierarchy the extraction of subjects of embedded (finite) clauses, giving evidence that cross-linguistically these are the least common of all. It is probably true, also, that they occur less often in English than other extractions do. If so, the embedded nominative gap in (44a) might take the processor by surprise. Hence (44a) might show less priming than (44b), but for reasons having nothing to do with the presence or absence of WH-trace. To avoid this problem one can try to equate the rated 'naturalness' of the two versions of each sentence, and to boost the 'expectability' of nominative gaps by including plenty of them in the materials. As a check on these precautions, one can watch out for any sign of an increase in priming correlated with how many nominative gap examples went before. See also Pickering and Shillcock (in press) for evidence that subject extractions from finite subordinate clauses are not difficult.

This experiment has yet to be run. I have argued here only that it would be a profitable next step in sorting out the tangle of issues, linguistic and psycholinguistic, that centre around empty categories. If we had one secure end, perhaps we could unravel the rest.

ACKNOWLEDGEMENTS

I have several people to thank for their help as I made this foray into matters of which I was almost totally ignorant. Among them are Andrew Barss, Sharon Inkelas, Judy Klavans, Rick McKinnon, Sheila Meltzer, David Swinney, and Draga Zec.

REFERENCES

Aoun, J., & Lightfoot, D.W. (1984). Government and contraction. *Linguistic Inquiry, 15*, 465–473.
Aoun, J., Hornstein, N., Lightfoot, D., & Weinberg, A. (1987). Two types of locality. *Linguistic Inquiry, 18*, 537–577.
Berwick, R.C., & Weinberg, A.S. (1984). *The grammatical basis of linguistic performance: Language use and acquisition*, Cambridge, MA: Bradford Books.
Bever, T.B., & McElree, B. (1988). Empty categories access their antecedents during comprehension. *Linguistic Inquiry, 19*, 35–43.
Bever, T.G., Straub, K., Shenkman, K., Kim, J.J., & Carrithers, C. (in press). The psychological reality of NP-trace. In *Proceedings of the 1989 meeting of the Northeastern Linguistics Society*.
Bolinger, B. (1981). Consonance, dissonance, and grammaticality: The case of *wanna*. *Language and Communication, 1*, 189–206.
Bouchard, D. (1986). Empty categories and the contraction debate. *Linguistic Inquiry, 17*, 95–104.
Bresnan, J. (1971). *Contraction and the transformational cycle in English*. Unpublished MS, distributed by Indiana University Linguistics Club.
Bresnan, J. (1978). A realistic transformational grammar. In M. Halle, J. Bresnan, & G.A. Miller (Eds.), *Linguistic theory and psychological reality*, Cambridge, MA: MIT Press.
Bresnan, J., & Kaplan, R.M. (1982). Lexical-Functional Grammar: A formal system for grammatical representation. In J. Bresnan (Ed.), *The mental representation of grammatical relations*. Cambridge, MA: MIT Press.
Chierchia, G. (1984). *Topics in the syntax and semantics of infinitives and gerunds*. PhD. dissertation, University of Massachusetts, Amherst, MA.
Chomsky, N. (1981). *Lectures on government and binding*, Dordrecht, The Netherlands: Foris.
Chomsky, N. (1986a). *Knowledge of language: Its nature, origin, and use*, New York: Praeger.
Chomsky, N. (1986b). *Barriers*, Cambridge, MA: MIT Press.
Chomsky, N., & Lasnik, H. (1978). A remark on contraction, *Linguistic Inquiry, 9*, 268–274.

Chung, S., & McCloskey, J. (1983). On the interpretation of certain island facts in GPSG, *Linguistic Inquiry, 14*, 704–713.

Comrie, B. (1982/89). *Language universals and linguistic typology*, Chicago, Illinois: University of Chicago Press. First edition 1982; second edition 1989.

Dell, G., McKoon, G., & Ratcliff, R. (1983). Activation of antecedent information in the processing of anaphoric reference in reading. *Journal of Verbal Learning and Verbal Behavior, 22*, 121–132.

Dowty, D. (1985). On recent analyses of the semantics of control. *Linguistics and Philosophy, 8*, 291–331.

Emmorey, K., & Lillo-Martin, D. (1991). *Processing spatial anaphora: Referent activation with overt and null pronouns in ASL.* Paper presented at the Fourth Annual CUNY Conference on Sentence Processing, Rochester, USA.

Engdahl, E. (1983). Parasitic gaps. *Linguistics and Philosophy, 6*, 5–34.

Fodor, J.A., & Fodor, J.D. (1980). Functional structure, quantifiers, and meaning postulates. *Linguistic Inquiry, 11*, 759–770.

Fodor, J.D. (1972). Beware. *Linguistic Inquiry, 3*, 528–535.

Fodor, J.D. (1975). *Gapping gapped*, unpublished MS, University of Connecticut.

Fodor, J.D. (1985). Deterministic parsing and subjacency, *Language and Cognitive Processes, 1*, 3–42.

Fodor, J.D. (1989). Empty categories in sentence processing. *Language and Cognitive Processes, 4*, SI 155–209.

Fodor, J.D. (1991). Sentence processing and the mental grammar. In P. Sells, S.M. Shieber, & T. Wasow (Eds.), *Foundational issues in natural language processing*, Cambridge, MA: MIT Press.

Gazdar, G. (1981). Unbounded dependencies and coordinate structure. *Linguistic Inquiry, 12*, 155–184.

Gazdar, G., Klein, E., Pullum, G.K., & Sag, I.A. (1985). *Generalized phrase structure grammar*, Cambridge, MA: Harvard University Press.

Goodall, G. (1991). *Wanna*-contraction as restructuring. In C. Georgopoulos & R. Ishihara (Eds.), *Interdisciplinary approaches to language: Essays in honor of S.-Y. Kuroda*, Dordrecht: Kluwer Academic Publishers.

Greene, S., McKoon, G., & Ratcliff, R. (in press). Pronoun resolution and discourse models. *Journal of Experimental Psychology: Learning, Memory and Cognition.*

Hornstein, N. (1989). Verb raising in Icelandic infinitives. *Proceedings of the Northeastern Linguistics Society, 20.*

Hornstein, N. (1991). A primer on PRO (and other empty categories). *Journal of Psycholinguistic Research, 20.3*, 187–196.

Jacobson, P. (1982). Evidence for gaps. In P. Jacobson & G.K. Pullum (Eds.), *The nature of syntactic representation*, Dordrecht, Holland: D. Reidel Publishing Co.

Jaeggli, O. (1980). Remarks on *to* contraction. *Linguistic Inquiry, 11*, 239–246.

Kaplan, R.M., & Zaenen, A. (1989). Long-distance dependencies, constituent structure, and functional uncertainty. In M. Baltin & A. Kroch (Eds.), *Alternative conceptions of phrase structure.* Chicago: Chicago University Press.

Keenan, E.L., & Comrie, B. (1977). Noun phrase accessibility and universal grammar. *Linguistic Inquiry, 8*, 63–99.

King, H.V. (1970). On blocking the rules for contraction in English. *Linguistic Inquiry, 1*, 134–136.

Klavans, J.L. (1985). The independence of syntax and phonology in cliticization, *Language, 61*, 95–120.

Koopman, H., & Sportiche, D. (1991). The position of subjects. *Lingua, 85*, 211–258.

Lakoff, G. (1972). The arbitrary basis of transformational grammar. *Language, 48*, 76–87.

Langendoen, D.T. (1975). Finite-state parsing of phrase-structure languages and the status of readjustment rules in grammar. *Linguistic Inquiry, 6,* 533–554.

Lasnik, H., & Saito, M. (1984). On the nature of proper government. *Linguistic Inquiry, 15.*2, 235–289.

Lasnik, H., & Uriagereka, J. (1988). *A course in GB syntax: Lectures on binding and empty categories.* Cambridge, MA: MIT Press.

Lightfoot, D. (1976). Trace theory and twice–moved NPs. *Linguistic Inquiry, 7.* 4, 559–582.

MacDonald, M.C. (1989). Priming effects from gaps to antecedents. *Language and Cognitive Processes, 4,* 1–72.

May, R. (1985). *Logical form: Its structure and derivation.* Cambridge, MA: MIT Press.

McElree, B., & Bever, T.G. (1989). The psychological reality of linguistically defined gaps. *Journal of Psycholinguistic Research, 18,* 21–35.

Nicol, J. (1988). *Coreference processing during sentence comprehension.* PhD. dissertation, MIT, Cambridge, MA.

Nicol, J. (this volume). *Reconsidering re-activation.*

Nicol, J., & Swinney, D. (1989). The role of structure in coreference assignment during sentence compehension. *Journal of Psycholinguistic Research, 18,* 5–19.

Osterhout, L., & Swiney, G. (in preparation). *Activation of antecendents to NP-trace.*

Pesetsky, D. (1982). *Paths and categories,* PhD. dissertation, MIT, Cambridge, MA.

Pickering, M., & Shillcock, R. (in press). Processing subject extractions. In H. Goodluck & M. Rochemont (Eds.), *Island constraints: Theory, acquisition and processing,* Dordrecht: Kluwer Academic Press.

Pollard, C., & Sag, I.A. (1987). *Information-based syntax and semantics, Volume I: Fundamentals.* CSLI Lecture Notes Series No. 13. CSLI, Stanford, California.

Pollard, C., & Sag, I.A. (1993). *Head driven phrase structure grammar.* Chicago and Stanford: University of Chicago Press and CSLI Publications.

Postal, P.M.,& Pullum, G.K. (1978). Traces and the description of English complementizer contraction. *Linguistic Inquiry, 9,* 1–29.

Postal, P.M. & Pullum, G.K. (1982). The contraction debate. *Linguistic Inquiry, 13,* 122–138.

Postal, P.M., & Pullum, G.K. (1986). Misgovernment. *Linguistic Inquiry, 17,* 104–110.

Pullum, G.K., & Postal, P.M. (1979). On an inadequate defense of trace theory. *Linguistic Inquiry, 10,* 689–706.

Re, L., Taber, H., Fodor, J.D., & Swinney, D.A. (1991). *Priming and probing for empty categories.* Poster presentation at the Fourth Annual CUNY Conference on Sentence processing, Rochester, NY.

Rizzi, L. (1986). Null objects in Italian and the theory of *pro. Linguistic Inquiry, 17,* 501–557.

Rizzi, L. (1990). *Relativized minimality.* Cambridge, MA: MIT Press.

Rothstein, S., & Snyder, W. (1991). *Another look at 'wanna' contraction and case.* Unpublished MS, Massachusetts Institute of Technology.

Sag, I.A. (1983). On parasitic gaps. *Linguistics and Philosophy, 6,* 35–45.

Schachter, P. (1984). Auxiliary reduction: An argument for GPSG, *Linguistic Inquiry, 15,* 514–523.

Selkirk, E.O. (1972). *The phrase phonology of English and French,* PhD. dissertation, MIT, Cambridge, MA.

Selkirk, E.O. (1984). *Phonology and syntax: The relation between sound and structure,* Cambridge, MA: MIT Press.

Sells, P. (1985). *Lectures on contemporary syntactic theories: An introduction to Government-Binding Theory, Generalized Phrase Structure Grammar, and Lexical Functional Grammar.* Stanford, California: CSLI.

Sobin, N. (1987). The variable status of Comp-trace phenomena. *Natural Language and Linguistic Theory, 5*, 33–60.

Sproat, R., & Ward, G. (1987). Pragmatic considerations in anaphoric island phenomena. *Papers from the 23rd regional meeting of the Chicago Linguistic Society, 23*, 321–325.

Swinney, D., Ford, M., Bresnan, J., & Frauenfelder, U. (1988). Coreference assignment during sentence processing. In M. Macken (Ed.), *Language structure and processing*, Stanford, California: CSLI.

Wood, W. (1979). Auxiliary reduction in English: A unified account. In *Papers from the Fifteenth Regional Meeting of the Chicago Linguistic Society*, University of Chicago, Illinois.

Zwicky, A.M. (1970). Auxiliary reduction in English. *Linguistic Inquiry, 1*, 323–336.

Zwicky, A. (1982). Stranded *to* and phonological phrasing in English. *Linguistics, 20*, 3–57.

17 Transparency and Visibility: Sentence Processing and the Grammar of Anaphora

Andrew Barss
University of Arizona, USA

INTRODUCTION

In her stimulating chapter, Janet Fodor addresses the relation between grammatical theory and sentence processing research, making a number of concrete proposals concerning the degree of fit between recent experimental findings and contemporary syntactic theories. In these remarks, I would like to focus on two major arguments of Fodor's paper, and in doing this I will try to comment both on specific aspects of her analysis and on the general approach. I hope my discussion here will advance the integration of theoretical research in grammatical theory and empirical studies of language processing. My remarks here will in part be cautionary, however.

Fodor's article examines recent work in sentence processing, specifically reactivation of noun phrases at positions in the input string where (on some theories of grammar) a referentially dependent constituent occurs. The intent of the article is to assess the relative optimality of competing theories of grammar in characterising those constructions in which reactivation occurs, and those where it apparently does not occur. To advance this assessment, Fodor contrasts Government-Binding (GB) theory, which has a multiplicity of empty categories, with *lexicalist* theories, in which the sole empty category is WH-trace. Fodor's discussion is intended to show problems in characterising the experimental data in GB terms, and the advantages of adopting a grammatical system with a more restricted set of empty categories. Generalised Phrase Structure Grammar (GPSG) is chosen as the representative theory of the latter type. I will refer to the position Fodor advances as the 'GPSG analysis', although (as she observes) the general argument can equally well be cast in terms of the formalisms of Lexical Functional Grammar, Head-Driven Phrase Structure Grammar, and other lexicalist theories. I will, for the sake of detail, cast my more technical discussion in the first section of this chapter in terms of the formalism advanced by Gazdar, Pullum, Klein, and Sag, 1985, and other closely related work. However, it should be clearly kept in mind that the fundamental contrast Fodor establishes, and which I follow, is between GB and a group of lexicalist theories which advocate analyses of Passive, Raising, and Control structures that do not invoke empty categories.

A general theme underlying Fodor's work is that of *transparency*: the view that there is a direct correspondence between the grammar and the processor, and hence clusterings of effects exhibited in behavioural research have immediate bearing on the choice of competing grammatical analyses. It may be useful to distinguish two variants of this hypothesis. On the first, what we may call *computational transparency*, the rules, filters, and principles of the grammar are directly incorporated as structure-building rules in the processing system, and the processing system consists of little else besides these computational implementations of the grammar (the Strong Competence Hypothesis of Kaplan & Bresnan, 1982, is an explicit endorsement of this view of transparency—see later discussion). The second view—which I believe is more what Fodor has in mind—we may call *representational transparency*. On this view, the output representations of the processing system (however they may be constructed) are identical to those that are asserted to exist by the grammatical theory adopted.[1,2] (The mode by which these representations are assigned to

---

[1] There are many possible degrees of transparency. In its most extreme form, the Transparency Hypothesis would hold that the representations generated by the grammar and those assigned to input strings by the processing system are identical; that the construction of these representations by the processor is instantaneous and infallible; and that there is a strict isomorphy between the rules and principles of the grammar and the internal mechanisms of the processing system. To the best of my knowledge no one, Fodor included, holds so extreme a view. However, Fodor argues extensively for a very high degree of correspondence between the grammar's rules and representations and those of the processor, making it important to examine the linguistic underpinnings of her arguments in detail. This present commentary attempts to do so.

It may be noted here that two dominant approaches to parsing theory run counter to the strong form of transparency just defined. The first is serial parsing models (see especially Frazier, 1979), under which the class of representations immediately constructed for an input string can be a proper subset of those assigned by the competence grammar. The second is parsing models (see especially Bever, 1970) which assign to the input types of representations that are not defined by the competence grammar. In a sense, models of the latter type assign to perceived utterances either a superset or a partially disjoint set of representations from the competence grammar's assigned representations.

input strings may or may not have any direct correspondence to the rules of the grammar.) I will use the terms *transparency* and *transparent* in this latter sense throughout.

I shall focus here on Fodor's very interesting suggestion that the basic reactivation effect can serve as a diagnostic of the exact representations recovered by the parser; and, as a consequence of the Transparency Hypothesis, a demonstration of the relative utility of competing theories. The general format of this type of argument is the following. Suppose grammar G1 clusters a number of different syntactic constructions into two groups, and suppose grammar G2 clusters them into a different two groups. Suppose further that results from behavioural studies cluster these constructions in a way identical to the way grammar G2 does. This is taken as direct evidence against G1, and in favour of (or at least optimally consistent with) G2. If the Transparency Hypothesis is correct, one would expect many such examples, given appropriate and careful experimental design.

The first major section of Fodor's paper argues that the majority of relevant experimental results are consistent with the lexicalist models of syntax in this way, and militate somewhat against the GB model, assuming transparency (in the sense that GB offers no apparent transparency-consistent way of accounting for the facts; cf. Fodor's section on 'Levels of Representation'). The main thrust of this argument comes from cross-model priming studies. It is argued that the class of constructions in which priming of an antecedent occurs corresponds exactly to the class of constructions in which, in GPSG and other lexicalist models, there is a uniform type of syntactic dependency between two constituents. It is further argued that there is no simple account within a GB model of syntax for these results. I will assess the specifics of this argument in the first section here, paying particular attention to a recent experiment conducted by Fodor, McKinnon, and Swinney (reported in Fodor's chapter) whose results are taken by Fodor to be problematic for a GB-based parsing model.

The second major section of Fodor's paper discusses predicted results for cross-modal priming in sentences with WH-extraction[3] from embedded

---

[2] See Fodor, Fodor, and Garrett, 1975, and Tanenhaus, Carlson, and Seidenberg, 1985, for much careful discussion of the differences, theoretical and empirical, between the two classes of models, as well as alternatives that do not endorse transparency of either sort.

[3] I will use the term 'extraction' in a theory-independent way, to make reference to the general phenomenon in (i), whereby a WH-phrase appears in a syntactic position different from the position with respect to which it functions as the argument of a predicate.

(i) [which man] do you think Mary admires___?

subject position, as in *who do you think___is outside?* The GB analysis of such constructions posits a WH-trace in the extraction position. Given the WH-traces in object position have been shown in a number of studies (e.g. studies reported in Nicol, 1989; Nicol & Swinney, 1989; Swinney, Ford, & Bresnan, 1989) to produce strong priming for the antecedent, one would, assuming the GB analysis, expect priming to occur in cases of subject extraction too, in the extraction position. On a lexicalist analysis, there is no trace in subject position, hence one would (on the set of assumptions made) expect that no priming will result.[4] Fodor gives, in this section, a comprehensive review of the literature on contraction, and discusses the possibility that GB theory might offer up a transparent account of reactivation by supposing that it is the recovery of PF representations that gives rise to the effect. I will discuss this proposal in my second section, and will conclude with a discussion of Fodor's proposed experiment on priming with subject extraction, and some general remarks concerning Visibility as a methodological assumption.

PRIMING AS A WINDOW INTO SYNTAX

In the first major section of Fodor's paper, a number of studies of antecedent reactivation (occurring during the processing of sentences involving some type of anaphoric dependence) are reviewed. These studies use one of two experimental techniques: (1) cross-modal lexical decision or naming (henceforth 'lexical priming'); and (2) all-visual probe recognition facilitation (henceforth VPR). These two methodologies differ in a number of ways. In cross-modal presentation, the sentence is presented auditorily, at a regular speech rate. The probe word (either a semantic associate of a critical word in the sentence, or a length- and frequency-matched control) is presented visually; the subject's task is to make a lexical decision on the probe. In VPR, the sentence is presented visually, word-by-word or phrase-by-phrase; the probe is also presented visually (as

---

Similarly, I shall refer to this argumental position (indicated with the dash in (i)) as the 'extraction site'. Extraction of a WH-phrase is analysed in GB as involving movement of the WH-phrase from the extraction position, leaving a trace; I will refer to this specific analysis as 'movement'.

[4] This is, of course, predicated on the assumption that traces are responsible for priming, which is a standard view of the antecedent-priming effect (e.g. Bever et al., 1990; Bever & McElree, 1988; McElree & Bever, 1989). cf. Nicol, this volume; Tanenhaus, Garnsey & Boland, 1990; Tanenhaus, Boland, Garnsey & Carlson, 1989; Tanenhaus, Boland, Mauner & Carlson, this volume *inter alia*, for a contrasting view.

in cross-model presentation); the subject's task is to decide whether the probe word appeared in the preceding sentence or not. Thus the modality of sentence presentation, the relation of the probe to the preceding sentence, and the subjects' task in response to a probe item all differ between the two methodologies. To the extent that the differing methodologies produce divergent results, the question of the proper interpretation of the results is complicated, and thus interesting.

The class of constructions examined using one or both of these methodologies includes most of the standard cases of what is called *NP anaphora*—constructions where (on the standard transformational grammar model, and carried over into GB) a syntactically represented NP is referentially dependent on another NP, which precedes and c-commands it. Specific construction types include those in (1–7). For uniformity of presentation, the examples here have been made as similar as possible; each is similar in form to those sentences examined (using one, or both, of the two methodologies) in the studies discussed by Fodor.

1. Reflexives: The policeman thinks that the baker$_1$ will blame *himself*$_1$ for the accident
2. Pronouns: The baker$_1$ thinks that the policeman will blame *him*$_1$ for the accident
3. WH-trace (Relative clause): That is [the baker]$_1$ that the dentist from the new medical centre in town invited t$_1$ to the party
4. WH-trace (questions): I wonder which baker$_1$ the dentist from the new medical centre in town invited t$_1$ to the party
5. NP-trace (Passive): [The baker from the big city to the east]$_1$ was invited t$_1$ to the party
6. NP-trace (Raising): [The baker from the big city]$_1$ is certain [t$_1$ to go to the party]
7. Control:[5] [The baker from the big city]$_1$ promised [PRO$_1$ to go to the party]

---

[5] I here, and throughout, use the terms 'Control' and 'Control sentence' in their linguistic sense, namely as descriptive terms for sentences containing infinitival complements, for example:

   i) John promised Mary [to leave on time]
   ii) John asked Mary [to leave on time]
   iii) John tried [to leave on time]

On a GB analysis, these infinitivals are clausal, and have a phonologically unexpressed, but syntactic represented, NP subject (termed 'PRO'). On lexicalist theories, the infinitival is simply a VP, lacking a syntactic subject. I hope no confusion with the term 'control' as it is used in experimental design arises; that term is avoided throughout the present article.

The constructions in (1–7) are assigned quite different structures in lexicalist theories like GPSG. Specifically, there is no empty category in (5–7), so that the verb (5) is intransitive, and the verbs in (6) and (7) take VP complements.

What is striking about the results in the processing literature, as Fodor observes in her chapter (see also Fodor, 1990, for considerable discussion) is that the two methodologies apparently diverge in terms of what constructions produce apparent reactivation for the antecedent of the dependent position. Fodor summarises these results as follows

8) • Visual Probe Recognition experiments indicate that the antecedent is reactivated in all cases (Bever & McElree, 1988; Bever et al., 1990; MacDonald, 1989; McElree & Bever, 1989), by the end of the sentence.

• Cross-modal priming experiments show reactivation following reflexives (1), personal pronouns (2), and object WH-trace (3–4); there is no consistent reactivation in passives, Raising, or Control[6] sentences (5–7), at the point where GB would postulate an empty category. That is, NP-trace and PRO do not show clear reactivation effects.

The transparency hypothesis supposes that classes of experimental results should correspond to natural classes of grammatical phenomena. Given this, the question confronting the advocate of such a view is: *which* of the clusterings in (8) should one take to reflect *which* subsystem of grammar?

Fodor's assertion (which I explore in some detail later) is that the class of dependencies producing priming in the cross-modal task is exactly equivalent to those that GPSG independently classifies as syntactic

---

[6] Nicol (personal communication) has recently found evidence for immediate priming in Control sentences for the antecedent of the implicit subject PRO, for sentences like:

i) That's [the actress]₂ who₂ [the dentist]₃ had invited t₂ [PRO₂ to go # to the party].

Actress is primed at the probe point #. This is apparently re-activation, rather than continued activation of the overt noun *actress*, since no priming for actress was found in this study in examples like (ii):

ii) That's [the actress]₂ who₂ had invited [the dentist]₃ [PRO₃ to go # to the party].

This pattern of results is inconsistent with Fodor's premise that Control complements do not trigger priming. However, I assume this premise throughout my discussion, as my concern here is in examining the logic of Fodor's argument.

phenomena, and those that do not produce priming are dependencies that lie outside the syntactic component of the grammar in GPSG,[7] namely dependencies that only exist in the semantic representation of the sentence. Consequently, the cross-modal results are taken to be problematic for GB, since (1–4) do not form a natural grammatical class excluding (4–7).

As for the VPR results—which show antecedent reactivation for all NP anaphora—Fodor takes this methodology to be sensitive to semantic interpretation. Any semantic theory, she observes, must capture the fact that [the baker] is understood as the (semantic) object of *blame* in (1–2), as the object of *invite* in (3–5), and as the subject of *go* in (6–7). Thus, she suggests, the fact that the antecedent (*baker*, in my [1–7]) is reactivated in all these structure types is consistent with a view under which the VPR technique taps into post-syntactic semantic representations. As such, this technique would have little bearing on choice among syntactic theories.

Regardless of exact explanation, the fact that the methodologies produce different results is intriguing. It minimally indicates that one must proceed with care in choosing experimental techniques, and it would be important to pursue the exact reasons for these methodologies producing such divergent results. Fodor is to be commended for beginning to address the question, although it remains an interesting puzzle as to *why* VPR should be sensitive to semantics and only semantics, and why the cross-modal technique should be sensitive to (hypothetically, at least) all and only syntactic dependencies,[8] and not the reverse, for example. Nonetheless

---

[7] Specifically, Fodor claims that the cross-modal technique is sensitive to elements of purely syntactic representations, and that the VPR technique (which gives rise to antecedent activation in a broader set of construction types) is only sensitive to semantic representations, particularly interpreted argument positions which may or may not be represented structurally in the syntax. The fact that the VPR technique shows antecedent reactivation only sentence finally (McElree & Bever, 1989) seems supportive of this argument, since semantic representations plausibly take a certain amount of time to be constructed off the syntactic representations.

[8] I should be very clear here that this is not intended as a criticism of Fodor's proposals. She has offered up an explicit hypothesis that goes a considerable way toward resolving the differences in results obtained under the two methodologies, in a way that allows both sets of results to be of relevance to the issue of how linguistic representations are recovered by the processing system. I simply want to point out that it is a puzzle, surely resolvable, as to why the opposite situation does not hold—with all-visual probe recognition sensitive only to syntactic structures, and cross-modal lexical decision sensitive only to computed semantic representations of those structures. This question naturally emerges under Fodor's hypothesis.

she offers a hypothesis that seeks a grammatical characterisation of the two bodies of results, and it is this specific conjecture that I will explore here, particularly with regard to the Fodor, McKinnon, and Swinney experiment that she reports. Before turning to that set of results, I would like briefly to review what would have to be said about the results just discussed if we assume a GB model of syntax.

In all the constructions given earlier (1–7), GB asserts the existence of a dependent NP, one capable of receiving its interpretation by means of a syntactic link to its antecedent. With the sole exception of the pronoun in (2), all these dependent NPs necessarily take antecedents,[9] and the antecedent's position within the sentence is highly constrained. Putting pronouns aside for the moment, the antecedent must in all cases c-command the NP which depends on it. Further constraints apply. The antecedent of a reflexive must, roughly, be the subject or object of the sentence containing it; the antecedent of PRO (the empty subject of a Control structure) must be the subject or object of the next highest clause (with particular choice dictated by the matrix verb itself); the antecedent of NP-trace, as in passive or Raising, must be the closest subject that c-commands the trace; and the antecedent of a WH-trace must not in subject or object position, but, rather, in a sentence-external position[10] (e.g. COMP, or the Specifier of COMP; see Chomsky, 1986b, for discussion). Because of these different requirements on the position of the antecedent, the requirements holding of the various dependent NPs are stated in several distinct subsystems of the grammar.

What unifies all the syntactic dependencies in (1–7) is the formalism of *indexing*. Indices are assigned to all NPs in a sentence, and the antecedent requirements are stated as conditions on the distribution of indices. Thus, supposing a theory with this general shape, it is easy to characterise the VPR effect in syntactic terms: the antecedent is reactivated whenever a coindexed phrase is encountered. (Alternatively, one might suppose that the type of reactivation measured by the VPR experiments arises after the computation of the semantic relations—coreference and variable binding—encoded by indexing relations.)

But, then, why doesn't lexical priming occur in all these constructions? The lack of a reliable effect with the lexical priming technique in Raising, Passive, and Control sentences is puzzling from this standpoint; the partitioning of dependencies indicated by the priming results does not match up with any natural class of syntactic dependencies in GB. Thus, it

---

[9] That is, pronouns present a special case, in that a pronoun is not required to have a syntactic antecedent, as in the cases of deixis, ostention, and the like.

[10] The reader is referred to van Riemsdjik and Williams, 1986; Lasnik and Urigareka, 1988, for specifics.

would seem that GB syntax alone does not provide an explanation of why the priming effect should be so restricted. Consequently, if one assumes GB syntax, the lack of priming in Raising, Passive and Control will have to be explained in a way other than appealing to the grammar itself; its source must lie within the operations of the processor. (One such characterisation is offered by Nicol, 1988, and we return to it in the next section.) If one adopts a lexicalist theory, the possibility exists of giving an account of the reactivation measured by lexical priming studies on which such priming arises from correctly linking any dependent NP to its antecedent; such a dependency, the argument would go, exists in (1–4), but not (5–7).

If these initial results continue to be replicated, and if it is the case that these results can be given a parsimonious analysis in GPSG, then this is a most impressive result.

In the following discussion, I will examine a cleverly designed experiment conducted by Fodor, McKinnon, and Swinney which further explores this issue, the results of which Fodor takes to be problematic for GB (assuming transparency), and to be more (perhaps optimally) consistent with the lexicalist models (again adopting transparency). After reviewing this experiment and her interpretation of the results, I will suggest that there are problematic aspects of this interpretation, and that a transparent characterisation of the results in lexicalist terms is actually more complicated, and perhaps more elusive, than at first it appears.

Fodor, McKinnon, and Swinney's Experiment

The experiment by Fodor, McKinnon, and Swinney (henceforth FMS) examines sentences like (9) and (10), in which the deepest object NP is a pronoun or reflexive, and the second verb (*sure*) is a Raising predicate. This experiment was motivated by previous experiments reported by Nicol (1988), and Osterhout and Swinney (1992). Nicol's experiment found priming for the grammatically possible antecedents of reflexives and pronouns; Osterhout and Swinney's found non-significant priming of the antecedent of NP-trace at the trace site, although significant priming of this antecedent was observed downstream from the trace position. The FMS experiment probed for antecedent reactivation after the embedded object NP, using the lexical priming technique (# indicates probe point)

9) The boxer knew that the doctor for the team was sure to blame himself # for the injury

10) The boxer knew that the doctor for the team was sure to blame him # for the injury

Semantic associates of *boxer* and *doctor* (and appropriate controls) were visually presented at a probe point immediately after the pronoun or reflexive. The initial results as reported are given in Table 17.1. The licit antecedent of the reflexive and pronoun are primed; the non-antecedents are not.[11]

The sentences examined in this experiment included a Raising predicate (*sure*, in the examples given earlier) one clause higher than the pronoun and reflexive; and thus the subject of the clause in which the reflexive or pronoun occurred was not phonetically present. In a GB analysis, this subject is an NP-trace; on a GPSG analysis, there is no subject syntactically present, and the complement of a Raising verb is taken to be a VP.

Table 17.1
Priming in msec

	First NP (e.g. boxer)	Second NP (e.g. doctor)
Himself	8	26*
Him	46*	11

Priming in Fodor, McKinnon; and Swinney experiment (difference in mean RT for control words minus related words in different treatment conditions). * = significant, $p < 0.05$.

---

[11] The materials for this experiment were adapted from those used in an experiment reported by Nicol (1988). Nicol's study found robust priming for the antecedent of the reflexive, and for the possible antecedents of the pronoun, in sentences like the following:

i) The boxer told the skier that *the doctor for the team* would blame *himself #* for the recent injury

ii) *The boxer* told *the skier* that the doctor for the team would blame *him #* for the recent injury

The nouns for which significant priming was found are italicised. What is striking about these results is that no priming was found for any NP that could not, grammatically, corefer with the pronoun or reflexive. Thus, Nicol concluded, the grammatical conditions on reflexive and pronoun binding are utilised immediately by the processing system. A potential problem for this explanation is that the results are also consistent with the processor making use of a simple interpretational strategy, whereby the closest animate NP to a reflexive is taken (at least temporarily) as its antecedent, and any NP other than the closest one is taken as the antecedent of a pronoun. In current work, Janet Nicol, David Basilico and I explore this question, examining reactivation in examples like:

iii) [The carpenter working with [the prisoner]$_1$]$_2$ blamed him/himself for the injury

These examples dissociate the simply strategy (which would predict priming for *prisoner* after the reflexive, and for *carpenter* after the pronoun) from 'smart processing', where the processor, incorporating the grammatical conditions on binding, would reactivate *carpenter* after the reflexive, and *prisoner* after the pronoun. The simple strategy would give priming for NPs which cannot, grammatically, serve as antecedent of the proform.

I would like to review Fodor's interpretation of the results of the FMS experiment in two steps. First, I will review the significance of these results for NP-trace, if we were to assume GB theory; I will then take up her explanation of these effects within GPSG, presuming the overall conclusion about the sensitivity of priming to syntactic dependencies that she had earlier advanced. My critical remarks are primarily directed at the latter part of her interpretation.

GB and the FMS Results

The syntactic structure of · (9, 10) in GB theory is as follows (I have indicated the indexing in [12] which gives rise to a coreferential interpretation of *the boxer* and *him*):

11) (= (9)) $[_{S1}$ The boxer$_1$ knew that $[_{S2}$ $[_{NP}$ the doctor for the team]$_2$ was sure $[_{S3}$ *trace*$_2$ to blame himself$_2$ for the injury]]]
12) (= (10)) $[_{S1}$ The boxer$_1$ knew that $[_{S2}$ $[_{NP}$ the doctor for the team]$_2$ was sure $[_{S3}$ *trace*$_2$ to blame him$_1$ for the injury]]]

The Raising predicate *sure* takes an infinitival S complement, and assigns no thematic role to its subject position. The NP *the doctor for the team* moves from the lowest subject position to its surface position, leaving an NP-trace. This trace, as always, must be bound by the immediately c-commanding subject; hence *the doctor for the team* and the trace are coindexed. The reflexive in (11) must be bound locally as well; this forces coindexation of the reflexive· and the trace, which is the only NP close enough to the reflexive to satisfy this requirement. Therefore, the trace serves as the antecedent of the reflexive. By transitivity of indexing, then, the reflexive must corefer with *the doctor for the team*. The other NP with independent reference, *the boxer*, receives an index distinct from *the doctor for the team* and hence is disjoint from the reflexive. We presume the standard theory of the interpretation of indices, where coindexing must be interpreted as coreference, and contraindexing as disjointness of reference (see Fiengo & May, forthcoming; Higginbotham, 1983, 1985; Lasnik, 1989, for discussion). The hierarchical structure of (12) is identical to that of (11); the only difference is with respect to the pronoun, and its referential interaction with the other NPs. Pronouns have effectively the opposite binding requirements from reflexives; they cannot overlap in reference with NPs that very locally c-command them. This requirement is encoded in the syntax; the pronoun must be contraindexed from the NP positions which very locally c-command it. In this case, this requirement will force the pronoun to bear a distinct index from the trace (and thus from *the doctor for the team*). As a result, the pronoun cannot corefer with *the doctor for the team*. The pronoun is free to be coindexed with *the boxer*.[12]

The possible referential dependencies between the pronoun and reflexive and the two higher NPs in (11, 12) are critically mediated by the NP-trace, on the analysis just reviewed. Recall Fodor's observation that it is difficult to characterise previous priming results in terms of any natural class of syntactic relations or structures within GB. If the processor accurately and immediately computes the structures in (11) and (12), and if priming arises when, and only when, a coindexation relation is identified, there should be priming of the antecedent of the trace at the point where trace would appear in the string. Fodor suggests that the current literature shows that this pattern of priming does not exist, and argues that the FMS experiment also demonstrates the inertness of NP-trace for priming.

In support of the latter conclusion, she draws our attention to the fourth cell of the matrix in Table 17.1—the amount of priming of associates of the second noun (e.g. *doctor*) after the pronoun *him* (which cannot be referentially dependent on the second NP) in sentences like (10, 12). This amount of priming is non-significant, and so it must be concluded that *the doctor for the team* is not active at the probe point, after the pronoun.

12') The boxer₁ knew that [the doctor for the team]₂ was sure [*trace* to blame him ## for the injury]

       |

     BOXER primed
     DOCTOR not primed

Fodor makes a crucial assumption at this point: if the putative trace triggers reactivation of NP_2 (e.g. *the doctor for the team*) at its point in the string, then it would remain reactivated three words later, after the pronoun. The lack of priming after the pronoun is then taken as inferential

---

[12] It is relevant to note that the pronoun's sole requirement is that it not corefer with *the doctor for the team*. It may be coindexed with *the boxer*, as in (12), or it may be contraindexed with both NPs, as in (i):

i) [s₁ The boxer₁ knew that [s₂ the doctor₂ for the team was sure [s₃t₂ to blame him₃ for the injury]]]

In such a case, the pronoun will refer to some third individual not mentioned in the sentence. This is always an option. Certainly, the interpretation on which *him* and *the boxer* corefer is dominant, but this preference has been quite conclusively shown to have nothing to do with the syntax of anaphora, and probably very little, if anything, to do with core sentential semantics. The determination of the final antecedent of the pronoun is thus the result of a number of factors; the contribution of the syntax is simply to rule out certain possibilities. Thus priming of some NP at a pronoun must be taken to reflect the *possibility* that the NP is the antecedent, not that the NP must be the antecedent. The import of this fact for Fodor's interpretation of the priming effect in sentences with pronouns is taken up later.

evidence that there was no activation earlier, at the trace position. (In making this assumption Fodor overlooks at least one possibility: that the NP-trace does immediately reactivate its antecedent but the antecedent is deactivated once the pronoun is reached, as a consequence of the processing of the pronoun. See the arguments put forth by Nicol, 1991, along these lines. I return to this possibility later.) The strongest interpretation of this lack of priming at the trace position is that there simply is no trace present. This is the conclusion Fodor draws.

However, as Fodor observes, there is significant priming of the second noun after *himself* (the second cell of Table 17.1) in sentences like (9, 11). What gives rise to this reactivation? And what import does it have for the conclusion that NP-trace is nonexistent?

Nicol (1988) suggests that a possible reason for why priming is not found immediately after NP-trace is that the presence of NP-trace is difficult for the processing system to detect. As Nicol observes, there are usually obvious cues that a WH-trace is upcoming in the input (namely, the morphological form and syntactic position of the WH-phrase itself), whereas NP-trace is not associated with such an obvious cue. Thus, lack of priming after NP-trace may simply reflect the fact that it has not yet been posited and indexed with its antecedent. Fodor terms this the 'processing difficulty' explanation, which stands as an alternative to her own syntactic explanation.

Fodor suggests that since there is priming of the second NP in (11) following the reflexive, an advocate of the processing difficulty explanation would have to take this as indicating that the NP-trace has been posited, and indexed with its antecedent, by the time the probe position (after the reflexive or pronoun) is reached. Thus, although it may take some time to establish the trace, it has been correctly posited and indexed by the time the reflexive is reached. The reflexive activates its ultimate antecedent (*the doctor for the team*), and the dependency between *the doctor for the team* and the reflexive is mediated by the trace; so, the binding of the reflexive by the trace is established by the processor by the probe point. Therefore, it is argued, we should also expect priming of *the doctor for the team* after the *pronoun* in (12), since it occupies the same temporal position as the reflexive does in (11), and the trace will have been processed in exactly the same way. Since there is no such priming in (12), Fodor concludes that the processing account of the lack of priming in the immediate context of NP-trace cannot be maintained. Since the processing difficulty account is the only one that has been offered that is consistent with GB syntax, it is further concluded (in the current absence of alternative GB-consistent explanations of those priming effects) that there is no such syntactic element as NP-trace, and lexicalist theories like GPSG have been supported as more optimal models of syntactic representation than movement-based analyses.

Evaluating the Argument

In evaluating this argument, note that it rests crucially on the *lack* of priming for the second NP at the probe point (occurring just after the pronoun) in sentences like (12). Only two explanations for the lack of this priming are considered: either there is no NP trace, in which case no priming is expected at the probe point; or there is a trace, but it has not yet been posited and assigned its antecedent. Since the existence of priming for the second NP in (11) eliminates the second possibility, we are left with only the first, the position Fodor advocates.

There is, however, a third interpretation of the FMS results, one fully consistent with GB and the transparency hypothesis: there is NP-trace, and it has been posited and assigned an antecedent by the time the pronoun is encountered, but some other property of the sentence (more accurately, some property of the processing of the sentence) causes the second NP to be de-activated after the pronoun is encountered. There are two plausible ways to think of this:

- Short-Term Activation: Reactivation due to NP trace is very short term, and it has simply died off by the time the pronoun is encountered.
- De-Activation: NP-trace reactivates its antecedent, but the subsequent processing of the pronoun, and the association of it with the first NP, suppresses the activation level of the second NP.

With regard to Short Term Activation, it characterises NP-trace as a rather ephemeral entity: it is perhaps difficult to detect, and once detected, it reactivates its antecedent for only a short time. That NP-trace should be associated with very short term activation is an unsatisfactory aspect of this analysis, since it means that some primitive property of NP-trace makes reactivation of the antecedent of NP-trace less durable than that of any other anaphoric item; and there is no apparent reason why this should be so.[13,14]

---

[13] As Janet Fodor has pointed out to me, there are relatively few (if any) studies that systematically probe downstream from a referentially dependent position, to see how long reactivation obtains. (See the experiment by Leiman reported in Tanenhaus, Carlson, & Seidenberg, 1985. Leiman's experiment found reactivation of the antecedent of a personal pronoun immediately after the pronoun, and 250msec downstream, but not 500msec after the pronoun.) This is, of course, an empirical question, and one of considerable interest. If it were found, for example, that antecedent reactivation due to the presence of WH-trace was more 'durable' than the reactivation induced by a reflexive or pronoun, this would be of considerable interest, as it would indicate another partitioning of the class of dependent elements in processing terms. The question of durability of reactivation interacts with the question of the strength of priming; if e.g. reflexives reactivate their antecedents more

With regard to the De-Activation account, it would tie the lack of priming of the second NP (after the pronoun in [12]) to the fact that, at the probe point used by FMS, the processor is actively computing antecedent possibilities for the pronoun. Essentially, on this view, the processor has shifted its attention to the pronoun, and as a side effect the activation level of NPs which were activated during previous anaphoric computations is suppressed. This characterisation in fact is very similar to the one proposed by Nicol (1991), on the basis of quite different results.

In sum, I do not find compelling the conclusion that there is no GB-compatible analysis of the FMS results. However, this experiment adds additional evidence to the view that the determination of antecedents for dependent NPs is more complex than previously thought. Under a GB analysis, one must invoke factors like ease of detection or limitations on the numbers of NPs that can simultaneously be active, factors that have no direct grammatical source. Each of the alternatives I have suggested here rely on assumptions about the processing system that have no clear counterpart in the formal syntactic theory. By contrast, Fodor proposes that there is a transparent explanation for lexical priming effects, including the FMS results, within the GPSG theory of grammar, one that invokes no processor-internal factors. I turn to this, and some evident complexities, in the next section. The rather complex line of argument, which goes through some technical details of GPSG, is set in a broader context at the end of this section.

GPSG and the FMS Results

Now I will evaluate the other half of Fodor's interpretation of the FMS results, namely the assertion that the results are fully consistent with a GPSG-like theory of syntax, particularly the GPSG treatment of Raising and its lack of NP-trace. Fodor does not detail the GPSG theory of

---

strongly than pronouns do (one possible interpretation of an experiment reported in Nicol, 1988), then it would be likely that the reflexive-induced priming would take long to die away.

[14] The other half of this account (that NP-trace might be difficult to detect) is readily understandable, since, as Nicol (1988) and Fodor observe, there simply are no cues that an NP-trace is forthcoming in the sentence; the deduction that an NP-trace is present in the input is quite complex. For example, as they observe, in some cases inferring the presence of an NP-trace is not deterministic. For example, a number of predicates are ambiguous between a Raising sense and a non-Raising sense (see Postal, 1971):

   i) John is certain [t to leave] (Raising)
   ii) John is certain that [Mary will leave] (Non-Raising)

By contrast, the presence of a WH-phrase is an infallible cue that a WH-trace occurs downstream.

Raising, reflexivisation, or pronominal coreference. I will do so in later sections to lay the foundations of my critical comments, in just enough detail to outline the basics of their system. In the present section I will quickly review the basic form of Fodor's argument, before turning to specifics.

In GPSG, like all lexicalist approaches to Raising (and Control and Passive), there is no such element as NP-trace; Raising constructions are generated with the Raising predicate taking a VP complement, with no syntactic subject position. Thus, (9) and (10) have the following constituent structure,[15] # indicates the probe point used by FMS:

13) [$_{S1}$ The boxer$_1$ [$_{VP1}$ knew that [$_{S2}$ [the doctor for the team]$_2$ [$_{VP2}$ was sure [$_{VP3}$ to blame himself$_2$ ##for the injury]]]

14) [$_{S1}$ The boxer$_1$ [$_{VP1}$ knew that [$_{S2}$ [the doctor for the team]$_2$ [$_{VP2}$ was sure [$_{VP3}$ to blame him$_1$ ##for the injury]]]

Fodor's argument concerning the FMS results (and previous lexical priming results) is the following. If it is assumed that priming occurs only as a result of the processor's establishing a syntactic dependency between two syntactic constituents, and if there is no syntactic subject of *to blame NP for the injury*, we should expect no reactivation of the raised NP after *to* in the lowest VP, or indeed in any position in a Raising sentence. Thus, the lack of priming for the second NP (*the doctor for the team*) during the processing of the complement *to blame him for the injury* in (14) is *expected*, since there is nothing to trigger reactivation of this NP. By contrast, the reflexive and pronoun are assigned the second and first NPs as their respective syntactic antecedents, and so priming occurs after these dependent NPs. I will show that there is an errant step in this argument.

Note a crucial aspect of this line of reasoning. The goal is to find a unified class of syntactic relations which map onto those constructions that give lexical priming. Let us call this class R (for 'reactivators'). Raising complements do not cause lexical priming[16] of their understood subjects (what is termed the *controller* in GPSG). Therefore the syntactic relation between a Raising complement and its controller is not a member of R.

---

[15] GPSG does not make use of indexing to track referential relations. I have simply used indexing in (16, 17) to mark the coreference relations relevant to the discussion.

[16] VPR is taken by Fodor to reflect semantic representation, in particular semantic dependencies between arguments. Hence, as a result of computing the *semantic* relationship between the understood subject of *blame* and its controller, the second NP (*the doctor*), the type of reactivation—whatever it is—that is measured by the VPR technique will arise. Thus, facilitation is seen in VPR experiments at the end of Raising sentences as a result of this *semantic* link being established.

Reflexives, and personal pronouns, do give rise to lexical priming; hence, the syntactic relation between proforms and their antecedents is a member of R.

A problem arises for GPSG in achieving this goal. The syntactic relation between the reflexive *himself* and its antecedent *the doctor for the team* in (13) is as much mediated by the syntax of Raising in GPSG as it is by the syntax of Raising in GB. This creates a genuine puzzle: *how can a relation giving rise to priming be parasitic on one which does not?*

What I shall show here is that, if the relation between *himself* and *the doctor* in (13) is a member of R so too is the relation between *to blame himself for the injury* and *the doctor*. Thus the pattern of priming supposed by Fodor does not map onto a clearly unified syntactic class. Specifically, if it is the case that there is *any* syntactic relation between *himself* and *the doctor* (a relation that must exist, given Fodor's hypothesis about the source of lexical reactivation), this relation is syntactically mediated by the relation between *to blame himself* (the complement of the Raising predicate) and *the doctor* (the subject NP). Thus, the fact that Raising complements do not (by Fodor's premise) cause priming is a complete mystery, no matter what theory of syntax, lexicalist or movement-based, one adopts.

In order to better explain the problems that arise from the GPSG analysis of lexical priming results, we will need to lay out the background mechanisms involved, and their interplay, in more detail than Fodor's discussion provides. I would like here to briefly review the GPSG characterisation of Raising, Control and reflexivisation, to indicate where I see the problem arising.

Agreement: GPSG on Raising, Control, and Reflexivisation

The most central property of the class of Raising constructions, one that must be captured in any syntactic framework, is the strong connection between the subject of the Raising predicate and the following VP. That is, in the scheme below, there are dependencies that hold between the italicised elements which elsewhere typically hold between the subject and predicate of a simplex clause:

15) *NP*   seems   to *VP*
     ″   appears   ″
     ″   is likely   ″
     ″   is certain   ″
     ″   is sure   ″
     ″   •   ″
     ″   •   ″
     ″   •   ″

As is well-known, predicates may impose a number of constraints on their subjects, as (16–18) show:

16)a. John is a happy man/ *happy men
   b. They are happy men/ *a happy man
17)a. Sincerity impresses/ *admires John
18)a. There is a riot going on/ *John is a riot going on
   b. John likes Mary/ *There likes Mary

In (16), we see that the singularity or plurality of the subject must match that of the predicate nominal. (17) illustrates the selectional restrictions of the verbs *admire* and *impress*; the first requires its subject to be animate, the second does not. The existential statement in (18a) requires a pleonastic (non-referential) subject, i.e. *there*, while the verb *likes* requires its subject to be referential (and animate), as (18b) shows.

In (19–21) are a number of examples of Raising, each showing a tight correspondence between the italicised phrases.

19)a. *John* seems [*to be a happy man*]/* [. . . *happy men*]
   b. *They* seem [*to be happy men*]/* [. . . *a happy man*]
20)a. *Sincerity* seems [*to impress*/* *to admire John*]
21)a. *There* seems [*to be a riot going on*]/* [*to like Mary*]
   b. *John* seems [*to like Mary*]/* [*to be a riot going on*]

Indeed, all the constraints imposed by the predicates in (16–18) on their subjects hold as well between the same predicates and the subjects of the Raising verb *seem*, and with the other Raising predicates. In (19), the singularity or plurality of the subject NP must match that of the embedded predicate nominal. In (20), the inverse selectional restrictions of *impress* and *admire* hold of the matrix subject. And in (21), the pleonastic/ referential contrast holds as well. It is this very tight parallel between simplex causes and Raising sentences that motivates a principled syntactic account of Raising. Following the sense of the term used in GPSG, let us call the various phenomena exhibited in (16–21) *agreement* effects, and take them to be syntactic in nature. Let us term the NP in question the *controller* of the VP.[17]

So, in a very important sense, the matrix subject NP in (19–21) functions as the subject of the embedded predicate. Any syntactic theory's account of Raising must formally capture this fact. Lexicalist theories express it as a dependency between the complement VP and the matrix subject;

---

[17] This is a different use of the term than in GB. In GB, the antecedent of PRO is its controller; nothing else is termed this.

movement theories as a dependency between (i) the complement VP and its empty category subject, and (ii) this trace and the matrix subject.

In GPSG, Raising structures are generated as described earlier, with the Raising verb taking a VP complement; no movement is involved. Thus, the bracketed material in (19–21) is a (tenseless) VP, with no syntactic subject. A similar approach is taken with Control constructions, as in (22, 23):

22) *John* promised Mary [$_{VP}$ *to go*]
23) John persuaded *Mary* [$_{VP}$ *to go*]

The Control verbs are generated with NP VP complement structures, as indicated. Agreement is manifest as well between the complement VP and one of the two NP arguments of the Control verb.

24) [The boys] promised John   [to be nice little fellows]
                             * [. . . a nice little fellow]
25) [The boys] persuaded John * [to be nice little fellows]
                               [. . . a nice little fellow]

The basic mechanism used in GPSG to characterise the *syntactic* relation between the complement VP and the NP with which it is associated—its controller—is agreement. The agreement relationship between the controller and the controlled VP is handled by assigning to both the NP and the VP a set of features; conditions are imposed on the appearance of features in syntactic trees in such a way as to capture the agreement facts just reviewed. All the ungrammatical cases in (19–21) are treated as mismatches in features, since the ultimate problem is a clash between the embedded verb or noun and the controller. For example, the ungrammatical (26) is assigned the feature matrices indicated:

26)a. * They seem to be a happy man
   b. [$_{NP1}$[HEAD: 3 plural] [$_{N1}$ They[HEAD: 3 plural.]]][$_{VP1}$[HEAD: 3pl] [$_{V1}$[HEAD: 3 plural] seem] [$_{VP2}$[HEAD: 3 sg.] to be [$_{NP2}$[HEAD: 3 sg.] a happy [$_{N2}$[HEAD: 3 sg.] man]]

(The features in these cases, which originate on the head of the relevant phrases, are termed HEAD features.) The embedded predicate nominal *a happy man* is marked third-person singular (as a result ultimately of the properties of its head noun); these features are passed up to the dominating VP2 *to be a happy man*. The subject NP *they*, itself plural, is required to agree with the matrix VP1 *seems to be a happy man*. This VP does agree with the subject, since the head verb *seem* is inflected for plural, and a VP always inherits the features of its head. The clash arises between the matrix (plural) subject and the embedded (singular) VP. The basic syntax of Raising in GPSG is to require agreement (for HEAD features) between the matrix subject and the embedded VP in all structures similar to (19–21).

Any mismatch along the way will result in a feature clash, and unacceptability. This is the syntax of Raising in GPSG. There is no trace, but keep in mind that there is a syntactic dependency (of agreement) between the subject NP and its associated embedded VP, critically involving the matching of HEAD features. This syntactic dependency— enforced agreement—is mapped onto a semantic dependency in all cases, assigning the property denoted by the controlled VP to the controller NP. Thus 'coreference' between the overt subject of a Raising predicate and the implicit subject of the controlled predicate is established only in the semantic representation, but is foreshadowed by the obligatory feature matching in the syntax (see Jacobson, 1987, for discussion).

Similarly, the complement VP in a Control construction (27, 28) is required to agree with either the subject or the object (depending on lexical choice) of the Control verb.

27) (Subject Control): [*The boy*] promised them [$_{VP}$ *to be a nice fellow*]
28) (Object Control): They persuaded [*the boy*] [$_{VP}$ *to be a nice fellow*]

The relevant semantic relation between the controller NP and (the implicit subject of) the complement VP is computed out in the semantics, much as it is for Raising.

GPSG on Reflexives: BINDING Features

There is little analogue in GPSG to the theory of binding in GB; there are rather few GPSG studies that examine anaphora in a detailed way, and anaphora does not have the central position that it does within GB. However, in what discussion there is of reflexivisation in GPSG work, the mechanism of enforced agreement is invoked to distinguish grammatical cases of reflexivisation like (29) from unacceptable cases like (30):

29 [$_{NP}$ The boy] [$_{VP}$ admires [$_{NP}$ himself]]
30) *[$_{NP}$ The boy] [$_{VP}$ admires [$_{NP}$ herself]]

The reflexives bear feature matrices. These, like HEAD features, percolate up from their origin position (e.g. the nominal 'himself') through the tree.[18] Let us assume, for illustration, that they percolate up to any dominating VP (see Sells, 1985, Chapter 3). Let us term these the *binding features*, and use the abbreviation *BF* to refer to the binding features, including the feature specifications for reflexives. Thus (29) is partially characterised as:

31) [$_{NP[HEAD: 3sg\ masc]}$ the boy] admires [$_{NP[BF:\ 3\ sg\ masc]}$ himself]

(30) will then have something like the following feature assignment, and will be ruled out by a clash of features, as the VP cannot simultaneously agree with both the masculine subject and the feminine reflexive:

32) [$_{NP[HEAD:\ 3\ sg\ masc]}$ The boy] [$_{VP[HEAD:\ 3\ sg\ masc]}$ [BF: 3 sg fem] admires [HEAD: 3 sg] [$_{NP[BF:\ 3\ sg\ fem]}$ herself]]

The VP is required to agree with the masculine subject, but the VP is marked feminine, due to the features inherited from the reflexive.

Thus Raising and reflexivisation have almost identical syntactic treatments in GPSG. The sole difference between them is the fact that Raising

---

[18] I rely here primarily on the analysis sketched in Sells, 1985, Chapter 3. My remarks here are addressed primarily to any lexicalist theory of Control, Raising, and reflexivisation, and are not meant to be quibbles about particular notations. Such analyses all involve treating the complement of Raising and Control verbs as a VP; the referential relation between the implicit subject of this VP and its 'controller' as one computed out directly in the semantics (translation into intensional logic in GPSG, f-structure in LFG); and the syntactic reflexive-antecedent connection mediated by some featural 'passing up' of the reflexive's presence into the dominating structure, from which point the reflexive's connection to the antecedent NP is subsumed under that holding between the VP and its controller.

In the Head-Driven Phrase Structure Grammar analysis of Pollard and Sag, 1983, things work out slightly differently from what I sketch here, although I believe my general remarks to hold for this approach as well. Briefly, their analysis holds that the binding features cannot pass up to a VP node in English-type languages; from this constraint the local nature of reflexivisation (whereby the antecedent must be structurally local to the reflexive) follows. So, the featural structure is roughly:

i) [$_{NP[HEAD: 3sg\ masc]}$ the boy] admires [$_{NP[BF:\ 3\ sg\ masc]}$ himself]

The semantic rule for interpreting the BFs will interpret the VP in such a way as to identify the referential values of the object position (occupied by the reflexive) and the next argument to be taken by the predicate (i.e. the subject). Thus coreference is ensured. Coreference between a controller NP and a controlled VP (as in Raising or Control constructions) is handled identically in the semantics. Whether or not the syntactic agreement between the reflexive and its antecedent is marked out by passing the BF features totally up through the tree is subject to debate; see Kang, 1988; Pollard and Sag, 1983; Sells, 1985, for discussion. My point here is that whatever syntactic relation is taken to hold between the reflexive and antecedent, it is mediated through the syntactic relation of the containing VP and the antecedent in cases like (9, 11, 13, 34, 43–45).

is treated via HEAD features, whereas reflexivisation is treated by invoking FOOT features, of which binding features are a subcase (this class also includes the SLASH feature involved in unbounded gap dependencies; see later comments). FOOT features are simply features that originate on a non-head element of a subtree; they percolate upwards, like HEAD features.

Now, let us return to the problem raised at the beginning of this section. As outlined, classical GPSG uses fundamentally the same formalism to characterise NP–VP relations in Raising and Control sentences, and the relation between a reflexive and its antecedent. I see no principled explanation why only the latter should give rise to lexical priming. In each case, a syntactic constituent—either a controlled VP, or a reflexive—is required to match in features a previously occurring NP. The problem becomes even worse in sentences—like those used in the FMS experiment—in which a reflexive is contained within the controlled predicate; for the ultimate syntactic relation of the reflexive to its antecedent is determined via the syntactic relation between the controlled complement and the antecedent. In the next subsection, I will note a similar problem with the fact that WH-trace reactivates its antecedent.

WH-Extraction and SLASH Features.   WH-traces occurring in object position have been examined in a number of studies using the cross-modal methodology, and reliably show immediate and strong antecedent reactivation. The GPSG analysis of WH-extraction (and related unbounded constructions, including relative clauses, Topicalisation, and so on) is rather similar to its analysis of reflexivisation, both syntactically and semantically. Syntactically, each node in the tree between the extraction site and the WH-phrase bears a SLASH feature matrix (similar to the Binding Feature matrix induced by the reflexives); the extraction site itself (in object extraction) is occupied by a non-overt category (a trace), and the antecedent and the SLASH matrices are required to agree.

33) I wonder [which man [$_S$ John likes]]

The entire syntax of WH-extraction (and other unbounded dependencies) is handled via these SLASH features.

Like the binding features used to account for reflexive agreement, the SLASH features are FOOT features: they originate from a non-head daughter of the category that bears them. Consequently, a generalisation emerges: lexical priming arises for those obligatory agreement relations expressed through FOOT features (reflexivisation, and WH-extraction),

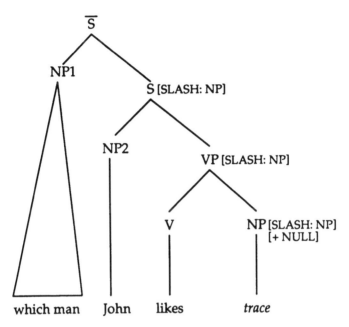

and the effect does not arise for obligatory HEAD agreement relations
(Raising).[19]

Reflexives in Raising Structures.   Let us return to the FMS sentences,
like (34):

34) The boxer told the skier that [[the doctor for the team] [$_{VP1}$ is sure
[$_{VP2}$ to blame himself for the recent injury]]]

Two syntactic agreement relations are manifest: (i) the agreement between
the reflexive and *the doctor*; and (ii) the agreement between the complement VP2 and *the doctor* (the syntax of Raising). Recall Fodor's basic
analysis of the lexical priming effect: it arises only when there is a syntactic
dependency between two constituents in the string. In such a case, the
second position will give rise to reactivation of the content of the first (the
antecedent or controller). For the strong version of that argument to be
maintained, in light of the results obtained so far, it must be shown that

---

[19] In this section, as throughout, I have assumed Fodor's partitioning of the data. See Nicol
(this volume) for evidence that the subjects of Raising verbs *are* reactivated immediately after
the Raising verb is encountered.

there is a syntactic dependency between the reflexive and its controller in (34), and *not* one between the controlled VP and its controller. As we have just seen, however, this is not the case: in both cases, there is a relation of formal feature agreement between the dependent constituent—the complement VP, and the reflexive—and the higher NP. The requirement of feature matching between the reflexive and its controller is the *only* syntactic constraint governing that pair of constituents. For example, no syntactic indexing theory is incorporated into GPSG. Furthermore, the ultimate matching between the reflexive and its controller is *parasitic* on the NP–VP agreement, consequently, it is unexplained why the former should give rise to reactivation and the latter not.

What I mean by 'parasitic' is the following: The binding features of the reflexive are registered at the level of the complement VP (e.g. being passed on up to the VP; see Sells, 1985, p. 114). From that point onwards, this feature bundle is incorporated into the group of features that is required to match between a VP and its controller.

Is there an amended version of Fodor's analysis that can be offered, which would maintain the notion that GPSG immediately offers a parsimonious syntactic explanation of the lexical priming effect? The only alternatives I can see of this form would be to maximise the difference between NP–VP agreement on the one hand, and NP-reflexive and WH-antecedent-WH-gap agreement on the other. One would have to suppose that, for some reason, the establishment of agreement relations concerning SLASH and Binding Features somehow gives rise to antecedent reactivation, whereas the establishment of agreement relations concerning HEAD features does not. There are two ways to split the relations.

Let us list three precise formulations of Fodor's conjecture concerning the lexical priming effect. (35) expresses the hypothesis I have just argued against; (36) and (37) weaken it in separate directions.

35) *The Strong Version. The lexical priming technique is sensitive to all syntactic dependencies on an NP.* That is, lexical priming will arise for some NP α immediately after the processor encounters a syntactic constituent that is syntactically dependent on α. Syntactic dependencies take the form of obligatory feature agreement, including the following (obligatorily agreeing constituents italicised):

   a. The boxer told the skier that *the doctor for the team* would blame *himself ##*for the recent injury (reflexivisation)

   b. I wonder *which doctor for the team* [the skier who won a medal] will blame *trace* for the recent injury (WH-extraction)

   c. *The doctor for the team* is sure *to be blamed for the accident* (Raising)

d. *The doctor for the team* promised the skier *to buy a car* (subject Control)

e. The doctor for the team persuaded *the skier to buy a car* (object Control)

As we saw earlier, this hypothesis is apparently contradicted by the presumed lack of lexical priming in (c–e).

36) *The NP–NP Agreement Hypothesis: The lexical technique is sensitive to all syntactic dependencies between pairs of NPs.* That is, lexical priming will arise for some NP α immediately after the processor encounters an NP β which is syntactically dependent on α. These syntactic dependencies take the form of obligatory FOOT-feature agreement, including these subcases (obligatorily agreeing constituents italicised):

a. The boxer told the skier that the *doctor for the team* would blame *himself* ##for the recent injury (reflexivisation)

b. I wonder *which doctor for the team* [the skier who won a medal] will blame *trace* for the recent injury (WH-extraction of NP)

c. This is *the doctor for the team* that [the skier who won a medal] will blame *trace* for the recent injury (relativisation of NP)

d. *the doctor for the team*, [the skier who won a medal] will blame *trace* for the recent injury (topicalisation of NP)

e. It's *the doctor for the team* that [the skier who won a medal] will blame *trace* for the recent injury (clefting of NP)

37) *The Non-Head Agreement Hypothesis: The lexical priming effect is sensitive to all obligatory syntactic dependencies involving the non-head feature types BF and SLASH.* That is, lexical priming will arise for some antecedent constituent α immediately after the processor encounters a syntactically present constituent β which is syntactically dependent on α. These syntactic dependencies take the form of obligatory FOOT-feature agreement, but with no restriction to NP, including (36a–e) and the following subcases (obligatorily agreeing constituents italicised):

a. I wonder *to which artist* the doctor will give the package [$_{PP}$ *trace*] (WH-extraction of PP)

b. This is *the artist to whom* the doctor will give the package [$_{PP}$ *trace*] (relativisation with PP-category gaps)

c. [$_{VP}$ *sell his car*], I believe that John will [$_{VP}$ *trace*]. (VP-preposing)

d. *Tired* though the baker may be [$_{AP}$ *trace*], the donuts will be made on time!

As we have seen, the Strong Hypothesis (35) is too strong, since it incorrectly predicts priming as a result of processing Raising constructions (contradicted directly by Fodor's interpretation of the FMS results) and Control constructions. The two weaker versions of Fodor's claim, the NP–NP Hypothesis and the Non-Head Agreement Hypothesis, make differing predictions: the latter predicts priming in a variety of constructions which the NP–NP hypothesis does not. There is little current evidence that bears on the choice between the competitors. However, the experiments reported by Nicol (this volume) examined antecedent activation in PP-extraction—case (37b)—and found priming for the antecedent at the trace position. These results are inconsistent with the NP–NP Agreement Hypothesis, and consistent with the Non-HEAD Feature Hypothesis. So, empirically, we are left with only (37) as a candidate, holding to the premises adopted earlier.

The Weak Hypotheses and Transparency

Let us now evaluate the conclusion that the Strong Hypothesis and the NP–NP Hypothesis are empirically inadequate, within the context of the Transparency Hypothesis. Fodor's original assertion concerning the relative optimality of GPSG and GB to account for the lexical priming results was quite straightforward. Reflexivisation and WH-extraction fall into one class (constructions involving an obligatory *syntactic* referential dependency), Raising and Control fall into another (constructions on which the referential dependency is only semantic, not syntactic). The lexical antecedent-reactivation effect occurs immediately and robustly in the former class of constructions, not the latter. Hence, the lexical priming technique can be taken as sensitive to syntactic representations (and dependencies defined over them), only if we accept the corollary that Raising and Control sentences have no such syntactic dependency. But this is not correct: I have shown that even within the GPSG theory, Raising and Control *do* involve a syntactic dependency on an antecedent. Critically, the relation in Raising between the subject NP and the embedded predicate is constrained by syntactic feature agreement, just as the syntactic relation between a reflexive and its antecedent is. And in the FMS materials, the reflexive-antecedent relation is partially subsumed under the VP-controller relation. This leads to either of the two weaker hypotheses, in which the lexical priming technique is sensitive to a *subclass* of syntactic dependencies.

The NP–NP Hypothesis (36) is inconsistent with the Transparency Hypothesis, because it requires the stipulation that the only relevant syntactic dependencies are those involving pairs of NPs; this restriction has no independent grammatical motivation. Further, it is incapable of characterising why PP-gaps should give priming, as they do in Experiment 1 of Nicol's chapter in this volume. Hence, the only hypothesis concerning the origin of the antecedent-reactivation effect that is both consistent with Transparency and simultaneously able to account for the restrictive nature of the phenomenon is (37), the Non-Head Feature Agreement Hypothesis.

The Non-Head Feature Agreement Hypothesis is consistent with the Transparency Hypothesis, since the class of constructions producing lexical-priming antecedent reactivation falls into a formal natural class, a class that excludes those constructions that do not produce such antecedent activation—namely the class of syntactic agreement relations excluding HEAD features. This is somewhat less appealing, I believe, than the initial hypothesis considered. Fodor's original suggestion was that the differences between the lexical priming effects and the VPR results correlates with the distinction between syntax and semantics: processing of syntactic constituents (and dependencies between them) produces robust lexical priming; semantic processing produces VPR reactivation. The arguments I have presented here constitute a complication for this suggestion, since now the basic partitioning must be viewed, not as a processing of syntactic vs semantic elements, but rather processing of non-head agreement vs all other processing, syntactic or semantic. Although this partitioning is coherent, and still allows a transparent relation between the grammatical construction types and the processing effects, it lacks the elegance of Fodor's original partitioning, and leaves the phenomenon of selective lexical priming largely unexplained. In the next section I re-examine the results concerning the reactivation of the antecedents of pronouns, which I will show to be inconsistent with (37) as formulated, and to raise a final problem for locating a transparent, GPSG-based characterisation of the priming results.

The Problem of Pronouns. Hypothesis (37) holds that the lexical reactivation effect is restricted to constructions in which two constituents obligatorily agree in FOOT features. The two core constructions falling into this class are bound reflexives and WH-traces in unbounded dependencies (cases of obligatory HEAD agreement, like Raising, Control, and normal Subject–Predicate constructions are thus excluded). However, there is a third construction type in which rapid, robust activation arises: sentences containing personal pronouns, like FMS's example given as (38), or the similar sentence in (39), from Nicol (1988).

38) (from FMS): *The boxer* knew that the doctor for the team was sure to blame *him* ##for the injury

39) (from Nicol (1988)): The *boxer* told *the skier* that the doctor for the team would blame *him* ## for the recent injury

In both studies, the grammatically possible antecedents of the pronoun were reactivated (e.g. *boxer* in (38) and *boxer* and *skier* in (39)), and the NP which could not grammatically serve as antecedent (*doctor* in both sentences) was not. This has two implications: (1) In order to maintain the hypothesis in (37), the Non-Head Agreement account of the lexical priming effect, it would have to be argued that *him* is required *by the syntax* to agree with *the boxer or the skier*; (2) In order to maintain the Transparency Hypothesis, all three constructions (those containing co-referent pronouns, reflexivisation, and unbounded extraction) would have to fall into a natural class excluding Raising and Control structures.

With regard to the first point, it is unanimously accepted by researchers on anaphora that there is no grammatical principle that forces some NP to be the antecedent of a pronoun. This argument was initially made by Lasnik (1976), who argued that the sole grammatical constraint holding of pronouns is a disjointness of reference condition, requiring (in the terminology of Chomsky, 1981) that a pronoun cannot be bound in a local domain. This leaves the question of the final determination of the antecedent of a pronoun entirely outside the grammar, subject to discourse and pragmatic factors.

Furthermore, there are well-known cases of referential dependencies in which there is a *mismatch* of morphological features between an element and its antecedent. These include split antecedents (40), overlapping reference (41), and the modern use of *they/them* as a gender-neutral singular (42):

40) Every courier told some double agent [that they were being observed]
41) John thinks that we ought to go to the movies (where *we* includes John).
42) Every student in this class is required to hand in their homework by the end of today!

Referential dependencies can exist in the absence of feature matchings.

Consequently, there can, in principle, be *no* obligatory syntactic relation between *him* and *the boxer* in (38). This is quite desirable, as the sentences are in fact ambiguous (with the ambiguity due to indeterminacy of the reference of the pronoun). Certainly, with the sentences in isolation, the preferred reading of the pronoun is where it corefers with *the boxer*, but this is not obligatory. The sentence is ambiguous, with the other reading one in which the pronoun refers to some (singular masculine) entity unmentioned in the sentence. Thus, the Non-Head Feature Hypothesis incorrectly predicts that there should be no priming for (semantic associates of) *boxer* after the pronoun in (38) or (39). That there is such priming falsifies the hypothesis. More generally, the existence of antecedent priming in both cases of obligatory anaphora (reflexivisation and unbounded extraction) and with pronouns seriously compromises any attempt to assert full isomorphy between the grammar and the processing system.

Is there a possible modification of (37) that would accurately describe the lexical priming results, and maintain the Transparency Hypothesis? I suggest not. We have already shown (36), the NP–NP Hypothesis to be inconsistent with the Transparency Hypothesis. And no other classification of the dependencies that give rise to antecedent reactivation seems available, without appealing to non-grammatical factors.

This is not to say that the lexical priming results constitute a 'mishmash' of unrelated phenomena. There exists one account of these results that combines principles of grammar with specific conjectures about the internal operations of the processor: the similar accounts advanced in Cowart and Cairns (1987), and Nicol (1988). On this model, a dedicated subprocessor (or *Coreference Processor*) builds up sets of candidate antecedents for each dependent constituent encountered. The construction of such antecedent sets is highly constrained by the grammar, so that, for example, reflexives and pronouns will be assigned disjoint sets of preceding NPs as possible antecedents. All the members of the set will be reactivated on construction of the set, that is, at the point where the dependent element is detected by the processor. For dependent constituents that are easily detected—reflexives, pronouns, and object WH-traces—immediate and robust reactivation of the candidate antecedents will arise. For elements that are not as easily detected—by hypothesis, NP-trace, and PRO—there may be no such robust reactivation, for obvious reasons.[20]

This view departs from strict Transparency in two ways: (1) the supposition that a candidate set of antecedents is constructed for each detected dependent element, with only one member to be chosen for ultimate interpretation; and (2) the hypothesis that, effectively, only one candidate set can be active at one time. Neither of these has an analogue in the syntactic grammar itself. Nonetheless, they are compatible with it.

The discussion here has been rather technical, and I wish to summarise it briefly, and put it in a broader, more schematic context. The crucial

---

[20] The one fact discussed by Fodor that does not easily fall under this account is the lack of priming for the second NP after the pronoun in cases like (10) (repeated here), in which there was non-significant priming for *doctor* (see Table 17.1):

10) The boxer knew that the doctor for the team was sure to blame him ##for the injury

This result is consistent with the view (advanced by Nicol, 1991) that reactivation is *suppressable*—specifically, that the reactivation of the candidate antecedent set for the pronoun (e.g. reactivation of *the boxer*) will suppress all previously reactivated constituents.

representations are those in which a reflexive is contained within a Raising or Control predicate; descriptively, the referential antecedent of the reflexive must be the NP of the matrix clause which fixes the interpretation of the implicit subject of the complement. Let us assume that there is a syntactic dependency, ultimately, between the reflexive and the matrix NP, as all current theories hold, and that semantic coreference is tied to this relation. Thus any theory of syntax must capture the following dependencies, where the links on the bottom of each example represent the syntactic dependencies, and those on top represent the semantic relations.

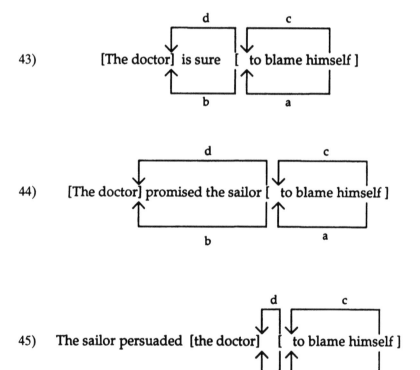

43)   [The doctor] is sure   [to blame himself]

44)   [The doctor] promised the sailor [to blame himself]

45)   The sailor persuaded [the doctor]   [to blame himself]

In GB, the *a* and *b* relations are coindexing, and the complement subject position is represented as a trace in (43) and as PRO in (44, 45). The *c* and *d* relations are coreference, as dictated by the indexing. In GPSG, the *a* and *b* relations are obligatory feature agreement. In LFG (see the papers in Bresnan [Ed.], 1982), the *a*, *b* relations are 'control equations', quite similar ultimately to feature agreement; neither lexicalist theory structurally represents the embedded subject. But, as in GB, the *c, d* relations come out as coreference in these lexicalist approaches, influenced by the respective syntactic relations. On Fodor's characterisation, visual probe recognition results are taken to reflect recovery, by the processor, of the semantic relations *c* and *d*. And this is a sensible interpretation: from a semantic standpoint, *a* and *b* (at least for the Control Sentences (44) and (45)) are virtually identical, serving to equate the referential value of two argument positions.

The problem I have outlined in this section amounts to the observation that there is no *direct* syntactic connection, *on any theory of syntax*, between the reflexive and *the doctor* in (43–45); all theories characterise the relation as the sum of the pair *a, b*. Consequently, there is no obvious reason why the processor would reactivate *the doctor* after recovering the syntactic relations *a* and *b*, and not reactivate the same NP just after recovering the syntactic relation *b*. This is *the piggyback problem*: on any current theory of syntax, the relation between the reflexive in (43–45) and its overt antecedent piggybacks on the relation of the controlled complement and its controller. Both *a* and *b* are syntactic dependencies of the same type (feature agreement, coindexing, or control equation resolution), holding between two syntactic maximal constituents (NP and NP, or VP and NP). (Given that dependencies between PP-gaps and their antecedents yield lexical priming, as Nicol's discussion shows, we cannot maintain that it is only NP–NP syntactic dependencies that create priming.) So, if recovering a pair of such relations gives reactivation, recovering either member of the pair should as well. It is not processing the *reflexive* which gives reactivation, surely; it is processing the relationship between it and its antecedent/controller. And in GPSG, LFG, and other lexicalist theories, this relation is, in (43–45), critically dependent on the complement-VP control relation, as much as it is in GB.

This leaves the advocate of a lexicalist theory in about the same position as the advocate of a movement-based theory—either the processor is selecting some particular subgroup of syntactic dependencies, a subgroup lacking independent grammatical motivation, or other non-grammatical factors are intruding. In neither case is the transparency hypothesis clearly supported in its strictest form.

Now, suppose one were to offer up a lexicalist theory on which the reflexive and *the doctor* are coindexed, in the syntax, and maintain that lexical priming arises through the discovery of such an indexed element in the input. To make such an analysis interestingly different from the approaches schematised earlier, this binding relation would have to be direct, sidestepping the Control/Raising relation entirely. That is, there would have to be a direct syntactic link (*a'* in 46) between the reflexive and its binder:

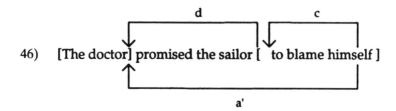

46)   [The doctor] promised the sailor [to blame himself]

a'

The problem with any such theory is that there is no way to capture the overwhelming generalisation about the interaction between lexical anaphors and Control/Raising predicates: the binder of the reflexive is always the same NP as the controller of the complement VP. The piggyback problem would be solved, at the expense of losing a fundamental generalisation known since the early days of generative grammar. And it would do no good to suppose that the syntactic dependency a' is licensed in virtue of the semantic referential dependencies c and d; this would get the relationship between syntax and semantics exactly backwards.

PF VISIBILITY AND CROSS-MODAL PRIMING EFFECTS

In the second major section of her article, Fodor suggests a way in which the cross-modal results could be interpreted within the GB framework without giving up the Transparency Hypothesis (or the GB framework itself). Fodor observes that the Phonetic Form (PF) level of representation in GB is often taken to only selectively represent empty categories. Specifically, a number of authors (Chomsky 1986a; Chomsky & Lasnik, 1977; Jaeggli, 1980; *inter alia*) have suggested that of the three GB empty categories that can occupy argument positions in English—WH-trace, NP-trace, and PRO—only WH-trace is mapped into a PF representation. The central notion here is that of *PF-Visibility*—the basic idea is that WH-trace is Casemarked, and NP-trace and PRO are not, and that only Casemarked arguments are visible (present) at PF. The main motivation for this idea— originally due to Jaeggli (1980)—comes from the differing effects of WH-trace and PRO and NP-trace on function-word contraction in English.

Fodor suggests that the way in which GB can provide a transparent analysis of the cross-modal antecedent-reactivation results is to attribute the effect to the postulation, by the processor, of the PF representation. In the PF structure, WH-trace (which gives rise to reactivation) is present, but PRO and NP-trace (which do not produce reactivation effects) are not present. In short, Fodor offers proponents of movement-based theories of syntax a way out of the dilemma posed by the selective nature of lexical priming. Let us call this the PF-Visibility account.

Fodor presents some alternatives to, and some problems for, the foundation of this line of argument. Specifically, she presents a series of arguments concerning the various sorts of function word contraction present in English, arguing first (following Schachter, 1984) that the standard GB analysis of *wanna*-contraction does not easily extend to the full range of contraction phenomena in English[21], and arguing second that lexicalist theories might provide a full accounting of the contraction effects (based on the account of Schachter, 1984), placing them all squarely in the syntax. If this latter position is adopted, the PF-visibility account of cross-modal priming is somewhat undermined, in the sense that it has plausible alternatives that do not require the existence of nominative trace, as GB theory does. I actually agree with Fodor's position that the PF-visibility account of priming is not tenable, although for somewhat different reasons.

In this section, I will make two points. First, I will demonstrate that the PF-Visibility account of antecedent reactivation cannot be maintained, for quite a simple reason: although lexical anaphors and (at least some) empty categories are carried over from the syntax into PF, their anaphoric relation to an antecedent is not. Second, I will briefly show (as Fodor does, in her discussion of non-syntactic analyses of function word contraction) that Schachter's argument against a trace-theoretic analysis of embedded subject extraction may plausibly be dismissed, in light of existing arguments (chiefly due to Selkirk, 1984) that auxiliary contraction is prosodically, not syntactically, constrained. Following Fodor, I will thus conclude that contraction may not bear as strongly on the nature of PF representation as it was once believed; and so parsing theory should advance with considerable care both in placing too much weight on the Jaeggli proposal concerning the differential representation at PF of the empty categories, and in placing too much weight on Schachter's argument in favour of lexicalist theories of complement structure.

---

[21] Fodor does not argue that GB is unable to account for the full range of contraction phenomena. Rather, she observes that a modification of the analysis of contraction is necessary to accommodate all the data; and that once this is done, one is left with the possibility that Jaeggli's original analysis—on which the notion that WH-trace, but not other empty categories, are present at PF—has plausible alternatives. This in turn, as Fodor observes, somewhat weakens the independent evidence for the PF-Visibility Hypothesis.

PF and Anaphora

The PF-visibility account of cross-modal priming has three parts:

A. *wanna*-contraction takes place in the post-syntactic level PF.
B. As is shown by those contexts that permit and those that prevent *wanna*-contraction, WH-trace is present in PF, and neither PRO nor NP-trace is so represented.
C. WH-trace gives immediate cross-modal priming for its antecedent; neither NP-trace nor PRO gives such reactivation.

Again, I presume the truth of thesis C for purposes of discussion, with the continuing caveat that I believe more work needs to be done before we can justifiably draw this conclusion. A and B together constitute a general view taken in the GB literature, and was originally argued by Lightfoot (1976), Chomsky and Lasnik (1977), and Jaeggli (1980). What I view as dubious is taking B as the source of C. The problem is simply that, although WH-trace may be categorically represented at PF, its anaphoric relation to the WH-antecedent is not: on the received view of that level of representation, indexing has absolutely no PF representation.

PF is an interface level, mediating between syntax proper and the phonological rule system; its input is S-structure, and its output must be stated in the vocabulary of the motor and perceptual systems. Those aspects of syntactic structure that are relevant to phonological/phonetic interpretation are carried over into the PF module—the most obvious example being broad syntactic constituency, and lexical category labelling, which exert influence on stress and prosodic phrasing (see Chomsky & Halle, 1968; Chomsky & Lasnik, 1991; Hayes, 1980; Selkirk, 1984; *inter alia*, for discussion). Chomsky has recently advanced a view (see Chomsky, 1991; Chomsky & Lasnik, 1991) according to which the only elements that can be so carried over are those which have a primitive effect on phonological computations. By this 'Full Interpretation' principle (FI), many aspects of syntactic structure cannot be mapped onto PF representation, as a general property of derivations.

Certainly one central syntactic relation that, plausibly, cannot be carried over into PF is anaphoric dependency (however formally represented in the syntax, whether by indexing, linking [Higginbotham, 1983; 1985], control equations [Bresnan, 1982], or whatever formalism). Thus, the S-structure (47a) can have a PF representation no richer than (47b); (47a) violates FI as a PF representation:

47)a. $[_{CP} [_{NP} [_{Det}$ which$] [_{N'} [_N$ rebel$]]]_1 [_{C'} [_C [_V$ will$]_2 [_{IP} [_{NP}$ you$] [_{INFL'}][_{INFL} e_2 [_{VP} [_{V'} [_V$ see$] t_1]]]]]]]$

b. $[_{CP} [_{NP} [_{Det}$ which$] [_{N'} [_N$ rebel$]]]][_C [_V$ will$] [_{IP} [_{NP}$ you$] [_{INFL}][_{VP} [_V$ see$] [_{NP} t]]]]]$

Fodor has suggested the PF-visibility account as a possible transparency-consistent GB answer to the selective cross-modal priming pattern C. Under this interesting hypothesis (which, as Fodor observes, permits GB to maintain a clearcut analysis of the differences between WH-trace and other empty categories) such priming might arise as a direct consequence of the recovery of such PF representations as (47b).

However, this cannot be the case, unless we radically change the standing view of PF in a very deep way. The object trace in (47b) is represented, at PF, as (1) lacking a phonetic matrix; (2) being of category NP; and (3) following 'see' in the string. The indexical dependency between the trace and [$_{NP}$ which rebel]—indicating that the NP is the antecedent of the trace—is not PF-represented. Consequently, no specialised relation to the WH-phrase can be recovered through the PF-representation alone; the 'gap' has no antecedent at this level of representation. Consequently, we must view antecedent reactivation as a result of the processor's recovery of syntactic, or semantic, representations. And so the PF-visibility account of cross-modal priming is not tenable, as it would rest on the perception of relations not defined at this level.

I take the problem just noted to be the strong argument against Fodor's hypothesis that antecedent reactivation might result from the processor's recovery of PF representations. In the next section, I will turn to other considerations concerning the phenomena that motivate the standard analysis of the representation of empty categories at PF. These considerations will raise questions about whether there is representation of some (WH-trace) and not other (NP-trace, PRO) empty categories at PF, by considering the underlying nature of contraction. My remarks in that section partially reiterate some of Fodor's thorough discussion of contraction, especially her review of syntactic and prosodic accounts of these phenomena.

Constraints on Contraction and PF Visibility

The initial argument made concerning the relevance of *wanna*-contraction to syntactic theory was introduced by Lightfoot (1976), and Chomsky and Lasnik (1977), who observed that the process is blocked when extraction has occurred from the complement subject position.

48)a. who$_1$ do you want [$_S$ t$_1$ to leave town by sunset]?
   b. * who do you wanna leave town by sunset?

Descriptively, the site of Wh-extraction blocks this type of contraction. This stands in sharp contrast to the pair (49a, b), which demonstrate that the non-overt subject of this control structure does not block contraction.

49) *wanna*-contraction:
a. I₁ want [$_s$ PRO₁ to leave now]
b. I wanna leave now.

In terms of the GB theory of empty categories, WH-trace blocks contraction, PRO does not. To fully round out the paradigm, one further case is of relevance: contraction across NP-trace. There is a variant of *want* that appears to act as a Raising verb, as in (50) (example from van Riemsdjik & Williams, 1986, p. 150).

50) These papers want to be finished by tomorrow.

This example receives the analysis in (51a), and, as van Riemsdjik and Williams observe, *wanna*-contraction may occur (51b):

51)a. [$_{NP}$ These papers]₁ want [$_s$ NP-trace₁ to be finished by tomorrow]
b. These papers wanna be finished by tomorrow.[22]

So, descriptively, NP-trace does not block *wanna*-contraction, nor the similar Verb+infinitival-to contractions above.

Thus, WH-trace in subject position is the sole empty category to block leftward *to* contraction onto the preceding verb. Jaeggli (1980) proposes what has become the standard GB analysis of this effect. Jaeggli observes

---

[22] Closely related to (51b) are the examples given here, in which in each case infinitival *to* may contract onto the preceding verb, across NP-trace (see Jaeggli, 1980):

i) a. I have [$_s$ t₁ to go]
   b. I hafta go.

ii) a. I ought [$_s$ t₁ to go]
    b. I oughta go.

iii) a. I used [$_s$ t₁ to go to the movies every Saturday morning]
     b. I usta go to the movies . . .

iv) a. I am supposed [$_s$ t₁ to go to the movies every Saturday morning]
    b. I am supposta [$_s$ t₁ to go to the movies every Saturday morning]

Observe that the sequence 'used to' cannot contract across an intervening WH-trace:

v) a. John used [the hammer] to open the window
   b. [which hammer]₁ did John use t₁ to open the window?
   c. *[which hammer] did John usta open the window?

As expected, contraction of *use+to* is selectively blocked by WH-trace, not by NP-trace.

that there is an independent property holding of WH-trace in argument position, but not of any other empty category in English. Alone among the empty categories, WH-trace in argument position must be assigned abstract Case. In the standard theory of Case assignment, Case is assigned only to overt NPs and WH-trace occupying argument positions. PRO is never governed (a property that follows theorematically from the Binding Theory), and government is a precondition on Case assignment; thus PRO is never Casemarked. NP-trace is also not Casemarked; it is the lack of Case in the complement subject position of (51a), for example, which forces Raising. Thus, the descriptive conditions on contraction may be stated as follows, following Jaeggli:

52) *wanna*-contraction is blocked by a Casemarked category.

Jaeggli further suggests that Casemarked elements (including all overt NPs, and WH-trace occurring in argument position) are mapped into the PF representation of a sentence, whereas non-casemarked elements (NP-trace, PRO) are not. Certain syntactic elements have a corresponding representation in the PF structure, and others do not. Granting this hypothesis (see Chomsky, 1986a; Chomsky & Lasnik, 1991; Jaeggli, 1980; for discussion), a casemarked empty category may be expected to have an effect on rules applying in the PF component, whereas non-Casemarked empty categories cannot, since they have no PF representation.

This yields a rather simple account of the contraction effects mentioned earlier: *to* may optionally contract to the left, onto *a left-adjacent* occurrence of the verbs *want, supposed, ought* and *used*. Specifically, the PF component will include the following rules of suppletion:

53)a. want+to——▶wanna
　　b. supposed+to——▶supposta
　　c. used+to——▶usta
　　d. ought+to——▶oughta

The fact that the site of WH-extraction blocks contraction follows an automatic consequence of the requirement that Casemarked elements be formally represented at PF. In (48), for example, the WH-trace must be represented at PF, making *want* and *to* non-adjacent, so the rule (53a) cannot apply.

Schachter's Argument.　Schachter (1984) argues against the basic trace-theoretic account of the constraints on *wanna*-contraction, based on the fact that subject WH-trace does not block *auxiliary contraction*. Fodor's argument against the PF-visibility account of priming depends in large part on Schachter's analysis.

54)a. Who₁ do you think [t₁ is here]?
   b. Who do you think's here?

Fodor is correct to emphasise that the existence of this type of contraction is seemingly problematic. If subject WH-trace blocks contraction of *to* onto *want* in (48b), then why does it not similarly block contraction of *is* leftward onto *think* in (54b)?

Several approaches have been taken to this problem. Schachter uses the asymmetry in the two types of contraction to argue in favour of a GPSG analysis of subject extraction, in which no trace is present. On his account, (54a) is assigned structure (55), whereas (48a) is assigned (56):

55) who do you think [$_{VP}$ is here]?
56) who₁ do you want [$_{NP}$ trace] [$_{VP}$ to leave town by sunset]?

Thus both wanna contraction and auxiliary contraction may be viewed as subject to exactly the same constraint: the function word may contract onto the verb only when they are string-adjacent. Since, crucially, GB does not allow any such analysis as (55), Schachter concludes that the existence of auxiliary contraction across a subject extraction site is a strong argument against GB's trace theory. It is this particular analysis that Fodor adopts.

Fodor calls to our attention the observation made by King (1970) and Bresnan (1971), namely that auxiliary contraction is seemingly sensitive to (i.e. blocked by) the presence of an empty category to the *right* of the auxiliary:

57)b. Who's hungry? John is [$_{VP}$ ø].
     * John's [$_{VP}$ ø]

Schachter's approach has no immediate account of this right-context effect.

However, a distinct type of analysis of aux-contraction is given by Selkirk (1984), who offers a detailed theory of the interaction between prosody (principally stress) and syntactic structure. In her theory, the differences between *wanna*-contraction and auxiliary contraction follow from general (and different) properties of the two rule types, thus vitiating Schachter's argument against trace theory. Crucially, Selkirk's theory gives an immediate explanation of both properties of auxiliary contraction noted earlier.

Selkirk on Prosodic Contraction.   Selkirk (1984) develops a comprehensive theory of the relationship between syntactic constituent structure, prosodic phrasing, and phonological stress. The central formal construct of Selkirk's stress theory is the *metrical grid* (originally introduced by Liberman & Prince, 1977; Prince, 1983) an alignment of syllable strings with grid columns of varying height. The grid encodes assignment of relative prominence (to be interpreted phonologically and phonetically as relative stress) to syllables aligned with the grid. The metrical grid, and the rules that construct and modify it, is the central link in her theory between syntax and phonology.

Prosodic contraction—including auxiliary contraction—is (on her view) a particular subcase of a fundamental alteration in the surface appearance of function words: such words have a strong and a weak form, and the weak form is licensed only under certain circumstances, in particular those where the syntax-sensitive rule of *Monosyllabic Destressing* may apply.

In Selkirk's theory, extending in part work by Liberman (1975) and Liberman and Prince (1977), the fundamental rhythmic pattern of speech, and in particular the tendency to alternate strong and weak syllables, and the capability of a syllable to be uttered with greater or lesser prominence than its neighbours, is captured by associating the syllable sequence with the metrical grid.

```
58)        x                    [level 4] ⎫
    x      x       x            [level 3] ⎬      (beats)
  x x x x  x  x x x             [level 2] ⎭
  x x x x  x  x x x             [level 1]        (demibeats)
the baker is laughing outside
```

The horizontal levels are the *metrical levels*; the points on the lowest level (level 1) are *demibeats*, and those that occupy level 2 or higher are *beats*. The height of the column dictates the relative stress prominence of the associated syllable—the higher the column, the greater the stress. The grid is also a timing representation, in that phonological elements associated with grid columns will (tend to) be articulated at a steady rate. The marks at level 2 are *basic beats*; a word must be assigned at least a basic beat if it is to surface with pronounced stress. Thus *destressing* is the operation of removing all grid marks for a syllable except for the lowest (the demibeat), whose function is to indicate timing in the utterance; since the syllable then has no grid mark at level 2 or higher, it will be pronounced without stress.

Various pause and timing phenomena are formally indicated by the assignment of a demibeat with no associated phonological material, what Selkirk terms a *silent demibeat*. Silent demibeats are added to a grid in accordance with the following rule:

59) *Silent Demibeat Addition*: Add a silent demibeat at the right edge of the portion of the grid aligned with:
   a) a content word

b) a content word which is the head of a non-adjunct constituent
c) a phrase
d) a major constituent of the sentence
e) a string preceding or constituting a focus
f) a string preceding or constituting an appositive

The basic grid phonology of function words is as follows. Function words are initially aligned with the grid, by assigning them a demibeat; they are also assigned a basic beat (a level 2 grid prominence), as are all words. Thus, in the absence of any destressing process, a function word will surface with a moderate degree of stress. Destressing is effected by the rule of Monosyllabic Destressing:

60) Monosyllabic Destressing

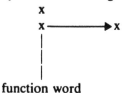

function word

Constraint: the grid column may not be followed by a silent demibeat.

Application of this rule will cause the syllable to surface without stress, and in some cases will allow the syllable to undergo further phonological processes, including vowel reduction. For our (58), Monosyllabic Destressing can apply to the auxiliary, allowing vowel reduction (a precondition for contraction), and aux-contraction onto the subject (see Selkirk, 1984, for details):

61)   x
        x   x   x
    x   x   x   x   x   x   x
    x   x   x   x   x   x   x   x
    the baker is laughing outside
    → 'the baker's laughing outside'

Since the weak forms of function words appear only in certain environments, the rule Monosyllabic Destressing is not free: it is blocked in certain circumstances. Specifically, it is blocked whenever the function word is followed by a silent demibeat; and the silent demibeats, in turn, are assigned based on syntactic constituency and other factors, by the rules given earlier. Now consider the examples below in this light:

62)a. Who₁ do you think [t₁ is laughing outside]?
  b. Who do you think's laughing outside?
63) Who's laughing outside?a. The baker is [$_{VP}$ φ].
               b. *The baker's [$_{VP}$ φ]

Both of these examples have an immediate explanation in Selkirk's theory. In (63a), the auxiliary is phonetically final in its phrase, and so a silent demibeat is added to the grid position immediately following the grid column of the auxiliary:

64)   x
    x x x x   x x x x
    x x x x   x x x x x
    the baker is   ⟶   the baker is
               Silent
               Demibeat
               Addition

Since the grid column over *is* is immediately followed by a silent demibeat in the output, Monosyllabic Destressing cannot apply, and hence (63b) is ungrammatical, for these essentially phonological reasons.

The reason why (62b) is grammatical is simply that nothing impedes Monosyllabic Destressing. The initial grid assigned to (62a) is approximately:

65)   x
             x   x
    x   x   x   x   x   x   x
    x   x   x   x   x   x   x
. . . you think is laughing outside

No silent demibeat follows the grid column over *is*, and hence Monosyllabic Destressing can apply, ultimately allowing the auxiliary to contract onto *think*. If Selkirk is right, auxiliary contraction applies late in the derivation, and is only indirectly sensitive to syntactic structure (via the subcases of (59)); and the process has nothing to do with empty categories *per se*.[23]

---

[23] There is another class of examples in which auxiliary contraction is prohibited for some (but not all) speakers (% indicates variability among speakers), where the auxiliary occurs before the deletion site in a Gapping construction or a comparative (Examples from Selkirk, 1984):

  i) Mary is dancing the rumba and Dan is____the cancan.
  i') *Mary is dancing the rumba and Dan's____the cancan.

As an additional example of the prosodic blocking of aux-contraction, observe that contraction may not precede an appositive:

66) *The baker, I think's, laughing outside.

On Selkirk's theory, the appositive is preceded (and followed by) a silent demibeat, and so the auxiliary cannot contract. Schachter's analysis has nothing immediately to say about this case either.

What is novel in Selkirk's theory is the focus on the phonology of contraction. There is nothing particularly special about gaps, except that they create environments in which the function word is phrase-final (in the relevant sense), and thus they trigger the rule of Silent Demibeat Addition, which in turn blocks Monosyllabic Destressing and reduction. The rule of Silent Demibeat Addition is independent of function words; it applies in a number of constructions in the environment of content words, and is the general principle by which syntactic and focus constituency are reflected in the timing of an utterance.

As a result of the success of Selkirk's theory in providing a comprehensive account of the left/right asymmetry in the sensitivity of prosodic contraction to the presence of a 'gap', Schachter's initial argument in favour of the GPSG traceless analysis of subject extraction is contravened. This permits us to uphold the classical GB characterisation the basic nature of PF structures, as containing WH-trace and not the other empty categories,[24] as Fodor notes. Given this alternative, one might continue to

---

ii) The table is longer than it is___wide.
ii') % The table's longer than it's___wide.

iii) Jane is a more promising lawyer than Harriet is a___brilliant doctor.
iii') *Jane is a more promising lawyer than Harriet's a___brilliant doctor.

Similar examples are discussed by Fodor. Selkirk suggests that, in both comparatives and Gapping, elements in the first and second clauses are paired up (*Mary* with *Dan*, *the rumba* with *the cancan* in (i), for example), and that each paired element is assigned prosodic focus, inducing the insertion of a silent demibeat after the auxiliary, thus blocking contraction. This process, she suggests, is subject to personal variation, accounting for the variation in judgments.

[24] See Barss, 1991, for a discussion of cases that pose a problem for a purely phonological prosodic analysis of auxiliary contraction. Many speakers report a consistent contrast between the examples in (i) and (ii):

i) Who do you think's available?

ii) ?? Who do you think's altruistic?

Apparently, such contraction is free when the following predicate (*available*, in (i)) denotes a temporary, or *stage-level*, property, whereas it is blocked before a predicate that denotes adopt the PF-visibility analysis as a way of explaining the pattern of cross-modal priming observed, with a GB-consistent, visibility-compatible analysis.

However, my demonstration (and Fodor's) of the continued validity of this view of PF does not contravene the argument I made earlier concerning the PF-Visibility account of lexical priming effects in sentence processing. To reiterate that point, which I believe stands regardless of what the proper analysis of contraction phenomena is: PF is not a level of representation at which core syntactic relations, including binding, are represented. Consequently, if lexical priming effects have anything at all to do with the relation of a dependent element to an antecedent, these effects must arise as a result of recovering either the syntactic or the semantic representation of a sentence. Similarly, if lexical priming is tied to the recovery of predicate-argument relations (as suggested by Nicol, this volume; Tanenhaus, Boland, Mauner, & Carlson, this volume; Tanenhaus & Carlson, 1989; Tanenhaus, Garnsey & Boland, 1990), again we must focus on syntactic and semantic representations and their computation, not on the recovery of PF representations.

Fodor's Proposed Experiment

At the end of her article, Fodor outlines a proposed experiment that will examine antecedent reactivation, using the cross-modal priming technique, in the environment of a subject WH-extraction site (relevant probe point

---

a permanent or *individual-level* property (the terminology is introduced by Carlson, 1977). Diesing (1990; 1992) presents a series of arguments that stage-level predicates have their subjects generated internal to the predicate's maximal projection, whereas the subjects of individual-level predicates are generated directly in clausal subject position. Thus (i) and (ii) have differing D-structures:

i)′ You think [$_{CP}$ [$_C$ [$_{IP}$ ∅ INFL [$_{VP}$ is $_{AP}$ [who] [$_{A'}$ available]]]]]?

ii)′ You think [$_{CP}$ [$_C$ [$_{IP}$ [who] INFL [$_{VP}$ is $_{AP}$[$_{A'}$ altruistic]]]]]

Barss argues that the contrasts in (i, ii) follow from the differences in syntactic extraction possibilities from the two positions; auxiliary contraction is taken to have a syntactic aspect, involving movement of *to* onto the higher verb, as an instance of head movement (see Baker, 1988, for much discussion of this general process). Roughly, the extracted subject in (ii) must leave a trace in clausal subject position; this trace in turn must be properly governed by C°, and it cannot be if the auxiliary is moved through COMP, as it would be on a head-movement analysis. However, the WH-phrase in (i)′ can come directly from its D-structure position inside the adjective phrase, and the resulting trace will be properly governed by INFL. The details of this analysis are quite complex, and I will not go into them here. However, it should be noted that this analysis presupposes that the verb+auxiliary complex is formed up in the syntax.

below indicated by ##). Experimental sentences to be tested include such cases as (67) and (68):

67) [NP Which lecture room]₁ does the art teacher at the night school [VP believe . . .
   a. [IP t₁ is ## restricted while the renovations are in progress]]? (GB analysis)
   b. [VP is ## restricted while the renovations are in progress]]? (lexicalist analysis)

68) [NP Which lecture room]₁ does the art teacher at the night school [VP understand . . .
   a. [IP [NP t₁] [[VP to be ## restricted while the renovations are in progress]? (GB analysis)
   b. [NP t₁] [VP to be ## restricted while the renovations are in progress]? (lexicalist analysis)

As Fodor observes, examining antecedent reactivation in such cases will be revealing for several reasons. She takes the outcome of the experiment to have direct bearing on the validity of the lexicalist or GB analysis of the complement structure (while noting two problems which I will review shortly). In the tensed complement case (67), GB and GPSG differ on whether or not a nominative trace is assumed to be present. Both theories agree that for the infinitival case (68) there is a post-verbal WH-trace.

If there is reactivation in (67), Fodor argues, GPSG will be at a loss to explain it within a strictly transparent approach to parsing, on which the exact representation in (67) is immediately recovered; and on this point I agree. Fodor further argues that if there is no antecedent reactivation in the complement constituent of (67), this result can be taken as problematic for GB theory. On this point I disagree. It is true that such a result (no reactivation) would be inconsistent with GB if we adopt strict Transparency: if object WH-traces produce reactivation, then subject traces should as well. However, one can easily imagine that, for reasons of detectability, subject traces should not produce immediate and robust reactivation, in spite of the fact that object traces do. Fodor raises this possibility, and observes that demonstrating the validity (or invalidity) of the transparency hypothesis and the optimality of particular grammatical models is difficult to do simultaneously. As she notes, it is quite plausible that detection of the presence of an object trace in the input string would be greatly facilitated by accessing the lexical properties of the verb, specifically its subcategorisation frame (see Fodor, 1990; Nicol 1989; Nicol & Swinney, 1989; Stowe, 1985/86; *inter alia*). Since subject traces are not subcategorised, this important cue is missing in sentences like (67); and thus it might take a longer period of time for the processor to detect the presence of this trace in the input. This is of course quite similar to Nicol's conjecture (reviewed in the first section here) that the lack of systematic and robust priming in the neighbourhood of PRO and NP-trace is due to difficulty of detectability. Such accounts, as I noted earlier, do not follow immediately from any properties of the grammar, but remain highly plausible.

Thus lack of reactivation at the probe point in (67) does not immediately disconfirm the GB syntactic analysis. As Fodor argues, there is a tradeoff— if no priming is found, either the GB analysis is disconfirmed, or this finding would indicate processing factors at hand other than immediate, infallible, and complete recovery of the set of correct structural representation(s) for the input string (thus posing a problem for strict transparency). As in many other cases, there is a tension between transparency, and the adoption of a particular structural analysis: if we were to find no priming at this position, *either* the GB analysis is wrong, *or* strict transparency is incorrect. In either case, of course, the results would be very revealing. (And, ideally, one would hope for experimental results that distinguish the two).

In the spirit of this part of Fodor's discussion, I would like to suggest that finding reactivation at the probe point in (67) does not necessarily disconfirm the lexicalist analysis. The verbs to be used in this experiment have to be able to take both a tensed complement clause (69), and an infinitival complement with an accusative subject argument (70); the latter is schematised in (71).

69) John believed that she was the best candidate
70) John believed/understood/wanted/expected her to be the best candidate
71) NP V NP-accusative to VP

As Fodor reminds us, verbs that can appear in the schema (71), also typically take NP direct objects:

72) John believed/understood/wanted/expected her.

Thus, the processor might be led, on hearing the input sequence (73a), to erroneously postulate a simple transitive structure, with a direct object trace (73b):

73)a. Which lecture room did the art teacher believe/understand/want/
     expect . . .
   b. [NP Which lecture room]₁ did [IP [NP the art teacher]₂ [VP believe/
      understand/want/expect [NP trace]₁?

This erroneously postulated object trace would reactivate its antecedent, as object traces do. Thus the hypothetical local garden path, and the priming it would induce, might give one the impression that a clausal subject trace has been postulated. Although the garden path is almost immediately disconfirmed (as Fodor notes in her discussion), its effects would be present at Fodor's indicated probe point, and thus the presence of priming at that point might be misleading for an experimental inquiry concerning the existence of subject traces. Since previous studies have suggested that such erroneous traces are in fact postulated in the course of sentence processing (e.g. Fodor, 1978), I think the suggested experiment is as likely to tell us something about the consistent (and very interesting) mistakes the parser makes as about the correct representations it postulates.

One possible way to address this problem—teasing apart transparency and the competing structural analyses—would be to probe further downstream, after the disambiguation point:

74) [NP Which lecture room]1 does the art teacher at the night school [VP believe . . .
   a. [IP t1 is ## restricted while ## the renovations are in progress]? (GB analysis)
   b. [VP is ## restricted while ## the renovations are in progress]? (lexicalist analysis)

75) [NP Which lecture room]1 does the art teacher at the night school [VP understand . . .
   a. [IP [NP t1] [[VP to be ## restricted while ## the renovations are in progress]? (GB analysis)
   b. [NP t1] [VP to be ## restricted while ## the renovations are in progress]? (lexicalist analysis)

Let us assume that the local garden path is resolved by the second probe point, and that the correct complement structure is (retroactively) assigned. (Intuitions tell us that these sentences are not robust garden paths.) Let us further presume that if a trace is postulated in complement subject position, the reactivation of *lecture room* will be maintained through the second probe point, four syllables later (this seems plausible, but of course it requires independent investigation, as noted in footnote 13). Then, by the second probe point, the local garden path effects will have been eliminated, and priming (or lack thereof) would perhaps give us a better clue as to the presence or absence of nominative trace than would priming at the first probe point.

CONCLUSION

I began this chapter by distinguishing two different versions of the Transparency Hypothesis, *computational transparency* and *representational transparency*. I have focused on the latter, the position urged by Janet Fodor in her chapter in this volume and elsewhere. A somewhat stronger version of transparency, falling under computational transparency, is the Strong Competence Hypothesis (Bresnan & Kaplan, 1982; Kaplan & Bresnan, 1982). According to Bresnan and Kaplan (1982, p. xxxi), a model of language processing 'satisfies the Strong Competence Hypothesis if and only if its representational basis is isomorphic to the competence grammar'. The representational basis of the processing model is the set of specifications of what structure it may assign to input strings. If a processing model satisfies the Strong Competence Hypothesis, it would also seem to be necessarily representationally transparent. This is so because, if the representational basis of the processing system and the competence grammar are isomorphic, the representations assigned to input in the course of sentence processing will be isomorphic to the representations assigned by the competence grammar. I have no idea what types of evidence empirically distinguish computational and representational transparency, since it would seem that what we have access to via results from behavioural experiments are the output representations.

In my specific discussion here, I initially examined the interpretation given by Fodor to the cross-modal lexical priming results, within the context of representational transparency, which asserts a close correspondence between the outputs of the processor and the structures assigned by the grammar. Fodor adopts a version of this hypothesis strong enough to motivate taking processing results as confirming particular structural analyses otherwise motivated on purely linguistic grounds. I have tried to show that such use of processing results to confirm and disconfirm details of competing syntactic theories is fraught with difficulty, and in this particular case does not stand up under close scrutiny.

However, transparency (at least representational transparency) is, I believe, an important, and perhaps necessary, assumption in designing and interpreting empirical investigations into sentence processing. If one does not assume some version of representational transparency, one is left stranded with no vocabulary in which to couch descriptions of sentence representations, and no clue as to what structures and relations the processor is attempting to recover.

My remarks here have suggested that lexicalist and movement-based theories of syntax are more alike than different. It should prove fruitful, in trying to answer the question of what representations are initially postulated by the processing system, and whether natural classes of phenomena identified on purely linguistic grounds also form natural processing classes, to capitalise on the major results of enquiry into syntactic structure and semantic interpretation that have emerged in the last 30 years of generative grammar.

Fodor has encouraged us to take very seriously the details of linguistic theory, and the details of careful psycholinguistic experimentation, in an exploration of the complex ways in which enquiry in either domain has significance for the other. Although I have disagreed with some of the particular conclusions of Fodor's article, I wholeheartedly endorse the spirit of the endeavour.

ACKNOWLEDGMENTS

I am very gratful to Tom Bever, Paul Bloom, Molly Diesing, Janet Fodor, Ken Forster, Merrill Garrett, Alec Marantz, Janet Nicol, and David Pesetsky for helpful discussion and advice. I am particularly indebted to Gerry Altmann, Janet Fodor, Janet Nicol, and an anonymous reviewer for very helpful written comments on an earlier draft of the work represented here. Portions of this work were presented at the 1991 CUNY Conference on Sentence Processing at the University of Rochester, and I would like to thank the organisers of that conference, particularly Tom Bever and Mike Tanenhaus, for the opportunity to present this work publicly. Finally, I would like to thank Gerry Altmann for being a most helpful and encouraging editor, and for helping a question posted to Janet Fodor at the 1990 Sperlonga Workshop on Cognitive Models of Speech Processing grow into the present chapter.

REFERENCES

Baker, M. (1988) *Incorporation*. Chicago: The University of Chicago Press.

Barss, A. (1991). *Contraction, head movement, and the stage-individual contrast.* Unpublished MS, University of Arizona.

Bever, T.G. (1970) The cognitive basis for linguistic structures. In J.R. Hayes, (Ed.), *Cognition and the development of language*, 279–362. New York: John Wiley & Sons.

Bever, T.G., & McElree, B. (1988). Empty categories access their antecedents during comprehension. *Linguistic Inquiry, 19*, 35–43.

Bever, T.G., Straub, K., Shenkman, K., Kim, J.J., & Carrithers, C. (1990). The psychological reality of NP-trace. *Proceedings of NELS 20*. GLSA, University of Massachusetts.

Bresnan, J. (1971). *Contraction and the transformational cycle.* Unpublished MS.

Bresnan, J. (1982). (Ed.) *The mental representation of grammatical relations*. Cambridge, MA: MIT Press.

Bresnan, J., & Kaplan, R. (1982). Introduction. In J. Bresnan (Ed.), *The mental representation of grammatical relations*. Cambridge, MA: MIT Press.

Carlson, G.N. (1977). *Reference to kinds in English.* Unpublished doctoral dissertation, University of Massachusetts, Amherst.

Chomsky, N. (1970). Remarks on nominalization. In R.A. Jacobs & P.S. Rosenbaum (Eds.), *Readings in English transformational grammar.* Waltham, MA: Ginn & Co.

Chomsky, N. (1981). *Lectures on Government and Binding.* Dordrecht: Foris.

Chomksky, N. (1986a). *Knowledge of language: Its nature, origin, and use.* New York: Praeger Publishers.

Chomsky, N. (1986b). *Barriers.* Cambridge, MA: MIT Press.

Chomsky, N. (1991). Some notes on economy of derivation and representation. In R. Freidin (Ed.), *Principles and parameters in comparative grammar.* pp. 417–454. Cambridge, MA: MIT Press.

Chomsky, N., & Halle, M. (1968). *The sound pattern of English.* New York: Harper & Rowe.

Chomsky, N., & Lasnik, H. (1977). Filters and control. *Linguistic Inquiry, 11,* 1–46.

Chomsky, N., & Lasnik, H. (1991). Principles and parameters theory. In J. Jacobs, A. von Stechow, W. Sternefeld, & T. Vennemann (Eds.), *Syntax: An international handbook of contemporary research.* Berlin: Walter de Gruyter.

Cowart, W., & Cairns, H. (1987). Evidence for an anaphoric mechanism within syntactic processing: Some reference relations defy semantic and pragmatic constraints. *Memory and Cognition 15,* 318–331.

Diesing, M. (1990). *The syntactic roots of semantic partition.* Unpublished doctoral dissertation, UMASS, Amherst.

Diesing, M. (1992). *Indefinites.* Cambridge, MA: MIT Press.

Fiengo, R., & May, R. (forthcoming). *Indices and identity.* Cambridge, MA: MIT Press.

Fodor, J.D., Fodor, J.A., & Garrett, M.F. (1975). The psychological unreality of semantic representations. *Linguistic Inquiry 6,* 515–31.

Fodor, J.D. (1978). Parsing strategies and constraints on transformations. *Linguistic Inquiry 9,* 427–473.

Fodor, J.D. (1990). Processing empty categories: Distinguishing syntactic and semantic reactivation effects. In G.T.M. Altmann (Ed.), *Cognitive models of speech processing: Psycholinguistic and computational perspectives.* Cambridge, MA & London, UK: MIT Press.

Fodor, J.D. (this volume). *Empty categories in sentence processing: A question of visibility.*

Ford, M., Bresnan, J., & Kaplan, R.M. (1982). A competence-based theory of syntactic closure. In J. Bresnan (Ed.), *The mental representation of grammatical relations, 11,* (pp. 727–796). Cambridge, MA: MIT Press.

Frazier, L. (1979). *On comprehending sentences: Syntactic parsing strategies.* Bloomington, Indiana: Indiana University Linguistics Club.

Gazdar, G., Pullum, G., Klein, E., & Sag, I. (1985). *Generalized phrase structure grammar.* Cambridge, MA: Harvard University Press.

Hayes, B. (1980). *A metrical theory of stress rules.* Unpublished doctoral dissertation, MIT, Cambridge, MA.

Higginbotham, J. (1983). Logical form, binding, and nominals. *Linguistic Inquiry, 14,* 395–420.

Higginbotham, J. (1985). On semantics. *Linguistic Inquiry, 16,* 547–93.

Jacobson, P. (1987). [Review of Gazdar, Pullum, Klein, & Sag, Generalised Phrase Structure Grammar.] *Linguistics and Philosophy 10,* 389–426.

Jaeggli, O.A. (1980). Remarks on *to* contraction. *Linguistic Inquiry, 11,* 239–245.

Kang, B.-M. (1988). Unbounded reflexives. *Linguistics and Philosophy, 11,* 415–456.

Kaplan, R.M., & Bresnan, J. (1982). Lexical-functional grammar: A formal system for grammatical representation. In J. Bresnan (Ed.), *The mental representation of grammatical relations, 4,* (pp. 173–281). Cambridge, MA: MIT Press.

King, H.V. (1970). On blocking the rules for contraction in English. *Linguistic Inquiry, 1*, 239–246.

Lasnik, H. (1976). Remarks on Coreference. *Linguistic Analysis, 2*, 1–22.

Lasnik, H. (1989). *Essays on anaphora*. Dordrecht: Kluwer Academic Publishers.

Lasnik, H., & Uriagereka, J. (1988). *A course in GB syntax: Lectures on binding and empty categories*. Cambridge, MA: MIT Press.

Liberman, M. (1975). *The intonational system of English*. Unpublished doctoral dissertation, MIT, Cambridge, MA.

Liberman, M., & Prince, A. (1977). On stress and linguistic rhythm. *Linguistic Inquiry, 8*, 249–336.

Lightfoot, D. (1976). Trace theory and twice-moved NPs. *Linguistic Inquiry, 7*, 559–582.

MacDonald, M.C. (1989). Priming effects from gaps to antecedents. *Language and Cognitive Processes, 4*, 35–56.

McElree, B. & Bever, T.G. (1989). The psychological reality of linguistically defined gaps. *Journal of Psycholinguistic Research, 18*, 21–35.

Nicol, J. (1988). *Coreference processing during sentence comprehension*. Unpublished doctoral dissertation, MIT, Cambridge, MA.

Nicol, J. (1989). What the parser knows about the grammar: Psycholinguistic evidence. In M. Barlow, D. Flickinger, & M. Wescoat (Eds.), *Proceedings of the Second West Coast Conference on Formal Linguistics, 8*, 289–302, Centre for the Study of Language and Information: Stanford, CA.

Nicol, J. (1991). *Reactivation reconsidered*. Unpublished MS, University of Arizona.

Nicol, J. (this volume). *Reconsidering reactivation*.

Nicol, J., & Swinney, D. (1989). The role of structure in coreference assignment during sentence comprehension. *Journal of Psycholinguistic Research, 18*, (1), 5–19.

Osterhout, L., & Swinney, D. (1992, March). *Time course of antecedent availability following NP-trace*. Poster presented at the 1992 CUNY Conference on Sentence Processing.

Pollard, C., & Sag, I. (1983). Reflexives and reciprocals in English: An alternative to the binding theory. *Proceedings of the Second West Coast Conference on Formal Linguistics, 2*.

Postal, P. (1971). *On Raising*. Cambridge, MA: MIT Press.

Prince, A. (1983). Relating to the grid. *Linguistic Inquiry, 14*, 19–100.

Schachter, P. (1984). Auxiliary reduction: An argument for GPSG. *Linguistic Inquiry, 15*, 514–523.

Selkirk, E. (1984). *Phonology and syntax: The relation between sound and structure*. Cambridge, MA: MIT Press.

Sells, P. (1985). *Lectures on contemporary syntactic theories*. Center For the Study of Language and Information (CSLI), Lecture Notes 3. (distributed by the University of Chicago Press).

Stowe, L. (1985/86). Parsing WH-constructions: Evidence for on-line gap location. *Language and Cognitive Processes, 1.3*, 227–245.

Swinney, D., Ford, M., & Bresnan, J. (1989). On the temporal course of gap-filling and antecedent assignment during sentence comprehension. In B. Grosz, R. Kaplan, M. Macken, & I. Sag (Eds.), *Language structure and processing*, Stanford, CA: CSLI.

Tanenhaus, M.K., Boland, J.E., Garnsey, S.M., & Carlson, G.N. (1989). Lexical structure in parsing long-distance dependencies. *Journal of Psycholinguistic Research, 18*, 37–50.

Tanenhaus, M.K., Boland, J.E., Mauner, G.A., & Carlson, G. (this volume). *More on combinatory lexical information: Thematic structure in parsing and interpretation*.

Tanenhaus, M., & Carlson, G. (1989). Lexical structure and language comprehension. In W.D. Marslen-Wilson (Ed.), *Lexical representation and process*. Cambridge, MA: MIT Press.

Tanenhaus, M.K., Carlson, G.N., & Seidenberg, M.S. (1985). Do listeners compute syntactic representations? In D.R. Dowty, L. Karttunen, & A.M. Zwicky (Eds.), *Natural language parsing: Psychological, computational and linguistic perspectives*. Cambridge, UK: Cambridge University Press.

Tanenhaus, M.K., Garnsey, S.M., & Boland, J. (1990). Combinatory lexical information and language comprehension. In G.T.M. Altmann (Ed.), *Cognitive models of speech processing: Psycholinguistic and computational perspectives*. Cambridge, MA & London, UK: MIT Press.

van Riemsdjik, H., & Williams, E. (1986). *Introduction to the theory of grammar*. Cambridge, MA: MIT Press.

18 Agreement, Coindexing and Reactivation: A Reply to Barss

Ivan A. Sag
Stanford University, USA

Janet Dean Fodor
Graduate Center, CUNY, USA

Of the many interesting issues raised by Barss (this volume) in his reply to Fodor's paper, we will address just one. This is his objection to Fodor's proposed explanation, based on phrase structure grammar (Generalised Phrase Structure Grammar, Head-Driven Phrase Structure Grammar), for the results of the cross-modal priming experiments on antecedent reactivation by empty categories. It is agreed on all sides that the experimental data are still incomplete and uncertain in various ways. But Barss is prepared to accept, for the purposes of this argument, the generalisation over the data suggested by Fodor: when the task is cross-modal on-line lexical decision or naming, reactivation is rapid and accurate for overt pronouns and anaphors and for WH-trace, but is slow and possibly inaccurate for passive, raising, and controlled complement constructions, which are analysed within Government Binding theory in terms of NP-trace and PRO.[1] Fodor argued that the weak effects for NP-trace and PRO are understandable if the cross-modal task addresses the syntactic structure of a sentence, and if GPSG/HPSG is right about the inventory of empty categories in natural language. Overt pronouns and anaphors are present in syntactic structures, and so is WH-trace. But PSG theories do not recognise NP-trace and PRO as syntactic constituents; the facts of passive, raising, and control constructions are explained in PSG without positing empty categories. (See, *inter alia*, Gazdar, Klein, Pullum, & Sag, 1985; Klein & Sag, 1985; Pollard & Sag, 1987, 1993; Sag & Pollard, 1991).

---

[1] Here, as in Fodor's paper, we use transformational terms (e.g. 'raising') for convenience, though they do not apply literally to PSG analyses.

Barss agrees with Fodor that (setting aside questions of PF) GB cannot account for the pattern of experimental data without invoking some sort of processing factors that do not follow from the mental grammar or the representations assigned to sentences. But Barss also challenges the ability of PSG to provide a linguistically transparent account of the data. The question he asks is: is the class of constructions that exhibit robust cross-modal antecedent reactivation a *natural* class in PSG? Fodor implies that it is; Barss attempts to show that it is not. He argues that even though PSG accepts the existence of WH-trace and denies the existence of NP-trace, it treats the two kinds of construction uniformly; hence it does not explain why they behave differently with respect to antecedent activation.

Barss sketches the GPSG derivations of a raising construction, a WH-question, and a reflexive pronoun construction. He says (p. 21 ms) that to maintain a strong version of the PSG explanation, 'it must be shown that there is a syntactic dependency between the reflexive and its antecedent . . . and not one between the raising structure and its a-controller' (= the matrix subject). In fact, as Barss correctly points out, all three constructions involve the matching of syntactic features between mother and daughter nodes, along a tree path extending from one member of the syntactic dependency to the other. However, this can hardly be hailed as a significant similarity between these constructions, since *all* constructions involve featural dependencies in PSG. The principles that determine these feature paths are very general, in fact universal. From the fact that these principles of PSG apply to all types of constructions, it obviously doesn't follow that PSG analyses all constructions identically. This would be just as absurd as arguing that GB fails to distinguish between different constructions because their derivations all involve principles and para-meters. GB just *is* a system of principles and parameters. The principles are various: they concern government, case, theta assignment, etc. A judgement as to whether the theory treats two constructions alike must presumably be based on *which* principles are invoked by their respective derivations. Similarly, PSG just *is* a system of rule schemata and principles, which determine the distribution of features in trees, and thereby the distribution of words and phrases. Here too, if we want to know which constructions are classed as similar by theory, we must ask *which* features and *which* principles are involved in their derivations. As we will show here, GSPG draws some interesting distinctions between constructions.

The question to be addressed, then, is whether PSG draws a *natural* distinction between the two classes of constructions that behave differently in the cross-modal antecedent reactivation experiments, i.e., between WH-extraction and pronoun anaphor binding, on one hand, and passive, raising and control on the other. At one point in his paper, Barss allows that there *is* a natural division between these construction types, based on the kind of feature that is used to characterise them. In GPSG, WH-extraction and anaphor binding involve foot features, but passive, raising and control do not.[2] Barss dubs this foot feature distinction a 'weak' PSG explanation of the data, by contrast with an explanation that would treat the constructions differently with respect to more than their feature types; but as we've seen, the latter is a chimera.[3] Thus if the foot feature hypothesis fits the facts neatly, it would seem to provide exactly the kind of account that Fodor had in mind: an independently motivated linguistic division of cases, which correlates with the psycholinguistic results.

In fact, the foot feature distinction appears *not* to be descriptively correct; as Barss points out, it fails to group pronouns with anaphors and WH-trace, though these are similar with respect to on-line antecedent activation. (Foot features are also not what is common to anaphors and WH-trace in more recent versions of PSG; see Pollard & Sag 1992; 1993). But this poses no problem for Fodor's PSG account of the experimental findings, as that account was not based on the distinction between foot and non-foot features at all. It was based on an even more fundamental property, which does distinguish WH-extraction and pronoun/anaphor constructions from raising, passive and control constructions, in all past and current versions of PSG that we know of.[4] This is simply whether the construction contains a syntactic constituent that is coindexed with an antecedent.[5]

---

[2] We have constructed here the generalisation that Barss presumably has in mind. His own exposition confuses matters by sometimes calling foot features 'non-head' features, and referring to SLASH as a non-head feature. It is in fact a central aspect of GPSG theory that SLASH is doubly classified as both a foot feature and a head feature.

[3] To add to the confusion, the version that Barss dubs 'strong' is *not* the one that says the difference must be existence *vs* non-existence of a featural dependency, but one that says the difference is existence *vs* non-existence of a *featural dependency 'on an NP'* (i.e. such that NP is the catgory of the antecedent). And he later says that what little experimental evidence we have on this matter suggests that WH-extracted PPs show antecedent reactivation, just as WH-extracted NPs do; so the 'strong' explanation would be explaining something that doesn't occur. We will ignore this 'dependency on an NP' idea, since it is not clear where it comes from, or why it is any 'stronger' than the 'dependency of foot features' idea. For the same reason we also ignore yet another alternative account that Barss contemplates (but rejects as non-transparent), which involves dependencies where both the antecedent and the dependent item are of category NP.

[4] But see the traceless analysis considered in the final chapter of Pollard and Sag 1993, which is not obviously compatible with the conclusions we draw here.

[5] It should be noted that Barss' paper repeatedly misreports Fodor's proposal. Fodor proposes (FN 7, p. 51) that 'what elicits the interpretive processes that feed [cross-modal] priming [of a target word by a reactivated antecedent phrase] is all and only constituents that exist at the syntactic level', and similarly (p. 13) 'that cross-modal priming [of target by antecedent] occurs only for elements present in syntactic structure' (continuing: 'and that NP-trace is not among them'). By contrast, Barss (p. 21) paraphrases 'Fodor's basic analysis of

Pronouns and anaphors are referentially dependent constituents.[6] So is WH-trace, which PSG and GB agree in positing for long-distance filler-gap constructions. WH-trace is lacking in inherent content and needs to be bound by an antecedent, just as a lexical anaphor needs to be bound by an antecedent. The NP-trace and PRO (when not *arb*) posited by GB are also referentially dependent constituents, whose interpretation depends on association with an antecedent. Note that this notion of interpretive dependence on an antecedent is not something we have imported *post hoc* in an attempt to make sense of embarrassing data; it is embedded in the very logic of the psycholinguistic experiments that have been conducted. From the earliest studies (MacDonald, 1989; McElree & Bever, 1989; Bever & McElree, 1988; Nicol, 1988), the experimental paradigms have been designed to find out whether empty categories *reactivate their antecedents* during sentence processing, as overt constituents that have antecedents have been shown to do. Though some more subtle interpretation no doubt could be imposed on these experiments, taken at their face value they are about the antecedence relation.

Linguistic theories give rise to predictions about outcomes of these experiments if the assumption is made that any element which *has* an antecedent will *reactivate* that antecedent in on-line processing. Then (other things being equal) GB clearly predicts that the hypothesised constituents NP-trace and PRO, as well as WH-trace and overt pronouns/anaphors, will exhibit on-line antecedent reactivation effects. PSG predicts that there will be a reactivation effect for WH-trace as for overt pronouns/anaphors, but none for control, raising, and passive constructions, where no referentially dependent constituents are posited. On current showing at least, it is the PSG prediction that is best supported by the cross-modal priming results.

Of course it is possible to tell a more complicated story that reconciles the results with GB predictions. One could assume, as Barss does, that

---

the lexical priming effect' as the proposal that 'it arises only when there is a syntactic *dependency* between two constituents in the string' [our emphasis]. Later, (p. 23) he portrays it, in similar vein, as distinguishing between 'constructions involving an obligatory *syntactic referential* dependency' and 'constructions in which the referential dependency is only semantic, not syntactic'. These formulations are inaccurate; they muddy the distinction between (a) the nature of the entities that trigger reactivation of their antecedents (obviously: only entities with antecedents, and by Fodor's hypothesis, only syntactic constituents), and (b) the nature of the antecedence relationship. We contend that even with respect to (b) WH-dependencies cannot be assimilated to raising in PSG in the way Barss suggests, but in any case it is clear that the two construction types differ sharply in PSG with respect to (a).

[6] On deictic pronouns see footnote 8. Also, the relation of referential dependence intended here, which is commonly characterised in terms of coindexation or 'linking' (Higginbotham, 1983), must be defined so that it does not exclude the binding of pronouns by quantifiers or other operators. See Pollard and Sag (1993: Chapter 2) for discussion.

NP-trace and PRO fail to show clear cross-modal reactivation effects for some other reason, such as a greater difficulty in detecting them on-line. This is addressed by the Fodor, McKinnon, and Swinney study reported in Fodor's paper. To account for the results of that experiment, Barss then needs to make the further assumption that only one item at a time can activate its potential antecedents. But without resort to these or any other special performance-theoretic assumptions, simply on its most straight-forward construal as the information base for sentence processing, PSG predicts these findings exactly.

Or so we claim. But Barss argues to the contrary, as we have noted, on the basis of the patterns of feature matching that GPSG employed to capture syntactic dependencies. He observes that though the PSG analysis of a raising construction contains no empty *noun phrase* whose interpretation is dependent on that of the matrix subject, it does exhibit a featural dependency between the embedded *verb phrase* and the matrix subject.[7] This is not surprising. It is just a matter of fact that there is a dependency in raising constructions, and any theory of grammar must provide an adequate means for describing it. Consider (1), with the raising verb *tends*:

(1) Kim tends to shout.

Informally, the raising dependency takes the form of a requirement that the subject of the matrix clause must be a phrase that *would* be suitable as the subject of the subordinate VP, *if* that VP had an overt subject. In (1), this condition is met, but it wouldn't be if we replaced *Kim* by the expletive *there*, or replaced *to shout* with the VP *to be nothing to do on Sundays*, which needs an expletive subject. So a raising dependency exists in the language. The only question, then, is whether Barss can make the case that the means by which PSG captures this raising dependency is so like the PSG mechanisms for capturing long-distance filler-gap dependencies that it follows that they should behave alike in the cross-modal priming experiments.

In attempting to make such a case, Barss misconstrues the formal representation of agreement in GPSG in one small, but crucial aspect. He assumes that NPs and VPs bear formally comparable feature specifications for person, number, etc., and that GPSG principles require identity of such features between a subject and its agreeing VP. Thus Barss' reconstruction of

---

[7] The analysis Barss cites is the GPSG analysis from Gazdar et al. (1985); the details differ slightly but inessentially from those of the HPSG analysis that we will sketch here. GPSG's feature matching (i.e. *type* identity of feature structures at different nodes) has given way in HPSG to structure sharing (i.e. *token*-identity of feature structures associated with different nodes). This is illustrated later.

GPSG assumes categories such as NP[PLU–,PER 3] and VP[PLU–,PER3]. In fact the distinction drawn by Gazdar et al. (1985) is between, e.g. NP[PLU–, PER 3] and VP[AGR NP[PLU–, PER 3]]. That is, whereas a noun phrase has *inherent* person and number features, a verb phrase has an *agreement* feature in the real sense of the term, i.e. a category-valued feature (AGR) whose value reflects the properties of the noun phrase it agrees with. Barss overlooks this distinction between nominal and verbal encoding of agreement information, and thus perceives a (non-existent) formal similarity in GPSG between subject–verb agreement and antecedent-pronoun agreement. This misunderstanding seems to be at the heart of Barss' critique of Fodor's paper: he fails to distinguish between a VP, whose interpretation is incomplete in one way (in the absence of a subject) and a referentially dependent expression whose interpretation is incomplete in quite a different way (in requiring some other element—typically a coindexed antecedent phrase—to provide its reference). In PSG, VP complements have no PRO or NP-trace subjects, hence they have no constituents that enter into *anaphoric* relations. *Kim* in example (1) is not the antecedent of the verb phrase *to shout*. In GB, VP complements *are* treated in terms of phonetically unrealised referential elements (PRO and NP-trace). *Kim* in (1) *is* the antecedent of the empty subject of *to shout*.

To summarise so far: Barss notes that 'raising' in PSG consists of a dependency of subject–verb agreement, mediated by agreement features on intervening nodes. He assumes that this agreement dependency is formally just like the agreement dependency between a pronoun or anaphor and its antecedent NP, and concludes that raising constructions should therefore behave—according to PSG as well as to GB—just like overt pronoun/anaphor constructions in sentence processing studies. But this is wrong.

The distinction between an agreeing predicate and an agreeing pronoun/ anaphor is even more clearly drawn in HPSG (See Pollard & Sag, 1993, Chapter 2). Let us consider prenominal agreement first. A referential expression (typically an NP, but also other arguments such as 'case marking PPs) in HPSG has as part of its semantic content an *index*, which consists of feature specifications for number, gender, and person. This is illustrated in (2), which shows the feature specification appropriate for the pronoun *she*.

(2)   INDEX $\begin{bmatrix} \text{PER } 3rd \\ \text{NUM } sing \\ \text{GEND } fem \end{bmatrix}$

We abbreviate NPs so specified as in (3)a, b.

(3)a. NP[PER *3rd*, NUM *sing*, GEND *fem*]

  b. NP[*3rd, sing, fem*]

Note that the index here is not a number or numerical variable. Coindexation in HPSG consists of *token*-identity of two agreement feature structures. An occurrence of *she* and the NP that binds it are associated with one and the same agreement feature complex.

This theory of agreement entails immediately that two expressions that are coindexed must agree with respect to all index features, though not with respect to other features that are external to index, such as CASE. A proform such as a pronoun is an element that has no content other than its index. We assume that in a felicitous discourse, an index must somehow be grounded. This can be achieved by association with a linguistic antecedent (anaphora), with an entity in the speaker's environment (deixis), or else with an entity that has been evoked into the discourse model implicitly by the prior text (as proposed, for example, by Webber (1978)). It is natural to assume that this grounding of an index is what causes reactivation effects in sentence processing.[8]

Now consider verb agreement. In HPSG this also involves indices, but otherwise it is quite different from coindexation agreement (just as in GPSG). Indeed, the HPSG treatment ties verb agreement even more closely into the general phenomenon of argument selection by predicates. HPSG does not use the AGR feature of GPSG, but extends the SUBCAT feature to subjects as well as objects. A verb or other predicator bears a SUBCAT feature whose value is a list of the syntactic arguments it needs to form a complete (or *saturated*) clause. This is illustrated in (4), which shows the SUBCAT feature for an intransitive verb like *walks*:

(4) walks

  SUBCAT < NP [*nom*][*sing,3rd*]>

This represents that *walks* is subcategorised for a single element, of syntactic category NP, with nominative case, and content whose index is specified as [NUM *sing*] and [PER *3rd*]. A very general principle of HPSG theory (the Head Feature Principle) ensures that as a head is associated

---

[8] It is not known whether semantic activation occurs on-line in cases of deictic interpretation of a pronoun, though this seems plausible (e.g. priming of 'snow' at the position of a pronoun used to refer demonstratively to a skier who is present in the discourse situation, but not previously mentioned in the discourse). Activation of an antecedent in a prior sentence in discourse has been reported for pronouns in Spanish by Meltzer (1992), and for unexpressed subjects (PRO) in English control by Fodor, Garrett, and Swinney (unpublished MS).

in a tree with appropriate arguments, the specifications for those arguments are cancelled from the head daughter's SUBCAT value. This *Subcategorisation Principle* thus has much the same effect in HPSG as functional application in Categorial Grammar (from which it is derived). It is illustrated in (5).

(5)

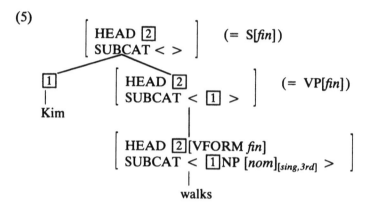

Here the boxed integers denote token identity of category-content complexes. Thus the highest node in (5) denotes a finite clause since it inherits the HEAD value of the verb, but has an empty SUBCAT list, indicating a saturated predicate. The feature identification between the subject and the category specified in the SUBCAT feature of the verb ensures that the subject has nominative case and a third singular index. The linguistic reasons for extending subcategorisation to encompass subject agreement in this way are documented in Pollard and Sag (1987; 1993). Though no part of its motivation, one consequence of this decision is that in HPSG, as in the GPSG analysis, the features of the verb are formally quite distinct from those of the NP it agrees with: nominals bear indices, verbs bear SUBCAT specifications for nominals with indices.

Now let us consider 'raising' and control. HPSG allows the embedding of an incomplete clause, e.g. an infinitival VP complement. Hence not all subjects on SUBCAT lists correspond to subject constituents in trees. The SUBCAT list for a control verb like *try*, for example, is as shown in (6), where the identity of boxed integers shows that two distinct NPs are required to be coindexed.

(6) *try*
SUBCAT <NP [3], VP[*inf*, SUBCAT <NP [3]>]>

The same rule schemata and universal principles that project phrases like (5) in HPSG also project structures like (7) from lexical heads whose SUBCAT list is (6).

(7)

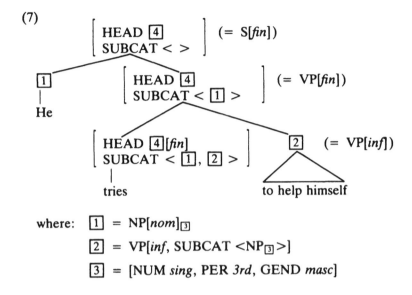

where: $\boxed{1}$ = NP[*nom*]$_{\boxed{3}}$

   $\boxed{2}$ = VP[*inf*, SUBCAT <NP$_{\boxed{3}}$>]

   $\boxed{3}$ = [NUM *sing*, PER *3rd*, GEND *masc*]

Here the complement VP's SUBCAT value corresponds to no nominal constituent in the tree. However, an element of that SUBCAT list is co-indexed with the expressed matrix subject *he*, and hence is interpretationally linked to it.

Let's now look inside the VP complement in (7). In (8) the infinitive VP is shown as a projection of the verb *help*, which has an unexpressed subject (specified only as a member of a SUBCAT list), and a reflexive anaphor object *himself* coindexed with it (obligatorily, by Principle A of the HPSG binding theory presented in Pollard & Sag 1992).[9]

(8)   (as in 7))

$$\left[\begin{array}{l} \text{HEAD } \boxed{5} \\ \text{SUBCAT} < \boxed{1} > \end{array} \right] \quad (= \text{VP}[\textit{inf}])$$

$$\left[\begin{array}{l} \text{HEAD } \boxed{5} \\ \text{SUBCAT} < \boxed{1}\text{NP }[\textit{nom}]_{\boxed{3}}, \boxed{6} > \end{array} \right] \qquad \boxed{6} \text{ NP}[\textit{acc}]_{\boxed{3}}$$

(to)   help   himself

where: $\boxed{3}$ = [NUM *sing*, PER *3rd*, GEND *masc*]

---

[9] For expository convenience, we are ignoring the treatment of the auxiliary element *to* in this discussion.

Between them, the various principles of HPSG theory induce patterns of covariance that look like long-distance agreement. The properties of the reflexive object in (7)/(8) affect the range of possible matrix subjects, because of a chain of index identities through the tree that are determined by Principle A, the Head Feature Principle, SUBCAT features in lexical entries, the Subcategorisation Principle, and so forth. Ungrammatical examples like (9) are thereby blocked:

(9)   *He tries to improve herself.

In this case the index of the reflexive pronoun *herself* must be [GEND *fem*] (specified by the lexicon), and yet it must also be identical to the index of the unexpressed subject of *help* (by Binding Principle A), which in turn is required (through a cascade of identities imposed by the Subcategorisation Principle) to be identical to the index of the subject *he*, which is [GEND *masc*] (from the lexicon). Since no index can be both [GEND *masc*] and [GEND *fem*], the example is determined to be ill-formed.

The treatment of raising in HPSG is similar to the treatment of control, except that in addition to index sharing, syntactic information (e.g. part of speech, case) is shared between the upstairs controller and the initial SUBCAT member of the downstairs verb as well. An example is shown in (10):

(10)

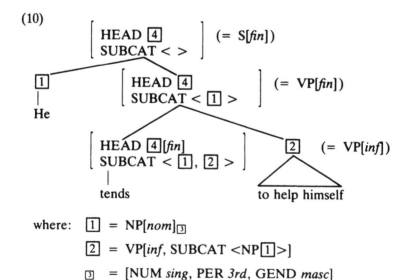

where: $\boxed{1}$ = NP[*nom*]$_{\boxed{3}}$

   $\boxed{2}$ = VP[*inf*, SUBCAT <NP$\boxed{1}$>]

   $\boxed{3}$ = [NUM *sing*, PER *3rd*, GEND *masc*]

Again we see the long-distance matching of indices, composed out of a series of local index agreement relations, each of which is required by a lexical entry or a general principle. But here, unlike in (7) the entire category-content complex (labelled $\boxed{1}$ in the SUBCAT list of the lower VP) is identified with that of the matrix subject.

The HPSG account of control and raising that we have sketched here differs in only inessential respects from the GPSG account that Barss addresses. And like the GPSG account, it clearly does distinguish what Barss says it fails to distinguish. A VP complement has the feature [SUBCAT < NP[. . .]>], with specifications of various properties of the NP. This feature of VPs is needed for many reasons other than control/raising constructions. But it makes control/raising constructions possible, since a matrix verb that selects for a VP complement can impose conditions of identity on members of the VP's SUBCAT list. For example, it can specify that the index of the initial (and only) member of that list is identical to the index of some other argument on the verb's SUBCAT list, resulting in obligatory control. Alternatively, it can specify that the entire first member of the VP complement's SUBCAT list is identical to another of the verb's arguments, resulting in raising. But in these cases the complement subject itself does not appear in the syntactic structure of the sentence. There is no overt constituent whose own index is identified with that of another constituent.[10] Thus a control/raising dependency is unlike a pronoun binding (or WH-trace binding) dependency. And there is no reason to suppose that the same things happen inside the sentence processing mechanism when it encounters a VP[SUBCAT <NP$_{[sing, \; 3rd, masc]}$>] as when it encounters an NP $_{[sing, 3rd, masc]}$. Some experimental paradigms might show similar responses to pronouns and unexpressed subjects. But it is no surprise for PSG in general, or HPSG in particular, that there should be experimental paradigms that show a difference between them.

It is important in psycholinguistics to consider very carefully the relation between linguistic representations and processing phenomena, predicted or observed; we agree with Barss on this. But his particular comments on the nature of this relationship in current phrase structure theories leave untouched the contention of Fodor's original paper: modern PSG, whose inventory of empty categories (phonetically unexpressed syntactic constituents) is more restricted than that of GB, makes transparent predictions about similarities and differences in the interpretation of different types of 'missing' arguments in natural language sentences, and these predictions—as of this writing—are remarkably consistent with the experimental findings.

---

[10] Except irrelevantly, of course, if the construction happens *also* to contain a pronoun or anaphor, like the *himself* in (8).

REFERENCES

Barss, A. (this volume). *Transparency and visibility: Sentence processing and the grammar of anaphora.*

Bever, T.G., & McElree, B. (1988). Empty Categories Access Their Antecedents During Comprehension. *Linguistic Inquiry, 19,* 35–43.

Fodor, J.D. (this volume). *Processing empty categories: A question of visibility.*

Fodor, J.A., Garrett, M.F., & Swinney, D.A. *A modular effect in parsing.* Unpublished MS, CUNY & University of Arizona.

Gazdar, G., Klein, E., Pullum, G.K., & Sag, I.A. (1985). *Generalized Phrase Structure Grammar.* Cambridge, MA & Oxford, UK: Harvard University Press & Basil Blackwell.

Higginbotham, J. (1983) Logical Form, Binding, and Nominals. *Linguistic Inquiry, 14,* 395–420.

Klein, E., & Sag, I.A. (1985). Type-driven Translation. *Linguistics and Philosophy, 8,* 163–201.

MacDonald, M.C. (1989). Priming Effects From Gaps to Antecedents. *Language and Cognitive Processes, 4,* 1–72.

McElree, B., & Bever, T.G. (1989). The Psychological Reality of Linguistically Defined gaps. *Journal of Psycholinguistic Research, 18,* 261–303.

Meltzer, S. (1992). *Antecedent activation by empty pronominals in Spanish.* Paper presented at the International Conference on Spoken Language Processing, Banff, Alberta, Canada.

Nicol, J. (1988). *Coreference Processing During Sentence Comprehension.* Doctoral dissertation, MIT, Cambridge, MA.

Pollard, C., & Sag, I.A. (1987). *Information-based syntax and semantics; Volume One—Fundamentals.* CSLI Lecture Notes Series No. 13, Stanford: CSLI, distributed by University of Chicago Press.

Pollard, C., & Sag, I.A. (1993). *Head-driven phrase structure grammar.* Chicago & Stanford: University of Chicago Press & CSLI Publications.

Pollard, C., & Sag, I.A. (1992). Anaphors in English and the Scope of Binding Theory. *Linguistic Inquiry, 23,* 261–303.

Sag, I.A., & Pollard, C. (1991). An Integrated Theory of Complement Control. *Language, 67.1,* 63–113.

Webber, B.L. (1978). *A formal approach to discourse anaphora.* Doctoral dissertation, Harvard University. [published by Garland Publishers, NY, 1979].

VI Processing Written Words

19 Form-Priming and Temporal Integration in Word Recognition

Kenneth Forster
University of Arizona, USA

INTRODUCTION

The analysis of form-priming in word recognition aims to determine the extent to which the processing of one linguistic expression can *condition* or *prime* the processing of a subsequent linguistic expression, purely by virtue of similarity of *form*. The hope is that by studying the conditions under which form similarity controls priming, we will uncover some of the operating characteristics of the form-based recognition system. In general terms, we try to interpret priming as some kind of residual effect left over from the processing of the prime, that the processing of the target word can either take advantage of, or be disrupted by.

Two general principles guide the design of our priming experiments. First, there is a very close temporal proximity of the two stimuli. This allows us to pick up highly *transient* effects that may otherwise dissipate during the interval betwen the prime and the target. Second, we try to eliminate the possibility that the observed priming effects are the products of a conscious, retrospective appreciation of the relationship between the prime and the target. The simple fact that the items are perceived to be related in some way may totally change the way in which subjects respond to the target stimulus, without there being any effect at all on the *perceptual* processing of the target.

The experiments to be discussed in this chapter all deal with visually presented forms, and exploit visual masking effects. The central feature of these procedures is that the temporal interval between the onset of the priming stimulus and the subsequent target stimulus is very brief (50–60ms). In addition, subjects have no, or very little, direct conscious awareness of the prime. When forced, they can make slightly better-than-chance judgements about whether the prime contains the same sequence of letters as the subsequently presented target stimulus, but they are completely unable to judge whether the prime was a word or a nonword (e.g. Forster & Davis, 1984). Our assumption is that the priming stimulus is in fact perceptually processed, but because of the interrupting effect of the target stimulus, the properties of the prime are never encoded into episodic memory, and hence the subject is unable subsequently to report its identity. This means, of course, that the subject's response to the target word is unlikely to be influenced by strategic processes that rely on conscious awareness of the relationship between the prime and the target.

A BRIEF REVIEW OF FORM-PRIMING EFFECTS

Interest in the question of form-priming dates from the work of Meyer, Schvaneveldt, and Ruddy (1974). Using visual presentation, they manipulated the orthographic and phonological similarity of the prime and the target independently. Essentially, they found a weak facilitatory effect of orthographic similarity only when the prime and target were also similar phonologically (e.g. *bribe–TRIBE*).[1] When the prime and target were phonologically dissimilar (e.g. *couch–TOUCH*), an inhibitory effect was obtained. Meyer et al. interpreted this latter result in terms of a bias to encode the second word phonologically so that it rhymed with the first. Subsequent work by Hillinger (1980) suggested that orthographic similarity played little or no role in either of these effects. Hillinger found that the same pattern of results was obtained when the prime was presented auditorily rather than visually, and also that facilitation could be obtained for rhyming pairs with little orthographic overlap (e.g. *prune–MOON*).

These results can be interpreted if we assume that the critical factor for form-priming is overlap in terms of phonological representations rather than orthographic representations. However, subsequent attempts to reproduce facilitatory form-priming effects with print have been largely unsuccessful (Bradley, Savage, & Yelland, 1983; Martin & Jensen, 1988). This state of affairs is quite puzzling, given the flood of positive effects for a far more

---

[1] Throughout this paper, primes will be printed in lower case letters, and targets in upper case letters.

indirect form of priming, namely semantic or associative priming. If activation apparently spreads so readily from one word unit to another along associative links, surely it should do so for form-related words?

One possible reason why it has been difficult to obtain consistent form-priming effects is suggested by the work of Colombo (1986). She observed that the overall result is really a mixture of facilitatory and inhibitory effects. Colombo found an inhibitory effect of form-related primes on visual lexical decision times for high-frequency words, and a facilitatory effect for low-frequency words. The interpretation offered by Colombo was framed in terms of an adaptation of the interactive activation model (McClelland & Rumelhart, 1986), in which competitive processes play a critical role. The idea here is that the prime acts as a competitor for the target word, and the more similar the prime is to the target, the more vigorous is the competition, and the longer it takes for the activation of the target word to overcome the activation in the word-unit for the prime. The major difficulty for this explanation, however, is that high-frequency words produce a more vigorous response than low-frequency words, and hence should be better able to resist any inhibitory effects of the prime.

The picture changes dramatically, however, when a *masked* priming paradigm is used. In this case, the prime is preceded by a masking stimulus, and the time interval between the onset of the prime and the target is extremely short, so short that subjects are largely unaware of the prime's existence. Under these conditions, strong *facilitatory* effects of a form-related prime are readily obtained. Evett and Humphreys (1981) were the first to examine form-priming effects with extremely short prime-target interval. Both the prime and target were presented tachistoscopically, one in lower case, the other in upper case, and these stimuli were temporally flanked by masking stimuli, the subject's task being to report the target word. The sequence of stimuli in a typical item might then look like this:

mask	# # # #
prime	f i l e
target	T I LE
mask	# # # #

The durations of the stimuli were adjusted so that the subject was unaware that two words were presented. Under these conditions, strong facilitatory effects of orthographic similarity were obtained. That is, subjects could identify the target word *TILE* more accurately when it was preceded by a related prime such as *file*, compared to a baseline control condition in which the prime was unrelated to the target, e.g. *door*.

Very similar effects have been obtained with the lexical decision task (Forster & Davis, 1984; Forster, Davis, Schoknecht, & Carter, 1987). This paradigm differs from the Evett-Humphreys paradigm in that the target stimulus is presented in clear view, whereas the prime is masked. The experimental paradigm is illustrated as follows:

mask	# # # # # #	500ms
prime	m a t u r e	60ms
target	N A T U R E	500ms

The subject's task is to classify the target as a word or not as rapidly as possible. The prime is always in lower-case letters, and the target is always in upper-case letters. Because the prime is presented briefly, and is masked by a combinaton of forward and backward masking (the latter coming from the target), the prime itself is usually unavailable for report. Subjects can, however, do slightly better than chance when asked to guess whether the prime was the same as the target, but are quite unable to guess whether it was a word or not (Forster & Davis, 1984).

The extent of priming is measured by comparing performance in the primed condition with a baseline condition in which the prime is orthographically unrelated to the target (e.g. *system–NATURE*). The strongest priming effects are found when the prime contains exactly the same letters as the target, i.e. repetition, or identity priming (e.g. *nature-NATURE*). Initially, it was believed that this was the only type of priming effect that could be obtained, since Forster and Davis (1984) found that once any letter was changed, the effect was the same as if all letters were changed. However, it was subsequently shown that this was true only for short words (four to five letters in length). With longer words, very strong priming effects were obtained with non-identical primes (e.g. *salior–SAILOR, mature–NATURE*). Finally, none of these effects appear to occur reliably for nonword targets (e.g. *matune–MAZUNE*), suggesting that the priming effect depends crucially on the existence of a lexical representation.

The obvious question to ask is why it should be so much easier to demonstrate positive form-priming effects with masked primes than with unmasked primes. That this is indeed the case seems beyond dispute, since Humphreys, Evett, Quinlan, and Besner (1987) demonstrated that if the SOA was increased so that subjects became aware of the prime, then no form-priming effects were obtained, although clear repetition priming was obtained. That is, the identification of the target word *TILE* was enhanced by a prior presentation of *tile* regardless of SOA, but for a prior presentation of *file*, enhancement was produced only with the very short SOA. A similar result was also obtained by Veres (1986) for lexical decision using the Forster and Davis (1984) paradigm. Veres found that the facilitatory effect of a masked word prime with an SOA of 60ms was completely absent with an SOA of 500ms. In addition, Segui and Grainger (1990) showed that the pattern of priming observed by Colombo (1986) was completely reversed when masked primes with a short SOA were used.

These results all suggest that masking the prime completely changes the type of form-priming that can be observed. There are several possible reasons why this might be the case. First, it could be that the form-priming effect has two components with different time-courses, one facilitatory and the other inhibitory, the former being very short-lived. Neither component need be influenced by awareness of the prime. That is, it could be entirely coincidental that the short SOA necessary to detect the facilitatory effect also has the effect of making the prime apparently invisible. A second possibility is that the process of becoming aware of the identity of a word involves inhibiting alternative interpretations. So, perceiving the prime may inhibit perception of the target word when the two are closely related. However, masking the prime could have the effect of preventing this late inhibitory process from operating.

Still another alternative is that masking might prevent the prime from being perceived as a separate entity from the target, as suggested by Humphreys, Besner, and Quinlan (1988). This would mean that the information extracted from the prime is somehow integrated into the processing of the target, as if the masking had the effect of preventing a reset of the recognition system prior to the processing of the target.

Finally, it might be that the differences between the two procedures have little to do with perceptual processes, and more to do with the effect of the task conditions on the subject's decision processes. For example, one problem that seems particularly prevalent when the subject is aware of the prime, is that there is a strong tendency to make a same-different comparison between the prime and the target. Although the resulting 'same' or 'different' judgement is quite irrelevant to the task, it may still influence the selection of the correct lexical decision (e.g. a 'same' judgement may produce a bias in favour of a 'Yes' response). However, when the prime is masked, no such comparison process is initiated, and hence any biasing effect is eliminated.

LEXICAL AND PRE-LEXICAL EFFECTS

Most models assume that there are at least two separate mapping operations involved in word recognition. The first one maps perceptual features onto some kind of segmental representation (i.e. letters or phonemes), and the second maps the segmental representation onto a lexical representation. Clearly, it is important to establish whether form-priming effects occur during the first mapping operation (pre-lexical), or the second (lexical). Does form-priming occur during the setting up of the internal coding of the input, or does it occur during the activation of lexical representations? Or does it occur during both?

To show that form-priming is lexical, it must be established that purely lexical properties of the target play a role in determining the amount of form-priming. For the lexical decision paradigm, it has been observed in many different experiments that there are no reliable priming effects for nonword targets, which has been taken as evidence that the priming effects in this task are not pre-lexical (Forster & Davis, 1984; Forster et al., 1987). If the prime increased the efficiency of the feature-to-letter mapping, then it would be expected to improve performance for both words and nonwords alike. A possible weakness in this argument is the fact that a 'No' decision in the lexical decision task may be triggered by a deadline mechanism. That is, the subject responds 'No' when some internal clock indicates that a self-defined time limit has expired without a lexical representation being retrieved. Unfortunately, this mechanism for making decisions introduces a number of complications arising from uncertainty about when this time period begins. For example, if the clock is started as soon as the mapping from the perceptual features to graphemic representations has been completed (or when lexical activation commences), then we will be able to detect any pre-lexical priming effect for nonwords, since the sooner the first stage is completed, the sooner the clock is started, and the sooner the time limit expires. This is the logical place to start the clock, but subjects may not appreciate this fact, or may be unable to detect when one mapping operation ends and the other begins (assuming that it even makes sense to assume that such a moment exists). Instead, subjects may be forced to begin timing from the only reliable anchor point, namely stimulus onset. Since they are unaware of the prime's existence they cannot take it into account when deciding on a deadline, hence they must use the same deadline for primed and unprimed items alike. This means that any pre-lexical priming effects will go undetected for nonword targets.

Of course, this argument would predict that nonwords would never show priming effects, but there have been occasional reports of priming for nonwords (Masson, 1991; Sereno, 1991), which complicates the picture considerably. Until more is known about the circumstances under which these effects obtained, it would be unwise to treat the evidence from nonwords as anything but equivocal. Fortunately, there are other lines of evidence that can be brought to bear on the issue. For example, both associative and morphological relationships between the prime and the target appear to exert an influence on masked priming (Bradley, 1991; Forster et al., 1987; Grainger, Cole, & Segui, 1991). These effects could not be explained if it was assumed that the only interaction between the prime and the target was pre-lexical. In similar vein, it has recently been discovered (Forster & Yoshimura, 1992) that phonologically mediated priming effects exist in Japanese, despite the fact that the prime is in *Kanji* characters (an ideographic script), whereas the target is in *Kana* characters (a syllabic script). Although many scripts can be related at an abstract *orthographic* level (e.g. lower and upper case Roman letters, or Roman and Cyrillic letters), this is not the case with *Kanji* and *Kana*, which can only be related at a *lexical* level.

The next question is whether form-priming is the product of some kind of cross-activation, or 'spread of effect', as would be expected if the lexical mapping operation involved a network architecture. Or is it simply the case that form-priming reflects occasional misidentification of the prime, so that it is really a special case of repetition priming? What is needed to settle this question is a demonstration that a prime can be accurately processed, but still influence the processing of a form-related target. This is a difficult task, but there are several indirect sources of evidence that can be brought to bear. One is the fact that identity priming effects do not appear to be reduced for word targets that closely resemble other words, compared with words that have no near neighbours (Forster et al., 1987). Presumably, the probability of misreading a word would be higher if it had many neighbours, and this should reduce the strength of identity priming. A similar inference can be drawn from the fact that a word can be equally well primed by a form-related word (e.g. *deadline–HEADLINE*) as a form-related nonword (e.g. *feadline–HEADLINE*) (Forster, 1987). It seems reasonable to suppose that the probability of misreading a nonword must be higher than the probability of misreading a word, and hence a nonword prime should be more effective than a word prime. The absence of any difference suggests that the primes were accurately read. Additional support for this assumption comes from the fact that primes that are morphologically related to the target, but do not resemble them closely (e.g. *kept–KEEP*) can be as effective as identity primes (e.g. *keep–KEEP*) (Forster et al., 1987). This suggests that the primes must have been accurately identified as morphological variants of the target word, and this gives them special priming powers. The alternative is to assume that *kept* is always misread as *keep*, which seems most unlikely.

FORM-PRIMING WITH SPEECH STIMULI

The physical differences between auditory and visual signals have consequences for the type of form-priming experiments that can be carried
out in the auditory modality. Since a spoken prime must necessarily be
extended in time, it is obviously difficult to manage very short SOAs. Also,
it is more difficult to prevent awareness of the prime without severely
degrading the signal. These differences suggest that form-priming effects
obtained in the auditory modality might be radically different from those
obtained in the visual modality.

The evidence appears to be equivocal. The initial attempt by Slowiaczek
and Pisoni (1986) to reproduce Hillinger's form-priming effects using
auditory presentation of both prime and target was not particularly
encouraging. Primes and targets shared three, two, or one phoneme(s).
However, there were no differences in lexical decision times to the target
word as a function of phonological overlap, although there was a strong
identity priming effect. That is, responses to the target word *BLACK* were
facilitated by prior presentation of the same word, but were unaffected by
prior presentation of *bland*. Slowiaczek and Pisoni speculate that the
reason they were unable to replicate Hillinger's results was because they
used non-rhyming stimuli. If this is correct, it suggests that the earlier
priming results depended more on rhyme-detection than form overlap. An
alternative possibility suggested by Slowiaczek and Pisoni was that form-
priming effects may be very transitory, and may have dissipated during the
relatively long inter-stimulus interval of 500ms used in this experiment.
However, they report that reducing the ISI to 50ms did nothing to improve
matters.[2]

The most puzzling feature of these results was the presence of equally
strong identity (repetition) priming effects for both word and nonword
targets, indicating an apparent pre-lexical source for the priming. The most
obvious explanation for this result would be that sub-lexical phonological
detectors are mediating the priming effect, and hence priming can take
place for targets that have no lexical representation (in contrast to the
situation for visual presentation). However, if sub-lexical detector units
can be primed, why is there no effect of partial phonological overlap?

One possibility is that these effects are in part the product of some type
of speaker normalisation process, in which the listener estimates parameters
of the speaker's vocal tract during the prime, and uses this information to
assist in identifying the target. Thus there is an advantage when the same
speaker produces both stimuli, and perhaps there is also an *extra* advantage

---

[2] Note that although the ISI is short, the SOA is not, since the SOA equals the duration
of the prime plus the ISI of 50ms.

when the prime and target are exactly the same phonetic expression, whether it is a word or a nonword. However, when the target differs in any way from the prime, this advantage may be lost.

However, the results obtained by Gagnon and Sawusch (1989), and Gagnon (1990), are inconsistent with this proposal. Like Slowiaczek and Pisoni, these investigators found priming effects for both word and nonword targets, but found no effect of variation in voice on priming. That is, the same priming effects were obtained whether the same voice was used, or two different voices. Significantly, strong facilitatory effects of partial phonological overlap were found in these studies, which is more consistent with the notion that sub-lexical units are involved. Gagnon and Sawusch propose that these units are position-specific phoneme detectors. Slowiaczek, Nusbaum, and Pisoni (1987) also obtained strong facilitatory effects of partial phonological overlap in an experiment that exactly parallels that of Slowiaczek and Pisoni (1986) which, as we have seen, produced no form-priming at all.

The overall picture for speech stimuli is somewhat clouded, although the preliminary indications are that the effects of form similarity are unlikely to have any purely *lexical* source. This may tell us something quite critical about how speech stimuli are recognised, or it may simply indicate that the appropriate experimental conditions for isolating a lexical effect have not yet been discovered. Maybe, for example, quite different patterns will emerge when procedures that allow for much shorter SOAs are developed, or when conditions that suppress awareness of the priming stimulus are employed. However, for the moment, it appears that spoken words do not show lexically mediated form-priming effects, but printed words do. In the next section we discuss how this effect is modulated by the existence of neighbouring form-related words.

THE NEIGHBOURHOOD DENSITY CONSTRAINT ON FORM-PRIMING

Perhaps the most interesting hypothesis about form-priming with visual stimuli is the notion that it is restricted to certain regions of lexical 'space'. If, following M. Treisman (1978), we represent the words of a language as points in a multidimensional orthographic space, so that very similar words are close together, and dissimilar words are far apart, then we would see that the words are not evenly distributed throughout this space. In some areas, words are very tightly bunched together, so that any given word has many close neighbours, while in other regions, the population density is very low. The similarity metric that defines this space is the one chosen by Coltheart, Davelaar, Jonasson, and Besner (1977), in which the distance between words is equal to the number of letters that would need to be changed in order to convert the spelling of one into the other. Word-pairs that are only one letter apart are defined as neighbours. Generally, shorter words have many more neighbours than longer words, and hence short words tend to be located in high-density neighbourhoods.

The density of the neighbourhood appears to control the pattern of interaction between neighbours in form-priming experiments (Forster et al., 1987). For longer neighbours, such as *headline* and *deadline*, strong facilitatory effects are obtained in a masked priming experiment, but for shorter neighbours such as *head* and *dead*, there is no facilitatory effect at all. Short words typically have a large number of neighbours. For example, *head* and *dead* each share a number of common neighbours (*lead, read, bead, mead*), as well as having non-shared neighbours (e.g. *held, heap, heal*, and *deal, dear, deaf, dean*, respectively). However, *headline* does not have a corresponding set of neighbours, nor does *deadline*. This is generally true for longer words. The reason for describing this distinction as a neighbourhood density effect rather than a length effect is the fact that short words with very few neighbours such as *able* and *axle* do show quite strong form-priming effects (Forster et al., 1987).

These results suggest that the existence of other neighbours somehow counteracts the tendency for similar forms to be excited by the same stimulus. Within a network model that allows for competitive processes at the word level, one could imagine that there is a balance between the excitation produced by cross-activation and the inhibitory effect of each word on its neighbours. In high-density regions, the inhibitory effects of the neighbours exactly balance the excitatory effects of the prime, but in low-density regions, the inhibition is weaker, and therefore facilitatory effects are observed. Strong support for this inhibitory interpretation is provided by the fact that in high-density regions, neighbours can have inhibitory effects. Segui and Grainger (1990) obtained clear inhibitory effects of a masked neighbour prime with four-letter words, but only when the prime was higher in frequency than the target. This finding suggests that high frequency words tend to dominate low frequency words in the competition between rival candidates.

Segui and Grainger show that the interactive activation model of McClelland and Rumelhart (1981) can explain the inhibitory effect of a prime that is higher in frequency than the target. Work in our own laboratory confirms this result (Forster, Dupoux, & Haan, 1990). This research uses a model in which there are inhibitory as well as excitatory links from letter nodes to word nodes. These inhibitory links make it possible for the network to perform the lexical decision task adequately, since without them, nonwords that are neighours of words (e.g. *fead*) are always eventually identified as words. The inhibitory form-priming effect stems from competitive processes between word nodes. When the target occurs, the node for a competitor (i.e. the prime) is already active, and this activation will tend to inhibit activation in the target node. When this competitor is unrelated to the target (i.e. the baseline control condition), this activation is rapidly suppressed by the target input, and hence there is relatively little interference from the prime. But when the prime is related to the target, the input from the target word continues to activate the competitor, thus prolonging the competition.

However, there are a number of problems with this explanation that need to be resolved. One problem is that *facilitatory* effects of a form-related prime should be obtained only under very limited circumstances, namely, when the prime activates the target without simultaneously activating any competitor of the target. For example, the prime *attifude* would have a positive effect on the target word *ATTITUDE* because the prime closely resembles the target word, but does not closely resemble any other word that might compete with the target (such as *ALTITUDE*). However, positive priming effects could never be obtained if the prime was itself a word, since it would be a competitor for the target. Thus, we would not expect the prime *altitude* to facilitate processing of *ATTITUDE*, since the prime would inhibit the target. However, these predictions are not supported (Forster, 1987), since the positive effect of a related prime in a low-density region appears to be unaffected by the lexical status of the prime. That is, *antitude* and *altitude* are equally effective as primes for *ATTITUDE*.

Another problem for this type of model is the fact that facilitatory effects ought to be obtained even in a high-density region if we ensure that the prime activates the target without simultaneously activating one of its competitors. This can be achieved if the target word has one letter-position that fails to generate any neighbours. For example, neighbours can be generated for the target word *WISE* at all positions except the second. Thus the prime *wose* would facilitate this target, since the only words it activates other than the target (e.g. *rose*) are not neighbours of the target, and hence do not compete as effectively. However, no priming effects at all are obtained in this condition, nor is there any difference between this type of prime and one that does activate competitors of the target, such as *wike* (Forster et al., 1990).

The alternative to a competitive account is to propose that for each separate word, there is an associated tuning function that specifies the weights associated with each letter in the word. These weights are positive if the letter is present in the stimulus, negative if it is not. To account for the density constraint, it is necessary to arrange those weights so that for high-density targets, one mismatching letter will cancel the effects of the matching letters, but for low-density targets, a net positive effect remains. Such a tuning function could operate equally well in a parallel activation model (the weights being the strength of the connections between letter units and word units) or in a lexical search model, where the tuning function defines what counts as a close match between the stimulus and a lexical entry. The problem here is to avoid simply restating the empirical facts in a slightly different way. This circularity could be avoided if some learning principle could be found that explained how the existence of neighbours changes the tuning function.

THE GENERALITY OF THE DENSITY
CONSTRAINT ACROSS TASKS

Current indications suggest that the phenomena associated with the neighbourhood density constraint may well prove to be one of the most challenging set of findings in the field, and therefore worthy of very close examination. However, there is one problem that makes the study of these phenomena somewhat problematic. Clearly, if the density constraint reflects very basic properties of the lexical retrieval system, then there should be absolutely no question about its generality across tasks. Unfortunately, the currently available evidence suggests that nothing could be further from the truth. In fact, it looks very much as though the lexical decision task might be the *only* task so far considered that is subject to the density constraint. For example, Evett and Humphreys (1981) found quite strong form-priming effects for short words using the tachistoscopic paradigm in which both the prime and target are briefly presented. Since short words are mostly located in high-density regions, it seems quite likely that this task does not show any density effects. Furthermore, Humphreys et al. (1988) refer to an unpublished paper by Manso de Zuniga, Quinlan, and Humphreys (1988), which found clear form-priming effects for similar materials using the naming task rather than the lexical decision task. Similar results have also been obtained in our own laboratory (Davis, 1990; Veres, 1986). Hence, neither the identification task nor the naming task are subject to the density constraint.

This lack of consistency across tasks creates a serious problem. Given that the lexical decision task appears to be the odd man out, the simplest solution would be to dismiss the lexical decision results as some kind of artifact introduced by the decision process (as argued in Humphreys et al., 1990), and to ignore the density constraint altogether. However we believe that this is the wrong move. The most important reason for resisting this line of argument is that there is no obvious mechanism that would explain how form-similarity effects could be obscured by the decision processes involved in the lexical decision task. The complaint with the lexical decision task is usually that it seems to be *overly* sensitive to the existence of prime-target relationships, not that it is *insensitive*. Given the great potential theoretical interest of the density constraint, it therefore seems worthwhile to take a closer look at the form-priming effects observed with these tasks.

FORM-PRIMING IN THE NAMING TASK

Forster and Davis (1991) specifically examined form-priming effects with the naming task in both high-density and low-density neighbourhoods, and they confirmed the earlier results, obtaining much the same priming effects in both types of regions. That is, equally strong priming effects were found for high-density pairs (e.g. *gord–GOLD*) as for low-density pairs (e.g. *zuro–ZERO*). However, in the course of these experiments, a quite unexpected phenomenon came to light that suggests an entirely different interpretation. What was observed was that there were a large number of errors in which the subject first produced the onset of the *prime*, and then immediately recovered, producing the target word. For example, the pair *pair–FILL* might have been pronounced '*p-fill*'. Occasionally, subjects actually produced the entire prime instead of the target, and on other occasions, they produced a blend of the two. The suggested interpretation was that these errors were the result of competing response tendencies to pronounce both the prime *and* the target. This would hardly be remarkable if the prime and target were, say, simultaneously visible, but in this case it must be remembered that the subject is entirely unaware of the nature of the prime. So essentially, it appears that the duration of the prime was long enough to initiate a naming response, but not long enough to support awareness of the prime.

Of more direct relevance for the present argument was that this interference effect seemed to be absent when the prime and target shared the same *onset*. That is, when the prime began with the same speech sound as the target (*belly–BREAK*), fewer false starts were recorded, and faster response times were obtained, compared with a control condition where there was no phonemic overlap at all (*merry–BREAK*). This *onset effect*, could, of course, generate a spurious form-priming effect, since in the form-related condition, there is a relatively high probability that the prime will have the same onset as the target (on average, three primes out of four will begin with the same letter), whereas this can never be the case in the control condition, where an all-letters-different prime was used. Forster and Davis speculated that the form-priming effect for high-density words might in fact be an onset effect. They tested this hypothesis by repeating the experiment, this time making sure that matching onsets were no more frequent in the form-related condition than in the control condition. Under these conditions, there was no longer any form-priming effect for high-density words, although the effect for low-density words remained.

Independent support for this analysis of response competition is provided by the fact that Stroop interference also appears to be minimised when the competing words have the same onset. Dalrymple-Alford (1972) found that saying 'red' to the word WRECK printed in red was much faster than responding 'green' to the same word printed in green. Similar results have been reported by Posnansky and Rayner (1978) for the picture-word interference task, where the subject must name a picture that has an irrelevant word printed beneath it. If these begin with the same letter (e.g. a picture of a ball with the word *basket* printed beneath it), then naming responses to the picture were much faster than when the initial letters differed.

So, evidently the naming task is not an ideal task to use with masked priming, since the prime activates a response that competes with the response to the target word. When the amount of competition is equated across conditions, then the naming task shows the same pattern of results as the lexical decision task. Hence we can infer that both lexical decision and naming are sensitive to the density constraint on form-priming.

FORM-PRIMING IN THE IDENTIFICATION TASK

The other task that appears to be insensitive to the density constraint is the identification task used by Evett and Humphreys (1981). As we have seen, this task differs from the lexical decision task in that the target word is also shown very briefly and is itself masked by a subsequent stimulus—a necessary procedure in order to generate sufficient errors for data analysis. Using this task, Evett and Humphreys obtained strong form-priming effects with four- and five-letter words which were definitely located in high-density regions. In many cases, their primes differed from the target by *more* than one letter, so there seems to be no question that this task is highly sensitive to orthographic overlap between the prime and the target.

In order to verify that there is indeed a difference between the tasks, we carried out a form-priming experiment using both procedures on the same set of items.[3] The stimulus presentation conditions for each task were as shown in Table 19.1. The durations of the stimuli were chosen to make the two tasks as comparable as possible, and in neither case was the prime clearly discernible as a separate stimulus from the target.

The items for this experiment were 32 items taken from the original Evett and Humphreys experiment. Half of the targets were primed by an identity prime (e.g. *tile–TILE*), half were primed by a form-related prime

---

[3] This experiment was carried out as an undergraduate research project by Fiona McKenzie-Smith, Jane Steinkamp, and Lisa Henry at Monash University.

TABLE 19.1
Presentation Conditions

		Identification	Lexical Decision
Mask	60ms	# # # #	500ms # # # #
Prime	60ms	f i l e	60ms f i l e
Target	60ms	T I L E	500ms T I L E
Mask	60ms	# # # #	

Presentation conditions used for comparison of form-priming effects in the tachistoscopic identification task and the lexical decision task.

that differed by one letter from the target (e.g. *file–TILE*). Performance in each of these conditions was compared with a baseline control condition in which there was no overlap between the prime and the target. Subjects in the lexical decision task were told to decide as rapidly as possible whether the item in upper-case letters was a word or not, whereas subjects in the identification task were told to write down the upper-case letters in the presented sequence. A total of 32 subjects were tested on the lexical decision task, and 10 subjects were tested on the identification task. The results of the experiment are shown in Table 19.2.

The results confirm our suspicion that the two tasks behave quite differently with respect to neighbourhood density. Both tasks show strong and significant priming in the repetition condition, but in the form-related condition, the lexical decision task shows a very weak facilitation effect of 16ms relative to the baseline condition, whereas the identification task shows a strong 21.2% facilitation.[4] The priming effect in the lexical decision task is not significant ($minF' < 1$), but in the identification task it was, $minF'$ (1,21) = 9.45, $p < 0.01$.

TABLE 19.2
Lexical Decision Times and Accuracy of Identification

Condition	Example	Lexical decision RT	Accuracy
Repeated	desk–DESK	487	78.8
Control	foot–DESK	525	43.8
Form-related	file–TILE	558	47.5
Control	hump–TILE	574	26.3

Lexical decision times (msec) and Accuracy of identification (percent) as a function of type of prime (items taken from Evett & Humphreys, 1981).

---

[4] There is a marked discrepancy between the baseline conditions, with better performance in both tasks for the items in the repeated condition. This is apparently due to item sampling errors (the target words in the repeated condition were not the same as in the form-related condition, nor were they matched in any way).

So, once again we are faced with a problem. Is the density constraint itself an artifact of the lexical decision task, or is there some aspect of form-priming in the identification task that makes the density constraint irrelevant? This is the same problem that we faced with the naming task earlier, and we resolved that problem by arguing that the masked priming procedure introduces a special effect in the naming task, namely response competition. Can a similar argument be made for the identification task? In the remaining sections, we argue that this is in fact the case.

FORM-INTEGRATION IN THE IDENTIFICATION TASK

The idea that we will explore is that form-priming occurs when information about the form characteristics of the prime is integrated with form-information about the target. That is, the processing of the target stimulus takes place against background activity defined by the interrupted processing of the priming stimulus. The idea here is that, normally, there is a system reset between two successive words. However, with very brief SOAs, this reset may not occur, and hence the processing of the target is superimposed on, or integrated with, the processing of the prime. Depending on the characteristics of the stimulus presentation, this integration may take many different forms. For example, integration of the prime and target could theoretically occur at a purely visible level in terms of the *physical* form of the two stimuli. Or, it could be that integration occurs at the more abstract level of *orthographic* form, where letter information derived from the prime is merged with letter information derived from the target. Or the integration could occur at a still more abstract level of *lexical* form.

Integration at the level of lexical form occurs if the prime alters the state of the *lexical* representation of the target word, and this change in state persists until processing of the target stimulus is well underway. Forster and Davis (1984) adopt such a theory, assuming that the prime 'opens' the entry for the target in a manner analogous to the way in which a disk operating system opens files. On the other hand, Humphreys et al. (1988) suggests that priming occurs at a lower level. They suggest that the conditions of presentation make it impossible for the subject to discern that *two* visual objects were presented rather than one. The second stimulus follows so closely after the first that the representations of the two stimuli are merged, and in fact compete with each other for a common representation. Where there is orthographic overlap between the two stimuli, this competition is less disruptive, compared with a case in which there is no overlap at all. An important feature of this theory is that the two stimuli are merged at a relatively abstract orthographic level, since the primes and targets are always presented in a different case.

There is still a third level at which integration could occur, and that is at a visual level in which details of physical form are critical. Since the prime and target are both presented very briefly in the identification task, the conditions for visual integration are ideal (DiLollo, 1980). On this story, the physical form of the prime and target are fused together briefly. The identifiability of the target stimulus then depends on how easily the target letters can be discriminated against the background of the prime letters, along the lines suggested by Eriksen's (1966) temporal luminance summation hypothesis.

It might seem that this proposal is obviously inadequate to explain form-priming, since it implies that there must be a systematic visual relation between lower and upper case versions of the same letter. Thus, to explain why *file* is a better prime for *TILE* than is *desk*, we would need to propose that the fusion of *e* with *E* will look more like an *E* than will the fusion of *k* with *E*. However, strange as it may seem, there does appear to be some truth to this proposal, as inspection of Fig. 19.1. should reveal. On the left we have superimposed lower and upper case versions of the same word on each other, while on the right we have superimposed lower and upper case versions of totally different words. It should be evident that the upper-case words in the left column are easier to read than those in the right column.

Humphreys et al. (1987) argue against this kind of interpretation by showing that various measures of similarity of form do not correlate with the amount of priming. However, ratings of the similarity of two forms may be quite irrelevant to the legibility of those forms when fused together. It has been shown (Davis, 1990; Davis & Forster, in press) that it is possible to

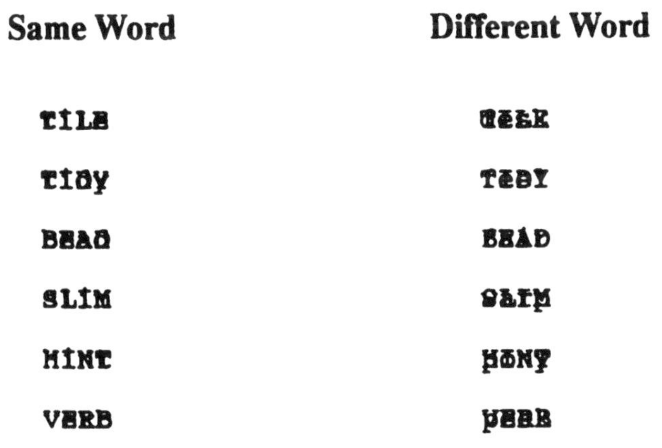

FIG. 19.1.   Legibility of superimposed lower- and upper-case versions of the same word, or of two completely different words.

create apparent priming effects in the identification task just by selecting primes that tend to obscure the target when fused with it. For example, the target *HATE* is better identified when preceded by the prime *bnff* than when it is preceded by the prime *xikk*, even though neither of these primes have any orthographic overlap with the target. At this point, it is worth noting that similar effects are not found in a lexical decision task using the same stimuli, presumably because the longer duration of the target in this task prevents fusion.

These results show that fusion effects need to be taken into account in the identification task, but they do not necessarily show that form-priming effects are *solely* the result of fusion. To investigate this issue, we need to take a different approach. The method we adopt here is to try to filter out the effects of fusion by comparing priming effects for *nonword* targets with those for words. If low-level fusion effects occur, then they should be present for nonword targets as well as word targets. Further, if fusion effects are solely responsible for priming, then it should be the case that the pair *fibe–TIBE* will show just as much priming as the pair *file–TILE*.

Our initial hypothesis then, is that the identification task shows the same lexical effects as the lexical decision task, but in addition is also sensitive to pre-lexical effects that are solely responsible for the form-priming observed with high-density words. The next experiment to be reported tested this hypothesis. The presentation conditions were as shown in Table 19.1 for the identification task. The target items were 48 four-letter words drawn from a high-density region, the average number of neighbours being 8.7. Also included were 48 four-letter nonword targets (e.g. *BENK, FLIB, TERP*). Each of these targets was presented in one of three priming conditions: (1) where it was preceded by an identical prime, i.e. repetition priming (e.g. *desk–DESK, benk–BENK*); (2) where it was preceded by a one-letter-different form-related prime (e.g. *delk–DESK, belk–BENK*); and (3) where it was preceded by a completely different word (e.g. *pain–DESK, type–BENK*). This last condition defined the baseline condition. In the form-related conditions, the primes were always nonwords. All primes were presented in lower-case letters, whereas the targets were in upper-case letters. Three different lists of items were prepared so that each target item appeared in each of the three priming conditions, but always in a different list. Six subjects were tested on each list, making a total of 18 subjects. The subjects were instructed to write down the upper-case letters only, and their responses were scored as correct only if they accurately reproduced all four letters in the correct sequence. The stimuli were presented in white letters on a black background using an IBM-style PC, with a Hercules monochrome graphics card displaying the standard IBM font. Each stimulus was centred in the screen and superimposed on the previous stimulus with no delay intervening.

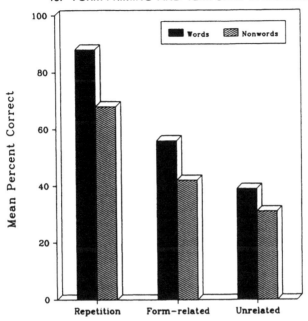

FIG. 19.2.   Identification accuracy for target words and nonwords as a function of type of prime.

Figure 19.2 shows the mean percentage of correctly reported targets as a function of the priming condition. The most striking feature of these results is that both word and nonword targets show very similar patterns of priming. In each case, the repetition priming condition produces the best performance, and there is a clear priming effect in the form-related condition as well, when compared with the baseline condition. The overall effect of priming was significant, $minF'$ $(2,67) = 35.80$, $p < 0.001$, and as might be expected, word targets were more accurately reported than nonword targets, $minF'$ $(1,51) = 12.76$, $p < 0.001$. However, there was no significant interaction between these main effects, $minF' < 1$.

The absence of any interaction between priming and lexical status suggests that the same priming effects occur for both words and nonwords. The most important effect for present purposes is the form-priming effect for nonword targets. This effect (11%) was significant by itself, $minF'$ $(1,45) = 4.56$, $p < 0.05$, and did not differ significantly from the corresponding effect for word targets (17%).

The existence of form-priming effects for nonword targets indicates that the identification task is markedly sensitive to pre-lexical effects. If we attempt to filter these pre-lexical effects out by subtracting the nonword effects from the word effects, we are left with a weak effect (6%), which is not significant. Hence it seems safe to conclude that the strong form-priming effects observed for words in this experiment are not lexical in nature. Surprisingly, much the same conclusion appears also to apply to the repetition priming effect, since there was no significant difference between the repetition effect for words (49%) and nonwords (37%). Either we conclude that the identification task does not produce any lexical effects at all (i.e. effects restricted to word targets), or we conclude that there is insufficient power in the experiment to distinguish between lexical and non-lexical effects.

Two follow-up experiments were conducted with the same materials in order to investigate further the nature of these non-lexical priming effects. The first of these experiments attempted to eliminate the possibility of *iconic* fusion of the prime and target by interpolating an energy mask between the two stimuli. If the priming effects observed in the first experiment were purely visual in nature, then an energy mask should at least reduce fusion, and hence reduce the priming effects for nonwords.

The energy mask used in this experiment consisted simply of a blank field four characters in width, presented in reverse video (white on black) for 60ms. All other conditions were exactly as in the previous experiment. The results for 30 subjects are shown in Fig. 19.3. Once again we find a very similar pattern for both word and nonword targets. The form-priming effect for nonwords (16.2%) is again significant, and is in fact slightly enhanced rather than reduced, compared with the previous experiment.

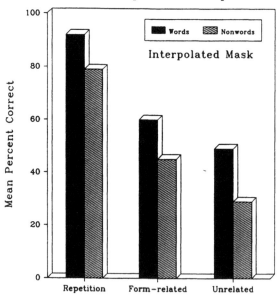

FIG. 19.3.   Identification accuracy for target words and nonwords when an energy mask is interpolated between the prime and the target.

It seems clear that an interpolated energy mask has no effect at all on the priming effects. This could mean that iconic fusion was not responsible for the original effect, or it could mean that the energy mask did not prevent fusion from occurring. Unfortunately, the latter possibility cannot be ruled out, since the experiment did not include any independent test of the effectiveness of the energy mask.

The second follow-up experiment attempted to rectify this problem by laterally displacing the prime relative to the target. This was done by inserting a non-alphabetic character ('=') at the beginning of the target (e.g. =TILE), and inserting a corresponding character at the end of the prime (e.g. file=). This produces a display in which the repeated letters no longer occupy the same spatial positions, as shown in Fig. 19.4(a). Since the two words are no longer aligned, there is no correlation at all between the letters occupying the same spatial positions, and the result is that fused displays are no longer any easier to read when the same word is fused with itself, as illustrated in Fig. 19.4(b). So, although fusion still occurs, it no longer favours one condition over another. The results for 36 subjects are shown in Fig. 19.5. As is readily apparent, this manipulation had very little impact, other than to lower overall performance. Both word and nonword targets still show strong form-priming effects.

This failure of misalignment to remove or modify the priming effects for nonword targets indicates fairly clearly that iconic fusion cannot possibly be the correct explanation, since iconic fusion is presumably defined in terms of retinal coordinates. This suggests that temporal integration must

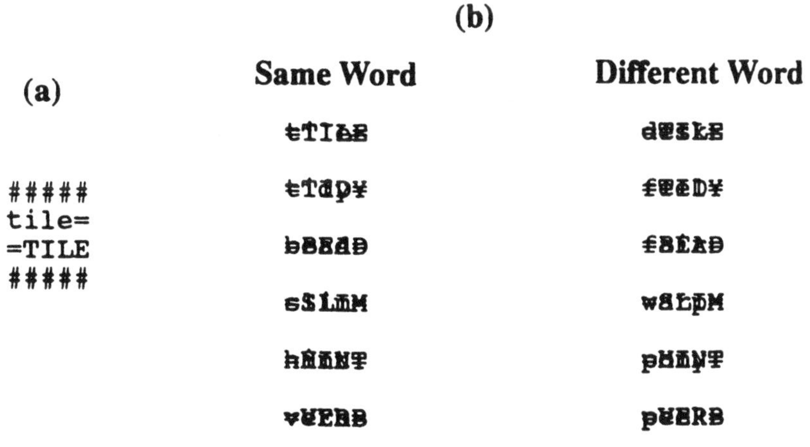

FIG. 19.4.   (a) Illustration of misalignment, and (b) legibility of fusion of prime and target when they are the same word, or different words.

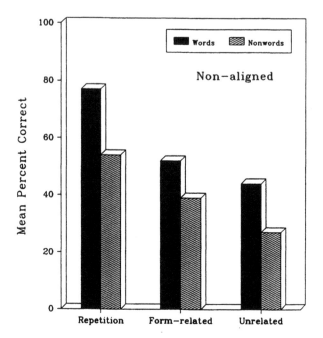

FIG. 19.5. Identification accuracy for target words and nonwords when the prime and target are misaligned by one character space.

occur at a higher level. Given that the displacement is defined in terms of character spaces, it seems that the lowest level at which this integration could occur would be at a level of letter *position*. That is, the coordinates used to specify the positions of the stimulus elements are *object-centred*. Thus, if the irrelevant character at the beginning of the target word is discarded (i.e. it is not taken as being the first character of the word), then the prime and target are essentially brought into alignment once again.

This theory proposes that temporal integration occurs over object-centred coordinates rather than spatial coordinates. Since this involves abstracting away from spatial location, one might want to question whether the two stimuli are integrated in terms of low-level visual properties, as proposed by Davis (1990), or whether they are amalgamated at a more abstract orthographic level, i.e. after letter identification has taken place. Essentially, we are dealing here with the problem of identifying a moving stimulus, and how information about such a stimulus is accumulated over time (and across different spatial positions of the object). Is it possible, for instance, that purely featural information can be accumulated while the object is moving, or must the segments of the object be identified first? One way to explore these notions would be to test whether the 'pseudopriming' observed by Davis (1990) occurs with misaligned stimuli.[5]

These issues are clearly of interest to a theory of the perception of motion, but go well beyond the scope of the present paper. Whatever the precise nature of the mechanism that is responsible for integration may be, it seems clear that the form-priming effects we have observed in the identification task are not lexical in nature, and therefore the existence of form-priming effects in a high-density region should not to be taken as a disproof of the generality of the lexical density constraint. Such a disproof requires the demonstration of form-priming for high-density word targets in the absence of any priming for comparable nonword targets.

As indicated earlier, it is not clear that the identification task shows any lexical involvement at all, even with identity priming. The best indicator of a lexical effect would be a much stronger repetition effect for words than nonwords. In the aligned experiment (Fig. 19.2), there was a trend in this direction (49% for words, 37% for nonwords), but this difference was not significant. Furthermore, in the energy mask experiment (Fig. 19.3), this difference disappeared altogether (32% for words, 33% for nonwords). These results are not encouraging for the view that the identification task taps both lexical and pre-lexical priming effects.

It appears then, that the analysis offered by Humphreys et al. (1990) is the correct view. Priming effects in the tachistoscopic identification task occur prior to lexical activation.[6] Hence it is hardly surprising that neighbourhood density is irrelevant, since this is, by definition, a lexical property. However, we now have to consider the question raised by Humphreys et al. (1990). If pre-lexical orthographic effects occur with very short SOAs, then why do these effects not appear with high-density words in the lexical decision task? Humphreys et al. (1990) suggest that the decision component of the lexical decision task is responsible, but do not offer any details. As we remarked earlier, it is hard to explain why the decision process would selectively filter out form-priming effects for high-density words only, and yet permit identity priming effects to be observed for the same words.

One way in which the tasks might differ is that satisfactory performance in the identification task can be obtained merely by attending to the letter

---

[5] Considerable care is required to design the appropriate experiment. In our initial attempts, misaligned pairs produced exactly the same results as aligned pairs. That is, *bnff* interfered with *HATE* whether it was aligned with it or not. However, this may just indicate that *b* interferes not only with *H*, but also with *A*, and with most other letters. What is needed is a prime that produces an illegible pattern when it is aligned with a particular target, but not when it is misaligned with it.

[6] It should be noted, however, that earlier work by Evett and Humphreys (1981) using this task showed semantic priming effects, which is not at all compatible with this view.

level, whereas lexical decision requires processing at higher levels. Orthographic effects do take place in both tasks, but are masked by lexical
processing, and are hence observable only in tasks that tap processing at
the orthographic level.

A more likely place to look for the answer, we feel, is in the differences
in stimulus presentation conditions, rather than the task requirements. The
tachistoscopic task involves two briefly presented stimuli, whereas the
lexical decision version involves only one brief stimulus. The SOAs in the
two tasks are quite similar, but the durations of the targets are not. The
relevance of this feature is simply that visual integration effects are far
more likely to occur when both stimuli are presented briefly (DiLollo,
1980). If either the first or the second stimulus is presented for a longer
duration, integration effects tend to disappear. Thus, in a lexical decision
task with a long exposure time target, there is no visual integration
between the prime and the target, and therefore the only way that form
overlap can produce priming is via the lexical activation system. By
hypothesis, this type of priming is influenced by lexical density, and hence
form-priming is only observed in low-density regions.

Further support for this analysis is provided by the observation of
Humphreys et al. (1988) that in the tachistoscopic task, there is no
orthographic priming if the *prime* is presented for a longer duration. This
would also be attributed to the absence of visual integration effects. Thus,
the presence or absence of orthographic priming appears to be controlled
by stimulus duration, not the type of task. This point could be made more
dramatically by running a further experiment using the same briefly
presented stimuli, but using lexical decision rather than identification as
the response measure. Assuming that the error rate is low enough to get
reasonable RT measures, we would expect to find orthographic priming,
despite the change in task. (Note: Such an experiment has in fact been
carried out by Davis & Forster (in press), with the expected result).

Finally, it should be noted that there is an interesting correspondence
between the form-priming effects observed with speech stimuli and the results
obtained with the tachistoscopic task. In the speech case, strong priming
effects are also observed for nonword targets, even when lexical decision is
used (Gagnon, 1990). It is interesting to speculate whether this implies that
there are no purely lexical form-priming effects in the speech modality.

INTEGRATION EFFECTS IN OTHER TASKS

Our general view is that form-priming can reflect integration of processing
at any one of a number of levels. The identification task seems to reflect
low-level integration, although we cannot yet say how low. Lower-level
integration effects of the sort we have been discussing here might also

occur in a new priming paradigm called *summation* priming (Forster, 1989b). This procedure resembles the lexical decision priming paradigm, except that *three* primes are presented in rapid succession (20ms per prime) rather than just one. The target word is nine letters in length (e.g. *SALVATION*), and each prime differs from the target word by three letters (e.g. *palratuon, sarvadiot,* and *sulvotiun*). Such a large difference would normally have made each prime quite ineffective in its own right. However, the combination of all three is extremely powerful, producing an effect that is equivalent to a 60ms presentation of a target neighbour as a prime (e.g. *salvotion*). The experimental conditions are illustrated in Table 19.3. The theoretical interest in this phenomenon stems from the fact that at first glance this priming appears to be produced by a non-linear summation over the separate effects of the individual primes.

However, the crucial property of the prime sequence appears to be that at each letter position, the correct letter is presented twice, but an incorrect letter is presented only once. Thus, if it were possible to integrate temporally across the three primes, the correct letter at each position would have a stronger representation than the incorrect letter, and hence it should be possible to simply read off the correct sequence of letters by taking only the most strongly represented letter. As might be expected from this analysis, this procedure is highly sensitive to display parameters such as alignment, size of display, and visual overlap, all of which suggests some kind of visual integration. So it may not be the case that there is a non-linear summation of three separate lexical activations, but rather there is an amalgamation of the three primes to form a new, and more effective priming stimulus.

As would be expected from a visual integration model, misalignment of these primes relative to each other completely eliminates the summation priming effect, in contrast to the misalignment experiment reported earlier in this paper. However, this holds only when the primes are presented for 20ms. When the duration of each prime is increased to 40ms, the summation effect returns. What this suggests is that integration across

TABLE 19.3
Experimental Conditions used in the Summation
Priming Paradigm

Mask	500ms	#	#	#	#	#	#	#	#	#
Prime	60ms	p	a	l	r	a	t	u	o	n
Prime	60ms	s	a	r	v	a	d	i	o	t
Prime	60ms	s	u	l	v	o	t	i	u	n
Target	500ms	S	A	L	V	A	T	I	O	N

Each prime differs by three letters from the target, but no
two primes differ at the same positions

different spatial locations can only occur at presentation rates as slow as 40ms per stimulus, which might explain why misalignment had no effect in the experiment reported here, since the presentation rate used was slower still (60ms per stimulus). This in turn suggests that it takes at least 40ms to develop a representation of the stimulus coded in terms of letter-positions rather than absolute spatial locations.

LETTER-POSITION CHANNELS

The evidence presented in this paper is compatible with the notion that activation can persist in a position-specific letter code. Thus, if the prime is the word *coffee*, then activation occurs in the 'F/3' channel, so that a benefit accrues to any target word or nonword that also contains *F* in the same position, regardless of spatial or retinal location. So, after the target moves to a new spatial location, the coordinates of each letter position must be redefined, much as if there were a movable grid that specified letter positions. If the task allows the subject to read off the information in the letter channels (as the identification task may well do), then we would expect a benefit to occur in the recognition of the target, no matter how small the overlap. This is in fact what the evidence reported by Humphreys et al. (1990) strongly suggests.

The question now arises of how this position-specific code is to be implemented in a word recognition model. In early network models such as the interactive activation model (McClelland & Rumelhart, 1981), it is assumed that there are multiple banks of letter-detectors, one bank for each letter-position. Thus the letter *A* in first position is assumed to be detected by a different processing unit to *A* in second position. Although this accounts nicely for graphemic priming effects, it is not a particularly appealing proposal, as becomes clear when we ask how many such letter-position channels are required. Four channels will obviously suffice for four-letter words, but what about five-letter words? If we go to five channels, what do we do about six-letter words? Given the amount of circuitry required to add another channel, it seems that there ought to be a fixed limit to the number of channels. Just because a person learns to recognise the word *antifloccinaucinihilipilificationistically* (the longest English word), we shouldn't have to postulate a 42-channel system to account for that ability.

On way around this problem is to postulate that a long word must be broken up into parts before it can be recognised. This allows us to adopt a small number of letter-position channels, but at a price, since we must now give an account of how the input is 'parsed', and how the constituents are eventually reassembled to form an intact word. A similar method is to use context-sensitive coding, in which relative position rather than absolute position is coded (Mozer, 1987). This is the solution adopted by Humphreys et al. (1990). What they suggest is that orthographic priming effects are mediated by sublexical units that correspond to letter clusters. Thus instead of producing activation in the *F/3* channel, the prime *coffee* might produce activation in an (*OFF*) unit, as well as a (*COF*) unit, a (*FFE*) unit, etc. This will assign unique codings to each word just so long as no word contains repeated clusters. Note that this code would eliminate the problem of redefining spatial location in the case of a moving stimulus. The *OFF* unit will continue to be excited no matter where the word *coffee* appears.

It should perhaps be pointed out that the problem of how to code letter position is by no means confined to network models. The same issues arise whether an input letter string is compared with all words in parallel, or serially, as in lexical search models (e.g. Forster, 1989a). What is perhaps more relevant to the parallel/serial debate is whether the comparison is supposed to occur across all letter positions simultaneously, or whether some serial component to the comparison is permitted (e.g. comparing the first syllables before considering the second syllables).

CONCLUSION

The major concern in this paper has been the generality of the neighbour-hood density constraint across different tasks. The data reported by Evett and Humphreys (1981) for the identification task clearly violate this constraint, in that strong form-priming is obtained in a high-density region of the lexicon. The experiments reported here have demonstrated that precisely the same form-priming effects can be found for nonword targets, suggesting that the priming effects are not lexical in nature. This means that the density constraint is not violated, since this constraint can only apply to lexically mediated form-priming.

The similarity of both form-priming and repetition priming for word and nonword targets raises the further question of whether the identification task shows any purely lexical effects at all. As suggested by Humphreys et al. (1988), it could be that this task reveals purely *orthographic* priming effects, in which the visual representations of the prime and target the compete with each other for an orthographic representation, prior to lexical access. If this is indeed the case, then there would be no reason to expect the results to conform to the density constraint.

The secondary concern of this paper is to raise the issue of how this pre-lexical priming effect might occur. Some version of temporal integration must be correct, but it is not clear what kinds of representations get integrated. We have examined the possibility that integration occurs at a purely visual level, and the fact that integration occurs despite an intervening energy mask, and despite spatial misalignment, and argues strongly against such an interpretation. The most likely hypothesis is that integration occurs over something like letter-position channels, which are independent of absolute spatial location.

REFERENCES

Bradley, D.C. (1991). *Masked priming studies of episodic and lexical representation.* Paper presented at the 32nd Annual Meeting of The Psychonomic Society, San Francisco.

Bradley, D.C., Savage, G.R., & Yelland, G.W. (1983). *Form-priming or not?* Paper delivered at the Fourth Language and Speech Conference, Monash University, Melbourne, Australia.

Colombo, L. (1986). Activation and inhibition with orthographically similar words. *Journal of Experimental Psychology: Human Perception and Performance, 12*, 226–234.

Coltheart, M., Davelaar, E., Jonasson, J.T., & Besner, D. (1977). Access to the internal lexicon. In S. Dornic (Ed.), *Attention and performance VI.* London: Academic Press.

Dalrymple-Alford, E.C. (1972). Sound similarity and color-word interference in the Stroop task. *Psychonomic Science, 28*, 209–210.

Davis, C. (1990). *Masked priming effects in speeded classification tasks.* Unpublished doctoral dissertation, Department of Psychology, Monash University, Melbourne, Australia.

Davis, C., & Forster, K.I. (in press). Masked orthographic priming: The effect of prime-target legibility. *Quarterly Journal of Experimental Psychology.*

DiLollo, V. (1980). Temporal integration in visual memory. *Journal of Experimental Psychology: General, 1*, 75–97.

Eriksen, C.W. (1966). Temporal luminance summation effects in backward and forward masking. *Perception and Psychophysics, 1*, 87–92.

Evett, L.J., & Humphreys, G.W. (1981). The use of abstract graphemic information in lexical access. *Quarterly Journal of Experimental Psychology, 33*, 325–350.

Forster, K.I. (1987). Form-priming with masked primes: The best-match hypothesis. In M. Coltheart (Ed.), *Attention & performance XII*, (pp. 127–146). Hillsdale, NJ: Lawrence Erlbaum Associates Inc.

Forster, K.I. (1989a). Basic issues in lexical processing. In W. Marslen-Wilson (Ed.), *Lexical representation and process*, (pp. 75–107) Cambridge, MA: MIT Press.

Forster, K.I. (1989b, November). *Summation effects in lexical form-priming with masked primes: Direct evidence for activation models?* Paper presented at the 30th Annual General Meeting of the Psychonomics Society, Atlanta, Georgia.

Forster, K.I., & Davis, C. (1984). Repetition priming and frequency attenuation in lexical access. *Journal of Experimental Psychology: Learning, Memory, and Cognition, 10*, 680–698.

Forster, K.I., & Davis, C. (1991). The density constraint on form–priming in the naming task: Interference effects from a masked prime. *Journal of Memory and Language, 30*, 1–25.

Forster, K.I., Davis, C., Schoknecht, C., & Carter, R. (1987). Masked priming with graphemically related forms: Repetition or partial activation? *Quarterly Journal of Experimental Psychology, 39*, 211–251.

Forster, K.I., Dupoux, E., & Haan, R. (1990, November). *The neighborhood density constraint on masked form priming.* Paper presented at the 31st Annual Meeting of the Psychonomics Society, New Orleans.

Forster, K.I., & Yoshimura, K. (1992). *Masked form-priming from Kanji to Kana: Evidence for automatic phonological recoding.* Paper presented at the CUNY Conference, New York.

Gagnon, D.A. (1990). *Phonetic priming in spoken word recognition: Task comparisons.* Paper presented at the 119th meeting of the Acoustical Society of America.

Gagnon, D.A., & Sawusch, J.R. (1989). *Gaining insight into the representational unit for spoken words with a naming task.* Paper presented at the 117th meeting of the Acoustical Society of America.

Grainger, J., Cole, P., & Segui, J. (1991). Masked morphological priming in visual word recognition. *Journal of Memory and Language, 30,* 370–384.

Hillinger, M.L. (1980). Priming effects with phonemically similar words: The encoding-bias hypothesis reconsidered. *Memory & Cognition, 8,* 115–123.

Humphreys, G.W., Besner, D., & Quinlan, P.T. (1988). Event perception and the word repetition effect. *Journal of Experimental Psychology: General, 117,* 51–67.

Humphreys, G.W., Evett, L.J., & Quinlan, P.T. (1990). Orthographic processing in visual word identification. *Cognitive Psychology, 22,* 517–560.

Humphreys, G.W., Evett, L.J., Quinlan, P.T., & Besner, D. (1987). Orthographic priming: Qualitative differences between priming from identified and unidentified primes. In M. Coltheart (Ed.), *Attention and performance XII,* (pp. 201–219) Hillsdale, NJ: Lawrence Erlbaum Associates Inc.

Manso de Zuniga, C.M., Quinlan, P.T., & Humphreys, G.W. (1988). *Task constraints on priming with masked primes.* Paper presented to the Experimental Psychology Society, Reading, UK.

Martin, R.C., & Jensen, C.R. (1988). Phonological priming in the lexical decision task: A failure to replicate. *Memory & Cognition, 16,* 505–521.

Masson, M.E.J. (1991). *Word repetition as eyes see it.* Paper presented at the 32nd Annual Meeting of The Psychonomic Society, San Francisco.

McClelland, J.L., & Rumelhart, D.E. (1981). An interactive activation model of context effects in letter perception: Part 1. An account of basic findings. *Psychological Review, 88,* 375–407.

McClelland, J.L., & Rumelhart, D.E. (1986). *Parallel distributed processing: explorations in the microstructures of cognition. Volume 2: Psychological and biological models.* Cambridge, MA: MIT Press.

Meyer, D.M., Schvaneveldt, R.W., & Ruddy, M.G. (1974). Functions of graphemic and phonemic codes in visual word-recognition. *Memory & Cognition, 2,* 309–321.

Mozer, M.C. (1987). Early parallel processing in reading: A connectionist approach. In M. Coltheart (Ed.), *Attention and performance XII.* London: Lawrence Erlbaum Associates Ltd.

Posnansky, C.J., & Rayner, K. (1978). Visual vs. phonemic contributions to the importance of the initial letter in word identification. *Bulletin of the Psychonomic Society, 11,* 188–190.

Segui, J., & Grainger, J. (1990). Priming word recognition with orthographic neighbors: Effects of relative prime-target frequency. *Journal of Experimental Psychology: Human Perception and Performance, 16,* 65–76.

Sereno, J.A. (1991). Graphemic, associative, and syntactic priming effects at a brief stimulus onset asynchrony in lexical decision and naming. *Journal of Experimental Psychology: Learning, Memory, and Cognition, 17,* 459–477.

Slowiaczek, L.M., & Pisoni, D.G. (1986). Effects of phonological similarity on priming in auditory lexical decision. *Memory & Cognition, 14,* 230–237.

Slowiaczek, L.M., Nusbaum, H.C., & Pisoni, D.G. (1987). Phonological priming in auditory word recognition. *Journal of Experimental Psychology: Learning, Memory, and Cognition, 13,* 64–75.

Treisman, M. (1978). Space or lexicon? The word frequency effect and the error response frequency effect. *Journal of Verbal Learning and Verbal Behavior, 17,* 37–59.

Veres, C. (1986). *Factors affecting word selection in a masked prime paradigm.* Unpublished honors thesis, Monash University, Melbourne, Australia.

20 An Overview of Neighbourhood Effects in Word Recognition

Juan Segui and Jonathan Grainger
Laboratoire de Psychologie Expérimentale, C.N.R.S. and René Descartes University, Paris, France.

INTRODUCTION

In recent years the characteristics of a given word's similarity neighbour-hood (words that are orthographically and/or phonologically similar) have become a topic of increasing interest in the word recognition literature. Prior to this, much of the enormous quantity of research on word recognition had been devoted to studying how a given word's internal characteristics, such as its printed frequency, syntactic category, concreteness, bigram frequency etc., can influence the recognition of that word. It is only relatively recently, however, that the formal relationships between different words have become a major topic.

The theoretical precursors of this new orientation are the different models of word recognition developed over the last two decades (Forster, 1976; Marslen-Wilson & Welsh, 1978; McClelland & Rumelhart, 1981; Morton, 1969; Paap, Newsome, McDonald, & Schvaneveldt, 1982). All these models stress the fact that recognising a word involves isolating the correct lexical representation in memory from among a set of possible candidates defined by the input characteristics of the model. Perhaps one of the principal defining characteristics of these different models, apart from their different input mechanisms, is the particular mechanism invoked to perform this selection task. These different mechanisms will be discussed in the light of the empirical results to be presented here (see Bard, 1990 for an excellent theoretical discussion of some possible mechanisms). Nevertheless, the principal aim of this chapter is to summarise the empirical data concerning the effects of similarity neighbourhoods in word

497

recognition. This analysis will be presented in two sections dealing separately with isolated word recognition and primed word recognition.

NEIGHBOURHOOD EFFECTS IN THE RECOGNITION OF ISOLATED WORDS

The neighbourhood characteristics of a given word can be described on at least two dimensions: (1) the number of similar words, or neighbourhood density; and (2) the frequencies of these similar words, or neighbourhood frequency. The empirical evidence available at present suggests that both these factors can influence ease of word recognition.

Neighbourhood Density

Coltheart, Davelaar, Jonasson, and Besner (1977) proposed a metric for orthographic similarity between words now referred to as the N metric. N is the number of orthographic neighbours of a given letter string calculated in the following manner: any word of the same length that can be generated by replacing one letter of the string with another letter in the same position. Thus the word *COOK* has neighbours such as *BOOK, LOOK, CORK, COOL*. Neighbourhood density refers to the number of orthographic neighbours of a given letter string, and therefore corresponds to Coltheart et al.'s N value when applying their metric. Most of the research in the visual modality has in fact applied this metric, it is only in the auditory modality that (understandably) different computations have been used (e.g. Luce, 1986).

The research on isolated word recognition, although not totally consistent, has generally shown that the neighbourhood density does not affect positive responses in the lexical decision task (Coltheart et al., 1977; Grainger, O'Regan, Jacobs & Segui, 1989), but does have an interfering effect on nonword rejection latencies in this task (Andrews, 1989; Coltheart et al., 1977; Luce, 1990), and has a facilitatory effect on naming latencies to written words (Andrews, 1989; Grainger, 1990; Gunther & Greese, 1985; Scheerer, 1987). Let us now look at each of these results more closely (see Table 20.1).

Perhaps the most robust and easily replicable result is the interfering effect of neighbourhood density on nonword decision latencies in the lexical decision task. In line with a large quantity of research using the lexical decision task, this result basically demonstrates that the more 'wordlike' a nonword is, the harder it is to reject it in this task. This principle applies not only to orthographic resemblance but also to phonological similarity, pseudohomophones (e.g. *BLOO*) being harder to reject than orthographic controls (e.g. *BLON*, Coltheart et al., 1977). The latter

TABLE 20.1
Neighbourhood Density Effects on Response
Latencies to Nonword Targets

	Small N	Large N
Andrews (1989)		
LDT	788	833*
Coltheart et al. (1977)		
LDT	617	654*
Gunther & Greese (1985)		
LDT	709	797*

Neighbourhood density effects on response latencies (in milliseconds) to nonword targets in the lexical decision task (LDT). * Significant differences ($p<0.05$).

result is nevertheless highly sensitive to the type of word stimuli used, the interference only appearing when homophone stimuli are present in the experimental lists (but see Scheerer, 1987 as a counterexample). In addition, research by Martin (1982) and Taft (1982) suggests that much (if not all) of this pseudohomophone interference can be attributed to orthographic similarity with words.

These results with nonword stimuli can be explained by a variable deadline (Coltheart et al., 1977), or temporal threshold, set by subjects when doing the lexical decision task. If no word has reached the identification threshold after a given time delay determined by the temporal threshold then a 'no' response is triggered. In order to accommodate these results, this temporal threshold would have to be set as a function of general activity in the lexical system; the greater the activity the more likely it is that there is a word present, and therefore the higher the threshold should be set. An alternative means of accommodating these results is in terms of the number of erroneous verifications executed in a serial verification mechanism. If a nonword decision is only taken after all possible candidates have been checked and rejected, then the more neighbours a nonword has the longer it will take to respond 'no'. One line of future research that may help test these two interpretations would be to independently vary the number of neighbours and their frequencies. The deadline model predicts that a few high frequency neighbours would produce just as much interference as many low frequency neighbours, whereas an exhaustive verification explanation predicts that number of neighbours (assuming they are all frequent enough) is the unique determining factor.

The observed absence of an effect of neighbourhood density on responses to word stimuli in visual lexical decision (Table 20.2) is consistent with models of word recognition that describe the recognition process as a horse race among independent competitors to reach an identification threshold (Coltheart et al., 1977; Morton, 1969). Andrews (1989) has nevertheless published data showing a facilitatory effect of neighbourhood density on lexical decision latencies to words. Perhaps the major problem with this study is the absence of any control of bigram frequency across the different neighbourhood densities. It is clear that these two factors are highly correlated, and that words with large neighbourhoods will tend to have high bigram frequencies. Although admittedly the evidence for facilitatory effects of bigram frequency in lexical decision is rather weak (Gernsbacher, 1984) it is still necessary to control for this factor if one wishes to ascribe the observed effects to neighbourhood density. Bigram frequency may also be responsible for the facilitatory effect of number of higher frequency neighbours observed by Grainger et al. (1989) in the gaze duration data. It is only between these two categories of words that we failed to provide an adequate control of bigram frequency, the words with more high frequency neighbours having a higher bigram frequency.

There is, however, another possible confounding factor present in Andrews' experiments that is directly related to the problem of bigram frequency. In these experiments the facilitatory effects of neighbourhood

TABLE 20.2
Neighbourhood Density Effects on Word Recognition Latencies (in milliseconds)

		Small N	Large N
Andrews (1989)			
LDT high freq		608	60ʻ
Experiment 1 low freq		733	696*
high freq		561	568
Experiment 2 low freq		682	637*
Coltheart et al. (1977)			
LDT		563	560
Grainger et al. (1989)			
1) Low frequency neighbours only.			
LDT		602	596
Gaze Duration		392	405
2) With high frequency neighbours.			
LDT		643	653
Gaze Duration		457	421
Gunther & Greese (1985)			
LDT		698	691

* Significant differences ($p<0.05$).

density were only observed with low frequency words, and were only robust in the item analyses when nonwords with low frequency bigrams were used as distractors. Now, it so happens that it is only in the low frequency, low density words that similar low frequency bigrams occur (e.g. *coax, fizz, flax*). The pattern of lexical decision latencies to word targets observed in Andrews' experiments could therefore be due to varying word/nonword discriminability across the stimulus categories. In other words, the low frequency/low density words may have looked more like nonwords than the other stimulus categories.

It should be noted that all the other studies cited in Table 20.2 show an absence of an effect of neighbourhood density on word responses in lexical decision. The majority of these studies provided strict controls not only of bigram frequency but also of the frequency characteristics of the neighbourhood (the presence or not of high frequency neighbours). It will be seen, however, in the discussion of neighbourhood frequency effects that follows, that facilitatory effects on word recognition may arise as the result of a combination of neighbourhood density and frequency.

The effects of neighbourhood density on word naming latencies are, on the other hand, extremely clear cut. Words with large neighbourhoods are named more rapidly than words with a small number of lexical neighbours (Table 20.3). This result is obtained with appropriate controls for bigram frequency, and cannot be attributed to differences in articulatory difficulty since the effect disappears in delayed naming (subjects pronounce a word as fast as possible on a given signal that appears a fixed time after stimulus

TABLE 20.3
Neighbourhood Density Effects on Word and Nonword Naming Latencies (in milliseconds)

		Small N	Large N
Word stimuli			
Andrews (1989)			
Naming	high freq	590	580
	low freq	643	594*
Delayed Naming	high freq	496	499
	low freq	510	513
Gunther & Greese (1985)			
Naming		730	707*
Delayed Naming		388	389
Nonword stimuli			
Gunther & Greese (1985)			
Naming		812	776*
Delayed Naming		414	409

* Significant differences ($p < 0.05$).

presentation). This effect of neighbourhood density on word naming latencies should not, however, be taken as evidence that neighbourhood density affects word recognition processes. The effect must be specifically interpreted within models of how written words are read aloud.

In particular, this result would appear to provide strong support for lexical pooling or analogy models of word naming (Glushko, 1979; Henderson, 1982; Kay & Marcel, 1981). According to these models, a word is named by a synthesisation process where the phonological representations of all activated words are pooled together to provide the final pronunciation. This synthesisation process will also be adopted in the naming aloud of nonword stimuli. The fact that facilitatory effects of neighbourhood density are also observed in nonword naming (Gunther & Greese, 1985) therefore adds further support to this position. Also, the facilitatory effect of neighbourhood density on word naming has been shown to interact with word frequency, much larger effects being observed with low frequency words (Andrews, 1989; see Monsell, Doyle, & Haggard, 1989, for a similar result). This once again adds support to analogy models of word naming, since the lower the target word's frequency the greater the weight attributed to the pronunciations of its neighbours in the synthesisation process. On the other hand, dual route models of word naming (Coltheart, 1978) have difficulty in accommodating such effects. It is not, however, impossible to provide modified versions of this type of model (e.g. Norris & Brown, 1985) that can handle the data (see Grainger, 1990, for a discussion on this point).

To conclude this section on neighbourhood density effects, the data clearly indicate interference effects of this factor in nonword rejection latencies and facilitatory effects on word and nonword naming latencies. On the other hand, the effects of neighbourhood density on lexical decision latencies to words remains to be clarified. One likely reason why contradictory data exists on this point is that some studies failed to control for bigram frequency and the frequency characteristics of the neighbourhoods. It is to this latter point that we now turn.

Neighbourhood Frequency

It is peculiar that much experimental work has focused on examining the effects of neighbourhood density in word recognition (ignoring the frequencies of these neighbours) when the majority of word recognition models predict that the frequencies of these neighbours relative to stimulus word frequency should be the determining factor. The early work of Havens and Foote (1963) on visual duration thresholds, and Savin (1963) on auditory thresholds of word stimuli, had already provided a clear indication of the importance of competitor frequency. Havens and Foote

(1963, p. 6) conclude on the basis of their results that '. . . visual duration thresholds are not primarily a function of the frequency of prior usage of stimuli but of the ability or inability of the stimuli to evoke high frequency competitive responses'.

There is now evidence, essentially from work in our own laboratory, (see Table 20.4) indicating that competitor or neighbourhood frequency also influences word recognition performance in tasks such as lexical decision and progressive demasking (see Grainger & Segui 1990, for a description of this technique). At present it appears that words that have at least one higher frequency neighbour are harder to recognise than words with no higher frequency neighbours (Grainger, 1990; Grainger et al., 1989; Grainger & Segui, 1990; Marslen-Wilson, 1990).

The interactive activation model (McClelland & Rumelhart, 1981) and the activation verification model (Paap et al., 1982) provide two distinct explanations of this phenomenon. In the interactive activation model, the word node corresponding to the stimulus word inhibits and receives inhibition from all other activated word nodes. The inhibitory output of a given node increases as its activation level rises, and is therefore a function of its resting level activation (calculated from printed frequency) and orthographic similarity with the stimulus. Higher frequency neighbours will therefore provide a stronger inhibitory effect on the stimulus word than lower frequency neighbours. In the activation verification model, all words that are orthographically similar to the stimulus will figure in the candidate set of representations that are submitted to a

TABLE 20.4
Neighbourhood Frequency Effects on Word Recognition Latencies (in milliseconds)

		high Nfreq	low Nfreq
Grainger et al. (1989)			
LDT		647	599*
Gaze Duration		439	399*
Grainger & Segui (1990)			
LDT	med freq	604	588*
	low freq	624	608*
Progressive demasking	med freq	2028	1906*
	low freq	2295	1982*
Grainger (1990)			
LDT	med freq	638	610*
	low freq	650	622*
Marslen-Wilson (1990)			
LDT		655	602*

* Significant differences ($p<0.05$).

frequency ordered verification process. The more frequent a candidate is relative to the stimulus word the more likely it is that this candidate will be checked and rejected before correctly selecting the stimulus word representation. Since this checking process will take a certain time, word recognition will be slower compared to the situation where the stimulus word itself is first in the verification queue.

In the experiments cited earlier, stimulus word frequency is kept quite low, and the higher frequency neighbours of the word stimuli generally have a high frequency of occurrence. This means that, in the majority of cases where a stimulus word is defined as having a higher frequency neighbour, the frequency difference between the stimulus word and its higher frequency neighbour is quite large. Just how this frequency difference affects the observed interference needs to be investigated in future experimentation. Such data would help discriminate between continuous mutual inhibition type explanations of neighbourhood interference, and discrete verification type explanations.

Similar effects of neighbourhood frequency have been obtained in auditory word recognition by Luce (1986). In a perceptual identification task using spoken words embedded in noise, Luce demonstrated that monosyllabic words with many high frequency neighbours were identified less accurately than words with few low frequency neighbours. More recently, inhibitory effects of neighbourhood frequency have been observed in auditory lexical decision, perceptual identification, and naming (Luce, 1990; Perea, Gotor, & Algarabel, 1990).

Taken together, this research suggests that it is neighbourhood frequency rather than neighbourhood density that is the principal factor determining ease of word recognition. A similar conclusion was recently drawn by Jared, McRae, and Seidenberg (1990) on the basis of experiments on word naming. Until now our discussion of neighbourhood effects on word naming has ignored the phonological characteristics of the stimulus word's orthographic neighbourhood. What appears critical in determining naming latencies, however, is the relative frequencies of 'friends' and 'enemies' in the target word's orthographic neighbourhood. Friends are orthographically similar words that are also pronounced similarly (e.g. SAVE, GAVE), and enemies are orthographically similar words with different pronunciations (e.g. SAVE, HAVE). Jared et al. (1990) found that low frequency words with frequent enemies and infrequent friends were harder to pronounce than low frequency words with infrequent enemies and frequent friends. The fact that lexical decision performance remained unaffected by these manipulations suggests that they are genuine phonological effects particular to the process of reading printed words aloud.

Jared et al. (1990) also demonstrated that total number of higher frequency orthographic neighbours did not affect lexical decision performance, thus replicating the results of Grainger (1990). Nevertheless, one recent result from our own laboratory (Paquotte, 1990) suggests an interesting interaction between the effects of neighbourhood frequency and neighbourhood density. Words that have a large number of high frequency neighbours appear to be easier to recognise than words with only one higher frequency neighbour. This effect has been observed in lexical decision error rates, and in masked identification latencies obtained with the progressive demasking paradigm. This result is particularly difficult for a serial verification mechanism to accommodate. Such a mechanism predicts that increasing the number of higher frequency neighbours should lead to a subsequent rise in recognition latencies. On the other hand, a mutual inhibition mechanism as implemented in the interactive activation model (McClelland & Rumelhart, 1981) successfully accounts for this result. The larger the number of high frequency neighbours the greater the internal inhibition between these competitors. This then reduces the total inhibition on the stimulus word.

NEIGHBOURHOOD EFFECTS IN FORM PRIMING

Unmasked Neighbourhood Priming

In the first part of this chapter we presented experimental data suggesting that words that have higher frequency neighbours are harder to recognise than those that do not. In order to accommodate this result, it was proposed that these higher frequency neighbours compete with the stimulus word, either by imposing themselves as the best initial candidate in a verification process, or by directly inhibiting the stimulus word representation via within-level inhibitory connections. One direct consequence of the verification hypothesis is that for the stimulus word to be successfully identified, these strong competitors must be verified and subsequently rejected. If this hypothesis is correct, then one might expect the higher frequency neighbours of the stimulus word to be in an inhibitory state immediately after stimulus word recognition, and therefore momentarily harder to recognise.

It is possible to test this hypothesis using the orthographic priming paradigm where a target word is directly preceded by an orthographically related (e.g. *slack–BLACK*) or unrelated prime (e.g. *crowd–BLACK*). According to the verification explanation of neighbourhood interference in isolated word recognition, if the target is a higher frequency neighbour of the prime (e.g. *blur-BLUE)* then it will be checked and rejected during the processing of the prime. On the other hand, if the target is a lower frequency neighbour of the prime (e.g. *blue–BLUR*) then it will not figure as a strong candidate during prime word processing, and therefore will not be checked and rejected. This explanation therefore predicts inhibitory effects of orthographic priming dependent on relative prime-target frequency.

Segui and Grainger (1990a) tested these predictions in an orthographic priming experiment with a 350ms SOA. In this study pairs of orthographically related French words, one high frequency the other low frequency (e.g. *CHAT-CHAR*) were used as prime and target, with the high frequency member serving as prime in one condition and the low frequency member serving as prime in another condition. Lexical decision latencies to the same target word were compared in the orthographically related condition and an unrelated condition where primes did not share letters with the target. The results are shown in Table 20.5.

Segui and Grainger (1990a) observed significant inhibitory effects when primes were lower frequency neighbours of the target, whereas a non-significant facilitation was observed when primes were higher frequency neighbours of the target. The results therefore support the verification–rejection explanation of neighbourhood interference in isolated word recognition. During the processing of the prime word (when sufficient time is available) any strong competitors will be verified as plausible candidates, and subsequently rejected when a mismatch between lexical and sensory information is detected. Higher frequency orthographically similar words constitute such strong competitors and therefore suffer the consequences of this verification–rejection process.

TABLE 20.5
Response Latencies

	Prime–Target freq	Related	Unrelated
Segui & Grainger, 1990a (Exp 1) LDT	Low–High High–Low	630 687	598* 702
Lukatela & Turvey, 1990 (Exp 4) LDT	Low–High High–Low	674 768	631* 764
Segui & Grainger, 1990a (Exp 3) LDT	Low–Medium High–Medium	639 609	605* 611
Grainger, 1990 (Exp 2) LDT	Low–High Medium–High	609 614	592* 594*
Grainger, 1990 (Exp 2) Naming	Low–High Medium–High	532 527	522* 520*
Grainger & Segui, 1992 LDT	Nonword–High Nonword–Low	648 683	625* 662*

Response latencies (in milliseconds) to word targets preceded by orthographically related or unrelated primes presented for approximately 350 milliseconds.
* Significant differences (p<0.05).

An alternative interpretation may be proposed within the framework of the interactive activation model (McClelland & Rumelhart, 1981). In order to accommodate these priming effects, one has to add the assumption that when a word is recognised then the activation levels of all words units are reset to their resting level. High frequency primes are more likely to be identified after 350ms of processing than are low frequency primes. Thus, whether a high frequency prime is orthographically related to the target word or not will generally not affect target recognition, since all word units will have been reset before target processing is initiated. Low frequency primes, on the other hand, will generally not trigger this global system reset, and will therefore remain activated during target processing. The activation level of orthographically related primes will then be sustained during target processing, and will therefore produce more inhibition on the target representation than unrelated primes.

Using a similar experimental procedure Lukatela and Turvey (1990, Experiment 4) have recently observed comparable results in phonological priming. When prime and target are phonologically similar, inhibition is observed compared to an unrelated condition when primes are low frequency and targets high frequency (Table 20.5). These results are therefore compatible with the hypothesis described earlier, according to which relative prime-target frequency will determine the relative strength of the target as a competitor during prime processing. Nevertheless, in these and in our own experiments, relative prime-target frequency is confounded with absolute prime and target frequency. This confound is particularly problematical in that other authors (Colombo, 1986; Lukatela & Turvey, 1990) interpret these inhibitory form priming effects in terms of absolute frequency. According to these authors, any lexical representations that are strongly activated during the processing of the prime word (except the most strongly activated representation) will be inhibited. Thus, independently of prime word frequency, any high frequency related targets will be inhibited according to this explanation. In agreement with this, Lukatela and Turvey (1990) observed inhibition between phonologically related high frequency prime-target pairs. That is, high frequency phonologically related primes inhibited high frequency targets.

This latter result stands in contradiction to our explanation within the interactive activation framework proposed earlier. According to this explanation, low frequency primes should inhibit low frequency targets, but high frequency primes should not inhibit high frequency targets. It is still possible, however, for a verification mechanism to explain such a result. Even when the stimulus word has a high printed frequency, its high frequency neighbours may still, on a non-negligible proportion of trials, be verified before the stimulus word. This explanation of the high frequency prime–high frequency target inhibitory effect predicts that in isolated word recognition, high frequency targets with high frequency neighbours should be harder to recognise than high frequency targets with only low frequency neighbours.

Nevertheless, it should be noted that our own results on orthographic priming suggest that absolute target frequency is not the critical factor for determining inhibition. In further experimentation (Segui & Grainger, 1990a, Experiment 3) we held target frequency constant and varied prime frequency, comparing high frequency prime–medium frequency target and low frequency prime–medium frequency target conditions (Table 20.5). Significant inhibition was observed on medium frequency targets only when primes were orthographically related lower frequency words. The same medium frequency targets were not affected by higher frequency primes. In a complementary study, Grainger (1990) demonstrated that comparable inhibitory effects of orthographic priming are obtained with low and medium frequency primes on the same set of high frequency targets. It is important to note that inhibitory effects were observed in both lexical decision and naming latencies to the same set of stimuli in this experiment. Also, in an auditory word identification experiment Goldinger, Luce, and Pisoni (1989) observed inhibitory effects of low frequency primes on high frequency targets, and an absence of inhibition when primes were high frequency and targets low frequency.

The data therefore appear to indicate that relative prime–target frequency is the best predictor of inhibitory effects of orthographic (and perhaps phonological) priming with unmasked, identifiable primes. Target words are inhibited by the prior presentation of an orthographically related prime of lower frequency. If this hypothesis is correct, then one should observe inhibitory orthographic priming effects of nonword primes independently of target word frequency. By definition a nonword has a frequency of occurrence close to zero. A nonword prime will therefore have a lower frequency than both low frequency and high frequency word targets. We therefore predict inhibitory orthographic priming on both low and high frequency targets in this situation. This hypothesis was tested in a recent experiment in our laboratory (Grainger & Segui, 1992).

The results (shown in Table 20.5) indicate clear inhibitory effects of approximately the same magnitude on both low and high frequency targets preceded by orthographically related nonword primes. According to an activation-verification explanation of inhibitory effects in unmasked ortho-graphic priming, when the prime is a nonword, both high and low frequency word neighbours reach a sufficiently high activation level to be entertained as plausible candidates and subsequently rejected. The inter-active activation framework has difficulty in accommodating this result since, as it stands, it can only predict facilitatory effects of orthographically related nonword primes. It could be argued, however, that the processing of nonword primes at relatively long prime stimulus durations involves mechanisms that are not usually employed in normal reading. The inhibitory effects of orthographic priming with unmasked primes are therefore most successfully interpreted at present in terms of a verification–rejection mechanism operating during the processing of the prime. This is basically a checking process that serves to eliminate strong competitors from the pool of candidates for identification, thus allowing the stimulus word itself to be successfully identified. This inhibitory mechanism should be operating only during the later stages of word recognition, and should therefore not be observable when primes are presented extremely briefly.

Masked Repetition Priming

In the masked priming paradigm, primes are preceded by a forward pattern mask and briefly presented (typically for about 60ms) before target presentation. This renders the prime extremely difficult to identify and indeed estimations of prime word reportability in these conditions rarely exceed 30%. Even in such extreme prime presentation conditions, there is evidence that lexical representations are activated during prime word processing and can subsequently affect the processing of the target.

Forster and Davis (1984) showed that recognition of a target word presented in upper case is facilitated when the prime is the same word presented in lower case (Table 20.6). These repetition effects observed with masked primes are qualitatively distinct from those obtained with unmasked primes. First, with masked primes the facilitation is short-lived and disappears with inter-stimulus intervals of more than two seconds, whereas with unmasked primes extremely long term facilitatory effects are observed. Second, masked repetition effects do not interact with word frequency (Forster & Davis, 1984; Segui & Grainger, 1990a; 1990b) whereas unmasked repetition effects do; low frequency words benefiting more from repetition than high frequency words. Finally, no effect of nonword repetition is observed in the masked priming paradigm (Forster & Davis, 1984), whereas there is evidence for facilitatory repetition effects for nonwords with unmasked primes (Feustel, Shiffrin, & Salasoo, 1983). The facilitatory nature of masked repetition priming effects were further tested by Segui and Grainger (1990b), by comparing the repeated condition with both an unrelated word prime and a neutral prime (xxxx) condition. Equivalent facilitatory repetition priming effects are obtained when measured against both baseline conditions (see Table 20.6).

Moreover, using a primed perceptual identification task, Humphreys and his colleagues (Evett & Humphreys, 1981; Humphreys, Besner, & Quinlan, 1988; Humphreys, Evett, & Quinlan, 1990; Humphreys, Evett,

TABLE 20.6
Response Latencies

	Item frequency	Repeated	Unrelated
Forster & Davis,	High	550	595*
1984 (Exp 1) LDT	Low	646	684*
	Nonwords	687	679
Segui & Grainger	High	553	595*
1990a (Exp 3) LDT	Low	659	704*
Segui & Grainger,	Medium	541	597*
1990b (Exp 1) LDT	Low	570	626*
Segui & Grainger,	Medium	585	630*
1990b (Exp 2) LDT	Low	601	659*
(unrelated condition = xxxx)			

Response latencies (in milliseconds) to word targets preceded by same word or orthographically
unrelated masked primes presented for 64 milliseconds.
* Significant differences ($p < 0.05$).

Quinlan, & Besner, 1987; Humphreys, Evett, & Taylor, 1982) have
systematically demonstrated that percent correct identification of upper
case targets is higher when the same word is presented very briefly in lower
case immediately before target presentation.

The results summarised here favour a lexical level explanation of
masked repetition priming. The briefly presented masked prime produces
a rise in the activation level of its lexical representation, so that when target
processing is initiated the target's lexical representation already has a
higher activation level than when a different word was presented as prime.
If some form of activation threshold must be reached during word
recognition (either to initiate a verification procedure or for word identification to occur), then the higher the starting activation level the faster
the word will be recognised. Thus, both the activation verification model
(Paap et al., 1982) and the interactive activation model (McClelland &
Rumelhart, 1981) can accommodate this phenomenon.

Masked Neighbourhood Priming

If this preactivation account of masked repetition priming is correct, then
the masked presentation of an orthographic neighbour of the target should
have very different effects from the repetition priming condition. The prior
presentation of an orthographic neighbour should produce a rise in
activation level of the corresponding lexical representation in memory.
This should then increase the competitivity of this representation during
processing of the target word. If competing units must reach a relatively
high activation level in order to produce noticeable interference (by

reaching a verification threshold or by producing sufficient intralevel inhibition), then it is likely that priming with higher frequency neighbours will cause the greatest interference. When targets are primed with lower frequency neighbours, the preactivation of the prime's lexical representation may not be great enough to render this representation sufficiently competitive to produce noticeable interference in target processing. We are therefore led to predict exactly the opposite pattern of effects of masked neighbourhood priming compared to those obtained with unmasked primes.

Using exactly the same stimuli as in the unmasked priming conditions, Segui and Grainger (1990a) confirmed these predictions. As can be seen in Table 20.7, significant inhibitory effects of orthographic priming were observed when low frequency targets were preceded by high frequency primes, whereas a non-significant facilitatory trend was observed with low frequency primes and high frequency targets. As with the unmasked priming situation, in a second experiment we tested the effects of relative prime-target frequency against absolute target frequency, by using medium frequency targets preceded by low and high frequency primes. The results clearly indicate that inhibitory effects of masked neighbour priming only obtain when the prime is more frequent than the target (see Table 20.7).

A further test of the relative frequency account of these masked neighbour priming effects was performed using nonword primes (Grainger & Segui, 1992). Once again, the same experimental stimuli as the unmasked condition were used in this experiment, with the same nonword primes for both high (e.g. *avel–AVEC*) and low frequency (e.g. *avel– AVEU*) word neighbours (an English example would be: *blut–BLUE, blut–BLUR*). The results (Table 20.7) indicate that neither high nor low frequency targets are inhibited by the prior presentation of a nonword neighbour in the masked priming paradigm. Nonword primes apparently do not sufficiently preactivate any single lexical representation for there to be noticeable interference during target processing.

TABLE 20.7
Response Latencies

	Prime–Target Freq	Related	Unrelated
Segui & Grainger,	Low–High	598	608
1990a (Exp 2) LDT	High–Low	709	661*
Segui & Grainger,	Low–Medium	643	631
1990a (Exp 3) LDT	High–Medium	662	621*
Grainger & Segui,	Nonword–High	579	571
1992 LDT	Nonword–Low	632	631

Response latencies (in milliseconds) to word targets preceded by orthographically related or unrelated masked primes presented for 64 milliseconds.
* Significant differences ($p<0.05$).

It is nevertheless important to note that Forster (1987) and Forster, Davis, Schoknecht, and Carter (1987) have observed significant facilitatory effects of nonword neighbour priming with much longer words (e.g. *bontrast–CONTRAST*). In these conditions, percent prime–target overlap is greatly increased (from 75% with four-letter words to 88% in the example given here), and therefore the target word will be receiving much more preactivation from the prime than in our experiments. Moreover, since *BONTRAST* is not a neighbour of any other English word, it is only the target word *CONTRAST* that will be receiving any preactivation. These nonword neighbour priming conditions used by Forster et al. (1987) therefore approximate the conditions of masked repetition priming reported earlier. The lexical representation of the target word itself is the only representation to be receiving much preactivation from the prime in these conditions.

Finally, when prime-target pairs are morphologically related (e.g. *ring–RUNG*) then facilitatory effects are obtained in the masked priming paradigm (Forster et al., 1987; Grainger, Colé, & Segui, 1991). This morphological facilitation was shown to be independent of prime-target frequency, facilitation occurring with primes that are more frequent than targets, and primes that are less frequent than targets (Grainger et al., 1991). Moreover, in the same experiments, Grainger et al. (1991) showed that low frequency targets that are facilitated by a more frequent morphologically related prime (e.g. *mural–MURET*) are inhibited by a more frequent orthographically related prime (e.g. *murir–MURET*). These results suggest that morphological information is represented explicitly in the word recognition system in a way that allows morphologically related words to be linked by facilitatory connections. This could be achieved by word units from the same morphological family being linked together via sublexical or supralexical morphological units.

CONCLUSIONS

In this chapter we have summarised some recent experimental work aimed at testing a general conception of word recognition as essentially a competitional process between formally similar words. In the first part of the chapter we examined the results of experiments conducted with isolated words. It was shown how both the number and the frequencies of a given word's neighbours can influence the ease of recognition of this word. The results generally support activation based models of word recognition in which the competitivity of a given word is determined by that word's frequency of occurrence and its similarity with the stimulus. More specifically, the mechanism of mutual inhibition between activated lexical representations implemented in the interactive activation model

(McClelland & Rumelhart, 1981) appears best at accommodating some recent results in this field.

In the second part of the chapter it was shown how the use of a priming procedure with unmasked and masked prime presentations allows one to modify the hypothetical competitivity of the competing words. The mechanisms involved in these modifications appear to be radically different depending on whether primes are unmasked and identifiable, or whether they are masked and difficult to report. With unmasked neighbour primes, significant inhibitory effects are observed when target words are preceded by lower frequency neighbours but not when they are preceded by higher frequency neighbours. When the prime is a lower frequency neighbour of the target, then the target representation attains a relatively high activation level compared to that of the prime word representation during prime processing. This high activation level of the target word representation must be suppressed for the prime word to be successfully identified, and this suppression of activation level leaves the target word momentarily harder to recognise.

The results obtained with masked primes are most readily interpreted in terms of a preactivation of the prime word's lexical representation during prime processing. The briefly presented prime word produces a rise in the activation level of its lexical representation. This preactivation of the prime facilitates target recognition when these two items are ortho-graphically identical (repetition priming), but inhibits target recognition when the target corresponds to a lower frequency neighbour of the prime. In the latter case the preactivation of the prime enhances its 'natural' competitivity. However, when the prime word corresponds to a lower frequency neighbour of the target, its prior presentation does not produce a great enough increase in activation level for it to affect target identification.

As noted in the previous sections, most of the results obtained in these experiments are compatible with predictions derived from the interactive activation or activation verification models. However, some modifications of these models are necessary to explain the complete set of current empirical data (see on this point, Grainger, 1990; Grainger & Segui, 1990; Segui & Grainger, 1990a). Nevertheless, even if more empirical and theoretical work is clearly necessary in order to specify the nature of the mechanisms involved in neighbourhood interference, the studies examined in the present chapter are globally favourable towards an activation based account where competitivity is determined by orthographic overlap and relative frequency.

REFERENCES

Andrews, S. (1989). Frequency and neighborhood effects on lexical access: Activation or search. *Journal of Experimental Psychology: Learning Memory and Cognition, 15*, 802–814.

Bard, E.G. (1990). Competition, internal inhibition, and frequency: Comments on the papers of Frauenfelder and Peeters, Marslen-Wilson, and others. In G. Altmann (Ed.), *Cognitive models of speech processing: Psycholinguistic and computational perspectives*, Cambridge, MA: MIT Press.

Colombo, L. (1986). Activation and inhibition with orthographically similar words. *Journal of Experimental Psychology: Human Perception and Performance, 12*, 226–234.

Coltheart, M. (1978). Lexical access in simple reading tasks. In G. Underwood (Ed.), *Strategies of information processing*, London: Academic Press.

Coltheart, M., Davelaar, E., Jonasson, J.T., & Besner, D. (1977). Access to the internal lexicon. In S. Dornic (Ed.), *Attention and performance VI*. New York: Academic Press.

Evett, L.J., & Humphreys, G.W. (1981). The use of abstract graphemic information in lexical access. *Quarterly Journal of Experimental Psychology, 33A*, 325–350.

Feustel, T.C., Shiffrin, R.M., & Salasoo, A. (1983). Episodic and lexical contributions to the repetition effect in word identification. *Journal of Experimental Psychology: General, 112*, 309–346.

Forster, K.I. (1976). Accessing the mental lexicon. In R.J. Wales & E.W. Walker (Eds.), *New approaches to language mechanisms*. Amsterdam: North-Holland.

Forster, K.I. (1987). Form-priming with masked primes: The best match hypothesis. In M. Coltheart (Ed.), *Attention and performance, XII*, (pp. 128–145), Hillsdale, NJ: Lawrence Erlbaum Associates Inc.

Foster, K.I., & Davis, C. (1984). Repetition priming and frequency attenuation in lexical access. *Journal of Experimental Psychology: Learning, Memory, and Cognition, 10*, 680–690.

Forster, K.I., Davis, C., Schoknecht, C., & Carter, R. (1987). Masked priming with graphemically related forms: Repetition or partial activation? *Quarterly Journal of Experimental Psychology, 39A*, 211–251.

Gernsbacher, M.A. (1984). Resolving 20 years of inconsistent interaction between lexical familiarity and orthography, concreteness and polysemy. *Journal of Experimental Psychology: General, 113*, 256–281.

Glushko, R.J. (1979). The organization and activation of orthographic knowledge in reading aloud. *Journal of Experimental Psychology: Human Perception and Performance, 5*, 674–691.

Goldinger, S.D., Luce, P.A., & Pisoni, D.B. (1989). Priming lexical neighbours of spoken words: Effects of competition and inhibition. *Journal of Memory and Language, 28*, 501–518.

Grainger, J. (1990). Word frequency and neighborhood frequency effects in lexical decision and naming. *Journal of Memory and Language, 29*, 228–244.

Grainger, J., Colé, P., & Segui, J. (1991). Masked morphological priming in visual word recognition: Evidence from masked priming. *Journal of Memory and Language, 30*, 370–384.

Grainger, J., O'Regan, J.K., Jacobs, A.M., & Segui, J. (1989). On the role of competing word units in visual word recognition: The neighborhood frequency effect. *Perception & Psychophysics, 45*, 189–195.

Grainger, J., & Segui, J. (1990). Neighborhood frequency effects in visual word recognition: A comparison of lexical decision and masked identification latencies. *Perception and Psychophysics, 47*, 191–198.

Grainger, J., & Segui, J. (1992). *Priming word recognition with orthographic neighbors: Effects of nonword primes*. Manuscript submitted for publication.

Gunther, H., & Greese, B. (1985). Lexical hermits and the pronunciation of visually presented words. *Forschungsberichte des Instituts fur Phonetik und Sprachliche Kommunikation des Universitat Munchen, 21*, 25–52.

Havens, L.L., & Foote, W.E. (1963). The effect of competition on visual duration threshold and its independence of stimulus frequency. *Journal of Experimental Psychology, 65*, 6–11.

Henderson, L. (1982). *Orthography and word recognition in reading.* London: Academic Press.

Humphreys, G.W., Besner, D., & Quinlan, P.T. (1988). Event perception and the word repetition effect. *Journal of Experimental Psychology: General, 117*, 51–67.

Humphreys, G.W., Evett, L.J., Quinlan, P.T., & Besner, D. (1987). Orthographic priming: Qualitative differences between priming from identified and unidentified primes. In M. Coltheart (Ed.), *Attention and performance XII*, London: Lawrence Erlbaum Associates Ltd.

Humphreys, G.W., Evett, L.J., & Quinlan, P.T. (1990). Orthographic processing in visual word identification. *Cognitive Psychology, 22*, 517–560.

Humphreys, G.W., Evett, L.J., & Taylor, D.E.T. (1982). Automatic phonological priming in visual word recognition. *Memory and Cognition, 10*, 576–590.

Jared, D., McRae, K., & Seidenberg, M.S. (1990). The basis of consistency effects in word naming. *Journal of Memory and Language, 29*, 687–715.

Kay, J., & Marcel, A. (1981). One process, not two, in reading aloud: Lexical analogies do the work of non-lexical rules. *Quarterly Journal of Experimental Psychology: Human Experimental Psychology, 33A*, 397–413.

Luce, P.A. (1986). *Neighborhoods of words in the mental lexicon.* Unpublished doctoral dissertation, Indiana University.

Luce, P.A. (1990). Similarity neighborhoods of spoken words. In G.T.M. Altmann (Ed.), *Cognitive models of speech perception: Psycholinguistic and computational perspectives*, Cambridge MA: MIT Press.

Lukatela, G., & Turvey, M.T. (1990). Phonemic similarity effects and prelexical phonology. *Memory & Cognition, 18*, 128–152.

Marslen-Wilson, W.D. (1990). Activation, competition, and frequency in lexical access. In G.T.M. Altmann (Ed.), *Cognitive models of speech processing: psycholinguistic and computational perspectives*, Cambridge, MA: MIT Press.

Marslen-Wilson, W.D., & Welsh, A. (1978). Processing interactions and lexical access during word recognition in continuous speech. *Cognitive Psychology, 10*, 29–63.

Martin, R.C. (1982). The pseudohomophone effect: The role of visual similarity in nonword decisions. *Quarterly Journal of Experimental Psychology, 34A*, 395–410.

Monsell, S., Doyle, M.C., & Haggard, P.N. (1989). Effects of frequency on visual word recognition tasks: Where are they?, *Journal of Experimental Psychology: General, 118*, 43–71.

Morton, J. (1969). Interaction of information in word recognition. *Psychological Review, 76*, 165–178.

McClelland, J.L., & Rumelhart, D.E. (1981). An interactive-activation model of context effects in letter perception, part 1: An account of basic findings. *Psychological Review, 88*, 375–405.

Norris,. D., & Brown, G. (1985). Race models and analogies theories: A dead heat? Reply to Seidenberg. *Cognition, 20*, 155–168.

Paap, K.R., Newsome, S.L., McDonald, J.E., & Schvaneveldt, R.W. (1982). An activation-verification model for letter and word recognition: The word superiority effect. *Psychological Review, 89*, 573–594.

Paquotte, M.-L. (1990). *L'effet de la fréquence relative des mots et la fréquence du voisinage dans la reconnaissance visuelle de mots.* Unpublished masters dissertation, Université René Descartes, Paris.

Perea, M., Gotor, A., & Algarabel, S. (1990, September). *Uniqueness point and competition in spoken word recognition.* Paper presented at the 4th Conference of the European Society for Cognitive Psychology, Como, Italy.

Savin, H.B. (1963). Word frequency effects and errors in the preception of speech. *The Journal of the Acoustical Society of America, 35,* 200–206.

Scheerer, E. (1987). Visual word recognition in German. In D.A. Allport, D. Mackay, W. Prinz, & E. Scheerer (Eds.), *Language perception and production: Shared mechanisms in listening, speaking, reading and writing,* (pp. 227–244), London: Academic Press.

Segui, J., & Grainger, J. (1990a). Priming word recognition with orthographic neighbors: Effects of relative prime-target frequency. *Journal of Experimental Psychology: Human Perception and Performance, 16,* 65–76.

Segui, J., & Grainger, J. (1990b). Masquage et effet de répétition du mot: sa nature et sa localisation fonctionnelle. *L'Année Psychologique, 90,* 345–357.

Taft, M. (1982). An alternative to grapheme–phoneme conversion rules? *Memory and Cognition, 10,* 465–474.

Author Index

Subject Index

www.ingramcontent.com/pod-product-compliance
Ingram Content Group UK Ltd.
Pitfield, Milton Keynes, MK11 3LW, UK
UKHW020435010325

455677UK00029B/1169